Ninth Edition

READINGS ABOUT

The Social Animal

Edited by

Elliot Aronson
University of California, Santa Cruz

Worth Publishers

Senior Sponsoring Editor: Laura Pople
Executive Marketing Manager: Renée Altier
Art Director: Babs Reingold
Project Management: Print Matters, Inc.
Production Manager: Sarah Segal
Composition: Compset
Printing and Binding: R. R. Donnelley and Sons
Cover drawing by Tom Durfee

Library of Congress Cataloging-in-Publication Number: 2003107775

ISBN: 0-7167-5966-7

Printed in the United States of America

First printing 2003

Worth Publishers
41 Madison Avenue
New York, NY 10010
www.worthpublishers.com

To my bigger, smarter brother,
Jason Aronson (1929–1961)

"The most incomprehensible thing about the world
is that it's comprehensible."   —Albert Einstein

Contents

VI.   HUMAN AGGRESSION   311

VII.   PREDJUDICE   385

VIII. LIKING, LOVING AND INTERPERSONAL SENSITIVITY   445

Preface

In my textbook *The Social Animal,* I attempt to paint a clear picture of the current state of our social-psychological knowledge and how such knowledge might be applied to alleviate some problems plaguing us in the world today. *The Social Animal* is intended to be concise, brisk, and lively. It is almost totally unencumbered by graphs, charts, tables, statistical analysis, or detailed methodological discussions. Although that kind of presentation provides an easy and even enjoyable introduction to the world of social psychology, many readers express a need to delve more deeply into the details of the research that forms the backbone of *The Social Animal.* To meet that need, I have edited this book, *Readings About the Social Animal.*

I have selected the readings that appear in this book in such a way that they both complement and supplement the material contained in the eighth edition of *The Social Animal.* Not only are the sections organized so as to coincide with chapters in *The Social Animal*, but the specific readings also represent an attempt to amplify and elaborate on the major themes covered in that book. Moreover, I have been especially careful to choose readings that provide a mixture of classic and contemporary research. Some of the articles were already classics when I first read them as a student. At the other end of the continuum are articles I encountered in the form of prepublication reports. This combination will provide the reader with a historical sweep as well as with the most contemporary ideas in the field.

There is another way of classifying the articles in this collection. Most of the articles are reports of specific research as originally published in technical journals; others are more general pieces summarizing several studies on a given topic written by one of the major contributors to that area. A specific report, though not always easy to read, has the advantage of providing the detail necessary for enabling the reader to gain some understanding of exactly what goes into a piece of research. The summary article is usually less technical and, therefore, easier to read, offering a more panoramic overview of the area by the people who know it best. In effect, it enables the reader to look over an investigator's shoulder and see how he or she views an array of research on a given topic.

For this, the ninth edition, I have benefited from the wise consultation of my friends and colleagues, Anthony Pratkanis, Carol Tavris, and Joshua Aronson (my son, the social psychologist!). We have continued the process of blending the classic with the contemporary—and the specific with the panoramic. As the years roll by, it is gratifying to note that some of the articles I first selected as contemporary in 1972 have now taken their place as genuine classics in 1999. My hope is that *today's* contemporaries will likewise take their place as classics in the decades to come.

Elliot Aronson

An Open Letter to the Reader

Welcome backstage. As mentioned in the Preface, there are two kinds of articles contained in this volume. Some selections are descriptions of research programs. These make exciting reading in that they describe in some detail a series of experiments aimed at explicating or extending a single idea. Other selections are reports of individual pieces of empirical research. These are equally exciting but sometimes get rather technical. I'm sure some of you (teachers, graduate students, statisticians, and other dedicated types) will want to understand thoroughly every sentence of every article on the following pages, perhaps in the hope of planning some research of your own. *Bon voyage!* For your benefit, I have not abridged or changed a line of the original.

My guess is that most of you do not require that amount of detail. Chances are, what you would like to get out of these articles is an understanding of what the investigator was trying to find out, how he or she went about his or her task, and how successful the outcome was. There is no better way to understand the research process than to read original reports. The adventure of reading an original report lies in your ability as the reader to put yourself in the shoes of the investigator as he or she transforms an idea into a viable set of research operations and tries to make sense of the results, which occasionally do not conform precisely to the predictions. Each of the original research reports contains four principal sections: (1) First there is an *introduction,* in which the author states the idea, where it came from, and why it's important, and distills the idea down to a hypothesis or series of hypotheses. (2) This is followed by a *procedure* section, in which the author tests the hypothesis by translating the idea into a concrete set of operations. In social psychology this frequently becomes a full-blown scenario designed to provide the participant (or subject) with a reasonable justification for responding to events without being allowed to know the true purpose of the procedure. The procedure section of a good piece of research is often the most interesting part, because it requires a great deal of ingenuity for the investigator to achieve precision without sacrificing realism or impact. (3) In the *results* section the investigator states as clearly and succinctly as possible what the findings were. The investigator uses various statistical procedures to ascertain the extent to which the data are reliable. (4) Finally there is a *discussion* section, in which the researcher evaluates and interprets the data presented in the preceding section and tries to make sense of them in the context of previous research. The creative researcher can also use this section to speculate about the implications of the data and to point the way toward future research.

   To those of you who do not yet have much experience in reading research reports, I offer a few suggestions about which parts of the study to read carefully and which parts to skim. If the article contains a summary (either at the beginning or at the end), I would read that first in order to familiarize myself with the general idea behind the piece of research and to learn quickly what the results were. Next, I would read the introduction carefully in order to learn the history of the idea and to understand the hypothesis thoroughly. I would then read the procedure section pretty carefully. I would skim the results section just to see the extent to which the findings agreed with the predictions. If the findings did not fit the predictions, I would look closely at the discussion section to see how the author had made sense of the results he or she did get and whether or not the explanation seemed plausible to me. Unless you are adept at and/or intrigued by statistical analyses, I would advise you to skim that section. For those of you who have little or no knowledge of statistical procedures, it would be terribly frustrating and would serve no useful purpose to bog yourself down in some of the details of the statistical analyses. These articles were selected because they were well done. It is probably safe for you to accept on faith that the analysis was performed competently.

I

INTRODUCTION: REFLECTIONS ON THE RESEARCH PROCESS

1

Research in Social Psychology
as a Leap of Faith

Elliot Aronson

It is an honor and a pleasure to be here among such a distinguished group of dedicated experimental social psychologists. When I was asked to deliver an Invited Address at this meeting, the suggested topic was: "What Ever Became of Elliot Aronson?" I'm sure the committee selecting the title had their tongues at least partly in their cheeks. At the same time, I think there may have been a kernel of seriousness embedded in that choice of a title. Because I haven't published a laboratory experiment in a few years, I suspect that there may be a feeling abroad that I might have decided to abandon the laboratory in favor of doing research in the imprecise domain of what some of us laughingly call "the real world." And I suppose that the folks who invited me might have been tweaking my nose about that alleged decision. Well, whether or not my nose was being tweaked, I decided to take the request seriously. Initially, my decision was to describe the research project in the "real world" that has me so excited that it has occupied a large proportion of

This chapter was delivered as an invited address at the 1976 Meeting of the Society of Experimental Social Psychologists at the University of California at Los Angeles. A slightly modified version appeared in *Personality and Social Psychology Bulletin,* Vol. 3, No. 2, Spring 1977, pp. 190–195, by permission of Division 8 of the American Psychological Association and of the Publisher, Sage Publications, Inc.

my research time for the past four or five years. This is an action research project aimed at exploring the consequences of building cooperative learning groups in elementary schools, and is a project I'm very excited about: Among other things, we are finding that the loss of self-esteem among ethnic children following desegregation (discovered by Gerard and Miller, 1975) is largely a function of the competitiveness of the traditional classroom. When we placed kids in cooperative learning groups (of a special kind) we reversed this trend and produced sharp increases in self-esteem and test performance among black and Chicano children (Aronson et al., 1975; Lucker et al., 1976; Aronson et al., 1966).

But after I arrived here, I realized that a heavy dose of data would be inappropriate for an after-dinner speech. My data might be too heavy a dessert. Besides, ever since I've been here, several of you have been urging me to keep it light and perhaps even to make it humorous. So, I decided to talk to you about the philosophy of science. After all, graduate students consider my approach to the philosophy of science to be extraordinarily light and some even find it to be hilarious.

In 1968 Merrill Carlsmith and I wrote a chapter in *The Handbook of Social Psychology* on experimentation in social psychology. We spent most of that chapter talking about sticky problems: the trials and tribulations involved in designing and conducting an experiment in this area. We wrote about ethical issues, about experimenter bias, about random samples, experimental realism, debriefing, and all kinds of things to watch out for. After we finished it, we read the thing over and we realized that it made experimentation sound like a terrible drag. Further, we realized that this impression didn't reflect our own excitement and enthusiasm about doing research in social psychology. So we included another paragraph in which we said, in effect, "Hey, it *does* sound like doing research in social psychology is difficult, problematical, and occasionally a pain in the ass—and this is all true—but we will have really misled you if we don't convey our major feeling about doing research in social psychology—and that is that, all things considered, it is great fun."

It's now several years since that chapter was published, and I think that it's about time that I explained at least some of what we meant by the statement that experimentation is fun. And I'd like to do it in terms of a metaphor.

The metaphor I'd like to make use of occurs in a novel by Camus called *The Plague.* The backdrop of the novel involves bubonic plague that is ravaging a town on the coast of Algeria. One of the major characters is Monsieur Grand—an amiable sort of man who is writing a book. He wants that book to be absolutely perfect. He wants every sentence to be flawless, every paragraph to be magnificent, every page to be fantastically beautiful. He wants it to be perfect to the extent that, when he sends it to a publisher, the publisher will read the first sentence and be so struck by it that he will stand up and say to his colleagues, "Ladies and Gentlemen, hats off."

Monsieur Grand spends a lot of time writing that first sentence—the sentence is about a woman riding a horse in the park, but not just any woman, horse, or park. "One fine morning in the month of May an elegant young horsewoman might have been seen riding a handsome sorrell mare along the flowery avenues of the Bois de Boulogne."

But he's not satisfied. Does each noun have too many qualifiers? Too fe' qualifier convey precisely what he intends? Does each word properl rhythm of a cantering horse? Would "flower-strewn" be preferable to "flowery ... ... or nine months go by and he's still working on that first sentence—he has 50 manuscript pages all on that first sentence, because, as you know, he wants to be so good that the publisher will say to his colleagues, "Ladies and Gentlemen, hats off."

One day as he is working on his manuscript, he becomes ill; as his symptoms develop, it soon becomes clear that he has contracted bubonic plague. His physician—who is also his friend—examines him and says, "I'm really sorry to have to tell you this, but you're going to die; you don't have much longer to live." So Monsieur Grand orders his physician to destroy his manuscript. He issues this order with such assertiveness and such strength that the physician immediately takes the manuscript—this 50 pages of one sentence meticulously honed and sharpened— and throws it into the fire.

The next day Monsieur Grand recovers. And he says to his friend, "I think I acted too hastily." This is incredibly ironic, of course; the one action on his part that was spontaneous was in the interest of *destroying* the thing that he had created with anything but spontaneity.

So much for the metaphor. Basically, I believe that there are two very different ways to do science. One is in the slow, methodical, one-step-at-a-time manner exemplified by Monsieur Grand. This involves a great deal of meticulous honing, sharpening, and polishing of the design and operations. This may require several months. When the researcher is ready to leave the drawing board, he runs the study, and after he runs a few subjects he realizes that there are some things about it that are not perfect. So he stops and brings it back to the drawing board and works some more, sharpening and honing. He then runs a few more subjects and notices something else that can be improved. Several years later he may have the kind of experiment that, when he submits it to the journal, the editor will say to his colleagues, "Ladies and Gentlemen, hats off."[1]

There's another way to do science. This involves, in effect, sketching a study in quick, broad strokes, pilot testing it—seeing where you went wrong, recasting it, and then running it as best as you can at the moment. As you finish the study and begin to write it up, you may realize that if you had it all to do over again you would have done it better. Of course; learning always takes place as a function of experience—even in the researcher. But in this approach, instead of going back to the drawing board to design that mythical "perfect" study that will produce a "hats off" response, you finish the writeup and submit it for publication—relying on the notion that science is a self-corrective enterprise. Self-corrective in the following sense: I know that if I do a study that *isn't* perfect, it will soon be improved upon by others. Thus, my goal is to get it into the literature to give my colleagues a chance to look at it, be stimulated by it, be provoked by it, annoyed by it, and then go ahead and do it better—even if their intent

---

[1] Even under these circumstances the "hats off" response is unlikely; chances are the editor will find some flaws that the author overlooked.

is to prove me wrong, and even if they succeed in proving me wrong. That's the exciting thing about science; it progresses by people taking off on one another's work. This is what William James (1956) called the "leap of faith." I have faith that if I do an imperfect piece of work, someone will read it and will be provoked to demonstrate this imperfection in a really interesting way. This will almost always lead to a greater understanding of the phenomenon under investigation. And maybe, after that other person does his research, the editor and the publisher and the world at large will say, "Hey, hats off." And that's OK.

Needless to say, I prefer the second way—as those of you who are familiar with my imperfect research can readily gather. And this "leap of faith" forms a vital aspect of my philosophy of science. Namely, that we don't have to make things perfect before we expose them to other people's thinking, criticism, and actions. It's more exciting, it's more yeasty, it's more provocative to treat science in big, broad brush strokes rather than meticulously polishing and honing and taking several years before coming out with a finished product. Since I believe that science is a self-correcting enterprise, I would prefer to be provocative than right. Of course, it goes without saying that I do not attempt to be wrong or sloppy. I attempt to do the best I can at the moment and share that less than perfect product with you—my colleagues and critics. William James maintains that there is an immense class of cases where faith creates its own verification. To use one of James' examples—if while climbing a mountain you must leap over a precipice, your belief that you can do it increases the probability of a successful outcome. To extrapolate our confidence that others will be excited by our research and provoked to carry it further or prove it wrong induces us to conduct research in a manner and publish it at a time that maximizes the probability of the research providing the yeast for this kind of empirical convocation.

It is now several years since Carlsmith and I wrote that chapter in the *Handbook* in which we very blithely announced that experimentation in social psychology was fun. And as I read the journals, it seems to me that a lot of the fun has gone out of social psychology. One of the reasons for this, I think, is that we've gotten much too cautious, much too careful, much too afraid to be wrong, and it's taken a lot of the zest and a lot of the yeast out of the research in social psychology.

One of the by-products of excessive caution is excessive self-consciousness. Indeed, one of the most characteristic aspects of contemporary social psychology is a recent trend toward discipline-wide self-consciousness, handwringing, and "kvetching." By conservative estimate, in the past five or six years I must have been invited to at least a half dozen symposia with titles like "Where is Social Psychology Heading?" or "What Must We Do About Social Psychology?" or "Whither Social Psychology?" (with or without the "h" in whither). This kind of self-consciousness is a bore. Let me be clear. I'm not opposed to a certain degree of self-consciousness on an individual level. Indeed, I believe that any individual scientist should take stock of herself every few years and give herself the opportunity to re-order her priorities. Every few years it is probably quite useful to ask: What is important? What are my ethical and societal concerns? Although this process is important for an individual, when an entire discipline does it, the implication is that there is a particular place we should all be going, a particular methodology we should all be using, particular topics we should all be studying. I think that that kind of self-consciousness is deadly and stultifying. The proper question is "What might *individuals* be doing?", not "What should the *field* be doing?" I like to think of the discipline of social psychology as a really large circus tent where a lot of different acts are going on and the acts occasionally cross, intermingle, and overlap. In that way each individual is doing what that person thinks is the most interesting or useful thing to do *and* is being challenged all the time by the existence of other people in the science who are engaged in overlapping topics employing different methods or different topics employing overlapping methods.

Watch out—I feel another metaphor coming on. There is a short story by J. D. Salinger entitled *Seymour: An Introduction* in which Buddy Glass, who is a budding writer, presents his short stories as he writes them to his older brother, Seymour, for criticism. Seymour, who is a wise and good man, generally writes these criticisms in the form of a letter. After one story, Seymour writes Buddy a letter (which Buddy keeps for many years afterwards) in which he says, in effect:

> You really are a terrific craftsman. You really know how to write. You really know how to put a sentence together; you've mastered the technique. You know how to take these sentences and string them together into paragraphs. Your stories are constructed beautifully. The one thing you haven't learned yet is what to write about, and that's a really important problem. As I was thinking about it, I came up with a solution that was so simple and so direct and so "obvious" that it boggles the mind. The solution is this: Just remember that before you were a writer you were a reader. Then, all you have to do is think about the one story, the one thing that you always wanted to read, and then sit down and write it.

As a scientist, I continually find myself trying to make some use of Seymour's advice. In effect, I say to myself: "Hey, remember that before you were a researcher you were a consumer of research. If you want to know what to do research on, just think of the one experiment on human social behavior that you always wanted to read about, and then go out and do it." I have always tried to follow my translation of Seymour's advice, and occasionally I have succeeded. It would be very dangerous to say to a group like this that I always succeed—that every experiment I do involves the one question that I always wanted to know the answer to—because that would open me up to ridicule. I can just hear you saying, "You mean the one thing you always wanted to know about human nature is what happens when people spill coffee all over themselves?" (Aronson, Willerman, and Floyd, 1966). It's quite a dangerous statement even if it were true—and it's not true.

But I've had my moments and I can tell when I'm following Seymour's advice because I can feel my excitement rise, and I think I'm onto one of those questions now. My current research questions are: How can we turn the educational experience of millions of elementary school children into a less dehumanizing experience? How can we counteract the trend in American education toward lowering self-concepts of minority group people? How can we teach skills of cooperation painlessly and easily in the ordinary classroom situation? How can we make learning an exciting, interesting, social psychological, as well as educational, venture? Since public schools are institutions that 95 percent of us and 95 percent of our children and 95 percent of our grandchildren are going to be going through, I see these as important issues.

But I promised you I wouldn't dwell on the research itself. What I do want to dwell on are my failures as a scientist—the times when I don't follow Seymour's advice. Occasionally I do research that I'm not particularly excited about. How come? Sometimes I find myself between ideas. Or sometimes the research I'm interested in is too hard to do or is taking a lot of time to set up. When this happens, instead of doing nothing, I get scared. Scared of what? Let me backtrack. Yesterday when we had a symposium about the editorial policy of our journals, my friend and former student, Darwyn Linder, talked to us eloquently about what he thought the major function of journals should be. He presented a discussion of three separate functions: One is the archival function; the journal serves as a permanent body of knowledge so that 50 years from now when people want to know what was going on in social psychology in the 1970s, they can look in the back issues of the journals. A second function it serves is as a way of exchanging information; if you want to know what is going on in various labs across the country right now at this moment, or at least what went on three years ago when the researchers did the experiment that finally got published, you can look in the current journal. The third function that Linder mentioned was that for the younger social psychologists—people who are teaching at universities without tenure—it serves a pragmatic function. That is, publishing in journals convinces deans that the young social psychologist is doing his job by piling up vast numbers of publications. But what I want to say is that the third function is not one that is limited to younger people who are desirous of tenure. I think it is something that afflicts some of us old guys, too, in a very different way. Whereas our jobs aren't dependent on publications, something else is. And that something—for a lack of a better word—I would call collegial esteem. What keeps me from consistently doing research on the one thing that I always wanted to find out about is that I get scared once in a while that if I'm not always active, not always producing things—anything—then perhaps some of my colleagues might think that I've lost it, and they may begin to ask questions like "Whatever became of Elliot Aronson?" which was indeed the suggested topic of this talk. It is conceivable to me that I'm not the only person here who has experienced that fear. If my suspicion is correct, then perhaps by discussing that hobgoblin we can, if nothing else, get rid of what Harry Stack Sullivan called "the fallacy of uniqueness." This may help us all to lay the hobgoblin to rest and get on with our proper business: for each of us in his own way to pursue as best as we can the answer to the one question he always wanted to know.

References

ARONSON, E., BLANEY, N., SIKES, J., STEPHAN, C., AND SNAPP, M. Busing and racial tension: The jig-saw route to learning and liking. *Psychology Today,* 1975, **8,** 43–50.

ARONSON, E., AND CARLSMITH, M. Experimentation in social psychology. In G. Lindzey and E. Aronson (eds.), *Handbook of social psychology.* Vol. 2 (2nd ed.). Reading, Mass,: Addison-Wesley, 1968.

ARONSON, E., WILLERMAN, B., AND FLOYD, J. The effect of a pratfall on increasing interpersonal attractiveness. *Psychonomic Science,* 1966, **4,** 227–228.

BLANEY, N., ROSENFIELD, R., STEPHAN, C., ARONSON, E., AND SIKES, J. Interdependence in the classroom: A field study. *Journal of Educational Psychology,* 1977, **69,** 139–146.

GERARD, H., AND MILLER, N. *School desegregation.* New York: Plenum Press, 1975.

JAMES, W. *The will to believe.* New York: Dover, 1956.

LUCKER, W., ARONSON, E. ROSENFIELD, D., AND SIKES, J., Performance in the interdependent classroom: A field study. *American Educational Research Journal,* 1976, **13,** No. 2, 115–123.

2

On Baseball and Failure*

Elliot Aronson

Acceptance Speech, SESP Distinguished Scientific Achievement Award, October, 1994

I am deeply touched by this honor. I cannot imagine a more meaningful honor for a social psychologist than having one's scientific research recognized by *this* group. I have always believed that experimentation in social psychology is a family business. And, if that's true, then you are the family. The people in this room are the best scientists in this business. No one knows better than you about what it takes to do a good experiment in this area. Every person in this room is well aware that there is an art to this wonderful science of ours. And it is a demanding art, indeed.

It is arguably more difficult to do an experiment in social psychology than in any other scientific discipline for one simple and powerful reason: In social psychology, we are testing our theories and hypotheses on participants who are almost always intelligent, curious, experienced human beings who have spent their entire lives in a social environment—and have, therefore, formed their own theories and hypotheses about precisely the behaviors we are trying to study in the laboratory. That is to say, everyone in the world, including the participants in our experiments, is a social psychological theorist. That simple fact makes doing experiments in social psychology both challenging and exciting.

Our challenge is to find a way to circumvent or neutralize the theories that our participants walk in with—so that we can observe their true behavior—not how they think they should behave if their own theory were true. Our excitement? Ahhh, that's what the rest of this so-called speech is about! Actually, it's not a speech at all. As a chronic and habitual story-teller, it seems appropriate for me to

*This speech was prepared for delivery at the annual convention of the Society of Experimental Social Psychologists, in 1994 by the recipient of its 12th annual Distinguished Scientific Achievement Award. Portions of this speech were published in *Dialogue* (a publication of the Society for Personality and Social Psychology) Spring 1995, 4–5.

tell you a story. The story takes place early in 1941, when I was nine years old. That was an important year for me; it was the year I discovered social psychology.

I grew up in Revere, Massachusetts—a small, run-down, blue collar city near Boston. Ours was the only Jewish family in a rough, passionately anti-Semitic neighborhood. When I was a child, my parents insisted that I attend Hebrew school, in addition to public school. The Hebrew classes were held very late in the afternoon, four days a week. Alas, the Hebrew school building was located clear on the other side of town, which meant that I used to have to walk through my own hostile neighborhood carrying my Hebrew books. I was like a walking advertisement, a beacon to the anti-Semitic kids: "Hey, look at me—I'm Jewish!" Simply getting to and from Hebrew school every day was something of an adventure: I was forever trying to find creative routes, zig-zag paths that would take me away from the greatest areas of danger. But, in spite of my best efforts, I was frequently waylaid, pushed around, and occasionally roughed up by gangs of teen-aged tough guys who yelled anti-Semitic slogans.

One of my most vivid childhood memories involves sitting on a curb, nursing a bloody nose and a split lip, and wondering how these kids could possibly hate me so much when they didn't even know me. I wondered if they were born hating Jews, or if they needed to be taught such hatred; I wondered if there might be any way to get them to hate me less—like, if they had gotten to know me better as a person, before they knew I was Jewish, would that have diminished their hatred.

I didn't realize it at the time, of course, but these were profound social psychological questions. And some ten years later, as an economics major at Brandeis, I wandered into an Intro. Psych. class being taught by Abraham Maslow—quite by accident. As it happened, Maslow was lecturing on the social psychology of prejudice, and I was astonished and delighted to discover that there was an entire profession where people actually got paid for thinking about those things and raising the same kinds of questions that I had raised when I was nine years old. I could hardly believe my ears! Wow, I thought, what a racket! And I immediately switched my major to psychology. And I've been thinking, Wow, what a racket, ever since! For over 35 years, I have been having so much fun doing social psychology that I keep expecting to hear a knock on my door in the middle of the night; the cops are going to arrest me for accepting money under false pretenses!

What's more, to my great personal satisfaction, some 30 years after I was sitting on that curb nursing my bloody nose and my split lip, I was able to invent a social psychological strategy for reducing prejudice in the schools—a strategy that not only teaches us something about human nature and human behavior, but one that really works—that really reduces prejudice and violence and thereby improves human lives. I feel blessed.

One of the things I love about social psychology is precisely that: It affords us the opportunity of doing both of those things simultaneously—of illuminating something important about human nature and doing some good in the world.

In my judgment, it is part and parcel of the mission of social psychology to uncover a lot of unappetizing things about human behavior—about mindless conformity, about blind obedience to authority, about violence, about prejudice, and the like. This could be depressing if it were not for the fact that this discipline of ours offers us the opportunity for redemption in the form of application: in the form of finding ways to reduce mindless conformity, blind obedience, prejudice and violence. And, of course, this redemption—this applied research—if it is done well, comes full circle and informs our theories and basic research. That is what I love about social psychology.

Needless to say, social psychology was not my first love. When I was nine years old, sitting on that curbstone in Revere, I sure as hell did not want to be a social psychologist. I did not even know there *was* such a thing. But even if I had known about social psychology, at that time I wanted to be a professional baseball player. Actually, my desire was much more specific than that: I wanted to play center field for the Boston Red Sox. (Of course, the Sox already had a center fielder at that time; but I was not greedy or impatient: I was willing to wait until he retired; I figured that would take about 10 years, and, by then, I would be ready!)

When I was a little kid, I worked hard at achieving my dream. Every spring, starting in late February, even before the snow had completely melted off the baseball field, a few of us were out there, shagging flies—hour, after hour, after hour.

And, with all that practice, I got pretty good at shagging flies—but I have a confession: In spite of hundreds of hours of practice, I never made the Red Sox. As a matter of fact, I could not even get to play center field on my high school team. I was much too slow a runner for that, and besides, I could not hit a curve ball to save my life. Indeed, as a ballplayer, I reached my peak at about the age of 14, since then, it has been downhill all the way! It is kind of sad to reach a peak at anything at age 14, but there you have it.

Fortunately, as I said, I eventually discovered social psychology. As a social psychologist, I expect to reach my peak any time now—or as we Red Sox fans are fond of saying, maybe next year!

Although I never made it as a ballplayer, I learned a few things playing baseball that proved to be useful to me as a social psychologist. It goes without saying that the game of baseball is vastly overused as a metaphor—but what the hell, why should I let a little thing like *that* stop me?

One of the things I like most about baseball is contained in the box score of a game: In baseball, they tally runs, hits, and errors. I like that because, generally speaking, we live in a society that is contemptuous of failure and punishes mistakes of all kinds. Because of this, we are under enormous pressure to deny our mistakes or minimize their importance. The danger of this attitude is that it makes people afraid to make mistakes and when people are afraid to make mistakes, they usually do not take many risks but play it close to the vest. Aronson's second law: People who are afraid to make mistakes are unlikely to make anything of great value. Moreover, if we are unselfconscious about our mistakes, we can look at them carefully and perhaps learn something important from them.

Playing baseball taught me how to deal with failure. It was a lesson I learned well when I was very young and for that, I will always be grateful. It goes without saying that I've made more than my share of mistakes—in life and in social psychology. (I will spare you my confessions of all my important failures as a human being and simply make reference to my failures in the lab.) In doing experiments, I screw up a lot—usually because I'm not as smart or skillful as I would like to be. Occasionally, I screw up merely because I'm trying to tackle a hypothesis that is elusive or difficult to test. I don't ever want to be deterred from trying to tackle a difficult hypothesis by my fear of screwing up.

In baseball, by including errors in the box score, they are saying, in effect, that it's not such a terrible thing to screw up—it's not desirable, of course, but screwing up is part of the game: a part of the game of baseball, a part of the game of life, a part of the game of social psychology. I've often thought that we should have a journal devoted to publishing interesting ideas that didn't work—and that people should submit these interesting failures with pride.

There are at least three good reasons for this: (1) Someone else may be able to pick up our fumble and run with it. (Whoops, a mixed athletic metaphor!) (2) It would be good for the self-confidence of our graduate students if they saw some of our failures on display as well as our successes. When grad students read the current journals, it creates the illusion that we old-timers are much more clever than we are. This would be harmless, except for the fact that they might get discouraged by this—concluding, erroneously, that they themselves would have a lot of difficulty measuring up. (3) Most important, it would make failure a legitimate part of the social psychology game—not just success. Like in baseball, errors are certainly not sought out—they are not desirable, per se—but the fear of error should not keep us from going after the difficult problems.

In the baseball box score, errors are tallied in the fielding part of the game—but the same kind of tolerance for imperfection is reflected in hitting. Consider this: If, as a batter, a ballplayer screws up two out of three times at bat, that will give him a lifetime batting average of .333; with a batting average of .333, he is likely to make it to the Hall of Fame!

When I thought about that for a little while, I realized that while I could never do nearly that well in hitting a baseball, .333 is just about my average as an experimentalist—that is, in designing and conducting experiments, I fail about twice as often as I succeed. If this honor you have so graciously given me today can be considered social psychology's equivalent of baseball's Hall of Fame, then I guess that means that I made it after all—even though I still can't hit a curve ball to save my life! I am very grateful that you found a way to make the dreams of a nine-year-old kid come true—after a fashion!

II

CONFORMITY AND OBEDIENCE

3

Opinions and Social Pressure

Solomon E. Asch

Exactly what is the effect of the opinions of others on our own? In other words, how strong is the urge toward social conformity? The question is approached by means of some unusual experiments.

That social influences shape every person's practices, judgments and beliefs is a truism to which anyone will readily assent. A child masters his "native" dialect down to the finest nuances; a member of a tribe of cannibals accepts cannibalism as altogether fitting and proper. All the social sciences take their departure from the observation of the profound effects that groups exert on their members. For psychologists, group pressure upon the minds of individuals raises a host of questions they would like to investigate in detail.

How, and to what extent, do social forces constrain people's opinions and attitudes? This question is especially pertinent in our day. The same epoch that has witnessed the unprecedented technical extension of communication has also brought into existence the deliberate manipulation of opinion and the "engineering of consent." There are many good reasons why, as citizens and as scientists, we should be concerned with studying the ways in which human beings form their opinions and the role that social conditions play.

Studies of these questions began with the interest in hypnosis aroused by the French physician Jean Martin Charcot (a teacher of Sigmund Freud) toward the end of the nineteenth century. Charcot believed that only hysterical patients could be fully hypnotized, but this view was soon challenged by two other physicians, Hyppolyte Bernheim and A. A. Liébault, who demonstrated that they could put most people under the hypnotic spell. Bernheim proposed that hypnosis was but an extreme form of a normal psychological process which became known as "suggestibility." It was shown that monotonous reiteration of instructions could induce in normal persons in the waking state involuntary bodily changes such as swaying or rigidity of the arms, and sensations such as warmth and odor.

It was not long before social thinkers seized upon these discoveries as a basis for explaining numerous social phenomena, from the spread of opinion to the formation of crowds and the following of leaders. The sociologist Gabriel Tarde summed it all up in the aphorism: "Social man is a somnambulist."

When the new discipline of social psychology was born at the beginning of this century, its first experiments were essentially adaptations of the suggestion demonstration. The technique generally followed a simple plan. The subjects, usually college students, were asked to give their opinions or preferences concerning various matters; some time later they were again asked to state their choices, but now they were also informed of the opinions held by authorities or large groups of their peers on the same matters. (Often the alleged consensus was fictitious.) Most of these studies had substantially the same result: confronted with opinions contrary to their own, many subjects apparently shifted their judgments in the direction of the views of the majorities or the experts. The late psychologist Edward L. Thorndike reported that he had succeeded in modifying the esthetic preferences of adults by this procedure. Other psychologists reported that people's evaluations of the merit of a literary passage could be raised or lowered by ascribing the passage to different authors. Apparently the sheer weight of numbers or authority sufficed to change opinions, even when no arguments for the opinions themselves were provided.

Now the very ease of success in these experiments arouses suspicion. Did the subjects actually change their opinions, or were the experimental victories scored only on paper? On grounds of common sense, one must question whether opinions are generally as watery as these studies indicate. There is some reason to wonder whether it was not the investigators who, in their enthusiasm for a theory, were suggestible, and whether the ostensibly gullible subjects were not providing answers which they thought good subjects were expected to give.

The investigations were guided by certain underlying assumptions, which today are common currency and account for much that is thought and said about the operations of propaganda and public opinion. The assumptions are that people submit uncritically and painlessly to external manipulation by suggestion or prestige, and that any given idea or value can be "sold" or "unsold" without reference to its merits. We should be skeptical, however, of the supposition that the power of social pressure necessarily implies uncritical submission to it: independence and the capacity to rise above group passion are also open to human beings. Further, one may question on psychological grounds whether it is possible as a rule to change a person's judgment of a situation or an object without first changing his knowledge or assumptions about it.

FIGURE 3.1
Experiment is repeated in the Laboratory of Social Relations at Harvard University. Seven student subjects are asked by the experimenter *(right)* to compare the length of lines *(see Fig. 3.2)*. Six of the subjects have been coached beforehand to give unanimously wrong answers. The seventh *(sixth from the left)* has merely been told that it is an experiment in perception. (Photograph by William Vandivert.)

In what follows I shall describe some experiments in an investigation of the effects of group pressure which was carried out recently with the help of a number of my associates. The tests not only demonstrate the operations of group pressure upon individuals but also illustrate a new kind of attack on the problem and some of the more subtle questions that it raises.

A group of seven to nine young men, all college students, are assembled in a classroom for a "psychological experiment" in visual judgment. The experimenter informs them that they will be comparing the lengths of lines. He shows two large white cards. On one is a single vertical black line—the standard whose length is to be matched. On the other card are three vertical lines of various lengths. The subjects are to choose the one that is of the same length as the line on the other card. One of the three actually is of the same length; the other two are substantially different, the difference ranging from three quarters of an inch to an inch and three quarters.

The experiment opens uneventfully. The subjects announce their answers in the order in which they have been seated in the room, and on the first round every person chooses the same matching line. Then a second set of cards is exposed; again the group is unanimous. The members appear ready to endure politely another boring experiment. On the third trial there is an unexpected disturbance. One person near the end of the group disagrees with all the others in his selection of the matching line. He looks surprised, indeed incredulous, about the disagreement. On the following trial he disagrees again, while the others remain unanimous in their choice. The dissenter becomes more and more worried and

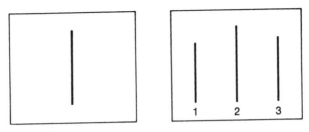

FIGURE 3.2
Subjects were shown two cards. One bore a standard line. The other bore three lines, one of which was the same length as the standard. The subjects were asked to choose this line.

hesitant as the disagreement continues in succeeding trials; he may pause before announcing his answer and speak in a low voice, or he may smile in an embarrassed way.

What the dissenter does not know is that all the other members of the group were instructed by the experimenter beforehand to give incorrect answers in unanimity at certain points. The single individual who is not a party to this prearrangement is the focal subject of our experiment. He is placed in a position in which, while he is actually giving the correct answers, he finds himself unexpectedly in a minority of one, opposed by a unanimous and arbitrary majority with respect to a clear and simple fact. Upon him we have brought to bear two opposed forces: the evidence of his senses and the unanimous opinion of a group of his peers. Also, he must declare his judgments in public, before a majority which has also stated its position publicly.

The instructed majority occasionally reports correctly in order to reduce the possibility that the naive subject will suspect collusion against him. (In only a few cases did the subject actually show suspicion; when this happened, the experiment was stopped and the results were not counted. There are 18 trials in each series, and on 12 of these the majority responds erroneously. How do people respond to group pressure in this situation? I shall report first the statistical results of a series in which a total of 123 subjects from three institutions of higher learning (not including my own, Swarthmore College) were placed in the minority situation described above.

Two alternatives were open to the subject: he could act independently, repudiating the majority, or he could go along with the majority, repudiating the evidence of his senses. Of the 123 put to the test, a considerable percentage yielded to the majority. Whereas in ordinary circumstances individuals matching the lines will make mistakes less than 1 percent of the time, under group pressure the minority subjects swung to acceptance of the misleading majority's wrong judgments in 36.8 percent of the selections.

Of course individuals differed in response. At one extreme, about one quarter of the subjects were completely independent and never agreed with the erroneous judgments of the majority. At the other extreme, some individuals went with the majority nearly all the time. The performances of individuals in this experiment tend to be highly consistent. Those who strike out on the path of independence do not, as a rule, succumb to the majority even over an extended series of trials, while those who choose the path of compliance are unable to free themselves as the ordeal is prolonged.

The reasons for the startling individual differences have not yet been investigated in detail. At this point we can only report some tentative generalizations from talks with the subjects, each of whom was interviewed at the end of the experiment. Among the independent individuals were many who held fast because of staunch confidence in their own judgment. The most significant fact about them was not absence of responsiveness to the majority but a capacity to recover from doubt and to reestablish their equilibrium. Others who acted independently came to believe that the majority was correct in its answers, but they continued their dissent on the simple ground that it was their obligation to call the play as they saw it.

Among the extremely yielding persons we found a group who quickly reached the conclusion: "I am wrong, they are right." Others yielded in order "not to spoil your results." Many of the individuals who went along suspected that the majority were "sheep" following the first responder, or that the majority were victims of an optical illusion; nevertheless, these suspicions failed to free them at the moment of decision. More disquieting were the reactions of subjects who construed their difference from the majority as a sign of some general deficiency in themselves, which at all costs they must hide. On this basis they desperately tried to merge with the majority, not realizing the longer-range consequences to themselves. All the yielding subjects underestimated the frequency with which they conformed.

Which aspect of the influence of a majority is more important—the size of the majority or its unanimity? The experiment was modified to examine this question. In one series the size of the opposition was varied from one to fifteen persons. The results showed a clear trend. When a subject was confronted with only a single individual who contradicted his answers, he was swayed little: he continued to answer independently and correctly in nearly all trials. When the opposition was increased to two, the pressure became substantial: minority subjects now accepted the wrong answer 13.6 percent of the time. Under the pressure of a majority of three, the subjects' errors jumped to 31.8 percent. But further increases in the size of the majority apparently did not increase the weight of the pressure substantially. Clearly the size of the opposition is important only up to a point.

Disturbance of the majority's unanimity had a striking effect. In this experiment the subject was given the support of a truthful partner—either another individual who did not know of the prearranged agreement among the rest of the group, or a person who was instructed to give correct answers throughout.

The presence of a supporting partner depleted the majority of much of its power. Its pressure on the dissenting individual was reduced to one-fourth: that is, subjects answered incorrectly only one-fourth as often as under the pressure of a unanimous majority (Fig. 3.6). The weakest persons did not yield as readily. Most interesting were the reactions to the partner. Generally the feeling toward him was one of warmth and closeness; he was credited with inspiring confidence. However, the subjects repudiated the suggestion that the partner decided them to be independent.

Was the partner's effect a consequence of his dissent, or was it related to his accuracy? We now introduced into the experimental group a person who was instructed to dissent from the majority but also to disagree with the subject. In some experiments the majority was always to choose the worst of the comparison lines and the instructed dissenter to pick the line that was closer to the length of the standard one; in others the majority was consistently intermediate and the dissenter most in error. In this manner we were able to study the relative influence of "compromising" and "extremist" dissenters.

Again the results are clear. When a moderate dissenter is present, the effect of the majority on the subject decreases by approximately one-third, and extremes of yielding disappear. Moreover, most of the errors the subjects do make are moderate, rather than flagrant. In short, the dissenter largely controls the choice of errors. To this extent the subjects broke away from the majority even while bending to it.

On the other hand, when the dissenter always chose the line that was more flagrantly different from the standard, the results were of quite a different kind. The extremist dissenter produced a remarkable freeing of the subjects; their errors dropped to only 9 percent. Furthermore, all the errors were of the moderate variety. We were able to conclude that dissent *per se* increased independence and moderated the errors that occurred, and that the direction of dissent exerted consistent effects.

In all the foregoing experiments each subject was observed only in a single setting. We now turned to studying the effects upon a given individual of a change in the situation to which he was exposed. The first experiment examined the consequences of losing or gaining a partner. The instructed partner began by answering correctly on the first six trials. With his support the subject usually resisted pressure from the majority: eighteen of twenty-seven subjects were completely independent. But after six trials the partner joined the majority. As soon as he did so, there was an abrupt rise in the subjects' errors. Their submission to the majority

FIGURE 3.3
Experiment proceeds as follows: In the top picture, the subject *(center)* hears rules of experiment for the first time. In the second picture, he makes his first judgment of a pair of cards, disagreeing with the unanimous judgment of the others. In the third, he leans forward to look at another pair of cards. In the fourth, he shows the strain of repeatedly disagreeing with the majority. In the fifth, after twelve pairs of cards have been shown, he explains that "he has to call them as he sees them." This subject disagreed with the majority on all twelve trials. Seventy-five percent of experimental subjects agree with the majority in varying degrees. (Photographs by William Vandivert.)

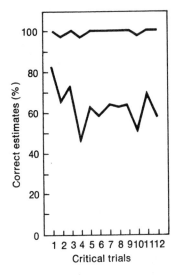

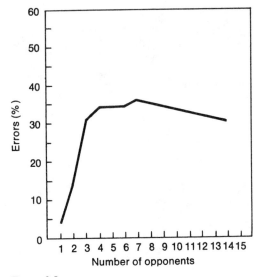

FIGURE 3.4
Error of 123 subjects, each of whom compared lines in the presence of six to eight opponents, is plotted in the gray curve. The accuracy of judgment not under pressure is indicated in black.

FIGURE 3.5
Size of majority that opposed them had an effect on the subjects. With a single opponent, the subject erred only 3.6 percent of the time; with two opponents he erred 13.6 percent; with three, 31.8 percent; with four, 35.1 percent; with six, 35.2 percent; with seven, 37.1 percent; with nine, 35.1 percent; with fifteen, 31.2 percent.

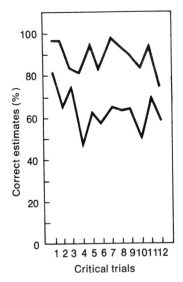

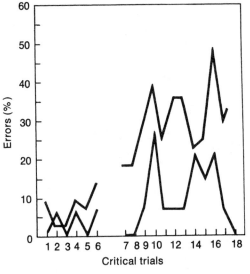

FIGURE 3.6
Two subjects supporting each other against a majority made fewer errors *(gray curve)* than one subject did against a majority *(black curve).*

FIGURE 3.7
Partner left subject after six trials in a single experiment. The gray curve shows the error of the subject when the partner "deserted" to the majority. The black curve shows error when partner merely left the room.

was just about as frequent as when the minority subject was opposed by a unanimous majority throughout.

It was surprising to find that the experience of having had a partner and of having braved the majority opposition with him had failed to strengthen the individuals' independence. Questioning at the conclusion of the experiment suggested that we had overlooked an important circumstance; namely, the strong specific effect of "desertion" by the partner to the other side. We therefore changed the conditions so that the partner would simply leave the group at the proper point. (To allay suspicion it was announced in advance that he had an appointment with the dean.) In this form of the experiment, the partner's effect outlasted his presence. The errors increased after his departure, but less markedly than after a partner switched to the majority.

In a variant of this procedure the trials began with the majority unanimously giving correct answers. Then they gradually broke away until on the sixth trial the naive subject was alone and the group unanimously against him. As long as the subject had anyone on his side, he was almost invariably independent, but as soon as he found himself alone, the tendency to conform to the majority rose abruptly.

As might be expected, an individual's resistance to group pressure in these experiments depends to a considerable degree on how wrong the majority is. We varied the discrepancy between the standard line and the other lines systematically, with the hope of reaching a point where the error of the majority would be so glaring that every subject would repudiate it and choose independently. In this we regretfully did not succeed. Even when the difference between the lines was seven inches, there were still some who yielded to the error of the majority.

The study provides clear answers to a few relatively simple questions, and it raises many others that await investigation. We would like to know the degree of consistency of persons in situations which differ in content and structure. If consistency of independence or conformity in behavior is shown to be a fact, how is it functionally related to qualities of character and personality? In what ways is independence related to sociological or cultural conditions? Are leaders more independent than other people, or are they adept at following their followers? These and many other questions may perhaps be answerable by investigations of the type described here.

Life in society requires consensus as an indispensable condition. But consensus, to be productive, requires that each individual contribute independently out of his experience and insight. When consensus comes under the dominance of conformity, the social process is polluted and the individual at the same time surrenders the powers on which his functioning as a feeling and thinking being depends. That we have found the tendency to conformity in our society so strong that reasonably intelligent and well-meaning young people are willing to call white black is a matter of concern. It raises questions about our ways of education and about the values that guide our conduct.

Yet anyone inclined to draw too pessimistic conclusions from this report would do well to remind himself that the capacities for independence are not to be underestimated. He may also draw some consolation from a further observation: those who participated in this challenging experiment agreed nearly without exception that independence was preferable to conformity.

References

ASCH, S. E. Effects of group pressure upon the modification and distortion of judgments. *Groups, leadership, and men,* Harold Guetzdow (ed.). Carnegie Press, 1951.

ASCH S. E. *Social psychology.* Prentice-Hall, Inc., 1952.

MILLER, N. E. AND DOLLARD, J. *Social learning and imitation.* Yale University Press, 1941.

4

Behavioral Study of Obedience

Stanley Milgram

This chapter describes a procedure for the study of destructive obedience in the laboratory. It consists of ordering a naive S to administer increasingly more severe punishment to a victim in the context of a learning experiment. Punishment is administered by means of a shock generator with thirty graded switches ranging from Slight Shock to Danger: Severe Shock. The victim is a confederate of the E. The primary dependent variable is the maximum shock the S is willing to administer before he refuses to continue further. Twenty-six Ss obeyed the experimental commands fully, and administered the highest shock on the generator. Fourteen Ss broke off the experiment at some point after the victim protested and refused to provide further answers. The procedure created extreme levels of nervous tension in some Ss. Profuse sweating, trembling and stuttering were typical expressions of this emotional disturbance. One unexpected sign of tension—yet to be explained—was the regular occurrence of nervous laughter, which in some Ss developed into uncontrollable seizures. The variety of interesting behavioral dynamics observed in the experiment, the reality of the situation for the S, and the possibility of parametric variation within the framework of the procedure, point to the fruitfulness of further study.

Obedience is as basic an element in the structure of social life as one can point to. Some system of authority is a requirement of all communal living, and it is only the man dwelling in isolation who is not forced to respond, through defiance or submission, to the commands of others. Obedience, as a determinant of behavior, is of particular relevance to our time. It has been reliably established that from 1933–1945 millions of innocent persons were systematically slaughtered on command. Gas chambers were built, death camps were guarded, daily quotas of corpses were produced with the same efficiency as the manufacture of appliances. These inhumane policies may have originated in the mind of a single person, but they could only be carried out on a massive scale if a very large number of persons obeyed orders.

Reprinted with permission from the author and *The Journal of Abnormal and Social Psychology,* Vol. 67, No. 4, 1963. Copyright © 1963 by the American Psychological Association. Copyright renewed © 1991 by Alexandra Milgram.

This research was supported by a grant (NSF G-17916) from the National Science Foundation. Exploratory studies conducted in 1960 were supported by a grant from the Higgins Fund at Yale University. The research assistance of Alan E. Elms and Jon Wayland is gratefully acknowledged.

Obedience is the psychological mechanism that links individual action to political purpose. It is the dispositional cement that binds men to systems of authority. Facts of recent history and observation in daily life suggest that for many persons obedience may be a deeply ingrained behavior tendency, indeed, a prepotent impulse overriding training in ethics, sympathy, and moral conduct. C. P. Snow (1961) points to its importance when he writes:

> When you think of the long and gloomy history of man, you will find more hideous crimes have been committed in the name of obedience than have ever been committed in the name of rebellion. If you doubt that, read William Shirer's "Rise and Fall of the Third Reich." The German Officer Corps were brought up in the most rigorous code of obedience . . . in the name of obedience they were party to, and assisted in, the most wicked large scale actions in the history of the world [p. 24].

While the particular form of obedience dealt with in the present study has its antecedents in these episodes, it must not be thought all obedience entails acts of aggression against others. Obedience serves numerous productive functions. Indeed, the very life of society is predicated on its existence. Obedience may be ennobling and educative and refer to acts of charity and kindness, as well as to destruction.

General Procedure

A procedure was devised which seems useful as a tool for studying obedience (Milgram, 1961). It consists of ordering a naive subject to administer electric shock to a victim. A simulated shock generator is used, with 30 clearly marked voltage levels that range from 15 to 450 volts. The instrument bears verbal designations that range from Slight Shock to Danger: Severe Shock. The responses of the victim, who is a trained confederate of the experimenter, are standardized. The orders to administer shocks are given to the naive subject in the context of a "learning experiment" ostensibly set up to study the effects of punishment on memory. As the experiment proceeds the naive subject is commanded to administer increasingly more intense shocks to the victim, even to the point of reaching the level marked Danger: Severe Shock. Internal resistances become stronger, and at a certain point the subject refuses to go on with the experiment. Behavior prior to this rupture is considered "obedience," in that the subject complies with the commands of the experimenter. The point of rupture is the act of disobedience. A quantitative value is assigned to the subject's performance based on the maximum intensity shock he is willing to administer before he refuses to participate further. Thus for any particular subject and for any particular experimental condition the degree of obedience may be specified with a numerical value. The crux of the study is to systematically vary the factors believed to alter the degree of obedience to the experimental commands.

The technique allows important variables to be manipulated at several points in the experiment. One may vary aspects of the source of command, content and form of command, instrumentalities for its execution, target object, general social setting, etc. The problem, therefore, is not one of designing increasingly more numerous experimental conditions, but of selecting those that best illuminate the *process* of obedience from the sociopsychological standpoint.

Related Studies

The inquiry bears an important relation to philosophic analyses of obedience and authority (Arendt, 1958; Friedrich, 1958; Weber, 1947), an early experimental study of obedience by Frank (1944), studies in "authoritarianism" (Adorno, Frenkel-Brunswik, Levinson, and Sanford, 1950; Rokeach, 1961), and a recent series of analytic and empirical studies in social power (Cartwright, 1959). It owes much to the long concern with *suggestion* in social psychology, both in its normal forms (e.g., Binet, 1900) and in its clinical manifestations (Charcot, 1881). But it derives, in the first instance, from direct observation of a social fact; the individual who is commanded by a legitimate authority ordinarily obeys. Obedience comes easily and often. It is a ubiquitous and indispensable feature of social life.

METHOD

Subjects

The subjects were 40 males between the ages of 20 and 50, drawn from New Haven and the surrounding communities. Subjects were obtained by a newspaper advertisement and direct mail solicitation. Those who responded to the appeal believed they were to participate in a study of memory and learning at Yale University. A wide range of occupations is represented in the sample. Typical subjects were postal clerks, high school teachers, salesmen, engineers, and laborers. Subjects ranged in educational level from one who had not finished elementary school, to those who had doctorate and other professional degrees. They were paid $4.50 for their participation in the experiment. However, subjects were told that payment was simply for coming to the laboratory, and that the money was theirs no matter what happened after they arrived. Table 4.1 shows the proportion of age and occupational types assigned to the experimental condition.

Personnel and Locale

The experiment was conducted on the grounds of Yale University in the elegant interaction laboratory. (This detail is relevant to the perceived legitimacy of the

TABLE 4.1
Distribution of age and occupational types in the experiment

Occupations	20–29 years *n*	30–39 years *n*	40–50 years *n*	Percentage of total (occupations)
Workers, skilled and unskilled	4	5	6	37.5
Sales, business, and white-collar	3	6	7	40.0
Professional	1	5	3	22.5
Percentage of total (age)	20	40	40	

Note: Total $N = 40$.

experiment. In further variations, the experiment was dissociated from the university, with consequences for performance.) The role of experimenter was played by a 31-year-old high school teacher of biology. His manner was impassive, and his appearance somewhat stern throughout the experiment. He was dressed in a gray technician's coat. The victim was played by a 47-year-old accountant, trained for the role; he was of Irish-American stock, whom most observers found mild-mannered and likable.

Procedure

One naive subject and one victim (an accomplice) performed in each experiment. A pretext had to be devised that would justify the administration of electric shock by the naive subject. This was effectively accomplished by the cover story. After a general introduction on the presumed relation between punishment and learning, subjects were told:

> But actually, we know very *little* about the effect of punishment on learning, because almost no truly scientific studies have been made of it in human beings.
>
> For instance, we don't know how *much* punishment is best for learning—and we don't know how much difference it makes as to who is giving the punishment, whether an adult learns best from a younger or an older person than himself—or many things of that sort.
>
> So in this study we are bringing together a number of adults of different occupations and ages. And we're asking some of them to be teachers and some of them to be learners.
>
> We want to find out just what effect different people have on each other as teachers and learners, and also what effect *punishment* will have on learning in this situation.

> Therefore, I'm going to ask one of you to be the teacher here tonight and the other one to be the learner.
>
> Does either of you have a preference?

Subjects then drew slips of paper from a hat to determine who would be the teacher and who would be the learner in the experiment. The drawing was rigged so that the naive subject was always the teacher and the accomplice always the learner. (Both slips contained the word "Teacher.") Immediately after the drawing the teacher and learner were taken to an adjacent room and the learner was strapped into an "electric chair" apparatus.

The experimenter explained that the straps were to prevent excessive movement while the learner was being shocked. The effect was to make it impossible for him to escape from the situation. An electrode was attached to the learner's wrist, and electrode paste was applied "to avoid blisters and burns." Subjects were told that the electrode was attached to the shock generator in the adjoining room.

In order to improve credibility the experimenter declared, in response to a question by the learner: "Although the shocks can be extremely painful, they cause no permanent tissue damage."

Learning task.   The lesson administered by the subject was a paired-associate learning task. The subject read a series of word pairs to the learner, and then read the first word of the pair along with four terms. The learner was to indicate which of the four terms had originally been paired with the first word. He communicated his answer by pressing one of four switches in front of him, which in turn lit up one of four numbered quadrants in an answer-box located atop the shock generator.

Shock generator.   The instrument panel consists of 30 lever switches set in a horizontal line. Each switch is clearly labeled with a voltage designation that ranges from 15 to 450 volts. There is a 15-volt increment from one switch to the next going from left to right. In addition, the following verbal designations are clearly indicated for groups of four switches going from left to right: Slight Shock, Moderate Shock, Strong Shock, Very Strong Shock, Intense Shock, Extreme Intensity Shock, Danger: Severe Shock. (Two switches after this last designation are simply marked XXX.)

Upon depressing a switch: a pilot light corresponding to each switch is illuminated in bright red; an electric buzzing is heard; an electric blue light, labeled "voltage energizer," flashes; the dial on the voltage meter swings to the right; various relay clicks are sounded.

The upper left-hand corner of the generator is labeled Shock Generator, Type ZLB, Dyson Instrument Company, Waltham, Mass. Output 15 Volts—450 Volts.

Details of the instrument were carefully handled to insure an appearance of authenticity. The panel was engraved by precision industrial engravers, and all components were of high quality. No subject in the experiment suspected that the instrument was merely a simulated shock generator.[1]

Sample shock.   Each naive subject is given a sample shock on the shock generator, prior to beginning his run as teacher. This shock is always 45 volts, and is applied by pressing the third switch of the generator. The shock is applied to the wrist of the naive subject, and has its source in a 45-volt battery wired into the generator. This further convinces the subject of the authenticity of the generator.

Shock instructions.   The subject is told to administer a shock to the learner each time he gives a wrong response. Moreover—and this is the key command— the subject is instructed to "move one lever higher on the shock generator each time the learner flashes a wrong answer." He is also instructed to announce the voltage level before administering a shock. This serves to continually remind subjects of the increasing intensity of shocks administered to the learner.

Preliminary and regular run.   Pretests revealed that the procedure of reading words and administering shocks requires some practice before it can be handled smoothly. Therefore, immediately preceding the regular run, the teacher is given a preliminary series of 10 words to read to the learner. There are 3 neutral words in the practice series (i.e., words that the learner answers correctly), so that shocks are administered for 7 of the words, with the maximum shock at 105 volts (moderate shock). Almost all subjects master the procedure by the time the preliminary run is over.

Subjects are then presented with a second list, and are told that the procedure is the same as for the first list; the experimenter adds, however:

> When you get to the bottom of the list, repeat it over again, and continue giving shocks, until the learner has learned all the pairs correctly.

The experimenter instructs the subject to

> start from 15 volts and increase the shock level one step each time the learner gives a wrong answer.

Feedback from the victim.   In all conditions the learner gives a predetermined set of responses to the word pair test, based on a schedule of approximately three wrong answers to one correct answer. In the present experimental condition

---

[1]A related technique, making use of a shock generator, was reported by Buss (1961) for the study of aggression in the laboratory. Despite the considerable similarity of technical detail in the experimental procedures, each investigator proceeded in ignorance of the other's work. Milgram provided plans and photographs of his shock generator, experimental procedure, and first results in a report to the National Science Foundation in January 1961. This report received only limited circulation. Buss reported his procedure six months later, but to a wider audience. Subsequently, technical information and reports were exchanged. The present article was first received in the editor's office on December 27, 1961; it was resubmitted with deletions on July 27, 1962.

no vocal response or other sign of protest is heard from the learner until Shock Level 300 is reached. When the 300-volt shock is administered, the learner pounds on the wall of the room in which he is bound to the electric chair. The pounding can be heard by the subject. From this point on, the learner's answers no longer appear on the four-way panel.

At this juncture, subjects ordinarily turn to the experimenter for guidance. The experimenter instructs the subject to treat the absence of a response as a wrong answer, and to shock the subject according to the usual schedule. He advises the subjects to allow 5–10 seconds before considering no response as a wrong answer, and to increase the shock level one step each time the learner fails to respond correctly. The learner's pounding is repeated after the 315-volt shock is administered; afterwards he is not heard from, nor do his answers reappear on the four-way signal box.

Experimenter feedback. At various points in the experiment the subject may turn to the experimenter for advice on whether he should continue to administer shocks. Or he may indicate that he does not wish to go on. It was important to standardize the experimenter's responses to these inquiries and reactions.

If the subject indicated his unwillingness to go on, the experimenter responded with a sequence of "prods," using as many as necessary to bring the subject into line.

> Prod 1: Please continue. *or* Please go on.
> Prod 2: The experiment requires that you continue.
> Prod 3: It is absolutely essential that you continue.
> Prod 4: You have no other choice, you *must* go on.

The prods were always made in sequence: Only if Prod 1 had been unsuccessful, could Prod 2 be used. If the subject refused to obey the experimenter after Prod 4, the experiment was terminated. The experimenter's tone of voice was at all times firm, but not impolite. The sequence was begun anew on each occasion that the subject balked or showed reluctance to follow orders.

Special prods. If the subject asked if the learner was liable to suffer permanent physical injury, the experimenter said:

> Although the shocks may be painful, there is no permanent tissue damage, so please go on. [Followed by Prods 2, 3, and 4 if necessary.]

If the subject said that the learner did not want to go on, the experimenter replied:

> Whether the learner likes it or not, you must go on until he has learned all the word pairs correctly. So please go on. [Followed by Prods 2, 3, and 4 if necessary.]

Dependent Measures

The primary dependent measure for any subject is the maximum shock he administers before he refuses to go any further. In principle this may vary from 0 (for a subject who refuses to administer even the first shock) to 30 (for a subject who administers the highest shock on the generator). A subject who breaks off the experiment at any point prior to administering the thirtieth shock level is termed a *defiant* subject. One who complies with experimental commands fully, and proceeds to administer all shock levels commanded, is termed an *obedient* subject.

Further records.   With few exceptions, experimental sessions were recorded on magnetic tape. Occasional photographs were taken through one-way mirrors. Notes were kept on any unusual behavior occurring during the course of the experiments. On occasion, additional observers were directed to write objective descriptions of the subjects' behavior. The latency and duration of shocks were measured by accurate timing devices.

Interview and dehoax.   Following the experiment, subjects were interviewed; open-ended questions, projective measures, and attitude scales were employed. After the interview, procedures were undertaken to assure that the subject would leave the laboratory in a state of well being. A friendly reconciliation was arranged between the subject and the victim, and an effort was made to reduce any tensions that arose as a result of the experiment.

RESULTS

Preliminary Notions

Before giving an account of the experimental results, it is instructive to consider how persons predict others will perform when commanded to administer powerful shocks to another person. Fourteen Yale seniors, all psychology majors, were provided with a detailed description of the experimental situation. They were asked to reflect carefully on it, and to predict the behavior of 100 hypothetical subjects. More specifically, they were instructed to plot the distribution of obedience of "100 Americans of diverse occupations, and ranging in age from 20 to 50 years," who were placed in the experimental situation.

There was considerable agreement among the respondents on the expected behavior of hypothetical subjects. All respondents predicted that only an insignificant minority would go through to the end of the shock series. (The estimates ranged from 0 to 3 percent; i.e., the most "pessimistic" member of the class predicted that of 100 persons, 3 would continue through to the most potent shock available on the shock generator—450 volts.) The class mean was 1.2 percent. The question was also posed informally to colleagues of the author, and the most general feeling was that few if any subjects would go beyond the designation Very Strong Shock.

Result of Experiment I

Subjects accept situation. With few exceptions subjects were convinced of the reality of the experimental situation, that they were administering shocks to another person, and the most potent shocks were extremely painful. In the post-experimental interview subjects were asked: "How painful to the learner were the last few shocks that you administered to him?" Subjects were instructed to indicate their answers on a printed 14-point scale ranging from "Not at all painful" to "Extremely painful." The modal response was 14 (Extremely painful) with the mean at 13.42.

Signs of extreme tension. Many subjects showed signs of nervousness in the experimental situation, and especially upon administering the more powerful shocks. In a large number of cases the degree of tension reached extremes that are rarely seen in sociopsychological laboratory studies. Subjects were observed to sweat, tremble, stutter, bite their lips, groan, and dig their fingernails into their flesh. These were characteristic rather than exceptional responses to the experiment.

One sign of tension was the regular occurrence of nervous laughing fits. Fourteen of the 40 subjects showed definite signs of nervous laughter and smiling. The laughter seemed entirely out of place, even bizarre. Full-blown, uncontrollable seizures were observed for 3 subjects. On one occasion we observed a seizure so violently convulsive that it was necessary to call a halt to the experiment. The subject, a 46-year-old encyclopedia salesman, was seriously embarrassed by his untoward and uncontrollable behavior. In the post-experimental interviews subjects took pains to point out that they were not sadistic types, and that the laughter did not mean they enjoyed shocking the victim.

Distribution of scores. It had been conjectured that persons would not, in general, agree to administer shocks beyond the level designated as Very Strong Shock. The distribution of maximum shocks for this experiment is shown in Table 4.2. The obtained distribution of scores deviates radically from the prediction.

Upon command of the experimenter, each of the 40 subjects went beyond the expected breakoff point. No subject stopped prior to administering Shock Level 20. (At this level—300 volts—the victim kicks on the wall and no longer provides answers to the teacher's multiple-choice questions.)

Of the 40 subjects, 5 refused to obey the experimental commands beyond the 300-volt level. Four more subjects administered one further shock, and then refused to go on. Two broke off at the 330-volt level, and 1 each at 345, 360, and 375 volts. Thus a total of 14 subjects defied the experimenter. It is instructive to reprint their remarks at the point of defiance, as transcribed from the tape recordings:

> [0124] I think he's trying to communicate, he's knocking . . . Well it's not fair to shock the guy . . . these are terrific volts. I don't think this is very humane . . . Oh, I

TABLE 4.2
Distribution of breakoff points

Verbal designation and voltage indication	Number of subjects for whom this was maximum shock
Slight Shock	
15	0
30	0
45	0
60	0
Moderate Shock	
75	0
90	0
105	0
120	0
Strong Shock	
135	0
150	0
165	0
180	0
Very Strong Shock	
195	0
210	0
225	0
240	0
Intense Shock	
255	0
270	0
285	0
300	5
Extreme Intensity Shock	
315	4
330	2
345	1
360	1
Danger: Severe Shock	
375	1
390	0
405	0
420	0
XXX	
435	0
450	26

can't go on with this; no, this isn't right. It's a hell of an experiment. The guy is suffering in there. No, I don't want to go on. This is crazy. [Subject refused to administer more shocks.]

[0123] He's banging in there. I'm gonna chicken out. I'd like to continue, but I can't do that to a man . . . I'm sorry I can't do that to a man. I'll hurt his heart. You take your check . . . No really, I couldn't do it.

These subjects were frequently in a highly agitated and even angered state. Sometimes, verbal protest was at a minimum, and the subject simply got up from his chair in front of the shock generator, and indicated that he wished to leave the laboratory.

Of the 40 subjects, 26 obeyed the orders of the experimenter to the end, proceeding to punish the victim until they reached the most potent shock available on the shock generator. At that point, the experimenter called a halt to the session. (The maximum shock is labeled 450 volts, and is two steps beyond the designation: Danger: Severe Shock.) Although obedient subjects continued to administer shocks, they often did so under extreme stress. Some expressed reluctance to administer shocks beyond the 300-volt level, and displayed fears similar to those who defied the experimenter; yet they obeyed.

After the maximum shocks had been delivered, and the experimenter called a halt to the proceedings, many obedient subjects heaved sighs of relief, mopped their brows, rubbed their fingers over their eyes, or nervously fumbled cigarettes. Some shook their heads, apparently in regret. Some subjects had remained calm throughout the experiment, and displayed only minimal signs of tension from beginning to end.

DISCUSSION

The experiment yielded two findings that were surprising. The first finding concerns the sheer strength of obedient tendencies manifested in this situation. Subjects have learned from childhood that it is a fundamental breach of moral conduct to hurt another person against his will. Yet, 26 subjects abandon this tenet in following the instructions of an authority who has no special powers to enforce his commands. To disobey would bring no material loss to the subject; no punishment would ensue. It is clear from the remarks and outward behavior of many participants that in punishing the victim they are often acting against their own values. Subjects often expressed deep disapproval of shocking a man in the face of his objections, and others denounced it as stupid and senseless. Yet the majority complied with the experimental commands. This outcome was surprising from two perspectives: first, from the standpoint of predictions made in the questionnaire described earlier. (Here, however, it is possible that the remoteness of the respondents from the actual situation, and the difficulty of conveying to them the concrete details of the experiment, could account for the serious underestimation of obedience.)

But the results were also unexpected to persons who observed the experiment in progress, through one-way mirrors. Observers often uttered expressions of disbelief upon seeing a subject administer more powerful shocks to the victim. These persons had a full acquaintance with the details of the situation, and yet systematically underestimated the amount of obedience that subjects would display.

The second unanticipated effect was the extraordinary tension generated by the procedures. One might suppose that a subject would simply break off or continue as his conscience dictated. Yet, this is very far from what happened. There were striking reactions of tension and emotional strain. One observer related:

> I observed a mature and initially poised businessman enter the laboratory smiling and confident. Within 20 minutes he was reduced to a twitching, stuttering wreck, who was rapidly approaching a point of nervous collapse. He constantly pulled on his earlobe, and twisted his hands. At one point he pushed his fist into his forehead and muttered: "Oh God, let's stop it." And yet he continued to respond to every word of the experimenter, and obeyed to the end.

Any understanding of the phenomenon of obedience must rest on an analysis of the particular conditions in which it occurs. The following features of the experiment go some distance in explaining the high amount of obedience observed in the situation.

1. The experiment is sponsored by and takes place on the grounds of an institution of unimpeachable reputation, Yale University. It may be reasonably presumed that the personnel are competent and reputable. The importance of this background authority is now being studied by conducting a series of experiments outside of New Haven, and without any visible ties to the university.

2. The experiment is, on the face of it, designed to attain a worthy purpose—advancement of knowledge about learning and memory. Obedience occurs not as an end in itself, but as an instrumental element in a situation that the subject construes as significant, and meaningful. He may not be able to see its full significance, but he may properly assume that the experimenter does.

3. The subject perceives that the victim has voluntarily submitted to the authority system of the experimenter. He is not (at first) an unwilling captive impressed for involuntary service. He has taken the trouble to come to the laboratory presumably to aid the experimental research. That he later becomes an involuntary subject does not alter the fact that, initially, he consented to participate without qualification. Thus he has in some degree incurred an obligation toward the experimenter.

4. The subject, too, has entered the experiment voluntarily, and perceives himself under obligation to aid the experimenter. He has made a commitment, and to disrupt the experiment is a repudiation of this initial promise of aid.

5. Certain features of the procedure strengthen the subject's sense of obligation to the experimenter. For one, he has been paid for coming to the laboratory. In part this is canceled out by the experimenter's statement that:

> Of course, as in all experiments, the money is yours simply for coming to the laboratory. From this point on, no matter what happens, the money is yours.[2]

6. From the subject's standpoint, the fact that he is the teacher and the other man the learner is purely a chance consequence (it is determined by drawing lots) and he, the subject, ran the same risk as the other man in being assigned the role of

---

[2]Forty-three subjects, undergraduates at Yale University, were run in the experiment without payment. The results are very similar to those obtained with paid subjects.

learner. Since the assignment of positions in the experiment was achieved by fair means, the learner is deprived of any basis of complaint on this count. (A similar situation obtains in Army units, in which—in the absence of volunteers—a particularly dangerous mission may be assigned by drawing lots, and the unlucky soldier is expected to bear his misfortune with sportsmanship.)

7. There is, at best, ambiguity with regard to the prerogatives of a psychologist and the corresponding rights of his subject. There is a vagueness of expectation concerning what a psychologist may require of his subject, and when he is overstepping acceptable limits. Moreover, the experiment occurs in a closed setting, and thus provides no opportunity for the subject to remove these ambiguities by discussion with others. There are few standards that seem directly applicable to the situation, which is a novel one for most subjects.

8. The subjects are assured that the shocks administered to the subject are "painful but not dangerous." Thus they assume that the discomfort caused the victim is momentary, while the scientific gains resulting from the experiment are enduring.

9. Through Shock Level 20 the victim continues to provide answers on the signal box. The subject may construe this as a sign that the victim is still willing to "play the game." It is only after Shock Level 20 that the victim repudiates the rules completely, refusing to answer further.

These features help to explain the high amount of obedience obtained in this experiment. Many of the arguments raised need not remain matters of speculation, but can be reduced to testable propositions to be confirmed or disproved by further experiments.[3]

The following features of the experiment concern the nature of the conflict which the subject faces.

10. The subject is placed in a position in which he must respond to the competing demands of two persons: the experimenter and the victim. The conflict must be resolved by meeting the demands of one or the other; satisfaction of the victim and the experimenter are mutually exclusive. Moreover, the resolution must take the form of a highly visible action, that of continuing to shock the victim or breaking off the experiment. Thus the subject is forced into a public conflict that does not permit any completely satisfactory solution.

11. While the demands of the experimenter carry the weight of scientific authority, the demands of the victim spring from his personal experience of pain and suffering. The two claims need not be regarded as equally pressing and legitimate. The experimenter seeks an abstract scientific datum; the victim cries out for relief from physical suffering caused by the subject's actions.

12. The experiment gives the subject little time for reflection. The conflict comes on rapidly. It is only minutes after the subject has been seated before the

---

[3]A series of recently completed experiments employing the obedience paradigm is reported in Milgram (1965).

shock generator that the victim begins his protests. Moreover, the subject perceives that he has gone through but two-thirds of the shock levels at the time the subject's first protests are heard. Thus he understands that the conflict will have a persistent aspect to it, and may well become more intense as increasingly more powerful shocks are required. The rapidity with which the conflict descends on the subject, and his realization that it is predictably recurrent may well be sources of tension to him.

13. At a more general level, the conflict stems from the opposition of two deeply ingrained behavior dispositions: first, the disposition not to harm other people, and second, the tendency to obey those whom we perceive to be legitimate authorities.

References

ADORNO, T., FRENKEL-BRUNSWIK, ELSE, LEVINSON, D. J., AND SANFORD, R. N. *The authoritarian personality.* New York: Harper, 1950.

ARENDT, H. What was authority? In C. J. Friedrich (ed.), *Authority.* Cambridge: Harvard Univer. Press, 1958. Pp. 81–112.

BINET, A. *La suggestibilité.* Paris: Schleicher, 1900.

BUSS, A. H. *The psychology of aggression.* New York: Wiley, 1961.

CARTWRIGHT, S. (ed.) *Studies in social power.* Ann Arbor: University of Michigan Institute for Social Research, 1959.

CHARCOT, J. M. *Oeuvres complètes.* Paris: Bureaux du Progrès Médical, 1881.

FRANK, J. D. Experimental studies of personal pressure and resistance. *J. gen. Psychol.,* 1944, **30,** 23–64.

FRIEDRICH, C. J. (ed.) *Authority.* Cambridge: Harvard Univer. Press, 1958.

MILGRAM, S. Dynamics of obedience. Washington: National Science Foundation, 25 January 1961. (Mimeo)

MILGRAM, S. Some conditions of obedience and disobedience to authority. *Hum. Relat.,* 1965, **18,** 57–76.

ROKEACH, M. Authority, authoritarianism, and conformity. In I. A. Berg and B. M. Bass (eds.), *Conformity and deviation.* New York: Harper, 1961. Pp. 230–257.

SNOW, C. P. Either-or. *Progressive,* 1961 (Feb.), 24.

WEBER, M. *The theory of social and economic organization.* Oxford: Oxford Univer. Press, 1947.

5

"From Jerusalem to Jericho": A Study of Situational and Dispositional Variables in Helping Behavior

John M. Darley and C. Daniel Batson

The influence of several situational and personality variables on helping behavior was examined in an emergency situation suggested by the parable of the Good Samaritan. People going between two buildings encountered a shabbily dressed person slumped by the side of the road. Subjects in a hurry to reach their destination were more likely to pass by without stopping. Some subjects were going to give a short talk on the parable of the Good Samaritan, others on a nonhelping relevant topic; this made no significant difference in the likelihood of their giving the victim help. Religious personality variables did not predict whether an individual would help the victim or not. However, if a subject did stop to offer help, the character of the helping response was related to his type of religiosity.

Helping other people in distress is, among other things, an ethical act. That is, it is an act governed by ethical norms and precepts taught to children at home, in school, and in church. From Freudian and other personality theories, one would expect individual differences in internalization of these standards that would lead to differences between individuals in the likelihood with which they would help others. But recent research on bystander intervention in emergency situations (Bickman, 1969; Darley & Lantané, 1968; Korte, 1969; but see also Schwartz & Clausen, 1970) has had bad luck in finding personality determinants of helping behavior. Although personality variables that one might expect to correlate with helping behavior have been measured (Machiavellianism, authoritarianism, social

Reprinted with permission of the authors and *The Journal of Personality and Social Psychology,* Vol. 27, No. 1, 1973. Copyright © 1973 by The American Psychological Association.

For assistance in conducting this research thanks are due Robert Wells, Beverly Fisher, Mike Shafto, Peter Sheras, Richard Detweiler, and Karen Glasser. The research was funded by National Science Foundation Grant GS-2293.

desirability, alienation, and social responsibility), these were not predictive of helping. Nor was this due to a generalized lack of predictability in the helping situation examined, since variations in the experimental situation, such as the availability of other people who might also help, produced marked changes in rates of helping behavior. These findings are reminiscent of Hartshorne and May's (1928) discovery that resistance to temptation, another ethically relevant act, did not seem to be a fixed characteristic of an individual. That is, a person who was likely to be honest in one situation was not particularly likely to be honest in the next (but see also Burton, 1963).

The rather disappointing correlation between the social psychologist's traditional set of personality variables and helping behavior in emergency situations suggests the need for a fresh perspective on possible predictors of helping and possible situations in which to test them. Therefore, for inspiration we turned to the Bible, to what is perhaps the classical helping story in the Judeo-Christian tradition, the parable of the Good Samaritan. The parable proved of value in suggesting both personality and situational variables relevant to helping.

> "And who is my neighbor?" Jesus replied, "A man was going down from Jerusalem to Jericho, and he fell among robbers, who stripped him and beat him, and departed, leaving him half dead. Now by chance a priest was going down the road; and when he saw him he passed by on the other side. So likewise a Levite, when he came to the place and saw him, passed by on the other side. But a Samaritan, as he journeyed, came to where he was; and when he saw him, he had compassion, and went to him and bound his wounds, pouring on oil and wine; then he set him on his own beast and brought him to an inn, and took care of him. And the next day he took out two dennarii and gave them to the innkeeper, saying, "Take care of him; and whatever more you spend, I will repay you when I come back." Which of these three, do you think, proved neighbor to him who fell among the robbers? He said, "The one who showed mercy on him." And Jesus said to him, "Go and do likewise." [Luke 10: 29–37 RSV]

To psychologists who reflect on the parable, it seems to suggest situational and personality differences between the nonhelpful priest and Levite and the helpful Samaritan. What might each have been thinking and doing when he came upon the robbery victim on that desolate road? What sort of persons were they?

One can speculate on differences in thought. Both the priest and the Levite were religious functionaries who could be expected to have their minds occupied with religious matters. The priest's role in religious activities is obvious. The Levite's role, although less obvious, is equally important: The Levites were necessary participants in temple ceremonies. Much less can be said with any confidence about what the Samaritan might have been thinking, but, in contrast to the others, it was most likely not of a religious nature, for Samaritans were religious outcasts.

Not only was the Samaritan most likely thinking about more mundane matters than the priest and Levite, but, because he was socially less important, it seems likely that he was operating on a quite different time schedule. One can imagine the priest and Levite, prominent public figures, hurrying along with little black books full of meetings and appointments, glancing furtively at their sundials. In contrast, the Samaritan would likely have far fewer and less important people counting on him to be at a particular place at a particular time, and therefore might be expected to be in less of a hurry than the prominent priest or Levite.

In addition to these situational variables, one finds personality factors suggested as well. Central among these, and apparently basic to the point that Jesus was trying to make, is a distinction between types of religiosity. Both the priest and Levite are extremely "religious." But it seems to be precisely their type of religiosity that the parable challenges. At issue is the motivation for one's religion and ethical behavior. Jesus seems to feel that the religious leaders of his time, though certainly respected and upstanding citizens, may be "virtuous" for what it will get them, both in terms of the admiration of their fellowmen and in the eyes of God. New Testament scholar R. W. Funk (1966) noted that the Samaritan is at the other end of the spectrum:

> The Samaritan does not love with side glances at God. The need of neighbor alone is made self-evident, and the Samaritan responds without other motivation [pp. 218–219].

That is, the Samaritan is interpreted as responding spontaneously to the situation, not as being preoccupied with the abstract ethical or organizational do's and don'ts of religion as the priest and Levite would seem to be. This is not to say that the Samaritan is portrayed as irreligious. A major intent of the parable would seem to be to present the Samaritan as a religious and ethical example, but at the same time to contrast his type of religiosity with the more common conception of religiosity that the priest and Levite represent.

To summarize the variables suggested as affecting helping behavior by the parable, the situational variables include the content of one's thinking and the amount of hurry in one's journey. The major dispositional variable seems to be differing types of religiosity. Certainly these variables do not exhaust the list that could be elicited from the parable, but they do suggest several research hypotheses.

Hypothesis 1. The parable implies that people who encounter a situation possibly calling for a helping response while thinking religious and ethical thoughts will be no more likely to offer aid than persons thinking about something else. Such a hypothesis seems to run counter to a theory that focuses on norms as determining helping behavior because a normative account would predict that the increased salience of helping norms produced by thinking about religious and ethical examples would increase helping behavior.

Hypothesis 2. Persons encountering a possible helping situation when they are in a hurry will be less likely to offer aid than persons not in a hurry.

Hypothesis 3. Concerning types of religiosity, persons who are religious in a Samaritan-like fashion will help more frequently than those religious in a priest or Levite fashion.

Obviously, this last hypothesis is hardly operationalized as stated. Prior research by one of the investigators on types of religiosity (Batson, 1971), however, led us to differentiate three distinct ways of being religious: *(a)* for what it will gain one (cf. Freud, 1927, and perhaps the priest and Levite), *(b)* for its own intrinsic value (cf. Allport and Ross, 1967), and *(c)* as a response to and quest for meaning in one's everyday life (cf. Batson, 1971). Both of the latter conceptions would be proposed by their exponents as related to the more Samaritanlike "true" religiosity. Therefore, depending on the theorist one follows, the third hypothesis may be stated like this: People *(a)* who are religious for intrinsic reasons (Allport and Ross, 1967) or *(b)* whose religion emerges out of questioning the meaning of their everyday lives (Batson, 1971) will be more likely to stop to offer help to the victim.

The parable of the Good Samaritan also suggested how we would measure people's helping behavior—their response to a stranger slumped by the side of one's path. The victim should appear somewhat ambiguous—ill-dressed, possibly in need of help, but also possibly drunk or even potentially dangerous.

Further, the parable suggests a means by which the incident could be perceived as a real one rather than part of a psychological experiment in which one's behavior was under surveillance and might be shaped by demand characteristics (Orne, 1962), evaluation apprehension (Rosenberg, 1965), or other potentially artifactual determinants of helping behavior. The victim should be encountered not in the experimental context but on the road between various tasks.

METHOD

In order to examine the influence of these variables on helping behavior, seminary students were asked to participate in a study on religious education and vocations. In the first testing session, personality questionnaires concerning types of religiosity were administered. In a second individual session, the subject began experimental procedures in one building and was asked to report to another building for later procedures. While in transit, the subject passed a slumped "victim" planted in an alleyway. The dependent variable was whether and how the subject helped the victim. The independent variables were the degree to which the subject was told to hurry in reaching the other building and the talk he was to give when he arrived there. Some subjects were to give a talk on the jobs in which seminary students would be most effective, others, on the parable of the Good Samaritan.

Subjects

The subjects for the questionnaire administration were 67 students at Princeton Theological Seminary. Forty-seven of them, those who could be reached by telephone, were scheduled for the experiment. Of the 47, 7 subjects' data were not included in the analyses—3 because of contamination of the experimental procedures during their testing and 4 due to suspicion of the experimental situation. Each subject was paid $1 for the questionnaire session and $1.50 for the experimental session.

Personality Measures

Detailed discussion of the personality scales used may be found elsewhere (Batson, 1971), so the present discussion will be brief. The general personality construct under examination was religiosity. Various conceptions of religiosity have been offered in recent years based on different psychometric scales. The conception seeming to generate the most interest is the Allport and Ross (1967) distinction between "intrinsic" versus "extrinsic" religiosity (cf. also Allen and Spilka, 1967, on "committed" versus "consensual" religion). This bipolar conception of religiosity has been questioned by Brown (1964) and Batson (1971), who suggested three-dimensional analyses instead. Therefore, in the present research, types of religiosity were measured with three instruments which together provided six separate scales: *(a)* a *doctrinal orthodoxy* (D-O) scale patterned after that used by Glock and Stark (1966), scaling agreement with classic doctrines of Protestant theology; *(b)* the Allport-Ross *extrinsic* (AR-E) scale, measuring the use of religion as a means to an end rather than as an end in itself; *(c)* the Allport-Ross *intrinsic* (AR-I) scale, measuring the use of religion as an end in itself; *(d)* the *extrinsic external* scale of Batson's Religious Life Inventory (RELI-EE), designed to measure the influence of significant others and situations in generating one's religiosity; *(e)* the *extrinsic internal* scale of the Religious Life Inventory (RELI-EI), designed to measure the degree of "driveness" in one's religiosity; and *(f)* the *intrinsic* scale of the Religious Life Inventory (RELI-I), designed to measure the degree to which one's religiosity involves a questioning of the meaning of life arising out of one's interactions with his social environment. The order of presentation of the scales in the questionnaire was RELI, AR, D-O.

Consistent with prior research (Batson, 1971), a principal-component analysis of the total scale scores and individual items for the 67 seminarians produced a theoretically meaningful, orthogonally rotated three-component structure with the following loadings:

Religion as means received a single very high loading from AR-E (.903) and therefore was defined by Allport and Ross's (1967) conception of this scale as measuring religiosity as a means to other ends. This component also received moderate negative loadings from D-O ($-.400$) and AR-I ($-.372$) and a moderate positive loading from RELI-EE (.301).

Religion as end received high loadings from RELI-EI (.874), RELI-EE (.725), AR-I (.768), and D-O (.704). Given this configuration, and again following Allport and Ross's conceptualization, this component seemed to involve religiosity as an end in itself with some intrinsic value.

Religion as quest received a single very high loading from RELI-I (.945) and a moderate loading from RELI-EE (.75). Following Batson, this component was conceived to involve religiosity emerging out of an individual's search for meaning in his personal and social world.

The three religious personality scales examined in the experimental research were constructed through the use of complete-estimation factor score coefficients from these three components.

Scheduling of Experimental Study

Since the incident requiring a helping response was staged outdoors, the entire experimental study was run in 3 days, December 14–16, 1970, between 10 A.M. and 4 P.M. A tight schedule was used in an attempt to maintain reasonably consistent weather and light conditions. Temperature fluctuation according to the *New York Times* for the 3 days during these hours was not more than 5 degrees Fahrenheit. No rain or snow fell, although the third day was cloudy, whereas the first two were sunny. Within days the subjects were randomly assigned to experimental conditions.[1]

Procedure

When a subject appeared for the experiment, an assistant (who was blind with respect to the personality scores) asked him to read a brief statement which explained that he was participating in a study of the vocational careers of seminary students. After developing the rationale for the study, the statement read:

> What we have called you in for today is to provide us with some additional material which will give us a clearer picture of how you think than does the questionnaire material we have gathered thus far. Questionnaires are helpful, but tend to be somewhat oversimplified. Therefore, we would like to record a 3–5-minute talk you give based on the following passage. . . .

Variable 1: Message.   In the task-relevant condition the passage read,

> With increasing frequency the question is being asked: What jobs or professions do seminary students subsequently enjoy most, and in what jobs are they most effective? The answer to this question used to be so obvious that the question was not

---

[1]An error was made in randomizing that increased the number of subjects in the intermediate-hurry conditions. This worked against the prediction that was most highly confirmed (the hurry prediction) and made no difference to the message variable tests.

even asked. Seminary students were being trained for the ministry, and since both society at large and the seminary student himself had a relatively clear understanding of what made a "good" minister, there was no need even to raise the question of for what other jobs seminary experience seems to be an asset. Today, however, neither society nor many seminaries have a very clearly defined conception of what a "good" minister is or of what sorts of jobs and professions are the best context in which to minister. Many seminary students, apparently genuinely concerned with "ministering," seem to feel that it is impossible to minister in the professional clergy. Other students, no less concerned, find the clergy the most viable profession for ministry. But are there other jobs and/or professions for which seminary experience is an asset? And, indeed, how much of an asset is it for the professional ministry? Or, even more broadly, can one minister through an "establishment" job at all?

In the helping-relevant condition, the subject was given the parable of the Good Samaritan exactly as printed earlier in this article. Next, regardless of condition, all subjects were told,

> You can say whatever you wish based on the passage. Because we are interested in how you think on your feet, you will not be allowed to use notes in giving the talk. Do you understand what you are to do? If not, the assistant will be glad to answer questions.

After a few minutes the assistant returned, asked if there were any questions, and then said:

> Since they're rather tight on space in this building, we're using a free office in the building next door for recording the talks. Let me show you how to get there [draws and explains map on 3 × 5 card]. This is where Professor Steiner's laboratory is. If you go in this door [points at map], there's a secretary right here, and she'll direct you to the office we're using for recording. Another of Professor Steiner's assistants will set you up for recording your talk. Is the map clear?

Variable 2: Hurry. In the high-hurry condition the assistant then looked at his watch and said, "Oh, you're late. They were expecting you a few minutes ago. We'd better get moving. The assistant should be waiting for you so you'd better hurry. It shouldn't take but just a minute." In the intermediate-hurry condition he said, "The assistant is ready for you, so please go right over." In the low-hurry condition he said, "It'll be a few minutes before they're ready for you, but you might as well head on over. If you have to wait over there, it shouldn't be long."

The incident. When the subject passed through the alley, the victim was sitting slumped in a doorway, head down, eyes closed, not moving. As the subject went by, the victim coughed twice and groaned, keeping his head down. If the subject stopped and asked if something was wrong or offered to help, the victim, startled and somewhat groggy, said, "Oh, thank you [cough]. . . . No, it's all right. [Pause] I've got this respiratory condition [cough]. . . . The doctor's given me these pills to take, and I just took one. . . . If I just sit and rest for a few minutes I'll be O.K. . . . Thanks very much for stopping though [smiles weakly]." If the subject persisted, insisting on taking the victim inside the building, the victim allowed him to do so and thanked him.

Helping ratings.   The victim rates each subject on a scale of helping behavior as follows:

> 0 = failed to notice the victim as possibly in need at all; 1 = perceived the victim as possibly in need but did not offer aid; 2 = did not stop but helped indirectly (e.g., by telling Steiner's assistant about the victim); 3 = stopped and asked if victim needed help; 4 = after stopping, insisted on taking the victim inside and then left him.

The victim was blind to the personality scale scores and experimental conditions of all subjects. At the suggestion of the victim, another category was added to the rating scales, based on his observations of pilot subjects' behavior:

> 5 = after stopping, refused to leave the victim (after 3–5 minutes) and/or insisted on taking him somewhere outside experimental context (e.g., for coffee or to the infirmary).

(In some cases it was necessary to distinguish Category 0 from Category 1 by the postexperimental questionnaire and Category 2 from Category 1 on the report of the experimental assistant.)

This 6-point scale of helping behavior and a description of the victim were given to a panel of 10 judges (unacquainted with the research) who were asked to rank order the (unnumbered) categories in terms of "the amount of helping behavior displayed toward the person in the doorway." Of the 10, 1 judge reversed the order of Categories 0 and 1. Otherwise there was complete agreement with the ranking implied in the presentation of the scale above.

The speech.   After passing through the alley and entering the door marked on the map, the subject entered a secretary's office. She introduced him to the assistant who gave the subject time to prepare and privately record his talk.

Helping behavior questionnaire.   After recording the talk, the subject was sent to another experimenter, who administered "an exploratory questionnaire on personal and social ethics." The questionnaire contained several initial questions about the interrelationship between social and personal ethics, and then asked three key questions: *(a)* "When was the last time you saw a person who seemed to be in need of help?" *(b)* "When was the last time you stopped to help someone in need?" *(c)* "Have you had experience helping persons in need? If so, outline briefly." These data were collected as a check on the victim's ratings of whether subjects who did not stop perceived the situation in the alley as one possibly involving need or not.

When he returned, the experimenter reviewed the subject's questionnaire, and, if no mention was made of the situation in the alley, probed for reactions to it and then phased into an elaborate debriefing and discussion session.

Debriefing

In the debriefing, the subject was told the exact nature of the study, including the deception involved, and the reasons for the deception were explained. The subject's reactions to the victim and to the study in general were discussed. The role of situational determinants of helping behavior was explained in relation to this particular incident and to other experiences of the subject. All subjects seemed readily to understand the necessity for the deception, and none indicated any resentment of it. After debriefing, the subject was thanked for his time and paid, then he left.

RESULTS AND DISCUSSION

Overall Helping Behavior

The average amount of help that a subject offered the victim, by condition, is shown in Table 5.1. The unequal-N analysis of variance indicates that while the hurry variable was significantly ($F = 3.56$, $df = 2/34$, $p < .05$) related to helping behavior, the message variable was not. Subjects in a hurry were likely to offer less help than were subjects not in a hurry. Whether the subject was going to give a speech on the parable of the Good Samaritan or not did not significantly affect his helping behavior on this analysis.

TABLE 5.1
Means and analysis of variance of graded helping responses

	M			
		Hurry		
Message	Low	Medium	High	Summary
Helping relevant	3.800	2.000	1.000	2.263
Task relevant	1.667	1.667	.500	1.333
Summary	3.000	1.818	.700	

Analysis of variance				
Source	SS	df	MS	F
Message (A)	7.766	1	7.766	2.65
Hurry (B)	20.884	2	10.442	3.56*
A × B	5.237	2	2.619	.89
Error	99.633	34	2.930	

Note: $N = 40$.
*$p < .05$.

TABLE 5.2
Stepwise multiple regression analysis

| | Help vs. no help | | | | Graded helping | | | |
| | Individual variable | | Overall equation | | Individual variable | | Variable equation | |
Step	r^a	F	R	F	r	F	R	F
1. Hurry[b]	−.37	4.537*	.37	5.884*	−.42	6.665*	.42	8.196**
2. Message[c]	.25	1.495	.41	3.834*	.25	1.719	.46	5.083*
3. Religion as quest	−.03	.081	.42	2.521	−.16	1.297	.50	3.897*
4. Religion as means	−.03	.003	.42	1.838*	−.08	.018	.50	2.848*
5. Religion as end	.06	.000	.42	1.430	−.07	.001	.50	2.213

Note: $N = 40$. Helping is the dependent variable. $df = 1/34$.
[a]Individual variable correlation coefficient is a point biserial where appropriate.
[b]Variables are listed in order of entry into stepwise regression equations.
[c]Helping-relevant message is positive.
*$p < .05$.
**$p < .01$.

Other studies have focused on the question of whether a person initiates helping action or not, rather than on scaled kinds of helping. The data from the preset study can also be analyzed on the following terms: Of the 40 subjects, 16 (40%) offered some form of direct or indirect aid to the victim (Coding Categories 2–5), 24 (60%) did not (Coding Categories 0 and 1). The percentages of subjects who offered aid by situational variable were, for low hurry, 63% offered help, intermediate hurry 45%, and high hurry 10%; for helping-relevant message 53%, task-relevant message 29%. With regard to this more general question of whether help was offered or not, an unequal-N analysis of variance (arc sine transformation of percentages of helpers, with low- and intermediate-hurry conditions pooled) indicated that again only the hurry main effect was significantly ($F = 5.22, p < .05$) related to helping behavior; the subjects in a hurry were more likely to pass by the victim than were those in less of a hurry.

Reviewing the predictions in the light of these results, the second hypothesis, that the degree of hurry a person is in determines his helping behavior, was supported. The prediction involved in the first hypothesis concerning the message content was based on the parable. The parable itself seemed to suggest that thinking pious thoughts would not increase helping. Another and conflicting prediction might be produced by a norm salience theory. Thinking about the parable should make norms for helping salient and therefore produce more helping. The data, as hypothesized, are more congruent with the prediction drawn from the parable. A person going to speak on the parable of the Good Samaritan is not significantly more likely to stop to help a person by the side of the road than is a person going to talk about possible occupations for seminary graduates.

Since both situational hypotheses are confirmed, it is tempting to stop the analysis of these variables at this point. However, multiple regression analysis procedures were also used to analyze the relationship of all of the independent variables of the study and the helping behavior. In addition to often being more statistically powerful due to the use of more data information, multiple regression analysis has an advantage over analysis of variance in that it allows for a comparison of the relative effect of the various independent variables in accounting for variance in the dependent variable. Also, multiple regression analysis can compare the effects of continuous as well as nominal independent variables on both continuous and nominal dependent variables (through the use of point biserial correlations, r_{pb}) and shows considerable robustness to violation of normality assumptions (Cohen, 1965, 1968). Table 5.2 reports the results of the multiple regression analysis using both help versus no help and the graded helping scale as dependent measures. In this table the overall equation Fs show the F value of the entire regression equation as a particular row variable enters the equation. Individual variable Fs were computed with all five independent variables in the equation. Although the two situational variables, hurry and message condition, correlated more highly with the dependent measure than any of the religious dispositional variables, only hurry was a significant predictor of whether one will help or not (column 1) or of the overall amount of help given (column 2). These results corroborate the findings of the analysis of variance.[2]

Notice also that neither form of the third hypothesis, that types of religiosity will predict helping, received support from these data. No correlation between the various measures of religiosity and any form of the dependent measure ever came near statistical significance, even though the multiple regression analysis procedure is a powerful and not particularly conservative statistical test.

Personality Difference among Subjects Who Helped

To further investigate the possible influence of personality variables, analyses were carried out using only the data from subjects who offered some kind of help to the victim. Surprisingly (since the number of these subjects was small, only 16) when this was done, one religiosity variable seemed to be significantly related to the kind of helping behavior offered. (The situational variables had no significant effect.) Subjects high on the religion as quest dimension appear likely, when they stop for the victim, to offer help of a more tentative or incomplete nature than are subjects scoring low on this dimension ($r = -.53, p < .05$).

This result seemed unsettling for the thinking behind either form of Hypothesis 3. Not only do the data suggest that the Allport-Ross–based conception of religion as *end* does not predict the degree of helping, but the religion as quest component is a significant predictor of offering less help. This latter result seems counterintuitive and out of keeping with previous research (Batson, 1971), which found that this type of religiosity correlated positively with other socially valued characteristics. Further data analysis, however, seemed to suggest a different interpretation of this result.

It will be remembered that one helping coding category was added at the suggestion of the victim after his observation of pilot subjects. The correlation of religious personality variables with helping behavior dichotomized between the added category (1) and all of the others (0) was examined. The correlation between religion as quest and this dichotomous helping scale was essentially unchanged ($r_{pb} = -.54, p < .05$). Thus, the previously found correlation between the helping scale and religion as quest seems to reflect the tendency of those who score low on the quest dimension to offer help in the added helping category.

What does help in this added category represent? Within the context of .he experiment, it represented an embarrassment. The victim's response to persistent offers of help was to assure the helper he was all right, had taken his medicine, just needed to rest for a minute or so, and, if ultimately necessary, to request the helper

---

[2]To check the legitimacy of the use of both analysis of variance and multiple regression analysis, parametric analyses, on this ordinal data, Kendall rank correlation coefficients were calculated between the helping scale and the five independent variables. As expected τ approximated the correlation quite closely in each case and was significant for hurry only (hurry, $\tau = -.38, p < .001$).

to leave. But the *super* helpers in this added category often would not leave until the final appeal was repeated several times by the victim (who was growing increasingly panicky at the possibility of the arrival of the next subject). Since it usually involved the subject's attemping to carry through a preset plan (e.g., taking the subject for a cup of coffee or revealing to him the strength to be found in Christ), and did not allow information from the victim to change that plan, we originally labeled this kind of helping as rigid—an interpretation supported by its increased likelihood among highly doctrinal orthodox subjects ($r = .63$, $p < .01$). It also seemed to have an inappropriate character. If this more extreme form of helping behavior is indeed effectively less helpful, then the second form of Hypothesis 3 does seem to gain support.

But perhaps it is the experimenters rather than the super helpers who are doing the inappropriate thing; perhaps the best characterization of this kind of helping is as different rather than as inappropriate. This kind of helper seems quickly to place a particular interpretation on the situation, and the helping response seems to follow naturally from this interpretation. All that can safely be said is that one style of helping that emerged in this experiment was directed toward the presumed underlying needs of the victim and was little modified by the victim's comments about his own needs. In contrast, another style was more tentative and seemed more responsive to the victim's statements of his need.

The former kind of helping was likely to be displayed by subjects who expressed strong doctrinal orthodoxy. Conversely, this fixed kind of helping was unlikely among subjects high on the religion as quest dimension. These latter subjects, who conceived their religion as involving an ongoing search for meaning in their personal and social world, seemed more responsive to the victim's immediate needs and more open to the victim's definitions of his own needs.

CONCLUSION AND IMPLICATIONS

A person not in a hurry may stop and offer help to a person in distress. A person in a hurry is likely to keep going. Ironically, he is likely to keep going even if he is hurrying to speak on the parable of the Good Samaritan, thus inadvertently confirming the point of the parable. (Indeed, on several occasions, a seminary student going to give his talk on the parable of the Good Samaritan literally stepped over the victim as he hurried on his way!)

Although the degree to which a person was in a hurry had a clearly significant effect on his likelihood of offering the victim help, whether he was going to give a sermon on the parable or on possible vocational roles of ministers did not. This lack of effect of sermon topic raises certain difficulties for an explanation of helping behavior involving helping norms and their salience. It is hard to think of a context in which norms concerning helping those in distress are more salient than for a person thinking about the Good Samaritan, and yet it did not significantly increase helping behavior. The results were in the direction suggested by the norm salience hypothesis, but they were not significant. The most accurate conclusion seems to be that salience of helping norms is a less strong determinant of helping behavior in the present situation than many, including the present authors, would expect.

Thinking about the Good Samaritan did not increase helping behavior, but being in a hurry decreased it. It is difficult not to conclude from this that the frequently cited explanation that ethics becomes a luxury as the speed of our daily lives increases is at least an accurate description. The picture that this explanation conveys is of a person seeing another, consciously noting his distress, and consciously choosing to leave him in distress. But perhaps this is not entirely accurate, for, when a person is in a hurry, something seems to happen that is akin to Tolman's (1948) concept of the "narrowing of the cognitive map." Our seminarians in a hurry noticed the victim in that in the postexperiment interview almost all mentioned him as, on reflection, possibly in need of help. But it seems that they often had not worked this out when they were near the victim. Either the interpretation of their visual picture as a person in distress or the empathic reactions usually associated with that interpretation had been deferred because they were hurrying. According to the reflections of some of the subjects, it would be inaccurate to say that they realized the victim's possible distress, then chose to ignore it; instead, because of the time pressures, they did not perceive the scene in the alley as an occasion for an ethical decision.

For other subjects it seems more accurate to conclude that they decided not to stop. They appeared aroused and anxious after the encounter in the alley. For these subjects, what were the elements of the choice that they were making? Why were the seminarians hurrying? Because the experimenter, *whom the subject was helping,* was depending on him to get to a particular place quickly. In other words, he was in conflict between stopping to help the victim and continuing on his way to help the experimenter. And this is often true of people in a hurry; they hurry because somebody depends on their being somewhere. Conflict, rather than callousness, can explain their failure to stop.

Finally, as in other studies, personality variables were not useful in predicting whether a person helped or not. But in this study, unlike many previous ones, considerable variations were possible in the kinds of help given, and these variations did relate to personality measures—specifically to religiosity of the quest sort. The clear light of hindsight suggests that the dimension of kinds of helping would have been the appropriate place to look for personality differences all along; *whether* a person helps or not is an instant decision likely to be situationally controlled. How a person helps involves a more complex and considered number of decisions, including the time and scope to permit personality characteristics to shape them.

References

ALLEN, R. O., AND SPILKA, B. Committed and consensual religion. A specification of religion-prejudice relationships. *Journal for the Scientific Study of Religion,* 1967, **6**, 191–206.

ALLPORT, G. W., AND ROSS, J. M. Personal religious orientation and prejudice. *Journal of Personality and Social Psychology,* 1967, **5,** 432–443.

BATSON, C. D. Creativity and religious development: Toward a structural-functional psychology of religion. Unpublished doctoral dissertation, Princeton Theological Seminary, 1971.

BICKMAN, L. B. The effect of the presence of others on bystander intervention in an emergency. Unpublished doctoral dissertation, City College of the City University of New York, 1969.

BROWN, L. B. Classifications of religious orientation. *Journal for the Scientific Study of Religion,* 1964, **4,** 91–99.

BURTON, R. V. The generality of honesty reconsidered. *Psychological Review,* 1963, **70,** 481–499.

COHEN, J. Multiple regression as a general data-analytic system. *Psychological Bulletin,* 1968, **70,** 426–443.

COHEN, J. Some statistical issues in psychological research. In B. B. Wolman (Ed.), *Handbook of clinical psychology.* New York: McGraw-Hill, 1965.

DARLEY, J. M., AND LATANÉ, B. Bystander intervention in emergencies: Diffusion of responsibility. *Journal of Personality and Social Psychology,* 1968, **8,** 377–383.

FREUD, S. *The future of an illusion.* New York: Liveright, 1953.

FUNK, R. W. *Language, hermeneutic, and word of God.* New York: Harper & Row, 1966.

GLOCK, C. Y., AND STARK, R. *Christian beliefs and anti-Semitism.* New York: Harper & Row, 1966.

HARTSHORNE, H., AND MAY, M. A. *Studies in the nature of character.* Vol. 1. *Studies in deceit.* New York: Macmillan, 1928.

KORTE, C. Group effects on help-giving in an emergency. *Proceedings of the 77th Annual Convention of the American Psychological Association,* 1969, **4,** 383–384. (Summary)

ORNE, M. T. On the social psychology of the psychological experiment: With particular reference to demand characteristics and their implications. *American Psychologist,* 1962, **17,** 776–783.

ROSENBERG, M. J. When dissonance fails: On eliminating evaluation apprehension from attitude measurement. *Journal of Personality and Social Psychology,* 1965, **1,** 28–42.

SCHWARTZ, S. H., AND CLAUSEN, G. T. Responsibility, norms, and helping in an emergency. *Journal of Personality and Social Psychology,* 1970, **16,** 299–310.

TOLMAN, E. C. Cognitive maps in rats and men. *Psychological Review,* 1948, **55,** 189–208.

6

A Focus Theory of Normative Conduct: Recycling the Concept of Norms to Reduce Littering in Public Places

Robert B. Cialdini and Raymond R. Reno
Carl A. Kallgren

Past research has generated mixed support among social scientists for the utility of social norms in accounting for human behavior. We argue that norms do have a substantial impact on human action; however, the impact can only be properly recognized when researchers (a) separate 2 types of norms that at times act antagonistically in a situation—injunctive norms (what most others approve or disapprove) and descriptive norms (what most others do)—and (b) focus Ss' attention principally on the type of norm being studied. In 5 natural settings, focusing Ss on either the descriptive norms or the injunctive norms regarding littering caused the Ss' littering decisions to change only in accord with the dictates of the then more salient type of norm.

Although social norms have a long history within social psychology, support for the concept as a useful explanatory and predictive device is currently quite mixed. Some researchers have used and championed the concept as important to a proper understanding of human social behavior (e.g., Berkowitz, 1972; Fishbein & Ajzen, 1975; McKirnan, 1980; Pepitone, 1976; Sherif, 1936; Staub, 1972; Triandis, 1977). Others have seen little of value in it, arguing that the concept is vague and overly general, often contradictory, and ill-suited to empirical testing (e.g., Darley & Latané, 1970; Krebs, 1970; Krebs & Miller, 1985; Marini, 1984). In addition, a

The authors thank Lisa Cramer, Cathy Daly, Ann Hazan, Bethel Kaminski, and Kim Whiting for their help in conducting Study 5, which served as the master's thesis for Raymond R. Reno.

Correspondence concerning this article should be addressed to Robert B. Cialdini, Department of Psychology, Arizona State University, Tempe, Arizona 85287 1104.

parallel controversy has developed within academic sociology where eth- nomethodological and constructionist critics have faulted the dominant normative paradigm of that discipline (Garfinkel, 1967; Mehan & Wood, 1975).

The effect of these criticisms has been positive in pointing out problems that must be solved before one can have confidence in the utility of normative explanations. One such problem is definitional. Both in common parlance and academic usage, *norm* has more than one meaning (Shaffer, 1983). When considering normative in- fluence on behavior, it is crucial to discriminate between the *is* (descriptive) and the *ought* (injunctive) meaning of social norms, because each refers to a separate source of human motivation (Deutsch & Gerard, 1955). The descriptive norm describes what is typical or *normal.* It is what most people do, and it motivates by providing evidence as to what will likely be effective and adaptive action: "If everyone is doing it, it must be a sensible thing to do." Cialdini (1988) has argued that such a presump- tion offers an information-processing advantage and a decisional shortcut when one is choosing how to behave in a given situation. By simply registering what most oth- ers are doing there and by imitating their actions, one can usually choose efficiently and well. Researchers have repeatedly found that the perception of what most others are doing influences subjects to behave similarly, even when the behaviors are as morally neutral as choosing a consumer product (Venkatesan, 1966) or looking up at the sky (Milgram, Bickman, & Berkowitz, 1969). The injunctive meaning of norms refers to rules or beliefs as to what constitutes morally approved and disapproved conduct. In contrast to descriptive norms, which specify what is done, injunctive norms specify what ought to be done. That is, rather than simply informing one's ac- tions, these norms enjoin it through the promise of social sanctions. Because what is approved is often what is typically done, it is easy to confuse these two meanings of norms. However, they are conceptually and motivationally distinct, and it is impor- tant for a proper understanding of normative influence to keep them separate, espe- cially in situations where both are acting simultaneously.

A second source of confusion surrounding the concept of social norms is that, although they are said to characterize and guide behavior within a society, they should not be seen as uniformly in force at all times and in all situations. That is, norms should motivate behavior primarily when they are activated (i.e., made salient or otherwise focused on); thus, persons who are dispositionally or temporarily fo- cused on normative considerations are most likely to act in norm-consistent ways (Berkowitz, 1972; Berkowitz & Daniels, 1964; Gruder, Romer, & Korth, 1978; Miller & Grush, 1986; Rutkowski, Gruder, & Romer, 1983; Schwartz & Fleishman, 1978). Of course, salience procedures should be effective for both descriptive and in- junctive norms. In fact, in situations with clear-cut descriptive and injunctive norms, focusing individuals on *is* versus *ought* information should lead to behavior change that is consistent only with the now more salient type of norm.

One purpose of this research was to test this assertion as it applies to individu- als' decisions to litter in public places. The choice of littering behavior for this study occurred for several reasons: (a) it provides a clearly observable action that is governed by a widely held injunctive norm (Bickman, 1972; Heberlein, 1971; Keep America Beautiful, Inc., 1968) and (b) it constitutes a growing social problem of considerable aesthetic, financial, and health-related costs to the culture. In California alone, for example, litter has increased by 24% over a recent span of 15 years, requiring $100 million annually in cleanup costs (California Waste Management Board, 1988) and posing health threats to humans and wildlife through water pollution, fire hazards, rodent and insect infestations, highway accidents, and thousands of injuries suffered from discarded cans and broken bottles (Geller, Winett, & Everett, 1982). Thus, a better understanding of the normative factors moderating deliberate littering would be of both conceptual and practical value.

A common finding in the literature on littering is that the act is significantly more likely in a littered setting than in a clean setting (e.g., Finnie, 1973; Geller, Witmer, & Tuso, 1977; Heberlein, 1971; Krauss, Freedman, & Whitcup, 1978; Reiter & Samuel, 1980). Although this finding is congruent with the normative view that, in most settings, individuals tend to act in accordance with the clear behavioral norm there (Krauss et al., 1978), it is also consistent with other motivational accounts. For example, it might be argued that the tendency to litter more in a littered environment is due to simple imitation. Or, it might be argued that individuals are more likely to litter into a littered environment because they perceive that their litter will do less damage to the state of the environment than if it were clean.

STUDY 1

In our first experiment, subjects were given the opportunity to litter into either a previously clean or a fully littered environment after witnessing a confederate who either littered into the environment or walked through it. By varying the state of the environment (clean vs. littered), we sought to manipulate the perceived descriptive norm for littering in the situation. By manipulating whether the confederate dropped litter into the environment, we sought to affect the extent to which subjects were drawn to focus attention on the state of the environment and, consequently, on the relevant descriptive norm there.

We had two main predictions: First, we expected that subjects would be more likely to litter into an already littered environment than into a clean one. This expectation is consistent with the findings of prior research on littering (e.g., Krauss et al., 1978; Reiter & Samuel, 1980) and with the view that, in most settings, individuals are at least marginally aware of the existing norms and tend to act in accordance with them. Second, and more important, we expected the effect of the descriptive norm for littering in the situation (as indicated by the state of the environment) to be significantly enhanced when subjects' attention was drawn to the environment by a littering other. This expectation was predicated on considerable prior evidence (see Fiske & Taylor, 1984, for a review) indicating that substantial psychological impact can result from salience procedures involving simple shifts in the visual prominence of stimulus information, including normative information (Feldman, Higgins, Karlovac, & Ruble, 1976; Ferguson & Wells, 1980; Manis, Dovalina, Avis, & Cardoze, 1980; Ruble & Feldman, 1976; Trope & Ginnosar, 1986). Specifically, then, we predicted an interaction such that subjects who saw the confederate litter into a fully littered environment would litter more than those who saw no such littering; whereas subjects who saw the confederate litter into a clean environment would litter less than those who saw no such littering.

Should we obtain this interaction, we would have good support for our focus model of normative conduct. It should be noted that the second component of this predicted interaction adds important conceptual weight to our test in that it is contrary to what would be anticipated by rival accounts. It is opposite to what would be expected if subjects were motivated simply by a greater reluctance to litter into a clean versus littered environment because of the greater relative damage to the respective environments that such littering would cause; by that account, subjects should be more likely to litter after observing littering in a clean environment because the environment will have already been damaged. Similarly, the second component of our predicted interaction pits the norm focus/salience interpretation against a straightforward imitation formulation, in which an unpunished litterer would be expected to increase the littering tendencies of observers in either type of environment. By postulating that a littering other will concentrate attention on evidence of what the majority of people have done, thereby highlighting normative considerations, only the (descriptive) norm focus/salience account predicts that observed littering will reduce subsequent littering in a clean environment.

METHOD

Subjects and Procedure

Norm salience.   Subjects were 139 visitors to a university-affiliated hospital who were returning to their cars in an adjacent, multilevel parking garage during the daylight hours of 5 days within a period of 8 consecutive days. Approximately 5 s after emerging from an elevator, subjects encountered an experimental confederate of college age walking toward them. In half of the instances, the confederate appeared to be reading a large, 21.6 × 35.6 cm (8½ × 14 in.) handbill, which he or she dropped into the environment approximately 4.5 cm (5 yd) before passing the subjects (high norm salience). A second confederate judged whether a subject had noticed the littering incident and, consequently, had deflected his or her attention at least momentarily to the parking garage floor. The great majority (93%) were judged to have done so, and only they were examined as to their subsequent littering behavior. In the other half of the instances, the confederate merely walked past the subject without carrying a handbill, so as to provide an equivalent degree of social contact (low norm salience).

Existing descriptive norm.   For some of the subjects, the floor of the parking structure had been heavily littered by the experimenters with an assortment of handbills, candy wrappers, cigarette butts, and paper cups (existing prolittering norm). For the remaining subjects, the area had been cleaned of all litter (existing antilittering norm). The state of the environment (littered or clean) was alternated in 2-hr blocks, with the initial state determined randomly at the start of each day. On arriving at their cars, subjects encountered a large handbill that was tucked under the driver's side windshield wiper so as to partially obscure vision from the driver's seat. The handbill, identical to that dropped by the confederate, carried a stenciled message that read, "THIS IS AUTOMOTIVE SAFETY WEEK. PLEASE DRIVE CAREFULLY." A similar handbill had been placed on all other cars in the area as well.

Measure of littering.   From a hidden vantage point, an experimenter noted the driver's sex, estimated age, and whether the driver littered the handbill. Littering was defined as depositing the handbill in the environment outside of the vehicle. Because there were no trash receptacles in the area, all subjects who failed to litter did so by taking and retaining the handbill inside their vehicles before driving away.

Analyses

Analyses in this and subsequent studies were conducted using the SPSS-X loglinear program, wherein tests for effects within dichotomous data are examined through the nesting of hierarchical models. This technique allows the testing of individual parameters by comparing the differences in the likelihood ratio chi-square of a pair of nested models. The differenced likelihood ratio is reported as a chi-square.

RESULTS AND DISCUSSION

Gender and age differences in littering have sometimes been found in past research (see Geller et al., 1982, for a review). Therefore, before proceeding to tests of our theoretical hypotheses, we explored the data for gender or age differences. None were found; consequently, neither variable was included in subsequent analyses.

Figure 1 depicts the amount of littering that occurred in each of the four experimental conditions. Loglinear analysis of those data produced a set of results that conforms to that predicted by our norm focus model. First, as expected, there was a main effect for the existing descriptive norm, in that subjects littered more in a littered environment than in a clean environment (41% vs. 11%), $\chi^2(1, N = 139) = 17.06$, $p < .001$. Second, this effect occurred to a much greater extent under conditions of high norm salience, when subjects' attention was drawn to the existing descriptive norm for the environment. That is, the size of the existing descriptive-norm effect when the confederate littered (6% vs. 54%), $\chi^2(1, N = 55) = 16.52, p < .001$, was significantly greater than when the confederate did not litter (14% vs. 32%), $\chi^2(1, N = 84) = 3.99, p < .05$; the resultant interaction was tested as a planned comparison that proved highly reliable, $\chi^2(1, N = 139) = 20.87, p < .001$. The significant interaction provides confirmation of our hypothesis that procedures designed to shift attention within a setting to just one type of operative norm—in this case, the descriptive norm—will generate behavior change that is consistent only with that type of norm. Apparently, this is so even when the behavior in question is governed by an injunctive norm—in this case, the antilittering norm—that is strongly and widely held in the society (Bickman, 1972; Heberlein, 1971; Keep America Beautiful, Inc., 1968).

The pattern of results also supported the directional predictions made from our model. That is, under conditions of high (descriptive) norm salience, subjects littered more in a littered environment (54% vs. 32%) but less in a clean one (6% vs. 14%), although neither simple effect was statistically significant, χ^2s = 2.76 and 1.18, respectively.

It is this latter finding, showing the least littering among subjects in the high norm salience/clean environment condition, that seems the most provocative of our study and, therefore, worthy of pursuit. After all, from an applied standpoint, we should be principally interested in strategies for litter abatement. Moreover, the fact that the least littering occurred among subjects who observed prior littering into a clean environment is of considerable conceptual interest, as it supports norm focus predictions over those that spring from a straightforward imitation or environmental damage account. Good reason exists, however, for caution in drawing strong conceptual conclusions from this finding. Although part of a theoretically

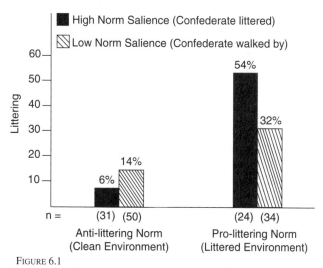

FIGURE 6.1
Percentages of subjects littering as a function of norm salience, and the direction of the descriptive norm regarding littering: Study 1.

predicted, significant interaction, the drop in littering due to high norm salience in the clean environment was far from significant by itself. Of course, this lack of significance might well have occurred because of a floor effect, owing to the low level of littering (14%) in the low norm salience/clean environment condition; nonetheless, in the interest of enhanced statistical confidence, a replication seemed warranted.

STUDY 2

In planning to replicate and extend our initial study, we recognized a pair of testable implications that flowed from our earlier analysis. First, consistent with the outcomes of Study 1, a subject who witnessed evidence of littering in an otherwise clean environment should litter less as a result; however, the evidence would not have to take the form, as it did in Study 1, of observed littering action. That is, the consequence of such action—a single piece of litter lying in an otherwise clean environment—should have the same effect, because of its conspicuousness, by drawing attention to an environment whose descriptive norm (except for one aberrant litterer) was clearly antilitter. Second, as the amount of litter increases progressively in a setting, so should the likelihood that a subject will litter into it because, by definition, that litter will change the descriptive norm for the setting. The upshot of this pair of implications of our normative analysis is a nonintuitive prediction: The likelihood that an individual will litter into an environment bearing various pieces of perceptible, extant litter will be described by a checkmark-shaped function. Little littering should occur in a clean environment; still less should occur with a sole piece of litter in an otherwise clean environment, but progressively greater littering should occur as litter accumulates and the descriptive norm for the situation changes from antilitter to prolitter.

METHOD

Subjects and Procedure

Subjects were 358 visitors to an amusement park in a large southwestern city during the evening hours of a pair of weekends in early summer. Immediately before turning a particular corner on a park walkway, subjects encountered a college-age experimental confederate passing out handbills that read "DON'T MISS TONIGHT'S SHOW," which referred to an entertainment program sponsored by the park on weekend nights. The confederate was instructed to give a handbill, at 1-min intervals, to the first passing adult walking alone or to one adult (the physically closest) in the first passing group. On turning the walkway corner, subjects, who were no longer visible to the confederate, faced a path of approximately 55 m (60 yd) from which no exit was possible except at its ends.

State of the environment.   All litter had been removed from the path except for varying numbers of handbills of the sort that subjects had just been given by a confederate. Depending on the experimental condition, the path contained 0, 1, 2, 4, 8, or 16 handbills that were visible from the path entrance.

Measurement of littering.   Because no litter receptacles were available on the path, a subject who deposited a handbill into the environment at any point along the path's length was considered a litterer. Subjects' littering behavior was covertly observed by a hidden, second experimental confederate, who also timed subjects' latency to litter (failure to litter was given a score of 100 s) and who removed any newly littered handbills from the path. On exiting the path, subjects turned a corner to find a pair of previously unseen litter receptacles; virtually all subjects who had not littered to that point dropped their handbills into one of the receptacles.

RESULTS AND DISCUSSION

As in Study 1, we first examined the littering data for age and gender differences. No significant effects were obtained because of subject age. However, we did find a significant tendency for men to litter more frequently than women (31% vs. 19%), $\chi^2(1, N = 358) = 7.41, p < .01$.

Figure 2 depicts the percentage of litterers in each of the experimental conditions of Study 2. The data pattern closely reflects the predicted checkmark shape of our normative analysis. The checkmark function hypothesis was tested in a two-step process. First, we constructed a planned comparison using trend weights that

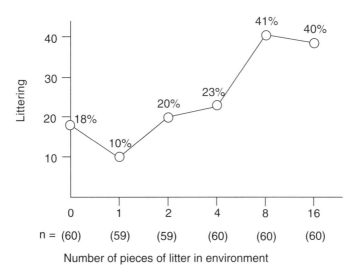

FIGURE 6.2
Percentages of subjects littering as a function of the number of pieces of litter in the environment: Study 2.

modeled the checkmark shape ($-2, -4, -1, 1, 2, 4$). It proved significant, $\chi^2(1, N = 358) = 21.80, p < .01$. A second planned comparison was then performed to test whether a difference in littering occurred between the zero littering condition and the one-piece-of-environmental-litter condition. No significant difference was found, $\chi^2(1, N = 229) = 1.64, p < .20$. Comparable analyses were conducted on the latency to litter data shown in Figure 3. As with frequency to litter, the first contrast proved significant, $F(1, 352) = 20.65, p < .01$, whereas the second did not ($F < 1$). There was no significant interaction between any of these contrasts and gender.

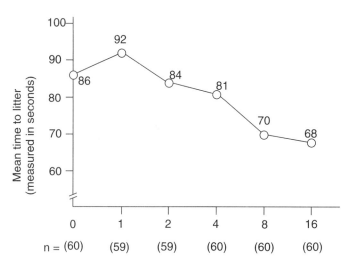

FIGURE 6.3
Mean latency to litter as a function of the number of pieces of litter in the environment: Study 2.

STUDY 3

Even though the general form of the findings of Study 2 confirmed our predictions, one crucial feature of the results offered only ambiguous support. The hypothesized decline in littering from the clean environment condition to the one-piece-of-litter condition of the study, although present (18% vs. 10%), was not conventionally significant, allowing the possibility that it may have been the overall linearity of the checkmark pattern, rather than its elbow-like bend, that accounted for the significance of our general planned comparison. This ambiguity is especially frustrating because, as in Study 1, it appears that a floor effect in the data may have prevented a clear demonstration of reduced littering under the circumstances predicted by our formulation. It is difficult to generate significantly less littering than that of a clean environment when the clean environment generates so little littering itself.

Consequently, we decided to conduct a conceptual replication of the theoretically relevant conditions of Study 2 that was designed to overcome the floor-effect problem. One way to deal with a floor effect of the sort that faced us is to increase the statistical power associated with our significance tests by increasing the number of subjects run in each condition. Thus, we used an experimental setting that would allow us to record the littering decisions of large numbers of subjects in a relatively short period of time. Additionally, in an attempt to sharpen the impact of our single-piece-of-litter manipulation, we chose a more conspicuous single piece of litter than we had used in Study 2.

Specifically, subjects were college dormitory residents who found a public service flier in their mailboxes. The environment in front of the mailboxes had been arranged so that it contained (a) no litter, (b) one piece of highly conspicuous litter (a hollowed-out, end piece of watermelon rind), or (c) a large array of various types of litter, including the watermelon rind. The dependent variable was subjects' tendencies to litter with the fliers. On the basis of our normative analysis and the pattern of results of Studies 1 and 2, we made a pair of predictions. First, we anticipated that subjects would litter more into a fully littered environment than into a clean one. Second, we expected that they would litter least into an otherwise clean environment that contained a single, attention-focusing piece of litter.

METHOD

Subjects

Subjects were 484 residents of a densely populated, high-rise women's dormitory on the campus of a large state university.

Procedure

The residents' mailboxes were located in rows at one corner of the dormitory's main lobby. The mailbox area was cut off visually from most of the lobby by a translucent partition. Once past the partition, subjects encountered an open area that fronted the mailboxes. During a 10 a.m. to 4 p.m. schoolday period, residents who opened their mailboxes to find a public service flier placed there as part of the experiment were counted as subjects, provided that no one else was simultaneously in the area getting her mail.

Depending on the experimental condition, subjects passing through the open area in front of their mailboxes encountered an environment that contained no litter or a single piece of litter (a hollowed-out, heel section of watermelon rind), or a large number of pieces of litter of various kinds (e.g., discarded fliers, cigarette butts, paper cups, candy wrappers, and soft drink cans), including the watermelon rind. A subject was considered to have littered if she deposited the flier anywhere in the environment (all waste containers had been removed) before exiting the lobby onto an elevator or through a set of doors leading to the campus. Of those subjects who littered, the great majority were observed by an unobtrusively placed experimenter to do so in the area in front of the mailboxes.

RESULTS AND DISCUSSION

The percentages of littering in the three experimental conditions are presented in Figure 4. Their pattern accords well with predictions based on our normative perspective; indeed, the expected quadratic trend was highly significant, $\chi^2(1, N = 484) = 23.12, p < .001$. Moreover, planned contrast tests of our two experimental predictions were supportive at conventional levels of significance. First, subjects were more likely to litter into a fully littered environment than into an unlittered one (26.7% vs. 10.7%), $\chi^2(1, N = 291) = 12.62, p < .001$. Second, subjects were less likely to litter into an environment when it contained a single, salient piece of litter than when it was unlittered (3.6% vs. 10.7%), $\chi^2(1, N = 335) = 6.79, p < .01$.

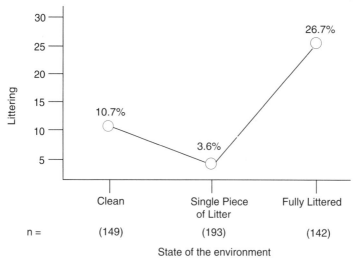

FIGURE 6.4
Percentages of subjects littering as a function of the amount of litter in the environment: Study 3..

Theoretical Implications

To this point, we have reported data from three experiments in three different natural settings that seem to converge sufficiently to allow the generation of statements about the conceptual and pragmatic value of those data. On the conceptual side, it appears that norms can be influential in directing human action; however, in keeping with the spirit of prior criticism of normative explanations, it is necessary for norm theorists to be specific about both the type of norm (injunctive or descriptive) thought to be acting in a situation and about the conditions under which it is likely to act. Distinguishing between injunctive and descriptive norms is crucial, because both types can exist simultaneously in a setting and can have either congruent or contradictory implications for behavior. For example, in Study 1 we showed that through procedures designed to highlight differing descriptive norms, we could enhance or undermine compliance with the societywide injunctive norm against littering. Such a finding should not be interpreted to mean that descriptive norms are, in this instance or in general, more powerful than injunctive norms. Rather, it is the differential focusing of attention on one or the other sort of norm that is the key. Indeed, even within the same type of norm, it seems to be the case from our findings that focus of attention is an important component. In all three experiments, exposing subjects to a single piece of litter in an otherwise clean environment—a procedure designed to draw subjects' attention to what most people had done in the setting (i.e., the descriptive norm)—reduced littering there.

Practical Applications

Because littering is a social problem, it is appropriate to consider the potential practical applications of our data as well. The finding of greatest applied value appears to be that subjects in three different settings littered least after encountering a single piece of litter in an otherwise unlittered place. At first glance, such a result might seem to suggest that individuals seeking to retard the accumulation of litter in a particular environment might affix a single, prominent piece of litter there. On closer consideration, however, it becomes clear that such an approach would be inferior to beginning with a totally clean environment. Examination of Figures 2 and 3, showing the average likelihood and latency of littering among subjects in our amusement park study, illustrates the point. Subjects who encountered a perfectly clean environment tended not to litter there, resulting in long delays before anyone despoiled it with a handbill. Once a single handbill appeared in the setting, subjects were even less likely to litter, generating even longer latencies before the second piece of litter appeared. At that point, with two pieces of litter visible in the environment, the descriptive norm began to change, and subjects' reluctance to litter into the setting began to deteriorate steadily, leading to shorter and shorter littering latencies with increasing accumulations of litter. Anyone wishing to preserve the state of a specific environment, then, should begin with a clean setting so as to delay for the greatest time the appearance of two pieces of litter there, because those two pieces of litter are likely to begin a slippery-slope effect that leads to a fully littered environment and to a fully realized perception that "everybody litters here." This logic further suggests that environments will best be able to retard littering if they are subjected to frequent and thorough litter pickups that return them to the optimal litter-free condition.

In considering the practical implications of our data, we recognized a weakness in our decision to focus subjects' attention on the descriptive rather than injunctive norm for littering: Procedures that focus subjects on the descriptive norm will only reduce littering when the environment is wholly or virtually unspoiled. Indeed, as was suggested in the data of Study 1, a descriptive norm focus when the environment is substantially littered will tend to increase littering there—hardly a desirable outcome for any but theory-testing purposes. A descriptive norm-focusing procedure, then, should only have socially beneficial effects in environments that do not need much help. The circumstances are different, however, when the injunctive norm is made salient and when, consequently, individuals are focused on what people typically approve and disapprove rather than on what they typically do in a situation. By making the injunctive norm against littering more prominent, we should expect reduced littering even in a heavily littered environment.

A test of this hypothesis seemed instrumental to a pair of potentially valuable goals. First, on the practical level, it might establish norm focus procedures that could be used for litter abatement in a variety of environments. Second, on the conceptual level, it would generate evidence for or against our contention that focusing attention on either *is* or *ought* information will lead to behavior change that is consistent only with the now more salient type of norm; to this point in the research program, we had examined only half of that contention by concentrating just on descriptive norms.

STUDY 4

Recall that in Study 1, we argued that a confederate's act of dropping a flier into the environment would draw subjects' attention to that environment and to clear evidence (that we had manipulated) concerning whether people typically littered there. In this way, we sought to manipulate focus of attention to the existing descriptive norm regarding littering in the setting. Presumably, if instead the environment were to give clear evidence of what is societally approved or disapproved there, the same attention-focusing device would function as an injunctive norm activator, because societally based approval or disapproval is the distinguishing characteristic of injunctive norms (Birnbaum & Sagarin, 1976; Marini, 1984; Sherif & Sherif, 1969).

The question of what clear approval/disapproval cue could be placed effectively in a natural environment to test our formulation was answered serendipitously while conducting Study 1. That study was run in a parking garage whose walls rose only halfway from the floor to the roof at each level. On one especially windy day, the litter we had distributed all around the garage floor in the fully littered environment condition was blown against an inside wall, as if someone had swept it there in a neat line. When a confederate dropped a handbill into that environment, virtually no subjects littered, whereas, on previous days the majority of subjects in that experimental condition had littered. In the course of puzzling over the discrepancy, we realized that the littering tendency of windy-day subjects may have declined when attention was called to the considerable litter in the environment because that litter gave the (mistaken) impression of having been swept—a clear disapproval cue.

Armed with this potential insight, we decided to conduct a partial replication and extension of Study 1, in which subjects saw a confederate who either did or did not drop a handbill into an environment that contained a large amount of either swept or unswept litter. In the case of unswept litter, we expected to replicate the data pattern of Study 1 for the comparable experimental cells; that is, we anticipated that by dropping a handbill, the confederate would focus subjects' attention on the environment and its evidence that people typically litter there, which should cause littering to increase. By dropping a handbill into a setting where prior litter had been swept (into piles), we anticipated that the confederate would once again focus subjects' attention on the environment. But in this instance, subjects would encounter a mixed message, composed of a descriptive norm cue (abundant litter) that would incline them toward littering and an injunctive norm cue (swept litter) that would incline them against it. Accordingly, we predicted that the difference in littering found in the unswept conditions would be reversed or at least reduced. Statistically, then, we expected an interaction between our two independent variables of whether a confederate dropped a handbill into the environment (high or low norm salience) and whether the environment contained swept or unswept litter (presence or absence of an injunctive norm cue). Furthermore, we expected a specific form for that interaction, such that any difference in littering found between the swept and unswept litter conditions under low-norm salience procedures would be significantly enhanced under high-norm salience procedures. That is, it was our belief that, under the low salience conditions, the normative forces present would be registered only minimally by subjects, resulting in only a minimal swept/unswept difference. However, under high salience conditions with normative issues now focal, the effect would be magnified.

METHOD

Subjects and Procedure

Norm salience. Subjects were 127 visitors to a university-affiliated hospital during the late afternoon and early evening hours of 6 days within a 13-day period. They underwent the same norm salience procedures as subjects in Study 1. That is, after emerging from a parking garage elevator, they encountered a college-age confederate who either dropped a distinctively colored handbill onto the floor in subjects' view or simply walked past without carrying a handbill.

Presence of an injunctive norm cue. For some subjects, the floor of the parking structure had been heavily littered by the experimenters, with the litter distributed across the environment in a fashion identical to that of Study 1. For the remaining subjects, all of this ambient litter had been swept into three large piles situated approximately 9 m (10 yd) apart in a line. In the high-norm salience/swept litter condition, the confederate dropped a handbill onto the floor approximately 1.5 m (5 ft) after passing the piles of litter. It was decided to have the confederate drop the handbill immediately in front, but in full view, of the litter piles to avoid an imitation explanation for our predicted effect. That is, if subjects had seen the confederate drop a handbill into one of the piles, then the predicted reduction in subjects' subsequent littering could be interpreted as simple modeling of a decision not to litter. The swept or unswept litter conditions were run in alternating 2-hr blocks, with the first run of the day determined randomly.

Measure of littering.   Littering was assessed as it was in Study 1.

RESULTS AND DISCUSSION

The influence of age and gender on littering rates was examined in an initial analysis; no significant effects occurred. Thus, these variables were not included in further analyses.

The percentage of subjects who littered in each of the experimental conditions of our design is displayed in Figure 5. Those percentages occurred in a pattern consistent with the form of the interaction that we were led to anticipate from our norm focus formulation. Using loglinear analyses, we tested that interaction with a planned comparison that contrasted the difference between the two low-norm salience cells (29% vs. 33%), $\chi^2(1, N = 68) = 0.18$, *ns,* against the difference be-

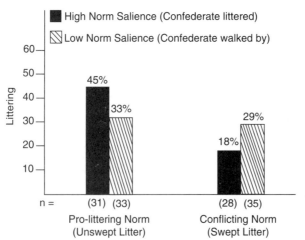

FIGURE 6.5
Percentages of subjects littering as a function of norm salience, and the configuration of litter in the environment: Study 4.

tween the two high-norm salience cells (18% vs. 45%), $\chi^2(1, N = 59) = 5.19$, $p < .02$. That interaction test proved significant, $\chi^2(1, N = 127) = 4.91, p < .03$.

Looking at the interaction pattern in another way, we can see that it is composed of two opposing trends—neither significant by itself, but significantly different in contrast to one another—both instigated by the same attention-focusing procedure. That is, when a dropped handbill drew attention to an unswept environment that, by its fully littered nature, gave evidence of a clear descriptive norm favoring littering there, littering tendencies rose (33% vs. 45%). However, when the same device drew attention to an environment that included a clearly conflicting injunctive norm cue as well, littering tendencies were reversed (29% vs. 18%). This pattern of effects accords well with each of the goals we set for Study 4. First, it supports our theoretical assertion that both descriptive and injunctive norms can elicit behavior change, with the prominence of one or the other type of norm accounting for the direction of the change. Second, it offers grounds for hope that certain kinds of undesirable action (littering, drinking and driving, tax cheating, highway speeding, etc.) can be restrained by the use of procedures that temporarily focus individuals on injunctive norms in the settings where the action is most likely to take place.

STUDY 5

To this point in our research program, we have examined the validity of our norm focus formulation by using an attention-focusing procedure designed to make subjects mindful of a specific descriptive norm (Studies 1–3) or of conflicting descriptive and injunctive norms (Study 4) governing littering in a situation. The first three studies found resultant behavior changes wholly in line with the descriptive norm. The fourth study, which added evidence of a contradicting injunctive norm to the perception of the existing descriptive norm, broke the dominance of the descriptive norm over subjects' behavior; it actually produced a (nonsignificant) reduction of littering in an environment where a clear, prolittering descriptive norm existed. It seemed to us that the logical next step in this progression was to conduct one additional study that removed any prolittering descriptive norm focus and that concentrated subjects exclusively on the injunctive, antilittering norm. It was our expectation that such an uncontaminated, injunctive norm focus would then lead to a significant reduction in littering.

We saw another reason for conducting an additional experiment. In Studies 1 through 4, our norm-focusing manipulation involved the dropping of a noticeable piece of litter into an environment (either by a seen or an unseen individual) so as to draw subjects' attention to the normative information present in that environment. There were several advantages of using that particular attention-focusing device, including the ability to make certain nonintuitive predictions that would not have flowed from rival theoretical accounts. We also recognized, however, that there would be certain drawbacks to using the same procedure yet again.

First, the generality of our conceptual argument could be seen as untested beyond the range of our specific norm salience manipulation. More important, though, using littering to highlight the norms related to littering could create interpretational ambiguities. That is, the littering act itself is not neutral. It carries social meanings (depending on the situation in which it occurs) that are likely to generate various kinds of perceptions of the littering agent. It is possible that one or another of these perceptions could have acted to incline subjects to follow or reject the litterer's lead. For instance, although it is unlikely that someone who littered into a fully littered environment, as occurred in Study 4, would be seen positively by subjects, someone who littered into an environment of neatly swept litter might be seen in an especially negative light; it is possible that this more negative view may have accounted for the reduction in littering among such subjects in Study 4. Similarly, it is conceivable that subjects in Studies 1 through 3 may have had an unpleasant reaction to any litterer who would litter into a previously clean setting and, hence, may have failed to litter so as to distance themselves from such an unsavory person.

To avoid interpretations of this sort, which are based on subjects' perceptions of a litterer, it was necessary to design a focus shift manipulation that would draw subjects' attention to the injunctive norm against littering but would do so without the action of a littering agent. To this end, in Study 5 we relied on the device of cognitive priming, wherein one concept can be activated in an individual by focusing that individual's attention on a related concept (see Higgins & Bargh, 1987, for a review). Most, although not all (cf. Ratcliff & McKoon, 1988), explanations of priming effects incorporate the notion of spreading activation, which posits that similar concepts are linked together in memory within a network of nodes and that activation of one concept results in the spreading of the activation along the network to other related concepts (Anderson, 1976, 1983; Collins & Loftus, 1975; McClelland & Rumelhart, 1981). A key determinant of whether the presentation of one concept will cause activation of another is their semantic or conceptual proximity.

If, as research by Harvey and Enzle (1981) indicates, norms are concepts stored in a network format, then focusing subjects on a particular norm should activate other norms that are perceived to be semantically close to it. Moreover, the greater the semantic proximity, the stronger should be the resultant activation. To test this possibility, we first had a large number of norms rated as to their similarity to the antilittering norm. Next, on the basis of those ratings, we selected three norms that, although alike in rated normativeness, differed in their perceived similarity (conceptual proximity) to the antilittering norm. Finally, we included reference to one or another of the norms on handbills that we placed on car windshields in a local library parking lot. We expected that the handbills containing a message reminding subjects of the most distant norm from the antilittering norm (voting) would be littered relatively often but that as the handbill messages referred to norms rated closer (energy conservation) and closer (recycling) to the antilittering norm, fewer and fewer subjects would litter them. We also expected that handbills containing no normative message would be littered most of all, whereas handbills containing the target, antilittering message would be littered least.

METHOD

Preliminary Ratings Study

A list of 35 norms that had been generated by the researchers and their colleagues (e.g., "Driving at a safe speed," "Recycling," "Paying taxes," and "Not littering") were shown to 95 undergraduate psychology students during a class session at a large state university. The students were asked to indicate the extent to which they found each item on the list to be normative or nonnormative on 9-point scales, anchored by the labels *extremely normative* (1) and *not at all normative* (9); the scale midpoint was labeled *somewhat normative* (5). A definition of norms was provided at the top of the list that read "Norms are shared beliefs within a culture as to what constitutes socially appropriate conduct."

A second list was shown to a different class of 87 undergraduate psychology students at the same university during a meeting of their class. In addition to the definition of norms at the top of the list, this list contained comparisons of each of the selected norms with the norm against littering. Subjects were asked to "indicate how closely related you believe each of the pairs of norms are" on 9-point scales anchored by the labels *identical* (1) and *unrelated* (9); the scale midpoint was labeled *somewhat close* (5). Examples of the comparison items are "The norm against littering and the norm for recycling" and "The norm against littering and the norm for returning library books on time."

Selection of the experimental norms.   Means for both types of ratings were computed. The norm for not littering was rated as 4.25 on the 9-point normativeness scale. We then limited our choices for the additional experimental norms to those that had means for both male and female subjects within one scale point of 4.25 on rated normativeness. From this pool and on the basis of the similarity scale ratings, we selected three norms to be close to, moderately close to, and far from the norm against littering. Those three norms and their rated distances from the norm against littering were, respectively, the norm for recycling (3.57), the norm for turning off lights when last to leave a room (5.74), and the norm for voting (7.12).

Generating the normative messages.   For each of the four experimental norms, a message was constructed that was suitable for presentation on a handbill. For the antilittering norm (identical to the target norm), it read, "April is Keep Arizona Beautiful Month. Please Do Not Litter." For the recycling norm (close to the target norm), it read, "April is Preserve Arizona's Natural Resources Month. Please Recycle." For the turning off lights norm (moderately close to the target norm), it read, "April is Conserve Arizona's Energy Month. Please Turn Off Unnecessary

Lights." For the voting norm (far from the target norm), it read, "April is Arizona's Voter Awareness Month. Please Remember That Your Vote Counts." Finally, a control message was constructed that carried no injunctive norm; it read, "April is Arizona's Fine Art's Month. Please Visit Your Local Art Museum."

Subjects and Procedure

Participants were 133 female patrons and 126 male patrons of a municipal public library branch who parked their cars in the library lot. After leaving the library and returning to their cars, subjects found on the driver's side of the windshield a handbill that had been placed there by an experimenter. The handbill carried one of the five experimental messages designed to focus subjects differentially on the norm against littering. Drivers' decisions to litter the handbill were recorded by an unobtrusively placed observer. Typically, subjects who littered did so immediately after reading the handbill message and virtually always within 5 s of having done so. Consequently, we felt confident that the priminglike effects we anticipated were well within the range of priming-effect durations found by other investigators (see Higgins & Bargh, 1987, for a review). No efforts were made to change the moderate amount of naturally occurring litter on the library grounds and parking lot, which consisted of a variety of cigarette butts and an occasional paper cup or soft drink can.

RESULTS AND DISCUSSION

In tests for gender effects within the data, only the main effect was significant, $\chi^2(1, N = 259) = 3.92$, $p < .05$, indicating that men littered more frequently than women (22% vs. 14%). To examine our hypothesis that as the conceptual distance between the antilittering norm and the handbill messages increased, littering rates would increase commensurately, we conducted a trend analysis. Only the predicted, linear trend (displayed in Figure 6) proved significant, $\chi^2(1, N = 259) = 5.48$, $p < .02$. Within the five experimental message means, only one comparison was significant, that between the target, antilittering norm (10%) and the no-norm control message (25%), $\chi^2(1, N = 118) = 4.87$, $p < .03$.

As in Study 4, focusing subjects differentially on the injunctive norm against littering, this time through the processes of priming and spreading activation, led to littering rates corresponding to the predicted degree of injunctive norm focus. Thus, as expected, subjects in Study 5 (a) littered least after encountering a message focusing them directly on the antilittering norm, (b) littered progressively more frequently as the encountered (equally normative) messages directed focus progressively away from the antilittering norm, and (c) littered most when the encountered message was not normative.

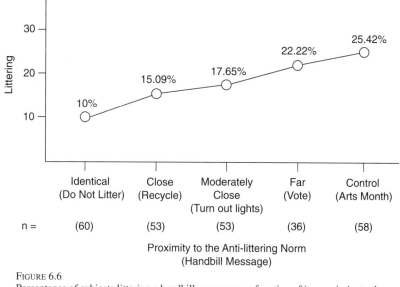

FIGURE 6.6
Percentages of subjects littering a handbill message as a function of its proximity to the injunctive norm against littering: Study 5.

GENERAL DISCUSSION

We began this article by reporting the mixed support for the utility of social norms in accounting for much of human behavior; the claim that the concept, as traditionally conceived, possesses great explanatory power currently has strong proponents and equally strong opponents. From the perspective of the research we have presented, it would appear that both camps are right. Norms clearly do have a considerable impact on behavior, but the force and form of that impact can only be usefully understood through conceptual refinements that have not been traditionally or rigorously applied. That is, to predict properly the likelihood of norm-consistent action requires, first, that one specify the type of norm—descriptive or injunctive—said to be operating. Second, one must take into account the various conditions that would incline individuals to focus attention on or away from the norm.

We have argued that our experimental manipulations worked to focus subjects on descriptive norms in Studies 1 through 3, on descriptive and injunctive norms in Study 4, and on injunctive norms in Study 5. Although the patterns of results in those studies are consistent with that argument, there is certainly room for alternative views. For example, it could be contended that, for subjects in Studies 1 through 3, seeing litter in an otherwise clean environment did not simply engage the descriptive norm against littering but engaged the injunctive norm as well. That is, a single piece of litter may have reminded subjects of societal objections to littering, and thus it may have been the activation of the injunctive norm that produced reduced littering in those studies. Alternative accounts of this sort for specific segments of our data, although not parsimonious in explaining the overall pattern of results, remain conceivable nonetheless.

That is so in part because our work was conducted in naturally occurring field settings where it was not possible to assess the precision and effectiveness of our norm-focus manipulations through the methods typically available to laboratory investigators. Detailed checks on the strength, specificity, and functional impact of a subject's attentional focus could not have been practicably administered in our research situations. The consequent absence of such measures allows questions to arise as to whether our experimental manipulations worked as planned. Without the corroboration of these measures, one may have less confidence that the type of norm we intended to be functional actually mediated our findings. Fortunately, the effectiveness of injunctive social norms, about which there has been doubt in the scientific community (Darley & Latané, 1970; Garfinkel, 1967; Krebs, 1970; Krebs & Miller, 1985; Marini, 1984), has the clearest support in our data. That is, although it does seem possible to explain our data patterns without recourse to the well-established concept of descriptive norms, it does not seem plausible to do so without recourse to the more disputed and interesting concept of injunctive social norms, especially in Studies 4 and 5. Nonetheless, future research should be done in ways that allow direct assessments of the mediating processes presumed to be active in the present work.

Throughout this research program, we have exposed subjects to acute situational conditions designed to focus them on or away from particular norms. We recognize, however, that enduring cultural and dispositional conditions may also influence one's normative focus. This distinction among cultural, situational, and dispositional factors strikes us as important in the realm of norms. In thinking about the concept, we have been led to speculate that norms function at the cultural/societal level, the situational level, and the individual level. Although they may not have developed such a tripartite conceptualization, norm theorists have recognized normative influences at each of these levels. At the first (cultural/societal) level, the influence of global norms on behavior within a culture or social group has often been noted (Birnbaum & Sagarin, 1976; Paicheler, 1976; Pepitone, 1976; Triandis, 1977; Triandis, Marin, Lisansky, & Betancourt, 1984). Indeed, many definitions of norms refer exclusively to this level. For example, Ross (1973) considered norms to be "cultural rules that guide behavior within a society" (p. 105). At the second level, others have recognized that cultural norms may not apply equally to all situations (Peterson, 1982). Consequently, definitions of norms often include an explicit situational component. For example, Popenoe (1983) defined social norms as expectations "of how people are supposed to act, think, or feel in specific situations" (p. 598). Finally, other social scientists have evidence that norms exist at the individual level as well. Most notable in this regard is the groundbreaking work of Schwartz (1973, 1977) on the concept of personal norms.

Our view is that what is normative (i.e., most often done or approved or both) in a society, in a setting, and within a person will, in each case, have demonstrable impact on action, but that the impact will be differential depending on whether the actor is focused on norms of the culture, the situation, or the self. Research is planned to test the implications of this conception.

References

ANDERSON, J. R. (1976). *Language, memory, and thought.* Hillsdale, NJ: Erlbaum.

ANDERSON, J. R. (1983). *The architecture of cognition.* Cambridge, MA: Harvard University Press.

BERKOWITZ, L. (1972). Social norms, feelings, and other factors affecting helping and altruism. In L. Berkowitz (Ed.), *Advances in experimental social psychology* (Vol. 6, pp. 63–108). San Diego, CA: Academic Press.

BERKOWITZ, L., & DANIELS, L. R. (1964). Affecting the salience of the social responsibility norm. *Journal of Abnormal and Social Psychology, 68,* 275–281.

BICKMAN, L. (1972). Environmental attitudes and actions. *Journal of Social Psychology, 87,* 323–324.

BIRNBAUM, A., & SAGARIN, E. (1976). *Norms and human behavior.* New York: Praeger.

CALIFORNIA WASTE MANAGEMENT BOARD. (1988). *The California litter problem.* Sacramento, CA: Author.

CIALDINI, R. B. (1988). *Influence: Science and practice* (2nd ed.). Glenview, IL: Scott, Foresman.

COLLINS, A. M., & LOFTUS, E. F. (1975). A spreading-activation theory of semantic processing. *Psychological Review, 82,* 407–428.

DARLEY, J. M., & LATANÉ, B. (1970). Norms and normative behavior: Field studies of social interdependence. In J. Macaulay & L. Berkowitz (Eds.), *Altruism and helping behavior* (pp. 83–102). San Diego, CA: Academic Press.

DEUTSCH, M., & GERARD, H. B. (1955). A study of normative and informational social influence upon individual judgment. *Journal of Abnormal and Social Psychology, 51,* 629–636.

FELDMAN, N. S., HIGGINS, E. T., KARLOVAC, M., & RUBLE, D. N. (1976). Use of consensus information in causal attributions as a function of temporal presentation and availability of direct information. *Journal of Personality and Social Psychology, 34,* 694–698.

FERGUSON, T. J., & WELLS, G. L. (1980). Priming of mediators in causal attribution. *Journal of Personality and Social Psychology, 38,* 461–470.

FINNIE, W. C. (1973). Field experiments in litter control. *Environment and Behavior, 5,* 123–144.

FISHBEIN, M., & AJZEN, L. (1975). *Belief, attitude, invention, and behavior.* Reading, MA: Addison-Wesley.

FISKE, S. T., & TAYLOR, S. E. (1984). *Social cognition.* Reading, MA: Addison-Wesley.

GARFINKEL, H. (1967). *Studies in ethnomethodology.* Englewood Cliffs, NJ: Prentice-Hall.

GELLER, E. S., WINETT, S., & EVERETT, P. B. (1982). *Preserving the environment.* New York: Pergamon Press.

GELLER, E. S., WITMER, J. F., & TUSO, M. A. (1977). Environmental interventions for litter control. *Journal of Applied Psychology, 62,* 344–351.

GRUDER, C. L., ROMER, D., & KORTH, B. (1978). Dependency and fault as determinants of helping. *Journal of Experimental Social Psychology, 14,* 227–235.

HARVEY, M. D., & ENALA, M. E. (1981). A cognitive model of social norms for understanding the transgression-helping effect. *Journal of Personality and Social Psychology, 41,* 866–875.

HEBERLEIN, T. A. (1971). Moral norms, threatened sanctions, and littering behavior. *Dissertation Abstracts International, 32,* 5906A. (University Microfilms No. 72-2639)

HIGGINS, E. T., & BARGH, J. E. (1987). Social cognition and social perception. *Annual Review of Psychology, 38,* 369–425.

KEEP AMERICA BEAUTIFUL, INC. (1968). *Who litters and why.* New York: Public Opinion Surveys.

KRAUSS, R. M., FREEDMAN, J. L., & WHITCUP, M. (1978). Field and laboratory studies of littering. *Journal of Experimental Social Psychology, 14,* 109–122.

KREBS, D. L. (1970). Altruism: An examination of the concept and a review of the literature. *Psychological Bulletin, 73,* 258–302.

KREBS, D. L., & MILLER, D. T. (1985). Altruism and aggression. In G. Lindzey & E. Aronson (Eds.), *The handbook of social psychology* (3rd ed.). New York: Random House.

MANIS, M., DOVALINA, L., AVIS, N. E., & CARDOZE, S. (1980). Base rates can affect individual prediction. *Journal of Personality and Social Psychology, 38,* 231–248.

MARINI, M. M. (1984). Age and sequencing norms in the transition to adulthood. *Social Forces, 63,* 229–244.

McCLELLAND, J. L., & RUMELHART, D. E. (1981). An interactive activation model of context effects in letter perception. *Psychological Review, 8,* 375–407.

McKIRNAN, D. J. (1980). The conceptualization of deviance: A conceptualization and initial test of a model of social norms. *European Journal of Social Psychology, 10,* 79–93.

MEHAN, H., & WOOD, H. (1975). *Reality of ethnomethodology.* New York: Wiley.

MILGRAM, S., BICKMAN, L., & BERKOWITZ, O. (1969). Note on the drawing power of crowds of different size. *Journal of Personality and Social Psychology, 13,* 79–82.

MILLER, L. E., & GRUSH, J. E. (1986). Individual differences in attitudinal versus normative determination of behavior. *Journal of Experimental Social Psychology, 22,* 190–202.

PAICHELER, G. (1976). Norms and attitude change: Polarization and styles of behavior. *European Journal of Social Psychology, 6,* 405–427.

PEPITONE, A. (1976). Toward a normative and comparative biocultural social psychology. *Journal of Personality and Social Psychology, 34,* 641–653.

PETERSON, L. (1982). An alternative perspective to norm-based explanations of modeling and children's generosity. *Merrill Palmer Quarterly, 28,* 283–290.

POPENOE, D. (1983). *Sociology* (5th ed.). Englewood Cliffs, NJ: Prentice-Hall.

RATCLIFF, R., & McKOON, G. (1988). A retrieval theory of priming in memory. *Psychological Review, 95,* 385–408.

REITER, S. M., & SAMUEL, W. (1980). Littering as a function of prior litter and the presence or absence of prohibitive signs. *Journal of Applied Social Psychology, 10,* 45–55.

ROSS, H. L. (1973). *Perspectives on social order.* New York: McGraw-Hill.

RUBLE, D. N., & FELDMAN, N. S. (1976). Order of consensus, distinctiveness, and consistency information and causal attributions. *Journal of Personality and Social Psychology, 34,* 930–937.

RUTKOWSKI, G. K., GRUDER, C. L., & ROMER, D. (1983). Group cohesiveness, social norms, and bystander intervention. *Journal of Personality and Social Psychology, 44,* 545–552.

SHAFFER, L. S. (1983). Toward Pepitone's vision of a normative social psychology: What is a social norm? *Journal of Mind and Behavior, 4,* 275–294.

SCHWARTZ, S. H. (1973). Normative explanations of helping behavior: A critique, proposal, and empirical test. *Journal of Experimental Social Psychology, 9,* 349–364.

SCHWARTZ, S. H. (1977). Normative influences on altruism. In L. Berkowitz (Ed.), *Advances in experimental social psychology* (Vol. 10, pp. 221–279). San Diego, CA: Academic Press.

SCHWARTZ, S. H., & FLEISHMAN, J. A. (1978). Personal norms and the mediation of legitimacy effects on helping. *Social Psychology, 41,* 306–315.

SHERIF, M. (1936). *The psychology of social norms.* New York: Harper.

SHERIF, M., & SHERIF, C. W. (1969). *Social psychology.* New York: Harper & ROW.

STAUB, E. (1972). Instigation to goodness: The role of social norms and interpersonal influence. *Journal of Social Issues, 28,* 131–150.

TRIANDIS, H. C. (1977). *Interpersonal behavior.* Monterey, CA: Brooks/Cole.

TRIANDIS, H. C., MARIN, G., LISANSKY, J., & BETANCOURT, H. (1984). *Simpatia* as a cultural script of Hispanics. *Journal of Personality and Social Psychology, 47,* 1363–1375.

TROPE, Y., & GINNOSAR, Z. (1986). On the use of statistical and nonstatistical knowledge. In D. Bar Tal & A. Kruglanski (Eds.), *The social psychology of knowledge.* New York: Cambridge Press.

VENKATCSAN, M. (1966). Experimental study of consumer behavior, conformity, and independence. *Journal of Marketing Research, 3,* 384–387.

7

Making Sense of the Nonsensical:
An Analysis of Jonestown

Neal Osherow

> Those who do not remember the past are condemned to repeat it.
>
> —quotation on placard over Jim Jones's rostrum
> at Jonestown

Close to one thousand people died at Jonestown. The members of the Peoples Temple settlement in Guyana, under the direction of the Reverend Jim Jones, fed a poison-laced drink to their children, administered the potion to their infants, and drank it themselves. Their bodies were found lying together, arm in arm; over 900 perished.

How could such a tragedy occur? The image of an entire community destroying itself, of parents killing their own children, appears incredible. The media stories about the event and full-color pictures of the scene documented some of its horror but did little to illuminate the causes or to explain the processes that led to the deaths. Even a year afterwards, a CBS Evening News broadcast asserted that "it was widely assumed that time would offer some explanation for the ritualistic suicide/murder of over 900 people. . . . One year later, it does not appear that any lessons have been uncovered" (CBS News, 1979).

The story of the Peoples Temple is not enshrouded in mystery, however. Jim Jones had founded his church over twenty years before, in Indiana. His preaching stressed the need for racial brotherhood and integration, and his group helped feed the poor and find them jobs. As his congregation grew, Jim Jones gradually increased the discipline and dedication that he required from the members. In 1965, he moved to northern California; about 100 of his faithful relocated with him. The membership began to multiply, new congregations were formed, and the headquarters was established in San Francisco.

I am very grateful to Elliot Aronson for his assistance with this essay. His insights, suggestions, and criticism were most valuable to its development. Also, my thanks to Elise Bean for her helpful editing.

Behind his public image as a beloved leader espousing interracial harmony, "Father," as Jones was called, assumed a messiah-like presence in the Peoples Temple. Increasingly, he became the personal object of the members' devotion, and he used their numbers and obedience to gain political influence and power. Within the Temple, Jones demanded absolute loyalty, enforced a taxing regimen, and delivered sermons forecasting nuclear holocaust and an apocalyptic destruction of the world, promising his followers that they alone would emerge as survivors. Many of his harangues attacked racism and capitalism, but his most vehement anger focused on the "enemies" of the Peoples Temple—its detractors and especially its defectors. In mid-1977, publication of unfavorable magazine articles, coupled with the impending custody battle over a six-year-old Jones claimed as a "son," prompted emigration of the bulk of Temple membership to a jungle outpost in Guyana.

In November, 1978, Congressman Leo Ryan responded to charges that the Peoples Temple was holding people against their will at Jonestown. He organized a trip to the South American settlement; a small party of journalists and "Concerned Relatives" of Peoples Temple members accompanied him on his investigation. They were in Jonestown for one evening and part of the following day. They heard most residents praise the settlement, expressing their joy at being there and indicating their desire to stay. Two families, however, slipped messages to Ryan that they wanted to leave with him. After the visit, as Ryan's party and these defectors tried to board planes to depart, the group was ambushed and fired upon by Temple gunmen—five people, including Ryan, were murdered.

As the shootings were taking place at the jungle airstrip, Jim Jones gathered the community at Jonestown. He informed them that the Congressman's party would be killed and then initiated the final ritual: the "revolutionary suicide" that the membership had rehearsed on prior occasions. The poison was brought out. It was taken.

Jonestown's remoteness caused reports of the event to reach the public in stages. First came bulletins announcing the assassination of Congressman Ryan along with several members of his party. Then came rumors of mass-deaths at Jonestown, then confirmations. The initial estimates put the number of dead near 400, bringing the hope that substantial numbers of people had escaped into the jungle. But as the bodies were counted, many smaller victims were discovered under the corpses of larger ones—virtually none of the inhabitants of Jonestown survived. The public was shocked, then horrified, then incredulous.

Amid the early stories about the tragedy, along with the lurid descriptions and sensational photographs, came some attempts at analysis. Most discussed the charisma of Jim Jones and the power of "cults." Jones was described as "a character Joseph Conrad might have dreamt up" (Krause, 1978), a "self-appointed messiah" whose "lust for dominion" led hundreds of "fanatic" followers to their demise (Special Report: The Cult of Death, *Newsweek*, 1978a).

While a description in terms of the personality of the perpetrator and the vulnerability of the victims provides some explanation, it relegates the event to the category of being an aberration, a product of unique forces and dispositions. Assuming such a perspective distances us from the phenomenon. This might be comforting, but I believe that it limits our understanding and is potentially dangerous. My aim in this analysis is not to blunt the emotional impact of a tragedy of this magnitude by subjecting it to academic examination. At the same time, applying social psychological theory and research makes it more conceivable and comprehensible, thus bringing it closer (in kind rather than in degree) to processes each of us encounters. Social psychological concepts can facilitate our understanding: The killings themselves, and many of the occurrences leading up to them, can be viewed in terms of obedience and compliance. The processes that induced people to join and to believe in the Peoples Temple made use of strategies involved in propaganda and persuasion. In grappling with the most perplexing questions—Why didn't more people leave the Temple? How could they actually kill their children and themselves?—the psychology of self-justification provides some insight.

CONFORMITY

The character of a church . . . can be seen in its attitude
toward its detractors.

—Hugh Prather, *Notes to Myself*

At one level, the deaths at Jonestown can be viewed as the product of obedience, of people complying with the orders of a leader and reacting to the threat of force. In the Peoples Temple, whatever Jim Jones commanded, the members did. When he gathered the community at the pavilion and the poison was brought out, the populace was surrounded by armed guards who were trusted lieutenants of Jones. There are reports that some people did not drink voluntarily but had the poison forced down their throats or injected (Winfrey, 1979). While there were isolated acts of resistance and suggestions of opposition to the suicides, excerpts from a tape, recorded as the final ritual was being enacted, reveal that such dissent was quickly dismissed or shouted down:

> JONES: I've tried my best to give you a good life. In spite of all I've tried, a handful of people, with their lies, have made our life impossible. If we can't live in peace then let's die in peace. (Applause) . . . We have been so terribly betrayed. . . .
>
> What's going to happen here in the matter of a few minutes is that one of the people on that plane is going to shoot the pilot—I know that. I didn't plan it, but I know it's going to happen. . . . So my opinion is that you be kind to children, and be kind to seniors, and take the potion like they used to in ancient Greece, and step over quietly, because we are not committing suicide—it's a revolutionary act. . . . We can't go back. They're now going back to tell more lies. . . .
>
> FIRST WOMEN: I feel like that as long as there's life, there's hope.
>
> JONES: Well, someday everybody dies.
>
> CROWD: That's right, that's right!

JONES: What those people gone and done, and what they get through will make our lives worse than hell. . . . But to me, death is not a fearful thing. It's living that's cursed. . . . Not worth living like this.

FIRST WOMAN: But I'm afraid to die.

JONES: I don't think you are. I don't think you are.

FIRST WOMAN: I think there were too few who left for 1,200 people to give them their lives for those people who left. . . . I look at all the babies and I think they deserve to live.

JONES: But don't they deserve much more—they deserve peace. The best testimony we can give is to leave this goddam world. (Applause)

FIRST MAN: It's over, sister. . . . We've made a beautiful day. (Applause)

SECOND MAN: If you tell us we have to give our lives now, we're ready. (Applause)
[*Baltimore Sun,* 1979.]

Above the cries of babies wailing, the tape continues, with Jones insisting upon the need for suicide and urging the people to complete the act:

JONES: Please get some medication. Simple. It's simple. There's no convulsions with it. . . . Don't be afraid to die. You'll see people land out here. They'll torture our people. . . .

SECOND WOMAN: There's nothing to worry about. Everybody keep calm and try to keep your children calm. . . . They're not crying from pain; it's just a little bitter tasting . . .

THIRD WOMAN: This is nothing to cry about. This is something we could all rejoice about. (Applause)

JONES: Please, for God's sake, let's get on with it. . . . This is a revolutionary suicide. This is not a self-destructive suicide. (Voices praise "Dad." Applause)

THIRD MAN: Dad has brought us this far. My vote is to go with Dad. . . .

JONES: We must die with dignity. Hurry, hurry, hurry. We must hurry. . . . Stop this hysterics. Death is a million times more perferable to spending more days in this life. . . . If you knew what was ahead, you'd be glad to be stepping over tonight . . .

FOURTH WOMAN: It's been a pleasure walking with all of you in this revolutionary struggle. . . . No other way I would rather go than to give my life for socialism. Communism, and I thank Dad very much.

JONES: Take our life from us. . . . We didn't commit suicide. We committed an act of revolutionary suicide protesting against the conditions of an inhuman world [*Newsweek,* 1978b, 1979].

If you hold a gun at someone's head, you can get that person to do just about anything. As many accounts have attested,[1] by the early 1970s the members of the Peoples Temple lived in constant fear of severe punishment—brutal beatings

---

[1]The reports of ex-Peoples Temple members who defected create a very consistent picture of the tactics Jim Jones employed in his church. Jenane Mills (1979) provides the most comprehensive personal account, and there are affidavits about the Peoples Temple sworn to by Deborah Blakey (May 12, 1978 and June 15, 1978) and Yolanda Crawford (April 10, 1978). Media stories about the Peoples Temple, which usually rely on interviews with defectors, and about Jonestown, which are based on interviews with survivors, also corroborate one another. (See especially Kilduff and Tracy (1977), *Newsweek* (1978a), Lifton (1979), and Cahill (1979).

coupled with public humiliation—for committing trivial or even inadvertent offenses. But the power of an authority need not be so explicitly threatening in order to induce compliance with its demands, as demonstrated by social psychological research. In Milgram's experiments (1963), a surprisingly high proportion of subjects obeyed the instructions of an experimenter to administer what they thought were very strong electric shocks to another person. Nor does the consensus of a group need be so blatantly coercive to induce agreement with its opinion, as Asch's experiments (1955) on conformity to the incorrect judgments of a majority indicate.

Jim Jones utilized the threat of severe punishment to impose the strict discipline and absolute devotion that he demanded, and he also took measures to eliminate those factors that might encourage resistance or rebellion among his followers. Research showed that the presence of a "disobedient" partner greatly reduced the extent to which most subjects in the Milgram situation (1965) obeyed the instructions to shock the person designated the "learner." Similarly, by including just one confederate who expressed an opinion different from the majority's, Asch (1955) showed that the subject would also agree far less, even when the "other dissenter's" judgment was also incorrect and differed from the subject's. In the Peoples Temple, Jones tolerated no dissent, made sure that members had no allegiance more powerful than to himself, and tried to make the alternative of leaving the Temple an unthinkable option.

Jeanne Mills, who spent six years as a high-ranking member before becoming one of the few who left the Peoples Temple, writes: "There was an unwritten but perfectly understood law in the church that was very important: 'No one is to criticize Father, his wife, or his children' " (Mills, 1979). Deborah Blakey, another long-time member who managed to defect, testified:

> Any disagreement with [Jim Jones's] dictates came to be regarded as "treason."
> . . . Although I felt terrible about what was happening, I was afraid to say anything
> because I knew that anyone with a differing opinion gained the wrath of Jones and
> other members. [Blakey, June 15, 1978.]

Conditions in the Peoples Temple became so oppressive, the discrepancy between Jim Jones's stated aims and his practices so pronounced, that it is almost inconceivable that members failed to entertain questions about the church. But these doubts went unreinforced. There were no allies to support one's disobedience of the leader's commands and no fellow dissenters to encourage the expression of disagreement with the majority. Public disobedience or dissent was quickly punished. Questioning Jones's word, even in the company of family or friends, was dangerous—informers and "counselors" were quick to report indiscretions, even by relatives.

The use of informers went further than to stifle dissent; it also diminished the solidarity and loyalty that individuals felt toward their families and friends. While Jones preached that a spirit of brotherhood should pervade his church, he made it clear that each member's personal dedication should be directed to "Father." Families were split: First, children were seated away from parents during services; then, many were assigned to another member's care as they grew up; and ultimately, parents were forced to sign documents surrendering custody rights. "Families are part of the enemy system," Jones stated, because they hurt one's total dedication to the "Cause" (Mills, 1979). Thus, a person called before the membership to be punished could expect his or her family to be among the first and most forceful critics (Cahill, 1979).

Besides splitting parent and child, Jones sought to loosen the bonds between wife and husband. He forced spouses into extramarital sexual relations, which were often of a homosexual or humiliating nature, or with Jones himself. Sexual partnerships and activities not under his direction and control were discouraged and publicly ridiculed.

Thus, expressing any doubts or criticism of Jones—even to a friend, child, or partner—became risky for the individual. As a consequence, such thoughts were kept to oneself, and with the resulting impression that nobody else shared them. In addition to limiting one's access to information, this "fallacy of uniqueness" precluded the sharing of support. It is interesting that among the few who successfully defected from the Peoples Temple were couples such as Jeanne and Al Mills, who kept together, shared their doubts, and gave each other support.

Why didn't more people leave? Once inside the Peoples Temple, getting out was discouraged; defectors were hated. Nothing upset Jim Jones so much; people who left became the targets of his most vitriolic attacks and were blamed for any problems that occurred. One member recalled that after several teen-age members left the Temple, "We hated those eight with such a passion because we knew any day they were going to try bombing us. I mean Jim Jones had us totally convinced of this" (Winfrey, 1979).

Defectors were threatened: Immediately after she left, Grace Stoen headed for the beach at Lake Tahoe, where she found herself looking over her shoulder, checking to make sure that she hadn't been tracked down (Kilduff and Tracy, 1977). Jeanne Mills reports that she and her family were followed by men in cars, their home was burglarized, and they were threatened with the use of confessions they had signed while still members. When a friend from the Temple paid a visit, she quickly examined Mills' ears—Jim Jones had vowed to have one of them cut off (Mills, 1979). He had made ominous predictions concerning other defectors as well: Indeed, several ex-members suffered puzzling deaths or committed very questionable "suicides" shortly after leaving the Peoples Temple (Reiterman, 1977; Tracy, 1978).

Defecting became quite a risky enterprise, and, for most members, the potential benefits were very uncertain. They had little to hope for outside of the Peoples Temple; what they had, they had committed to the church. Jim Jones had vilified previous defectors as "the enemy" and had instilled the fear that, once outside of the Peoples Temple, members' stories would not be believed by the "racist, fascist" society, and they would be subjected to torture, concentration camps, and execution. Finally, in Guyana, Jonestown was surrounded by dense jungle, the few trails patrolled by armed security guards (Cahill, 1979). Escape was not a viable option. Resistance was too costly. With no other alternatives apparent, compliance became the most reasonable course of action.

The power that Jim Jones wielded kept the membership of the Peoples Temple in line, and the difficulty of defecting helped to keep them in. But what attracted them to join Jones's church in the first place?

PERSUASION

Nothing is so unbelievable that oratory cannot make it acceptable.

—Cicero

Jim Jones was a charismatic figure, adept at oratory. He sought people for his church who would be receptive to his messages and vulnerable to his promises, and he carefully honed his presentation to appeal to each specific audience.

The bulk of the Peoples Temple membership was comprised of society's needy and neglected: the urban poor, the black, the elderly, and a sprinkling of ex-addicts and ex-convicts (Winfrey, 1979). To attract new members, Jones held public services in various cities. Leaflets would be distributed:

> PASTOR JIM JONES . . . Incredible! . . . Miraculous! . . . Amazing! . . . The Most Unique Prophetic Healing Service You've Ever Witnessed! Behold the Word Made Incarnate In Your Midst!
> God works as tumorous masses are passed in every service. . . . Before your eyes, the crippled walk, the blind see! [Kilduff and Javers, 1978.]

Potential members first confronted an almost idyllic scene of blacks and whites living, working, and worshipping together. Guests were greeted and treated most warmly and were invited to share in the group's meal. As advertised, Jim Jones also gave them miracles. A number of members would recount how Jones had cured them of cancer or other dread diseases; during the service Jones or one of his nurses would reach into the member's throat and emerge with a vile mass of tissue—the "cancer" that had been passed as the person gagged. Sometimes Jim Jones would make predictions that would occur with uncanny frequency. He also received revelations about members or visitors that nobody but those individuals could know—what they had eaten for dinner the night before, for instance, or news about a far-off relative. Occasionally, he performed miracles similar to more well-established religious figures:

> There were more people than usual at the Sunday service, and for some reason the church members hadn't brought enough food to feed everyone. It became apparent that the last fifty people in line weren't going to get any meat. Jim announced, "Even though there isn't enough food to feed this multitude, I am blessing the food that we have and multiplying it—just as Jesus did in biblical times."

> Sure enough, a few minutes after he made this startling announcement, Eva Pugh came out of the kitchen beaming, carrying two platters filled with fried chicken. A big cheer came from the people assembled in the room, especially from the people who were at the end of the line.
>
> The "blessed chicken" was extraordinarily delicious, and several of the people mentioned that Jim had produced the best-tasting chicken they had ever eaten. [Mills, 1979.]

These demonstrations were dramatic and impressive; most members were convinced of their authenticity and believed in Jones's "powers." They didn't know that the "cancers" were actually rancid chicken gizzards, that the occurrences Jones "forecast" were staged, or that sending people to sift through a person's garbage could reveal packages of certain foods or letters of out-of-town relatives to serve as grist for Jones' "revelations" (Kilduff and Tracy, 1977; Mills, 1979). Members were motivated to believe in Jones; they appreciated the racial harmony, sense of purpose, and relief from feelings of worthlessness that the Peoples Temple provided them (Winfrey, 1979; Lifton, 1979). Even when suspecting that something was wrong, they learned that it was unwise to voice their doubts:

> One of the men, Chuck Beikman . . . jokingly mentioned to a few people standing near him that he had seen Eva drive up a few moments earlier with buckets from the Kentucky Fried Chicken stand. He smiled as he said, "The person that blessed this chicken was Colonel Sanders."
>
> During the evening meeting Jim mentioned the fact that Chuck had made fun of his gift. "He lied to some of the members here, telling them that the chicken had come from a local shop," Jim stormed. "But the Spirit of Justice has prevailed. Because of his lie Chuck is in the men's room right now, wishing that he was dead. He is vomiting and has diarrhea so bad he can't talk!"
>
> An hour later a pale and shaken Chuck Beikman walked out of the men's room and up to the front, being supported by one of the guards. Jim asked him, "Do you have anything you'd like to say?"
>
> Chuck looked up weakly and answered, "Jim, I apologize for what I said. Please forgive me."
>
> As we looked at Chuck, we vowed in our hearts that we would never question any of Jim's "miracles"—at least not out loud. Years later, we learned that Jim had put a mild poison in a piece of cake and given it to Chuck. [Mills, 1979.]

While most members responded to presentations that were emotional, one-sided, and almost sensational in tone, those who eventually assumed positions of responsibility in the upper echelons of the Peoples Temple were attracted by different considerations. Most of these people were white and came from upper-middle-class backgrounds—they included lawyers, a medical student, nurses, and people representing other occupations that demanded education and reflected a strong social consciousness. Jones lured these members by stressing the social and political aspects of the church, its potential as an idealistic experiment with integration and socialism. Tim Stoen, who was the Temple's lawyer, stated later, "I wanted utopia so damn bad I could die" (Winfrey, 1979). These members had the information and intelligence to see through many of Jones's ploys, but, as Jeanne Mills explains repeatedly in her book, they dismissed their qualms and dismissed Jones's deception as being necessary to achieve a more important aim—furthering the Cause: "For the thousandth time, I rationalized my doubts. 'If Jim feels it's necessary for the Cause, who am I to question his wisdom?' " (Mills, 1979).

It turned out to be remarkably easy to overcome their hesitancy and calm their doubts. Mills recalls that she and her husband initially were skeptical about Jones and the Peoples Temple. After attending their first meeting, they remained unimpressed by the many members who proclaimed that Jones had healed their cancers or cured their drug habits. They were annoyed by Jones' arrogance, and they were bored by most of the long service. But in the weeks following their visit, they received numerous letters containing testimonials and gifts from the Peoples Temple, they had dreams about Jones, and they were attracted by the friendship and love they had felt from both the black and the white members. When they went back for their second visit, they took their children with them. After the long drive, the Mills's were greeted warmly by many members and by Jones himself. "This time . . . my mind was open to hear his message because my own beliefs had become very shaky" (Mills, 1979). As they were driving home afterwards, the children begged their parents to join the church:

> We had to admit that we enjoyed the service more this time and we told the children that we'd think it over. Somehow, though, we knew that it was only a matter of time before we were going to become members of the Peoples Temple. [Mills, 1979.]

Jim Jones skillfully manipulated the impression that his church would convey to newcomers. He carefully managed its public image. He used the letter-writing and political clout of hundreds of members to praise and impress the politicians and press that supported the Peoples Temple, as well as to criticize and intimidate its opponents (Kasindorf, 1978). Most importantly, Jones severely restricted the information that was available to the members. In addition to indoctrinating members into his own belief system through extensive sermons and lectures, he inculcated a distrust of any contradictory messages, labelling them the product of enemies. By destroying the credibility of their sources, he inoculated the membership against being persuaded by outside criticism. Similarly, any contradictory thoughts that might arise within each member were to be discredited. Instead of seeing them as having any basis in reality, members interpreted them as indications of their own shortcomings or lack of faith. Members learned to attribute the apparent discrepancies between Jones's lofty pronouncements and the rigors of life in the Peoples Temple to their personal inadequacies rather than blaming them on any fault of Jones. As ex-member Neva Sly was quoted: "We always blamed ourselves for things that didn't seem right" (Winfrey, 1979). A unique and distorting language developed within the church, in which "the Cause" became anything that Jim Jones said (Mills, 1979). It was spoken at Jonestown, where a guard tower was called the "playground" (Cahill, 1979). Ultimately, through the clever use of oratory, deception, and language, Jones could speak of death as "stepping over," thereby camouflaging a hopeless act of self-destruction as a noble and brave act of "revolutionary suicide," and the members accepted his words.

SELF-JUSTIFICATION

Both salvation and punishment for man lie in the fact
that if he lives wrongly he can befog himself so as not
to see the misery of his position.

—Tolstoy, "The Kreutzer Sonata"

Analyzing Jonestown in terms of obedience and the power of the situation can help
to explain why the people *acted* as they did. Once the Peoples Temple had moved to
Jonestown, there was little the members could do other than follow Jim Jones's dictates. They were comforted by an authority of absolute power. They were left with few
options, being surrounded by armed guards and by the jungle, having given their pass-
ports and various documents and confessions to Jones, and believing that conditions
in the outside world were even more threatening. The members' poor diet, heavy
workload, lack of sleep, and constant exposure to Jones's diatribes exacerbated the
coerciveness of their predicament; tremendous pressures encouraged them to obey.

By the time of the final ritual, opposition or escape had become almost impossible for most of the members. Yet even then, it is doubtful that many *wanted* to resist or to leave. Most had come to believe in Jones—one woman's body was found
with a message scribbled on her arm during the final hours: "Jim Jones is the only
one" (Cahill, 1979). They seemed to have accepted the necessity, and even the
beauty, of dying—just before the ritual began, a guard approached Charles Garry,
one of the Temple's hired attorneys, and exclaimed, "It's a great moment . . . we all
die" (Lifton, 1979). A survivor of Jonestown, who happened to be away at the den-
tist, was interviewed a year following the deaths:

> If I had been there, I would have been the first one to stand in that line and take that
> poison and I would have been proud to take it. The thing I'm sad about is this; that I
> missed the ending. [Gallagher, 1979.]

It is this aspect of Jonestown that is perhaps the most troubling. To the end, and
even beyond, the vast majority of the Peoples Temple members *believed* in Jim
Jones. External forces, in the form of power or persuasion, can exact compliance.
But one must examine a different set of processes to account for the members' in-
ternalizing those beliefs.

Although Jones's statements were often inconsistent and his methods cruel,
most members maintained their faith in his leadership. Once they were isolated at
Jonestown, there was little opportunity or motivation to think otherwise—resistance or escape was out of the question. In such a situation, the individual is motivated to rationalize his or her predicament; a person confronted with the inevitable
tends to regard it more positively. For example, social psychological research has
shown that when children believe that they will be served more of a vegetable they
dislike, they will convince themselves that it is not so noxious (Brehm, 1959), and

when a person thinks that she will be interacting with someone, she tends to judge a description of that individual more favorably (Darley and Berscheid, 1967).

A member's involvement in the Temple did not begin at Jonestown—it started much earlier, closer to home, and less dramatically. At first, the potential member would attend meetings voluntarily and might put in a few hours each week working for the church. Though the established members would urge the recruit to join, he or she felt free to choose whether to stay or to leave. Upon deciding to join, a member expended more effort and became more committed to the Peoples Temple. In small increments, Jones increased the demands made on the member, and only after a long sequence did he escalate the oppressiveness of his rule and the desperation of his message. Little by little, the individual's alternatives became more limited. Step by step, the person was motivated to rationalize his or her commitment and to justify his or her behavior.

Jeanne Mills, who managed to defect two years before the Temple relocated in Guyana, begins her account, *Six Years With God* (1979), by writing: "Every time I tell someone about the six years we spent as members of the Peoples Temple, I am faced with an unanswerable question: 'If the church was so bad, why did you and your family stay in for so long?'" Several classic studies from social psychological research investigating processes of self-justification and the theory of cognitive dissonance (see Aronson, 1980, chapter 4; Aronson, 1969) can point to explanations for such seemingly irrational behavior.

According to dissonance theory, when a person commits an act or holds a cognition that is psychologically inconsistent with his or her self-concept, the inconsistency arouses an unpleasant state of tension. The individual tries to reduce this "dissonance," usually by altering his or her attitudes to bring them more into line with the previously discrepant action or belief. A number of occurrences in the Peoples Temple can be illuminated by viewing them in light of this process. The horrifying events of Jonestown were not due merely to the threat of force, nor did they erupt instantaneously. That is, it was *not* the case that something "snapped" in people's minds, suddenly causing them to behave in bizarre ways. Rather, as the theory of cognitive dissonance spells out, people seek to *justify* their choices and commitments.

Just as a towering waterfall can begin as a trickle, so too can the impetus for doing extreme or calamitous actions be provided by the consequences of agreeing to do seemingly trivial ones. In the Peoples Temple, the process started with the effects of undergoing a severe initiation to join the church, was reinforced by the tendency to justify one's commitments, and was strengthened by the need to rationalize one's behavior.

Consider the prospective member's initial visit to the People's Temple, for example. When a person undergoes a severe initiation in order to gain entrance into a group, he or she is apt to judge that group as being more attractive, in order to justify expending the effort or enduring the pain. Aronson and Mills (1959) demonstrated that students who suffered greater embarrassment as a prerequisite for being allowed to participate in a discussion group rated its conversation (which actually was quite boring) to be significantly more interesting than did those students who experienced little or no embarrassment in order to be admitted. Not only is there a tendency to justify undergoing the experience by raising one's estimation of the goal—in some circumstances, choosing to experience a hardship can go so far as to affect a person's perception of the discomfort or pain he or she felt. Zimbardo (1969) and his colleagues showed that when subjects volunteered for a procedure that involves their being given electric shocks, those thinking that they had more choice in the matter reported feeling less pain from the shocks. More specifically, those who experienced greater dissonance, having little external justification to account for their choosing to endure the pain, described it as being less intense. This extended beyond their impressions and verbal reports; their performance on a task was hindered less, and they even recorded somewhat lower readings on a physiological instrument measuring galvanic skin responses. Thus the dissonance-reducing process can be double-edged: Under proper guidance, a person who voluntarily experiences a severe initiation not only comes to regard its ends more positively, but may also begin to see the means as less aversive: "We begin to appreciate the long meetings, because we were told that spiritual growth comes from self-sacrifice" (Mills, 1979).

Once involved, a member found ever-increasing portions of his or her time and energy devoted to the Peoples Temple. The services and meetings occupied weekends and several evenings each week. Working on Temple projects and writing the required letters to politicians and the press took much of one's "spare" time. Expected monetary contributions changed from "voluntary" donations (though they were recorded) to the required contribution of a quarter of one's income. Eventually, a member was supposed to sign over all personal property, savings, social security checks, and the like to the Peoples Temple. Before entering the meeting room for each service, a member stopped at a table and wrote self-incriminating letters or signed blank documents that were turned over to the church. If anyone objected, the refusal was interpreted as denoting a "lack of faith" in Jones. Finally, members were asked to live at Temple facilities to save money and to be able to work more efficiently, and many of their children were raised under the care of other families. Acceding to each new demand had two repercussions: In practical terms, it enmeshed the person further into the Peoples Temple web and made leaving more difficult; on an attitudinal level, it set the aforementioned processes of self-justification into motion. As Mills (1979) describes:

> We had to face painful reality. Our life savings were gone. Jim had demanded that we sell the life insurance policy and turn the equity over to the church, so that was gone. Our property had all been taken from us. Our dream of going to an overseas mission was gone. We thought that we had alienated our parents when we told them we were leaving the country. Even the children whom we had left in the care of Carol and Bill were openly hostile toward us. Jim had accomplished all this in such a short time! All we had left now was Jim and the Cause, so we decided to buckle under and give our energies to these two.

Ultimately, Jim Jones and the Cause would require the members to give their lives.

What could cause people to kill their children and themselves? From a detached perspective, the image seems unbelievable. In fact, at first glance, so does the idea of so many individuals committing so much of their time, giving all of their money, and even sacrificing the control of their children to the Peoples Temple. Jones took advantage of rationalization processes that allow people to justify their commitments by raising their estimations of the goal and minimizing its costs. Much as he gradually increased his demands, Jones carefully orchestrated the members' exposure to the concept of a "final ritual." He utilized the leverage provided by their previous commitments to push them closer and closer to its enactment. Gaining a "foot in the door" by getting a person to agree to a moderate request makes it more probable that he or she will agree to do a much larger deed later, as social psychologists—and salespeople—have found (Freedman and Fraser, 1966). Doing the initial task causes something that might have seemed unreasonable at first appear less extreme in comparison, and it also motivates a person to make his or her behavior appear more consistent by consenting to the larger request as well.

After indoctrinating the members with the workings of the Peoples Temple itself, Jones began to focus on broader and more basic attitudes. He started by undermining the members' belief that death was to be fought and feared and set the stage by introducing the possibility of a cataclysmic ending for the church. As several accounts corroborate (see Mills, 1979; Lifton, 1979; Cahill, 1979), Jones directed several "fake" suicide drills, first with the elite Planning Commission of the Peoples Temple and later with the general membership. He would give them wine and then announce that it had been poisoned and that they would soon die. These became tests of faith, of the members' willingness to follow Jones even to death. Jones would ask people if they were ready to die and on occasion would have the membership "decide" its own fate by voting whether to carry out his wishes. An ex-member recounted that one time, after a while

> Jones smiled and said, "Well, it was a good lesson. I see you're not dead." He made it sound like we needed the 30 minutes to do very strong, introspective type of thinking. We all felt strongly dedicated, proud of ourselves. . . . [Jones] taught that it was a privilege to die for what you believed in, which is exactly what I would have been doing. [Winfrey, 1979.]

After the Temple moved to Jonestown, the "White Nights," as the suicide drills were called, occurred repeatedly. An exercise that appears crazy to the observer was a regular, justifiable occurrence for the Peoples Temple participant. The reader might ask whether this caused the members to think that the actual suicides were merely another practice, but there were many indications that they knew that the poison was truly deadly on that final occasion. The Ryan visit had been climatic, there were several new defectors, the cooks—who had been excused from the prior drills in order to prepare the upcoming meal—were included, Jones had been growing increasingly angry, desperate, and unpredictable, and, finally, everyone could see the first babies die. The membership was manipulated, but they were not unaware that this time the ritual was for real.

A dramatic example of the impact of self-justification concerns the physical punishment that was meted out in the Peoples Temple. As discussed earlier, the threat of being beaten or humiliated forced the member to comply with Jones's orders: A person will obey as long as he or she is being threatened and supervised. To affect a person's *attitudes,* however, a mild threat has been demonstrated to be more effective than a severe threat (Aronson and Carlsmith, 1963) and its influence has been shown to be far longer lasting (Freedman, 1965). Under a mild threat, the individual has more difficulty attributing his or her behavior to such a minor external restraint, forcing the person to alter his or her attitudes in order to justify the action. Severe threats elicit compliance, but, imposed from the outside, they usually fail to cause the behavior to be internalized. Quite a different dynamic ensues when it is not so clear that the action is being imposed upon the person. When an individual feels that he or she played an active role in carrying out an action that hurts someone, there comes a motivation to justify one's part in the cruelty by rationalizing it as necessary or by derogating the victim by thinking that the punishment was deserved (Davis and Jones, 1960).

Let's step back for a moment. The processes going on at Jonestown obviously were not as simple as those in a well-controlled laboratory experiment; several themes were going on simultaneously. For example, Jim Jones had the power to impose any punishments that he wished in the Peoples Temple, and, especially towards the end, brutality and terror at Jonestown were rampant. But Jones carefully controlled how the punishments were carried out. He often called upon the members themselves to agree to the imposition of beatings. They were instructed to testify against fellow members, bigger members told to beat up smaller ones, wives or lovers forced to sexually humiliate their partners, and parents asked to consent to and assist in the beatings of their children (Mills, 1979; Kilduff and Javers, 1978). The punishments grew more and more sadistic, the beatings so severe as to knock the victim unconscious and cause bruises that lasted for weeks. As Donald Lunde, a psychiatrist who has investigated acts of extreme violence, explains:

> Once you've done something that major, it's very hard to admit even to yourself that you've made a mistake, and subconsciously you will go to great lengths to rationalize what you did. It's very tricky defense mechanism exploited to the hilt by the charismatic leader. [*Newsweek,* 1978a.]

A more personal account of the impact of this process is provided by Jeanne Mills. At one meeting, she and her husband were forced to consent to the beating of their daughter as punishment for a very minor transgression. She relates the effect this had on her daughter, the victim, as well as on herself, one of the perpetrators:

> As we drove home, everyone in the car was silent. We were all afraid that our words would be considered treasonous. The only sounds came from Linda, sobbing quietly in the back seat. When we got into our house, Al and I sat down to talk with Linda. She was in too much pain to sit. She stood quietly while we talked with her. "How do you feel about what happened tonight?" Al asked her.

"Father was right to have me whipped," Linda answered. "I've been so rebellious lately, and I've done a lot of things that were wrong. . . . I'm sure Father knew about those things, and that's why he had me hit so many times."

As we kissed our daughter goodnight, our heads were spinning. It was hard to think clearly when things were so confusing. Linda had been the victim, and yet we were the only people angry about it. She should have been hostile and angry. Instead, she said that Jim had actually helped her. We knew Jim had done a cruel thing, and yet everyone acted as if he were doing a loving thing in whipping our disobedient child. Unlike a cruel person hurting a child, Jim had seemed calm, almost loving, as he observed the beating and counted off the whacks. Our minds were not able to comprehend the atrocity of the situation because none of the feedback we were receiving was accurate. [Mills, 1979.]

The feedback one received from the outside was limited, and the feedback from inside the Temple member was distorted. By justifying the previous actions and commitments, the groundwork for accepting the ultimate commitment was established.

CONCLUSION

Only months after we defected from Temple did we realize the full extent of the cocoon in which we'd lived. And only then did we understand the fraud, sadism, and emotional blackmail of the master manipulator.

—Jeanne Mills, *Six Years with God*

Immediately following the Jonestown tragedy, there came a proliferation of articles about "cults" and calls for their investigation and control. From Synanon to Transcendental Meditation, groups and practices were examined by the press, which had a difficult time determining what constituted a "cult" or differentiating between those that might be safe and beneficial and those that could be dangerous. The Peoples Temple and the events at Jonestown make such a definition all the more problematic. A few hours before his murder, Congressman Ryan addressed the membership: "I can tell you right now that by the few conversations I've had with some of the folks . . . there are some people who believe this is the best thing that ever happened in their whole lives" (Krause, 1978). The acquiescence of so many and the letters they left behind indicate that this feeling was widely shared—or at least expressed—by the members.

Many "untraditional"—to mainstream American culture—groups or practices, such as Eastern religions or meditation techniques, have proven valuable for the people who experience them but may be seen as very strange and frightening to others. How can people determine whether they are being exposed to a potentially useful alternative way of living their lives or if they are being drawn to a dangerous one?

The distinction is a difficult one. Three questions suggested by the previous analysis, however, can provide important clues: Are alternatives being provided or taken away'? Is one's access to new and different information being broadened or denied? Finally, does the individual assume personal responsibility and control or is it usurped by the group or by its leader?

The Peoples Temple attracted many of its members because it provided them an alternative way of viewing their lives; it gave many people who were downtrodden a sense of purpose, and even transcendence. But it did so at a cost, forcing them to disown their former friendships and beliefs and teaching them to fear anything outside of the Temple as "the enemy." Following Jones became the *only* alternative.

Indeed, most of the members grew increasingly unaware of the possibility of any other course. Within the Peoples Temple, and especially at Jonestown, Jim Jones controlled the information to which members would be exposed. He effectively stifled any dissent that might arise within the church and instilled a distrust in each member for contradictory messages from outside. After all, what credibility could be carried by information supplied by "the enemy" that was out to destroy the Peoples Temple with "lies"?

Seeing no alternatives and having no information, a member's capacity for dissent or resistance was minimized. Moreover, for most members, part of the Temple's attraction resulted from their willingness to relinquish much of the responsibility and control over their lives. These were primarily the poor, the minorities, the elderly, and the unsuccessful—they were happy to exchange personal autonomy (with its implicit assumption of personal responsibility for their plights) for security, brotherhood, the illusion of miracles, and the promise of salvation. Stanley Cath, a psychiatrist who has studied the conversion techniques used by cults, generalizes: "Converts have to believe only what they are told. They don't have to think, and this relieves tremendous tensions" (*Newsweek,* 1978a). Even Jeanne Mills, one of the better-educated Temple members, commented:

> I was amazed at how little disagreement there was between the members of this church. Before we joined the church, Al and I couldn't even agree on whom to vote for in the presidential election. Now that we all belonged to a group, family arguments were becoming a thing of the past. There was never a question of who was right, because Jim was always right. When our large household met to discuss family problems, we didn't ask for opinions. Instead, we put the question to the children, "What would Jim do?" It took the difficulty out of life. There was a type of "manifest destiny" which said the Cause was right and would succeed. Jim was right and those who agreed with him were right. If you disagreed with Jim, you were wrong. It was as simple as that. [Mills, 1979.]

Though it is unlikely that he had any formal exposure to the social psychological literature, Jim Jones utilized several very powerful and effective techniques for, controlling people's behavior and altering their attitudes. Some analyses have compared his tactics to those involved in "brainwashing," for both include the control of communication, the manipulation of guilt, and dispensing power over people's existence (Lifton, 1979), as well as isolation, an exacting regimen, physical pressure, and the use of confessions (Cahill, 1979). But using the term brainwashing makes the process sound too esoteric and unusual. There *were* some unique and scary elements in Jones' personality—paranoia, delusions of grandeur, sadism, and a preoccupation with suicide. Whatever his personal motivation, however, having formulated his plans and fantasies, he took advantage of well-established social psychological tactics to carry them out. The decision to have a community destroy itself was crazy, but those who performed the deed were "normal" people who were subjected to a tremendously impactful situation, the victims of powerful internal forces as well as external pressures.

POSTSCRIPT

Within a few weeks of the deaths at Jonestown, the bodies had been transported back to the United States, the remnants of the Peoples Temple membership were said to have disbanded, and the spate of stories and books about the suicide/murders had begun to lose the public's attention. Three months afterwards, Michael Prokes, who had escaped from Jonestown because he was assigned to carry away a box of Peoples Temple funds, called a press conference in a California motel room. After claiming that Jones had been misunderstood and demanding the release of a tape recording of the final minutes [quoted earlier], he stepped into the bathroom and shot himself in the head. He left behind a note, saying that if his death inspired another book about Jonestown, it was worthwhile (*Newsweek,* 1979).

POSTSCRIPT

Jeanne and Al Mills were among the most vocal of the Peoples Temple critics following their defection, and they topped an alleged "death list" of its enemies. Even after Jonestown, the Mills's had repeatedly expressed fear for their lives. Well over a year after the Peoples Temple deaths, they and their daughter were murdered in their Berkeley home. Their teen-aged son, himself an ex-Peoples Temple member, has testified that he was in another part of the large house at the time. At this writing, no suspect has been charged. There are indications that the Mills's knew their killer—there were no signs of forced entry, and they were shot at close range. Jeanne Mills had been quoted as saying, "It's going to happen. If not today, then tomorrow." On the final tape of Jonestown, Jim Jones had blamed Jeanne Mills by name, and had promised that his followers in San Francisco "will not take our death in vain" (*Newsweek,* 1980).

References

ARONSON, E. *The social animal* (3rd ed.) San Francisco: W. H. Freeman and Company, 1980.

ARONSON, E. The theory of cognitive dissonance: A current perspective. In L. Berkowitz (ed.), *Advances in experimental social psychology.* Vol. 4. New York: Academic Press, 1969.

ARONSON, E., AND CARLSMITH, J. M. Effect of the severity of threat on the devaluation of forbidden behavior. *Journal of Abnormal and Social Psychology,* 1963, **66,** 584–588.

ARONSON, E., AND MILLS, J. The effects of severity of initiation on liking for a group. *Journal of Abnormal and Social Psychology.* 1959, **59,** 177–181.

ASCH, S. Opinions and social pressure. *Scientific American,* 1955, 193. (Also reprinted in this volume.)

Tape hints early decision by Jones on mass suicide. *Baltimore Sun,* March 15, 1979.

BLAKEY, D. Affidavit: Georgetown, Guyana. May 12, 1978.

BLAKEY, D. Affidavit: San Francisco. June 15, 1978.

BREHM, J. Increasing cognitive dissonance by a *fait-accompli. Journal of Abnormal and Social Psychology,* 1959, **58,** 379–382.

CAHILL, T. In the valley of the shadow of death. *Rolling Stone.* January 25, 1979.

Committee on Foreign Affairs, U.S. House of Representatives, Report of a staff investigative group. *The assassination of Representative Leo J. Ryan and the Jonestown, Guyana tragedy.* Washington, D.C.: Government Printing Office, May 15, 1979. (Many of the other press reports are reprinted in this volume.)

CRAWFORD, Y. Affidavit: San Francisco. April 10, 1978.

DARLEY, J., AND BERSCHEID, E. Increased liking as a result of the anticipation of personal contact. *Human Relations,* 1967, **20,** 29–40.

DAVIS, K., AND JONES, E. Changes in interpersonal perception as a means of reducing cognitive dissonance. *Journal of Abnormal and Social Psychology,* 1960, **61,** 402–410.

"Don't be afraid to die" and another victim of Jonestown. *Newsweek,* March 10, 1980.

A fatal prophecy is fulfilled. *Newsweek,* MARCH 10, 1980.

FREEDMAN, J. Long-term behavioral effects of cognitive dissonance. *Journal of Experimental Social Psychology,* 1965, **1,** 145–155.

FREEDMAN, J., AND FRASER, S. Compliance without pressure: The foot-in-the-door technique. *Journal of Personality and Social Psychology,* 1966, **4,** 195–202.

GALLAGHER, N. Jonestown: The survivors' story. *New York Times Magazine,* November 18, 1979.

KASINDORF, J. Jim Jones: The seduction of San Francisco. *New West,* December 18, 1978.

KILDUFF, M., AND JAVERS, R. *The suicide cult.* New York: Bantam, 1978, and *San Francisco Chronicle.*

KILDUFF, M., AND TRACY, P. Inside Peoples Temple. *New West,* August 1, 1977.

KRAUSE, C. *Guyana massacre.* New York: Berkley, 1978, and *Washington Post.*

LIFTON, R. J. Appeal of the death trip. *New York Times Magazine,* January 7, 1979.

MILGRAM, S. Behavioral study of obedience. *Journal of Abnormal and Social Psychology,* 1963, **67,** 371–378. (Also reprinted in E. Aronson (ed.), *Readings about the social animal.*)

MILGRAM, S. Liberating effects of group pressure. *Journal of Personality and Social Psychology,* 1965, **1,** 127–134.

MILLS, J. *Six years with God.* New York: A & W Publishers, 1979.

REITERMAN, T. Scared too long. *San Francisco Examiner,* November 13, 1977.

The sounds of death. *Newsweek,* December 18, 1978b.

Special report: The cult of death. *Newsweek,* December 4, 1978a.

TRACY, P. Jim Jones: The making of a madman. *New West,* December 18, 1978.

WINFREY, C. Why 900 died in Guyana. *New York Times Magazine,* February 25, 1979.

YOUNG, S. Report on Jonestown. *The CBS Evening News with Walter Cronkite.* November 16, 1979.

ZIMBARDO, P. *The cognitive control of motivation.* Glenview, Ill.: Scott Foresman, 1969.

ZIMBARDO, P., EBBESON, E., AND MASLACH, C. *Influencing attitudes and changing behavior* (2nd ed.). Reading, Mass.: Addison-Wesley, 1977.

III

MASS COMMUNICATION, PROPAGANDA, AND PERSUASION

8

Effects of Varying the Recommendations in a Fear-Arousing Communication

James M. Dabbs, Jr. and Howard Leventhal

It has been suggested that divergent effects of fear arousal on attitude change can be caused by variations in the recommendations in a persuasive communication. In a three-way factorial design Ss were presented with communications manipulating fear of tetanus and the perceived effectiveness and painfulness of inoculation against tetanus. Inoculation was recommended for all Ss. It was expected that more Ss would take shots described as highly effective and not painful, and that this tendency would change as level of fear was increased. The manipulations of effectiveness and painfulness were perceived as intended, but they did not affect intentions to take shots or shot-taking behavior. The fear manipulation influenced both intentions and behavior, with higher fear producing greater compliance with the recommendations.

A number of studies have investigated the effects of fear arousal on persuasion. Although the majority report that fear increases persuasion, the picture is not completely clear. Facilitating effects of fear on persuasion have been reported in studies of dental hygiene practices (Haefner, 1965; Leventhal and Singer, 1966; Singer, 1965), tetanus inoculations (Leventhal, Jones, and Trembly, 1966; Leventhal, Singer, and Jones, 1965), safe driving practices (Berkowitz and Cottingham, 1960; Leventhal and Niles, 1965), and cigarette smoking (Insko, Arkoff, and Insko, 1965; Leventhal and Watts, 1966; Niles, 1964). However, under increasing levels of fear Janis and Feshbach (1953) observed no increase in acceptance of beliefs

Reprinted with permission from the authors and *The Journal of Personality and Social Psychology,* Vol. 4, No. 5, 1966. Copyright © 1966 by the American Psychological Association.

The present study was supported in part by United States Public Health Service Grant CH00077-04 to Howard Leventhal. The authors wish to thank John S. Hathaway and James S. Davie of the Yale University Department of University Health for their many contributions to the research.

about the proper type of toothbrush to use, and Leventhal and Niles (1964) observed some decrease in acceptance of a recommendation to stop smoking. All these results are based on verbal measures of *attitude* change.

The picture is even less clear when one considers actual *behavior* change. The study on tetanus by Leventhal et al. (1965) reports that some minimal amount of fear is necessary for behavior change, but that further increases in fear do not affect change. The later study by Leventhal et al. (1966) reports a slight tendency for increases in fear to increase behavior change. In the studies of dental hygiene practices, Janis and Feshbach (1953) reported decreased behavior change under high fear, while Singer (1965) found no main effect of fear. In the study on smoking by Leventhal and Watts (1966) high fear simultaneously increased compliance with a recommendation to cut down on smoking and decreased compliance with a recommendation to take an X-ray.

The present study attempted to account for some of these divergent findings. It is reasonable to expect that the behavior being recommended by a persuasive communication is of critical importance (Leventhal, 1965). Recommendations that are seen as effective in controlling danger may be accepted more readily as fear is increased, while ineffective recommendations may be rejected rationally or may produce reactions of denial (Janis and Feshbach, 1953) or aggression (Janis and Terwilliger, 1962). Additionally, rejection of a recommended behavior may occur if subjects have become afraid of the behavior itself (Leventhal and Watts, 1966).

Recommendations presented as part of fear-arousing communications vary in their effectiveness in controlling danger and in the unpleasantness associated with them. For example, brushing the teeth offers no guarantee of preventing decay, while taking a chest X-ray can lead to the unpleasant discovery of lung cancer. An audience might well reject recommendations which are ineffective in warding off danger or which are difficult, painful, or apt to bring unpleasant consequences. Recommendation factors have been invoked post hoc to explain research findings, but have not been manipulated and studied directly.

In the present study fear was manipulated by presenting differing discussions of the danger of tetanus. Inoculations and booster shots were recommended for protection against tetanus. Under high and low levels of fear, inoculation was portrayed so that it would be seen as more or less *effective* in preventing tetanus and more or less *painful* to take (these manipulations were orthogonal). Subjects' intentions to take shots and their actual shot-taking behavior were used to measure compliance with the recommendations.

It was expected that compliance would be greater when shots were highly effective or not painful. These factors might produce simple main effects or they might interact with level of fear. It seemed more likely that the latter would be the case— that increased fear would make subjects either more or less sensitive to differences in the recommendations.

METHOD

Subjects and Design

Letters were sent to all Yale College seniors asking them to participate in a study to be conducted jointly by the John Slade Ely Center, a local research organization, and the Department of University Health. The study was presented as a survey of student health practices at Yale and an evaluation of some health-education materials. An attempt was then made to contact all seniors by telephone for scheduling.

Of approximately 1000 students who received letters, 274 were scheduled and run in the experiment. Seventy-seven of these were excluded because they had been inoculated since the preceding academic year, and 15 were excluded because of suspicion, involvement in compulsory inoculation programs, allergic reactions to inoculation, or religious convictions against inoculation. The final usable N was 182.

Each subject received a communication which was intended to manipulate perceived effectiveness and painfulness of inoculation. Three levels of fear (including a no-fear control level), two levels of effectiveness, and two levels of pain were combined in a $3 \times 2 \times 2$ factorial design. The n's for the resulting 12 conditions ranged from 11 to 20, with smaller n's in the no-fear control conditions.

Procedure

Experimental sessions were conducted in a classroom with groups ranging in size from 1 to 12. Subjects within each session were randomly assigned to conditions. Control (no-fear) conditions were run separately because of the brevity of the control communications.

Questionnaires containing medical items and personality premeasures were administered at the beginning of the session. Subjects then read a communication on tetanus and gave their reactions to it in a second questionnaire. They were assured that all their responses would be kept confidential.

Communications

Communications were ten-page pamphlets which discussed the danger of tetanus and the effectiveness and painfulness of inoculation.[1] All pamphlets gave spe-

---

[1]Communications have been deposited with the American Documentation Institute. Order Document No. 9011 from ADI Auxiliary Publications Project, Photoduplication Service, Library of Congress, Washington, D.C. 20540. Remit in advance $2.00 for microfilm or $3.75 for photocopies and make checks payable to: Chief, Photoduplication Service, Library of Congress.

cific instructions on how to become inoculated and were similar in style and content to those used by Leventhal et al. (1965) and Leventhal et al. (1966).

Fear.   Low-fear material described the very low incidence of tetanus and indicated that bleeding from a wound usually flushes the poison-producing bacilli out of the body. A case history was included which reported recovery from tetanus following mild medication and throat-suction procedures. High-fear material indicated that tetanus can be contracted through seemingly trivial means and that if contracted the chances of death are high. A high-fear case history was included which reported death from tetanus despite heavy medication and surgery to relieve throat congestion. Black-and-white photographs were included in the low-fear material and color photographs in the high-fear material. The discussion of tetanus and case history were omitted entirely from control (no-fear) communications.

Effectiveness.   The effectiveness manipulation stressed either the imperfections or the unusual effectiveness of inoculation. Low-effectiveness material stated that inoculation is generally effective and about as adequate as the measures available to deal with other kinds of danger. It pointed out, however, that no protection is perfect and that there is a possibility that even an inoculated person will contract tetanus. High-effectiveness material described inoculation as almost perfect and as far superior to methods available to deal with other kinds of danger. It emphasized that inoculation reduces the chances of contracting tetanus, for all practical purposes, to zero. All communications reported that a new type of inoculation was available at the Department of University Health which would provide protection against tetanus for a period of 10 years.

Pain.   To produce fear of the recommended behavior, it was pointed out that inoculation against tetanus has always been painful. Subjects were told that the new inoculation requires a deep intramuscular injection of tetanus toxoid and alum precipitate, making the injection even more painful than before and the local reaction longer lasting. The discussion of pain was presented to subjects as a forewarning so that the discomfort would not take them by surprise. This discussion was omitted from pamphlets in the no-pain conditions.

Specific instructions on how to get a shot and a map showing the location of the Department of University Health were included in all pamphlets. Subjects were encouraged to get a shot or at least to check on whether or not they needed one.

Measures

Most questions on the pre- and postcommunication questionnaires were answered on 7-point rating scales. The precommunication questionnaire contained medical questions and four personality measures (susceptibility, coping, anxiety, and self-esteem). The susceptibility measure was made up of three items which asked subjects how susceptible they felt toward common illnesses, toward unusual diseases, and toward illness and disease in general. Three items used to measure coping asked subjects whether they tended to tackle problems actively or to postpone dealing with them. The problems concerned subjects' health habits, their everyday lives as students, and their decisions regarding summer activities. The anxiety scale was made up of 10 true-false items from the Taylor (1953) Manifest Anxiety scale.

The self-esteem measure was similar to that used by Dabbs (1964). Subjects rated themselves on 20 adjectives and descriptive phrases and then rated each of the 20 items as to its desirability. Eight items were classified as desirable and 12 as undesirable on the basis of mean ratings from the entire sample of subjects. Using this group criterion of desirability, each subject's self-esteem score was defined as the sum of his ratings on the desirable items. (It was subsequently discovered that 12 subjects in the present study had participated in the earlier study by Dabbs, and the correlation between their self-esteem scores in the two studies was .62, $p < .01$. This correlation, despite a lapse of 3 years and changes in the measuring instrument, suggests this type of measure is reasonably stable.)

The postcommunication questionnaire included checks on each of the experimental manipulations, a 10-item mood adjective check list, and questions on intentions to take shots, the importance of shots, and the likelihood of contracting tetanus. The subject's evaluation of the pamphlet and the date and place of his last tetanus shot were obtained on this questionnaire.

A measure of behavioral compliance with the recommendations was obtained from shot records of the Department of University Health. Subjects were counted as complying if they took tetanus shots between the experimental sessions and the end of the semester, about one month later. When contacted by letter and phone, no subjects reported receiving shots at places other than the Department of University Health. A few reported that they had tried to take shots and had been told they did not need any. These subjects were counted as having taken shots but their data are presented separately in footnote 2.

TABLE 8.1
Compliance with recommendations

	Control (no fear)	Low fear	High fear
Mean intentions to take shots	4.12	4.73	5.17
Proportion of Ss taking shots	.06	.13	.22
N	48	62	72

RESULTS

Main Effects of the Manipulations

Compliance with the recommendations was unaffected by the manipulations of effectiveness and pain. The manipulation of fear, however, influenced both intentions to take shots ($F_{2,179} = 4.85$, $p < .01$) and actual shot-taking behavior[2] ($F = 3.39$, $p < .05$). The effects were linear (Table 8.1), with compliance being greatest under high fear. The consistency of subjects' responses is indicated by high biserial correlations between intention and behavior measures within high-fear ($r_b = .62$, $p < .01$) and low-fear ($r_b = .68$, $p < .01$) conditions; no correlation was computed for the control conditions since only three control subjects took shots.

Table 8.2 shows that the fear manipulation increased feelings of fear, as it was intended to do. It also increased feelings of interest and nausea, belief in the severity of

TABLE 8.2
Other reactions to fear manipulation

	Control	Low fear	High fear	F[a]
Fear[b]	7.74	9.25	12.19	21.50**
Feelings of nausea	1.27	1.24	1.90	7.95**
Feelings of interest	4.48	4.70	5.39	6.12**
Evaluation of the severity of tetanus	4.64	4.83	5.34	3.86*
Feelings of susceptibility to tetanus	3.46	3.99	4.25	3.31*
Evaluation of the importance of shots	5.85	6.16	6.52	6.44**
Desire for more information about tetanus	3.08	2.68	3.57	3.90*

[a]F ratios are computed from three-way analyses of variance. In each analysis $df = 2/170$ (approximately).
[b]"Fear" represents the sum of three items: feelings of fear, fear of contracting tetanus, and fear produced by the pamphlet.
*$p < .05$.
**$p < .01$.

---

[2]"Shot-taking behavior" combines 20 subjects who took shots and 7 who reported trying to take shots. These two categories are distributed similarly across the fear treatment conditions: 2, 6, and 12 subjects took shots and 1, 2, and 4 subjects tried to do so.

An arc sine transformation of the proportions in Table 8.1 was used (Winer, 1962). This made it possible to test the significance of the differences between groups against the *baseline variance* of the transformation (see Gilson and Abelson, 1965). Base-line variance has a theoretical value which does not depend on computations from observed data. In the present case this value is given by the reciprocal of the harmonic mean number of cases on which each proportion is based, or $1/59 = .0169$.

tetanus and the importance of taking shots, and desire to have additional information. None of these measures were affected by the manipulations of effectiveness or pain.

Both effectiveness and pain were successfully manipulated. Check questions showed that subjects in the high-effectiveness conditions felt inoculation was more effective than did those in the low-effectiveness conditions ($\bar{X}_{high} = 6.7$, $\bar{X}_{low} = 5.8$, $F_{1,170} = 105.85$, $p < .01$). Subjects in the pain conditions felt shots would be more painful ($\bar{X}_{pain} = 4.1$, $\bar{X}_{no\ pain} = 2.3$, $F_{1,170} = 74.56$, $p < .01$) and reported more "mixed feelings" about taking shots ($F_{1,170} = 7.20$, $p < .01$) than did subjects in the no-pain conditions. But the clear perception of differences in effectiveness did not affect subjects' intentions to take shots, nor did increasing the anticipated painfulness of shots decrease intentions to take them. In fact, there was a slight tendency for painfulness to strengthen intentions to be inoculated ($F_{1,170} = 2.72$, $p = .10$).

Correlations Among Responses

Only within the high-fear condition did reported fear correlate with intentions to take shots ($r = .23$, $p < .01$). A scatterplot of scores revealed that the high-fear condition increased the range of reported fear and that the positive correlation could be attributed to subjects in the extended portion of the range (those scoring higher than 13 on a 19-point composite scale). These extreme subjects all showed strong intentions to take shots, while other subjects in the high-fear condition sometimes did and sometimes did not intend to take shots. This pattern suggests that fear and acceptance of a recommendation are more closely associated when fear is relatively high, though acceptance may occur at any level of reported fear.

Unlike fear, anger was negatively associated with intent to take shots. The overall within-class correlation between anger and intentions was $-.18$ ($p < .05$). This correlation remained essentially the same within different levels of the fear treatment, but became increasingly negative as the recommendation was portrayed as less effective and more painful (Table 8.3). Both the row and column differences in

TABLE 8.3
Correlations between anger and intentions to take shots
under varying portrayal of recommendations

	Effectiveness	
	Low	High
Pain		
Low	$-.29$	.15
High	$-.52$	$-.18$

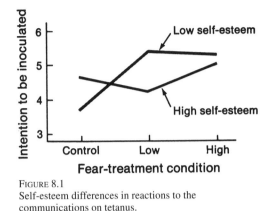

FIGURE 8.1
Self-esteem differences in reactions to the
communications on tetanus.

Table 8.3 are significant[3] (for rows, $CR = 2.02$, $p < .05$; for columns, $CR = 2.81$, $p < .01$). It should be emphasized that these are correlational differences only. Low effectiveness and high pain did not increase the mean level of anger or decrease intentions (or decrease actual shot taking). The ranges of anger and intention scores also did not differ among the four conditions.

Personality Differences

None of the premeasures on personality (susceptibility, coping, anxiety, self-esteem) were significantly correlated with intentions to take shots, nor did the correlations vary systematically across the 12 experimental conditions. However, differences were observed when subjects were split at the median into groups high and low on self-esteem subjects. Figure 8.1 shows intentions to take shots among high- and low-self-esteem subjects. The only significant effect within this data (other than the main effect of fear) is the interaction between self-esteem and fear level ($F_{2,166} = 4.74$, $p < .01$). Subjects low in self-esteem increased their intentions to take shots from control to low-fear conditions, then showed no further increase under high fear. Subjects high in self-esteem, on the other hand, showed increased intentions only from low- to high-fear conditions.

DISCUSSION

A positive relationship between fear arousal and persuasion was observed. Increases in the intensity of the fear manipulation were associated with increases in

---

[3]Significance of these differences was tested after applying Fisher's z' transformation to the correlation coefficients.

attitude and behavior change, with high correlations between intentions to take shots and actual shot taking. These findings are similar to those of Leventhal et al. (1966), who reported a slight tendency for shot taking to increase as fear was raised from low to high levels.

Subjects' beliefs about the effectiveness of inoculation did not affect their compliance; they responded equally well to recommendations portrayed as low and high in effectiveness. This may be because even the low-effective recommendation was rated relatively high in effectiveness (5.8 on a 7-point scale). However, the manipulation was sufficient for subjects to perceive significant differences between low and high effectiveness, and the failure of this variable to influence compliance suggests caution in using it to reconcile divergent results of studies on fear arousal and persuasion (Janis and Leventhal, 1967; Leventhal, 1965; Leventhal and Singer, 1966).

The description of pain produced mixed feelings about shots, but did not prevent subjects from taking them. Perhaps this is because the discomfort of inoculation is negligible in comparison with the pain of tetanus itself. A stronger manipulation of anticipated "painfulness" was unintentionally introduced in the study by Leventhal and Watts (1966), who created fear of smoking by showing a film in which a chest X-ray led to the discovery of cancer and to surgical removal of a lung. The authors suggested that decreased X-ray taking in this condition was more likely caused by fear of the consequences of an X-ray than by defensive reactions to the fear-arousing material on cancer. The present findings do not invalidate their conclusion, but they limit the range of situations to which such an explanation might apply. Subjects apparently do not respond to small variations in the effectiveness or unpleasantness of a recommended course of action. Unless a compelling deterrent exists, people who anticipate danger prefer to do something rather than nothing.

This last statement is qualified by differences in the behavior of high- and low-self-esteem subjects. Low-self-esteem subjects showed high compliance with the recommendations in both high- and low-fear conditions, while high-self-esteem subjects showed high compliance only in the high-fear condition. In addition, personality measures of self-esteem and coping were significantly correlated ($r = .49$, $p < .01$) in the present study, as they were in the study reported by Dabbs (1964). One might conclude that high-self-esteem subjects are more active and aggressive in dealing with their environment and have developed more skill in meeting dangers with appropriate protective actions. Thus, they may recognize inoculation to be more appropriate when the danger of tetanus is greater, while low-self-esteem subjects may accept the position of the communication that inoculation is appropriate regardless of the magnitude of danger. An alternative possibility is that some differences characteristically associated with self-esteem simply disappear when there is an urgent need to combat danger (as there was with the high-fear communication).

In the conditions where inoculation was depicted as ineffective or painful, anger was negatively associated with intentions to be inoculated. It is possible that increased anger in these conditions would have lowered compliance. But since anger and compliance did not covary as the fear treatment was increased, there appears to be no causal relationship between them. It seems more likely that anger does not decrease compliance, but that under certain conditions it provides the justification for noncompliance. Under other conditions—as when recommended behaviors are highly effective, not painful, and not a reasonable target for anger—noncompliance may have to be justified in some other manner.

All the present findings could have been influenced by several factors which were not varied. For example, all subjects received the manipulations of perceived danger, effectiveness, and pain in the same order. Learning about the dangers of tetanus first may have caused some subjects to ignore differences in the effectiveness and painfulness of inoculation. In addition, all subjects were asked after reading the communications whether or not they intended to be inoculated. One might expect that stating an intention to be inoculated would commit the subject to following this course of behavior later on. However, the findings of Leventhal et al. (1965) and Leventhal et al. (1966) indicate that specific instructions must be present before intentions will be translated into behavior. Since all subjects in the present study did receive specific instructions, the high correlations between intentions and behavior may be due to this factor.

Finally, while fear and persuasions were associated, the evidence of any causal relationship between them is tenuous. As in most studies of fear arousal and attitude change, the communications used were complex ones. They discussed the damage tetanus can cause and the likelihood of contracting it. They differed in fearfulness, interest, and feelings of nausea evoked. They also differed in length, type of language used, and amount of information about tetanus. With such confounding it is impossible to attribute increases in attitude change solely to increases in fear. This is an inherent difficulty when fear is manipulated by the use of differing descriptions of danger. Another approach should be developed by anyone wishing to manipulate fear independently of other aspects of a persuasive communication.

References

BERKOWITZ, L., AND COTTINGHAM, D. R. The interest value and relevance of fear-arousing communications. *Journal of Abnormal and Social Psychology,* 1960, **60,** 37–43.

DABBS, J. M., JR. Self-esteem, communicator characteristics, and attitude change. *Journal of Abnormal and Social Psychology,* 1964, **69,** 173–181.

GILSON, C., AND ABELSON, R. P. The subjective use of inductive evidence. *Journal of Personality and Social Psychology,* 1965, **2,** 301–310.

HAEFNER, D. P. Arousing fear in dental health education. *Journal of Public Health Dentistry,* 1965, **25,** 140–146.

INSKO, C. A., ARKOFF, A., AND INSKO, V. M. Effects of high and low fear-arousing communications upon opinions toward smoking. *Journal of Experimental Social Psychology,* 1965, **1,** 256–266.

JANIS, I. L., AND FESHBASH, S. Effects of fear-arousing communications. *Journal of Abnormal and Social Psychology,* 1953, **48,** 78–92.

JANIS, I. L., AND LEVENTHAL, H. Human reactions to stress. In E. Borgatta and W. Lambert (eds.), *Handbook of personality theory and research.* New York: Rand McNally, 1967.

JANIS, I. L., AND TERWILLIGER, R. An experimental study of psychological resistances to fear-arousing communications. *Journal of Abnormal and Social Psychology,* 1962, **65,** 403–410.

LEVENTHAL, H. Fear communications in the acceptance of preventive health practices. *Bulletin of the New York Academy of Medicine,* 1965, **41,** 1144–1168.

LEVENTHAL, H., JONES, S., AND TREMBLY, G. Sex differences in attitude and behavior change under conditions of fear and specific instructions. *Journal of Experimental Social Psychology,* 1966, **2,** 387–399.

LEVENTHAL, H., AND NILES, P. A field experiment on fear arousal with data on the validity of questionnaire measures. *Journal of Personality,* 1964, **32,** 459–479.

LEVENTHAL, H., AND NILES, P. Persistence of influence for varying durations of threat stimuli. *Psychological Reports,* 1965, **16,** 223–233.

LEVENTHAL, H., AND SINGER, R. P. Affect arousal and positioning of recommendations in persuasive communications. *Journal of Personality and Social Psychology,* 1966, **4,** 137–146.

LEVENTHAL, H., SINGER, R. P., AND JONES, S. Effects of fear and specificity of recommendations upon attitudes and behavior. *Journal of Personality and Social Psychology,* 1965, **2,** 20–29.

LEVENTHAL, H., AND WATTS, J. C. Sources of resistance to fear-arousing communications on smoking and lung cancer. *Journal of Personality,* 1966, **34,** 155–175.

NILES, P. The relationships of susceptibility and anxiety to acceptance of fear-arousing communications. Unpublished doctoral dissertation, Yale University, 1964.

SINGER, R. P. The effects of fear-arousing communications on attitude change and behavior. Unpublished doctoral dissertation, University of Connecticut, 1965. *Dissertation Abstracts,* 1966, **26,** 5574.

TAYLOR, J. A. A personality scale of manifest anxiety. *Journal of Abnormal and Social Psychology,* 1953, **48,** 285–290.

WINER, B. J. *Statistical principles in experimental design.* New York: McGraw-Hill, 1962.

9

Attribution Versus Persuasion as a Means for Modifying Behavior

Richard L. Miller, Philip Brickman, and Diana Bolen

The present research compared the relative effectiveness of an attribution strategy with a persuasion strategy in changing behavior. Study 1 attempted to teach fifth graders not to litter and to clean up after others. An attribution group was repeatedly told that they were neat and tidy people, a persuasion group was repeatedly told that they should be neat and tidy, and a control group received no treatment. Attribution proved considerably more effective in modifying behavior. Study 2 tried to discover whether similar effects would hold for a more central aspect of school performance, math achievement and self-esteem, and whether an attribution of ability would be as effective as an attribution of motivation. Repeatedly attributing to second graders either the ability or the motivation to do well in math proved more effective than comparable persuasion or no-treatment control groups, although a group receiving straight reinforcement for math problem-solving behavior also did well. It is suggested that persuasion often suffers because it involves a negative attribution (a person should be what he is not), while attribution generally gains because it disguises persuasive intent.

Despite the volume of research on attitude change and persuasion, there is surprisingly little evidence that persuasion can be effective, particularly if a criterion of persistence of change over time is applied (Festinger, 1964; Greenwald, 1965b;

Reprinted with permission from the authors and *The Journal of Personality and Social Psychology,* Vol. 31, No. 3, 1975. Copyright © 1975 by the American Psychological Association.

This research was carried out as a master's thesis by the first author under the supervision of the second author and was partially supported by National Science Foundation Grant GS-28178. We are grateful to Donald Campbell and Thomas Cook for serving on the thesis committee and to Lawren ɔ Becker and Glenn Takata for help with the data analysis. Thanks are also due to Susan Bussey and Charlotte Yeh, who served as experimenters, and to Bobbe Miller, who did much of the initial coding and typed the early drafts of this article.

This work would have been impossible without the enthusiasm, cooperation, and enlightened support of Irene Timko, principal of Anderson Elementary School. Great thanks are also due to the teachers who participated in this project. In Study 1, thanks go to Catherine Lebenyi, Wendy Weiss, and Ira Mizell for willingly helping to initiate a new behavioral modification technique. In Study 2, where an incredible number of experimental manipulations were administered by the teachers, special thanks go to Margaret Paffrath, Ronnie Briskman, June Butalla, and Susan Levie. Thanks are also due to the eighth-grade assistants who administered our tests.

Rokeach, 1968; Zimbardo and Ebbesen, 1969; Cook, 1969). The failure of persuasive efforts to produce lasting change may be taken as evidence that subjects have not integrated the new information into their own belief systems (Kelman, 1958) or taken it as the basis for making an attribution about themselves (Kelley, 1967). We might expect that a persuasive communication specifically designed to manipulate the attributions a person made about himself would be more effective in producing and maintaining change. This research was designed to test the relative importance of attribution manipulations to persuasive attempts by comparing a normal persuasion treatment and an attribution treatment.

   The persuasion conditions of the present research were designed to be maximally effective through their use of a variety of techniques which have been found to be helpful, at least on occasion, in past research. Past research has shown that an optimal persuasive manipulation should involve a high-credibility source (Hovland and Weiss, 1951) delivering a repeated message (Staats and Staats, 1958) with an explicitly stated conclusion (Hovland and Mandell, 1952) which is supported by arguments pointing out the benefits of change (Greenwald, 1965a) and overlearned by the audience (Cook and Wadsworth, 1972). Face-to-face communication by the source (Jecker, Maccoby, Breitrose, and Rose, 1964), reinstatement of the source at the time of attitude assessment (Kelman and Hovland, 1953), and active role playing or participation by the audience in the message (Janis and King, 1954) are also helpful.

   The attribution techniques were also designed to be maximally effective through their use of all three factors specified by Kelley (1967) as conducive to making a stable attribution: consistency of the evidence over time, consistency of the evidence over modalities, and consistency or consensus across sources.

STUDY 1: LITTERING BEHAVIOR

Study 1 attempted to modify children's littering behavior. Behavior was monitored before and after treatment and again after a 2-week period of nontreatment. It was hypothesized that both the attribution and the persuasion conditions would result in initial posttreatment behavioral change but that the attribution condition would show greater persistence as a result of altering the basic self-concept of the subjects in a direction inconsistent with littering.

METHOD

Participants

   The research took place in three fifth-grade classrooms in an inner-city Chicago public school. Two fifth-grade classrooms were randomly assigned to the experimental conditions, while a third was designated a control group. Three female experimenters, all undergraduate psychology majors at Northwestern University, were randomly assigned to a different classroom for each test.

Experimental Manipulations

There were a total of 8 days of attribution and persuasion treatments dealing with littering, with discussion intended to average about 45 minutes per day.

Attribution condition.   On Day 1, the teacher commended the class for being ecology-minded and not throwing candy wrappers on the auditorium floor during that day's school assembly. Also on Day 1, the teacher passed on a comment ostensibly made by the janitor that their class was one of the cleanest in the building. On Day 2, after a visiting class had left the classroom, the teacher commented that paper had been left on the floor but pointed out that "our class is clean and would not do that." The students at this point disagreed pointedly and remarked that they would and did indeed litter. On Day 3, one student picked up some paper discarded on the floor by another and after disposing it in the wastebasket was commended by the teacher for her ecology consciousness. On Day 4, Row 1 was pointed out as being the exceptionally neat row in the room by the teacher. Also on Day 4, the principal visited the class and commented briefly on how orderly it appeared. After the principal left the room, the students castigated the teacher for her desk being the only messy one in the room. On Day 5, a large poster of a Peanuts character saying "We are Andersen's Litter-Conscious Class" was pinned to the class bulletin board. Also on Day 5, the teacher gave a lesson on ecology and talked about what we "the class" are doing to help. On Day 6, the principal sent the following letter to the class: "As I talked to your teacher, I could not help but notice how very clean and orderly your room appeared. A young lady near the teacher's desk was seen picking up around her desk. It is quite evident that each of you are very careful in your section." On Day 7, the teacher talked about why "our class" was so much neater. In the interchange the students made a number of positive self-attributions concerning littering. On Day 8, the janitors washed the floor and ostensibly left a note on the blackboard saying that it was easy to clean.

Persuasion condition.   On Day 1 during a field trip, the children were told about ecology, the dangers of pollution, and the contribution of littering to pollution. They were then asked to role play being a trash collector and to pick up litter as they came across it. On Day 2, inside the school lunchroom the teacher talked about garbage left by students and gave reasons why it should be thrown away: it looked terrible, drew flies, and was a danger to health. On Day 3, the teacher gave a lecture on ecology, pollution, and litter and discussed with the class how the situation could be improved. Also on Day 3, the teacher passed on a comment ostensibly from the school janitor that they needed help from the students in keeping the floors clean, implying here as elsewhere that nonlittering would lead to approval and commendation by various adult authorities. On Day 4, the teacher told the students that everyone should be neat, mentioning aesthetics among other reasons for neatness. Also on Day 4, the principal visited the class and commented briefly about the need for clean and tidy classrooms. On Day 5, the teacher told the students that they should not throw candy wrappers on the floor or the playground but should dispose of them in trash cans. Also on Day 5, a large poster of a Peanuts character saying "Don't be a litterbug" with "Be neat" and "Don't Litter" bordering it was pinned to the class bulletin board. On Day 6, the principal sent the following letter to the class: "As I talked to your teacher, I could not help but notice that your room was in need of some cleaning. It is very important that we be neat and orderly in the upkeep of our school and classrooms. I hope each of you in your section will be very careful about litter." On Day 7, the teacher appointed several children in each row to watch and see if people were neat outside the building as well as in the classroom. On Day 8, a note was left on the board ostensibly from the janitors to remind the children to pick up papers off the floor.

Measurement of Littering

Pretest. To discover any existing differences among the three classrooms with respect to their tendency to litter, a specially marked reading assignment which had previously been turned in to the teachers was returned to the students 5 minutes before the end of the school day. The students were then instructed to throw the assignment away after the bell rang for dismissal. After school the experimenters counted the number of assignments thrown in the wastebasket versus left on the floor or on the shelf under the students' seats. Less than 20% of the students in each class disposed of their assignments in the wastebaskets. The precise percentages were 20% for the control group ($n = 31$), 16% for the persuasion group ($n = 26$), and 15% for the attribution group ($n = 27$).

Posttest. A two-part behavioral test was designed to tap the two aspects of the ecology-littering problem, nonlittering and cleaning up the litter of others.

On the morning of the tenth day, minutes before the first recess, each teacher introduced the experimenter for her classroom as a marketing representative of a local candy manufacturing firm and left the experimenter in charge of the room. The experimenter explained that she was testing the tastiness of a new brand of candy and passed out one piece of candy to each student. The candy was wrapped in colored cellophane with a different color used for each classroom. Following the taste test, the class was dismissed for recess. During recess the experimenters counted the number of candy wrappers in the wastebaskets, on the floor, and in the desk seats. The experimenters then relittered the classroom entrance area with seven specially marked candy wrappers. After recess the experimenters checked the hallway and playground for discarded candy wrappers. During the lunch break, which came 1 hour after recess, the experimenters reentered the classroom and determined the disposition of the specially marked candy wrappers.

The second posttest followed the first by a period of 2 weeks. During this time no mention of ecology or littering was permitted in any of the classrooms. The second test was very similar to the first except that this time, the experimenters did not interact with the students. Ten minutes before the afternoon recess the teacher passed out toy puzzles as Christmas presents from the Parent Teachers Association. The students were asked to try to work the puzzles before recess. Each puzzle was wrapped in a color-coded container with a different color assigned to each class. During recess the experimenters entered the classroom and determined the disposition of the containers left there. They then relittered the entrance way. After recess the experimenters searched the hallway and playground for other containers. After school the experimenters reentered the classroom and determined the disposition of the relittered containers.

RESULTS AND DISCUSSION

Littering Behavior

Figure 9.1 charts the percentage of items in each group which were discarded in the wastebasket on each test. A chi-square test was used to compare frequency of littering in the three groups on the immediate and delayed posttests. Although the measures directly reflect items of litter rather than individual subjects, it was observed by the experimenters that subjects independently discarded their own candy wrappers in the wastebaskets. The three groups were significantly different at both the immediate posttest, $\chi^2 (2) = 18.14, p < .001$, and at the delayed posttest, $\chi^2 (2) = 20.99, p < .001$. The attribution group was significantly superior to the persuasion group on both the immediate posttest, $\chi^2 (1) = 7.19, p < .01$, and the delayed posttest, $\chi^2 (1) = 16.15, p < .01$. Although the persuasion group appeared to show an immediate increase in litter-conscious behavior, it was not significantly different from the control group even on the immediate posttest, $\chi^2 (1) = 2.57, ns$.

Cleanup Behavior

All seven items were picked up by members of the attribution group on both the immediate and the delayed posttest. Persuasion group members picked up four items on the immediate posttest and two on the delayed posttest, while control group members picked up two items on the immediate posttest and three on the delayed test. Since the total number of wrappers left was only seven and more than one wrapper may sometimes have been picked up by a single individual, a chi-

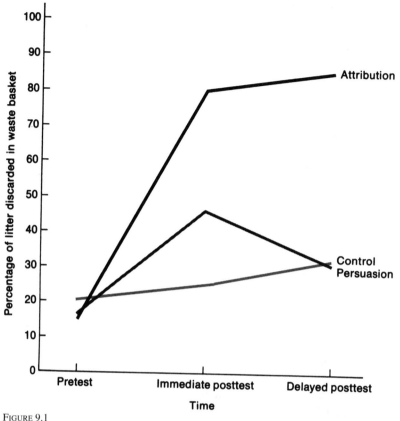

FIGURE 9.1
Nonlittering behavior of the attribution, persuasion, and control groups over time (Study 1).

square test is not fully appropriate. Nonetheless, such a test would be significant at the .05 level at each posttest, which supports the appearance of differences favoring the attribution group.

After this study the attribution teacher was advised that the nonlittering behavior could perhaps be maintained if the students were occasionally reminded of the attribution "You are neat." Three months later the teacher reported that her class was still significantly neater than it had been prior to treatment.

The results for both the littering test and the cleanup test support the hypothesis that attribution is a more effective technique than persuasion for inducing stable behavioral change. We would like to show, however, that this effect holds for other kinds of behavior. Furthermore, it would be desirable to overcome a weakness in Study 1 that arose from the fact that treatments were nested within classrooms. It is possible, if relatively unlikely, that the differences emerging over time were due to teacher differences rather than treatment differences. Study 2 avoids this by including all treatment and control conditions in each classroom.

STUDY 2: MATH ACHIEVEMENT

The results of Study 1 are certainly encouraging for an attributional approach to modifying behavior. However, while ecology consciousness and nonlittering are of some social importance, they are not the primary focus of the schools, which is, at least theoretically, to teach skills. Will attribution and persuasion techniques show the same pattern of effectiveness in generating a skilled behavior, like math achievement, as they have in generating a socially desirable but unskilled behavior, like disposing of trash in wastebaskets? Furthermore, littering behavior would certainly be only a weakly valenced aspect of self, while most of the skills taught in schools would be highly valenced and of considerable import for a student's self-concept. Will attribution be an aspect? The first purpose of Study 2 was to answer just these questions. It might also be noted that attributions in Study 2, in addition to being more central to self-concept, are specifically directed to particular individuals rather than addressed to a group as a whole.

The second purpose of Study 2 was to test the relative effectiveness of attributions of motivation versus attributions of ability in changing behavior. Both perceptions of ability and motivation are essential to the belief that a person will attain a given goal (Heider, 1958). Study 1, however, would seem to have involved primarily the attribution of motivation, since the children presumably began with a common belief that they had the ability to be neat. In the case of a skilled behavior like arithmetic, however, it would seem more likely that motivation and belief in one's motivation to do well are more common than ability and belief in one's ability to do well (Katz, 1964), so that attributions of ability would be of greater value than attributions of motivation. Nonetheless, enhancing people's perceptions of their motivation for a task may also benefit their performance. Study 2 attempts to separate ability and motivation as the bases of attribution and the targets of persuasive appeal.

So far we have only considered cognitive strategies for modifying attitudes and behavior. Staats (1965) has shown that even young children will engage in complex learning tasks if they are simply given appropriate reinforcement. According to Bandura (1969), a successful reinforcement strategy for behavior modification requires a valued reinforcer which is contingent upon the desired behavior and a reliable procedure for eliciting the desired behavior. In the present study both verbal praise and extrinsic rewards were used as reinforcers for efforts at mathematical achievement, and a number of overlapping procedures were used to elicit these efforts.

To compare the relative efficacy of the attribution and reinforcement techniques with standard attitude change approaches, a persuasive manipulation was devised similar to the one used in Study 1. The only changes were that audience participation and role playing were deleted, since neither was appropriate to the treatment conditions, while public labeling was added. It appears from the study of deviance (Becker, 1963) that public labeling of a person can lead that person to redefine himself along the lines of the label. While it was felt in Study 1 that children had to be convinced of the benefits of nonlittering in the persuasion condition, the advantages of math achievement as a means for obtaining rewards in school seemed too obvious to need pointing out.

The present study attempted to modify children's math-related self-esteem and their math scores on skill tests. The six conditions were attribution ability, attribution motivation, persuasion ability, persuasion motivation, reinforcement control, and a no-message control. It was hypothesized that all three basic techniques (attribution, persuasion, and reinforcement) should have an initial positive effect on the self-esteem and math behavior of the subjects but that attribution should have the most enduring effect over time.

METHOD

Participants

The research took place in four second-grade classrooms of the same inner-city Chicago public school involved in Study 1. Second-grade students were picked, since it was felt on the basis of Rosenthal and Jacobson (1968) that their school-related self-concepts would be more malleable than at a later age. In all, 96 students took part in the study. All five experimental conditions and one control condition were present in each of the four classrooms. From each class list of approximately 30 students, 24 were randomly assigned to the six possible conditions. Thus 4 students in each classroom appeared in each condition.

Overview of Procedure

All subjects first received a mathematics pretest and a self-esteem pretest. Subsequent treatments consisted of 8 days of attribution, persuasion, or reinforcement. Immediately following the treatment, math and self-esteem posttests were administered. Delayed posttests were given after a 2-week period of no treatment. The control group received the pretests and the immediate and delayed posttests but no treatment. Student absences for both treatments and tests were made up on the day the student returned to school.

Experimental Manipulations

Five treatment techniques were used with all groups: verbal comments, written comments, letters from the teacher, letters from the principal, and medals. The above order is followed in discussing these techniques for each experimental condition. It should also be noted that in the attribution and persuasion conditions, students were initially called to the principal's office in groups of eight, where they received a treatment-related message. The principal discontinued these treatments after the third day of the experiment, however, on the grounds that they were too time-consuming for her and that she found the false attribution treatments too difficult to deliver.

All treatment techniques were prepackaged. Before the experiment began, teachers' treatment packages were prepared which listed the treatment techniques and their recipients for each day. The order in which each subject received the treatments was randomized for classroom "A" and repeated in each of the other classrooms.

Attribution ability.   The general focus of this treatment was attributing to the students skill and knowledge in mathematics. Three different verbal comments were made by the teacher to each student on different days: "You are doing very well in arithmetic," "You are a very good arithmetic student," and "You seem to know your arithmetic assignments well." Three different written notes were tied to assignments on different days and handed back to the students: "You're doing very well," "excellent work," and "very good work." The letters from the teachers and principal underscored the students' excellent work in math and were sent home on days when a verbal or written note was not scheduled. The letter from the teacher included the phrases "very good student," "does all his assignments well," and "excellent arithmetic ability." The letter from the principal used the phrases "excellent ability," "knows his assignments," and "very good student." The medals awarded to the attribution ability students featured the words "good student—math."

Attribution motivation.   The general focus of this treatment was attributing hard work and consistent trying to the student. Three appropriate verbal comments were made by the teacher to each child privately, and three written notes were appended to a test or assignment. The verbal comments were the following: "You really work hard in arithmetic," "You're working harder in arithmetic," and "You're trying more in arithmetic." The written comments were as follows: "You're working harder, good!" "You're trying more, keep at it!" and "Keep trying harder!" The letters from the teacher and principal underscored the child's application in math. The teacher's letter used the phrases "working hard," "trying," and "applying himself." The principal's letter used the phrases "working harder," "applying himself," and "trying harder." The medals awarded to the attribution motivation students featured the words "hard worker—math."

Persuasion ability.   The general focus of this treatment was to persuade the student that he should be good in arithmetic and doing well in that subject. Three verbal comments and three written comments summarizing that message were made in the same manner as that for the attribution messages. The three verbal comments were "You should be good at arithmetic," "You should be a good arithmetic student," and "You should be doing well in arithmetic." The three written comments were "should be better," "should be good at arithmetic," and "should be getting better grades." The letters from the teacher and principal used ostensible "aptitude test scores" to inform parents that their child should be making good grades in math. The teacher's letter included the injunctions "should be doing well," "should be getting high grades," and "should be becoming a good arithmetic student." The principal's letter used the phrases "should get good grades," "should do very well," and "should be a good arithmetic student." The medals awarded to these students contained the words "do better—math."

Persuasion motivation.   The general focus of this treatment was to persuade the student that he should be working harder and spending more time on math. The three verbal and the three written comments asked the child to try more at math and were made in the same way as they were in the other treatment conditions. The three verbal comments were "You should spend more time on arithmetic," "You should work harder at arithmetic," and "You should try more on arithmetic." The three written notes were "Try harder," "Work more on arithmetic," and "Work harder." The letters from the teachers and the principal informed parents that their child should spend more time on math and to pass that idea along to him. The teachers' letter included the injunctions "should be trying harder," "should spend more time on arithmetic," and "should be applying himself." The principal's letter used the phrases "spend more time" and "try harder." The medals awarded the persuasion motivation students contained the words "work harder—math."

Reinforcement.   The reinforcement condition also followed the same format as the attribution and persuasion conditions except that it added two additional methods and deleted the principal's comments. Three verbal comments indicating pride in the student's good work were made by the teacher. They were as follows: "I'm proud of your work," "I'm pleased with your progress in arithmetic," and "very good." Three written comments of simple praise were appended to the student's math work. They were "excellent" "very good," and "I'm very happy with your work." The letters from the teachers and principal indicated pride and satisfaction in the child's work to the parent. The teacher's letter used the phrases "proud of his work" " good grades," and "happy with his work." The principal's letter used the phrases "excellent progress," "doing very well," and "proud of him." The medals awarded those students contained the words "math award." On Days 2, 5, and 7, students were praised verbally if they chose to work on an extra math problem rather than a reading exercise. On two other days the students received silver stars by solving a problem from a math assignment.

Control.   The control condition received no treatment whatsoever but took part in all tests of mathematical ability and self-esteem.

MEASUREMENTS

Self-Esteem

The self-esteem pretest was an adaptation of the questionnaire originally developed by Rogers and Dymond (1954) that includes items which measure self-esteem with regard to peers and parents, school interests, and personal interests. Four new items were added which dealt specifically with math-related self-esteem. All items were declarative sentences generally of the "I am ——" form, from which the children were asked to say whether it was "like me" or "unlike me." The self-esteem pretest and posttest were both administered individually to each student by one of a dozen eighth-grade assistants, who asked each question privately to the second graders and personally recorded the subject's answer. The self-esteem posttest was given in the morning on the day after treatment ended.

Mathematics

The pretest and all subsequent math tests were 20-item tests consisting of 25% review questions, 50% current material, and 25% new material. The math pretest was administered by the teachers as a regular arithmetic quiz. The immediate posttest was administered in the afternoon on the day after treatment ceased. The final posttest was administered after a 2-week period in which no treatment took place.

RESULTS

Self-Esteem

The mean math self-esteem scores for all six conditions on the pretest and the posttest are presented in Figure 9.2. Analysis of variance of the pretest scores indicated that there were no significant differences among the five treatment groups and the control group in math self-esteem before treatment began, $F(5, 90) = .79$, *ns*.

The major analysis of the math self-esteem scores was a repeated measures analysis of variance using the six experimental conditions and the two times of

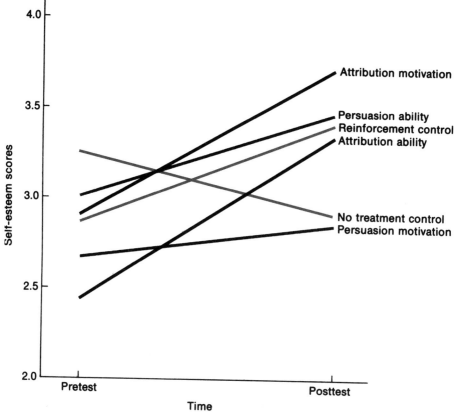

FIGURE 9.2
Self-esteem scores for the attribution, persuasion, and control groups over time (Study 2).

measurement as factors. Results indicated both a main effect of time, $F (1, 90) =$ 10. 84, $p < .01$, and a significant Time $\times$ Treatment interaction, $F (5, 90) = 2.41$, $p < .05$. As can be seen from Figure 9.2, all treatment groups show an increase in self-esteem, while the control group shows a decrease, which is probably due to the lack of any treatment for control students in the face of a number of public treatments visible to them in their classroom.

A subsidiary analysis of variance was performed using only the attribution and the persuasion groups, with mode of treatment (attribution vs. persuasion), basis of treatment (ability manipulation vs. motivation manipulation), and time as the three independent variables. Results again indicated a main effect of time, $F (1, 60) = 19.02, p < .001$, and a significant Time $\times$ Mode of Treatment interaction, $F (1, 60) = 4.76, p < .05$. The math self-esteem of the attribution groups increased more sharply from pretest (2.66) to posttest (3.50) then did the math self-esteem of the persuasion groups (2.84 at pretest, 3.13 at posttest). Only the attribution ability and attribution motivation groups were significantly different from the no-treatment control group in their change from pretest to posttest, $F (1, 30) = 7.58$,

$p < .01$ for attribution ability, $F (1, 30) = 7.66$, $p < .01$ for attribution motivation. This difference approached but fell short of significance for the persuasion ability group, $F (1, 30) = 3.12$, $p < .11$. Similar analyses showed no significant effects on general school-related and non-school-related self-esteem.

Mathematics

The mean total math scores for all six conditions on the pretest, the immediate posttest, and the delayed posttest are presented in Figure 9.3. Analysis of variance of the pretest scores indicated that there were no significant differences among the five treatment groups and the control group in their total math scores before treatment began, $F (5, 90) = .54$, *ns*.

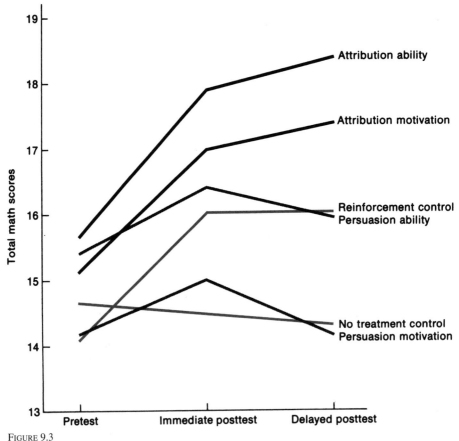

FIGURE 9.3
Total math scores of the attribution, persuasion, and control groups over time (Study 2).

The major analysis of the math test scores was a repeated measures analysis of variance using the six experimental conditions and the three times of measurement as factors. The results show both a main effect of time, $F (2, 180) = 36.69, p < .001$, and a significant Time $\times$ Treatment interaction, $F (10, 180) = 5.57, p < .001$. From Figure 9.3 it can be seen that both attribution conditions show marked increases on the immediate posttest followed by a slight tendency to enlarge that increase after the 2-week delay. Both persuasion conditions appear to show an increase on the immediate posttest but fail to maintain that increase over the 2-week delay. The reinforcement condition shows a pattern similar to that of the attribution conditions but with a lesser degree of improvement.

To assess the extent to which attribution and persuasion differed in their initial effectiveness versus the extent to which they differed in their ability to maintain their effectiveness over time, separate analyses were made of changes from the pretest to the immediate posttest and from the immediate posttest to the delayed posttest. Mode of treatment (attribution vs. persuasion) and basis of treatment (ability vs. motivation) were used as factors along with time of test. For change from pretest to the immediate posttest, a significant Mode $\times$ Time interaction, $F (1, 60) = 11.97, p < .001$, indicated that attribution was significantly more effective than persuasion in inducing change. Only the attribution ability and attribution motivation groups were significantly different from the no-treatment control group in their change from pretest to immediate posttest, $F (1, 30) = 14.75, p < .01$ for attribution ability; $F (1, 30) = 11.42, p < .01$ for attribution motivation. This difference approached but fell short of significance for the persuasion ability group, $F (1, 30) = 2.92, p < .10$.

For change from the immediate posttest to the delayed posttest, another significant Mode $\times$ Time interaction, $F (1, 60) = 13.67, p < .001$, indicated that the attribution treatments were also superior to the persuasion treatment in maintaining what change they produced. The attribution treatments show an increase of .50 from the immediate to the delayed posttest, while the persuasion treatments show a decrease of .63.

Finally, to make a preliminary test as to whether attribution and persuasion were similar in their effects on high- and low-ability students, subjects in each condition were divided at the cell median according to their math pretest performance. An analysis of variance on posttest math scores was conducted using pretest ability (high vs. low), treatment (attribution vs. persuasion, ignoring basis of treatment), and posttest time (immediate vs. delayed) as factors. Initially more able students continued to outperform initially less able students, $F (1, 60) = 46.01, p < .001$, on the posttests. Attribution was more effective than persuasion for both groups, $F (1, 60) = 19.39, p < .001$, but the attribution-persuasion difference was significantly larger for the low-ability students than for the high-ability students, interaction $F (1, 60) = 5.66, p < .05$. Average posttest scores for the high-ability students were 18.8 for attribution and 17.8 for persuasion, while for low-ability students they were 16.5 for attribution and 13.0 for persuasion.

DISCUSSION

In both studies the attribution treatments caused a significant change which persisted over time. These treatments were strong enough to overcome counterarguing by subjects in Study 1 and a history of at best modest success among many subjects in Study 2. Both attributions based upon subjects' ability to do something and those based upon subjects' motivation to do it appeared effective. The effects of persuasion were, in general, insignificant and dissipated over time.

The fact that the superiority of attribution treatments over persuasion treatments was demonstrated in two different field experiments using different behaviors (nonlittering and math problem solving), two different subject populations (fifth graders and second graders), and two different designs (a between-classroom design and a within-classroom design) gives us some confidence that these effects are real and generalizable. Neither study is without weakness. The nesting of treatments within classrooms in Study 1 leaves teacher or group differences as a possible, if unlikely, alternative explanation for the treatment effects that emerged over time. The public nature of the treatments in each classroom in Study 2 means that treatment effects may have been aided by implicit comparisons students were making between their own condition and other treatments, a process which must lie behind the unexpected drop in math self-esteem shown by the no-treatment control group. (This last result must also be counted among the ethical costs of a within-classroom design.) The weaknesses of the two studies, however, are quite different, while their effects are quite similar, which suggests that the results are not due to idiosyncrasies of design.

The present research provides a general framework into which previous work concerning the effects of teacher expectancies on pupil performance (Beez, 1968; Rosenthal and Jacobson, 1968; Seaver, 1973) can be fit. The means by which teacher expectancies are communicated is at best a dependent variable in previous studies (Meichenbaum, Bowers, and Ross, 1969) and often mysteriously unobserved. The present study made the communication of expectancies, in the form of attributions, its central manipulation. The fact that this programmed communication of expectancies worked as it did provides some support for the essential validity of the often elusive teacher expectancy effect.

Effects of Attribution

That attributions based upon ability and attributions based upon motivation did not differ in their effectiveness implies that direct linkage of skill-specific attributions to the self-system is more important than the basis on which this linkage is made. The message "You are a particular kind of person" is more important than the specification of "why." It should be noted, however, that the present research contrasted only two kinds of internal attributions, ability and motivation. Attributions made to a person on the basis of external factors ("You are neat because I am watching you") would presumably be less effective in producing lasting change.

Attribution can, of course, involve elements of persuasion. As we have seen, the statement "You are a neat person" may be a most effective means of persuading someone to be neat. Nonetheless, such attributional statements need not involve persuasive intent but may instead be simple statements of fact. Indeed, their guise as truth statements may be thought of as their most effective advantage. Not only does this enable them to work directly on a person's self-concept, as noted, but it may also enable them to slip by the defenses a person ordinarily employs against persuasive attempts effective because it is less easily recognized as persuasion, and hence less likely to arouse resistance, counterarguing, or reactance.

In Study 1 the attribution treatment did elicit counterarguing by the students, which suggests a possible reactance (Brehm, 1972) or boomerang effect (McGuire, 1969), but there was no evidence of such an effect by the end of the experiment. It is possible that reactance, like other attitude-change forces, dissipates over time as the issue is worked through and the treatment is maintained. It is also possible that the elementary school students who were subjects in the present studies are less likely to perceive the manipulative intent of an attribution treatment and less likely to show reactance than a comparable adult group.

Attribution and Persuasion

In accounting for the relative ineffectiveness of persuasion, we may note first of all that persuasive communications urging a person to do something do not necessarily tap the internal self-concept of their target. Worse yet, to the extent that they do implicate self-concept, they may involve the negative attribution that the person is not the kind of individual who engages in the recommended behavior. An appeal to be neat or an appeal to work hard can involve the implicit attribution that the person is not currently the sort of individual who is neat or works hard. If convincing people that they are neat or hard working is the key to making them neat or hard working, a naive persuasive attempt can cancel out its own message. At best it attributes to its target the potential for becoming the sort of person recommended, but this is clearly much weaker than the attribution that the person already embodies the desired behavior.

In this study, moreover, the persuasive messages implied something negative about the subjects, while the attribution treatments implied something positive. Although blame as well as praise has been shown to be effective in eliciting improved performance (see Kennedy and Willcutt, 1964, for a review of the mixed results in this area), one of the best designed studies (Hurlock, 1925) found that the improvement elicited by blame dissipated over time, while that elicited by praise persisted. It may be speculated that persuasion and punishment both remain effective in motivating behavior only so long as the actors feel that they can accomplish what is being called for. As they accept the implicit negative attributions of a persuasive message, the effectiveness of the message diminishes. This may explain why persuasion was relatively more effective for high-ability students than for low-ability students. The high-ability students may have been better able to respond to the appeal to do better without becoming discouraged by the implicit attribution (which they could to some extent discount) that they were not currently demonstrating appropriate accomplishment.

The implicit attributions of the persuasion treatments in this study were negative because the behaviors they were calling for (which the subjects were presumably not emitting) were positive. Likewise, the attribution treatments were positive because the behaviors they attributed to the subjects were positive. For practical and ethical reasons, all of the treatments in the present study were aimed at producing positive or socially desirable behaviors. It is our idea that the implicit or explicit labeling itself, and not merely the rewardingness or punishingness of the labels, made the present attribution treatments effective and the persuasion treatments ineffective. This can only be known for sure, however, by a study that aims at producing undesirable behavior, in which case attributions of the behavior would have negative implications, which persuasion to the behavior would have implicit positive implications for the present self-concept. If people were responding to the attributions in the present experiment only because they were rewarding, we would expect that attributions of an undesirable behavior would have reverse effects and, indeed, that persuasion under these circumstances might even be more effective. The sociological literature on deviance (e.g., Schur, 1971), however, suggests that negative attributions (e.g., labeling as delinquent) can indeed produce or support the attributed behavior, as does a recent experimental study of labeling "charitable" or "uncharitable" behaviors (Kraut, 1973). We may suspect, then, that the positive implications of the attributions in the present study were not the sole key to their effectiveness and that if a suitable experiment could be designed in which the target behavior were socially undesirable, attribution would continue to be more effective than persuasion in generating that behavior.

Attribution and Reinforcement

A straightforward reward contingency program seems to modify behavior because it makes that behavior worthwhile to the subject. However, the separation between reinforcement and attribution seems somewhat confounded. Symbolic reinforcement, as used in the present study, has some attributional aspects. Simple praise is often interpreted as a "You are X" statement. Furthermore, attribution can contain elements of reinforcement especially when socially desirable behaviors are the focus of the attributional process. Thus to some extent a reinforcement procedure that produces enduring change may require elements of attribution, while a successful attribution treatment may involve elements of reinforcement.

The remaining feature distinguishing attribution from reinforcement would seem to be the noncontingent nature of the attribution. In this regard it is interesting to note that Kazdin (1973) has recently found that under circumstances where the desired behavior was emitted at a fairly high base rate and subjects believed that reinforcement was contingent, noncontingent reinforcements were as effective as contingent ones in modifying behavior. Attribution treatments, however, may have the very important further advantage over simple reinforcement of serving to elicit behavior (like modeling; see Bandura, 1969) as well as to maintain it.

Practical and Ethical Implications

The present study supports the idea that an effort to improve the child's academic self-concept will help improve academic performance, if only because the improved self-image will make actual success less inconsistent, less unexpected, and less likely to be discounted or rejected (Brickman, 1972). A distinguishing feature of the present attribution treatments is that they focused on raising self-esteem in a specific area of skill rather than raising global or general self-esteem. The failure of more general "cultural enrichment" or general "self-concept enhancement" programs may be due in part to the fact that these global manipulations have only vague and diffuse implications for particular areas of academic performance (but cf. deCharms, 1972).

Nonetheless, there are a number of reasons to be cautious about considering these results as the basis for a solution to any social problem. It is unlikely that long-standing individual differences in accomplishment will be overcome by short-term manipulation of motivation, incentive, or self-regard. A gain of three problems solved after a week of treatment is not very substantial in terms of life chances; and there is no reason to assume that 10 weeks of treatment will necessarily result in a gain of 30 problems. Second, the attribution treatments in Study 2 were difficult to administer and, unlike the treatments in Study 1, did not produce any immediate and visible indications of success to sustain teacher enthusiasm. While the teachers involved in Study 1 were quite positive toward the study, those involved in Study 2 had decidedly mixed feelings about the value of the time and energy involved. More seriously, the false attributions came increasingly to be felt by at least one teacher and by the principal as an intolerable risk to their credibility. As indicated, the principal terminated her office meetings with the students after the third day of treatment mainly on these grounds. While future research could tailor attributions not to be too discrepant from individual pretest baselines, the practical and ethical difficulties involved in maintaining such attributions will not thereby be eliminated. All of these matters warn against an uncritical application of the present results to matters of educational importance.

References

BANDURA, A. *Principles of behavior modification.* New York: Holt, Rinehart & Winston, 1969.

BECKER, H. S. *Outsiders: Studies in the sociology of deviance.* New York: Free Press, 1963.

BEEZ, W. V. Influence of biased psychological reports on teacher behavior and pupil performance. *Proceedings of the 76th Annual Convention of the American Psychological Association,* 1968, **3,** 605–606. (Summary)

BREHM, J. *Responses to loss of freedom: A theory of psychological reactance.* Morristown, N.J.: General Learning Press, 1972.

BRICKMAN, P. Rational and non-rational elements in reactions to disconfirmation of performance expectancies. *Journal of Experimental Social Psychology,* 1972, **8,** 112–123.

COOK, T. D. *The persistence of induced attitude change: A critical review of pertinent theories.* Unpublished manuscript, Northwestern University, 1969.

COOK, T. D., AND WADSWORTH, A. Attitude change and the paired-associate learning of mimal cognitive elements. *Journal of Personality,* 1972, **40,** 50–61.

DECHARMS, R. Personal causation training in the schools. *Journal of Applied Social Psychology,* 1972, **2,** 95–113.

FESTINGER, L. Behavioral support for opinion change. *Public Opinion Quarterly,* 1964, **28,** 404–417.

GREENWALD, A. G. Behavior change following a persuasive communication. *Journal of Personality,* 1965a, **33,** 370–391.

GREENWALD, A. G. Effects of prior commitment on behavior change after a persuasive communication. *Public Opinion Quarterly,* 1965b, **29,** 595–601.

HEIDER, F. *The psychology of interpersonal relations.* New York: Wiley, 1958.

HOVLAND, C. I., AND MANDELL, W. An experimental comparison of conclusion drawing by the communicator and the audience. *Journal of Abnormal and Social Psychology,* 1952, **47,** 581–588.

HOVLAND, C. I., AND WEISS, W. The influence of source credibility on communication effectiveness. *Public Opinion Quarterly,* 1951, **15,** 635–650.

HURLOCK, E. B. An evaluation of certain incentives used in school work. *Journal of Educational Psychology,* 1925, **16,** 145–159.

JANIS, I. L., AND KING, B. T. The influence of role playing on opinion change. *Journal of Abnormal and Social Psychology,* 1954, **49,** 211–218.

JECKER, J., MACCOBY, N., BREITROSE, H. S., AND ROSE, E. D. Teacher accuracy in assessing cognitive visual feedback from students. *Journal of Applied Psychology,* 1964, **48,** 393–397.

KATZ, I. Review of evidence relating to effects of desegregation on the intellectual performance of Negroes. *American Psychologist,* 1964, **19,** 381–399.

KAZDIN, A. E. The role of instructions and reinforcement in behavior changes in token reinforcement programs. *Journal of Educational Psychology,* 1973, **64,** 63–71.

KELLEY, H. H. Attribution theory in social psychology. *Nebraska Symposium on Motivation,* 1967, **14,** 192–238.

KELMAN, H. C. Compliance, identification, and internalization: Three processes of opinion change. *Journal of Conflict Resolution,* 1958, **2,** 51–60.

KELMAN, H. C., AND HOVLAND, C. I. "Reinstatement" of the communicator in delayed measurement of opinion change. *Journal of Abnormal and Social Psychology,* 1953, **48,** 327–335.

KENNEDY, W. A., AND WILLCUTT, H. C. Praise and blame as incentives. *Psychological Bulletin,* 1964, **62,** 323–332.

KRAUT, R. E. Effects of social labeling on giving to charity. *Journal of Experimental Social Psychology,* 1973, **9,** 551–562.

McGUIRE, W. J. The nature of attitudes and attitude change. In G. Lindzey and E. Aronson (eds.), *Handbook of social psychology* (2nd ed.). Reading, Mass.: Addison-Wesley, 1969.

MEICHENBAUM, D. H., BOWERS, K. S., AND ROSS, R. R. A behavioral analysis of teacher expectancy effect. *Journal of Personality and Social Psychology,* 1969, **13,** 306–316.

ROGERS, C., AND DYMOND, R. *Psychotherapy and personality change.* Chicago: University of Chicago Press, 1954.

ROKEACH, M. *Beliefs, attitudes, and values.* San Francisco: Jossey-Bass, 1968.

ROSENTHAL, R., AND JACOBSON, L. *Pygmalion in the classroom: Teacher expectation and pupils' intellectual development.* New York: Holt, Rinehart & Winston, 1968.

SCHUR, E. M. *Labeling deviant behavior.* New York: Harper & Row, 1971.

SEAVER, W. B. Effects of naturally induced teacher expectancies. *Journal of Personality and Social Psychology,* 1973, **28,** 333–342.

STAATS, A. W. A case in and a strategy for the extension of learning principles to problems of human behavior. In L. Krasner and L. P. Ullman (eds.), *Research in behavior modification,* New York: Holt, Rinehart & Winston, 1965.

STAATS, A. W., AND STAATS, C. K. Attitudes established by classical conditioning. *Journal of Abnormal and Social Psychology,* 1958, **57,** 37–40.

ZIMBARDO, P., AND EBBESEN, E. B. *Influencing attitudes and changing behavior.* Reading, Mass.: Addison-Wesley, 1969.

10

The Impact of Mass Violence on U.S. Homicides

David P. Phillips

The impact of mass media violence on aggression has almost always been studied in the laboratory; this paper examines the effect of mass media violence in the real world. The paper presents the first systematic evidence indicating that a type of mass media violence triggers a brief, sharp increase in U.S. homicides. Immediately after heavyweight championship prize fights, 1973–1978, U.S. homicides increased by 12.46 percent. The increase is greatest after heavily publicized prize fights. The findings persist after one corrects for secular trends, seasonal, and other extraneous variables. Four alternative explanations for the findings are tested. The evidence suggests that heavyweight prize fights stimulate fatal, aggressive behavior in some Americans.

Since 1950 more than 2500 studies have attempted to discover whether mass media violence triggers additional aggressive behavior (Comstock et al., 1978; Murray and Kippax, 1979; Roberts and Bachen, 1981; National Institutes of Mental Health, 1982). With few exceptions (reviewed in Phillips, 1982b), researchers have studied aggression *in the laboratory,* and there is consensus that media violence can trigger additional aggression in the laboratory setting. However, policy makers, unlike researchers, have been primarily concerned with violence *outside* the laboratory, particularly with serious, fatal violence like homicide. Studies of media effects on homicide have been extremely rare and there is no systematic evidence to date indi-

Reprinted with permission of the author and *American Sociological Review,* Vol. 48, 1983.

Direct all correspondence to: David P. Phillips, Department of Sociology, University of California, La Jolla, CA 92093.

This paper benefited very substantially from technical discussions with H. White and C. Granger (Economics Department) and N. Beck (Political Science Department). I am grateful to these colleagues for leading me beside the still waters of time-series regression analysis. I am also grateful to M. Cole and M. Schudson (Communications Department), V. Konecni (Psychology Department), and B. Berger, A. Cicourel, F. Davis, C. Mukerji, and C. Nathanson (Sociology Department), all at the University of California at San Diego. Finally, I would like to thank two anonymous referees for helpful comments.

cating that mass media violence elicits additional murders.[1] As Andison has noted (1980:564), we do not know whether "there are deaths and violence occurring in society today because of what is being shown on the TV screen."

This paper presents what may be the first systematic evidence suggesting that some homicides are indeed triggered by a type of mass media violence. The current study builds on earlier research (Phillips, 1974, 1977, 1978, 1979, 1980, 1982a) which showed that: (1) U.S. suicides increase after publicized suicide stories. This finding has been replicated with American (Bollen and Phillips, 1982) and Dutch (Ganzeboom and de Haan, 1982) data. (2) The more publicity given to the suicide story, the more suicides rise thereafter. (3) The rise occurs mainly in the geographic area where the suicide story is publicized. (4) California (Phillips, 1979), Dutch (Ganzeboom and de Haan, 1982), and Detroit (Bollen and Phillips, 1981) auto fatalities all increase just after publicized suicide stories. (5) The more publicity given to the stories, the greater the increase, and (6) the increase occurs mainly in the area where the story is publicized. (7) Single-car crash fatalities increase more than other types, and (8) the driver in these crashes is significantly similar to the person described in the suicide story, while the passengers are not. These results are statistically significant and persist after correction for day-of-the-week and seasonal fluctuations, holiday weekends, and linear trends. After testing alternative explanations, Phillips concluded that suicide stories appear to elicit additional suicides, some of which are disguised as auto accidents.

It would be interesting to discover whether *homicide* stories elicit additional homicides. But it is difficult to conduct such a study because, unlike suicide stories, homicide stories occur so often that it is very difficult to separate the effect of one story from the effect of the others. However, some other types of violent stories occur much less often, and it is possible to discover whether these types of stories trigger a rise in U.S. homicides.

MASS MEDIA VIOLENCE AND U.S. HOMICIDES

In reviewing the literature on media effects, Comstock (1977) concluded that violent stories with the following characteristics were most likely to elicit aggression: When the violence in the story is presented as (1) rewarded, (2) exciting, (3) real, and (4) justified; when the perpetrator of the violence is (5) not criticized for his behavior and is presented as (6) intending to injure his victim.[2]

One type of story that meets all of these criteria is the heavyweight prize fight, which is almost universally presented as highly rewarded, exciting, real, and

---

[1] Some anecdotal data link a particular murder with subsequent murders or murder attempts (e.g., the Tylenol "copycat" crimes). But I know of only one *systematic* study of the topic (Berkowitz and Macaulay, 1971). This study found no increase in homicides after three publicized murder stories.

[2] Comstock also notes that a story is more likely to be imitated if the aggressor in the story is like the person exposed to the story, and if the victim in the story is like the imitator's victim. These points will be taken up later in this paper.

justified. Furthermore, the participants are not criticized for their aggressive behavior and are presented as trying to injure each other.

In a well-known series of studies, Berkowitz and various associates (1963, 1966, 1967, 1973) examined the impact of a filmed prize fight in the laboratory. They found that angered laboratory subjects behaved more aggressively after seeing a filmed prize fight scene. In contrast, angered laboratory subjects exposed to a track meet film displayed a significantly lower level of aggression.

In sum, the heavyweight prize match is a promising research site because (1) it meets Comstock's criteria for stories most likely to elicit aggression, and (2) it is known to elicit aggression in the laboratory.

DATA SOURCES

An exhaustive list of championship heavyweight prize fights and their dates was obtained from *The Ring Book Boxing Encyclopedia,* which is the standard reference on the topic. The period 1973–1978 has been chosen for analysis because, for this period, daily counts of all U.S. homicides are publicly available from the National Center for Health Statistics.[3]

METHOD OF ANALYSIS

A standard time-series regression analysis is used.[4] Homicides are known to fluctuate significantly by day of the week, by month, and by year (Conklin, 1981). In addition, as we will see, homicides rise markedly on public holidays. All these "seasonal" effects must be corrected before one can assess the effect of prize fights on homicides.

A 0–1 dummy variable was constructed for all days that were Mondays, another dummy variable was coded for Tuesdays, and in general a different dummy variable was assigned to each day of the week, with Sunday being the omitted variable. Similarly, a 0–1 variable was coded for each month of the year (with January being the omitted variable), and for each year (with 1978 being the omitted variable). In

---

[3]Data for 1973–1977 consist of computerized death certificates generated by the National Center for Health Statistics and made available by the Inter-University Consortium for Political Science Research. As of this writing, 1978 computerized death certificates are not yet publicly available. Consequently, for 1978, a published table (National Center for Health Statistics, 1978: Table I-30) has been used instead. A 50 percent sample of 1972 deaths is also available but will not be analyzed, because its inclusion with the complete, 100 percent sample data for 1973–1978 would violate the assumption of homoscedasticity required in the analysis that follows. It is theoretically possible to correct for this type of heteroscedasticity and then include the 1972 data in the analysis. But it was judged unnecessary to do so, because the data set is already very large even without the 1972 information. In all, there are 2192 data points for the daily data, 1973–1978.

[4]For the application of this approach to daily mortality data, see Bollen and Phillips (1981, 1982). For general introductions to time-series regression techniques, see Ostrom (1978), Rao and Miller (1971) and Johnston (1972).

addition, a dummy variable was assigned to each of the public holidays (New Year's Day, Memorial Day, Independence Day, Labor Day, Thanksgiving, and Christmas). Finally, a dummy variable, PFIGHT(X), was used to indicate the presence of a championship prize fight. The regression coefficient of PFIGHT(X) gives the effect of a prize fight on homicides X days later (i.e., the effect of a prize fight lagged X days). Initially, the effect of the prize fight is examined for the ten-day period following it; later, a longer period is studied.

RESULTS

Table 10.1 (page 136) gives the size and statistical significance of each coefficient.[5] This table shows that, after the average championship prize fight, homicides increase markedly on the third day (by 7.47) and on the fourth day (by 4.15), for a total increase of 11.62.[6] The rise in homicides after the prize fight is statistically significant.[7]

---

[5]These statistical significances are biased if there is serial correlation among the regression residuals. The conventional test for serial correlation, the Durbin-Watson test, is appropriate when a lagged dependent variable is included in the regression model (Nerlove and Wallis, 1966), as is the case in Table 10.1. A common alternative test, using Durbin's h statistic, cannot be used here for reasons described in Bollen and Phillips (1982: fn. 7). Consequently, another test for serial correlation proposed by Durbin (1970) was used instead. This test reveals no evidence of first-order autocorrelation. Autocorrelation of higher orders was sought by the methods described in Bollen and Phillips (1982), with no evidence of serial correlation being uncovered. One other feature of Table 1 should be mentioned briefly. The table shows that homicides increase markedly on all U.S. public holidays except Memorial Day. To my knowledge, this finding has not been previously demonstrated with U.S. daily homicide data.

[6]The coefficient of .12 for HOMICIDE(1) indicates that there is a small, lagged endogenous effect. This implies, for example, that each of the lagged prize fight dummies has its impact distributed over more than one day. Therefore, the effect of prize fights on homicides one day later (for example) does not take place one day later, but is realized over a longer period of time. The small coefficient for the endogenous variable (.12) means that the long-run effects of PFIGHT(X) and other variables decay very rapidly and aren't much more than their immediate ones, but the distributed effects do exist. Thus, the pattern of lags is more complicated than is immediately apparent from Table 10.1. In sum, because of small, lagged endogenous effects, the impact of one PFIGHT(X) variable overlaps to a small extent with the impact of another. However, the presence of the lagged endogenous variable does not affect the validity of the statistical tests of the hypotheses (see also footnote 7).

[7]In Table 10.1 we are examining the series of eleven coefficients, PFIGHT(0), PFIGHT(1), . . . PFIGHT(10). Under the null hypothesis, none of these eleven prize fight coefficients is likely to be very large. On the other hand, under the alternative hypothesis that prize fights trigger homicides, one or more of these eleven coefficients is likely to be large and positive. If one or more of the PFIGHT(X) coefficients is sufficiently large, we can reject the null hypothesis in favor of the alternative. One way to discover whether H_0 can be rejected is to proceed as follows. Because the covariance matrix indicates that the estimates of the coefficients for PFIGHT(X) are uncorrelated, and because of the asymptotic normality of the coefficient estimates, it follows that these coefficient estimates are in fact independent. This in turn implies that the t-statistics for each of these coefficients are independent. Under these circumstances, one can use the binomial test to evaluate the probability of finding that r or more of the PFIGHT(X) coefficients are statistically significant at a given level. Table 10.1 indicates that there are two PFIGHT(X) coefficients — PFIGHT(3), PFIGHT(4) — which are statistically significant at .025 or better. For $n = 11$, $P = 0.25$, $r \geq 2$, the binomial test indicates that the probability of finding two or more significance levels of .025 in 11 independent trials is .0296. Thus, we can reject the null hypothesis on the joint evidence provided by the eleven PFIGHT(X) coefficients.

TABLE 10.1
U.S. HOMICIDES regressed on heavyweight prize fight, controlling for daily, monthly, yearly, and holiday effects, 1973–1978

Regressand HOMICIDES	R^2 .671	$\bar{R}^2$ .665	D.F. 2148	N 2190	Regressand HOMICIDES	R^2 .671	$\bar{R}^2$ .665	D.F. 2148	N 2190
Regressor	Regression coefficient		t-statistic		Regressor	Regression coefficient		t-statistic	
Intercept	55.34*		30.16		April	.43		.46	
HOMICIDE(1)	.12*		5.64		May	−.69		−.73	
PFIGHT(−1)	1.97		.94		June	1.61		1.74	
PFIGHT(0)	1.95		.93		July	4.16*		4.46	
PFIGHT(1)	−.26		−.13		August	4.46*		4.83	
PFIGHT(2)	1.32		.63		September	3.91*		4.16	
PFIGHT(3)	7.47***		3.54		October	2.79*		3.02	
PFIGHT(4)	4.15†		1.97		November	3.04*		3.25	
PFIGHT(5)	−.60		−.29		December	5.86*		6.30	
PFIGHT(6)	3.28		1.57		1973	−1.11		−1.70	
PFIGHT(7)	.35		.17		1974	1.71*		2.62	
PFIGHT(8)	.99		.47		1975	1.28		1.96	
PFIGHT(9)	3.10		1.48		1976	−3.01*		−4.60	
PFIGHT(10)	2.28		1.09		1977	−1.73*		−2.62	
Monday	−16.46*		−21.74		New Year's Day	41.08*		10.29	
Tuesday	−16.71*		−17.97						
Wednesday	−18.42*		−19.13		Memorial Day	−1.05		−.28	
Thursday	−15.81*		−15.88		Independence Day	21.61*		5.89	
Friday	−8.02*		−8.41						
Saturday	14.54*		16.95		Labor Day	16.92*		4.56	
February	1.88**		1.99		Thanksgiving	18.34*		4.98	
March	1.13		1.23		Christmas	10.25*		2.79	

Note: The variable HOMICIDE(1) indicates homicides lagged one day. Two-tailed t-tests are used for all seasonal variables; one-tailed t-tests for prize fight variables. *Significant at .01 or better. **Significant at .05 or better. ***Significant at .0002. †Significant at .025.

Table 10.1 shows that the third day displays by far the largest peak in homicides. It is interesting to note that this "third-day peak" appears not only in the present study but also, repeatedly, in several earlier investigations: California auto fatalities peak on the third day after publicized suicide stories (Phillips, 1979), as do Detroit auto fatalities (Bollen and Phillips, 1981) and U.S. noncommercial airplane crashes (Phillips, 1978, 1980). At present we do not know the precise psychosocial mechanisms producing the third day lag, but this phenomenon has now been replicated so often in different data sets that it seems to be a relatively stable effect which will repay future investigation.

The observed peak in homicides after a prize fight cannot be ascribed to day-of-the-week, monthly, yearly, or holiday effects, because all of these "seasonal" variables were corrected for in the regression analysis. In addition, one cannot plausibly ascribe the homicide peak to random fluctuations, because the peak is statistically significant.

SOME ALTERNATIVE EXPLANATIONS FOR THE PEAK IN HOMICIDES

Two different explanations can be tested with the data in Table 10.2 (page 138). For each fight, this table indicates: (1) The number of homicides observed three days after the prize fight. (2) The number of homicides expected on the third day, under the null hypothesis that prize fights have no effect on homicides.[8] (3) The difference between the observed and expected number of homicides. (A positive difference indicates that homicides are higher than expected just after the prize fight.) (4) Whether the fight was held outside the United States. (5) Whether the fight was discussed on the network evening news.

"Personal Experience" hypothesis.   Perhaps the prize fight affects only those actually attending the fight, not those experiencing it through the mass media. If this is so, one cannot claim that *mass media* violence is triggering a rise in homicides.

If one must personally experience the prize fight in order to be affected by it, then prize fights occurring outside the United States should trigger few if any U.S. homicides. In contrast, prize fights held inside the United States should elicit much larger rises in homicides. The evidence in Table 10.2 contradicts these predictions. After the average "foreign" fight, U.S. homicides rise by 12.128, while a much *smaller* rise, 2.862, occurs after the average U.S. fight.[9] Thus, the "personal experience" hypothesis does not seem plausible.

"Modeling" hypothesis—first test.   A different hypothesis can also be tested with the data in Table 10.2 (page 138). Prize fights may trigger some homicides through some type of modeling of aggression. If this is so, then prize fights receiving much publicity should have a greater effect than prize fights receiving less publicity.

One way to test this hypothesis is to see whether prize fights discussed on the network evening news are followed by relatively large increases in homicides, while relatively small increases occur after the remaining, less-publicized prize

---

[8]Under the null hypothesis, PFIGHT(X) has no impact on the number of homicides; thus, for Table 10.2 the expected number of homicides under H_0 is calculated by omitting PFIGHT(X) from the regression variables and rerunning the regression equation.

[9]At present, we do not know why U.S. homicides rise so much more after foreign than domestic fights. Perhaps a detailed study of the characteristics of these fights would help to resolve this question.

TABLE 10.2
Fluctuation of U.S. homicides three days after each heavyweight prize fight, 1973–1978

Name of fight	Observed no. of homicides	Expected no. of homicides	Observed minus expected	Fight held outside U.S.?	On network evening news?
Foreman/Frazier	55	42.10	12.90	yes	yes
Foreman/Roman	46	49.43	−3.43	yes	no
Foreman/Norton	55	54.33	.67	yes	no
Ali/Foreman	102	82.01	19.99	yes	yes
Ali/Wepner	44	46.78	−2.78	no	yes
Ali/Lyle	54	47.03	6.97	no	yes
Ali/Bugner	106	82.93	23.07	yes	no
Ali/Frazier	108	81.69	26.31	yes	yes
Ali/Coopman	54	45.02	8.98	yes	no
Ali/Young	41	43.62	−2.62	no	no
Ali/Dunn	50	41.47	8.53	yes	yes
Ali/Norton	64	52.57	11.43	no	yes
Ali/Evangelista	36	42.11	−6.11	no	no
Ali/Shavers	66	66.86	−.86	no	no
Spinks/Ali	89	78.96	10.04	no	yes
Holmes/Norton*	53	48.97	4.03	no	no
Ali/Spinks	59	52.25	6.75	no	yes
Holmes/Evangelista*	52	50.24	1.76	no	no

*Sponsored by World Boxing Council; all other fights sponsored by the World Boxing Association.

fights.[10] The evidence in Table 10.2 is consistent with this "modeling" explanation. Homicides rise by 11.127 after the average "publicized" fight, and by only 2.833 after the average unpublicized one. The difference between these two figures is statistically significant at .0286 (two-sample *t*-test, one-tailed).[11]

It is perhaps worth noting that the most touted of all the prize fights in this period, the so-called "Thrilla in Manilla" between Ali and Frazier, displays the largest third-day peak in homicides.

"Modeling" hypothesis—second test.   The modeling hypothesis can also be tested in another way. The laboratory literature on the modeling of mass media aggression (see footnote 2) repeatedly suggests that (1) a person is more likely to imitate an aggressor on the screen if he is similar to that aggressor; (2) a person is more likely to aggress against a target victim if his target is similar to the victim on the screen.[12] In sum, the laboratory literature suggests that there is modeling of both the *aggressor and* of the aggressor's *victim*.

---

[10]A thorough analysis of this topic is desirable but would be extremely laborious. Future studies might attempt to measure the additional publicity derived from advertisements in all the media, not only at the time of the fight, but also in the weeks and months preceding it. In addition, one might wish to measure closed circuit television receipts, corrected for inflation.

[11]The formula used for this particular *t*-test does not require that the two compared populations have equal variances. For a description of this test, see Brownlee (1965:299–303). One might prefer to substitute the Mann-Whitney for the *t*-test. When this is done, $P = .0211$.

[12]Berkowitz and associates (1963, 1966, 1967, 1973) have shown this in a series of ingenious studies particularly relevant to this paper. They showed that laboratory subjects were most likely to inflict shocks on a target if that target had the same name as the losing boxer on the screen.

If *aggressor* modeling exists after a prize fight, then after a young, black male wins a boxing match, murders by young, black males should increase (but murders by young, *white* males should not). Conversely, after a young, white male wins a boxing match, the opposite findings should occur. Unfortunately, *aggressor* modeling cannot be studied with the death certificates examined in this paper, because these certificates do not reveal the identity of the murderer, only of the victim.

However, it is possible to use these death certificates to discover whether *victim* modeling exists after a heavyweight prize fight. If such modeling occurs, then, just after a prize fight, homicide victims should be unusually similar to the losing boxer. Specifically, after a young, *white* male is beaten in a prize fight, the homicide deaths of young, white male victims should increase; no such increase should appear for young, *black* male victims. Conversely, after a young, *black* male is beaten in a prize fight, the homicide deaths of young, *black* male victims should increase, while the homicide deaths of young, white males should not.

These predictions can be tested with the information in Tables 10.3 (page 140) and 10.4 (page 141), which distinguish between the impact of "black loser" prize fights (in which a black is beaten) and "white loser" prize fights (in which a white is beaten).[13] The detailed mortality data necessary to generate these tables can be found only in the computerized death certificates cited in footnote 3. These are available only for 1973–1977. Thus, it should be stressed that the period to be examined in the remainder of this paper is 1973–1977, not 1973–1978, as in Tables 10.1 and 10.2.

Table 10.3 (page 140) examines the impact of "white loser" and "black loser" prize fights on the homicides of young, *white* male victims. The evidence supports the hypothesis of victim modeling. *White* loser prize fights are followed by significant increases in young, white male homicide deaths; in contrast, *black* loser prize fights do not seem to trigger young, white male homicide deaths.[14]

White homicides increase significantly on the day of the prize fight (by 3.86 per fight), two days thereafter (by 3.14 per fight), and eight days after the fight (by 2.97 per fight). Thus young, white male homicides rise by a total of 9.97 (= 3.86 + 3.14 + 2.97)

---

[13]In the period under study (1973–1977) nearly all the losing boxers were 20–34.9; consequently I have defined "young males" as men in this age range. Nearly all the losing boxers were white (Wepner, Bugner, Coopman, Dunn) or black (Frazier, Norton, Foreman, Lyle, Young, Shavers). However, two of the losing boxers were Hispanic Americans (one Uruguayan and one Puerto Rican). There is no separate classification for Hispanic Americans on the computerized death certificate, and it is unclear whether one can treat these fighters as either white or black. Consequently, these two fights have been excluded from the analysis that follows.

[14]The analysis described in footnote 7 (and applied to Table 10.1) can be reapplied to the results in Table 10.3. Examining the coefficients, WL(0), . . . WL(10), we see that three are statistically significant at .0251 or better. The covariance analysis indicates that the estimates of the coefficients WL(X) are uncorrelated. Because of this and the asymptotic normality of the coefficient estimates, we can treat as independent the t-statistics for WL(0), . . . WL(10). Using the binomial test, with $n = 11$, $P = .0251$, $r \geq 3$, one finds that the probability of finding three or more coefficients significant at .0251 in eleven independent trials is .0022. Hence, the homicides of young, white males increase significantly just after "White Loser" prize fights.

TABLE 10.3
Impact of "White Loser" (WL) and "Black Loser" (BL) prize fights
on the homicides of young, white male victims, U.S., 1973–1977[a]

Regressand	R^2 $\bar{R}^2$	D.F. N
HOMICIDES	.3781 .360	1772 1825

Regressor	Regression coefficient	t-statistic
Intercept	10.43*	23.78
HOMICIDE(1)	.01	.23
WL(−1)	.70	.46
WL(0)	3.86**	2.54
WL(1)	.30	.20
WL(2)	3.14**	2.07
WL(3)	.48	.31
WL(4)	.57	.37
WL(5)	−.29	−.19
WL(6)	.93	.61
WL(7)	.35	.23
WL(8)	2.97[†]	1.96
WL(9)	.53	.35
WL(10)	.58	.39
BL(−1)	1.36	1.27
BL(0)	.04	.03
BL(1)	−1.44	−1.34
BL(2)	−.59	−.55
BL(3)	1.20	1.11
BL(4)	.69	.64
BL(5)	−1.06	−.99
BL(6)	1.61	1.50
BL(7)	−.14	−.13
BL(8)	.32	.30
BL(9)	.28	.26
BL(10)	−.53	−.49

[a]As in Table 10.1 the effect of prize fight variables is calculated, controlling for seasonal variables. For reasons of clarity, the coefficients for these seasonal variables have not been displayed in Table 10.2 since the prime purpose of this table is to contrast the impact of "White Loser" and "Black Loser" prize fights. One-tailed t-tests are used for the prize fight variables; two-tailed t-tests for all other variables.
*Significant at less than .001; **significant at .006; ***significant at .019; [†]significant at .0251.

per white loser prize fight. Interestingly, the typical white loser prize fight has a larger total impact (9.97) than almost any other variable in the table. Of the 27 "seasonal" variables examined, only one (New Year's Day) has a larger impact on young, white male homicides.[15] This suggests that the impact of a white loser prize fight is not only statistically significant, but practically significant as well. At present, it is not known why this type of prize fight seems to exert so large an effect.

---

[15]The coefficient for this holiday is 15.75. Although the effect of any given prize fight is large compared with the effect of seasonal variables, the cumulative effect of all prize fights combined is not large compared with the cumulative effect of all seasonal variables combined. This is because there are relatively few prize fights.

TABLE 10.4
Impact of "White Loser" (WL) and "Black Loser" (BL)
prize fights on the homicides of young, black male
victims, U.S., 1973–1977

Regressand HOMICIDES	R^2 $\bar{R}^2$ .452 .436	D.F. N 1772 1825
Regressor	Regression coefficient	t-statistic
Intercept	10.59*	20.79
HOMICIDE(1)	.04	1.63
WL(−1)	.83	.48
WL(0)	−1.30	−.75
WL(1)	−1.60	−.93
WL(2)	.19	.11
WL(3)	2.82	1.59
WL(4)	−.82	−.47
WL(5)	−1.19	−.69
WL(6)	−1.66	−.96
WL(7)	2.80	1.62
WL(8)	−.78	−.45
WL(9)	1.62	.94
WL(10)	.59	.34
BL(−1)	−.25	−.21
BL(0)	1.19	.98
BL(1)	−.60	−.49
BL(2)	.18	.15
BL(3)	.67	.54
BL(4)	2.68**	2.19
BL(5)	2.28***	1.86
BL(6)	−.22	−.18
BL(7)	.04	.03
BL(8)	−.76	−.62
BL(9)	1.50	1.23
BL(10)	.30	.25

*Significant at less than .001; **significant at .014; ***significant at .032.
See also Footnotes to Table 10.3.

Table 10.4 examines the impact of "white loser" and "black loser" prize fights on the homicides of young, *black* male victims. Once again, the evidence supports the hypothesis of victim modeling. Black loser prize fights are followed by significant increases in young, black male homicide deaths. In contrast, white loser prize fights do not trigger significant increases in black male homicides.

Black homicides rise significantly on the fourth and fifth days after black loser fights by a total of 4.96 (= 2.68 + 2.28) per fight.[16] The total impact of the black loser prize fight exceeds the impact of almost all seasonal variables. Only New

---

[16]The analysis of Table 10.4 is parallel to that of Table 10.3. Once again, statistical theory and the covariance analysis justify treating as independent the eleven t-statistics for BL(0), . . . BL(10). We observe two BL(X) coefficients significant at .032 or better. The probability of finding two or more BL(X) coefficients significant at this level in eleven independent trials is .0465. Hence, young, black male homicide deaths increase significantly just after "Black Loser" prize fights.

Year's Day and Thanksgiving trigger larger increases in homicides (the coefficients for these holidays being 8.88 and 8.00, respectively). Evidently, a black loser prize fight has a significant, substantive effect on young, black male homicides.

Precipitation hypothesis.   The above evidence is consistent with the notion that prize fights sometimes serve as aggressive models and trigger some U.S. homicides. But perhaps the prize fight merely precipitates a murder that would have occurred anyway, even in the absence of the prize fight.

If a prize fight merely "moves up" a murder so that it occurs a little sooner than it otherwise would have, then the peak in homicides after a prize fight should be followed by a *dip* in homicides soon after. An examination of the three-week period following the prize fight reveals no significant dip in homicides. None of the negative coefficients for PFIGHT(1), PFIGHT(2), . . . , PFIGHT(21) is significant, even at the .10 level. Hence, the precipitation hypothesis seems to be implausible.

Gambling hypothesis.   Perhaps the prize fight provokes no aggressive modeling whatsoever. It merely triggers an increase in gambling, which in turn provokes anger, fighting, and murder. If this explanation is correct, then homicides should rise not only after prize fights but also after other occasions that provoke a great deal of gambling. In the United States, the Super Bowl probably provokes more gambling than any other single event. Yet homicides do *not* rise significantly after these occasions.

One can construct a variable, SUPERBOWL(X), to assess the impact of the Super Bowl on homicides X days later, and one can include this variable in the regression model specified in Table 10.1. The coefficients for SUPERBOWL(X) are listed in Table 10.5. There is some weak evidence that homicides actually *decrease* on the day of the Super Bowl and one day later, and then rise above the expected rate on the third day. Even if one considers these coefficients to be statistically significant (which they are not), it is evident that the Super Bowl is associated with a net drop in homicides rather than a rise. This is not what one would expect if the gambling hypothesis were correct. This hypothesis is also rendered implausible by some of the other evidence presented above: If the gambling hypothesis were true, then it is difficult to see why the traits of the homicide victims should be similar to the traits of the losing boxer.[17]

---

[17]The evidence presented does not support the notion that the gambling hypothesis is a necessary and sufficient explanation for the rise in homicides after a prize fight. But it remains possible that gambling *in combination with* aggressive modeling is helping to provoke the increase in homicides. One way to test this hypothesis is to examine police case histories of murders occurring three and four days after a prize fight. These case histories would have to be compared with case histories taken from control periods.

TABLE 10.5
Impact of the Superbowl on U.S. homicides, controlling
for the effect of seasonal and prize fight variables, U.S.,
1973–1977

Regressor	Regression coefficient	t-statistic
SUPERBOWL(-1)	2.78	.68
SUPERBOWL(0)	-5.03	-1.22
SUPERBOWL(1)	-6.36	-1.55
SUPERBOWL(2)	2.26	.55
SUPERBOWL(3)	6.00	1.46
SUPERBOWL(4)	-1.41	$-.34$
SUPERBOWL(5)	1.10	.27
SUPERBOWL(6)	-1.67	$-.41$
SUPERBOWL(7)	-2.24	$-.54$
SUPERBOWL(8)	3.61	.87
SUPERBOWL(9)	-4.82	-1.17
SUPERBOWL(10)	2.16	.52

Note: The coefficients for the other regressor variables (i.e.,
prize fight and seasonal variables) are not displayed.

In sum, we have now assessed four possible explanations for the rise in homicides after a heavyweight prize fight. At present, the best available explanation is that the prize fight provokes some imitative, aggressive behavior, which results in an increase in homicides. The size of this increase will be considered in the next section.

Size of the increase in homicides after prize fights. Column 3 of Table 10.3 gives the amount by which homicides increase on the third day after each prize fight. The sum of the numbers in this column is 125.64, indicating that U.S. homicides rose by this amount on the third day after championship heavyweight prize fights, 1973–1978. The sum of the numbers in column 2 gives the total number of homicides expected on the third day—1008.36. Dividing 125.64 by 1008.36 gives the percentage increase in homicides on the third day—12.46 percent. Thus, whether one considers the percentage increase or the absolute increase, it appears that homicides rise by a nontrivial amount on the third day after a championship heavyweight prize fight.

The rise in homicides on the fourth day is smaller but still not negligible. Employing calculations similar to those in Table 10.2, one can determine that homicides increase by 67.97 on the fourth day. The percentage increase is 6.58 percent (= 67.97/1033.03). For the third and fourth days combined, homicides increase by a little less than 200 (193.61 = 125.64 + 67.97). The percentage increase for the two-day period is 9.48 percent (= 193.61/[1008.36 + 1033.03]).

This paper has presented evidence which suggests that heavyweight prize fights provoke a brief, sharp increase in homicides. Some implications of this evidence will be briefly considered in the final section of this paper.

SUMMARY

Many researchers have claimed that one cannot generalize with confidence from the impact of mass media violence *in the laboratory* to the impact of mass media violence *in the real world*.[18] These critics point out that laboratory experiments have been set in highly artificial contexts. Typically, the sorts of aggression studied in a laboratory (like hitting plastic dolls or inflicting electric shocks) have not been representative of serious, real-life violence, such as murder or rape. In almost all studies, the laboratory subjects have been nursery school children or college students and thus not representative of the U.S. television audience. Typically, the laboratory subject is presented with a brief, violent excerpt of a television program. In contrast, the "real-life" viewer may watch several hours of television at a sitting, and the violence may be interspersed with humor, commercials, and trips to the bathroom. In contrast to the laboratory subject, who watches television alone, the real-life viewer may well be surrounded by family or friends. Their comments may distract from the television or shape the perception of its many messages. For these reasons, it is inappropriate to generalize from the laboratory to the real world.

The above argument appears to be seriously challenged by the evidence provided in this paper. The data presented in this paper indicate that mass media violence *does* provoke aggression in the real world as well as in the laboratory. In contrast to laboratory studies, the present investigation assesses the effect of mass media violence in a natural context. Unlike laboratory studies, the present study examines a type of violence which is of serious concern to policy makers. Finally, the present investigation does not focus exclusively on a mass media audience consisting of college students and nursery school children. The laboratory study, with its great potential for rigor, has always been capable of establishing the internal validity of findings. The present study has helped to establish that these findings have external validity as well.

---

[18]Comstock (1975:30–40) provides a valuable summary of the debate on this topic. In addition, see Phillips ("Behavioral impact," 1982), who also indicates why it is difficult to generalize from the few field experiments that exist.

References

ANDISON, E. S. Television violence and viewer aggression: A cumulation of study results 1956–1976. In G. C. Wilhoit, and H. de Bock (eds.), *Mass Communication Review Yearbook*. Vol. I. Beverly Hills, Cal.: Sage, 1980.

BERKOWITZ, L., AND RAWLINGS, E. Effects of film violence on inhibitions against subsequent aggression. *Journal of Abnormal and Social Psychology,* 1963, **66,** 405–12.

BERKOWITZ, L., AND GEEN, R. Film violence and the cue properties of available targets. *Journal of Personality and Social Psychology,* 1966, **3,** 525–30.

BERKOWITZ, L., AND GEEN, R. Stimulus qualities of the target of aggression: A further study. *Journal of Personality and Social Psychology,* 1967, **5,** 364–68.

BERKOWITZ, L., AND ALIOTO, J. T. The meaning of an observed event as a determinant of its aggressive consequences. *Journal of Personality and Social Psychology,* 1973, **28,** 206–17.

BERKOWITZ, L., AND MACAULAY, J. The contagion of criminal violence. *Sociometry,* 1971, **34,** 238–60.

BOLLEN, K. A., AND PHILLIPS, D. P. Suicidal motor vehicle fatalities in Detroit: A replication. *American Journal of Sociology,* 1981, **87,** 404–12.

BOLLEN, K. A., AND PHILLIPS, D. P. 1981, Imitative suicides: A national study of the effects of television news stories. *American Sociological Review,* 1982, **47,** 802–809.

BORNLEE, K. A. *Statistical theory and methodology in science and engineering.* New York: Wiley, 1965.

COMSTOCK, G. *Television and human behavior: The key studies.* Santa Monica, Cal.: Rand, 1975.

COMSTOCK, G. Types of portrayal and aggressive behavior. *Journal of Communication,* 1977, **26,** 189–98.

COMSTOCK, G., CHAFFEE, S., KATZMAN, N., McCOMBS, M., AND ROBERTS, D. *Television in America.* Beverly Hills, Cal.: Sage, 1978.

CONKLIN, J. *Criminology.* New York: Macmillan, 1981.

DURBIN, J. Testing for serial correlation in least-squares regression when some of the regressors are lagged dependent variables. *Econometrica,* 1970, **38,** 410–21.

GANZEBOOM, H. B. G., AND DE HAAN, D. Gepubliceerde zelfmoorden en verhoging van sterfte door zelfmoord en ongelukken in Nederland 1972–1980. *Mens en Maatschappij,* 1982, **57,** 55–69.

JOHNSTON, J. *Econometric methods.* New York: McGraw-Hill, 1972.

MURRAY, J., AND KIPPAX, S. From the early window to the late night show: international trends in the study of television's impact on children and adults. *Advances in Experimental Social Psychology,* 1979, **12,** 253–320.

NATIONAL CENTER FOR HEALTH STATISTICS. *Vital statistics of the United States.* Washington, D.C.: U.S. Government Printing Office, 1978.

NATIONAL INSTITUTES OF MENTAL HEALTH. *Television and behavior: Ten years of scientific progress and implications for the eighties.* vol. 1: summary report. Washington, D.C.: U.S. Government Printing Office, 1982.

NERLOVE, M., AND WALLIS, K. F. Use of the Durbin-Watson statistic in inappropriate situations. *Econometrica,* 1966, **34,** 235–38.

OSTROM, C. W. *Time series analysis: Regression techniques.* Beverly Hills, Cal.: Sage, 1978.

PHILLIPS, D. P. The influence of suggestion on suicide: Substantive and theoretical implications of the Werther effect. *American Sociological Review,* 1974, **39,** 340–54.

PHILLIPS, D. P. Motor vehicle fatalities increase just after publicized suicide stories. *Science,* 1977, **196,** 1464–65.

PHILLIPS, D. P. Airplane accident fatalities increase just after stories about murder and suicide. *Science,* 1978, **201,** 148–50.

PHILLIPS, D. P. "Suicide, motor vehicle fatalities, and the mass media: Evidence toward a theory of suggestion." *American Journal of Sociology,* 1979, **84,** 1150–74.

PHILLIPS, D. P. Airplane accidents, murder, and the mass media: Towards a theory of imitation and suggestion. *Social Forces,* 1980, **58,** 1001–24.

PHILLIPS, D. P. The impact of fictional television stories on U.S. adult fatalities: New evidence on the effect of the mass media on violence. *American Journal of Sociology,* 1982, **87,** 1340–59.

PHILLIPS, D. P. The behavioral impact of violence in the mass media: A review of the evidence from laboratory and nonlaboratory investigations. *Sociology and Social Research,* 1982, **66,** 387–98.

RAO, P., and MILLER, R. L. *Applied econometrics.* Belmont, Cal.: Wadsworth, 1971.

THE RING BOOK SHOP. *The Ring boxing encyclopedia and record book.* New York: The Ring Book Shop, 1980.

ROBERTS, D. F., AND BACHEN, C. M. Mass communication effects. In M. R. Rosenzweig and L. W. Parker (eds.), *Annual Review of Psychology.* Palo Alto, Cal.: Annual Reviews, 1981.

IV

SOCIAL COGNITION

11

Contrast Effects and Judgments of Physical Attractiveness: When Beauty Becomes a Social Problem

Douglas T. Kenrick and Sara E. Gutierres

Three studies were conducted to test the hypothesis that judgments of average females' attractiveness or dating desirability will be adversely affected by exposing judges to extremely attractive prior stimuli (i.e., judgments will show a "contrast effect"). Study 1 was a field study in which male dormitory residents watching a popular television show, whose main characters are three strikingly attractive females, were asked to rate a photo of an average female (described as a potential blind date for another dorm resident). These subjects rated the target female as significantly less attractive than did a comparable control group. Two other studies demonstrated analogous effects in a more controlled laboratory setting. In addition, the third study indicated a direct effect of informational social influence on physical attractiveness judgments. Implications are discussed, with particular attention to mass media impact.

Within the past several years, social psychologists have gathered a wealth of data attesting to the central importance of physical attractiveness in interpersonal interaction (see Berscheid and Walster, 1974, for a review). This variable has been found to have a particularly profound effect in dating situations (e.g., Berscheid, Dion, Walster, and Walster, 1971; Brislin and Lewis, 1968; Byrne, Ervin, and Lamberth, 1970; Stroebe, Insko, Thompson, and Layton, 1971; Walster, Aronson, Abrahams, and Rottman, 1966). Brislin and Lewis (1968), for instance, found a correlation of .89 between perceived physical attractiveness and the "desire to date."

Reprinted with permission from the authors and *The Journal of Personality and Social Psychology,* Vol. 38, No. 1, 1980. Copyright © 1980 by the American Psychological Association.

The authors wish to express their appreciation to Guy Fosse, Joni Herzog, Jim Kulma, Debra Lorenz, Bill Patenaude, Bob Schartmann, and Dave Stringfield, who helped at various stages of the present endeavor. We would also like to thank Richard A. Block, Robert B. Cialdini, and John W. Reich for their helpful comments on an earlier version of this manuscript.

It has been noted that physical attractiveness has generally been used as an independent variable in social psychological research (Berscheid and Walster, 1974; Gross and Crofton, 1977). As Gross and Crofton (1977) put it, "beauty has been conceptualized as an invariant 'cause' in previous studies" (p. 86). Nevertheless, a number of studies have shown that judgments of attractiveness can be influenced by other information likely to affect interpersonal attraction in general, such as knowledge of a target person's attitudinal similarity (Walster, cited in Berscheid and Walster, 1974), information that she/he possesses positively valued traits (Gross and Crofton, 1977), actual acquaintance with the target person (Cavior, 1970), or association of the target person with a highly attractive other (Meiners and Sheposh, 1977). In addition to these situational variations, judgments of physical attractiveness have been found to vary across cultural and racial groups (e.g., Cross and Cross, 1971; Marshall and Suggs, 1971), although Berscheid and Walster (1974) suggest that modern mass media may soon obscure any such differences in favor of Western standards. These authors also suggest that socialization of romantic preference is accomplished through the mass media and that "few advertisements or popular movies and novels depict mundane levels of physical attractiveness" (p. 167). If the media do influence one's standards of attractiveness, while at the same time suggesting that only highly beautiful or handsome others are appropriate as love objects, one might expect an inverse relationship between exposure to mass media and the extent to which an individual's standards for the attractiveness of a romantic partner are "realistic."

In fact, if one can extrapolate the findings from research into other areas of perceptual judgment, there is reason to be concerned about even the short-term impact of mass media on our judgments of the attractiveness of the more mundane potential romantic partners around us. One consistently reported finding in perceptual judgments is a "contrast" effect, that is, judgments of moderate stimuli in a series are found to be displaced away from extreme or distant stimuli. This effect has been found for judgments of physical dimensions such as weight (e.g., Heintz, 1950; Sherif, Taub, and Hovland, 1958), length of lines (e.g., Krantz and Campbell, 1961); and shape (Helson and Kozaki, 1968); as well as social stimuli such as attitudes (Hovland, Harvey, and Sherif, 1957), pleasantness of facial expressions (Manis, 1971), criminal acts (Pepitone and DiNubile, 1976), and personality impressions (Simpson and Ostrom, 1976). If such effects can be presumed to generalize to judgments of physical attractiveness, prior exposure to highly unattractive individuals would result in an enhanced perception of the attractiveness of an "average" person, with the reverse being true of exposure to very attractive persons. Some additional implications would follow from the existence of such an effect in this realm. In our mass-media-oriented culture, where we are bombarded with highly attractive females, such exposure should produce a rather high "adaptation level" (Helson, 1964), resulting in lowered assessments of the beauty of average "real world" females. Given the particularly high relationship between such judgments and dating desirability, such exposure might also lead to an analogous decrement along this latter dimension as well.

It should be noted that in this case, there are at least two bodies of literature that might lead one to expect that such contrast effects would *not* hold in this realm. First, there is evidence that perceptual contrast will not be induced by stimuli that, although sufficiently distant from the stimulus along the relevant dimension, possess other characteristics that lead subjects to consider them to belong to different "universes of discourse" (Helson, 1971). Brown (1953), for instance, had subjects lift a tray between judgments of a series of weights. Although a similarly heavy anchor weight produced a contrast effect, lifting the tray had no effect on judgments. Similarly, Bevan and Pritchard (1963) found that shape judgments were not affected by grossly deviant or oversized stimuli. If media females are not considered to belong to the same category or "universe of discourse" as real-life females, their beauty might be discounted and fail to influence judgments of nonmedia females. Second, since physical attractiveness has been shown to have the qualities of a reinforcer (e.g., Byrne, Ervin, and Lamberth, 1970; Dion, 1977), and since contextual association with reinforcing events has been shown to enhance the attractiveness of a target person (Clore and Byrne, 1974; Lott and Lott, 1974), exposure to an average female in a context of highly attractive females might be expected to lead to a classical conditioning effect such that the average female would actually come to be judged more positively. Similarly, in a context of highly unattractive females, she should come to be judged more negatively if such a process applied here. Three studies were therefore performed to test the hypothesis that exposure to extreme attractiveness stimuli would produce contrasted judgments of a target person of average attractiveness.

Study 1 was a field study in which subjects were asked to judge a potential blind date for a fellow dormitory resident. One group of subjects was students who were watching the television program "Charlie's Angels" (whose main characters are three beautiful women), whereas controls consisted of residents of the same dormitory (sampled during the same night) who were not watching this show at the time.

STUDY 1

Method

Subjects. Subjects were 81 male dormitory residents at Montana State University. They participated in groups of 1 to 6 on the evening of February 1, 1977.

Procedure. Two male confederates entered a dormitory room during one of two time periods (during the hour preceding "Charlie's Angels," or during the hour at which "Charlie's Angels" was aired).[1] They explained to the students in the room:

---

[1]All subjects who were watching television during this time slot were tuned to this program, which was quite popular at the time of this study (sixth in the Nielsen ratings).

Confederate A: Listen, could I just interrupt you guys for 30 seconds? We're having a major philosophical dispute here and we need to do an informal survey to resolve the question. You see, we have a friend coming to town this week and we want to fix him up with a date, but we can't decide whether to fix him up with her or not, so we decided to conduct a survey.

Confederate B: You see, I don't think she looks very good.

Confederate A: But I think she looks pretty good. At any rate, we want you to give us your vote on how attractive you think she is. (Confederate A begins to hold up the picture, but it is faced away from subjects so they can't see it).

Confederate B: Right, on a scale of 1 to 7, with 1 being very unattractive, 4 being exactly average, and 7 being beautiful.

Confederate A: (turns over photo) Now, nobody say anything until everyone makes up his own mind, and be honest—give your honest opinion.

Confederate B: Remember, 1 is very unattractive, 4 is right in the middle, and 7 is very attractive.

Confederate A held up the picture, allowed each subject to make a silent judgment, and then had the subjects give their responses. They thanked the subjects, left the room, and immediately recorded the time, condition, and each subject's response independently. Agreement between the two confederates was 100 percent in all instances.

Stimulus photo.   The stimulus photo was an 8 cm $\times$ 5 cm. black-and-white yearbook snapshot taken from a series of slides presented in earlier research (Kenrick and Gutierres, Note 1). A group of 11 undergraduate males from the population used in the present research had given this photo a mean rating of 4.11 on a scale analogous to that used by the subjects in our field study.

Results

Subjects' data were broken down into four groups. Those watching "Charlie's Angels" constituted the "experimental" group, whereas those watching another television program earlier in the night were designated as control subjects. To control for the possibility that ratings by experimental subjects may have been due simply to their having been made at a later hour, two additional control groups were included. Subjects in these groups were not watching television but were sampled either during the "Charlie's Angels" time slot or during the preceding hour. The data from the group watching "Charlie's Angels" were plotted against the data from all control groups, using a planned orthogonal contrast. It was expected that the "Charlie's Angels" group would show lowest mean ratings of the target's attractiveness. Although subjects were cooperative in making silent independent judgments, the group mean was used as the unit of analysis in the contrast presented below.

In line with predictions, results indicated relatively lowest ratings by viewers of "Charlie's Angels" ($M = 3.43$, versus 4.00 combined M for the controls),[2] $F (1, 24) = 5.03, p < .03$. This contrast accounted for 84 percent of the between-groups variance. A similar test using the individual subject as the unit of analysis resulted in $F (1, 77) = 7.39, p < .01$.

Discussion

Results of Study 1 were directly in line with predictions, indicating relatively lowest ratings of an average female by subjects who were observing highly attractive media females. Nevertheless, since subjects were not randomly assigned to conditions, our results are open to several interpretations. First, "Charlie's Angels" viewers may have been more negative in their rating of the target female because of the immediate influence of the beautiful media stimuli. Second, the effect may have been due to the fact that these viewers were more negative because of a chronic tendency to expose themselves to highly attractive females depicted in the media. Both of these possibilities would be consistent with our hypotheses. A third possibility, however, is that some other difference may have existed to make "Charlie's Angels" viewers more generally negative in their judgments of females. Although we can offer no intuitively compelling reasons to assume this to be the case, it seems best to consider our hypothesis confirmation in Study 1 as suggestive evidence only at this point. Study 2 was designed to offer a more direct test of our hypothesis by manipulating exposure to media beauty in subjects randomly assigned to conditions.

STUDY 2

Method

Subjects.   Subjects were 48 male undergraduates enrolled in introductory psychology at Montana State University, who participated in small groups of 3 to 5.

Procedure.   Subjects arrived for an experiment entitled "personality" and were told:

> This is a study of first impression formation. We are interested in determining how much we can tell about a person from only a brief encounter or glance. Many people assume that we can tell quite a bit from a person's face alone. It is assumed that we can tell whether someone is honest or dishonest, sociable or unsociable, et cetera

---

[2]Five groups of subjects (19 total) were watching "Charlie's Angels." Respective means and number of groups were 4.31 ($n = 3$) for nontelevision watchers sampled during the "Charlie's Angels" time slot and 4.08 ($n = 8$) and 3.82 ($n = 12$) for television watchers and nontelevision watchers, respectively, who were sampled during the previous time slot. A test of the residual effects was not significant.

from their eyes or mouth, for instance. Advertisements, books, and magazines often include a certain type of face in an attempt to present a certain image to the public— of an intelligent scientist, an overworked housewife, a dedicated businessman, a vivacious and happy young model, and so on. As part of the present investigation we've given intensive psychological tests and interviews to a group of students and interviewed several of their friends and acquaintances as well. We've developed a personality profile for each of these persons. You will be seeing only a yearbook photo of one of these people, and your task will be to simply give your honest first impression of what that person is really like. You may not feel that you have enough information to respond to each dimension, but simply take your best guess, since accuracy or inaccuracy of impression formation is what we're interested in.

Following this, subjects were instructed not to communicate with one another verbally or nonverbally, since the experiment necessitated completely independent judgments. Seating was arranged so that observation of other subjects' written responses was not possible. For experimental subjects, a black and white slide of an attractive female in a magazine advertisement[3] was turned on during the verbal instructions, and the experimenter pointed to it (as if to give an example) as he mentioned the "young model." Control subjects heard the same instructions but were not exposed to the magazine ad. Following the instructions, all subjects were shown a slide of a female of average attractiveness (the same one used in the first study) and were given a "personality rating" sheet to fill out on her. The rating form contained several bipolar scales (likable–unlikable, reasonable–unreasonable, courteous–rude, selfish–unselfish, warm–cold, sincere–insincere, responsible–irresponsible, beautiful–ugly, kind–cruel). The rating of the target person along the dimension beautiful–ugly constituted the main dependent variable. It was predicted that she would be rated as significantly less beautiful following exposure to the attractive female advertisement.

Results

In line with predictions, ratings of the target person indicated that she was seen as significantly less beautiful by subjects exposed to the advertisement, $F(1, 46) = 7.10$, $p < .01$. Mean ratings were 4.41 for the experimental group and 3.52 for the controls (higher ratings indicate that the target person was seen as relatively *less* beautiful).[4] These results parallel those of the first study and cannot be explained as due to self-selection of subjects.

---

[3]This slide was an advertisement for Wella Balsam, depicting the popular model Farrah Fawcett-Majors. In pretesting, a group of 21 undergraduates (11 males, 10 females) from the same population used in the study proper gave this slide a mean rating of 6.67 on the 7-point scale analogous to that used in Study 1.

[4]None of the other adjectives showed any effect of the manipulation except "responsible–irresponsible." Subjects exposed to the advertisement saw the target as significantly more responsible. Although these results were not predicted, they may fit with Stephan, Berscheid, and Walster's (1971) finding that under some circumstances, males who judge a female as sexually attractive may also see her as relatively "careless" and "uninhibited."

STUDY 3

The first two studies were concerned with the indirect influence of contextual stimuli on judgments of attractiveness. They demonstrated that exposure to beautiful media females could result in lowered assessments of a female of average attractiveness. A third study was conducted to provide an additional test of the question addressed in the first two studies while also examining the more direct impact of informational social influence (Deutsch and Gerard, 1955) on judgments of attractiveness. We are often exposed to our peers' assessments of members of the opposite sex, and a number of classical social psychological findings suggest that peers' judgments can influence assessments even of "objective" reality (e.g., Asch, 1951; Crutchfield, 1955; Sherif, 1935). Given the interpersonal importance of attractiveness judgments, it is of some interest to determine the applicability of this classical effect in the present realm.

Also of some interest was the question of whether exposure to peer evaluations would influence judgments of persons not directly commented on. That is, would exposure to peer evaluations produce an alteration of *standards* that would generalize to judgments of other persons (not directly evaluated)?

Finally, the third study included female subjects as well as males. Since physical attractiveness judgments have been found to influence interpersonal behaviors between same-sex as well as opposite-sex persons (see Berscheid and Walster, 1974, for a review), it is of interest to determine the applicability of our findings to same-sex assessments.

Method

Subjects. Subjects were 98 undergraduates (49 males, 49 females) enrolled in introductory psychology at Montana State University who participated in groups of 2 to 7. One subject was deleted because of suspicion regarding the male confederates.

Procedure. Subjects arrived for an experiment entitled "pretesting stimuli" and were led to a small room containing several chairs and a slide projector. In half the conditions, two male confederates posed as subjects and always sat together in the back row of two rows of five chairs. The experimenter explained:

> As the sign-up sheets indicated, we're interested in having you help us pretest some stimuli for an experiment we'll be running at the start of next semester. What that experiment will involve is seeing how well people judge personality from only a small amount of information. We'll be showing people a photograph including only a person's face and asking them to judge the person's overall personality. We've found in the past, however, that these judgments are often influenced by other irrelevant factors, so we'll be asking you to make an objective judgment of several photographs so we can control for these irrelevant factors next semester. All right, for the first 6 photographs you'll be rating the physical attractiveness of each face.

Prior stimuli.   Subjects were then given a sheet containing six 9-point scales labeled 1 (extremely unattractive) and 9 (extremely attractive). They were further instructed to observe each slide carefully for 40 seconds, at which point a blank screen would appear that would signal them to make their judgment. For all conditions Slides 2, 3, and 5 were held constant. These slides showed black-and-white yearbook photographs of females previously judged to be "average" in attractiveness (Kenrick and Gutierres, Note 1). Half the subjects saw highly attractive slides in Slots 1, 4, and 6, whereas the other half saw unattractive slides in these positions. Attractive and unattractive slides were also yearbook photos selected in the same manner as the "average" photos.

Confederate comments.   Half of each group heard the confederates make comments about the third and fifth (average) slides. These comments were negative in the groups exposed to the high-attractive series (e.g., "What a dog," nonverbal utterances of displeasure) and positive in the groups exposed to the low-attractive series (e.g., "You can set me up with her," nonverbal utterances of attraction). After Slide 5 had been rated, the experimenter mentioned that any comments might influence the others in the room and asked that the subjects refrain from giving any public responses to the stimuli. (For controls, this request was made before Slide 1 was shown.)

Target person.   After Slide 6 had been rated, subjects were told that the next slide would be "evaluated on a completely different dimension" and were handed a sheet that asked them to check one of seven sentences ranging from "I would find this person extremely desirable as a date" to "I would find this person extremely undesirable as a date." Female subjects were instructed to evaluate the female as a potential date for a male friend. This final photo was selected in the same manner as the other "average" slides (2, 3, and 5) and was, like them, held constant for all subjects.[5]

Subjects were then fully debriefed and were probed for suspicion. All reported having clearly heard the confederates' comments (when they were made), and most generally reported in informal discussion that they found them obnoxious and did not feel they were influenced. Nevertheless, as might be expected, other males had in several cases spontaneously joined in verbal agreement with the confederates' comments during the experimental session. Data were therefore treated using the group as the unit of analysis.

---

[5]Although this photo was not rated on physical attractiveness within the context of the present study (as the other average photos used were) we did have it rated on a 7-point scale like that used in the first two studies (1 = extremely unattractive, 4 = average, 7 = extremely attractive) by 66 undergraduates (34 males, 32 females) from the same subject pool during the following academic year. The mean rating obtained was 4.42 for this group. Note that the polarity here is reversed from that of the 7-point "dating desirability" scale used in Study 3, and this should be read as 3.58 if one wishes to make direct comparison. We would suggest that the reader who chooses to do so should keep in mind that there may well be some slippage in making such a conversion.

Predictions

1. It was expected that exposure to attractive prior stimuli would lead to relatively decreased ratings of the target person's dating desirability.

2. It was further expected that subjects' ratings of the physical attractiveness of Slides 3 and 5 (the "average" slides for which comments were made) would be affected in the direction of the confederates' comments. Since this would have resulted in decreased ratings of these two slides in the attractive condition (since negative comments were made here) and increased ratings in the unattractive condition (since positive comments were made here), this would have shown up as an interaction between the confederate comment factor and the attractiveness factor.

3. In addition, we were interested in seeing whether confederates' comments would indirectly enhance the influence of the prior stimuli on ratings of the final target person (by further heightening standards in the attractive condition, and vice versa). This would also have shown up as an interaction effect, as indicated in Prediction 2 above.

Results

Manipulation check. Comparisons between attractive and unattractive slides in Positions 1, 4, and 6 yielded differences significant beyond the .001 level in each instance. Mean ratings of the three attractive slides were 7.00, 7.74, and 7.82 for the attractive and 4.24, 3.26 and 2.36 for the unattractive series, respectively. Discounting the effects of the independent variables (discussed below), the overall mean ratings for Slides 2, 3, and 5 (constant slides in series) were 5.18, 5.00, and 5.51, respectively.

Sex of subject. Prior to the analysis using the whole group mean as the unit of analysis, an analysis dividing each group into male and female subjects was performed. This analysis indicated that sex of subject yielded no main effects or interactions on any of the dependent variables, except for ratings of Slide 5, for which a main effect of subject sex was obtained, $F (1, 29) = 8.26, p < .01$. Females rated this slide as more attractive ($M = 5.91$) than did males ($M = 5.19$).

Main analyses. Ratings of the target person's "dating desirability" showed the predicted main effect of prior stimuli (P), $F (1, 14) = 15.01, p < .002$. As expected from our earlier results, subjects exposed to the attractive prior slides gave significantly lowered ratings of the target person (see Table 11.1). As indicated in the predictions section above, a significant interaction of prior stimuli and confederates' comments (C) would have indicated that the comments further enhanced the standards set by the prior stimuli. The F for the interaction term was less than 1, thus failing to support this suggestion. The C "main effect" was also nonsignificant, $F (1, 14) = 1.51$.

Prior stimuli and confederate comments. On the slides for which confederates made direct comments, ratings were, as predicted, lowered in the attractive

TABLE 11.1
Influence of stimulus attractiveness and confederate comments on ratings of prior stimuli and target person, Study 3

| | Attractiveness of prior stimuli | | | |
| | Attractive | | Unattractive | |
Item rated	Confederate comment	Control	Confederate comment	Control
Slide 3[a]	4.63	5.08	6.04	5.00
Slide 5[a]	4.30	5.02	6.96	6.08
Target person[b]	4.33	4.16	3.34	2.78

[a]Higher ratings indicate *more* positive ratings of female's beauty on a 9-point scale.
[b]Higher ratings indicate *less* desirability as a date on a 7-point scale.

condition (where negative comments were made) and enhanced in the unattractive condition (where positive comments were made). This showed up as a significant P × C interaction on Slide 5, $F (1, 14) = 4.66, p < .05$, and a marginally significant effect on Slide 3, $F (1, 14) = 4.41, p < .06$ (see Table 11.1). In addition, there was a significant main effect of prior stimuli on Slide 5, $F (1, 14) = 25.50, p < .001$, as well as a similar trend on Slide 3, $F (1, 14) = 3.91, p < .07$, indicating relatively lower ratings in the context of highly attractive stimuli.[6] Since confederates' comments should have canceled out for the C effect, Fs were, not surprisingly, less than 1 for ratings of both Slide 3 and Slide 5.

GENERAL DISCUSSION

The results of Study 3 were consistent with those of the first two studies in supporting the existence of a contrast effect phenomenon for judgments of physical attractiveness. This effect occurred despite the fact that the attractive stimuli in the first two studies were drawn from a different "universe of discourse" than that from which the target person was drawn. To the extent that the beauty of media females may have been "discounted" due to this factor, it was not sufficient to remove the adverse contrast effect. Similarly, the contrary prediction based on a simple application of classical conditioning principles (i.e., that reinforcement value of attractive photos would generalize to an average target photo in the same series) was not borne out. This result is consistent with other findings suggesting that simple generalization of affective reactions to attraction objects is often overruled by other (e.g., cognitive) factors (Kenrick and Johnson, 1979).

---

[6]Ratings of Slide 2 were also significantly more negative when it followed an attractive slide in Position 1, $F (1, 14) = 9.23, p < .01$.

Possible Implications

Media impact (the "Farrah factor").[7]   The present results support the suggestion that our initial impressions of potential romantic partners will be adversely affected if we happen to have been recently exposed to posters, magazines, television, or movies showing highly attractive individuals (or if such stimuli are concurrently present). Kenrick and Gutierres (Note 1) found analogous results to those obtained here, using stimuli randomly chosen from advertisements in best-selling magazines. Their results indicated, not surprisingly, that media females are indeed selected from a highly skewed distribution with regard to physical attractiveness.

Whether or not our obtained effects are long lasting cannot be determined from the present series of studies. Even if such effects are very short-lived, however, they could still be of some consequence, influencing the desirability of females who happen to meet a male immediately following or during exposure to such media. Of some interest in this regard is a recent study by Snyder, Tanke, and Berscheid (1977), which suggests that initial judgments of a target's attractiveness may function as a self-fulfilling prophecy. In the Snyder et al. study, targets who were perceived to be unattractive actually came to behave in a less friendly and likable manner than targets who were regarded as attractive. Further, there is other research showing that the judged physical attractiveness of a computer date actually determines the likelihood of seeking further interaction with that person (Walster et al., 1966).

Thus, let us imagine a scenario involving a college-age male who, like the subjects in our first study, is engrossed in an episode of a television show containing unusually beautiful females in the central roles (the examples are not hard to come by, especially given the recent conscious and concerted effort of TV network producers to place very highly attractive women in starring roles). He is briefly introduced to a neighbor who happens to be a female of average physical attractiveness. Our data suggest that his immediate assessment of her attractiveness and dating desirability will be lower than might otherwise be the case. Based on the findings of Dion (1977), he might be expected to subsequently reduce his visual attention to her (thus retarding any return of his "adaptation level" to mundane levels). He might also act in such a manner as to inhibit demonstrations of friendliness on her part, following Snyder et al. (1977), and also be less likely to seek to interact with her in the future, in line with the findings of Walster et al. (1966).

Individual differences in history of exposure.   Research on perceptual judgment in other areas suggests that the judgment of a stimulus is determined by both the immediate stimulus context and by a "pooled" estimate of the judge's past experience with stimuli in the same realm of discourse (Helson, 1964, 1971).

---

[7]This term was coined by the editors of *Human Behavior* magazine (February 1979 issue) for the effect we have been investigating in this series of studies.

Given the male college student's vast history of exposure to female facial stimuli, the manipulations in Studies 2 and 3 could only be seen as having a transitory impact, likely to be erased by relatively short exposure to real-world females. Nevertheless, given a tendency to selectively attend to and actively seek visual exposure to highly beautiful females (Dion, 1977), our results suggest the possibility that "chronic" standards for physical attractiveness may be somewhat inflated, particularly among individuals who are exposed to relatively more mass media (whose pooled estimate of a facial stimulus is based on a highly skewed and "nonrepresentative" sample). Note in this regard that there is evidence that the average adolescent in this society has spent more time watching television than in school (Gerbner and Gross, 1976).

We have focused our discussion thus far on the effects of media beauty, but it should also be pointed out that our results have potential implications for other realms as well. For instance, some individuals may be chronically exposed to unusually high levels of attractiveness by virtue of their occupation (e.g., airline pilots, bartenders in Playboy clubs, undergraduates at UCLA, and so on). If these individuals are themselves unattractive, the effects of such exposure may be particularly adverse, leading to the adoption of unrealistically high standards and consequent dissatisfaction with those females actually available to them and likely to be interested in them (at least according to the "matching" hypothesis; Berscheid and Walster, 1974).[8]

Cognitive influences. Social psychologists have recently shown renewed interest in studying subjects' phenomenological reconstructions of the social situations they are faced with. Social behavior seems to be influenced not simply by "objective" environmental stimuli but also by the subjects' tendency to interpret these stimuli, selectively attend to them, and selectively recall them (e.g., Berkowitz, 1978; Snyder and Uranowitz, 1978). When the present research is considered in the light of such findings, some additional researchable implications unfold. Given the rewarding nature of attractiveness, individuals may well selectively notice the atypically attractive persons in their environments and selectively recall them (perhaps even actively generating images of such persons in their absence). Thus, an individual whose everyday activities expose him or her to a "representative" sample of opposite-sex persons may nevertheless *construct* a "biased" adaptation level.

It should be noted at this point that we have not elucidated the cognitive mediators underlying our obtained effect. Although such a question is not relevant for the social implications we have touched on, it would be of some theoretical interest to investigate the cognitive processes responsible for our effect. It seems unlikely, for instance, that contrast effects obtained in this realm (and in other realms of social judgment) are due to "receptor fatigue," as the analogous effects obtained with purely sensory phenomena might be (Helson, 1964), unless one posits a relatively

---

[8]Our thanks to an anonymous reviewer for this suggestion.

central and higher order mechanism for such judgments. On the other hand, an explanation in terms of "scale usage" effects (e.g., Anderson, 1975; Parducci, 1965) cannot deal with the results of Studies 1 and 2 and must be stretched a great deal to account for the results of Study 3.

Influence of Peer Evaluations on Attractiveness Judgments

In addition to demonstrating indirect contextual influences on judgments of attractiveness, the results of the third study indicated that information regarding peer judgments will influence evaluations of physical beauty. Subjects' judgments tended to conform to evaluative comments expressed by confederates in this study. Since subjects' judgments were private in this case, these results would seem to be an instance of what Deutsch and Gerard (1955) have referred to as "informational" as opposed to "normative" social influence. This latter effect would also seem to have clear "real-life" analogues. It has been noted that initial preinteraction encounters are strongly influenced by visual characteristics (Levinger, 1974), and very often such first visual encounters are accompanied by friends' explicit evaluations of the target individual's attractiveness. In fact, students can often be observed actively seeking peer evaluations of the attractiveness of potential romantic partners with whom relationships have progressed to what Levinger (1974) has termed the level of "surface contact."

The results of Study 3 showed only a direct effect of confederates' comments on physical attractiveness judgments, whereas general "standards" for dating desirability were not influenced by these comments. It is possible that long-term exposure to peers with either very high or very low "standards" would result in a more general effect, but the present methodology (in which only two females were evaluated by the peer models) does not allow for any such determination.

Influence of Media Depictions of Males on Females' Judgment

The present series of studies used only female target persons. Although physical attractiveness has generally been found to be more important for females than for males (e.g., Berscheid et al., 1971; Efran, 1974; Stroebe et al., 1971; Walster et al., 1966), attractiveness has not been found to be insignificant for men, by any means. These same studies, for instance, have shown physical attractiveness to be significant in importance for males as well, and Berscheid and Walster (1974) point out that although females consistently *report* physical attractiveness to be less important in their judgments of males, the findings with regard to *behavioral* measures are sometimes contradictory (e.g., Byrne et al., 1970). It seems likely that the present findings would have similar implications for judgments of males, although this remains to be empirically verified.

Reference Note

1. KENRICK, D. T., AND GUTIERRES, S. E. Influences of mass media on judgments of physical attractiveness: The people's case against Farrah Fawcett. Paper presented at the meeting of the American Psychological Association, Toronto, August 1978.

References

ANDERSON, N. On the role of context effects in psychophysical judgment. *Psychological Review,* 1975, **82,** 462–482.

ASCH, S. E. Effects of group pressure upon the modification and distortion of judgment. In H. Guetzkow (Ed.), *Groups, leadership, and men.* Pittsburgh: Carnegie Press, 1951.

BERKOWITZ, L. *Cognitive theories in social psychology.* New York: Academic Press, 1978.

BERSCHEID, E., DION, K., WALSTER, E., AND WALSTER, G. W. Physical attractiveness and dating choice. *Journal of Experimental Social Psychology,* 1971, **7,** 173–189.

BERSCHEID, E., AND WALSTER, E. Physical attractiveness. In L. Berkowitz (Ed.), *Advances in experimental social psychology* (Vol. 7). New York: Academic Press, 1974.

BEVAN, W., AND PRITCHARD, J. R. The anchor effect and the problem of relevance in the judgment of shape. *Journal of General Psychology,* 1963, **69,** 147–161.

BRISLIN, R. W., AND LEWIS, S. A. Dating and physical attractiveness. *Psychological Reports,* 1968, **22,** 976.

BROWN, D. R. Stimulus similarity and the anchoring of subjective scales. *American Journal of Psychology,* 1953, **66,** 199–214.

BYRNE, D., ERVIN, C. R., AND LAMBERTH, J. Continuity between the experimental study of attraction and real-life computer dating. *Journal of Personality and Social Psychology,* 1970, **16,** 157–165.

CAVIOR, N. Physical attractiveness, perceived attitude similarity, and interpersonal attraction among fifth and eleventh grade boys and girls. Unpublished doctoral dissertation, University of Houston, 1970.

CLORE, G. L., AND BYRNE, D. A reinforcement-affect model of attraction. In T. L. Huston (Ed.), *Foundations of interpersonal attraction.* New York: Academic Press, 1974.

CROSS, J. F., AND CROSS, J. Age, sex, race, and the perception of facial beauty. *Developmental Psychology,* 1971, **5,** 433–439.

CRUTCHFIELD, R. A. Conformity and character. *American Psychologist,* 1955, **10,** 191–198.

DEUTSCH, M., AND GERARD, H. B. A study of normative and social influences upon individual judgment. *Journal of Abnormal and Social Psychology,* 1955, **51,** 629–636.

DION, K. K. The incentive value of physical attractiveness. *Personality and Social Psychology Bulletin,* 1977, **3,** 67–70.

EFRAN, M. G. The effect of physical appearance on the judgment of guilt, interpersonal attraction, and severity of recommended punishment in a simulated jury task. *Journal of Experimental Research in Personality,* 1974, **8,** 45–54.

GERBNER, G., AND GROSS, L. The scary world of TV's heavy viewer. *Psychology Today,* 1976, **9,** 41–45.

GROSS, A. E., AND CROFTON, C. What is good is beautiful. *Sociometry,* 1977, **40,** 85–90.

HEINTZ, R. K. The effect of remote anchoring points upon the judgments of lifted weights. *Journal of Experimental Psychology,* 1950, **40,** 584–591.

HELSON, H. *Adaptation-level theory: An experimental and systematic approach to behavior.* New York: Harper & Row, 1964.

HELSON, H. Adaptation-level theory: 1970 and after. In M. H. Appley (Ed.), *Adaptation-level theory: A symposium.* New York: Academic Press, 1971.

HELSON, H., AND KOZAKI, T. Effects of duration of series and anchor-stimuli on judgments of perceived size. *American Journal of Psychology,* 1968, **81,** 292–302.

HOVLAND, C., HARVEY, O., AND SHERIF, M. Assimilation and contrast effects in reactions to communication and attitude change. *Journal of Abnormal and Social Psychology,* 1957, **55,** 244–252.

KENRICK, D. T., AND JOHNSON, G. A. Interpersonal attraction in aversive environments: A problem for the classical conditioning paradigm? *Journal of Personality and Social Psychology,* 1979, **37,** 570–577.

KRANTZ, D. L., AND CAMPBELL, D. T. Separating perceptual and linguistic effects of context effect upon absolute judgment. *Journal of Experimental Psychology,* 1961, **62,** 35–42.

LEVINGER, G. A three-level approach to attraction: Toward an understanding of pair relatedness. In T. Huston (Ed.), *Foundations of interpersonal attraction.* New York: Academic Press, 1974.

LOTT, A., AND LOTT, B. The role of reward in the formation of positive interpersonal attitudes. In T. L. Huston (Ed.), *Foundations of interpersonal attraction.* New York: Academic Press, 1974.

MANIS, M. Context effects in communication: Determinants of verbal output and referential decoding. In M. H. Appley (Ed.), *Adaptation-level theory: A symposium.* New York: Academic Press, 1971.

MARSHALL, D. S., AND SUGGS, R. C. (Eds.), *Human sexual behavior: Variations in the ethnographic spectrum.* New York: Basic Books, 1971.

MEINERS, M. L., AND SHEPOSH, J. P. Beauty or brains: Which image for your mate? *Personality and Social Psychology Bulletin,* 1977, **3,** 262–265.

PARDUCCI, A. Category judgment: A range-frequency model. *Psychological Review,* 1965, **72,** 407–418.

PEPITONE, A., AND DINUBILE, M. Contrast effects in judgments of crime severity and the punishment of criminal violators. *Journal of Personality and Social Psychology,* 1976, **33,** 448–459.

SHERIF, M. A study of some social factors in perception. *Archives of Psychology,* 1935, **187.**

SHERIF, M., TAUB, D., AND HOVLAND, C. Assimilation and contrast effects of anchoring stimuli on judgments. *Journal of Experimental Psychology,* 1958, **55,** 150–156.

SIMPSON, D. D., AND OSTROM, T. M. Contrast effects in impression formation. *Journal of Personality and Social Psychology,* 1976, **34,** 625–629.

SNYDER, M., TANKE, E. D., AND BERSCHEID, E. Social perception and interpersonal behavior: On the self-fulfilling nature of social stereotypes. *Journal of Personality and Social Psychology,* 1977, **35,** 656–666.

SNYDER, M., AND URANOWITZ, S. W. Reconstructing the past: Some cognitive consequences of person perception. *Journal of Personality and Social Psychology,* 1978, **36,** 941–950.

STEPHAN, W., BERSCHEID, E., AND WALSTER, E. Sexual arousal and heterosexual perception. *Journal of Personality and Social Psychology,* 1971, **20,** 93–101.

STROEBE, W., INSKO, C. A., THOMPSON, V. D., AND LAYTON, B. D. Effects of physical attractiveness, attitude similarity, and sex on various aspects of interpersonal attraction. *Journal of Personality and Social Psychology,* 1971, **18,** 79–91.

WALSTER, E., ARONSON, V., ABRAHAMS, D., AND ROTTMANN, L. Importance of physical attractiveness in dating behavior. *Journal of Personality and Social Psychology,* 1966, **4,** 508–516.

12

The Effect of Attitude on the Recall
of Personal Histories

Michael Ross, Cathy McFarland, and Garth J. O. Fletcher

Two studies were conducted to examine the relation between attitudes and the recall of past behaviors. The same paradigm was utilized in both experiments. First, subjects' attitudes on an issue were manipulated. Subjects were then asked to recall past behaviors relevant to the newly formed attitude. The results indicated that attitudes can exert a directive influence on recall of personal histories. The implications of the results for investigations of the relations between attitudes, behavior, and recall are discussed.

The concept of attitude has had a variable status in social psychology. In one famous quote, attitude was described as the "primary building stone in the edifice of social psychology" (Allport, 1968, p. 63). In recent years, however, some social psychologists have been more inclined to agree with Wicker's (1971) suggestion that "it may be desirable to abandon the attitude concept" (p. 29). This disenchantment stems from the evidence that attitudes fail to predict behavior in a variety of circumstances (Calder and Ross, 1973; Wicker, 1969). Although this view is overly pessimistic (Ajzen and Fishbein, 1977; Fazio and Zanna, 1981), it seems clear that attitudes play a limited role in the etiology of many behaviors.

The importance of attitudes is not circumscribed by their role in predicting behavior, however. The function of attitudes examined in the present research was suggested by Bartlett (1932) in the context of his work on recall of pictures and prose passages. Bartlett proposed that attitudes influence memory: "Recall is . . . a

Reprinted with permission from the authors and *The Journal of Personality and Social Psychology,* Vol. 40, No. 4, 1981. Copyright © 1981 by the American Psychological Association.

This research was supported in part by a Social Sciences and Humanities Research Council research grant to Michael Ross. The studies were conducted while Cathy McFarland was receiving an SSHRC doctoral fellowship. The authors thank Susan Fiske, Jim Olson, and Mark Zanna for their comments on an earlier version of the manuscript.

construction, made largely on the basis of an attitude, and its general effect is that of a justification of the attitude" (p. 207). Bartlett deduced this from the content of subjects' recall and their self-reports of how they prodded their memories.

Following Bartlett, there has been a considerable amount of research relating cognitive schemata to recall that suggests, albeit indirectly, that attitudes might be expected to influence memory. This research demonstrates that recall can be biased by evaluations and impressions. For example, in a study testing Heider's (1958) balance theory, Zajonc and Burnstein (1965) found that errors in recall of hypothetical relationships tended to be in the direction of producing cognitively balanced rather than imbalanced structures. Also, memory of the characteristics of hypothetical individuals has been shown to be influenced by impressions of the target people formed after the characteristics have been described (Lingle, Geva, Ostrom, Leippe, and Baumgardner, 1979; Snyder and Uranowitz, 1978).

Research on the selective learning hypothesis is more directly relevant to the present concerns. This research has provided less compelling evidence for a relation between attitudes and recall. Levine and Murphy (1943) described the selective learning hypothesis as follows: An individual "notes and remembers material which supports his social attitudes better than material which conflicts with these attitudes" (p. 515). The paradigm utilized by Levine and Murphy and subsequent researchers consists of exposing subjects to material that is consistent or inconsistent with their attitudes and asking them to reproduce the material at a later time. Although early studies provided support for the hypothesis (e.g., Jones and Kohler, 1958; Levine and Murphy, 1943), subsequent research has often yielded inconsistent or negative results (e.g., Greenwald and Sakumura, 1967). There is some recent evidence that the selective learning hypothesis may hold only for certain kinds of people (Olson, 1980).

It is reasonable to expect that attitudes will at times affect the recall of prose passages or opinion statements. Anyone who has examined the complicated and esoteric passages employed by Bartlett, for example, will not be surprised to learn that subjects forgot the details quickly and reconstructed them using vague residual feelings or attitudes as guides.

For the social psychologist, however, a more interesting question concerns whether attitudes guide or shape the recall of events that occur in everyday life. Accordingly, in the present research we examined whether attitudes affect the recall of personal histories. We have been unable to locate any previous research that attempts to show that people's attitudes shape their memories of their own past behaviors. A possible cause of this neglect is that there are a number of reasons to believe that people may not base their recall on their attitudes. For example, many of our actions are well practiced, even routinized. As a result, we may be able to recall them without difficulty, not necessarily by remembering each instance but simply by remembering that the activities are performed habitually. Second, actions occur in social and environmental contexts that limit severely the range of potential behaviors. Thus, remembering the context may serve to evoke the behavior enacted. Third, many attitudes are related in a loose and multifaceted fashion to a network of behaviors rather than to one specific behavior (Fishbein and Ajzen,

1974). Moreover, a number of different attitudes may relate to the same behavior, and, alternatively, some behaviors may not be connected to any salient attitudes. In sum, attitudes often may appear to be indirect and unnecessary vehicles for recalling past actions.

With these concerns in mind, the following question was examined in the present research: Can attitudes be shown to exert a directive influence on individuals' recall of their past behaviors when the conditions are optimal for demonstrating such an effect? To answer this question, we changed subjects' attitudes on an issue. We then measured recall of past behaviors relevant to the newly formed attitudes.

There were a number of considerations that guided our selection of attitude issues and experimental design. First, for the hypothesis to receive a fair test, it is necessary to produce quite sizable shifts in attitude. It would hardly be surprising if recall of past behaviors were unaffected by a minor change in attitudes. McGuire (1964) has shown that beliefs that are widely shared and rarely questioned ("cultural truisms") are vulnerable to attack. For this reason, we chose to manipulate attitudes on two issues of this nature. Second, we selected issues for which we could identify unambiguously relevant and specifiable behaviors. Third, we incorporated procedures that were intended to reduce the possible experimental demands inherent in asking subjects to recall actions that may be related to their attitudes. Thus, we manipulated but did not assess the attitudes of subjects who answered the behavior recall questions. This procedure was designed to decrease the likelihood that subjects would view the experiment as a study of the relation between attitudes and recall. Also, the behavior recall items were imbedded in a lengthy questionnaire that was administered in a "second experiment." This second study was allegedly unrelated to the first one, in which attitudes were manipulated. Finally, to verify that the attitude manipulation was indeed effective, we ran an additional group of subjects whose attitudes were measured in the absence of behavior recall.

In summary, the purpose of the present study was to examine the effects of attitudes on the recall of personal histories. Would recall be biased by subjects' attitudes?

EXPERIMENT 1

Method

Subjects.   The subjects were 54 males and 47 females recruited from the voluntary subject pool at the University of Waterloo. Thirty-five of the subjects completed the questionnaire that assessed attitudes, and 66 of the subjects completed the questionnaire that assessed behavior recall. The data from 4 subjects were eliminated from the analysis. Three of these subjects were suspicious of the link between the two studies, and the other subject did not follow the instructions correctly in filling out the questionnaire. Of the 3 suspicious subjects, 1 was in the negative toothbrushing condition, attitude assessment; 1 was in the negative toothbrushing condition, recall assessment; and 1 was in the positive bathing condition, recall assessment.

Procedure.   A pretest was conducted to select the attitude issues for the study. Twenty-eight students were stopped on campus and asked for their opinions on a series of health-related issues; opinions were assessed on a 7-point scale (1 = strongly disagree; 7 = strongly agree). On the basis of this pretest, two items that showed reasonably high agreement were selected for the experiment: "It is important for health reasons to shower or bathe at least once a day" ($M = 5.41$, $SD = 1.07$), and "It is important for proper dental care to brush one's teeth after every meal" ($M = 5.83$, $SD = 1.34$). Toothbrushing was one of the cultural truisms employed by McGuire (1964).

In the experiment proper, some subjects were exposed to a communication that was either favorable or unfavorable toward toothbrushing; the remaining subjects were exposed to a communication that was either favorable or unfavorable toward bathing frequently. In the context of a second experiment, subjects were then asked to indicate either their attitudes on the relevant issues (toothbrushing and bathing) or to indicate how often they had brushed their teeth and bathed in the preceding 2 weeks.

Subjects were contacted for the experiment by telephone. The caller identified herself as a secretary for the psychology department. Subjects were informed that they would participate in two brief studies that were to be conducted one after the other due to scheduling ease. Subjects were told that the first study examined factors influencing the effectiveness of communications and that the second study concerned the relation of personality type to life-style.

Upon arrival at the first experiment, subjects were taken to a room in groups of 2 to 5 and told that they would be listening to tape recordings of a university radio program dealing with current health problems. They were informed that this show typically consisted of a brief interview with a medical or social scientist.

The subjects were told that they would listen to two of these interviews and write down the most important points. They were informed that the experimenter wanted to determine if there was agreement among nonexperts as to which were the key points. They would also be asked to generate an argument of their own that was consistent with the material being presented. They were told that their judgments and arguments would be used in the construction of health appeals that would eventually be presented to the Canadian public. They were asked to not put their names on their answer sheets; their responses were to be anonymous.

Subjects were taken to individual rooms to listen to the tape recordings through headphones. All subjects listened first to a filler tape arguing for higher seat belt usage in automobiles and then to either the positive or negative toothbrushing tape or the positive or negative bathing tape.

The interviews on the issues of toothbrushing and bathing were allegedly with officials of the Canadian Dental Association and the Canadian Medical Association, respectively. In the positive toothbrushing condition, the official described how frequent brushing strengthened tooth enamel and protected the teeth and gums against disease. In the negative toothbrushing condition, the same official argued the dangers of frequent brushing: Abrasive toothpastes cause erosion of the enamel, and frequent brushing may harm the gums, leading to infection and tooth loss. Further, it was emphasized that flossing was much superior to toothbrushing.

In the positive bathing condition, the official suggested that infrequent bathing can create skin complaints and that body odor can only be eliminated by frequent use of soap and water. In the negative bathing condition, he stated that frequent bathing removes a layer of skin that protects one against infection and that it also causes increased oil production in the skin, which can cause skin complaints.

The seat belt interview was allegedly with a representative of the Ontario Government Safety Division who argued for increased seat belt usage. We presented the seat belt tape to obscure the connection between the two studies. In the second study, there were no items on the questionnaire that pertained to the seat belt issue.

After listening to the tapes and making their evaluations, subjects were thanked and dismissed. They returned to the waiting area and were contacted by the experimenter for the second study. This experimenter took subjects to a large "survey research" room. They were told that they would anonymously complete a questionnaire designed to assess the relation between personality type and lifestyle. They were informed that previous studies relating personality to life-style had focused on the abnormal personality and the everyday activities he or she engaged in. The present study would be concerned with this relationship in normal individuals.

The behavior recall groups responded to a version of the questionnaire that contained questions asking them to estimate the frequency with which they had engaged in various activities during the past 2 weeks. The target questions, which were imbedded among many other health-related items, were "How many times have you brushed your teeth in the past two weeks? (a) after breakfast, (b) after lunch, (c) after dinner," and "How many baths (or showers) have you taken in the past 2 weeks? (a) in the morning, (b) between 10 A.M. and 6 P.M., (c) in the evening."

The attitude assessment groups responded to a questionnaire that asked them to give their opinions of the same everyday activities that appeared in the recall version of the questionnaire. Three 9-point semantic differential scales were used to assess attitudes on the two target issues. The items were worded as follows: "Brushing your teeth after every meal is: important–unimportant, healthy–unhealthy, beneficial–harmful," and "Taking showers and baths often is: healthy–unhealthy, hygienic–unhygienic, beneficial–harmful."

After answering either the recall or opinion questions, all subjects filled out the personality section of the questionnaire. The personality test was Snyder's (1974) self-monitoring scale. Finally, subjects were probed for suspiciousness. They anonymously completed a questionnaire that required them to describe the purposes of the study and to discuss any confusing or odd aspects of the procedures. The experimenter also asked subjects directly if they had noticed a connection between the two studies. Subjects were informed of the purposes of the experiment and fully debriefed following the suspiciousness probe.

Results

Attitude change. The three semantic differentials for each issue were summed, with higher scores reflecting more negative attitudes. All of the subjects responded to both the toothbrushing and bathing items on their attitude questionnaires. Accordingly, subjects who listened to the persuasive message on toothbrushing served as controls for subjects who heard the bathing message, and vice versa. The mean attitude in each condition is shown in Table 12.1. Subjects who listened to the positive messages were substantially more favorable toward toothbrushing and bathing than were subjects who heard the negative messages: For toothbrushing, $t(7.36) = 3.46$, $p < .002$; for bathing, $t(8.03) = 5.23$, $p < .001$.[1]

The attitudes of control subjects were similar to those of the pretest group, which were very positive. Not surprisingly, therefore, it was the negative message that exerted the stronger influence on attitudes. Subjects who heard the messages derogating toothbrushing and bathing held more negative attitudes toward these activities than did control subjects: For toothbrushing, $t(7.45) = 3.25$, $p < .01$; for bathing, $t(22) = 3.34$, $p < .003$. The tendency for subjects who heard the positive message to hold more favorable attitudes than control subjects approached significance on the bathing message only, $t(19.48) = 2.07$, $p < .052$.

TABLE 12.1
Mean attitude and behavior recall scores for Experiment 1

	Toothbrushing			Bathing		
	Positive message	Control	Negative message	Positive message	Control	Negative message
Attitude						
M	3.62	4.17	12.75	3.70	5.87	11.63
n	8	18	8	10	16	8
Behavior recall						
M	35.85	32.8	28.62	11.06	11.35	10.89
n	13	36[a]	13	18	26	19

Note: The higher the attitude score, the more negative the attitude. The behavior recall scores indicate the number of times subjects reported brushing their teeth or bathing in the preceding 2 weeks.

[a]The *n* in this condition is 36 rather than 37, because one of the subjects failed to answer the relevant control question.

---

[1]The degrees of freedom used were fractional, because the variances were heterogeneous and a separate variance *t* value was calculated. This procedure is described in Myers (1979).

Behavior recall.   Subjects who heard a message derogating toothbrushing reported brushing their teeth significantly fewer times in the preceding 2 weeks than did subjects who heard the positive message, $t(24) = 2.16$, $p < .05$ (means are shown in Table 12.1). However, the difference between the negative and positive bathing groups was slight and nonsignificant $(t < 1)$.[2]

Once again, subjects who listened to the persuasive message on one of the target issues could serve as controls for subjects who heard the persuasive message on the other issue. The control mean was intermediate to and nonsignificantly different from the mean behavior recall scores of subjects who heard the positive, $t(36.4) = 1.20$, $p < .24$, and negative, $t(47) = 1.20$, $p < .24$, toothbrushing messages. The control mean was virtually identical to the means obtained from subjects who heard the positive and negative bathing messages $(ts < 1)$.

Discussion

Relatively large shifts in attitudes toward toothbrushing and bathing were obtained. Behavior recall appeared to be biased by attitudes only on the toothbrushing issue, however.

There are a number of differences between the two types of events that may account for the discrepant behavior recall results. Bathing takes longer than toothbrushing and constitutes a more complex series of behaviors. Bathing is also usually carried out no more than once per day. Perhaps for these reasons, bathing is a more vivid and memorable event than toothbrushing and therefore less prone to memory distortion over relatively short periods of time.

On this basis, it appears plausible to suggest that a longer time period than 2 weeks may be necessary for changes in attitudes toward bathing to significantly influence behavior recall. To test this hypothesis, the bathing recall condition in the first experiment was replicated in Experiment 2, with subjects being asked to recall the number of times they had bathed or showered in the previous month rather than in the preceding 2 weeks.

EXPERIMENT 2

Method

Subjects.   The subjects were 12 females and 30 males obtained from the voluntary subject pool at the University of Waterloo. Four subjects (3 in the negative bathing condition and 1 in the positive bathing condition) were suspicious of the link between the two experiments; their data were therefore excluded from the analysis.

---

[2]The results are not altered when the data from the suspicious subjects are included in the analysis.

Procedure.   The positive and negative bathing tapes were identical to those used in the previous experiment. The bathing recall question was altered; subjects were asked how many baths or showers they had taken over the last month. The filler items in the questionnaire were also changed to assess recall over a 1-month period.

Results

Subjects who were exposed to the negative bathing message reported bathing fewer times in the preceding month ($M = 17.15$) than did subjects who were exposed to the positive message ($M = 25.33$), $t(36) = 2.51$, $p < .02$. Thus, the shift from a 2-week to a 1-month recall period produced the hypothesized effect (see Footnote 2). Because only one issue was used in this study, no control comparisons were derived.

SELF-MONITORING AND THE RELATION BETWEEN ATTITUDES AND RECALL

The self-monitoring scale was included largely to provide subjects with a rationale for distinguishing the second part of each study from the first part. Based on Snyder's (1979) characterization of low and high self-monitors, however, one might expect low self-monitors in particular to show the assimilation of behavior recall to current attitudes. As the behaviors of low self-monitors generally correspond to their attitudes, their attitudes may be a useful cue by which to recall their behaviors. The attitudes of high self-monitors should not serve this function to the same degree, because their behavior tends to be guided by the situation rather than by their attitudes (Snyder, 1979).

A median split on the self-monitoring dimension produced some support for this reasoning in both experiments. In the first experiment, low self-monitors who received the negative toothbrushing message ($M = 26.43$) reported brushing their teeth significantly fewer times than low self-monitors who received the positive toothbrushing message ($M = 38.00$), $t(22) = 2.29$, $p < .05$. This contrast was not significant among high self-monitors (for negative toothbrushing, $M = 31.1$; for positive toothbrushing, $M = 34.5$; $t < 1$). Similarly, in the second experiment, low self-monitors who received the negative bathing message ($M = 14.20$) reported bathing fewer times than low self-monitors who received the positive bathing message ($M = 27.40$), $t(27) = 2.28$, $p < .05$. High self-monitors who received the negative bathing message ($M = 19.20$) did not differ significantly in their recall from high self-monitors who received the positive bathing message ($M = 25.50$; $t = 1.16$, $p < .30$).[3]

---

[3]Note that there was no relation between self-monitoring and amount of attitude change (for bathing, $F = 1.69$, *ns;* for toothbrushing, $F < 1$) and that results from the control conditions revealed that high and low self-monitors did not differ in the frequency with which they reported brushing their teeth or bathing in the absence of persuasive messages (*t*s < 1).

These data should be considered with caution, however. The two-way interaction between self-monitoring and the direction of the persuasive message was not statistically significant in either experiment, $F(1, 22) = 1.44, p < .25$ (Experiment 1), and $F(1, 27) < 1$ (Experiment 2). Also, the cell ns were low, ranging from 5 to 10 subjects. The pattern is intriguing, though, and replication with higher ns seems warranted.

GENERAL DISCUSSION

The results indicate that attitudes can exert a directive influence on recall of personal histories under carefully controlled and specifiable conditions. Presumably, the attitude serves as a retrieval cue. Individuals either reconstruct their actions in light of the attitude, or they focus on the subset of their behaviors that is consistent with the attitude. The present research does not reveal whether this effect on retrieval can be explained purely in information processing terms (different cues, i.e., attitudes, prompting different retrieval) or whether motivational concerns need be posited. (Attitude-consistent material arouses positive affect, and attitude-inconsistent material evokes negative affect, resulting in selective attention to attitude-consistent material.) The quote from Bartlett presented earlier allows for both possibilities, which seems to be the most reasonable hypothesis at the moment.

The data also reveal that attitudes do not always affect the recall of past behaviors, even within the limits of our experimental paradigm. The results for the recall of bathing behavior in Experiment 1 suggest that attitudes may not influence reconstructive memory when the behavior is vivid or readily recalled. Note that this lack of effect argues against simple demand and self-presentation interpretations of the significant results. If subjects had formulated the experimental hypothesis and were responding to confirm it, or if subjects were responding on the behavior recall assessment to present themselves in a positive way, they were certainly free to do so on the 2-week bathing measure used in Experiment 1. Yet they did not.

There are two other reasons for disputing a self-presentation interpretation of the data. First, the anonymity of subjects' responses and the separation of the attitude and behavior recall portions of the study should have attenuated concerns for self-presentation. Second, Snyder's (1979) characterization of the self-monitoring dimension suggests that high self-monitors are more concerned about self-presentation than are low self-monitors. Thus, the impact of attitude on behavior should be greater with high self-monitors, assuming that the effect is mediated by a concern for self-presentation. If anything, though, the effect was stronger among low self-monitors, a result that is congruent with the hypothesis that attitudes rather than concerns for self-presentation guide recall.

The current research has shown that attitudes affect recall, whereas much of the research on selective learning has failed to demonstrate such selectivity (e.g., Greenwald and Sakumura, 1967). There are differences between the paradigms that could contribute to the discrepant results. In the typical selective learning study, subjects are provided with arguments on both sides of an issue. Although it might be expected that subjects will remember arguments consistent with their attitudes better than arguments inconsistent with their attitudes, the procedure introduces a number of factors that may influence memory and obscure the relation between attitudes and recall. For example, the relative familiarity or novelty of the arguments may be related to the subject's own position on the issue. For many subjects, the arguments that contradict their attitudes may be more novel and elicit greater attention than the arguments that support their attitudes (Greenwald and Sakumura, 1967). Because both attention and familiarity should enhance memory, there may not be a difference in recall between the familiar supporting arguments and the novel opposing arguments.

The current paradigm sidesteps this difficulty. The source of recall is the subject's personal history rather than material containing novel arguments provided by the experimenter. Furthermore, an inconsistency between attitudes and own behaviors may arouse more negative affect and, hence, greater motivation to reduce the disparity than an inconsistency between attitudes and information provided by an experimenter.

A series of studies by Feather (1969a, 1969b, 1969c) and a recent experiment by Weldon and Malpass (Note 1) offer some support for these contentions. Feather simply asked subjects to list the arguments pertinent to an issue. Subjects were able to report more arguments that supported their position than arguments that contradicted their position. Thus, selectivity is evidenced when recall is based on personal experience rather than on experimentally contrived materials. In addition, Weldon and Malpass (Note 1) demonstrated that attitudes are related to recall in a standard selective learning paradigm when factors such as familiarity with the arguments and intellectual skills are controlled for.

The current results complement those of past research on attitudes, behaviors, and recall of behaviors. Previous studies have shown that (a) attitudes can, at times, direct behavior (Ajzen and Fishbein, 1977; Fazio and Zanna, 1978), (b) behavior can affect attitudes (Bem, 1972), (c) current behaviors can affect the recall of past attitudes (Bem and McConnell, 1970), and (d) current attitudes are affected by the selective recall of past behaviors (Salancik, 1974). The present study adds another link. Attitudes can influence the recall of past behaviors.

It is intriguing to speculate about the possible associations among these causal sequences. For example, the results of the present experiment have methodological implications for the study of attitude–behavior relations. In some investigations of the effects of attitudes on behavior, subjects' recall of actions relevant to the attitude being investigated serves as the measure of behavior (e.g., Fishbein and Ajzen, 1974; Kahle and Berman, 1979; Ostrom, 1969). Our research suggests that behavioral recall may be biased by attitudes; as a result, the obtained degree of attitude–behavior consistency in such studies may be inflated spuriously (i.e., attitudes may exert a stronger influence over behavior recall than over behavior). The possibility of such a confound provides one more reason why actual behavior should be examined in studies of this kind, though we appreciate how difficult an investigative imperative this can be.

In addition, it is plausible to postulate a feedback loop between behavior recall and attitude. The present research indicates that attitudes may bias the recall of past behaviors. It follows that a review of previous behavior may lead individuals to conclude (perhaps inappropriately) that their past actions are consistent with their current attitudes and, hence, increase the confidence with which current attitudes are held.

The ramifications may not stop at this point, however. Fazio and Zanna (1981) have shown that the more confident individuals are of their attitudes, the better these attitudes predict future behavior. Thus, much like a self-fulfilling prophecy, the process of behavior review may increase the control that attitude exerts over future behavior and produce a genuine increase in attitude–behavior consistency.

In a more general vein, the current data support Greenwald's (1980) characterization of the self or ego as analogous to a totalitarian political regime in which history is revised and fabricated to suit present concerns. Individuals appear to be revisionist historians with respect to their personal memories.

Reference Note

1. WELDON, P. E., AND MALPASS, R. S. *The effects of attitudinal, cognitive, and situational variables on recall of biased communications.* Unpublished manuscript, University of Washington, 1980.

References

AJZEN, I., AND FISHBEIN, M. Attitude–behavior relations: A theoretical analysis and review of empirical research. *Psychological Bulletin,* 1977, **84,** 888–918.

ALLPORT, G. W. The historical background of modern social psychology. In G. Lindzey and E. Aronson (Eds.), *The handbook of social psychology* (Vol. 1). Reading, Mass.: Addison-Wesley, 1968.

BARTLETT, F. C. *Remembering: A study in experimental social psychology.* Cambridge, England: Cambridge University Press, 1932.

BEM, D. J. Self-perception theory. In L. Berkowitz (Ed.), *Advances in experimental social psychology* (Vol. 6). New York: Academic Press, 1972.

BEM, D. J., AND McCONNELL, H. K. Testing the self-perception explanation of dissonance phenomena: On the salience of premanipulation attitudes. *Journal of Personality and Social Psychology,* 1970, **14,** 23–31.

CALDER, B. J., AND ROSS, M. *Attitudes and behavior.* Morristown, N.J.: General Learning Press, 1973.

FAZIO, R. H., AND ZANNA, M. P. On the predictive validity of attitudes: The roles of direct experience and attitude. *Journal of Personality,* 1978, **46,** 228–243.

FAZIO, R. H., AND ZANNA, M. P. Direct experience and attitude–behavior consistency. In L. Berkowitz (Ed.), *Advances in experimental social psychology* (Vol. 14). New York: Academic Press, 1981.

FEATHER, N. T. Attitude and selective recall. *Journal of Personality and Social Psychology,* 1969, **12,** 310–319. (a)

FEATHER, N. T. Cognitive differentiation, attitude strength, and dogmatism. *Journal of Personality,* 1969, **37,** 111–126. (b)

FEATHER, N. T. Differentiation of arguments in relation to attitude, dogmatism, and tolerance of ambiguity. *Australian Journal of Psychology,* 1969, **21,** 21–29. (c)

FISHBEIN, M., AND AJZEN, I. Attitudes toward objects as predictors of single and multiple behavioral criteria. *Psychological Review,* 1974, **81,** 59–74.

GREENWALD, A. G. The totalitarian ego: Fabrication and revision of personal history. *American Psychologist,* 1980, **35,** 603–618.

GREENWALD, A. G., AND SAKUMURA, J. S. Attitude and selective learning: Where are the phenomena of yesteryear? *Journal of Personality and Social Psychology,* 1967, **7,** 387–397.

HEIDER, F. *The psychology of interpersonal relations.* New York: Wiley, 1958.

JONES, E. E., AND KOHLER, R. The effects of plausibility on the learning of controversial statements. *Journal of Abnormal and Social Psychology,* 1958, **57,** 315–320.

KAHLE, L. R., AND BERMAN, J. J. Attitudes cause behaviors: A cross-lagged panel analysis, *Journal of Personality and Social Psychology,* 1979, **37,** 315–321.

LEVINE, J. M., AND MURPHY, G. The learning and retention of controversial statements. *Journal of Abnormal and Social Psychology,* 1943, **38,** 507–517.

LINGLE, J. H., GEVA, N., OSTROM, T. M., LEIPPE, M. R., AND BAUMGARDNER, M. H. Thematic effects of person judgments on impression organization. *Journal of Personality and Social Psychology,* 1979, **37,** 674–687.

MCGUIRE, W. J. Inducing resistance to persuasion: Some contemporary approaches. In L. Berkowitz (Ed.), *Advances in experimental social psychology* (Vol. 1). New York: Academic Press, 1964.

MYERS, J. L. Fundamentals of experimental design. Boston: Allyn & Bacon, 1979.

OLSON, J. M. *Selective recall: Attitudes, schemata, and memory.* Unpublished doctoral dissertation, University of Waterloo, 1980.

OSTROM, T. M. The relationship between the affective, behavioral, and cognitive components of attitude. *Journal of Experimental Social Psychology,* 1969, **5,** 12–30.

SALANCIK, J. R. Inference of one's attitude from behavior recalled under linguistically manipulated cognitive sets. *Journal of Experimental Social Psychology,* 1974, **10,** 415–427.

SNYDER, M. Self-monitoring of expressive behavior. *Journal of Personality and Social Psychology,* 1974, **30,** 526–537.

SNYDER, M. Self-monitoring processes. In L. Berkowitz (Ed.), *Advances in experimental social psychology* (Vol. 12). New York: Academic Press, 1979.

SNYDER, M., AND URANOWITZ, S. W. Reconstructing the past: Some cognitive consequences of person perception. *Journal of Personality and Social Psychology,* 1978, **36,** 941–950.

WICKER, A. W. Attitudes versus actions: The relationship of verbal and overt behavioral responses to attitude objects. *Journal of Social Issues,* 1969, **25,** 41–78.

WICKER, A. W. An examination of the "other variables" explanation of attitude–behavior inconsistency. *Journal of Personality and Social Psychology,* 1971, **19,** 18–30.

ZAJONC, R. B., AND BURNSTEIN, E. The learning of balanced and unbalanced social structures. *Journal of Personality,* 1965, **33,** 570–583.

13

Attitude Accessibility as a Moderator of the Attitude-Perception and Attitude-Behavior Relations: An Investigation of the 1984 Presidential Election

Russell H. Fazio and Carol J. Williams

It was hypothesized that the extent to which individuals' attitudes guide their subsequent perceptions of and behavior toward the attitude object is a function of the accessibility of those attitudes from memory. A field investigation concerning the 1984 presidential election was conducted as a test of these hypotheses. Attitudes toward each of the two candidates, Reagan and Mondale, and the accessibility of those attitudes, as indicated by the latency of response to the attitudinal inquiry, were measured for a large sample of townspeople months before the election. Judgments of the performance of the candidates during the televised debates served as the measure of subsequent perceptions, and voting served as the measure of subsequent behavior. As predicted, both the attitude-perception and the attitude–behavior relations were moderated by attitude accessibility. The implications of these findings for theoretical models of the processes by which attitudes guide behavior, along with their practical implications for survey research, are discussed.

Research on the consistency between individuals' attitudes and behavior toward an object has focused on the identification of variables that moderate the extent of the observed relation. This approach, which has been referred to as the *When?* generation of research due to its focus on the issue of when attitude scores are predictive

Reprinted with permission from the authors and *The Journal of Personality and Social Psychology,* Vol. 51, No. 3, 1986. Copyright © 1986 by the American Psychological Association.

The present research was supported by Grant MH 38832 from the National Institute of Mental Health.

The authors thank David Brown, the manager of the shopping mall where the attitude data were collected, for his cooperation; Sheri Rieth for her skillful assistance with all the phases of data collection; and Michael Bailey for designing and building the apparatus that was used to measure and record attitudes and response latencies. In addition, the authors are grateful to Paget Gross, David Sanbonmatsu, and Steven Sherman for their comments on an earlier draft of the article.

of later behavior (Zanna and Fazio, 1982), has produced considerable progress. A variety of situational variables, personality factors, and qualities of the attitude itself have been identified as moderators of the attitude-behavior relation (see Fazio, 1986, for a recent review).

Yet another approach to the attitude-behavior issue has been initiated recently. This approach centers on the process(es) by which attitudes guide behavior, what Zanna and Fazio (1982) referred to as the *How?* question. Within this context, it has been suggested that the accessibility of an individual's attitude from memory assumes crucial importance. In fact, Fazio and his colleagues have proposed a model of the attitude-to-behavior process that focuses specifically on the chronic accessibility of the attitude from memory (Fazio, 1986; Fazio, Powell, and Herr, 1983). In brief, the model views behavior in any given situation as stemming from individuals' perceptions of the attitude object and the situation in which the attitude object is encountered. Consistent with the object appraisal function that attitudes presumably serve (Katz, 1960; Smith, Bruner, and White, 1956) and with the constructive nature of perception, individuals' attitudes may guide such perceptions. That is, selective processing of the qualities of the attitude object in the immediate situation can occur. However, selective processing in a manner that is congruent with the valence of the attitude is conceivable only given that the attitude has been activated from memory upon observation of the attitude object. Hence, the accessibility of the attitude is postulated to be a critical determinant of whether the attitude-to-behavior process is initiated. In this way, attitude accessibility is thought to affect both the attitude-perception and the attitude-behavior relations.

The present research involves both the *when* and the *how* approach in that it centers on attitude accessibility as a moderator of the attitude-behavior relation. Attitude accessibility was measured for each of the respondents in an attitude survey. The consistency between attitudes and later behavior toward the attitude object (as well as the consistency between attitudes and perceptions of the attitude object in a later situation) was examined as a function of attitude accessibility scores. In this way the present investigation serves as both a test of the proposed process model (the how question) and as an attempt to identify a variable that moderates the attitude-behavior relation (the when question).

According to the process model, the chronic accessibility of an attitude is a function of the associative strength of the attitude object and the evaluation that the individual holds of the object. That is, attitudes are characterized as object-evaluation associations and the strength of the association acts as a determinant of the accessibility of the attitude. The stronger the association, the greater the likelihood that the evaluation will be activated spontaneously upon the individual's encountering the attitude object. Support for this view stems from a number of experiments involving attempts to enhance the strength of the object-evaluation association by inducing individuals to note and express their attitudes repeatedly. Such repeated expression has been found to enhance both the speed with which individuals can respond to inquiries concerning their attitudes (Fazio, Chen, McDonel, and Sherman, 1982; Powell and Fazio, 1984) and the likelihood that the attitude will be activated automatically from memory upon the individual's mere observation of the attitude object (Fazio et al., 1983; Fazio, Sanbonmatsu, Powell, and Kardes, 1986).

The obvious implication of this view is that the attitudes of two individuals with identical scores from some attitude measurement instrument may still differ markedly. The strength of the object-evaluation association and, hence, the chronic accessibility of the attitude may differ. Consequently, when they encounter the attitude object in a given situation, the attitude of one individual may be activated automatically, whereas the attitude of the other may not be. Thus, the two individuals may construe any information that becomes available concerning the attitude object quite differently. Perceptions of the attitude object and, ultimately, behavior toward the object are more likely to be "guided" by the attitude in the case of the individual whose attitude has been activated.

To date, little research has been conducted linking attitude accessibility to attitude-behavior consistency. However, a number of findings suggest that such a moderating effect may occur. For example, the manner of attitude formation has been found to affect both attitude-behavior consistency (see Fazio and Zanna, 1981, for a review) and attitude accessibility (Fazio et al., 1982, Experiments 1 and 2; Fazio et al., 1983). In separate experiments, it has been observed that individuals who were introduced to a set of intellectual puzzles, via direct behavioral experience with example puzzles, formed attitudes that were both more accessible from memory and more predictive of their later behavior with those puzzles than did individuals who were provided only with indirect nonbehavioral experience. Enhancement of the strength of the object-evaluation association through repeated attitudinal expression has been found to produce similar effects. Again, in separate experiments, this manipulation has been observed to enhance both attitude accessibility, as mentioned earlier (Fazio et al., 1982, Experiment 3), and attitude-behavior consistency. The latter evidence is provided by an experiment in which repeated attitudinal expression increased the correspondence between attitudes toward a set of intellectual puzzles and subsequent behavior involving those puzzles (Fazio et al., 1982, Experiment 4).

Thus, although past findings are consistent with the hypothesis that attitude accessibility acts as a moderator of attitude-behavior consistency, no single investigation has examined this postulated relation directly. The present study does so by simultaneously assessing attitudes and the accessibility of those attitudes and then assessing relevant perceptions and relevant behavior at later points in time. Attitudes that are highly accessible from memory are hypothesized to be more predictive of subsequent perceptions of the attitude object and subsequent behavior toward the attitude object than are attitudes characterized by relatively poor accessibility.

In the present investigation, attitude accessibility was measured via the latency of response to an attitudinal inquiry. Hence, it is important to review what is known about this measure. First, as indicated by the research involving repeated attitudinal expression, latency of response to an attitudinal inquiry does appear to index the strength of an object-evaluation association satisfactorily. Second, the latency measure appears to be a fairly good approximation of the likelihood of automatic activation of the evaluation upon mere observation of the attitude object. Experiments have shown that attitude objects preselected on the basis of an individual's having responded quickly to an attitudinal inquiry are more likely to be activated automatically upon subsequent presentation of the attitude object than are attitudes characterized by relatively slow latencies of response to an attitudinal inquiry (Fazio et al., 1986). Thus, how long it takes to respond to an attitudinal inquiry is reflective of the likelihood that the attitude will be activated spontaneously upon one's encountering the attitude object.

The specific latency measure used in the present research differs only slightly from the operationalization involved in the research upon which the preceding inferences are drawn. In the previous work, the response whose latency was measured involved a dichotomous judgment. For example, upon presentation of an attitude object, subjects would press either a control button labeled *good* or one labeled *bad* as quickly as possible. In the present investigation, we were interested in simultaneously obtaining a scalar measure of the attitude and the response latency. Subjects heard a tape-recorded attitude statement and, as quickly as possible, responded by pressing one of five buttons labeled *strongly disagree* to *strongly agree*.

PILOT EXPERIMENT

Given this desired modification, we were somewhat concerned about the extent to which response latency would still reflect the strength of the object-evaluation association. Hence, we conducted a preliminary experiment, modeled after that by Powell and Fazio (1984), involving the repeated expression manipulation. Fifty-five subjects expressed attitudes toward each of three target issues a total of three times and did not evaluate another three target issues. The target issues that were used concerned gun control, school prayer, and the United Nations as one set, and Reaganomics, the space program, and mandatory retirement age as the other set. Which set of issues comprised the repeated expression versus control items was counterbalanced across subjects. Each time that an issue appeared on the questionnaire it was evaluated with respect to a different semantic differential scale. For example, subjects might have evaluated gun control on a support/oppose scale, then on a beneficial/harmful scale, and so on. After completing the questionnaires, subjects participated in the response time task. Response latencies were affected by the repeated expression manipulation. Subjects were significantly faster at indicating the extent of their agreement or disagreement with attitudinal statements that concerned issues toward which they had repeatedly expressed their attitudes ($M = 2.65$ s) than statements that concerned issues toward which they had not

$(M = 3.28)$, $t(54) = 3.55$, $p < .001$. This finding suggests that increasing the number of response options from two to five did not affect the sensitivity of the latency measure as an indicant of the strength of the object-evaluation association.

OVERVIEW

The present investigation concerned attitudes, perceptions, and behavior relevant to the 1984 presidential election. Specifically, both attitudes toward each of the candidates, Reagan and Mondale, and the accessibility of those attitudes were assessed for a large sample of townspeople in the summer of 1984. The perception and behavior measures were collected months later. The perception measure concerned respondents' judgments of the performance of the candidates during the nationally televised debates. The behavior measure was collected by telephoning respondents within a few days after the election and asking them to indicate whether they had voted in the election and, if so, for whom.

It was predicted that individuals whose attitudes toward a candidate were relatively accessible, that is, individuals who were able to respond relatively quickly to the attitudinal inquiry, would display perceptions of debate performance that were more congruent with their attitudes than would individuals whose attitudes were marked by relatively low accessibility, that is, those who responded relatively slowly to the attitudinal inquiry. Such differential selective processing of the debates and, although not measured, of other information about the candidates that became available during the course of the campaign, was expected to affect the stability of respondents' attitudes. As a result, the likelihood that voting behavior would be congruent with the attitude scores obtained months earlier also was expected to be moderated by the accessibility of the attitude.

METHOD

Subjects

A total of 245 voting age residents of the Bloomington, Indiana area participated in the initial part of the study. Twenty-five of these individuals responded to an advertisement in the local newspaper. Another 16 people were recruited and interviewed at the public library. The majority of the sample, the remaining 204 individuals, were shoppers at a local mall who agreed to participate in a political survey. The subjects were paid $3.00 for participating in the survey. All interviews were conducted during June and July of 1984. Participants were interviewed either singly or, more commonly, in pairs.

Of these 245 respondents, 136 provided perception data in the manner described later and 153 provided usable data regarding their voting behavior. Because occa-

sional missing values exist within the subsample of respondents for whom perception or voting data were available, the number of observations involved in the various analyses that were conducted is not always consistent. Sample sizes or degrees of freedom are reported for each analysis that was conducted.

Procedure

The initial part of the study was described to participants simply as a political
survey. No mention was made of the experimenters' affiliation with the psychology department. The survey consisted of 25 attitudinal statements recorded on a
cassette tape. Subjects were instructed to listen to each statement and indicate the
extent of their agreement with the statement by pressing one of five buttons labeled
strongly agree, agree, don't care, disagree, and *strongly disagree.* Subjects were
instructed to respond as quickly as possible while being sure that their response accurately reflected their opinion on each issue. Each recorded statement was pre-
ceded by a warning signal, the word *ready,* to ensure the respondents' full attention. A 15-s interval separated each statement on the tape.

The apparatus that was used for this survey was specially designed for the investigation. It was a battery-powered, portable unit consisting of a Timex-Sinclair microcomputer, a two-channel cassette recorder, and two subject stations. The attitudinal statements and the *ready* signals were recorded on one channel of the tape. At
the end of each statement, an electronic marker was recorded on the second channel. This marker served as a signal to the microcomputer to begin timing. Participants responded via a five-button control box. Two such response stations were attached to the apparatus. Subjects' responses stopped the timing. Both the responses
and the response latencies (to the nearest millisecond) were recorded by the microcomputer.

The first five statements were intended to serve as practice items to acquaint
subjects with the procedure. The experimenter monitored the subjects' performance during these trials to ensure that subjects did understand the procedure. Of
the remaining 20 statements, 5 were factual items[1] (e.g., "The capital of Indiana is
Terre Haute") and 15 were opinion items concerning attitudes toward such issues
as school prayer, gun control, and nuclear power plants in addition to the two ma-
jor-party candidates for the presidency. These two critical statements were "A good

---

[1]These factual fillers were included with the hope that they might provide a baseline measure of how
quickly individuals generally respond to a query and thus serve to reduce some of the measurement error involved in latency indications of attitude accessibility. However, response latency to the factual
items did not correlate substantially with latency to either of the target items. The average correlations
of the factual latencies with the Reagan latency and the Mondale latency were a mere .186 and .174, respectively. Furthermore, the average interitem correlations among the latencies to the 15 opinion issues
was an insubstantial .189. Thus, latencies of response within this data set appear to have been very content specific.

president for the next 4 years would be Ronald Reagan" and "A good president for the next 4 years would be Walter Mondale".[2]

When participants had finished, they were asked to complete a payment receipt, which involved their indicating their names, addresses, and telephone numbers. It was in this way that the information necessary to contact the respondents for the next two phases of the investigation was obtained.

The next phase concerned judgments of the candidates' performances during the nationally televised debates. The first debate involved the presidential candidates and was held on October 7; the second involved the vice-presidential candidates and was held on October 11. It was judgments of those two debates that served as our perception measures. A third debate in the series occurred on October 21, but was not included in our questionnaire because we were concerned that individuals might not complete and return the questionnaire prior to their actual casting of a vote on election day.

The day after the second debate, subjects were mailed a letter from the Political Behavior Research Laboratory on psychology department letterhead. (If two or more members of a household had participated in the initial survey, only one was sent this letter.) The letter asked for help in a study being conducted concerning public perceptions of the performance of the participants in the two debates that had been held thus far. It further explained that if individuals would complete and return the enclosed stamped postcard by October 25, they would receive a check for $2.00. In addition, subjects were urged to complete the postcard questionnaire regardless of whether they had only read or heard about the debates or whether they had actually watched the debates. The postcard contained an item concerning the presidential debate. Subjects were asked to endorse one of five statements: "Reagan was much more impressive," "Reagan was slightly more impressive," "The two candidates performed equally well," "Mondale was slightly more impressive," or "Mondale was much more impressive." A similarly worded item concerned the vice-presidential debate. In addition, subjects were asked to indicate whether they had watched each debate. Of the 216 letters that were mailed, 136 responses were received.

The final phase of the investigation concerned voting behavior. Beginning the day after the election, an attempt was made to contact by telephone all the individuals who had participated in the initial survey. One hundred sixty-three individuals were reached and were asked whether they had voted and, if so, for whom. Eight of these people chose not to reveal their votes. Two other respondents had voted for candidates other than Reagan or Mondale and their data were not included in subsequent analyses.

---

[2]The somewhat awkward wording of these statements was necessitated by a desire to have the name of the candidate appear at the end of the statement, which served as the location of the marker on the second channel of the tape that started the timing.

RESULTS

Presentation of the results will be divided into two major sections. We will consider first the relations between attitudes and perceptions and between attitudes and voting behavior among the respondents as a whole. We then will turn our attention to tests of the hypotheses and to how the overall relations vary as a function of attitude accessibility.

Relations Within the Overall Sample

As is to be expected, attitudes toward Reagan and Mondale were negatively correlated, $r(239) = -.657, p < .001.$[3] Response latencies for the two questions inquiring about Reagan and Mondale correlated only moderately, $r(239) = .273, p < .001$. The average latency for the Reagan item ($M = 1.983$ s) did not differ significantly from the average latency for the Mondale question ($M = 1.954$), $t < 1$, suggesting that the strength of object-evaluation associations for the two candidates was roughly equivalent within the sample.[4]

The attitude-perception relation.   It is commonly believed that preexisting attitudes toward the candidates color viewers' judgments of the candidates' performances during the debates. The data provide clear support for this belief. Attitude toward Reagan and attitude toward Mondale were each predictive of respondents' judgments of performance during the presidential debate. The upper portion of Table 13.1 presents the relevant correlation coefficients. On the assumption that attitudes toward the presidential candidates also would be relevant to the other member of the respective ticket, correlations were also computed concerning the performance of the vice-presidential candidates during their debate. Selective processing of candidate performance is again evident (see Table 13.1). The more positive the attitude toward Reagan, the more positively the performance of the Republican vice-presidential candidate, George Bush, was judged relative to the performance of the Democratic candidate, Geraldine Ferraro. Likewise, individuals with positive attitudes toward Mondale were more likely to judge Ferraro's performance to

---

[3]All significance levels reported in this article are two-tailed.

[4]In order to compare response latencies to the two questions, it was necessary to measure precisely the locations of the timing markers for the two questions. Using a storage oscilloscope, it was possible to determine the interval between the marker and the end of the acoustic signal for each statement to the nearest millisecond. These constants then were added to the recorded latencies. Thus, the response latencies reported refer to the interval between the precise conclusion of the acoustic signal and the subjects' responses.

TABLE 13.1
Correlations between attitudes and perceptions and attitudes and voting behavior

	Attitude toward		
Sample and measure	Reagan	Mondale	*t*
Perceptions			
All respondents			
Presidential debate	.474	.432	<1
	(134)	(134)	
Vice-presidential debate	.536	.398	2.21**
	(134)	(134)	
Both debates	.605	.496	1.88*
	(134)	(134)	
Watchers only			
Presidential debate	.458	.436	
	(101)	(101)	<1
Vice-presidential debate	.538	.358	
	(84)	(84)	2.28**
Both debates	.566	.486	
	(74)	(74)	<1
Voting behavior			
All respondents	.710	.565	2.96***
	(150)	(150)	
Voters only	.782	.632	3.28***
	(121)	(121)	

Note: The number of respondents upon which any given correlation is based is listed in parentheses. The *t* value refers to the significance test of the difference between two dependent correlation coefficients.
*p < .07, **p < .05, ***p < .005.

have been better than Bush's than were individuals with negative attitudes toward Mondale. Finally, an overall perception measure involving the sum of respondents' judgments regarding the two debates was also examined and revealed similar congruency between respondents' attitudes and judgments of the debate performances of the candidates. The pattern of relations that was observed on these three perception measures was essentially the same when we restricted the analyses to only those respondents who had indicated watching each debate (see Table 13.1).

Also presented in the upper portion of Table 13.1 is the *t* value of a statistical test of the difference between two correlation coefficients within the same sample (Cohen and Cohen, 1975). With respect to each of the three perception measures, when considering either all the respondents or only those who reported watching the debates, attitude toward Reagan was more predictive of judgments of debate performance than was attitude toward Mondale. In three of the six cases, this difference approached or reached statistical significance.

The attitude-voting behavior relation.   Of the 153 individuals who provided usable data regarding their voting behavior, 29 indicated that they had not voted. In one set of analyses that was conducted, those 29 individuals who indicated they had not voted were assigned a score of 0, and those who voted for Reagan or Mondale were assigned scores of +1 or −1, respectively. Thus, these analyses involved all the respondents. The correlation between each attitude measure and voting behavior is presented in the lower portion of Table 13.1. Despite having been assessed over 3 months prior to the election, attitudes toward Reagan and Mondale were each highly predictive of voting behavior. However, attitude toward Reagan was significantly more predictive of voting behavior than was attitude toward Mondale, suggesting that attitude toward Reagan might have been a more important determinant of voting behavior than attitude toward Mondale.

An additional set of analyses was performed only on the subsample of respondents who reported having voted. These analyses revealed similar but somewhat stronger relations between attitudes and voting behavior. Once again, the correlations between attitude toward Reagan and voting and between attitude toward Mondale and voting differed significantly, implying that feelings toward Mondale were less critical in determining how the respondents voted than were evaluations of Reagan.

Relations as a Function of Attitude Accessibility

Division into high and low accessibility groups.   Findings from previous research (Powell and Fazio, 1984) have indicated the existence of a small, but nonetheless statistically reliable, relation between attitude extremity and latencies of response to an attitudinal inquiry. In the present case, attitude extremity, scored as deviation from the neutral point, was associated with faster response latencies with respect to Reagan, $r(240) = .531, p < .001$, and to Mondale, $r(242) = .532, p < .001$.

As a consequence of this relation between attitude extremity and latency, dividing subjects at the overall median response time with respect to each candidate would have resulted in more extreme attitudes in the high accessibility group than in the low accessibility group. In order to ensure that any inferences drawn about attitude accessibility were not confounded by attitude extremity, a much more conservative procedure was followed in classifying subjects into high and low accessibility groups. Median splits were performed at each and every response level for each of the two attitudes in question. For example, in considering the accessibility of attitudes toward Reagan, the latencies of all subjects who had responded *strongly agree* to the item were examined. Those whose latency was faster than the median for this subsample were assigned to the high accessibility group and those with latencies slower than the median were assigned to the low accessibility group. The same procedure was followed for each of the other response levels. As a result, attitude distributions in our high and low accessibility groups were perfectly equivalent, and we could examine whether knowledge of attitude accessibility enhances predictive power over and above any effect of attitude extremity.[5] Such division into high and low accessibility groups was conducted anew on the specific set of respondents who provided data for each perception and voting measure that was examined.

The attitude-perception relation. The hypothesis that attitude accessibility moderates the extent to which perceptions of the candidates' debate performance are congruent with attitudes toward the candidates was examined by comparing attitude-perception correlations within high and low accessibility groups. Those individuals who had responded to the questionnaire regarding the debates were assigned to high and low accessibility groups in the manner just described. This was done for attitudes toward each of the candidates. The correlations that were computed once again involved judgments of the performance of the candidates in the presidential debate, judgments of the vice-presidential debate, and the overall measure mentioned earlier. The upper portion of Table 13.2 displays the correlation coefficients within each group, along with the z value of the statistical test of the difference between the correlations in the high and low accessibility groups, for both the sample of all respondents and the subsample that reported viewing the debate(s) on television. In each and every case, the attitude-perception correlation is stronger in the high accessibility group than in the low accessibility group. Differences as a function of attitude accessibility were particularly evident with respect to attitude toward Reagan, especially when considering the vice-presidential debate. It was in such cases that the differences approached or achieved a conventional level of statistical significance.

The stronger effects of attitude accessibility for perceptions of the vice-presidential debate than for judgments of the presidential debate might have been a consequence of differential ambiguity. Whereas the media seemed to have viewed Mondale as the clear victor in the presidential debate, the vice-presidential debate was viewed much more evenly. Our own subjects appear to have concurred. The average rating of the outcome of the presidential debate on the 5-point scale was 2.27, which was reliably different from the neutral point value of 3, $t(135) = 7.14$, $p < .001$, in the direction of Mondale having performed more impressively than Reagan. In contrast, the vice-presidential debate was viewed as more of a toss-up.

---

[5]Our procedure for controlling for attitude extremity involves observed attitude scores that obviously are not a perfect indication of true attitudes. Given that attitudes are measured with some error, it should be noted that underlying extremity differences may persist even when we equate individuals on the extremity of their measured responses. Ideally, we would have liked to control for error-free extremity by measuring extremity in multiple ways and controlling for an extremity latent variable. However, assessing the relevant attitudes in multiple ways was not feasible within the context of the present field situation. Thus, we focused on controlling for measured attitude extremity, which is clearly preferable to not attempting any control whatsoever for attitude extremity.

TABLE 13.2
Correlations between attitudes and perceptions and between attitudes and voting behavior within High Accessibility (HA) and Low Accessibility (LA) groups

| | Attitude toward | | | | | |
| | Reagan | | | Mondale | | |
Sample and measure	LA	HA	z	LA	HA	z
Perceptions						
All respondents						
Presidential debate	.471	.483	<1	.416	.468	<1
	(67)	(68)		(69)	(67)	
Vice-presidential debate	.409	.660	2.02**	.380	.448	<1
	(67)	(67)		(69)	(66)	
Both debates	.537	.673	1.23	.473	.546	<1
	(67)	(67)		(69)	(66)	
Watchers only						
Presidential debate	.394	.529	<1	.437	.438	<1
	(50)	(51)		(51)	(50)	
Vice-presidential debate	.410	.679	1.73*	.312	.403	<1
	(42)	(42)		(42)	(42)	
Both debates	.404	.738	2.13**	.381	.587	1.13
	(37)	(37)		(37)	(37)	
Voting behavior						
All respondents	.601	.816	2.73***	−.482	−.616	1.17
	(76)	(75)		(76)	(76)	
Voters only	.663	.891	3.39****	−.563	−.658	<1
	(61)	(61)		(62)	(61)	

Note: The number of respondents upon which any given correlation is based is listed in parentheses. The z value refers to the significance test of the difference between two independent correlation coefficients.
*$p < .10$, **$p < .05$, ***$p < .01$, ****$p < .001$.

Although the average rating of 3.21 did reveal a preference for Bush, $t(134) = 1.98$, $p = .05$, the extremity of this average judgment of the debate outcome was significantly less than had been the case for the presidential debate, $t(134) = 4.41$, $p < .001$. If, as these data suggest, the outcome of the presidential debate was less ambiguous than the vice-presidential debate, then it is not surprising that attitude accessibility appeared to exert a larger role with respect to the vice-presidential debate than the presidential debate.

With respect to attitude toward Mondale, a difference between high and low accessibility groups was evident consistently across the various samples and measures but in no case was the difference large enough to achieve statistical significance. As we shall see, this pattern of strong effects of accessibility for attitude toward Reagan and weaker effects for attitude toward Mondale was evident consistently in the data set. More shall be said about this pattern following the presentation of additional results.

An additional set of analyses was performed to examine the extent to which attitudes toward Reagan and Mondale jointly predicted perceptions. The multiple correlation using the two attitude measures as joint predictors of perceptions was computed within high and low accessibility groups. To create two accessibility groups with equivalent attitude distributions, the sample of individuals who had provided data on a given perception measure was first divided into a series of subsamples. Any given subsample consisted of individuals with identical responses to the question concerning Reagan and identical responses to the question concerning Mondale. For example, all individuals who had responded *strongly agree* to the Reagan item and *strongly disagree* to the Mondale item comprised one subsample; all who had responded *agree* to the Reagan item and *strongly disagree* to the Mondale item comprised another subsample, and so on. The average latency of response to the two attitudinal inquiries was computed for each respondent. Within each subsample, the median average latency served as the division point. Those whose average latency was faster than the median within the subsample were assigned to the high accessibility group, and those whose average latency was slower than the subsample median were assigned to the low accessibility group. Although cumbersome, this procedure ensured that any differences that were observed as a function of accessibility were not confounded by differential attitude distributions in the two groups.

The results of these analyses are depicted in the upper portion of Table 13.3. The multiple correlations predicting perceptions from attitudes toward Reagan and Mondale were stronger in the high accessibility group than in the low. In two of the cases, these differences approached statistical significance (see Table 13.3).

The attitude-voting behavior relation.
The hypothesis concerning the moderating role of attitude accessibility was examined by comparing the correlation between each attitude and voting behavior for groups displaying high versus low accessibility with respect to each attitude. Those individuals who had provided usable voting behavior data were divided into high and low accessibility groups in the manner described earlier. The correlation coefficients are presented in the lower portion of Table 13.2. In all cases, the relation between attitude and behavior is stronger, just as predicted, among subjects characterized by high attitude accessibility than among those characterized by low attitude accessibility. This was particularly true with respect to attitude toward Reagan. For both the entire sample and the subsample including only the voters, respondents whose attitudes toward Reagan were highly accessible displayed significantly greater attitude-behavior consistency than those whose attitudes were relatively less accessible. Indeed, among the voters in the high accessibility group, nearly 80 percent of the variance in voting behavior, as compared with 44 percent among low accessibility voters, was predicted by attitude toward Reagan. The high correlation evident among respondents with a highly accessible attitude toward Reagan is all the more astound-

TABLE 13.3
Multiple correlations using attitudes toward Reagan and Mondale as joint predictors
of perceptions and of voting behavior within high and low accessibility groups

	Accessibility group		
Sample and measure	Low	High	z
Perceptions			
All respondents			
Presidential debate	.440	.580	1.08
	(67)	(68)	
Vice-presidential debate	.432	.658	1.86*
	(67)	(67)	
Both debates	.530	.721	1.81*
	(67)	(67)	
Watchers only			
Presidential debate	.446	.558	
	(51)	(50)	<1
Vice-presidential debate	.488	.623	
	(42)	(42)	<1
Both debates	.513	.669	
	(37)	(37)	1.00
Voting behavior			
All respondents	.637	.823	2.48**
	(75)	(75)	
Voters only	.723	.879	2.46**
	(61)	(60)	

Note: The number of respondents is listed in parentheses. The z value refers to the significance test of the difference between two independent correlation coefficients.
  *$p < .075$, **$p < .025$.

ing when one keeps in mind that the attitude was measured via a single item some
3½ months prior to the election.

As with the findings concerning the attitude-perception relation, the moderating
role of attitude accessibility was less apparent when considering attitude toward
Mondale. Although the correlations between attitude toward Mondale and voting
were stronger in the high than in the low accessibility groups, the differences were
not as large as had been found for attitude toward Reagan and were not statistically
significant.

Attitudes toward Reagan and Mondale as joint predictors of voting behavior
were examined in the same way as had been done with respect to the perception
measures. As before, subsamples of individuals who had responded identically to
the Reagan question and identically to the Mondale question were divided into
high and low accessibility groups on the basis of the subsample's median average
response latency to the two questions. The multiple correlations predicting voting
behavior from the two attitude measures was significantly higher in the high accessibility group than in the low for both the sample that included all respondents and

the sample that included only voters. The lower portion of Table 13.3 presents the within-groups multiple correlations and the significance tests.

DISCUSSION

The results of this investigation essentially confirmed the initial predictions. The accessibility of the attitude from memory was found to moderate both the attitude-perception and the attitude-behavior relations. Individuals with relatively accessible attitudes, as indicated by relatively fast latencies of response to the attitudinal inquiry, displayed greater selective perception as a function of those attitudes and greater attitude-behavior consistency than did individuals with less accessible attitudes.

One unexpected finding concerned the relative weakness of the results when considering attitude toward Mondale singly. Although this attitude measure was consistently more predictive of subsequent perceptions and behavior among the high accessibility respondents than among the low, the differences were small and not statistically reliable. What may account for the lesser robustness of the results with respect to attitude toward Mondale than with attitude toward Reagan?

When considering attitude-perception and attitude-behavior relations within the overall sample, it was observed that attitude toward Mondale tended to be less predictive than attitude toward Reagan. This suggests that Mondale and attitudes toward him were relatively less important in determining perceptions of the debates and voting than were Reagan and attitudes toward him. How individuals felt toward Reagan appears to have influenced how they voted more so than how they felt about the alternative. Such differential influence may be typical of elections that involve an incumbent. Indeed, political scientists have shown that voting in such cases can be interpreted as a retrospective rewarding or punishing of the incumbent based on satisfaction or dissatisfaction with his first term (Fiorina, 1981; Key, 1966). If Mondale and attitudes toward him were less relevant to judgments of the outcomes of the debates and to the decision for whom to vote, then it is not surprising that consideration of the accessibility of this less relevant attitude did not produce robust benefits in the ability to predict the subsequent judgments and behavior.

The weakness of the results with respect to attitude toward Mondale should not detract from the strength and clarity of the other findings. The analyses involving attitude toward Reagan and the analyses using attitudes toward Reagan and Mondale as multiple predictors each revealed a substantial moderating role of attitude accessibility. As such, they provide excellent support for the hypotheses derived from the proposed model of the attitude-behavior process (Fazio, 1986). Just as suggested by the model, attitude accessibility acts as a determinant of both the attitude-perception and the attitude-behavior relations.

It should be noted, however, that within the context of the model perceptions that have been biased by an activated attitude are regarded as an immediate precursor of behavior. This is because the model is intended to address behavior that flows from one's definition of an event involving the attitude object. How one defines the event is viewed as the determinant of behavior. The critical issue is whether that definition is influenced by attitude, which in turn depends on whether the attitude is activated from memory or observation of the attitude object.

The present results provide support for the model's assertion that selective perception depends on the accessibility of the attitude from memory. Recent research documents that latency of response to a direct attitudinal inquiry is at least roughly indicative of the likelihood that the attitude will be activated automatically upon mere presentation of the attitude object (Fazio et al., 1986). In the present case, individuals with accessible attitudes (as indicated by relatively fast latencies) were more likely to judge the performance of the candidates during the debates in a manner that was congruent with their attitudes. Such individuals held attitudes that presumably involved relatively strong object-evaluations associations. Consequently, their attitudes were probably more likely to be activated while they were viewing the debates and, hence, were more likely to color their perceptions of the outcomes of the debates. However, unlike the context addressed by the postulated attitude-behavior process model, these perceptions were not an immediate precursor of the voting behavior of ultimate interest in the present case.

Instead, the influence of attitude accessibility upon the consistency between attitudes, as assessed months earlier, and voting behavior seems to have been a function of the stability of those attitudes. The act of voting in a presidential election is clearly a reasoned, intentional action in which individuals would actively retrieve the relevant attitudes from memory if they had not been activated automatically. Thus, there is no need for attitudes to be highly accessible from memory for the attitudes to exert an influence upon the act of voting. Indeed, most voters enter the voting booth with a definite intention to vote for a particular candidate. However, whether the attitudes that form the basis for the behavioral intention are equivalent to those assessed months earlier does depend on the accessibility of those initial attitudes.

Initial attitudes characterized by high accessibility were likely to have biased people's interpretations of any information about the candidates that came to their attention during the course of the campaign, including the outcome of the debates. The present data indicate that such selective processing was less likely for individuals whose attitudes were relatively less accessible. The amount of selective processing, as in the judgments of the debates, is apt to have determined the persistence of the attitude over time. Thus, greater selective processing on the part of those individuals with relatively accessible attitudes is likely to mean that their final voting decisions were affected by attitudinal positions more equivalent to the ones that they held months earlier than was the case for individuals with less accessible attitudes.

This reasoning implies that an association should exist between attitude-perception congruency and attitude-behavior correspondence. That is, individuals who held initial attitudes that were unlikely to bias their interpretations of subsequent information should display less attitude-behavior correspondence because those attitudes were potentially more subject to modification during the course of the campaign. Additional analyses of the present data revealed such an association. For the subset of respondents who had provided both perception and voting information (82 individuals when considering only voters, and 95 when also including those who reported not having voted), we computed two indices. The absolute value of the difference between standardized attitude scores and standardized perception scores served as an index of discrepancy between attitudes and perceptions. Similarly, the absolute value of the difference between standardized attitude scores and standardized voting scores served as an index of the discrepancy between attitudes and behavior.[6] These two indices were consistently and reliably associated. Regardless of whether the attitude examined concerned Reagan or Mondale, regardless of which of the three perception measures was used, and regardless of which of the two voting measures was examined, a significant correlation between attitude-perception and attitude-behavior discrepancies was apparent. The 12 correlation coefficients ranged from .264 to .523, with the average being .381 (all $ps < .02$).[7] Thus, the less the individual's attitude promoted selective processing of the debates, the less likely the individual was to vote in a manner that was consistent with that initial attitude.

These findings serve to illustrate the relevance of attitude accessibility and the likelihood of automatic attitudinal activation to behavioral decisions that are not themselves the immediate outcome of automatic processes but instead stem from conscious and deliberative reasoning. Fazio (1986) has discussed automatic versus controlled processing (see Schneider and Shiffrin, 1977; Shiffrin and Schneider, 1977) models of the attitude-behavior relation and has offered some thoughts about attempts to integrate the two into a more comprehensive model. The present investigation illustrates one such linkage. Voting behavior is most likely the result of a controlled process in which individuals reflect and arrive at a behavioral intention, conceivably in a manner consistent with Ajzen and Fishbein's (1980) theory of reasoned action. Yet, the sort of automatic processes that the model proposed by Fazio and his associates (Fazio, 1986; Fazio et al., 1983) focuses on are relevant to such decisions. Just as postulated by the automatic process model, a relatively accessible attitude is likely to bias interpretations of subsequently received information because it is likely to be activated automatically upon observation or mention of the attitude object. As a result, a relatively accessible attitude is apt to remain

---

[6]Just as one would expect, comparison of mean index scores in high versus low accessibility groups confirmed the findings reported earlier concerning the differences in correlation coefficients in the high versus low groups. Index scores were generally lower, indicating less discrepancy between attitudes and perceptions and between attitudes and behavior, within the high than within the low accessibility groups.

[7]This relation between attitude-perception discrepancy and attitude-behavior discrepancy also was evident within the high (average $r = .314$, $p < .05$) and within the low (average $r = .398$, $p < .01$) accessibility groups.

more persistent over time than one that is less accessible. Such greater persistence implies that the attitudinal position that is considered at the time that the controlled decision is made will be more equivalent to the initial position in the case of accessible than in the case of relatively inaccessible attitudes.

Our interpretation of the present findings rests on the validity of latency of response to an attitudinal inquiry as a measure of the chronic accessibility of the attitude. As indicated earlier, this measure has been found to relate to the likelihood of automatic activation of the attitude upon exposure to the attitude object (Fazio et al., 1986). Attitude objects concerning which an individual can indicate an attitude relatively quickly when faced with a direct inquiry are also likely to activate the attitude from memory automatically upon their presentation. In contrast, attitude objects for which response latencies to an inquiry are relatively slow are also unlikely to produce automatic attitudinal activation upon their presentation. Thus, we can be confident that the latency measure that was used in the present investigation does reflect the chronic accessibility of the attitude.

Nevertheless, the correlational nature of the present investigation should not be overlooked. Attitude accessibility may be related to other qualities of the attitude that are reflective of attitudinal "strength," such as attitude centrality, certainty, and affective-cognitive consistency (see Raden, 1985, for a review of such strength-related attitude dimensions). Indeed, precisely such covariation among the various indices of attitudinal strength has been hypothesized (e.g., Fazio et al., 1982; Fazio, 1986). It has been suggested that the attitudinal qualities that have been identified as moderators of the attitude-behavior relation all may do so because they reflect the strength of the object-evaluation association and, hence, in terms of the attitude-behavior process, the likelihood that the attitude will be activated from memory when the attitude object is encountered. Furthermore, it has been found that attitude accessibility is affected by the manner of attitude formation (Fazio et al., 1982; Fazio et al., 1983); attitudes based on direct behavioral experience are more accessible from memory than are those based on indirect experience. Also, attitude accessibility has been found to relate to the personality construct of self-monitoring (Snyder, 1974); low self-monitoring individuals possess attitudes that are generally more accessible from memory than do high self-monitors (Kardes, Sanbonmatsu, Voss, and Fazio, 1986). Both the manner of attitude formation and self-monitoring have been shown to moderate the attitude-behavior relation.

Thus, although we can be confident that our latency measure reflects attitude accessibility, a number of additional variables may be related to our classification of individuals in the present investigation as possessing attitudes of either high or low accessibility. Which single dimension or combination of dimensions is causally "responsible" for the moderating effects that were observed cannot be discerned given the correlational nature of the investigation. What we see as the advantage of focusing upon the construct of attitude accessibility is its clear relevance to the issue of the *process* by which attitudes influence perceptions and behaviour. Unlike other indicants of the "strength" of an attitude, attitude accessibility operates at an information processing level of analysis. Nonetheless, the present findings are most appropriately viewed as simply *consistent* with the implications of the theoretical model of the attitude-behavior process that has been proposed. As such, they provide a real-world corroboration of past experimental findings that have indicated that the strength of the object-evaluation association (and, hence, attitude accessibility) has a causal impact on attitude-behavior consistency (Fazio et al., 1982, Experiment 4). Additional experimental work is necessary to isolate the causal influence of attitude accessibility. Such work appears warranted on the basis of the present correlational findings stemming from an important, real-world context.

Regardless of any ambiguity concerning the causal mechanism that might be operating in the present case, two additional, more practical, implications of the findings are worth noting. The data clearly indicate that behavioral prediction can be improved by consideration of the accessibility of respondents' attitudes. Differences as large as 35 percent in the amount of behavioral variance explained by attitude were observed as a function of attitude accessibility. The very simplicity of the latency measure that was used to index attitude accessibility makes it attractive for use in surveys in which one is concerned with the prediction of individuals' behavior from their attitudes. Our findings indicate that such an approach is not only feasible but also beneficial. The accessibility of respondents' attitudes provides an indication of the degree to which attitudes are likely to guide subsequent behavior. Thus, one's ability to predict how a given individual will behave may be enhanced by the simultaneous measurement of attitude and attitude accessibility.

Although far more speculative, the technique also may be useful to a pollster interested not in the prediction of individual behavior but in the drawing of an inference about the future behavior of a population. A pollster who desires to obtain an estimate of the future behavior of some population by assessing the attitudes of a representative sample might achieve a more accurate estimate by also considering the accessibility of the respondents' attitudes. If those attitudes appear to be highly accessible, more faith could be placed in the validity of the sample's attitudes as an estimate of the population's future behavior. If those attitudes appear to involve rather weak object-evaluation associations and, hence, are less accessible, then the sample's attitudes are less likely to constitute a valid estimate of the population's behavior. One can easily imagine conducting research involving a large series of such polls and the collection of population behavioral data, in order to arrive at some weighting system by which a pollster might use the average accessibility of attitudes within a sample as an indication of the degree to which the sample attitudes provide a reasonable estimate of future behavior within the population.

The present data also suggest that the degree to which individual's interpretations of information follow from their attitudes is a function of the accessibility of those attitudes. This, too, has a practical implication. Because relatively inaccessible attitudes seem to promote less selective processing, individuals who possess attitudes of this sort would seem to be more easily swayed by information about the attitude object. It is for such people, as opposed to those with highly accessible attitudes, that persuasive communications have the best chance to be effective agents of attitude change. Consistent with this reasoning, Wood (1982) has found that attitude change in response to a persuasive communication is moderated by the degree to which individuals can rapidly retrieve beliefs about the attitude object from memory. Thus, whether the context be a political campaign, a marketing campaign, or whatever, the maximal use of resources might be made by targeting efforts at individuals whose attitudes are relatively low in accessibility. Especially in a situation in which various demographic variables are associated with attitude accessibility, such targeting would be possible. The measure of attitude accessibility used in the present study—latency of response to an attitudinal inquiry—would appear to provide a feasible means of identifying a target population for whom the campaigner's persuasive efforts might pay off.

References

AJZEN, I., AND FISHBEIN, M. *Understanding attitudes and predicting social behavior.* Englewood Cliffs, NJ: Prentice Hall, 1980.

COHEN, J., AND COHEN, P. *Applied multiple regression/correlation analysis for the behavioral sciences.* Hillsdale, NJ: Erlbaum, 1975.

FAZIO, R. H. How do attitudes guide behavior? In R. M. Sorrentino and E. T. Higgins (Eds.), *The handbook of motivation and cognition: Foundation of social behavior,* 204–243. New York: Guilford Press, 1986.

FAZIO, R. H., CHEN, J., McDONEL, E. C., AND SHERMAN, S. J. Attitude accessibility, attitude-behavior consistency, and the strength of the object-evaluation association. *Journal of Experimental Social Psychology,* 1982, **18,** 339–357.

FAZIO, R. H., POWELL, M. C., AND HERR, P. M. Toward a process model of the attitude-behavior relation: Accessing one's attitude upon mere observation of the attitude object. *Journal of Personality and Social Psychology,* 1983, **44,** 723–735.

FAZIO, R. H., SANBONMATSU, D. M., POWELL, M. C., AND KARDES, F. R. On the automatic activation of attitudes. *Journal of Personality and Social Psychology,* 1986, **50,** 229–238.

FAZIO, R. H., AND ZANNA, M. P. Direct experience and attitude-behavior consistency. In L. Berkowitz (Ed.), *Advances in experimental social psychology* (Vol. 14), 162–202. New York: Academic Press, 1981.

FIORINA, M. P. *Retrospective voting in American national elections.* New Haven, CT: Yale University Press, 1981.

KARDES, F. R., SANBONMATSU, D. M., VOSS, R., AND FAZIO, R. H. Self-monitoring and attitude accessibility. *Personality and Social Psychology Bulletin* 1986, **12,** 468–474.

KATZ, D. The functional approach to the study of attitudes. *Public Opinion Quarterly,* 1960, **24,** 163–204.

KEY, V. O. *The responsible electorate.* New York: Vintage, 1966.

POWELL, M. C., AND FAZIO, R. H. Attitude accessibility as a function of repeated attitudinal expression. *Personality and Social Psychology Bulletin,* 1984, **10,** 139–148.

RADEN, D. Strength-related attitude dimensions. *Social Psychology Quarterly,* 1985, **48,** 312–330.

SCHNEIDER, W., AND SHIFFRIN, R. M. Controlled and automatic human information processing: I. Detection, search, and attention. *Psychological Review,* 1977, **84,** 1–66.

SHIFFRIN, R. M., AND SCHNEIDER, W. Controlled and automatic human information processing: II. Perceptual learning, automatic attending, and a general theory. *Psychological Review,* 1977, **84,** 127–190.

SMITH, M. B., BRUNER, J. S., AND WHITE, R. W. *Opinions and personality.* New York: John Wiley & Sons, 1956.

SNYDER, M. The self-monitoring of expressive behavior. *Journal of Personality and Social Psychology,* 1974, **30,** 526–537.

WOOD, W. Retrieval of attitude-relevant information from memory: Effects on susceptibility to persuasion and on intrinsic motivation. *Journal of Personality and Social Psychology,* 1982, **42,** 798–810.

ZANNA, M. P., AND FAZIO, R. H. The attitude-behavior relation: Moving toward a third generation of research. In M. P. Zanna, E. T. Higgins, and C. P. Herman (Eds.), *Consistency in social behavior: The Ontario Symposium* (Vol. 2), 283–301. Hillsdale, NJ: Erlbaum, 1982.

14

Videotape and the Attribution Process: Reversing Actors' and Observers' Points of View

Michael D. Storms

Two actor subjects at a time engaged in a brief, unstructured conversation while two observer subjects looked on. Later a questionnaire measured the actors' attributions of their own behavior in the conversation either to dispositional, internal causes or to situational, external causes. Similarly, each observer attributed his matched actor's behavior. Videotapes of the conversation, replayed to subjects before the attribution questionnaire, provided an experimental manipulation of visual orientation. Some actors and observers saw no videotape replay, while other subjects saw a tape that merely repeated their original visual orientations. As predicted for both of these conditions, the actors attributed relatively more to the situation than the observers. A third set of subjects saw a videotape taken from a new perspective—some actors saw a tape of themselves, while some observers saw the other participant with whom their matched actor had been conversing. With this reorientation, self-viewing actors attributed relatively more to their own dispositions than observers. The results indicated the importance of visual orientation in determining attributional differences between actors and observers. Pragmatically, the theoretical framework and results of the study had relevance to the use of videotape self-observation in therapy and T groups.

When an individual observes a behavior and attempts to understand its causes, he is concerned with the relative importance of personal dispositions of the actor and the surrounding social and environmental context. Both an observer who wishes to explain another's behavior and an actor who tries to understand his own behavior attempt to make the appropriate causal attributions. There is reason to believe,

Reprinted with permission from the author and *The Journal of Personality and Social Psychology,* Vol. 27, No. 2, 1973. Copyright © 1973 by the American Psychological Association.

The research for this article was performed as part of the author's Ph.D. dissertation submitted to the Department of Psychology, Yale University. The author wishes to express his appreciation to Richard E. Nisbett, who served as advisor for the thesis and who has contributed many helpful criticisms of the present chapter.

however, that actors and observers do not always arrive at the same explanation of the actor's behavior. Jones and Nisbett (1971) have argued that when actors seek to explain their own behavior, they are inclined to give considerable weight to external, environmental (i.e., situational) causes. Observers, on the other hand, place considerably more emphasis on internal, personal (i.e., dispositional) causes of the actor's behavior.

Several studies (Jones and Harris, 1967; Jones, Rock, Shaver, Goethals, and Ward, 1968; McArthur, 1970, 1972; Nisbett, Caputo, Legant, and Marecek, 1973) have been cited in support of this general proposition, and Jones and Nisbett have discussed a variety of factors which might lead to such attributional differences between actors and observers. These factors include (a) differences in information about the event, behavior, and context which is *available* to actors and observers and (b) differences in how information is *processed* by actors and observers. Actors may have private information about some aspects of the event, including their own feelings and the historical context in which the event transpires, while observers may have more complete information about the behavior itself. Furthermore, in the interests of controlling events and predicting the future, actors may attend more to situational variables in an event, and observers may attend more to variations in the actor's behavior.

The present study examines a fundamental difference between actors and observers which may lead, in turn, to some of the information differences postulated by Jones and Nisbett (1971). Perhaps the most obvious difference between actors and observers is that they have, quite literally, different points of view. Actors cannot see themselves act; physically they cannot observe much of their own behavior. They may watch the antecedents of their own behavior, or its consequences, or both. But they do not normally view the behavior itself. In addition to the physical difficulty of watching oneself, there are temporal restrictions which contribute to a lack of self-observation. There may not be enough time or mental capacity to contemplate past behavior, monitor present behavior, and plan future behavior all at once. Finally, there are motivational reasons for avoiding an excess of self-observation. In the interest of acting unself-consciously and maintaining control over the immediate events taking place, the actor may learn that it is dysfunctional to be overly concerned with his own present and past behavior. Instead, it is reasonable to assume that most actors focus on the situation in which they find themselves. They look at, attend to, and think about various changing aspects of the environment in which and to which they must respond.

While the actor is watching the situation in which he finds himself, the observer is probably watching the actor. It is usually interesting and often important to watch the behavior of other people. Consequently, observers are often visually oriented toward the actor. Although an observer can take his eyes off the actor and view other aspects of the situation, he probably sees less of the situation than the actor does. As with actors, the observer's scope is also limited by time. Observers cannot simultaneously watch the actor and observe as much of the situation as the actor can. Moreover, observers may find it more efficient in terms of controlling and predicting the ongoing event to concentrate on the actor's behavior rather than on the actor's situation. Finally, the actor is, after all, part of the observer's situation. For the same reasons that an actor focuses on his own situation, the observer focuses on the behavior of the actor, which is part of his (the observer's) situation.

Thus, we postulate that there is a simple difference between actors and observers. Actors watch their environment (which includes the behavior of other people) more than they watch their own behavior. Observers watch the behavior of the actor more than they watch the actor's situation.

If it is true that attributions are largely influenced by point of view, it should be possible to change the way actors and observers interpret a behavior by changing their visual orientations.

A test of this hypothesis requires some means of changing actors' and observers' orientations. Fortunately, modern technology provides a simple and interesting means to accomplish this change—namely, the use of videotape. Videotapes of an event, taken from various camera angles, can be replayed to actors and observers to redirect their attention to other aspects of the event. Of particular interest is the case in which videotape presents a new visual orientation, that is, when actors are shown a tape of their own behavior from the observers' perspective and when observers are shown a tape of some key aspect of the actor's situation from the actor's perspective. Such reorientation should affect actors and observers so as to weaken (or even reverse) their original attributional biases. Actors who see themselves should make more dispositional attributions about their own behavior. Observers who see another aspect of the actor's situation should become more situational in attributing the actor's behavior.

Thus, the question to be answered by this study is whether actors' and observers' attributions can be significantly influenced, perhaps even reversed, by changing their visual orientation toward an event. The implications of such a question may go beyond immediate theoretical concerns. Discrepancies between actors' and observers' perceptions and interpretations of behavior are of paramount concern to therapists, group relations consultants, and T group trainers. Often such practitioners must attempt to bridge the interpretational gap between actor and observer, patient and therapist, and individual and group.

METHOD

Overview

The hypothesis was tested in an experiment that featured a simple interpersonal event, namely a brief getting-acquainted conversation between two strangers (actors). In addition, two other subjects (observers) were told to watch the conversation but not to participate in it.

Videotape replays of the conversation provided the experimental manipulation. The design made it possible to compare the effects of three orientation conditions: (a) one in which no visual reorientation was attempted (no videotape), (b) one in which videotape was used simply to repeat the subject's original orientations (same orientation), and (c) one in which videotape reversed the orientation of actor and observer (new orientation). In one set of conditions, actors and observers saw a videotape from essentially the same orientation as they had had in "real life." Actors saw a videotape replay of the other participant with whom they were conversing (actor—same orientation), and observers saw a videotape of the same actor they had been observing and about whom they would later answer questions (observer—same orientation). In another set of conditions, actors and observers received an entirely new orientation on videotape. Actors saw a videotape of themselves in the conversation (actor—new orientation), and observers saw a videotape of the other participant with whom their target actor had been conversing (observer—new orientation). In addition, a set of actors and observers were run with no videotape replay.

Subjects

One hundred and twenty Yale undergraduate male volunteers participated in 30 groups of 4. Subjects were solicited by sign-up sheets which specified that people who volunteered for the same session should not be previously acquainted.

Procedure

When each group of four subjects arrived at the experiment, they were told,

> This is a study in an area of social psychology called "interpersonal dynamics." More specifically, I'm interested in what I call "getting acquainted"—that is, what happens when two strangers meet for the first time and initiate their first conversation. Two of you in this study will be having a short, first conversation with each other. In addition, this study calls for two observers.

Subjects were randomly assigned to the role of actor (actually referred to as participant in the script) or observer. Two subjects were assigned to be actors and to have a getting-acquainted conversation together. Each of the remaining two observer subjects was assigned to observe his matched actor during the conversation.

The experimenter then mentioned,

> There is one thing I would like to add to the procedure today. I've gotten hold of some videotape equipment and I will be taping your conversation. My thought was that it might be useful to you in answering the questionnaires to see the conversation replayed on tape.

Subjects were then seated in the experimental room as shown in Figure 14.1. Actors sat at one end of the table, across from each other, with one camera focused on each. Observers sat at the other end of the table, diagonally across from and facing their matched actors. The experimenter reiterated that the conversation would

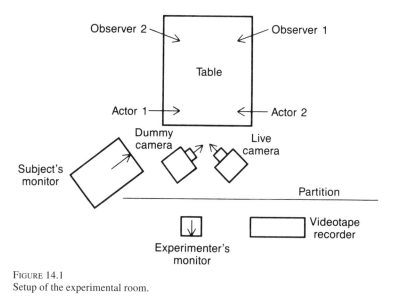

Figure 14.1
Setup of the experimental room.

last about 5 minutes, that the actors could talk about anything they wished, perhaps starting with their names and where they lived, and that observers should silently watch their matched actors.

After adjusting the equipment, the experimenter signaled to the participants to begin their conversation. Five minutes later, he asked them to stop and wait silently while the tapes were rewound. At this point, the experimental manipulation was performed. A random number table was consulted to determine whether the session would be a control session, in which case the subject would not see any tape, or an experimental session. If an experimental session was indicated, the experimenter continued, "I'm afraid only one camera was working very well and the other one is just too poor to see anything. So we'll only be able to see one of you on the videotape." Experimental subjects were always shown the tape of Actor 1.

Thus one actor, Actor 2, saw a tape of the same participant he had just seen in real life (Actor 1) and was the actor–same orientation subject. The other actor, Actor 1, viewed the tape of himself and was the actor–new orientation subject. Similarly, one observer, Observer 1, saw a tape of the same actor he had been observing in the conversation (Actor 1) and was the observer–same orientation subject. The other observer, Observer 2, saw a tape of the participant whom he had not been observing previously (Actor 1) and was the observer–new orientation subject. Thus each experimental session yielded one subject in each of the four experimental cells.

If a control session was indicated, the experimenter said the following instead: "I'm afraid this is lousy equipment. It just didn't take a good enough picture to be worth our while looking at it. So we'll just have to skip the tapes and go on to the questionnaire." These no-videotape control sessions produced two actor–no-videotape subjects and two observer–no-videotape subjects.

At this point, for control subjects, and after the videotape replay for experimental subjects, the experimenter introduced the questionnaire, stressing that it was confidential and that the subjects would not see each other's responses. When the subjects completed the questions, they were debriefed. At this time, the experimenter raised the issue of experimental deception, but no subject indicated suspicion that the videotape had been a deliberate manipulation or even an essential part of the experiment.

Measures

On the postexperimental questionnaire, actor subjects answered mostly questions about themselves, and observer subjects answered questions about their matched actor. After a few introductory filler items, a page of instructions and the key dependent measures of attribution were presented. The instructions informed subjects that in the next part of the questionnaire they would be asked to describe their own (their matched actor's) behavior along four standard dimensions: friendliness, talkativeness, nervousness, and dominance. Then, for each of the four behaviors, subjects were to indicate how much influence they thought the following two factors had in causing that behavior:

(A) *Personal characteristics* about yourself (your matched participant): How important were your (his) personality, traits, character, personal style, attitudes, mood, and so on in causing you (him) to behave the way you (he) did?

(B) *Characteristics of the situation:* How important were such factors as being in an experiment, the "getting acquainted" situation, the topic of conversation, the way the other participant behaved and so on in causing you (him) to behave the way you (he) did?

Thus, on each of the next four pages, three questions were presented. The first asked about the perceived level of behavior on one of the four dimensions, for example, "To what extent did you (your matched participant) behave in a friendly, warm manner?" The question was followed by a 9-point scale labeled extremely friendly (9) to extremely unfriendly (1). Presented next were the two attribution questions: "How important were personal characteristics about you (your matched participant) in causing you (him) to behave that way?" and "How important were characteristics of the situation in causing you (him) to behave that way?" Each of these questions was followed by a 9-point scale labeled extremely important (9) to extremely unimportant (1).

These last two questions, repeated over the four behavioral dimensions, provided the principal and most direct measure of subjects' attributions. These four dimensions were not selected on the basis of any particular theoretical or empirical considerations, but simply because it was anticipated that subjects would manifest behaviors along each of these dimensions and that subjects would be able to make judgments about them. Since the hypothesis was concerned with the relative strength of dispositional versus situational attributions and made no distinctions among the four behavioral dimensions, the appropriate measure was the difference between perceived importance of personal characteristics and perceived importance of situational characteristics in causing the actor's behavior, summed over all four behaviors. This difference score was referred to as the dispositional–situational index. A higher value on this index indicated that a subjects' attributions were relatively more dispositional and less situational. It is important to note this dual meaning of the dispositional–situational index. When an effect is described as "relatively more dispositional," it is equally valid to say "relatively less situational."

A second, less direct measure of the subjects' attributions appeared later in the questionnaire. The subjects were asked to report their estimates of the actor's level of behavior in *general* on each of the four behavioral dimensions, for example, "How friendly a person are you (is your matched participant) in general?" Responses were made on a scale from very friendly (9) to very unfriendly (1). It was then possible to compare these answers to the subjects' previous answers about the actor's level of behavior in the conversation. If a subject had perceived that the actor's behavior in the conversation was due to a stable personal disposition, then the subject would likely have predicted that the actor behaved the same way in general. Thus, dispositional attributions would lead to a low discrepancy between the subject's perception of the actor's behavior in the conversation and his behavior in general. On the other hand, if the subject had thought that the actor's behavior was caused by the situation, he would more likely have reported that the actor behaved differently in general. Thus, situational attributions would lead to greater discrepancy between the subjects' perceptions of the actor's present and general levels of behavior. The simplest measure of this discrepancy was the absolute value of the difference between the present level-of-behavior scores and the general level-of-behavior scores, summoned over all four behaviors. This measure was referred to as the present-behavior–general-behavior index. The higher the value of this discrepancy index, the more a subject made situational (or the less he made dispositional) attributions.

The remainder of the questionnaire contained items not directly related to present concerns.

RESULTS

Dispositional Versus Situational Attributions for Behavior

The main hypothesis of the present study concerns the effects of videotape reorientation on actors' and observers' causal attributions of the actor's behavior. Before considering the effects of reorientation, however, it is helpful to examine the evidence pertinent to the original Jones and Nisbett (1971) hypothesis that actors are characteristically inclined to attribute causality to aspects of the situation, while observers tend to attribute causality to the actor's disposition. Evidence for

TABLE 14.1
Dispositional, situational, and dispositional minus situational attribution scores totaled over all four behaviors

Attribution	Same orientation	No videotape	New orientation
Actors' attributions of own behavior			
Dispositional	26.10	27.35	27.50
Situational	25.95	25.10	20.70
Dispositional–situational	.15[a]	2.25[ab]	6.80[c]
Observers' attributions of matched actor's behavior			
Dispositional	27.10	27.30	25.75
Situational	22.20	22.50	24.15
Dispositional–situational	4.90[bc]	4.80[bc]	1.60[ab]

Note: Dispositional–situational means not sharing the same superscript are significantly different at the .05 level or beyond by Newman-Keuls tests.

this proposition is found in two conditions of the present experiment: the no-videotape cells in which the subjects did not receive any videotape replay, and the same-orientation cells in which the videotape merely repeated the subjects' original visual perspectives.

The relevant data are presented in Table 14.1. The key dependent measure, the total dispositional–situational index, reflects the relative strength of dispositional and situational attributions; a higher value on this index indicates relatively more dispositional (less situational) attributing. A comparison of the dispositional–situational means for actors and observers in the no-videotape and same-orientation cells reveals that, in both of these conditions, actors attributed relatively more to situational causes than did observers ($p < .12$, $p < .05$, respectively).[1] It is further noted from these data that a videotape which merely repeated the subjects' original orientation had little effect on either actors or observers. Dispositional–situational scores for actors in the same-orientation condition did not differ from those for actors in the no-videotape condition ($q = 1.79$, ns), and scores for observers in the two conditions were also similar ($q = 1$, ns). Thus, under conditions of no videotape and under conditions of repeated videotape orientation, the subject's role as actor or observer was an important determinant of attributions. Actors attributed their own behavior relatively more to situational causes, and observers attributed the behavior relatively more to dispositional causes.

The main hypothesis of the present study can be examined with the data presented in the last column of Table 14.1. It was anticipated that actors who saw themselves on videotape would become relatively less situational (more disposi-

---

[1]These comparisons, and all two cell comparisons in the present study, are based on the q statistic from the Newman-Keuls procedure from testing differences among several means (see Winer, 1962). The degrees of freedom, taken from the overall analysis of variance, equal 114; n equals 20 per cell. The Newman-Keuls is a more stringent test than the usual two-tailed t test.

tional) in attributions of their own behavior, while observers who saw a videotape of the other participant with whom the actor had been conversing would become relatively more situational (less dispositional) in their attributions of the actor's behavior. Since opposite effects of videotape reorientation were predicted for actors and observers, the hypothesis was properly tested by the interaction between subjects' roles (actor or observer) and videotape orientation. The predicted Role × Videotape Orientation interaction was obtained at beyond the .001 level of confidence ($F = 9.72$, $df = 2/114$, $p < .001$). Neither the main effect for role nor the main effect for videotape orientation was significant. The interaction reflected a complete reversal of the relative perspectives of actor and observer in the new-orientation condition. In the same-orientation and no-videotape conditions, the actors' attributions were more situational than the observers'. In the new-orientation condition, in contrast, the actors were relatively more dispositional than the observers. This reversed effect was significant in itself ($p < .05$).

Examining the simple dispositional and situational scores also presented in Table 14.1, it is apparent that reorientation had a stronger influence on the subjects' evaluation of situational factors than on their evaluation of dispositional factors. The array of means for attributions to dispositional causes was in the direction of the predicted interaction, but the effect did not reach significance ($F = 1.38$; $df = 2/114$, *ns*). The situational attribution scores showed the expected reverse pattern, and the interaction was significant ($F = 5.78$, $df = 2/114$, $p < .005$).

The hypothesis is thus strongly supported. Visual orientation has a powerful influence on the attributions of actors and observers. Indeed, the data in Table 14.1 suggest the strongest possible conclusion: Under some circumstances actual role as actor or observer is unimportant, and visual orientation is totally determinative of attributions.

Two other aspects of the dispositional–situational data are noteworthy. (a) Repetition on videotape of essentially the same information which had been presented in real life had little effect on either the actors or the observers. Actors in the same-orientation condition were only slightly and nonsignificantly more situational than no-videotape actors, and same-orientation observers were only slightly and nonsignificantly more dispositional than no-videotape observers. (b) The predicted experimental effects were not obtained with equal strength for all four of the behaviors on which the total dispositional–situational index was based.

The fact that videotape in the same-orientation cells had little effect on the subject's attributions suggests that mere repetition of information and the addition of time to review the event did not affect the subject's perceptions of the event. The subjects appear to have absorbed all relevant data about the event during its real-life occurrence. Of course, one would not necessarily expect this to be true of all events. If the episode were more complex or of longer duration, subjects could easily miss important information in vivo. A videotape replay would fill in these informational gaps and could, quite possibly, produce different attributions.

The most noteworthy difference among the four behavioral dimensions was the failure of the dominance dimension to contribute to the experimental effects. Considering each behavioral dimension separately, the Role × Videotape Orientation interaction was significant for friendliness, talkativeness, and nervousness, each at the .025 level of confidence, but was trivial for dominance ($F < 1$). Comments by subjects during the debriefing suggest a possible reason for the failure of dominance to contribute to the experimental effects. Subjects complained that dominance was a difficult dimension on which to judge people in the context of a simple, 5-minute getting-acquainted conversation. While friendliness, talkativeness, and nervousness are dimensions with concrete behavioral counterparts (such as smiling, talking, and fidgeting), apparently dominance is a more abstract dimension and requires a higher order of inference.

When the dominance question was excluded from the analysis, each of the experimental effects was strengthened. Across the remaining three dimensions, the interaction test of videotape reorientation was strengthened from an F of 9.72 to an F of 13.89 ($df = 2/114$, $p < .001$). Tests for the Jones and Nisbett (1971) hypothesis were also strengthened; the contrast between actors and observers in the no-videotape condition was significant at the .05 level, and the contrast between actors and observers in the same-orientation conditions was significant at the .01 level.

Perceived Level of Behavior and Perceived Discrepancy from General Behavior

In addition to the two attribution questions, the subjects also answered questions about the perceived level of behavior on each dimension. Past experiments in this area have typically created a specific, standardized behavior for subjects to attribute. The present experiment, with its unstructured conversations, did not furnish all subjects with the same behavior. This flexibility was desirable, in that it provided a more general test of the attribution hypotheses over several, naturally occurring behaviors. But it also created the possibility that perceptions of the perceived level or intensity of behavior could differ among experimental conditions and thus account for the different attributions. This does not appear to have been the case, however. There were two ways of calculating perceived level of behavior: (a) by taking the direct value from the 9-point scale for each level-of-behavior response and (b) since the scales were bipolar (for example, 9 = very friendly to 1 = very unfriendly), by taking the deviation of the subject's response from the midpoint of the scale (5). Neither of these measures yielded significant comparisons between any cells in the experiment, either for each behavior considered separately or for all four behaviors totaled. Furthermore, the overall correlations between the total dispositional–situational measure of attributions and the two measures of perceived level of behavior were trivial and nonsignificant ($r = -.049$, for the direct score; $r = -.021$, for the score of deviation from midpoint). Thus, it is apparent that differences in perceived level of behavior could not account for the attribution differences.

TABLE 14.2
Present behavior minus general behavior discrepancy scores
summed over all four behaviors

Subjects	Same orientation	No videotape	New orientation
Actors	7.15	5.00	4.25
Observers	5.45	4.90	5.90

Since there were no significant differences in perceived level of behavior, it is meaningful to examine the second measure of subjects' attributions, the present-behavior–general-behavior discrepancy scores. This index reflected the absolute difference between the subjects' perceptions of the actor's *present behavior* (in the conversation) and the actor's *general behavior,* summed over all four behaviors. A small discrepancy would indicate that a subject expected the actor's present behavior to generalize and was thus making a dispositional attribution. A greater discrepancy would indicate less generalization of the actor's behavior and thus a situational attribution.

The results of the present-behavior–general-behavior discrepancy measure, presented in Table 14.2, corroborated the findings on the dispositional–situational measure of attributions. The effects of videotape reorientation, as tested in the Role $\times$ Videotape Orientation interaction, reached significance at $p < .05$, ($F = 3.38$, $df = 2/114$). Again, neither the main effect for role nor the main effect for orientation was significant. Although the direction of differences between the actors and observers in the various conditions was as expected, none of the individual comparisons between cells reached significance on the present-behavior–general-behavior measure, even with the exclusion of the dominance dimension. It appears that the results for the present-behavior–general behavior measure followed the same pattern as, but were generally weaker than, the results for the dispositional–situational measure. The two measures were, incidentally, significantly correlated (overall $r = .361$, $p < .01$).

DISCUSSION

The present study demonstrates that visual orientation has a powerful influence on the inferences made by actors and observers about the causes of the actor's behavior. When videotape was not presented and subjects were left to assume their own orientations, or when videotape reproduced subjects' original orientations, actors attributed their behavior relatively more to situational causes than did observers. This finding supports the Jones and Nisbett (1971) hypothesis that actors' attributions are typically more situational than observers'. But under conditions of reorientation, when subjects saw a new point of view on videotape, the attributional differences between actors and observers were exactly reversed. Reoriented, self-viewing actors attributed their behaviors relatively less to situational causes than did observers. This effect was obtained on two very different measures of attribution across a variety of behavioral dimensions in an unstructured situation.

Mechanisms of Videotape Reorientation

Two important issues arise concerning the possible mechanisms by which video orientation affected attributions. The first issue, one crucial to any laboratory social psychology experiment, concerns experimenter demand characteristics. Demand characteristics could have influenced the results of the present study if the hypotheses had been communicated to subjects either by the experimenter's behavior or by the fact the subjects viewed only one videotape. Both of these possibilities depend on subjects' developing the expectation that videotape had importance for how they should respond. The possibility of communicating the hypotheses was avoided by leading subjects to believe that videotape was not an essential part of the experiment and that the experimenter had wanted to show both tapes but could not, due to circumstances beyond his control. During debriefing, subjects were questioned on their reactions to this hoax; they reported no suspicion that the videotape breakdown had been intentional or important. Moreover, if subjects had been responding to the attribution questions out of desire to support the experimenter's hypotheses, it is unlikely they could have produced the results of the indirect present-behavior–general-behavior measure. This index was derived from the absolute value of the difference between the four level-of-behavior questions and the four general-behavior questions. These questions were widely separated in the questionnaire, and subjects would have had to perform a rather elaborate calculus to produce these results deliberately. Thus, it does not seem likely that the reorientation effects can be accounted for by experimenter demand characteristics.

The second issue involves the possible mechanisms by which videotape caused the predicted attributions. This study was designed to demonstrate that a global manipulation (visual orientation) affects actors' and observers' attributions of the actors' behavior. The study was not designed to separate out the many possible mechanisms by which this might occur. However, some informed speculation is possible.

Jones and Nisbett (1971) proposed several factors that contribute to attributional differences between actors and observers, including differences in the information available about an event and differences in how that information is processed. These two categories are not mutually exclusive, and videotape orientation may have affected aspects of both information availability and information processing. When actors or observers saw a videotape of an event from a different point of view, they may have received some totally new information. The actor may have realized, for the first time, some new aspects of his own behavior; the observer may have seen new aspects of the situation or of the other participant. These new facts could have contributed to changes in subjects' inferences about the cause of behavior. Second, the salience of already available information may have changed for reoriented subjects. Changes in the salience of information have been shown to affect people's perceptions of the reasons for their behavior. For example, Kiesler, Nisbett, and Zanna (1969) found that subjects tended to adopt as explanations of their own behavior motives that were made salient by a confederate. Similarly, subjects in the present study might have formulated their attributions about the actor's behavior on the basis of potential causes which had just been made salient by the videotape. Finally, videotape reorientation may have produced new response sets for subjects. Actors who viewed themselves on tape may have been put into a "self-discovery" frame of mind and thus led to think about their own personality as revealed in their behavior. Similarly, observers who saw a videotape from the actor's point of view may have developed an "empathic" set, imagining themselves to be in the actor's shoes.

It is also of interest to consider the exact nature of the attributional changes evoked by videotape. Changes on the key dependent variable, the dispositional–situational index, were accounted for mostly by changed evaluations of situational causes. Actors assigned a great deal of causality to the situation unless videotape forced them to look away from the situation and toward their own behavior. Observers originally assigned less causality to the situation unless videotape impressed situational factors on them. Differences in attribution to dispositional causes, although in the expected direction, were much weaker than these differences in attribution to situational causes. It may be that the relatively greater amount of change on the situational dimension reflects people's general way of viewing the role of dispositions in causing behavior. People may characteristically assign fixed and fairly high importance to personal responsibility for behavior. Consequently, they may be left with only one means of modifying their relative assignment of causality and responsibility, namely by varying their evaluations of the situation. In line with this possibility, there may have been a ceiling effect for dispositional attributions in the present study; the overall mean importance assigned to dispositional causes equaled nearly 7 out of a possible 9 scale points. Subjects were thus left with little room to express enhanced dispositional influences.

Up to this point, discussion has been limited to information-related variables which may be modified by video exposure and may in turn affect attributions. Undoubtedly, motivational variables, such as the need to maintain self-esteem and particular self-concepts, could also be affected by videotape observations. One might expect the self-viewing actors in particular to be influenced by such motivations. It is important to note, however, that the present findings were obtained in a situation which was, in many respects, low-key. The behaviors elicited in the getting-acquainted conversations were routine and probably not highly relevant to actors' self-concepts, the interaction between subjects was fairly unemotional, and actors and observers did not have the opportunity to discuss their potentially opposing views of the actor's behavior. It is therefore important to consider whether the present findings would generalize to situations where actors and observers are more emotionally involved, such as in psychotherapy and T groups. There is reason to believe that the present findings have some applicability to the use of videotape even in such emotionally charged settings.

Videotape in Therapy and T Groups

There has been a recent and dramatic increase in the application of videotape feedback in therapy and human relations training. Alger and Hogan (1966a) asserted that "videotape recording represents a technological breakthrough with the kind of significance for psychiatry that the microscope has had for biology [p. 1]." In clinical practice, videotape is frequently used to increase a patient's knowledge of his own behavior (cf. Bailey and Sowder, 1970; Holzman, 1969), and this apparently leads to therapeutic gain. Reivich and Geertsma (1968) reported increased accuracy in patients' knowledge of their own behavior after videotape self-observation. They measured the disparity between a patient's self-ratings on clinical scales and the ratings given him by psychiatric nurses. After videotape self-observation, the ratings of the actor patient came to agree more with the ratings of the observer nurses. Alderfer and Lodahl (1971) found that videotape playback in T groups increased subjects' "openness." Openness was defined as willingness to explore the internal meaning of and accept personal responsibility for an attitude or behavior. Finally, case studies in marital therapy (Alger and Hogan, 1966a; Kagan, Krathwohl, and Miller, 1963) have reported that one or both marriage partners are more willing to assume the blame for a poor relationship after seeing themselves on videotape.

On the other hand, some negative consequences of self-observation have also been reported. For instance, Carrere (1954) used videotape to show alcoholics how they behaved when intoxicated, but he found it necessary to edit the more shocking scenes. The full presentation of their behavior when drunk was too stressful for many of his patients. Parades, Ludwig, Hassenfeld, and Cornelison (1969) similarly reported the lowering of alcoholic patients' self-esteem after viewing their own drunken behavior on tape. Leitenberg, Agras, Thompson, and Wright (1968) gave behavioral feedback (although not video) to phobic patients undergoing behavior modification. These authors found that feedback to patients about successful progress speeds their cure, but information about temporary setbacks interferes with the therapy. Finally, Geertsma and Reivich (1965) reported that some self-viewing depressive patients become more depressed, some schizophrenic patients engage in more bizarre behavior, and some neurotics show an increase in the symptoms characteristic of their particular disorder.

Research to date on the use of videotape in therapy is insufficient to indicate how and with whom it is a beneficial therapy adjunct. It may be possible, however, to apply the findings and the theoretical framework of the present study to the issue of videotape use in therapy. The present study demonstrates that self-observation can change the causal interpretation a person gives to his own behavior. The self-viewing actor (and possibly the self-viewing patient) is more likely to accept personal, dispositional responsibility for his behavior and is less likely to deflect responsibility to the situation.

This attributional consequence of self-observation may help to account for some of the effects of videotape in therapy. For example, the increased openness of T group participants after self-observation may reflect a tendency for each group member to assume more personal, dispositional responsibility for his behavior in the group. Similarly, in marital therapy, the husband or wife who sees himself or herself on videotape may realize for the first time his or her own behavioral contribution to the marital conflict and may be more willing to place a dispositional blame on himself or herself. Finally, the reported increase in agreement between a patient's clinical self-ratings after videotape self-observation and the ratings of observing psychiatric nurses closely parallels the present findings. Self-observation increases an individual's dispositional attributions, thus bringing him more in agreement with the observer's built-in bias for dispositional attributions.

It seems likely that this increase in dispositionality of a patient's attributions would prove to be sometimes therapeutic and sometimes distherapeutic. Successful therapy no doubt usually involves making a patient aware of his own behavior and convincing him to accept personal responsibility for that behavior. Self-observation apparently aids this process and, to that extent, should be therapeutic. However, two potentially negative outcomes of this process might be suggested. First, in becoming more dispositional about their own behavior, individuals who see themselves on videotape may actually underestimate real and viable situational explanations for their behavior. Actors in the present study who saw their own behavior on videotape had a higher mean for dispositional attributions and a lower mean for situational attributions than any other group of subjects. This suggests the possibility that self-viewing actors may have been "undersituational" in attributing their own behavior. That is, videotape may have reoriented these actors so much that they perceived situational causes for their behavior to be even less important than did others who viewed them. And if, as Jones and Nisbett (1971) have suggested, observers are themselves inclined to underattribute to the situation, this poses a disturbing possibility for therapy. Ironically, the therapist and the self-viewing patient could reach complete agreement about the patient's behavior, yet this agreement could result from a mutual underestimation of the importance of the patient's situation in causing his behavior. This collaborative illusion between patient and therapist could be especially harmful if the patient blames himself for behavior that is in fact due to some aspect of his environment.

Past research on attribution processes has uncovered another area where attributions to the self can have distherapeutic results. Storms and Nisbett (1970) and Valins and Nisbett (1971) have suggested that negative self-labeling which results from attributing uncomplimentary behaviors to dispositions within oneself often lead to a loss of self-esteem and an actual increase in the pathological behavior. For example, insomniacs who attribute their sleeplessness to some negative state within themselves may increase their anxiety and thus aggravate their original condition. Storms and Nisbett proposed that such exacerbation may result whenever self-attributions of a negative disposition increase the individual's anxiety and when anxiety is an irritant to the pathology, such as in impotence, stuttering, and other neurotic conditions. This exacerbation phenomenon may be occurring in some of the therapy cases where negative results have followed the use of videotapes. The finding that self-observation lowers the self-esteem of alcoholic patients might be an instance of this. An alcoholic patient who sees a tape of his own drunken behavior may become quite upset and depressed about himself. Such a traumatic experience may only increase the likelihood that the patient will drink to excess. Whenever a pathology is caused or influenced by a poor self-concept, self-observation of extremely uncomplimentary behavior may serve to retard therapeutic progress.

Research on attribution processes may help to create a theoretical framework for the area of videotape self-observation in therapy settings. The present study suggests that self-observation increases an individual's dispositional attributions of his own behavior and that this brings interpretation of his behavior more in line with an observer's interpretation. In most cases, this should be advantageous to the therapy process, but in certain cases self-attributions could lead to an exacerbation of the original pathology. Therapists would therefore be well advised to look critically at the potential consequences of self-observation. It seems especially important to consider whether a personal, dispositional attribution of the pathological behavior aids the patient to become aware of his problem and to deal with it, or whether self-attribution increases the patient's anxiety to the point of exacerbating his problem.

References

ALDERFER, C. P., AND LODAHL, T. M. A quasi experiment on the use of experiential methods in the classroom. *Journal of Applied Behavioral Science,* 1971, **7,** 43–69.

ALGER, I., AND HOGAN, P. The use of videotape recordings in conjoint marital therapy. Paper presented at the meeting of the American Psychoanalytic Association, Atlantic City, N.J., May 1966. (a)

ALGER, I., AND HOGAN, P. Videotape: Its use and significance in psychotherapy. Paper presented at the meeting of the Society of Medical Psychoanalysts, New York Academy of Medicine, New York, September 1966. (b)

BAILEY, K. G., AND SOWDER, W. T. Audiotape and videotape self-confrontation in psychotherapy. *Psychological Bulletin,* 1970, **74,** 127–137.

CARRERE, M. J. Le psychochoc cinématographique. *Annales Médico-Psychologiques,* 1954, **112,** 240–245.

GEERTSMA, R. H., AND REIVICH, R. S. Repetitive self-observation by videotape playback. *Journal of Nervous and Mental Disease,* 1965, **141,** 29–41.

HOLZMAN, P. S. On hearing and seeing oneself. *Journal of Nervous and Mental Disease,* 1969, **148,** 198–209.

JONES, E. E., AND HARRIS, V. A. The attribution of attitudes. *Journal of Experimental Social Psychology,* 1967, **3,** 1–24.

JONES, E. E., AND NISBETT, R. E. *The actor and the observer: Divergent perceptions of the causes of behavior.* Morristown, N.J.: General Learning Press, 1971.

JONES, E. E., ROCK, L., SHAVER, K. G., GOETHALS, G. R., AND WARD, L. M. Pattern of performance and ability attribution: An unexpected primacy effect. *Journal of Personality and Social Psychology,* 1968, **10,** 317–340.

KAGAN, N., KRATHWOHL, D. R., AND MILLER, R. Stimulated recall in therapy using videotape: A case study. *Journal of Counseling Psychology,* 1963, **10,** 237–243.

KIESLER, C. A., NISBETT, R. E., AND ZANNA, M. P. On inferring one's beliefs from one's behavior. *Journal of Personality and Social Psychology,* 1969, **11,** 321–327.

LEITENBERG, H., AGRAS, W. S., THOMPSON, L. E., AND WRIGHT, D. E. Feedback in behavior modification: An experimental analysis of two cases. *Journal of Applied Behavioral Analysis,* 1968, **1,** 131–137.

MCARTHUR, L. Appropriateness of the behavior and consensus and distinctiveness information as determinants of actors' and observers' attributions. Unpublished manuscript, Yale University, 1970.

MCARTHUR, L. A. The how and what of why: Some determinants and consequences of causal attribution. *Journal of Personality and Social Psychology,* 1972, **22,** 171–193.

NISBETT, R. E., CAPUTO, G. C., LEGANT, P., AND MARECEK, J. Behavior as seen by the actor and as seen by the observer. *Journal of Personality and Social Psychology,* 1973, **27,** 154–164.

PARADES, A., LUDWIG, K. D., HASSENFELD, I. N., AND CORNELISON, F. S. A clinical study of alcoholics using audio-visual self-image feedback. *Journal of Nervous and Mental Disease,* 1969, **148,** 449–456.

REIVICH, R. S., AND GEERTSMA, R. H. Experiences with videotape self-observation by psychiatric inpatients. *Journal of Kansas Medical Society,* 1968, **69,** 39–44.

STORMS, M. D., AND NISBETT, R. E. Insomnia and the attribution process. *Journal of Personality and Social Psychology,* 1970, **16,** 319–328.

VALINS, S., AND NISBETT, R. E. *Some implications of attribution process for the development and treatment of emotional disorders.* Morristown, N.J.: General Learning Press, 1971.

WINER, B. J. *Statistical principles in experimental design.* New York: McGraw-Hill, 1962.

15

Strangers to Ourselves: Discovering the Adaptive Unconscious

Timothy D. Wilson

Of all studies, the one he would rather have avoided was that of his own mind. He knew no tragedy so heartrending as introspection.

—*Henry Adams, The Education of Henry Adams*
(1918)

There is a lot about ourselves that is difficult to know, such as our nonconscious preferences, personality traits, goals, and feelings. How might people gain insight into the hidden corners of their minds? What better place to start than with introspection, which many of us assume opens an inner path that, if followed carefully, leads to important self-insights. Introspection can be quite useful, but not always in the way that most people think.

EVERYDAY INTROSPECTION

A few years ago some friends of mine, both research psychologists, moved to a new city and began looking for a house. They took a rather unusual approach to their house hunt. First, they made a list of all the attributes of a house they cared about, such as the neighborhood, school district, number of rooms, layout of the kitchen, and so on. The list was quite exhaustive, taking up several pages. Then, when they visited houses with their real estate agent, they took out a copy of the list and rated each house on every attribute. They used the familiar tool of the so-

---

This is an abridged version of Chapter 8 "Introspection and Self-Narratives" from *Strangers to Ourselves: Discovering the Adaptive Unconscious.*

cial psychologist, the 7-point scale. Is the kitchen in this house a 5 or a 6 on the scale? What about the broom closet? After seeing several houses, my friends figured, they would have a good way of quantifying and remembering how they had felt about each one. They could simply compute the average rating of each house and know which one to buy.

Contrast this to the way my real estate agent determines the kind of house her clients want. When she meets with her clients for the first time, she listens patiently as they describe their preferences, nodding her head sympathetically. Many people, like my psychologist friends, go into exhaustive detail. Then, my agent ignores everything the clients just said. She takes them to a wide variety of houses—some modern, some old; some with large yards, some with small; some in town, some in the country—even if the clients have just told her that they would never consider houses in some of these categories.

On the initial visits, the agent pays close attention to her clients' emotional reactions as they walk through the houses, trying to *deduce* what they are really looking for. Often, she says, she determines that people like something quite different from what they have described. One couple said they had to have an older house with charm and would not even consider a newer house. My agent noticed, however, that the couple perked up and seemed happiest when she took them to modern houses. The couple eventually bought a house in a new development outside of town, rather than the older house in the city they said they had always wanted. My agent's wisdom is shared by other real estate professionals, so much so that there is a common saying in the business: "Buyers Lie."

Buyers, of course, do not deliberately misrepresent what they want. Rather, they may not be fully aware of their preferences or have difficulty articulating them. One reason my real estate agent is so successful is that she is quite skilled at inferring what her clients want and often knows their preferences better than the clients themselves do.

Is there a way that people can introspect more carefully about these nonconscious states in order to figure them out? A lot of time would be saved if people could articulate their preferences exactly. Real estate agents would not have to drive clients around to different kinds of houses and figure out what they really wanted.

Perhaps my psychologist friends are onto something. If people approached their preferences more carefully and analytically, using 7-point scales to rate every attribute of a new house or car or potential mate, maybe they could determine better what they really liked. This strategy has been recommended by many very smart people, such as Benjamin Franklin, in a letter to the scientist Joseph Priestly:

> My way is to divide half a sheet of paper by a line into two columns, writing over the one Pro, and over the other Con. Then, during three or four days of consideration, I put down under the different heads short hints of the different motives, that at different times occur to me, for or against each measure . . . When each [reason] is thus considered, separately and comparatively, and the whole lies before me, I think I can judge better, and am less likely to make a rash step.

Other people have suggested that the analytic "pluses and minuses" approach is not very useful. Even worse, as the writer Mario Vargas Llosa discovered when he was a judge at the Berlin film festival, it might actually obscure how one really feels:

> I went to every screening with a fresh pack of notecards that I would dutifully cover with my impressions of each and every film. The result, of course, was that the movies ceased to be fun and turned into problems, a struggle against time, darkness and my own esthetic emotions, which these autopsies confused. I was so worried about evaluating every aspect of every film that my entire system of values went into shock, and I quickly realized that I could no longer easily tell what I liked or didn't or why.

A well-known social psychologist had a similar experience when trying to decide whether to accept a job offer from another university. It was a difficult decision, because there were many attractive features of both her current position and the new one—as well as some minuses. One of her colleagues, Irving Janis, had written a book advising people to complete detailed "balance sheets," listing the pros and cons of each alternative (much as Benjamin Franklin recommended), so she decided to give it a try. Here is her report of what happened: "I get half way through my Irv Janis balance sheet and say, 'Oh hell, it's not coming out right! Have to find a way to get some pluses over on the other side.'"

And finally, I should report on what happened to my psychologist friends who carried their exhaustive list of 7-point scales to every house they visited. After dutifully filling out the scales for a few houses, they found that they were even more confused than before about which houses they liked and why. "We finally threw away the list," they said, "and went with our gut feelings about which house we liked the best." They bought a lovely house in which they have been living happily for the past fifteen years. Perhaps introspection is not always fruitful, and may even mislead people about how they feel. As the poet Theodore Roethke put it, "Self-contemplation is a curse / That makes an old confusion worse."

Does this mean that introspection is a useless exercise that is best avoided? that we should advise against all navel-gazing, tell insight therapists to take down their shingles, and recommend that people focus on anything but themselves? It would be odd for a psychologist to tell people never to think about themselves, and this is not my message. The key is to understand that introspection does not open magic doors to the unconscious, but is a process of construction and inference. Once this is understood, the question becomes when this process of construction is likely to be helpful and when it is not.

Ours Is Not to Reason Why

Consider what happens when people engage in the Franklinesque type of introspection, whereby they analyze the reasons for their preferences. Sometimes people do this formally, as Franklin suggested, by making lists of the pluses and minuses of the alternatives. At other times they do it less formally, such as when they think, "Why do I feel the way I do about this person I'm dating, anyway?" My colleagues and I have investigated what happens when people introspect in this manner. We typically ask people to spend about ten minutes writing down their reasons for a particular feeling. We tell them that the purpose of this exercise is to organize their thoughts and that no one will read what they write, and then see what effect this introspection has on their subsequent attitudes.

We have asked people to analyze a wide range of attitudes, including their feelings toward someone they have just met, romantic partners, political candidates, social issues, consumer products, works of art, and college courses. We have been struck by the fact that people have no difficulty in coming up with a list of reasons for their feelings. Almost never has anyone said, "Sorry, I just don't know why I feel the way I do." Instead, people freely and readily write quite detailed reasons for their feelings.

The accuracy of people's reasons, however, is suspect. People are not always wrong—if they say they love their romantic partner because he is extremely kind, or because he has a great sense of humor, they might be right. People do not have access to all the determinants of their feelings, however, and their reasons are often a function of cultural or personal theories that can be wrong or, at best, incomplete. As Immanuel Kant put it, "We can never, even by the strictest examination, get completely behind the secret springs of action."

If people recognized that their explanations were sometimes inaccurate, there would be no danger in making a list of the reasons why they felt the way they did. "I'll do the best I can," they might say, "but keep in mind that my list is undoubtedly incomplete and that some of the things I put down are probably wrong. Hey, I took psychology in college, Doc." There is an illusion of authenticity, however, such that the reasons people give feel more accurate than they are.

Because people have too much faith in their explanations, they come to believe that their feelings match the reasons they list. If they generate several reasons why their dating partner is pretty unexciting ("He has really nice taste in upholstery"), they infer that they are not all that in love—even if they were in love before. In other words, they construct a story about how they feel that is based on reasons that are not entirely trustworthy. The story has the ring of truth to people, but because they have used faulty information (reasons that happened to be on their minds), it often misrepresents how they really feel.

We have found evidence of just this sequence of events. For example, Dolores Kraft and I asked college students involved in dating relationships to write down, privately and anonymously, why their relationship was going the way it was, and then to rate how happy they were with their relationship. Compared to people in a control condition who did not analyze reasons, these students tended to change their attitudes toward their relationship. Some became happier with it, some less happy.

Why? First, we assumed that people did not know exactly why they felt the way they did. It is not as if people can say with any accuracy, "Okay, here are my reasons: her basic integrity and kindness account for 43 percent of my love, her sense of humor 16 percent, her political views 12 percent, that endearing way she brushes the hair out of her eyes 2 percent, and the rest is pheromones." Instead, people brought to mind reasons that conformed to their cultural and personal theories about why people love others and that happened to be on their minds ("I was just looking at the paisley pattern on his couch and thinking about what a great decorator he is"). Because there is a certain arbitrariness to these reasons, they often do not match people's prior feelings perfectly. In fact the reasons people gave bore almost no relationship to how happy they said they were with their relationship a few weeks earlier. But because people do not recognize this fact, they assume that their reasons are an accurate reflection of their feelings, leading to attitude change. In short, people construct a new story about their feelings based on the reasons that happen to come to mind.

This is what seems to have happened to Proust's Marcel in *Remembrance of Things Past*. As seen in Chapter 1, Marcel becomes convinced that he no longer loves Albertine, after analyzing and introspecting about his feelings: "As I compared the mediocrity of the pleasures that Albertine afforded me with the richness of the desires which she prevented me from realizing . . . [I] concluded that I did not wish to see her again, that I no longer loved her."

I should point out that analyzing reasons does not always lead to attitude change in a negative direction. In our study of dating couples, not all people who listed reasons became more negative toward their relationship. Rather, the direction of the attitude change depended on the nature of the reasons that happened to come to each person's mind. People who found it easiest to think of positive reasons ("He's a great friend and easy to talk to") changed their attitude in a positive direction, whereas those who thought of lukewarm or negative reasons ("He has a fine fashion sense, though it would be nice if he didn't wear that pink shirt quite so often") changed in a negative direction. Marcel found it easiest to think of negative aspects of his relationship with Albertine, and thus concluded that he no longer loved her.

If Benjamin Franklin picked up a psychology journal and read about these findings, he might respond, "Just as I thought—when people step back and think about the pros and cons, they come up with a better-informed, more reasoned point of view. After people analyze reasons, their attitude is superior to the quick, possibly rash judgments they would have otherwise made."

The story people construct on the basis of their reasons analysis, however, can misrepresent how they really feel. Such was the case with Marcel, who discovers, only after learning that Albertine has left him, how wrong he was about his overanalyzed feelings. We have found that the feelings people report after analyzing reasons are often incorrect, in the sense that they lead to decisions that people later regret, do not predict their later behavior very well, and correspond poorly with the opinion of experts.

For example, in another study we compared people who were asked to list reasons about why their relationship was going the way it was with people who did not list reasons. Whose feelings did the best job of predicting the longevity of the relationship? It was the latter group, who did not analyze reasons. This is consistent with the notion that when people analyzed reasons, they constructed stories based on faulty data, such as which aspects of the relationship were easiest to put into words, were on their minds, or were consistent with their theories about how they should feel, leading to attitudes that were less well informed than those of people in the control group, who just gave their unanalyzed, gut feelings. As Goethe put it, "He who deliberates lengthily will not always choose the best."

A study of people's attitudes toward works of art tested Goethe's hunch. Some people analyzed exactly why they liked or disliked five art posters and some did not. Then, all participants chose one of the posters to take home. Two weeks later, we called people up and asked them how happy they were with the poster they had chosen. Benjamin Franklin might predict that the people who analyzed their reasons would make the best choices, by carefully laying out the pros and cons of each option. We found the opposite: the people who did not list reasons, and presumably based their choices on their unanalyzed gut feelings, were happier with their posters than were the people who had listed reasons. Like Mario Vargas Llosa, who found it difficult to tell how he felt about the films when he analyzed each one, the students in the reasons analysis group seemed to lose sight of which poster they really liked the best.

A few years ago I was interviewed by a reporter about this line of research. After we chatted for a while the reporter said she had one final question: "So, Dr. Wilson, I gather you are saying that people should never think about why they feel the way they do and should simply act on their first impulses?" I was horrified and had images of people following the reporter's conclusions about my research, leading to increases in teen pregnancy, drug relapses, and fistfights.

It is important to distinguish between informed and uninformed gut feelings. We should gather as much information as possible, to allow our adaptive unconscious to make a stable, informed evaluation rather than an ill-informed one. Most of us would agree that it would not be wise to marry the first person we are attracted to. If we spend a lot of time with someone and get to know him or her very well, and still have a very positive gut feeling, that is a good sign.

The trick is to gather enough information to develop an informed gut feeling and then not analyze that feeling too much. There is a great deal of information we need in order to know whether someone would make a good partner, much of it processed by our adaptive unconscious. The point is that we should not analyze the information in an overly deliberate, conscious manner, constantly making explicit lists of pluses and minuses. We should let our adaptive unconscious do the job of forming reliable feelings and then trust those feelings, even if we cannot explain them entirely.

Is It Always so Bad to Think about Reasons?

Another thing I told the reporter is that there are some exceptions to the danger of analyzing reasons, which follow from our explanation of why it can be harmful. As we have seen, people often change their minds about how they feel because the reasons they think of do not match their prior feelings very well. There is a group of people for whom this is not true, namely people who are quite knowledgeable about the topic they are analyzing. In the study with the art posters, for example, people who knew a lot about art—those who had taken high school and college art courses—tended to list reasons that matched their prior feelings well. Consequently, the act of listing reasons did not lead to any attitude change in this group. It was the unknowledgeable people who were most likely to bring to mind reasons that conflicted with their initial feelings, causing them to revise their stories about how they felt. Contrary to Benjamin Franklin's advice, the knowledgeable people in our studies do not seem to gain anything by analyzing reasons. The art experts did not like the posters they chose more than unknowledgeable people, but neither did they like them more.

But surely, you might argue, we have not done a fair test of the kind of introspection Franklin recommended. He suggested that people write down pros and cons "during three or four days consideration," whereas in our studies people typically write about reasons only once for ten minutes or so. Might people better decipher their feelings with a longer self-analysis? To find out, Dolores Kraft and I asked the people in our dating couples study to come back to our lab and analyze reasons again, once a week for four weeks. We found that a fair amount of attitude change occurred the first time people analyzed reasons (as discussed earlier), and then people tended to stick to this new attitude when they came back and analyzed reasons again. There did not seem to be any advantage to analyzing reasons more than once; rather, people brought to mind reasons that conflicted with their initial attitude, changed their attitudes to match those reasons, and then stuck to that new attitude.

It is possible, of course, that people would have benefited from an even longer reasons analysis or from one that was not spread out over so much time. My hunch, though, is that if people are not very knowledgeable about the topic they are analyzing, it is an exercise best avoided—at least in the way we have studied it, whereby people sit down by themselves and think about why they feel the way they do.

Recognizing Gut Feelings

Suppose you take my advice and let your adaptive unconscious develop feelings about somebody or something, and avoid the kind of introspection in which you try to put into words exactly why you feel the way you do. What if you are still not certain how you feel? Sometimes people have mistaken beliefs about the nature of their feelings, particularly when their feelings conflict with cultural feeling rules ("people love their ponies," "my wedding day will be the happiest time of my life"), personal standards ("I am not prejudiced at all toward African Americans"), or conscious theories ("I must love him because he conforms to my idea of Mr. Right"). Is there a kind of introspection by which you can gain access to feelings that are hidden in this manner?

Introspection should not be viewed as a process whereby people open the door to a hidden room, giving them direct access to something they could not see before. The trick is to allow the feelings to surface and to see them through the haze of one's theories and expectations.

A recent study by Oliver Schultheiss and Joachim Brunstein suggests one way people might accomplish this. They measured people's implicit motives, using the Thematic Apperception Test technique, whereby people make up stories about a set of standard pictures and these stories are coded for how people express motives such as the need for affiliation or power. They then told participants that they would play the role of a therapist who would use directive techniques to counsel a client. Because people were instructed to be directive and keep control of the situation, and to focus on ways of helping the client, those who were high in both the need for power and the need for affiliation were expected to react especially positively.

The question is, did people know that this was a situation that was well suited or not well suited to their implicit motives? The answer was no when the researchers simply described the counseling situation to participants, and then asked them how they would feel. Consistent with many studies that find that people are not very aware of their implicit motives, people who were high in the need for affiliation and power did not anticipate that the counseling session would make them any happier or feel more engaged than other participants.

In another condition, however, people first underwent a goal imagery procedure whereby they listened to a detailed, tape recorded description of the counseling session and imagined how they would be likely to feel in that situation. Under these circumstances people high in the need for affiliation and power were more likely to recognize that the situation would be one that they would enjoy, and they reported that they would be much happier and more engaged in that situation than other participants did.

Thus, hearing a detailed, image-laden description of the situation was sufficient to trigger feelings generated by people's implicit motives, and people were able to pay attention to these feelings and use them to predict how they would feel in the real situation. I would not call this "introspection" as normally defined, because people were not opening doors to hidden rooms in order to see feelings of which they were unaware. Instead, they were able to imagine a future situation well enough that the feelings it would invoke were actually experienced, and were able to avoid the kinds of introspection we have studied (analyzing reasons) that might obscure how they would really feel.

It remains to be seen how well people can use this technique in everyday life. The suggestion, at least, is that if people took the time to imagine future situations in great detail (e.g., "How would I feel if my housekeeper rushed in with the news that Albertine has left me?"), they might be better able to recognize the feelings generated by their adaptive unconscious, and to see through the smoke screen created by analyzing reasons or by the adoption of cultural feeling rules and conscious theories. They would have better data on which to base their narrative about their feelings and reactions.

INTROSPECTING ABOUT PERSONAL PROBLEMS

Although some of the studies on introspection considered so far dealt with topics that were very important to people, such as why a romantic relationship is going the way it is, they are generally not topics that are causing people distress (most of the participants in our studies were reasonably happy with their relationships). Perhaps people are more adept at introspecting about things that have gone wrong in their lives. There are many ways to introspect about one's source of distress, however, some of which are more helpful than others.

Ruminating When Distressed

One way is to ruminate about a problem, which Susan Nolen-Hoeksema defines as thinking about one's feelings and their causes repetitively without taking action to improve one's situation. In numerous studies, she has found that rumination leads to a negative, self-defeating pattern of thought that makes matters worse, especially when people are depressed or in bad moods to start with. Ruminators are worse at solving problems related to their distress, focus more on negative aspects of their past, explain their behavior in more self-defeating ways, and predict a more negative future for themselves.

In one study, for example, the participants were college students who were either moderately depressed or nondepressed. In the rumination condition, the students were asked to spend eight minutes thinking about their emotions and traits—that is, to try to understand their feelings, why they felt that way, their character, why they turned out the way they did, and who they strived to be. In a distraction condition, the students spent eight minutes thinking about mundane topics unrelated to themselves, such as "clouds forming in the sky" and "the shiny surface of a trumpet." People's moods were measured before and after they completed the rumination or distraction task. Rumination caused depressed participants to become even more depressed, whereas the distraction task made them less depressed. Rumination had little effect on people who were not depressed.

When the depressed students ruminated they focused on the negative side of things, as if their dysphoria was a filter that kept out any positive thoughts. Compared with the other groups—such as the nondepressed students who ruminated and the depressed students who did not ruminate—they brought to mind more negative memories from their pasts (e.g., "Everyone passed the test except me") and felt that negative events in their current lives, such as getting into arguments with their friends, were more common. In another study, people who reported that they often ruminated when they felt depressed were more likely to be depressed a year later, even after their initial levels of depression were controlled for. In short, unhappiness and ruminating about your unhappiness is a bad combination that leads to more depression.

Finding Meaning Through Introspection

Imagine that you received these instructions:

> For the next three days, I would like for you to write about your very deepest thoughts and feelings about an extremely important emotional issue that has affected you and your life. In your writing, I'd like you to really let go and explore your very deepest emotions and thoughts. You might tie your topic to your relationships with others, including parents, lovers, friends, or relatives; to your past, your present, or your future; or to who you have been, who you would like to be, or who you are now.

Jamie Pennebaker and his colleagues have given these instructions to hundreds of people, including college students, community members, maximum-security prisoners, people laid off from their jobs, and new mothers. Most people take it quite seriously and write about personal, often deeply troubling incidents, such as the death of a loved one, the end of a relationship, or sexual and physical abuse. Not surprisingly, people find it upsetting to write about such events and, right after doing so, report more distress than do control participants who write about superficial topics (such as their plans for their day).

As time goes by, however, people show remarkable benefits from the writing exercise. Compared with people in the control condition, those who write about emotional experiences report better moods, get better grades in college, miss fewer days of work, show improved immune system functioning, and are less likely to visit physicians. Writing about emotional experiences is distressing in the short run but has quite positive long-term effects.

Why does writing about emotional experiences—often very painful ones—have more beneficial effects than the other kinds of introspection we have discussed? One possibility is that people tend to hide or suppress their negative emotional experiences, and that the stress caused by constant inhibition takes its toll on their mental and physical health. Having the opportunity to express traumatic events might have a cathartic effect, improving people's well-being by removing the stress caused by inhibition. Although inhibition may well cause stress and contribute to health problems, there is no evidence that Pennebaker's writing exercise works by lowering inhibition. For example, people who write about events that they have already discussed with others do as well as people who write about events they have kept secret.

Rather, writing seems to work by helping people make sense of a negative event by constructing a meaningful narrative that explains it. Pennebaker has analyzed the hundreds of pages of writing his participants provided, and found that the people who improved the most were those who began with rather incoherent, disorganized descriptions of their problem and ended with coherent, organized stories that explained the event and gave it meaning.

Why is rumination harmful whereas Pennebaker's writing exercise is beneficial? One key is that people often ruminate when they are depressed, and the depression focuses their attention on negative thoughts and memories, making it difficult to construct a meaningful, adaptive narrative about the problems. Rumination is a repetitive, spiraling kind of thought whereby people can't stop thinking about things in a negative light, like Mr. Dimmesdale in *The Scarlet Letter:* "He kept vigils, likewise, night after night, sometimes in utter darkness; sometimes with a glimmering lamp; and sometimes, viewing his own face in a looking-glass, by the most powerful light which he could throw upon it. He thus typified the constant introspection wherewith he tortured, but could not purify, himself." In contrast, Pennebaker's participants, who are typically not depressed, are able to take a more objective look at their problems and to construct a narrative that helps explain it in a more adaptive manner. In fact, Pennebaker's technique does not work as well right after a severe trauma, when people are too upset to examine their situation objectively.

Constructing a meaningful narrative can also keep people from trying to suppress their thoughts about a distressing topic. If an event has no coherent explanation it is likely to keep coming to mind, leading to further rumination, or possibly to an attempt to push the thoughts away. Deliberate attempts at thought suppression is a losing exercise, as Daniel Wegner and his colleagues found. People may be able to succeed in not thinking about something for a short time, but often thoughts about the unwanted topic come flooding back. Under some circumstances, such as when people are tired or preoccupied, thought suppression backfires, leading to even more thought about the unwanted topic. An event that has been explained and assimilated into one's life story is less likely to keep coming to mind, triggering attempts to suppress it.

The narrative metaphor helps explain all the examples of everyday introspection we have considered. Analyzing reasons focuses people on bad "data," information that is easy to verbalize but may have little to do with true feelings. Consequently, people construct stories about their feelings from faulty information. Rumination and thought suppression can be harmful in at least two ways: they can make it difficult to engage in the construction of a new narrative, because people are preoccupied with uncontrollable, unwanted thoughts; and, to the extent that people do construct new narratives, they can focus people's attention on negative, pejorative thoughts. Pennebaker's writing exercise is the only kind of introspection we have seen so far in which people are able to construct meaningful stories that have beneficial effects.

V

SELF-JUSTIFICATION

16

Dissonance, Hypocrisy, and the Self-Concept

Elliot Aronson

Since its appearance some 40 years ago, Leon Festinger's theory of cognitive dissonance has enjoyed a prodigious and often controversial history. Its impact on the field of social psychology has been enormous—both in its capacity to account for a broad range of apparently disparate phenomena and in the innovative, high-impact methodology developed to test its propositions.

The theory is also very important to me, personally, because it played a pivotal role in my own professional development. As a first year graduate student at Stanford, I had zero interest in social psychology—what little I knew about that discipline seemed both boring and pedestrian. At the heart of social psychology was the issue of social influence—certainly an important topic—but, in the mid 1950s, the existing knowledge of social influence seemed fairly cut and dried and rather obvious. What did social psychologists know for sure about social influence at that time?

1. If you want people to go along with your position, offer tangible rewards for compliance and clear punishments for non-compliance.
2. Present an audience with a reasonable communication, attributing it to a highly credible communicator.
3. Present the individual with the illusion that everyone else in sight agrees with one another.

Paper presented at the special conference marking the fortieth anniversary of the theory of cognitive dissonance, University of Texas at Arlington, March 17th, 1997.

4. If a member of your discussion group disagrees with you, you will send him more messages (in an attempt to get him to see the light) than if he agrees with you. If he persists in being stubborn, you will try to eject him from the group.

In those days, the overwhelming trend in all of American empirical psychology was, "Let's find the reinforcer." If a person (or a rat) does something, there must be a reason, and that reason had to be the gaining of an identifiable reward such as food, money, or praise, or the removing of a noxious state of affairs such as pain, fear, or anxiety. If food will induce a hungry rat to press the lever of a Skinner box or turn left in a Y-maze, surely conceptually similar rewards can induce a person to adopt a given opinion. The classic experiment that seemed to epitomize experimental social psychology in the mid 1950s is the still classic Asch (1951) experiment in which a unanimous majority apparently disagrees with an individual on a simple, unambiguous perceptual judgment. Why do most people conform to this kind of group pressure? Perhaps it makes them anxious to be alone against a unanimous majority; they fear being considered crazy, being held in low esteem, and so on. It's comforting to be in agreement with others. That's the reward for conformity.

Or take the equally classic experiment done by Hovland and Weiss (1951). Why do people tend to believe a statement attributed to a credible source (like J. Robert Oppenheimer) rather than a non-credible one (like Pravda)? Perhaps it increases the probability of being right—and being right reduces anxiety and makes us feel good, smart, and esteemed. That's the reward for changing one's belief.

These data are true enough—but hardly worth getting excited about. My old "bobbeh" (grandmother), a fountainhead of folk wisdom, could have told me those things without having done an elaborate experiment to demonstrate the obvious. Then, in 1957, Leon Festinger invented the theory of cognitive dissonance—deftly combining cognition and motivation—and produced a revolution that revitalized social psychology—and changed it forever. I first read Festinger's book in the form of a pre-publication carbon copy that the author thrust into my hands (rather disdainfully!) after I told him I was trying to decide whether or not to enroll in his graduate seminar. Reading that manuscript was something of an epiphany for me. It was (and still is) the single most exciting book I have ever read in all of psychology.

The core proposition of the theory is a very simple one: If a person were to hold two cognitions that are psychologically inconsistent, he would experience dissonance. Because dissonance is an unpleasant drive state (like hunger, thirst, or pain), the person will attempt to reduce it—much like he would try to reduce hunger, thirst, or pain. Viewed more broadly, cognitive dissonance theory is essentially a theory about sense-making—how people try to make sense out of their environment and their behavior— and thus, try to lead lives that are (at least in their own minds) sensible and meaningful.

As I implied above, one of the theory's most important aspects was in the challenge it presented to the long-standing dominance of reinforcement theory as an all-purpose explanation for social-psychological phenomena. To illustrate this challenge (as well as its importance) consider the following scenario: A young man performs a monotonous, tedious task as part of an industrial relations experiment. After completing it, he is informed that his participation as a subject is over. The experimenter then appeals to him for help. He states that his research assistant was unable to be there and asks the subject if he would help run the experiment. Specifically, the experimenter explains that he is investigating the effect of people's preconceptions about their performance of a task—specifically, he wants to see if a person's performance is influenced by whether he's told either positive things about the task (in advance), negative things about the task (in advance), or nothing at all about the task. The next participant, who is about to arrive, is assigned to be in the "favorable information condition." The experimenter asks the subject if he would tell the incoming participant that he had just completed the task (which is true) and that he found it to be an exceedingly enjoyable one (which is not true, according to the subject's own experience). The subject is offered either $1 or $20 for telling this lie and for remaining on call in case the regular assistant cannot show up in the future.

The astute reader will recognize this as the scenario of the classic experiment by Leon Festinger and J. Merrill Carlsmith (1959). I regard this experiment, because of the enormous impact it had on the field, the single most important study ever done in social psychology. The results were striking. The subjects who said that they found the task enjoyable in order to earn the paltry payment of $1 came to believe that it actually *was* enjoyable to a far greater extent than those who said it to earn the princely payment of $20. The experiment was a direct derivation from the theory of cognitive dissonance. Needless to say, reinforcement theory would suggest that, if you reward individuals for saying something, they might become infatuated with that statement (through secondary reinforcement). But dissonance theory makes precisely the opposite prediction. If I were a subject in the Festinger-Carlsmith experiment, my cognition that the task I performed was boring is dissonant with the fact that I informed another person that it was enjoyable. If I were paid $20 for making that statement, this cognition would provide ample external justification for my action—thus reducing the dissonance. However, if I were paid only $1, I would lack sufficient external justification for having made the statement—I would be experiencing the discomfort of dissonance—and would be motivated to reduce it. In this situation, the most convenient way to reduce dissonance would be for me to try to convince myself that the task was somewhat more interesting than it seemed at first. In effect, in the process of persuading myself that the task was actually interesting, I would convince myself that my statement to the other student was not a great lie.

Similarly, in another early experiment aimed at testing dissonance theory, Aronson & Mills (1959) demonstrated that people who go through a severe initiation in order to gain admission to a group, come to like that group better than people who go through a mild initiation to get into the same group. Reinforcement theory would suggest that we like people and groups that are associated with reward; dissonance theory led Aronson and Mills to the prediction that we come to like things for which we suffer. All cognitions having to do with the negative aspects of the group are dissonant with the cognition that we suffered in order to be admitted to the group—and therefore, they get distorted in a positive direction, effectively reducing the dissonance.

Even in the early years, it was crystal clear that dissonance-generated attitude change was not limited to such trivial judgments as the dullness of a boring task or the attractiveness of a discussion group. The early researchers extended the theory to much more important opinions and attitudes, such as a striking reassessment of the dangers of smoking marijuana among students at the University of Texas (Nel, Helmreich, & Aronson, 1969), and the softening of Yale students' negative attitudes toward the alleged anti-student brutality of the New Haven police (Cohen, 1962).

IMPACT ON THE FIELD

It is hard to convey the impact these early experiments had on the social psychological community at the time of their publication. The findings startled a great many social psychologists largely because they challenged the general orientation accepted either tacitly or explicitly by the field. These results also generated enthusiasm among most social psychologists because, at the time, they represented a striking and convincing act of liberation from the dominance of a general reward-reinforcement theory. The findings of these early experiments demonstrated dramatically that, at least under certain conditions, reward theory was inadequate. In doing so, dissonance research sounded a clarion call to cognitively oriented social psychologists, proclaiming in the most striking manner that human beings *think;* they do not always behave in a mechanistic manner. It demonstrated that human beings engage in all kinds of cognitive gymnastics aimed at justifying their own behavior.

Perhaps most important, dissonance theory inspired an enormous number and variety of hypotheses that were specific to the theory and could be tested in the laboratory. The wide array of research that dissonance theory has produced is truly astonishing. Dissonance research runs the gamut from decision-making to color preferences; from the socialization of children to curing people's snake phobias; from interpersonal attraction to antecedents of hunger and thirst; from the proselytizing behavior of religious zealots to the behavior of gamblers at racetracks; from inducing people to conserve water by taking showers to selective informational exposure; from helping people curb their temptation to cheat at a game of cards to inducing people to practice safer sex.

The impact of dissonance theory went even beyond the generation of new and exciting knowledge. Given the nature of the hypotheses we were testing, dissonance researchers were forced to develop a new experimental methodology; a powerful, high-impact set of procedures that allowed us to ask truly important questions in a very precise manner. As we all know, the laboratory tends to be an artificial environment. But dissonance research made it necessary to overcome that artificiality by developing a methodology that would enmesh subjects in a set of events—a drama, if you will—which made it impossible for them to avoid taking these events seriously.

In my writing on research methods (Aronson & Carlsmith, 1968; Aronson, Ellsworth, Carlsmith, & Gonzales, 1990) I've called this tactic *experimental reality* where, within the admittedly phony confines of the lab, real things are happening to real people. Because of the nature of our hypotheses, we could not afford the luxury—so common in contemporary research—of having subjects passively look at a videotape of events happening to someone else and then make judgments about them. Rather, our research questions required the construction of an elaborate scenario in which subjects became immersed. Thus, what dissonance research brought into focus more clearly than any other body of work is the fact that the social psychological laboratory, with all of its contrivances and complex scenarios, can produce clear, powerful effects which are conceptually replicable in both the laboratory and in the real world.

DISSONANCE AND THE SELF:
THE POWER OF SELF-PERSUASION

Research has shown that the persuasive effects in the above experiments are more powerful and more persistent than those resulting from persuasion techniques based on rewards, punishments, or source credibility (e.g., see Freedman, 1965). The major reason is that the arousal of dissonance always entails relatively high levels of *personal involvement,* and therefore the reduction of dissonance requires some form of *self-justification.* Let me elaborate. From the very outset, some of us who were working closely with the theory felt that, at its core, it led to clear and unambiguous predictions—but around the edges it was a little too vague. Several situations arose where it wasn't entirely clear what dissonance theory would predict, or indeed whether or not dissonance theory even made a prediction. Around 1958, the standing joke among Leon's research assistants was, "If you really want to be sure whether A is dissonant with B, ask Leon!" While this was said with our tongues firmly planted in our cheeks, it reflected the fact that we argued a lot about whether or not dissonance theory applied in a wide variety of situations.

What comes to mind, most specifically, are two strenuous running arguments that Leon and I had about two of his classic examples. The first involved a person stepping out of doors in a rainstorm and not getting wet. Festinger was convinced this would arouse a great deal of dissonance, while I had considerable difficulty seeing it. My disagreement went something like this: "What's that got to do with *him?* It's a strange phenomenon, all right—but unless he feared he was losing his mind, I don't see the dissonance."

The second was Festinger's classic example of a situation where dissonance theory *didn't* apply. This was the case of a man driving, late at night, on a lonely country road and getting a flat tire (Festinger, 1957, pp. 277–278). Lo and behold, when he opened the trunk of his car, he discovered he didn't have a jack. Leon maintained that, while the person would experience frustration, disappointment, perhaps even fear—there are no dissonant cognitions in that situation. My argument was succinct: "Of course there is dissonance! What kind of idiot would go driving late at night on a lonely country road without a jack in his car?" "But," Leon countered, "where are the dissonant cognitions?"

It took me a couple of years, but it gradually dawned on me that what was at the heart of my argument in both of those situations was the self-concept. That is, when I said above that dissonance theory made clear predictions *at its core,* what I implicitly meant by "at its core" were situations where the individual's self-concept was at issue. Thus, in the raindrop situation, as far as I could judge, the self was not involved. In the flat tire situation, the self-concept *was* involved; what was dissonant was (A) the driver's cognition about his idiotic behavior with (B) his self-concept of being a reasonably smart guy. Accordingly, I wrote a monograph (Aronson, 1960), in which I argued that dissonance theory makes its strongest predictions when an important element of the self-concept is threatened, typically when an individual performs a behavior that is inconsistent with his or her sense of self. Initially, I did not intend this to be a major modification of the theory—but only an attempt to tighten the predictions a bit. That is, in my opinion, this "tightening" retained the core notion of inconsistency but shifted the emphasis to the self-concept—thus clarifying more precisely when the theory did or did not apply. I believe that this minor modification of dissonance theory turned out to have important ramifications inasmuch as it increased the predictive power of the theory without seriously limiting its scope.

In addition, this modification uncovered a hidden assumption contained in the original theory. Festinger's original statement—and all of the early experiments—rested on the implicit assumption that individuals have a reasonably positive self-concept. But, if an individual considered himself to be a "schnook," he might expect himself to do schnooky things—like go through a severe initiation in order to get into a group, or say things that he didn't quite believe. For such individuals, dissonance would not be aroused under the same conditions as for persons with a favorable view of themselves. Rather, dissonance would occur when negative self-expectancies were violated—that is, when the person with a poor self-concept engages in a behavior that reflects positively on the self.

To test this assumption, Merrill Carlsmith and I conducted a simple little experiment which demonstrated that, under certain conditions, college students would be made uncomfortable with success; that they would prefer to be accurate in predicting their own behavior, even if it meant setting themselves up for failure. Specifically, we found that students who had developed negative self-expectancies regarding their performance on a task showed evidence of dissonance arousal when faced with success on that task. That is, after repeated failure at the task, subjects who later achieved a successful performance actually changed their responses from accurate to inaccurate ones, in order to preserve a consistent, though negative, self-concept (Aronson & Carlsmith, 1962). [In recent years, Swann and his students have confirmed this basic finding in a number of experiments and quasi-experiments (Swann, 1984; Swann, 1991; Swann & Pelham, 1988; Swann & Read, 1981).]

A few years later, I carried this reasoning a step further (Aronson, 1968; Aronson, Chase, Helmreich, & Ruhnke, 1974), elaborating on the centrality of the self-concept in dissonance processes and suggesting that, in this regard, people generally strive to maintain a sense of self that is both consistent *and* positive. That is, because most people have relatively favorable views of themselves, they want to see themselves as:

(1) competent
(2) moral
(3) able to predict their own behavior.

In sum, efforts to reduce dissonance involve a process of self-justification because, in most instances, people experience dissonance after engaging in an action that leaves them feeling stupid, immoral, or confused (see Aronson, Chase, Helmreich, & Ruhnke, 1974). Moreover, the greater the personal commitment or self-involvement implied by the action and the smaller the *external* justification for that action, the greater the dissonance and, therefore, the more powerful the need for self-justification. Thus, in the Festinger-Carlsmith experiment, the act of deceiving another person would make one feel immoral or guilty. To reduce that dissonance, one must convince oneself that little or no deception was involved—in other words, that the task *was,* in fact, a rather interesting activity. By justifying one's actions in this fashion, one is able to restore a sense of self as morally good. In the Aronson & Mills experiment, going through hell and high water in order to gain admission to a boring discussion group is dissonance with one's self-concept as a smart and reasonable person who makes smart and reasonable decisions.

SCOPE VS. TIGHTNESS IN THEORY-BUILDING

All theories are lies. That is, all theories are only approximations of the empirical domain they are trying to describe. Accordingly, it is inevitable that theories will evolve and change in order to more accurately reflect new data that are being generated. Indeed, it is the *duty* of theorists to modify their theory in the face of new data and new ideas. Festinger understood this better than most scientists. At the same time, understandably, he was deeply enamored of both the elegant simplicity and the breadth of his original theoretical statement. Accordingly, when I first came out with the self-concept notion of dissonance, Festinger was not pleased. He felt that, although my revision had led to some interesting research, he also felt that, conceptually, I was limiting the scope of the theory far too much. I agreed that the scope was a bit smaller, but I believed that the increased accuracy of prediction (the added tightness) was worth the slightly more limited scope. In 1987, while serving as the discussant at an APA symposium on cognitive dissonance, Festinger acknowledged the dilemma of the theorist who has a hard time seeing his theory change—yet, who knows that change it must. (One might say that this is a situation bound to produce considerable dissonance in the theorist!) In typical fashion, Leon poked fun at himself for trying to cling to the original conceptualization even though he knew better:

> No theory is going to be inviolate. Let me put it clearly. The only kind of theory that can be proposed and ever will be proposed that absolutely will remain inviolate for decades, certainly centuries, is a theory that is not testable. If a theory is at all testable, it will not remain unchanged. It has to change. All theories are wrong. One doesn't ask about theories, can I show that they are wrong or can I show that they are right, but rather one asks, how much of the empirical realm can it handle and how must it be modified and changed as it matures.
>
> As a lot of people know, I ended up leaving social psychology, meaning dissonance theory, and I want to clarify that. Lack of activity is not the same as lack of interest. Lack of activity is not desertion. I left and stopped doing research on the theory of dissonance because I was in a total rut. The only thing I could think about was how correct the original statement had been—how every word in that book was perfect. So to me I did a good thing for cognitive dissonance by leaving it. I think if I had stayed in it I might have retarded progress for cognitive dissonance for at least a decade.

In theory building, there is always a tension between scope and precision; generally speaking, the more precise one usually gains precision at the price of scope. In my own (admittedly biased) opinion, the self-concept notion strikes exactly the right balance between scope and precision.

THE SELF-CONCEPT AND THE INDUCTION OF HYPOCRISY

In recent years, the self-concept notion of dissonance has led us into areas of investigation that would not have been feasible under the rubric of Festinger's initial formulation. One of these involves the induction of feelings of hypocrisy. This discovery came about quite by accident. At the time, I was not even thinking about theory development but was struggling to find an effective way to convince sexually active college students to use condoms in this, the era of AIDS. The problem is not an easy one to solve—because it transcends the simple conveying of information to rational people. College students already have the requisite information; that is, virtually all sexually active college students know that condoms are an effective way to prevent AIDS. The problem is that the vast majority are not using condoms—because they consider them to be a nuisance, unromantic and unspontaneous. In my research, I had run into a stone wall; I had tried several of the traditional, direct persuasive techniques (powerful videos, aimed at arousing fear or at eroticizing the condom) with very limited success. Whatever impact my videos did have was of very short duration; our subjects would try condoms once or twice and then stop using them.

Eventually, I thought about using the counter-attitudinal attitude paradigm. That is, why not try to get people to argue against their own attitudes—as in the Festinger-Carlsmith experiment? On the surface, it seemed like a great idea. After all, we had found that this strategy was powerful and, when judiciously applied, had long-term effects on attitudes and behavior—precisely what was needed in this societal situation. But wait a minute: In the condom-use situation, there were no counter-attitudinal attitudes to address. That is, our surveys and interviews had demonstrated that sexually active young adults already were in favor of people using condoms to prevent AIDS. *They simply weren't using them.* They seemed to be in a state of denial—denying that the dangers of unprotected sex applied to them— in the same way they applied to everyone else. How could we invoke the counter-attitudinal attitude paradigm if there was no counter-attitude to invoke?

It occurred to me that the solution had to come from the self-concept—because being in denial is not an attractive thing to be doing. The challenge was to find a way to place individuals in situations where the act of denial would be unfeasible because it would conflict, in some way, with their positive images of themselves. And then it struck me. Suppose you are a sexually active college student and, like most, (a) you do not use condoms regularly and (b) being in denial, you have managed to blind yourself to the dangers inherent in having unprotected sex. Suppose, on going home for Christmas vacation, you find that Charlie, your 16-year-old kid brother has just discovered sex and is in the process of boasting to you about his many and varied sexual encounters. What do you say to him? Chances are, as a caring, responsible older sibling, you will dampen his enthusiasm a bit by warning him about the dangers of AIDS and other sexually transmitted diseases, and urge him to, at least, take proper precautions—by using condoms.

Suppose that I am a friend of the family who was invited to dinner and who happened to overhear this exchange between you and your kid brother. What if I were to pull you aside and say, "That was very good advice you gave Charlie—I am very proud of you for being so responsible; by the way, how frequently do *you* use condoms?" In other words, by getting you to think about that, I am confronting you with your own hypocrisy. According to the self-concept version of the theory, this would produce dissonance because you are not practicing what you are preaching. That is, for most people, their self-concept does not include behaving like a hypocrite.

My students and I then proceeded to design and conduct a simple little experiment following the scenario outlined above (Aronson, Fried, & Stone, 1990). In a 2×2 factorial design, in one condition, college students were induced to make a videotape in which they urged their audience to use condoms; they were told that the video would be shown to high school students. In the other major condition, the college students simply rehearsed the arguments without making the video. Cutting across these conditions was the "mindfulness" manipulation: In one set of conditions, our subjects were made mindful of the fact that they themselves were not practicing what they were preaching; to accomplish this we asked them to think about all those situations where they found it particularly difficult or impossible to use condoms in the recent past. In the other set of conditions, we did nothing to make the students mindful of their past failures to use condoms.

The one cell where we expected to produce dissonance is the one high in hypocrisy—i.e., where subjects made the video and were given the opportunity to dredge up memories of situations where they failed to use condoms. Again, how did we expect them to reduce dissonance? By increasing the strength of their intention to use condoms in the future. And that is precisely what we got. Those subjects who were in the high dissonance (hypocrisy) condition showed the greatest intention to increase their use of condoms. Moreover, two months later, there was a tendency for the subjects in the high dissonance cell to report using condoms a higher percentage of the time than in any of the other three cells.

In a follow-up experiment (Stone, Aronson, Crain, Winslow & Fried, 1994) we strengthened the manipulations of the initial experiment and used a "behavioroid" measure of the dependent variable. Specifically, in each of the conditions described above, subjects were subsequently provided with an opportunity to purchase condoms at a very substantial discount (10 cents each). The results were unequivocally as predicted. Fully 83% of the subjects in the hypocrisy condition purchased condoms; this was a significantly greater percentage than in each of the other three conditions, none of which were reliably different from each other. The effect was a powerful and long lasting one: Three months after the induction of hypocrisy, a telephone survey indicated that 92% of the subjects in the hypocrisy condition were still using condoms regularly—a figure that was significantly different from the control conditions.

Subsequently, we increased our confidence in the efficacy of the "induction of hypocrisy" paradigm, testing the paradigm in a different situation, a situation where we could get a direct behavioral measure of the dependent variable. We found one in the shower room of our campus field house. As you may know, central California has a chronic water shortage. On our campus, the administration is constantly trying to find ways to induce students to conserve water. So we decided to test our hypothesis by using dissonance theory and the induction of hypocrisy to convince students to take shorter showers. What we discovered is that although it is impossible, within the bounds of propriety, to follow people into their bedrooms and observe their condom-using behavior, it was easily possible to follow people into the shower rooms and observe their shower-taking behavior.

In this experiment (Dickerson, Thibodeau, Aronson & Miller, 1992), we went to the university field house and intercepted college women who had just finished swimming in a highly chlorinated pool and were on their way to take a shower. Just like in the condom experiment, it was a 2 × 2 design in which we varied commitment and mindfulness. In the commitment conditions, each student was asked if she would be willing to sign a flyer encouraging people to conserve water at the field house. The students were told that the flyers would be displayed on posters; each was shown a sample poster—a large, colorful, very public display. The flyer read: "Take shorter showers. Turn off water while soaping up. If I can do it, so can you!" After she signed the flyer, we thanked her for her time, and she proceeded to the shower room, where our undergraduate research assistant (blind to condition) was unobtrusively waiting (with hidden waterproof stopwatch) to time the student's shower.

In the mindful conditions we also asked the students to respond to a water conservation "survey," which consisted of items designed to make them aware of their pro-conservation attitudes and the fact that their typical showering behavior was sometimes wasteful.

The results are consistent with those in the condom experiment: We found dissonance effects only in the cell where the subjects were preaching what they were not always practicing. That is, in the condition where the students were induced to advocate short showers and were made mindful of their own past behavior, they took very short showers. To be specific, in the high dissonance cell, the length of the average shower (which, because of the chlorine in the swimming pool, included a shampoo and cream rinse) averaged just over three and a half minutes (that's short!) and was significantly shorter than in the control condition.

How can we be certain that dissonance is involved in these experiments? Although the data are consistent with the self-concept formulation of dissonance theory, there is another plausible interpretation. It is conceivable that the effects of the hypocrisy manipulation may have been due to the effects of priming. The combination of pro-attitudinal advocacy and the salience of past behavior may have served, in an additive fashion, to make subjects' positive attitudes toward condom use or water conservation highly accessible, thus fostering a stronger correspondence between their attitudes and behavior (e.g., Fazio, 1986). What is needed to pin it down was evidence that the hypocrisy effect involves physiological arousal, thereby indicating the presence of dissonance rather than the mere influence of attitude salience.

An experiment by Fried & Aronson (1995) provide exactly this sort of evidence. Within the context of the hypocrisy paradigm, this experiment employed a "misattribution of arousal" manipulation, a strategy brilliantly developed in earlier research to document the existence of dissonance as an uncomfortable state of arousal by Zanna & Cooper (1974). Zanna & Cooper found that, when subjects are given an opportunity to misattribute their arousal to a source other than their dissonance-arousing behavior—for example, to an overheated room, a placebo, or glaring fluorescent lights—the attitude change typically associated with dissonance reduction no longer occurs.

Using a modified version of the earlier condom experiments, Fried and Aronson's study required subjects to compose and deliver pro-attitudinal, videotaped speeches advocating the importance of recycling. These speeches were ostensibly to be shown to various groups as part of a campaign to increase participation in recycling programs on campus and in the larger community. Hypocrisy was induced in half the subjects by asking them to list recent examples of times when they had failed to recycle; the other half simply wrote and delivered the speech, without being reminded of their wasteful behavior. In addition, half the subjects in each condition were given an opportunity to misattribute arousal to various environmental factors within the laboratory setting. Specifically, subjects were asked to answer questions regarding the room's lighting, temperature, and noise level, including how these ambient factors might have affected them. (This was accomplished under the guise of asking subjects to rate the room's suitability for use as laboratory space—a request that was made to appear unrelated to the activities in which subjects were participating.) To summarize, pro-attitudinal advocacy was held constant, and the salience of past behavior and the opportunity for misattribution were manipulated, yielding a 2×2 factorial design with the following conditions: (1) hypocrisy (high salience); (2) hypocrisy with misattribution; (3) no hypocrisy (low salience); and (4) no hypocrisy with misattribution. Dissonance reduction was measured by asking subjects to volunteer to help a local recycling organization by making phone calls soliciting support for recycling.

The results of this experiment revealed that arousal was indeed present within the hypocrisy conditions. Hypocrisy subjects who were not afforded the opportunity to misattribute the source of their arousal volunteered significantly more often, and for longer blocks of time, than subjects in the other experimental conditions. Moreover, volunteer behavior for hypocrisy subjects who were allowed to misattribute their arousal was no greater than for subjects who were not exposed to the hypocrisy manipulation.

HYPOCRISY: DISSONANCE IN THE ABSENCE OF AVERSIVE CONSEQUENCES

As I stated above, the initial reason for the development of the hypocrisy paradigm was couched in my attempt to apply dissonance theory to the solution of a societal problem. The hidden bonus was that it also sheds some light on an interesting theoretical controversy among dissonance theorists. I should say, at the outset, that dissonance research tends to be a family business—thus, the controversies are invariably friendly arguments—around the dinner table as it were. One such controversy involves the "new look" theory developed several years ago by Cooper and Fazio (1984). In examining the early forced compliance experiments, like the Festinger-Carlsmith experiment and the Nel, Helmreich & Aronson experiment,

Cooper and Fazio made an interesting discovery: In these experiments, not only was inconsistency present, but aversive consequences were also always present; that is, lying to another person is usually aversive because it does the recipient harm. Their next step was a bold one: Cooper and Fazio asserted that dissonance is not due merely to inconsistent cognitions at all—but rather, is aroused only when an individual feels personally responsible for bringing about an aversive or unwanted event. Or, to put it in my terms, dissonance is caused solely by harming another person—which is a threat to the person's self-concept as a morally good human being.

Although I always appreciated the boldness implicit in Cooper and Fazio's theorizing, I could never bring myself to buy into the notion that aversive consequences are essential for the existence of dissonance. Moreover, in terms of our earlier discussion of "scope vs. tightness," it seems to me that Cooper and Fazio's conception is limiting the scope of the theory enormously, while gaining nothing in tightness that wasn't already present in the self-concept notion.

The ultimate solution to a theoretical dispute is to do an experiment. How do you test this difference empirically? Several years ago, I was at a loss as to how to produce inconsistency in the Festinger/Carlsmith type of experiment without also producing aversive consequences for the recipient of one's message. After all, if you are misleading another person, by telling him something you believe is false, then you are always bringing about aversive consequences, aren't you? But, without quite realizing it, my students and I seem to have stumbled onto the solution with the hypocrisy experiments. In this procedure, the subjects are preaching what they are not practicing (and are therefore experiencing dissonance), but where are the aversive consequences for the audience in the condom experiment? There are none. Indeed, to the extent that the "hypocrites" succeed in being persuasive, far from producing aversive consequences for the recipients they may well be saving their lives. And still, it is clear from the data that our subjects were experiencing dissonance. For a fuller discussion of this theoretical controversy see Thibodeau & Aronson (1992).

SELF-JUSTIFICATION, SELF-ESTEEM, AND SELF-COMPASSION

From the very beginning I found dissonance theory to be a powerful explanation for a wide swath of human behavior. The scientist in me was always delighted by the exciting, nonobvious predictions generated by the theory, as well as the creative experimentation used to test these predictions. But, at the same time, the humanist in me was always a bit troubled by the rather bleak, rather unappetizing picture the theory painted of the human condition—forever striving to justify our actions after the fact. Over the past few years, my reasoning about dissonance and the self-concept has led me to speculate about how a person's self-esteem might interact with the experiencing and reduction of dissonance. These speculations might suggest a more complete picture of human nature. Let me begin this speculation by calling your attention to two intriguing experiments in the dissonance literature. First, let us consider an experiment I did a great many years ago with David Mettee (Aronson & Mettee, 1968), in which we demonstrated that, if we temporarily raised an individual's self-esteem, it would serve to insulate him from performing an immoral act like cheating. We found that the higher self-esteem served to make the anticipation of doing something immoral more dissonant than it would have been otherwise. Thus, when our subjects were put in a situation in which they had an opportunity to win money by unobtrusively cheating at a game of cards, they were able to say to themselves, in effect, "Wonderful people like me don't cheat!" And they succeeded in resisting the temptation to cheat to a greater extent than those in the control condition.

Now, let us consider an experiment performed by David Glass (1964). In this study, people were put in a situation where they were induced to deliver a series of electric shocks to other people. They then had an opportunity to evaluate their victims. Dissonance theory predicts that if individuals are feeling awful about having hurt someone, one way to reduce the dissonance is to convince themselves that their victim is a dreadful person who deserved to suffer the pain of electric shock. What Glass found was that it was precisely those individuals who had the highest self-esteem who derogated their victims the most. Consider the irony: It is precisely because I think I am such a nice person that, if I do something that causes you pain, I must convince myself you are a rat. In other words, because nice guys like me don't go around hurting innocent people, you must have deserved every nasty thing I did to you. On the other hand, if I already consider myself to be something of a scoundrel, then causing others to suffer does not introduce as much dissonance; therefore, I have less of a need to convince myself that you deserved your fate. The ultimate tragedy, of course, is that, once I succeed in convincing myself that you are a dreadful person, it lowers my inhibitions against doing you further damage.

Taking the two experiments together, Aronson & Mettee showed that high self-esteem can serve as a buffer against immoral behavior, while Glass showed that once a person commits an immoral action, high self-esteem leads him into a situation where he might commit further mischief. In pondering these two experiments, I have come to the conclusion that it is far too simplistic to think of self-esteem as a one-dimensional phenomenon—either high or low. I would like to suggest that self-esteem can be high or low *and* either fragile or well-grounded. "Well-grounded" in this context means that a positive self-image has been developed and held during a great deal of past behavior, whereas "fragile" suggests that a positive self-image has never been securely developed. People with high/well-grounded self-esteem need not be concerned with developing or verifying their self-images, and can enter situations with the confident knowledge that they are competent, moral people. On the other hand, because of their lack of a secure self-image, people with high/fragile self-esteem are overly concerned with trying to preserve images of themselves as being competent and moral at all costs.

Typically, people with high/fragile self-esteem in their zeal to maintain a belief in their terrificness, often boast about their achievements—trying desperately to convince themselves and others that they are terrific. But their boasting behavior, their misjudgments, their errors, the wrong turns they make because they are thinking more about themselves than the situation they are in—all this tends to shatter the fragile images they are trying to defend. As a result, they frequently feel like imposters, and are forever trying to prove that they aren't. Thus, they are always trying to win every possible argument, pushing themselves to believe they are always right, avoiding and explaining away failures and mistakes instead of attending to them long enough to learn from them, justifying their behavior to themselves at every turn.

In contrast, people with high/well-grounded self-esteem are not invested in winning arguments for winning's sake, don't need to believe they're always right, don't need to explain away failures and mistakes, and don't need to engage in the almost frantic self-justification in which high/fragile self-esteem people constantly engage. Instead, when they fail or make mistakes, people with high/well-grounded self-esteem can look at their failures and mistakes and learn from them. For example, a person with high, well-grounded self-esteem can look at his or her errors, and say, in effect, "Oh, my god, I screwed up—I did a stupid (or hurtful, or immoral) thing. But just because I did a stupid (or hurtful, or immoral) thing this time, this doesn't make me a stupid (or hurtful, or immoral) person. Let me look at it. How did it come about? How can I make it better? What can I learn from this situation so that I might decrease the possibility that I'll screw up in a similar way again?"

I would speculate that the majority of Glass's high self-esteem participants would have self-esteem that fits with my notion of high/fragile. This is why they rushed to derogate their victim. But if a person had high self-esteem that was well-grounded, that is, if she or he had a very secure, positive self-image, they would not use derogation of the victim as a way to reduce their dissonance caused by the psychological inconsistency between the cognitions "I just did a cruel thing" and "I am a warm, generous person."

Continuing my speculation, I would argue that the key to developing high/well-grounded self-esteem lies in the ability to look at one's shortcomings and mistakes and failures with full attention instead of turning away and trying to ignore them or explain them away. To be able to do this requires a good measure of constructive self-compassion. One must be able to look at one's errors with understanding and sympathy and have the ability to forgive oneself for not being perfect before picking up, learning from those errors, and going on. Self-compassion is not complacency. Rather, self-compassion implies the ability to examine one's imperfect behavior, feel truly bad about any harm one has done or any stupidities one has committed—and not rush to justify the behavior. People who have constructive self-compassion will examine their stupidities and failures, consider ways to atone for the hurt they have caused others, and eventually pick themselves up, brush themselves off, learn from their mistakes, and move on. In other words, people with constructive self-compassion avoid three kinds of mistakes: trying to write off all errors as the other guy's fault; glibly forgiving themselves for everything, and moving on without learning anything; and neurotic self-flagellation.

I believe that self-compassion can be taught. That is, I believe it is possible to teach people to become more self-compassionate by helping them see mistakes not as terrible things to be denied or justified, but rather, as inevitable at worst and, at best, as golden opportunities for learning. It is an uphill struggle—because our culture is a judgmental one that does not take kindly to human error. As I have written elsewhere (Fried & Aronson, 1995), I find it ironic that perhaps the most prominent place where the American culture recognizes error as something that is inevitable is in our national pastime, baseball, where the very box score consists of runs, hits, and errors. In short, in the box score, errors, although certainly not desirable, are seen as part of the game—a part of the game of baseball—and perhaps a part of the game of life, as well. As I write this, the news is full of General Joseph Ralston, who was President Clinton's top choice to become Chairman of the Joint Chiefs of Staff. He has just withdrawn his name from consideration after having been pilloried by congress and the media because apparently he had a love affair some thirteen years ago while separated from his wife. From the outcry, it would appear that most Americans consider his actions immoral. But are they unforgivable? Do his actions disqualify him from holding the position as our nation's top military officer? If so, in what way? These are questions that must be addressed seriously and with some compassion. It is at least conceivable that many of the people who are judging General Ralston most harshly are not, themselves, beyond reproach. How do we account for that hypocrisy?

Needless to say, it is risky for a writer to be referring to a very current event in an essay that he intends to be around for a few years; there is nothing as stale or forgettable as yesterday's scandal. But I wanted to mention the Ralston case because it is not an isolated incident; rather, I think it illustrates the kind of hypocritical witch-hunting that has become all too common in contemporary American life. I have a strong guess that if we can learn to become more adept at facing up to our own mistakes in order to learn from them, perhaps we can develop the kind of well-grounded self-esteem that will enable us to resist rushing to reduce dissonance in situations that result in harsh judgment and a high degree of cognitive distortion. At the same time, it may render us a bit more tolerant of the mistakes of others and perhaps a bit less hypocritical in our orientation to the less-than-perfect behavior of our public figures.

Admittedly, at this point, my reasoning in this entire section is purely speculative. At the same time, it is comforting to know that I am not alone in these kinds of speculations. Very recently, Meg Rohan (1996), a young Australian social psychologist has independently begun a research project on various aspects of self-esteem that seems headed in the same direction—attesting, among other things, to the continuing vitality of Festinger's revolutionary little theory.

References

ARONSON, E. The cognitive and behavioral consequences of the confirmation and disconfirmation of expectancies. Grant proposal submitted to the National Science Foundation. Harvard University, 1960.

ARONSON, E. Dissonance theory: Progress and problems. In R. P. Abelson, E. Aronson, W. J. Mcguire, T. M. Newcomb, M. J. Rosenberg, & P. H. Tannenbaum, (Eds.), *Theories of cognitive consistency: A sourcebook.* Skokie, IL: Rand-McNally, 1968.

ARONSON, E., & CARLSMITH, J. M. Performance expectancy as a determinant of actual performance. *Journal of Abnormal and Social Psychology,* 1962, **65,** 178–182.

ARONSON, E., & CARLSMITH, J. M. Experimentation in social psychology. In G. Lindzey & E. Aronson (Eds.) *The handbook of social psychology* (2nd Edition). Reading, Mass: Addison-Wesley, 1968.

ARONSON, E., CHASE, T., HELMREICH, R., & RUHNKE, R. A two-factor theory of dissonance reduction: The effect of feeling stupid or feeling awful on opinion change. *International Journal for Research and Communication,* 1974, **3,** 59–74.

ARONSON, E., ELLSWORTH, P., CARLSMITH, J. M., & GONZALES, M. H. *Methods of research in social psychology.* New York: McGraw Hill, 1990.

ARONSON, E., FRIED, C., & STONE, J. Overcoming denial and increasing the intention to use condoms through the induction of hypocrisy. *American Journal of Public Health,* 1991, **81,** 1636–1638.

ARONSON, E., & METTEE, D. Dishonest behavior as a function of differential levels of induced self-esteem. *Journal of Personality and Social Psychology,* 1968, **9,** 121–127.

ARONSON, E., & MILLS, J. The effect of severity of initiation on liking for a group. *Journal of Abnormal and Social Psychology,* 1959, **59,** 177–181.

ASCH, S. E. Effects of group pressure upon the modification and distortion of judgments. In H. Guetzkow (Ed.), *Groups, leadership and men,* pp. 177–190. Pittsburgh: Carnegie Press, 1951.

COHEN, A. R. An experiment on small rewards for discrepant compliance and attitude change. In J. W. Brehm & A. R. Cohen (Eds.), *Explorations in cognitive dissonance,* 1962, (pp. 73–78). New York: Wiley.

COOPER, J., & FAZIO, R. H. A new look at dissonance theory. In L. Berkowitz (Ed.), *Advances in experimental social psychology* (Vol. 17, pp. 229–266). Orlando, FL: Academic Press, 1984.

DICKERSON, C., THIBODEAU, R., ARONSON, E., & MILLER. Using cognitive dissonance to encourage water conservation. *Journal of Applied Social Psychology,* 1992, **22,** 841–854.

FAZIO, R. H. On the power and functionality of attitudes: The role of attitude accessibility. In A. R. Pratkanis, S. J. Breckler, & A. G. Greenwald (Eds.), *Attitude structure and function* (pp. 153–179). Hillsdale, NJ: Lawrence Erlbaum, 1989.

FESTINGER, L. *A theory of cognitive dissonance.* Evanston, Ill.: Row, Peterson, 1957.

FESTINGER, L., & CARLSMITH, J. M. Cognitive consequences of forced compliance. *Journal of Abnormal and Social Psychology,* 1959, **58,** 203–211.

FREEDMAN, J. Long term behavioral effects of cognitive dissonance. *Journal of Experimental Social Psychology,* 1965, **1,** 145–155.

FRIED, C., & ARONSON, E. Hypocrisy, misattribution, and dissonance reduction: A demonstration of dissonance in the absence of aversive consequences. *Personality and Social Psychology Bulletin,* 1995, **21,** 925–933.

GLASS, D. Changing in liking as a means of reducing cognitive discrepancies between self-esteem and aggression. *Journal of Personality,* 1964, **32,** 531–549.

HOVLAND, C. I., & WEISS, W. The influence of source credibility on communication effectiveness. *Public Opinion Quarterly,* 1951, **15,** 635–650.

NEL, E., HELMREICH, R., & ARONSON, E. Opinion change in the advocate as a function of the persuasibility of the audience: A clarification of the meaning of dissonance. *Journal of Personality and Social Psychology,* 1969, **12,** 117–124.

ROHAN, M. J. The Performance-Integrity Framework: A new solution to an old problem. Unpublished doctoral thesis. University of Waterloo, Ontario, Canada, 1996.

STONE, J., ARONSON, E., CRAIN, A. L., WINSLOW, M. P., & FRIED, C. B. Inducing hypocrisy as a means of encouraging young adults to use condoms. *Personality and Social Psychology Bulletin,* 1994, **20,** 116–128.

SWANN, W. B., JR. Quest for accuracy in person perception: A matter of pragmatics. *Psychological Review,* 1984, **91,** 457–477.

SWANN, W. B., JR. To be adored or to be known? The interplay of self-enhancement and self-verification. In R. M. Sorrentino & E. T. Higgins (Eds.) *Motivation and Cognition.* New York: Guilford, 1991.

SWANN, W. B., JR., & PELHAM, B. W. The social construction of identity: Self-verification through friend and intimate selection. Unpublished manuscript, University of Texas-Austin, 1988.

SWANN, W. B., JR., & READ, S. J. Acquiring self-knowledge: The search for feedback that fits. *Journal of Personality and Social Psychology,* 1981, **41,** 1119–1128.

THIBODEAU, R., & ARONSON, E. Taking a closer look: Reasserting the role of the self-concept in dissonance theory. *Personality and Social Psychology Bulletin,* 1992, **18,** 591–602.

ZANNA, M., & COOPER, J. Dissonance and the pill: An attribution approach to studying the arousal properties of dissonance. *Journal of Personality and Social Psychology,* 1974, **29,** 703–709.

17

Compliance Without Pressure:
The Foot-in-the-Door Technique

Jonathan L. Freedman and Scott C. Fraser

Two experiments were conducted to test the proposition that once someone has agreed to a small request he is more likely to comply with a larger request. The first study demonstrated this effect when the same person made both requests. The second study extended this to the situation in which different people made the two requests. Several experimental groups were run in an effort to explain these results, and possible explanations are discussed.

How can a person be induced to do something he would rather not do? This question is relevant to practically every phase of social life, from stopping at a traffic light to stopping smoking, from buying Brand X to buying savings bonds, from supporting the March of Dimes to supporting the Civil Rights Act.

One common way of attacking the problem is to exert as much pressure as possible on the reluctant individual in an effort to force him to comply. This technique has been the focus of a considerable amount of experimental research. Work on attitude change, conformity, imitation, and obedience has all tended to stress the importance of the degree of external pressure. The prestige of the communicator (Kelman and Hovland, 1953), degree of discrepancy of the communication (Hovland and Pritzker, 1957), size of the group disagreeing with the subject (Asch, 1951), perceived power of the model (Bandura, Ross, and Ross, 1963), etc., are the kinds of variables that have been studied. This impressive body of work, added to

Reprinted with permission from the authors and *The Journal of Personality and Social Psychology,* Vol. 4, No. 2, 1966. Copyright © 1966 by the American Psychological Association.

The authors are grateful to Evelyn Bless for assisting in the running of the second experiment reported here. These studies were supported in part by Grant GS-196 from the National Science Foundation. The first study was conducted while the junior author was supported by an NSF undergraduate summer fellowship.

the research on rewards and punishments in learning, has produced convincing evidence that greater external pressure generally leads to greater compliance with the wishes of the experimenter. The one exception appears to be situations involving the arousal of cognitive dissonance in which, once discrepant behavior has been elicited from the subject, the greater the pressure that was used to elicit the behavior, the less subsequent change occurs (Festinger and Carlsmith, 1959). But even in this situation one critical element is the amount of external pressure exerted.

Clearly, then, under most circumstances the more pressure that can be applied, the more likely it is that the individual will comply. There are, however, many times when for ethical, moral, or practical reasons it is difficult to apply much pressure when the goal is to produce compliance with a minimum of apparent pressure, as in the forced-compliance studies involving dissonance arousal. And even when a great deal of pressure is possible, it is still important to maximize the compliance it produces. Thus, factors other than external pressure are often quite critical in determining degree of compliance. What are these factors?

Although rigorous research on the problem is rather sparse, the fields of advertising, propaganda, politics, etc., are by no means devoid of techniques designed to produce compliance in the absence of external pressure (or to maximize the effectiveness of the pressure that is used, which is really the same problem). One assumption about compliance that has often been made either explicitly or implicitly is that once a person has been induced to comply with a small request he is more likely to comply with a larger demand. This is the principle that is commonly referred to as the foot-in-the-door or gradation technique and is reflected in the saying that if you "give them an inch, they'll take a mile." It was, for example, supposed to be one of the basic techniques upon which the Korean brainwashing tactics were based (Schein, Schneier, and Barker, 1961), and, in a somewhat different sense, one basis for Nazi propaganda during 1940 (Bruner, 1941). It also appears to be implicit in many advertising campaigns which attempt to induce the consumer to do anything relating to the product involved, even sending back a card saying he does not want the product.

The most relevant piece of experimental evidence comes from a study of conformity done by Deutsch and Gerard (1955). Some subjects were faced with incorrect group judgments first in a series in which the stimuli were not present during the actual judging and then in a series in which they were present, while the order of the memory and visual series was reversed for other subjects. For both groups the memory series produced more conformity, and when the memory series came first there was more total conformity to the group judgments. It seems likely that this order effect occurred because, as the authors suggest, once conformity is elicited at all it is more likely to occur in the future. Although this kind of conformity is probably somewhat different from compliance as described above, this finding certainly lends some support to the foot-in-the-door idea. The present research attempted to provide a rigorous, more direct test of this notion as it applies to compliance and to provide data relevant to several alternative ways of explaining the effect.

EXPERIMENT I

The basic paradigm was to ask some subjects (Performance condition) to comply first with a small request and then three days later with a larger, related request. Other subjects (One-Contact condition) were asked to comply only with the large request. The hypothesis was that more subjects in the Performance condition than in the One-Contact condition would comply with the larger request.

Two additional conditions were included in an attempt to specify the essential difference between these two major conditions. The Performance subjects were asked to perform a small favor, and, if they agreed, they did it. The question arises whether the act of agreeing itself is critical or whether actually carrying it out was necessary. To assess this a third group of subjects (Agree-Only) was asked the first request, but, even if they agreed, they did not carry it out. Thus, they were identical to the Performance group except that they were not given the opportunity of performing the request.

Another difference between the two main conditions was that at the time of the larger request the subjects in the Performance condition were more familiar with the experimenter than were the other subjects. The Performance subjects had been contacted twice, heard his voice more, discovered that the questions were not dangerous, and so on. It is possible that this increased familiarity would serve to decrease the fear and suspicion of a strange voice on the phone and might accordingly increase the likelihood of the subjects agreeing to the larger request. To control for this a fourth condition was run (Familiarization) which attempted to give the subjects as much familiarity with the experimenter as in the Performance and Agree-Only conditions with the only difference being that no request was made.

The major prediction was that more subjects in the Performance condition would agree to the large request than in any of the other conditions, and that the One-Contact condition would produce the least compliance. Since the importance of agreement and familiarity was essentially unknown, the expectation was that the Agree-Only and Familiarization conditions would produce intermediate amounts of compliance.

Method

The prediction stated above was tested in a field experiment in which housewives were asked to allow a survey team of five or six men to come into their homes for two hours to classify the household products they used. This large request was made under four different conditions: after an initial contact in which the subject had been asked to answer a few questions about the kinds of soaps she used, and the questions were actually asked (Performance condition); after an identical contact in which the questions were not actually asked (Agree-Only condition); after an initial contact in which no request was made (Familiarization condition); or after no initial contact (One-Contact condition). The dependent measure was simply whether or not the subject agreed to the large request.

Procedure.   The subjects were 156 Palo Alto, California, housewives, 36 in each condition, who were selected at random from the telephone directory. An additional 12 subjects distributed about equally among the three two-contact conditions could not be reached for the second contact and are not included in the data analysis. Subjects were assigned randomly to the various conditions, except that the Familiarization condition was added to the design after the other three conditions had been completed. All contacts were by telephone by the same experimenter who identified himself as the same person each time. Calls were made only in the morning. For the three groups that were contacted twice, the first call was made on either Monday or Tuesday and the second always three days later. All large requests were made on either Thursday or Friday.

At the first contact, the experimenter introduced himself by name and said that he was from the California Consumers' Group. In the Performance condition he then proceeded:

> We are calling you this morning to ask if you would answer a number of questions about what household products you use so that we could have this information for our public service publication, "The Guide." Would you be willing to give us this information for our survey?

If the subject agreed, she was asked a series of eight innocuous questions dealing with household soaps (e.g., "What brand of soap do you use in your kitchen sink?") She was then thanked for her cooperation, and the contact terminated.

Another condition (Agree-Only) was run to assess the importance of actually carrying out the request as opposed to merely agreeing to it. The only difference between this and the Performance condition was that, if the subject agreed to answer the questions, the experimenter thanked her, but said that he was just lining up respondents for the survey and would contact her if needed.

A third condition was included to check on the importance of the subject's greater familiarity with the experimenter in the two-contact conditions. In this condition the experimenter introduced himself, described the organization he worked for and the survey it was conducting, listed the questions he was asking and then said that he was calling merely to acquaint the subject with the existence of his organization. In other words, these subjects were contacted, spent as much time on the phone with the experimenter as the Performance subjects did, heard all the questions, but neither agreed to answer them nor answered them.

In all of these two-contact conditions some subjects did not agree to the requests or even hung up before the requests were made. Every subject who answered the phone was included in the analysis of the results and was contacted for the second request regardless of her extent of cooperativeness during the first contact. In other words, no subject who could be contacted the appropriate number of times was discarded from any of the four conditions.

The large request was essentially identical for all subjects. The experimenter called, identified himself, and said either that his group was expanding its survey (in the case of the two-contact conditions) or that it was conducting a survey (in the One-Contact condition). In all four conditions he then continued:

> The survey will involve five or six men from our staff coming into your home some morning for about two hours to enumerate and classify all the household products that you have. They will have to have full freedom in your house to go through the cupboards and storage places. Then all this information will be used in the writing of the reports for our public service publication, "The Guide."

If the subject agreed to the request, she was thanked and told that at the present time the experimenter was merely collecting names of people who were willing to take part and that she would be contacted if it were decided to use her in the survey. If she did not agree, she was thanked for her time. This terminated the experiment.

Results

Apparently even the small request was not considered trivial by some of the subjects. Only about two-thirds of the subjects in the Performance and Agree-Only conditions agreed to answer the questions about household soaps. It might be noted that none of those who refused the first request later agreed to the large request, although as stated previously all subjects who were contacted for the small request are included in the data for those groups.

Our major prediction was that subjects who had agreed to and carried out a small request (Performance condition) would subsequently be more likely to comply with a larger request than would subjects who were asked only the larger request (One-Contact condition). As may be seen in Table 17.1, the results support the prediction. Over 50 percent of the subjects in the Performance condition agreed to the

TABLE 17.1
Percentage of subjects complying
with large request in Experiment I

Condition	%
Performance	52.8
Agree-Only	33.3
Familiarization	27.8*
One-Contact	22.2**

Note: $N = 36$ for each group. Significance levels represent differences frorn the Performance condition.
*$p < .07$.
**$p < .02$.

larger request, while less than 25 percent of the One-Contact condition agreed to it. Thus it appears that obtaining compliance with a small request does tend to increase subsequent compliance. The question is what aspect of the initial contact produces this effect.

One possibility is that the effect was produced merely by increased familiarity with the experimenter. The Familiarization control was included to assess the effect on compliance of two contacts with the same person. The group had as much contact with the experimenter as the Performance group, but no request was made during the first contact. As the table indicates, the Familiarization group did not differ appreciably in amount of compliance from the One-Contact group, but was different from the Performance group ($\chi^2 = 3.70$, $p < .07$). Thus, although increased familiarity may well lead to increased compliance, in the present situation the differences in amount of familiarity apparently were not great enough to produce any such increase; the effect that was obtained seems not to be due to this factor.

Another possibility is that the critical factor producing increased compliance is simply agreeing to the small request (i.e., carrying it out may not be necessary). The Agree-Only condition was identical to the Performance condition except that in the former the subjects were not asked the questions. The amount of compliance in this Agree-Only condition fell between the Performance and One-Contact conditions and was not significantly different from either of them. This leaves the effect of merely agreeing somewhat ambiguous, but it suggests that the agreement alone may produce part of the effect.

Unfortunately, it must be admitted that neither of these control conditions is an entirely adequate test of the possibility it was designed to assess. Both conditions are in some way quite peculiar and may have made a very different and extraneous impression on the subject than did the Performance condition. In one case, a housewife is asked to answer some questions and then is not asked them; in the other, some man calls to tell her about some organization she has never heard of. Now, by themselves neither of these events might produce very much suspicion. But, several days later, the same man calls and asks a very large favor. At this point it is not at all unlikely that many subjects think they are being manipulated, or in any case that something strange is going on. Any such reaction on the part of the subjects would naturally tend to reduce the amount of compliance in these conditions.

Thus, although this first study demonstrates that an initial contact in which a request is made and carried out increases compliance with a second request, the question of why and how the initial request produces this effect remains unanswered. In an attempt to begin answering this question and to extend the results of the first study, a second experiment was conducted.

There seemed to be several quite plausible ways in which the increase in compliance might have been produced. The first was simply some kind of commitment to or involvement with the particular person making the request. This might work, for example, as follows: The subject has agreed to the first request and perceives that the experimenter therefore expects him also to agree to the second request.

The subject thus feels obligated and does not want to disappoint the experimenter; he also feels that he needs a good reason for saying "no"—a better reason than he would need if he had never said "yes." This is just one line of causality—the particular process by which involvement with the experimenter operates might be quite different, but the basic idea would be similar. The commitment is to the particular person. This implies that the increase in compliance due to the first contact should occur primarily when both requests are made by the same person.

Another explanation in terms of involvement centers around the particular issue with which the requests are concerned. Once the subject has taken some action in connection with an area of concern, be it surveys, political activity, or highway safety, there is probably a tendency to become somewhat more concerned with the area. The subject begins thinking about it, considering its importance and relevance to him, and so on. This tends to make him more likely to agree to take further action in the same area when he is later asked to. To the extent that this is the critical factor the initial contact should increase compliance only when both requests are related to the same issue or area of concern.

Another way of looking at the situation is that the subject needs a reason to say "no." In our society it is somewhat difficult to refuse a reasonable request, particularly when it is made by an organization that is not trying to make money. In order to refuse, many people feel that they need a reason—simply not wanting to do it is often not in itself sufficient. The person can say to the requester or simply to himself that he does not believe in giving to charities or tipping or working for political parties or answering questions or posting signs, or whatever he is asked to do. Once he has performed a particular task, however, this excuse is no longer valid for not agreeing to perform a similar task. Even if the first thing he did was trivial compared to the present request, he cannot say he never does this sort of thing, and thus one good reason for refusing is removed. This line of reasoning suggests that the similarity of the first and second requests in terms of the type of action required is an important factor. The more similar they are, the more the "matter of principle" argument is eliminated by agreeing to the first request, and the greater should be the increase in compliance.

There are probably many other mechanisms by which the initial request might produce an increase in compliance. The second experiment was designed in part to test the notions described above, but its major purpose was to demonstrate the effect unequivocally. To this latter end it eliminated one of the important problems with the first study which was that when the experimenter made the second request he was not blind as to which condition the subjects were in. In this study the second request was always made by someone other than the person who made the first request, and the second experimenter was blind as to what condition the subject was in. This eliminates the possibility that the experimenter exerted systematically different amounts of pressure in different experimental conditions. If the effect of the first study were replicated, it would also rule out the relatively uninteresting possibility that the effect is due primarily to greater familiarity or involvement with the particular person making the first request.

EXPERIMENT II

The basic paradigm was quite similar to that of the first study. Experimental subjects were asked to comply with a small request and were later asked a considerably larger request, while controls were asked only the larger request. The first request varied along two dimensions. Subjects were asked either to put up a small sign or to sign a petition, and the issue was either safe driving or keeping California beautiful. Thus, there were four first requests: a small sign for safe driving or for beauty, and a petition for the two issues. The second request for all subjects was to install in their front lawn a very large sign which said "Drive Carefully." The four experimental conditions may be defined in terms of the similarity of the small and large requests along the dimensions of issue and task. The two requests were similar in both issue and task for the small-sign, safe-driving group, similar only in issue for the safe-driving-petition group, similar only in task for the small "Keep California Beautiful" sign group, and similar in neither issue nor task for the "Keep California Beautiful" petition group.

The major expectation was that the three groups for which either the task or the issue was similar would show more compliance than the controls, and it was also felt that when both were similar there would probably be the most compliance. The fourth condition (Different Issue-Different Task) was included primarily to assess the effect simply of the initial contact which, although it was not identical to the second one on either issue or task, was in many ways quite similar (e.g., a young student asking for cooperation on a noncontroversial issue). There were no clear expectations as to how this condition would compare to the controls.

Method

The subjects were 114 women and 13 men living in Palo Alto, California. Of these, 9 women and 6 men could not be contacted for the second request and are not included in the data analysis. The remaining 112 subjects were divided about equally among the five conditions (see Table 17.2). All subjects were contacted between 1:30 and 4:30 on weekday afternoons.

Two experimenters, one male and one female, were employed, and a different one always made the second contact. Unlike the first study, the experimenters actually went to the homes of the subjects and interviewed them on a face-to-face basis. An effort was made to select subjects from blocks and neighborhoods that were as homogeneous as possible. On each block every third or fourth house was approached, and all subjects on that block were in one experimental condition. This was necessary because of the likelihood that neighbors would talk to each other about the contact. In addition, for every four subjects contacted, a fifth house was chosen as a control but was, of course, not contacted. Throughout this phase of the experiment, and in fact throughout the whole experiment, the two experimenters did not communicate to each other what conditions had been run on a given block nor what condition a particular house was in.

The small-sign, safe-driving group was told that the experimenter was from the Community Committee for Traffic Safety, that he was visiting a number of homes in an attempt to make the citizens more aware of the need to drive carefully all the time, and that he would like the subject to take a small sign and put it in a window or in the car so that it would serve as a reminder of the need to drive carefully. The sign was three inches square, said "Be a safe driver," was on thin paper without a gummed backing, and in general looked rather amateurish and unattractive. If the subject agreed, he was given the sign and thanked; if he disagreed, he was simply thanked for his time.

The three other experimental conditions were quite similar with appropriate changes. The other organization was identified as the Keep California Beautiful Committee and its sign said, appropriately enough, "Keep California Beautiful." Both signs were simply black block letters on a white background. The two petition groups were asked to sign a petition which was being sent to California's United States Senators. The petition advocated support for any legislation which would promote either safer driving or keeping California beautiful. The subject was shown a petition, typed on heavy bond paper, with at least twenty signatures already affixed. If she agreed, she signed and was thanked. If she did not agree, she was merely thanked.

The second contact was made about 2 weeks after the initial one. Each experimenter was armed with a list of houses which had been compiled by the other experimenter. This list contained all four experimental conditions and the controls, and, of course, there was no way for the second experimenter to know which condition the subject had been in. At this second contact, all subjects were asked the same thing: Would they put a large sign concerning safe driving in their front yard? The experimenter identified himself as being from the Citizens for Safe Driving, a different group from the original safe-driving group (although it is likely that most subjects who had been in the safe-driving conditions did not notice the difference). The subject was shown a picture of a very large sign reading "Drive Carefully" placed in front of an attractive house. The picture was taken so that the sign obscured much of the front of the house and completely concealed the doorway. It was rather poorly lettered. The subject was told that: "Our men will come out and install it and later come and remove it. It makes just a small hole in your lawn, but if this is unacceptable to you we have a special mount which will make no hole." She was asked to put the sign up for a week or a week and a half. If the subject agreed, she was told that more names than necessary were being gathered and if her home were to be used she would be contacted in a few weeks. The experimenter recorded the subject's response and this ended the experiment.

Results

First, it should be noted that there were no large differences among the experimental conditions in the percentages of subjects agreeing to the first request. Although somewhat more subjects agreed to post the "Keep California Beautiful" sign and somewhat fewer to sign the beauty petition, none of these differences approach significance.

The important figures are the number of subjects in each group who agreed to the large request. These are presented in Table 17.2. The figures for the four experimental groups include all subjects who were approached the first time, regardless of whether or not they agreed to the small request. As noted above, a few subjects were lost because they could not be reached for the second request, and, of course these are not included in the table.

It is immediately apparent that the first request tended to increase the degree of compliance with the second request. Whereas fewer than 20 percent of the controls agreed to put the large sign on their lawn, over 55 percent of the experimental subjects agreed, with over 45 percent being the lowest degree of compliance for any experimental condition. As expected, those conditions in which the two requests were similar in terms of either issue or task produced significantly more compliance than did the controls (X^2's range from 3.67, $p < .07$ to 15.01, $p < .001$). A somewhat unexpected result is that the fourth condition, in which the first request had relatively little in common with the second request, also produced more compliance than the controls ($X^2 = 3.40$, $p < .08$). In other words, regardless of whether or not the two requests are similar in either issue or task, simply having the first request tends to increase the likelihood that the subject will comply with a subsequent, larger request. And this holds even when the two requests are made by different people several weeks apart.

A second point of interest is a comparison among the four experimental conditions. As expected, the Same Issue-Same Task condition produced more compliance than any of the other two-contact conditions, but the difference is not signifi-

TABLE 17.2
Percentage of subjects complying with large request
in Experiment II

	Task[a]			
Issue[a]	Similar	N	Different	N
Similar	76.0**	25	47.8*	23
Different	47.6*	21	47.4*	19

One-Contact 16.7 ($N = 24$)

Note: Significance levels represent differences from the One-Contact condition.

[a]Denotes relationship between first and second requests.

*$p < .08$.

**$p < .01$.

cant (X^2's range from 2.7 to 2.9). If only those subjects who agreed to the first request are considered, the same pattern holds.

DISCUSSION

To summarize the results, the first study indicated that carrying out a small request increased the likelihood that the subject would agree to a similar larger request made by the same person. The second study showed that this effect was quite strong even when a different person made the larger request, and the two requests were quite dissimilar. How may these results be explained?

Two possibilities were outlined previously. The matter-of-principle idea which centered on the particular type of action was not supported by the data, since the similarity of the tasks did not make an appreciable difference in degree of compliance. The notion of involvement, as described previously, also had difficulty accounting for some of the findings. The basic idea was that once someone has agreed to any action, no matter how small, he tends to feel more involved than he did before. This involvement may center around the particular person making the first request or the particular issue. This is quite consistent with the results of the first study (with the exception of the two control groups which as discussed previously were rather ambiguous) and with the Similar-Issue groups in the second experiment. This idea of involvement does not, however, explain the increase in compliance found in the two groups in which the first and second request did not deal with the same issue.

It is possible that in addition to or instead of this process a more general and diffuse mechanism underlies the increase in compliance. What may occur is a change in the person's feelings about getting involved or about taking action. Once he has agreed to a request, his attitude may change. He may become, in his own eyes, the kind of person who does this sort of thing, who agrees to requests made by strangers, who takes action on things he believes in, who cooperates with good causes. The change in attitude could be toward any aspect of the situation or toward the whole business of saying "yes." The basic idea is that the change in attitude need not be toward any particular issue or person or activity, but may be toward activity or compliance in general. This would imply that an increase in compliance would not depend upon the two contacts being made by the same person, or concerning the same issue or involving the same kind of action. The similarity could be much more general, such as both concerning good causes, or requiring a similar kind of action, or being made by pleasant, attractive individuals.

It is not being suggested that this is the only mechanism operating here. The idea of involvement continues to be extremely plausible, and there are probably a number of other possibilities. Unfortunately, the present studies offer no additional data with which to support or refute any of the possible explanations of the effect. These explanations thus remain simply descriptions of mechanisms which might produce an increase in compliance after agreement with a first request. Hopefully, additional research will test these ideas more fully and perhaps also specify other manipulations which produce an increase in compliance without an increase in external pressure.

It should be pointed out that the present studies employed what is perhaps a very special type of situation. In all cases the requests were made by presumably nonprofit service organizations. The issues in the second study were deliberately noncontroversial, and it may be assumed that virtually all subjects initially sympathized with the objectives of safe driving and a beautiful California. This is in strong contrast to campaigns which are designed to sell a particular product, political candidate, or dogma. Whether the technique employed in this study would be successful in these other situations remains to be shown.

References

ASCH, S. E. Effects of group pressure upon the modification and distortion of judgments. In H. Guetzkow (ed.), *Groups, leadership and men; research in human relations.* Pittsburgh: Carnegie Press, 1951, pp. 177–190.

BANDURA, A., ROSS, D., AND ROSS, S. A. A comparative test of the status envy, social power, and secondary reinforcement theories of identificatory learning. *Journal of Abnormal and Social Psychology,* 1963, **67,** 527–534.

BRUNER, J. The dimensions of propaganda: German short-wave broadcasts to America. *Journal of Abnormal and Social Psychology,* 1941, **36,** 311–337.

DEUTSCH, M., AND GERARD, H. B. A study of normative and informational social influences upon individual judgment. *Journal of Abnormal and Social Psychology,* 1955, **41,** 629–636.

FESTINGER, L., AND CARLSMITH, J. Cognitive consequences of forced compliance. *Journal of Abnormal and Social Psychology,* 1959, **58,** 203–210.

HOVLAND, C. I., AND PRITZKER, H. A. Extent of opinion change as a function of amount of change advocated. *Journal of Abnormal and Social Psychology,* 1957, **54,** 257–261.

KELMAN, H. C., AND HOVLAND, C. I. "Reinstatement" of the communicator in delayed measurement of opinion change. *Journal of Abnormal and Social Psychology,* 1953, **48,** 327–335.

SCHEIN, E. H., SCHNEIER, I., AND BARKER, C. H. *Coercive pressure.* New York: Norton, 1961.

18

Reducing Weight by Reducing Dissonance: The Role of Effort Justification in Inducing Weight Loss

Danny Axsom and Joel Cooper

The role of effort justification in psychotherapy was examined. It was hypothesized that the effort involved in therapy, plus the conscious decision to undergo that effort, leads to positive therapeutic changes through the reduction of cognitive dissonance. An experiment was conducted in which overweight subjects attempted to lose weight through one of two forms of "Effort Therapy." These therapies were bogus in that they were based solely on the expenditure of effort on a series of cognitive tasks that were unrelated to any existing techniques or theory addressing weight loss. One of the therapies called for a high degree of effort, while the degree of effort in the second therapy was low. Decision freedom to enter into and continue with the study was also varied. It was predicted that weight loss would occur only when both effort and decision freedom were high. Results supported these predictions, although some ambiguity arose from the failure to clearly manipulate decision freedom. Over an initial three-week period, High Effort subjects lost slightly more weight than Low Effort subjects. A six-month follow-up revealed that the effects of effort on weight loss had increased and were highly significant. Internal analyses indicated a further influence of the decision freedom variable. Possible mechanisms mediating the dissonance effect were discussed, as were several alternative explanations.

Several theorists have noted that psychotherapy is potentially a fertile arena for the application of social psychological principles (Frank, 1961; Goldstein, Heller, and Sechrest, 1966; Brehm, 1976; Strong, 1978). Frank (1961), for example, has characterized therapy as a relationship between a sufferer and a socially sanctioned authority who attempts to produce certain changes in the emotions, attitudes, and behaviors of the sufferer. Clearly this implies the importance of social psychological processes dealing with attitude change and social influence. These would seem to have an important bearing on the interpersonal influence setting we call psychotherapy.

Reprinted by permission of the authors.

One approach that has been applied to the study of attitude change is the concept of effort justification derived from the theory of cognitive dissonance (Festinger, 1957). We believe that the notion of effort justification is also potentially important in understanding both the process and outcome of psychotherapy. Effort justification concerns the consequences of engaging in an effortful activity in order to obtain some goal. The fact that one has engaged in an effortful event is discrepant with the notion that one does not usually engage in such effort. And for what purpose? In the typical effort justification sequence, either the goal or the means for achieving that goal is not attractive at the outset of the sequence. Consider, for example, the classic experiment by Aronson and Mills (1959). Subjects in a High Effort condition were made to undergo an event that was difficult and embarrassing. Their goal was to join a sexual discussion group that was, in reality, dull, boring, and a general waste of time. Yet those subjects who underwent the highly effortful procedure came to indicate that the group and its members were generally interesting and enjoyable.

Why did such changes occur? The reason given by Aronson and Mills was based upon the tension state of dissonance that was created by the voluntary expenditure of effort. "Why did I undergo such embarrassment and effort?" a subject may have asked. "Because I really did like the discussion group," might be the reply. In other words, the goal was elevated in attractiveness as a way of justifying the expenditure of effort.

Cooper (forthcoming) argues that the effort justification sequence might lie at the basis of many psychotherapeutic systems. Typically, psychotherapy involves a patient volunteering for an effortful and sometimes emotionally draining process. A client may have a fear of certain objects, may find relationships with others unpleasant, or may find it noxious to behave in certain socially adaptable ways. Yet in any of the myriad of procedures generically called psychotherapy, clients often make changes in their attitudes, emotions, and behavior. The goal states—be they phobic objects, interpersonal relations, or particular behaviors—become more acceptable or attractive. At least part of this change may result from an attempt to justify the expenditure of effort, just as in Aronson and Mills's study the discussion group became more attractive.

Which systems of therapy are more effective in producing change? The answer does not appear to rest decisively with any school. Despite the fact that some systems of therapy rely upon the production of behavior, others on the arousal of anxiety and others on the discussion of emotionally traumatic events, none seems to be clearly superior in producing effective changes (e.g., Sloane et al., 1975). Frank (1961) has aptly noted that the commonalities in psychotherapeutic systems may be more germaine than their differences. And one of the common factors that would seem to underlie virtually all effective therapy systems is the expenditure of effort. Psychoanalytic schools rely upon emotional catharses, desensitization approaches evoke degrees of anxiety, and virtually all therapies rely upon the use of a considerable amount of time and often expense. To the degree that participation in the therapies is voluntary, they are conceptually similar to Aronson and Mills's study of the effort justification sequence.

Cooper (forthcoming) conducted a pair of experiments to test the role of effort justification in psychotherapy. He reasoned that if successful therapy outcomes were due to effort justification, the particular form of effort should not matter, as long as that effort is seen as related to the goal in question. In one experiment, college students who were afraid of snakes were recruited. They participated in one of two experimental therapies. One of the therapeutic procedures was a modified form of implosive therapy (Stampfl and Levis, 1976) that is based upon the learning theory notion of extinction. This therapy involves a high degree of effortful participation on the part of the participant. The other therapy was based solely on the expenditure of physical effort and was not based upon any existing theory of therapy. Subjects were asked to jump rope, run in place, and perform other physical exercises. Subjects in each therapy condition first attempted to come as close as they could to a six-foot boa constrictor. Half of the subjects in each condition then made an informed choice about participating in the effortful therapy; the other half participated without such a choice. According to dissonance theory, the effort justification sequence should be invoked only under conditions of an informed choice (e.g., Linder, Cooper, and Wicklund, 1968). Therefore it was predicted that, on the basis of dissonance theory, effort justification would be invoked by either therapy since both implosive therapy and the newly created physical exercise therapy involved high degrees of effort—but this would occur only under conditions of high decision freedom. It was found that subjects in either form of therapy made significant improvement in the degree to which they could approach the boa constrictor—if and only if they participated under conditions of free choice. Neither the exercise therapy nor implosive therapy was effective in the absence of choice.

The basic approach was repeated in a conceptual replication. Participants were university students who were nonassertive. Cooper (forthcoming) assigned half of them to a physical exercise therapy and half to a standard therapy for lack of assertiveness (i.e., behavior rehearsal; see Salter, 1949). Once again, it was found that either form of therapy was effective in increasing participants' assertiveness, as long as it was engaged in voluntarily.

The conclusion from Cooper's experiments is that the voluntary expenditure of effort is at least one of the effective ingredients in psychotherapy, regardless of whether that effort forms part of a traditional therapy or whether it is improvised in a series of physical exercises. Exercise therapies or traditional therapies may be effective in promoting change, as long as they are engaged in voluntarily. However, several important questions remain unanswered. First, the notion that effort leads to positive changes in psychotherapy has yet to receive a direct test. This is because neither of Cooper's experiments used *variations* in effort as an independent variable. To the extent that effort justification is involved in psychotherapy, it should be shown that variations in the degree of effort will lead to variations in the degree of change that ensues.

Equally important is the question of duration of change that occurs as a result of effort justification. Both of Cooper's experiments involved single-session therapies with change measured immediately after the session. While this is a typical procedure in laboratory experiments involving attitude change, it is not parallel to the desired outcome of psychotherapy. Change as a result of therapy is anticipated to be more long lasting, and an assessment of the effort justification procedure should be based not so much on an immediate assessment as on its long term consequence. There are only a few reports in the dissonance literature of cognitive changes lasting well beyond the experimental session (Freedman, 1965). So the question of duration of consequences takes on enormous significance in assessing the appropriateness of the conceptual analysis that is based upon the psychology of effort justification.

The focus of the present experiment was on weight loss. This problem offers many advantages for an experimental study of effort justification procedures. First, there are objective and nonreactive measurements available for body weight that can be easily and repeatedly sampled. Second, the dependent measure thoroughly defines the criterion of a successful therapy, since weight loss represents the specific goal of treatment (Wollersheim, 1970). In addition, the number of different approaches to weight loss that exist in society attests to the fact that there is, at present, no agreed upon effective treatment for the loss of weight. The present experiment uses the concept of effort justification to effect such a treatment.

METHOD

Subjects

Subjects were recruited via newspaper ads for an "Experiment concerning possible methods of weight reduction." They were contacted by phone for scheduling and were assured that the procedure would be safe and would not include any medication. The following restrictions applied: First, only those 18 years of age and older were solicited. Second, men were excluded from the final subject pool (this decision was made after the initial response to the ads was overwhelmingly female). A third step, which was also taken to increase homogeneity, restricted allowable weight deviations to include only those women who were 10 to 20 percent above "desirable body weight" (according to the Metropolitan Life Insurance Company statistics [1959]). The lower limit was similar to that used by Schachter and his colleagues in their studies of obesity (Schachter, 1971); the upper limit decreased the probability of there being a physiological etiology and complication associated with overweightness (Olson, 1964). Fourth, no one receiving therapy or medication for their weight was included. Fifth, potential subjects who participated in athletic activities that would greatly increase weight by increasing muscle size rather than body fat were excluded (Schachter, Goldman, and Gordon, 1968). Finally, only subjects who lived within twenty minutes' traveling time of the laboratory were included, since extraordinary distances could affect the manipulation of effort.

Sixty-eight subjects who fulfilled the above requirements began the experiment. Each was paid at the rate of one dollar per session. Fifteen subjects were lost through attrition. Chi-square analyses failed to reveal any relationship between experimental conditions and the decision to terminate.[1] In addition, data from one subject were omitted when she arrived at two consecutive sessions too late to complete the full procedure. Fifty-two subjects comprised the final sample.

Procedure

General overview.   A 2 (level of effort) × 2 (level of choice) between-subjects design with an external control group was utilized. Subjects attended five sessions over a three week period. They attended two sessions during each of the first two weeks and one during the final week. To minimize extraneous influences on weight change, sessions for each subject were scheduled at the same time of day and the same days of the week throughout. Six months after the experimental sessions were completed, a final weighing session was conducted.

The choice variable.   Subjects in the four experimental conditions were first met by a female experimenter who measured and recorded their weight.[2] She then administered the choice variable. Subjects in the *High Choice* conditions were told: "I have been instructed to advise you that although the procedures you will follow are perfectly safe and harmless, they may also be effortful and anxiety producing. If you like, you can stop the experiment now and you will be paid for this session. Would you like to continue?"

A Princeton University Informed Consent form was then given to be read and signed. This stated, in part, "I may withdraw my consent and discontinue participation in the project at any time." As the form was being read, the weigher emphasized, "As you notice on the form, you may withdraw your consent and stop at any time . . . you still have the prerogative to stop participation later. . . ."

Subjects in the *Low Choice* conditions were not asked whether they wanted to continue. Subjects were merely warned about the potential effort and anxiety and then told, "We'll go ahead and begin."

The second experimenter introduced himself and administered a "Life Pattern Questionnaire" concerning everyday eating and exercise patterns and other activities that might be useful in interpreting weight change data. It was also administered to increase the perceived legitimacy of the procedure. All subjects were then given a small booklet in which to monitor their eating over the three week period. This too was partly to increase the perceived legitimacy of the procedure.

---

[1]Reported reasons for dropping out included loss of interest, outside interference such as sudden job changes, and unexpected transportation problems, which prevented participation.

[2]Subjects were weighed in indoor clothing and without shoes.

The second experimenter explained the rationale for the study by noting that psychologists have frequently found strong correlations between heightened neurophysiological arousal and increased emotional sensitivity. The present researchers, he added, had been able to take advantage of this by presenting subjects with various tasks designed specifically to increase this neurophysiological arousal and thereby enhance emotional sensitivity in a way that helped lead to weight reduction. He then explained that although the procedure had been very successful in the preliminary investigations, the precise reasons for the weight loss obtained were still uncertain, and the present study aimed to make the process clearer.

The tasks were described as requiring much concentration and consequently being neurophysiologically arousing and sometimes stressful. The subject was assured that this arousal and stress would be brief and not last beyond any session. In keeping with the cover story, all subjects were attached to a galvanic skin response (GSR) apparatus (ostensibly to measure their level of arousal) while performing the tasks described below.

The effort variable.   Effort in the present experiment involved the degree of difficulty of a variety of cognitive tasks. Effort was manipulated by varying task difficulty and duration, the parameters chosen being established through pre-testing. Subjects in the High Effort conditions worked for 20 minutes at a 3-channel tachistiscope. Their task was to discriminate which of several near-vertical lines presented sequentially was most vertical. Each line was visible for only 350 milliseconds. Those in the Low Effort condition worked for 3 minutes and were given 1 second to view each line.

Subjects then moved to a delayed-auditory feedback apparatus. High Effort subjects were given 30 minutes of recitation, in which they attempted to recite nursery rhymes, read a short story, and recite the U.S. Pledge of Allegiance with their own voice reflected back to them via earphones at a delay of 316 milliseconds. The delay was similar to that used by Zimbardo (1965) in his manipulation of high effort. In addition, the voice of a woman attempting similar tasks during pretesting was overlayed onto the recorder so that the subject not only had to contend with the delay, but also with yet another voice. Low Effort subjects worked for only 10 minutes and the auditory delay was cut in half (158 milliseconds). This reduced delay, accomplished by increasing tape speed, also rendered the voice distraction incomprehensible and therefore less disruptive (Mackworth, 1970).

To avoid the potential confounding of session length with level of effort, subjects in the Low Effort condition, after completing the T-scope task, returned to the waiting room to relax for 40 minutes before finishing the session. This procedure, which is similar to that used by Wicklund, Cooper, and Linder (1967), was explained to Low Effort subjects as being necessary to allow the arousal due to the T-scope task to dissipate before beginning the next task.

Upon finishing the final task, the subject completed a brief questionnaire concerning her impression of the session. Most importantly, she was asked, "In general, how effortful would you describe the hour as a whole?" This was followed by a 7-point response scale labeled "Very little" and "Very much" at the end points. The subject then returned to the weighing room for the final choice manipulation. For High Choice subjects, the first experimenter stated, "I'll remind you again that you can still stop the experiment and be paid for what you've done so far. Would you like to continue?" When the subject acknowledged that she wished to continue, she was given an appointment card containing the time and date of the next session. Low Choice subjects were merely given the appointment card without any mention of a new decision.

Sessions two through four.   The following three sessions were similar to the first. The Life Pattern Questionnaire was not administered during these sessions and the cover story was not repeated. The sessions contained T-scope and DAF tasks that were of the same durations as those of Session One, although the content of the visual discriminations and DAF reading tasks was altered to relieve possible boredom.

The final experimental session.   Session Five contained the final assessment of weight change during the experimental period and was conducted by the second experimenter. Unaware of the subject's choice condition, he weighed the subject and then informed her that her participation in the study was completed. He asked the subject to fill out a questionnaire that covered various weight-related topics and the subject's perceptions of the study. Crucial were two final manipulation checks: "How effortful would you describe the experiment as a whole?" (1 = very little; 9 = very much); and "How free did you feel *not* to continue with the experiment at any time?" (1 = not free to choose; 9 = very free to choose). Next the Life Patterns Questionnaire was readministered. Finally, the subject was carefully questioned about any suspicions she may have had about the purpose of the study, fully debriefed, and paid for her participation. The need for deception and the importance and possible implications of the study were discussed at length.

Control group.   To provide a baseline indication of normal weight fluctuation among subjects in our sample, ten subjects from those who responded to the advertisement were randomly assigned to a control condition. When contacted to begin, they were told that they would be unable to participate as originally planned due to a change in the procedure that meant using less participants. They were then asked to engage in a project "to determine normal female weight fluctuation over time." Control subjects also participated in five sessions, scheduled in a similar fashion as the experimental subjects. They were simply greeted and weighed during each session. The Life Patterns Questionnaire was administered at the first and fifth sessions. A shortened version of the final questionnaire was also administered at the fifth session. It was emphasized that this was not a weight reduction study and that subjects should therefore simply carry on their normal daily activities. Dieting was left to their discretion.

The final assessment.   Six months after the fifth session was completed, participants were contacted for a follow-up weighing. The subjects were unaware that they would be re-contacted. Forty-two of the 52 subjects were able to return; nine had since moved from the area or were unable to be reached; one had become pregnant. At this follow-up, subjects were given a copy of the results from the original experiment.

RESULTS

Checks on the Manipulations

The amount of effort involved in the subjects' participation was assessed in two ways. First, at the end of the four experimental sessions, subjects were asked to rate the effortfulness of the preceding hour (1 = very little; 7 = very much). A 2 (choice) × 2 (effort) × 4 (sessions) repeated measures analysis of variance showed a significant main effect for Effort ($\bar{X}_{high}$ = 4.31 vs. $\bar{X}_{low}$ = 3.14), F (1, 37) = 10.21, $p < .005$. In addition, during the final session all subjects, including the control group, rated the effortfulness of the experiment as a whole (1 = very little; 9 = very much). Planned comparisons again confirmed that High Effort subjects rated the study as more effortful, F (1, 45) = 4.62, $p < .05$. Dunnett comparisons showed that only the High Effort–Low Choice groups differed significantly from the effortfulness ratings of the Control group ($p < .08$ and $p < .05$, respectively).

Results from the perceived choice manipulation checks revealed that the manipulation of this variable was not entirely effective. At the final session, the subjects were asked how free they felt not to continue with the experiment at any time. This primary measure of decision freedom was supplemented by three additional questions that related to perceived freedom (all scaled 1 = not free to choose; 9 = very free to choose). A multivariate analysis of variance on these questions revealed a marginal main effect for Choice, Wilkes Likelihood Ratio Exact F (4, 34) = 2.19, $p < .10$. Why this effect was only marginal can be seen by examining the primary choice measure. Of the 41 subjects in the experimental groups who responded to this question, 56 percent marked the highest level of choice. In fact, even 40 percent of the Low Choice subjects responded this way. This apparent ceiling effect was evident on all four questions. Although a univariate analysis of variance performed on the data from the primary choice measure showed that High Choice subjects felt significantly more freedom to discontinue the experiment than Low Choice subjects, F (1, 45) = 5.06, $p < .05$, the ceiling effect caused both the normality and homogeneity assumptions underlying the analysis of variance to be violated (F_{max} = 13.04, $p < .01$), which results in a positive bias in the test (Winer,

1971). The overwhelming proportion of extreme responses also rendered nonparametric analyses of little use, since the number of tied ranks was unacceptably high. We are thus left uncertain as to the statistical and psychological significance of the choice manipulation.

Weight loss: data from session five.   The amount of weight change at the immediate conclusion of the experimental sessions was measured in pounds.[3,4] As can be seen from Table 18.1, the effort justification hypothesis that there would be more weight loss in the High Effort–High Choice condition was not found. Planned comparisons revealed only a tendency toward a main effect for effort, $F (1, 47) = 2.28$, $p < .14$. Given the questionable effectiveness of the choice manipulation, these results are more understandable. If choice is considered high in all cells, then the effort justification prediction must be that subjects in the High Effort conditions would lose more weight than those in the Low Effort conditions. Although the evidence for this is marginal, additional data should be considered: Seven of the nine subjects who lost the most weight were from the High Effort conditions, while five of the six who gained the most weight were from the Low Effort

TABLE 18.1
Mean Weight Change Over the Initial Five Sessions (in pounds)

Group	Unadjusted	Internal Analysis
High Effort–High Choice	−1.75	−2.25
High Effort–Low Choice	−1.77	−1.20
Low Effort–High Choice	−1.16	−1.33
Low Effort–Low Choice	− .45	0
Control	+ .17	—

Note: For the internal analysis, subjects were grouped according to High vs. Low *assigned* Effort and High vs. Low *reported* Choice (obtained by a median split of responses to the choice manipulation check).

---

[3]For clarity of presentation, the weight change analyses reported are based on difference scores. The crucial assumptions behind the use of difference scores, namely, that within-group regression coefficients relating initial to final weight are homogeneous and equal to 1.00, are both satisfied (*b*'s for High Effort–High Choice; High Effort–Low Choice; Low Effort–High Choice; Low Effort–Low Choice; and the control were, respectively, 1.01, .95, 1.01, .99, and 1.02).

[4]Since the duration of this portion of the experiment was short and weight changes were expected to be small, data on each subject's menstrual cycle were also collected (during the fifth session). This was to ensure against any spurious weight change effects resulting from water retention (congestive dysmenorrhea) coinciding with menstruation. For example, if a subject began the experiment at or near menstruation, perhaps any weight loss obtained later would simply reflect a return to normal weight; likewise, legitimate losses could be concealed if the final session ended at menstruation. However, analyses of menstrual data showed that only a small number of subjects had either started or finished their sessions around menstruation and that these subjects were equally distributed across conditions.

conditions. In addition, *t* tests, adjusted for the number of possible comparisons, revealed that only in the combined High Effort conditions was weight deviation significantly different from zero, $t(20) = 4.11, p < .02$.

The equivocal success of the choice manipulation makes interpretations involving that variable difficult. To better understand the role of choice, an internal analysis was performed on the data. Specifically, the analysis used the subjects' report of how much freedom they experienced as the choice variable. Table 18.1 shows the weight lost by the subjects as a function of their *assigned* degree of effort and their *reported* experience of freedom, the latter variable obtained by a median split on the primary choice measure. A planned contrast shows a marginally significant difference between the High Effort–reported High Choice condition and the remaining three conditions, $F(1, 37) = 3.39, p < .08$. In addition, only the High Effort–reported High Choice condition showed weight deviations that were significantly different from zero, $t(9) = 4.26, p < .06$.

Weight loss: the final measure.   Encouraged by the direction if not the magnitude of the results, we proceeded with the final dependent measure: the six month follow-up. As Table 18.2 indicates, dramatic differences had developed over the six month period. High Effort subjects had lost an average of 6.5 additional pounds. Low Effort subjects, on the other hand, showed a slight gain in weight. The difference was highly significant, whether measured as change from the fifth session, $F(1, 30) = 20.30, p < .001$, or the beginning of the experiment, $F(1, 30) = 20.45, p < .001$. Of the 16 High Effort subjects who reported for the final measure, 15 had lost weight, whereas only 7 of the 18 Low Effort subjects and 4 of the 8 Control subjects lost weight. Once again, an internal analysis using a median split on the choice measure was performed. These results showed that subjects in the High Effort–reported High Choice group lost the most weight, although this

TABLE 18.2
Mean Weight Change With First Follow-up (in pounds)

Group	Over Follow-up Period	Overall	Internal Analysis: Over Follow-up Period	Internal Analysis: Overall
High Effort–High Choice	-6.46_a	-7.93_a	-7.21_a	-9.75_a
High Effort–Low Choice	-6.61_a	-9.03_a	-5.03_a	-6.61_a
Low Effort–High Choice	$-.14_b$	-1.47_b	$+1.10_b$	$-.48_b$
Low Effort–Low Choice	$+1.75_b$	$+1.33_b$	$+.44_b$	$+.44_b$
Control	$+.94_b$	$+.94_b$	—	—

Note: "Over follow-up period" indicates weight change from the conclusion of the initial sessions to the follow-up; "overall" indicates weight change from the beginning of the experiment to the follow-up. Within each column, means with different subscripts differ significantly from one another ($p < .05$ by Newman-Keuls).

group did not differ significantly from those in the High Effort–reported Low Choice condition.

Weight loss: one more time.   One year from the date of the initial experimental session, subjects were contacted once again. By this time, many had either moved or otherwise changed situations so that they could no longer return in person for the weighing. These subjects weighed themselves at home and reported their weight by phone. As a result, data were obtained for 50 of the 52 original subjects. Analyses using only those subjects who returned to be weighed were similar to findings based on the full subject pool, so only the latter are reported. Once again, the main effect for effort was highly reliable, $F (1, 45) = 7.79, p < .01$. The average weight loss for high effort subjects one year from their participation in the experimental session was 6.7 pounds whereas low effort subjects lost only .34 pounds (Control $\bar{X} = -1.86$ pounds). Ninety percent of the High Effort participants were below their initial weight whereas only 48 percent of the Low Effort and 56 percent of the Control subjects were below their initial weight. Once again, an internal analysis revealed that the High Effort–reported High Choice group had lost the most weight. An *a priori* contrast showed this group to be significantly different from the other three, $F (1, 36) = 5.26, p < .05$.

DISCUSSION

The weight loss observed in the High Effort cells was both substantial and consistent. Since subjects were initially an average of 17 pounds overweight, High Effort subjects—who lost an average of 8.55 pounds by the first follow-up—were able to achieve a 50 percent reduction in excess weight. The chief issue to be addressed, then, is not whether positive therapeutic change occurred but rather whether effort justification processes can account for this change.

The results offer clear support for the role of effort in instigating the weight reduction. But the weakness of the choice manipulation makes a final interpretation less clear than would be desired. The notion of effort justification predicts weight loss for participants who engaged in a high degree of effort and who perceived their freedom to participate to be high. Since an overwhelming proportion of subjects perceived their freedom to be high, the main effects found for the effort variable are consistent with the effort justification approach.

In retrospect, the problem with the manipulation of choice could have been expected. Subjects came to the university from various locations in the community. They returned for several sessions. Attempting to convince Low Choice subjects that they were not at all free to discontinue the experiment would have strained ethical considerations as well as credibility. Rather, we remained silent about choice considerations to Low Choice subjects and instead emphasized the high degree of decision freedom to those subjects assigned to the High Choice conditions.

Since freedom was apparently already assumed to be high by the participants, our manipulation did not have much differential impact. Because of this strong ceiling effect, even internal analyses could offer only slight assistance by showing tendencies for the High Effort–reported High Choice group to lose the greatest amount of weight.

What of those subjects who actually reported feeling low decision freedom? There were eight such subjects who checked points lower than the mid-point of the primary choice scale. For them, it would be predicted that, regardless of effort, weight loss would not occur. Indeed, six of the eight actually gained weight over the initial five sessions. The mean weight change for all eight was +.56 pounds. Seven returned for the first follow-up. Although their mean weight change was −1.75 pounds, this was largely due to one highly aberrant subject who had lost 13 pounds. The remaining six were virtually unchanged ($\bar{X}$ = +.13 pounds). By the second follow-up, overall weight change for the eight subjects reporting low choice was almost zero ($\bar{X}$ = −.06 pounds).

The dramatic amount of weight change that occurred during the six month period following the experimental session stands in marked contrast to the marginal degree of weight change that occurred immediately after the experiment. Of course, weight change takes time and it is not surprising that only a few pounds could be changed during the three weeks of the sessions. But this weight loss was not only maintained over the half-year period, it was markedly increased by those subjects in the High Effort conditions. Why should this have happened? Long-term changes as a function of laboratory intervention are not commonplace in the literature.

Our answer, based upon the concept of effort justification, must still be in the form of speculation. It would appear that effort justification worked to increase the attractiveness of the *goal* of weight loss. There is no evidence that subjects in the High Effort conditions found that they could be successful at losing weight during the experimental sessions and continued their method over the long period of time prior to the follow-up measure. The data show little relationship between weight lost during the initial experimental sessions and weight lost by the first follow-up. Our initial statement of effort justification principles is consistent with this lack of relationship, for it is the goal state that effort renders more attractive. Just as Aronson and Mills's (1959) subjects who underwent effort viewed the goal of belonging to the discussion group with greater attractiveness, so too did our subjects come to view the goal of losing weight with more zeal and fervor. As a result, subjects in the High Effort conditions pursued that goal *regardless* of how successful they might have been during the five experimental sessions. Subjects in the Low Effort conditions, on the other hand, did not view the goal as being more attractive. Regardless of whether they had shown any weight loss during the five experimental sessions, they showed no consistent pattern of weight loss during the succeeding six months. Thus, the data are consistent with the notion that the goal of weight loss became more attractive to High Effort subjects who then pursued that goal more vigorously during the intervening six months.

Alternative explanations for the data may still arise due to the equivocal nature of the choice manipulation. One such explanation is that High Effort subjects may have formed differentially higher expectations about the therapy's potential outcome. These high expectations may have led to stricter adherence to some self-prescribed regimen that resulted in weight loss. Those who initially lost weight might have formed what Ross, Lepper, and Hubbard (1975) have referred to as antecedent—consequent explanations for why they were losing weight. However, it is difficult for an expectation-based hypothesis to explain why those initially showing little or no weight loss would later lose. As we have already mentioned, the data reveal that High Effort subjects lost weight during the six month period regardless of whether they had initially lost or gained. This factor is more consistent with the effort justification hypothesis for it appears to be the goal of weight loss that becomes more attractive.

But this speculation should only emphasize the need for more work in the area. In particular, the specific processes producing the changes need more attention. Perhaps an attributional alternative—a self-perception process, for example—could account for our findings.

When combined with the two experiments reported by Cooper (forthcoming), the present experiment adds to the confidence with which the concept of effort justification can be applied to psychotherapy. In the present experiment, the concept of effort was expanded to include cognitive mental tasks, and the data showed that variations in this type of effort led to systematic differences in the amount of weight that participants lost. Although the findings were of a small magnitude at the conclusion of the five experimental sessions, the amount of weight lost after a six month period by subjects who had undergone a highly effortful procedure was considerable. The extension over time adds important new dimensions to research on effort justification as well as to research on psychotherapeutic outcomes.

The application of effort justification principles to psychotherapy would seem to call for serious consideration on the basis of the present data. Some therapists may feel uneasy applying effort justification because the principles have become associated with the use of deception (Brehm, 1976). Such deception is not endemic to effort justification. In fact, effort justification could be relied upon by initially advising clients very truthfully of the effort and unpleasantness that lie ahead. As Freud (1929) stated, "when we take a neurotic patient into psychoanalytic treatment . . . we point out the difficulties of the method to him, the long duration, the efforts and sacrifices it calls for . . ." (p. 15). Effort justification also stresses the client's personal responsibility for choosing to participate and remain in therapy. When viewed in this light, perhaps the effort justification principle emanating from the social psychological laboratory will become more palatable to therapists. We are not saying that effort justification is the only influence on therapy outcomes; nor are we necessarily advocating an "effort therapy." What we do believe is that effort justification influences outcomes. To the extent that therapists take advantage of this process they may enhance the efficacy of their therapies.

References

ARONSON, E., AND MILLS, J. The effects of severity of initiation on liking for a group. *Journal of Abnormal and Social Psychology,* 1959, **59,** 177–181.

BREHM, S. S. *The application of social psychology to clinical practice.* Washington, D.C.: Hemisphere, 1976.

COOPER, J. *Reducing fears and increasing assertiveness: The role of dissonance reduction.* Manuscript submitted for publication, 1979.

FESTINGER, L. *A theory of cognitive dissonance.* Stanford: Stanford University Press, 1957.

FRANK, J. D. *Persuasion and healing.* Baltimore: The Johns Hopkins Press, 1961.

FREEDMAN, J. L. Long-term behavioral effects of cognitive dissonance. *Journal of Experimental Social Psychology,* 1965, **1,** 145–155.

FREUD, S. *Introductory lectures on psychoanalysis.* New York: Norton, 1966.

GOLDSTEIN, A. P., HELLER, K., AND SECHREST, L. B. *Psychotherapy and the psychology of behavior change.* New York: Wiley, 1966.

LINDER, D. E., COOPER, J., AND WICKLUND, R. A. Pre-exposure persuasion as a result of commitment to pre-exposure effort. *Journal of Experimental Social Psychology,* 1968, **4,** 470–482.

MACKWORTH, J. F. *Vigilance and attention: A signal detection approach.* Harmondsworth: Penguin, 1970.

METROPOLITAN LIFE INSURANCE COMPANY OF NEW YORK. New weight standards for men and women. *Statistical Bulletin,* **40,** 1959.

OLSON, R. E. Obesity. In H. F. Conn (ed.), *Current therapy.* Philadelphia: W. B. Saunders, 1964.

ROSS, L., LEPPER, M. R., AND HUBBARD, M. Perseverance in self-perception and social perception: Biased attributional processes in the debriefing paradigm. *Journal of Personality and Social Psychology,* 1975, **32,** 880–892.

SALTER, A. *Conditioned reflex therapy: The direct approach to the reconstruction of personality.* New York: Creative Age Press, 1949.

SCHACHTER, S. *Emotion, obesity, and crime.* New York: Academic Press, 1971.

SCHACHTER, S., GOLDMAN, R., AND GORDON, A. Effects of fear, food deprivation, and obesity on eating. *Journal of Personality and Social Psychology,* 1968, **10,** 91–97.

SLOANE, R. B., STAPLES, F. R., CRISTOL, A. H., YORKSTON, N. J., AND WHIPPLE, K. *Short-term analytically oriented psychotherapy vs. behavior therapy.* Cambridge, Mass.: Harvard University Press, 1975.

STAMPFL, T., AND LEVIS, D. Essentials of implosive therapy: A learning theory based psychodynamic behavioral therapy. *Journal of Abnormal Psychology,* 1967, **72,** 496.

STRONG, S. R. Social psychological approach to psychotherapy research. In S. Garfield and A. Bergin (eds.), *Handbook of psychotherapy and behavior change.* New York: Wiley, 1978.

WICKLUND, R. A., COOPER, J., AND LINDER, D. E. Effects of expected effort on attitude change prior to exposure. *Journal of Experimental Social Psychology,* 1967, **3,** 416–428.

WINER, B. J. *Statistical principles in experimental design* (2nd ed.). New York: McGraw-Hill, 1971.

WOLLERSHEIM, J. Effectiveness of group therapy based upon learning principles on the treatment of overweight women. *Journal of Abnormal Psychology,* 1970, **76,** 462–474.

ZIMBARDO, P. G. The effect of effort and improvisation on self-persuasion produced by role playing. *Journal of Experimental Social Psychology,* 1965, **1,** 103–120.

19

Dishonest Behavior as a Function of Differential Levels of Induced Self-Esteem

Elliot Aronson and David R. Mettee

After taking a personality test, Ss were given false feedback aimed at temporarily inducing either an increase in self-esteem, a decrease in self-esteem, or no change in their self-esteem. They were then allowed to participate in a game of cards, in the course of which they were provided with opportunities to cheat under circumstances which made it appear impossible to be detected. Significantly more people cheated in the low self-esteem condition than in the high self-esteem condition. A chi-square evaluating cheater frequency among the high self-esteem, the no information (no change in self-esteem), and the low self-esteem conditions was significant at the .05 level. The results are discussed in terms of cognitive consistency theory.

Recent theorizing and experimentation have suggested that a person's expectancies may be an important determinant of his behavior. Working within the framework of the theory of cognitive dissonance, Aronson and Carlsmith (1962) conducted an experiment in which subjects were led to develop an expectancy of poor performance on a "social sensitivity" test. The subjects then proceeded to perform beautifully. Aronson and Carlsmith found that these subjects subsequently changed their superior performance to an inferior one when retested over the same material. Similarly, Wilson (1965) found that subjects were significantly more attracted to a negative evaluator than to a positive evaluator if the negative evaluations were in accord with a strong performance expectancy which had led the subjects to withdraw from a competitive event. Consistency theory thus has received some support in specific expectancies and performance directly related to these expectancies.

Reprinted with permission from the authors and *The Journal of Personality and Social Psychology,* Vol. 9, No. 2, 1968. Copyright © 1968 by the American Psychological Association.

This experiment was supported by a National Science Foundation Graduate Fellowship (NSF-26-1140-3971) to David R. Mettee and by grants from the National Science Foundation (NSF GS 750) and the National Institute of Mental Health (MH 12357-01) to Elliot Aronson. Authors are listed in alphabetical order.

But what about more pervasive expectancies such as those about the self? Bramel (1962) showed some evidence for the impact of self-esteem on subsequent behavior. In his study he temporarily raised or lowered the subjects' self-esteem by providing them with positive or negative information about their personalities. He then allowed them to discover irrefutable negative information about themselves. The individuals who held low self-concepts were more willing to accept this information; that is, they were not as prone as people who had been induced toward high self-esteem to project this specific negative attribute onto others. These results are consistent with the work of Rogers (1951), who argued that negative or maladaptive responses occur as the result of being consistent with a negative self-concept, and that such responses can be altered only by first changing the self-concept in a direction consistent with adaptive responses.

The prediction being tested in the present experiment is in accord with the experiments cited above. In addition, it carries our interest in the self-concept one step further in the direction Rogers has taken—toward greater generalization. What Aronson and Carlsmith showed is that people try to behave in a highly specific manner which will coincide with a highly specific self-expectancy; that is, people who believe that they are poor in a "social sensitivity" test will take action aimed at performing poorly on the test. But does this generalize? If we feel low and worthless on one or two dimensions do we behave generally in low and worthless ways—even if the behavior is not directly and specifically related to the low aspects of the self-concept? For example, if a person is jilted by his girlfriend (and thus feels unloved), is he more apt to go out and rob a bank, kick a dog, or wear mismatched pajamas?

In the present experimental situation we are predicting just that. Concretely, individuals who are provided with self-relevant information which temporarily causes them to lower their self-esteem (but does *not* specifically make them feel immoral or dishonest) are more apt to cheat than those who are made to raise their self-esteem—or those who are given no self-relevant information at all (control condition). Similarly, people who are induced to raise their self-esteem will be less likely to cheat than the controls. This hypothesis is based upon the assumption that high self-esteem acts as a barrier against dishonest behavior because such behavior is inconsistent. In short, if a person is tempted to cheat, it will be easier for him to yield to this temptation if his self-esteem is low than if it is high. Cheating is not inconsistent with generally low self-esteem; it *is* inconsistent with generally high self-esteem.

METHOD

General Procedure

The subjects were led to believe that they were participating in a study concerned with the correlation between personality test scores and extra-sensory perception (ESP). They were told that their personalities would be evaluated with the self-esteem scales of the California Personality Inventory (CPI) and that their ESP ability would be ascertained with the aid of a modified game of blackjack. Before participating in the blackjack game, subjects took the personality test and received false feedback (either positive, negative, or neutral) about their personalities. During the blackjack game subjects were faced with the dilemma of either cheating and winning or not cheating and losing in a situation in which they were led to believe (erroneously) that cheating was impossible to detect. The opportunity to cheat occurred when the subjects were "accidentally" dealt two cards at once instead of one. The rightful card put the subject over 21 and ensured defeat, whereas the mistakenly dealt extra card, if kept, provided the subject with a point total that virtually assured victory. The card which the subject kept constituted the dependent variable.

Subjects

The subjects were 45 females taken from introductory psychology classes at the University of Texas, who were randomly assigned to one of three self-esteem conditions: high, low, and neutral. In actuality, 50 subjects were run; the result of five subjects were discarded because of suspicion. Three of these were in the low self-esteem condition; two were in the high self-esteem condition. The criteria for elimination were determined a priori and were followed rigidly throughout the experiment. It was made explicit that the experimenter had no preconceptions as to how personality traits might be related to ESP ability, but simply wanted to determine whether or not, for example, people who are easily angered have more ESP than calm people.

Personality Test

All subjects came to the first session together and were given the self-esteem scales of the CPI. The CPI was administered by a person who introduced himself as a member of the University Counseling Center staff. Subjects were told at this session that the experiment was concerned with ESP and personality characteristics. They were informed that this session was to determine the personality traits of the subjects, with ESP ability to be measured in the second session.

A shortened version of the CPI was used to evaluate the personalities of the subjects. This version contained only the six scales related to self-esteem and, for our purposes, constituted a measure of the subjects' chronic self-esteem. However, the *primary* experimental purpose of this text was merely to provide the opportunity and rationale for situationally manipulating the subjects' self-esteem via preprogrammed feedback regarding subjects' personality test results.

In order to separate the experimenter as much as possible from the personality evaluation aspects of the experiment, subjects were told by the experimenter that Miss Jacobs,[1] a member of the University of Texas Counseling Center staff, had kindly consented to administer the personality tests. It was emphasized that she would score the personality inventories and that the experimenter's access to their scores would not be on a name basis but via a complicated coding process. It was indicated that, as a matter of convenience, subjects would be given feedback regarding their personality tests when they came for the second session of the experiment. Following this, the CPI's were distributed, subjects completed them, and before leaving were assigned a time to return for the second session with three subjects assigned to each specific time slot.

Personality Score

In the second session subjects were tested in groups of three. Upon arrival for the second session, subjects were greeted by Miss Jacobs and told to be seated in an outer office which provided access to three adjoining offices. After all three subjects had arrived, Miss Jacobs handed each subject a manila envelope bearing appropriate Counseling Center insignia and assigned each subject to a different office where she was to go to read the results of her personality test. In addition, Miss Jacobs told the subjects that she had been given a sheet of instructions to deliver to them. The sheet of instructions was handed to the subjects along with the manila envelope.

The personality test results consisted of three standard feedbacks unrelated to subjects' performance on the CPI. Each of the three subjects present at any one specific time was randomly assigned feedback of either high self-esteem (HSE = positive), no self-esteem (NSE = neutral), or low self-esteem (LSE = negative) in content.

The HSE and LSE personality reports were parallel in content except, of course, for the nature of the evaluation. For example, a portion of the HSE report stated:

> The subject's profile indicates she has a stable personality and is not given to pronounced mood fluctuations of excitement or depression. Her stableness does not seem to reflect compulsive tendencies, but rather an ability to remain calm and level-headed in almost any circumstance. Her profile does suggest she might be rather impulsive concerning small details and unimportant decisions. This impulsive tendency is probably reflected in a lack of concern with material things. In addition, it appears that material things are important to the subject only insofar as they enable her to express her generosity, good nature, and zest for living. . . . [she] is intellectually very mature for her age.

The corresponding portion of the LSE report stated:

> The subject's profile indicates that she has a rather unstable personality and is given to pronounced mood fluctuations of excitement or depression. Her instability seems

---

[1]The authors would like to express their appreciation to Sylvia Jacobs for her assistance in running the study.

to reflect compulsive tendencies and relative inability to remain calm and level-headed in circumstances which involve tension and pressure. Her profile does suggest she might be rather meticulous and careful concerning small details and when making unimportant decisions. In addition, it appears that material things are very important to the subject as an end in themselves. She appears to be a very selfish person who clings to material things as a source of personal gratification and as an emotional crutch.

In the NSE condition the subject was told that her report had not yet been evaluated due to a heavy backlog of work at the Counseling Center. Instead, she was presented with a sample profile which was described as a typical or average CPI profile such as one might find in a psychological textbook. The comments in this NSE report paralleled those of the HSE and LSE reports (e.g., "... fairly stable personality ... occasionally experiences mood fluctuations ..."). The contents of the rest of the reports was designed to be global in nature and contained comments concerning the person's ability to make friends, general impact of personality, and depth of thought. Since the dependent variable involved honesty, special care was taken to refrain from mentioning anything directly involving honesty. Similarly, nothing whatever was mentioned, either explicitly or implicitly about the person's moral behavior or "goodness" of conduct.

Warm-up Instructions

After reading their personality test results, subjects turned to their page of instructions. The instructions stated:

> The purpose of this experiment is to correlate extrasensory perception ability with personality characteristics. In order to get a true measure of a person's ESP ability, it is necessary that one's mind be primed for thinking. In order to accomplish this, I am having you engage in a period of cerebral warm-up. It's not important what you think about—anything will do—but the crucial point is that you are to use your mind, warm it up by thinking. You need not concentrate intensely, just keep your mind active and filled with thought. A few minutes of this will suffice to prepare you for the ESP experiment.

The purpose of this "warm-up" period was to provide an opportunity for the impact of our manipulations to sink in. Since the subjects had just received an evaluation of their personalities we were quite confident that they would be thinking about this material.

Following the warm-up period, the subjects were sent, one at a time, at intervals of approximately 30 seconds, from the second floor of the psychology building to a room on the fourth floor. Here they were met by the experimenter who was unaware of which subject had received which type of personality feedback. The subjects were placed in one of three cubicles which isolated them from each other. Thus it was impossible for subjects to converse with one another between the time they received their personality results and the time the dependent measure was collected.

Apparatus

The apparatus consisted of four booths or cubicles; the front panels of three of the cubicles bounded an area 1 foot square. Access to this area was available via the fourth cubicle which had no front panel. The experimenter, when sitting in the fourth cubicle, was thus able to receive and dispense playing cards to the subjects in the other three cubicles via slots in their front panels. Subjects in their cubicles had no means of communicating with their fellow subjects nor could they see the experimenter due to plywood panels on both sides and at the top of their booths.

Inside each booth there were two slots and two toggle switches. One switch was designated to be turned on to indicate a "no" answer and the other to indicate a "yes" answer. One of the slots was horizontal with the base of the booth, and was situated in the middle of the front panel one-half inch above the cubicle base. The other slot was vertical and was the slot through which subjects returned cards to the experimenter.

The experimenter's cubicle contained three inclined sheet-metal slides leading down to the horizontal slots of the subjects' booths, three vertical slots from each subject's booth which were shielded so that subjects could not see into the experimenter's compartment, three scoreboards (one for each subject), six small light bulbs, each connected to one of the subjects' "yes" and "no" switches. The experimenter's booth also contained a small electric motor. The motor was functionless except for sound effects, and was activated periodically during the experimental session.

Experimental Materials

The experimenter had two decks of cards. One deck was used for the general game of cards to be played; the other deck was divided into three stacks of cards (one stack for each subject) with a prearranged sequence. These were the crucial hands which a subject would be dealt on those occasions when she would be given the opportunity to cheat. The prearranged stacks consisted of four hands of blackjack with four cards in each hand. The first two cards in all hands totaled approximately 11–13 points with the third card sending the point total over 21. The fourth card, if substituted for the third, always brought the point total to between 19 and 21 points.

Each subject's cubicle contained, in addition to the two toggle switches, a 15-watt light bulb and 10 fifty-cent pieces (or $5). The half-dollars were used as "chips" and potential reward in the experimental task.

Experimental Instructions

After the subjects were seated, the experimenter recited the instructions. He described the results of some previous experiments concerning ESP. Rhine's conclusion that some persons do indeed possess ESP was presented; however, *no* indication was given that certain types of persons possess ESP while others do not. In order to make the cover story appear more credible, subjects were asked to read a recent newspaper article taped to a side panel of their cubicles, which told of how a young girl had been winning an astonishing number of raffle contests which, according to a research institute at Duke University, was perhaps due to her ESP powers. This article indicated that having ESP could be materially valuable, but no mention was made either in the article or in the instructions that having ESP was an intrinsically positive or valued trait to possess. Following this, subjects were told that their ESP ability was going to be evaluated in the context of a modified game of blackjack. It was clearly explained that the game was to be played among the three subjects and that the experimenter was not participating in the game as a contestant. The subjects were then informed of the presence and necessity of a "card-dealing machine." The experimenter said that the cards were to be dealt by a machine "in order to insure against possible interference with your ESP due to another person handling the cards." In actuality, the machine was used in order to provide an opportunity for the subjects to cheat, and to make it easier for subjects to cheat since the machine apparently removed the experimenter from the situation; this will be described below. According to the experimenter's description, the machine automatically dealt them a card on each round. In order to "stand pat," subjects had to switch on their "no" light so that the experimenter could divert the dealing machine from giving them a card on the next round. The use of light signals rather than verbal ones to inform the experimenter that the subject wanted to stand pat was justified by "the necessity of keeping talking at a minimum in order not to interfere with your ESP." The modifications and rules of the blackjack game were as follows:

Each subject was provided with $5 by the psychology department as a stake with which to play the game. Each subject was to "bet 50¢, no more or no less," on the outcome of each hand. Subjects were informed that at the conclusion of the experiment they would be allowed to keep all winnings over $5, but that subjects having less than $5 at the game's conclusion *would not* be required or obligated to make up the deficit out of their own pockets; this made it impossible for any subject to "lose" any of her own money.

We presented the following cover story regarding how ESP ability would be measured: The subjects were told to "concentrate for approximately 5 to 10 seconds before each hand," that is, to think about whether they would win or not win the upcoming hand. If they thought or felt they were going to win, they were to push the "yes" switch in front of them to the "on" position for 5 seconds, whereas if subjects felt they were not going to win the upcoming hand, they were to push the "no" switch to the "on" position for 5 seconds. The number of correct guesses *above chance* supposedly constituted a subject's ESP score. Prior to each guess, all subjects deposited a fifty-cent piece in the vertical slot, and it was explained to the subjects that on every hand they were trying to win a kitty with $1.50 in it.

A thorough explanation of the objectives of blackjack was given in order to equalize differential card game experience between the subjects. It was emphasized that point totals of 14–15 made the choice of whether or not to take another card especially difficult because of the high probability of going over 21 if another card was taken, and the low probability of winning by standing pat. The point totals of the various cards were also emphasized with the Ace counting only 11 points rather than 1 or 11 points, to simplify the experiment; also, all face cards were worth 10 points, and all numbered cards were worth their face values.

It was explained to subjects that:

> The card-dealing machine is a "home-made" affair. It has not as yet been perfected and at times makes mistakes. So far we've been able to iron out most of the mistakes, but occasionally the machine will deal two cards at a time instead of one. The machine is set up so that it deals from the top of the deck, as in a normal game of cards; when a person receives two cards, the top card is actually the card he should have gotten and the bottom card is the mistaken card. Now, the machine is fairly good, but at times will make this mistake. If it ever happens that you are dealt two cards, pick up the two cards and immediately return the bottom card to me by slipping it through the vertical slot. Remember, the top card is your card, the bottom card should be returned to me through the vertical slot.

Subjects were told that when all "no" switches were turned on, the experimenter would say "Game," which was a signal to subjects that they were to push all their cards through the vertical slot to the experimenter. Again, no talking was allowed under the pretext of not interfering with ESP. The experimenter then examined each player's hand, determined the winner, collected the three fifty-cent pieces and slid them down the slide of the winner. When the experimenter said "Begin," indicating that the next game was to start, the two subjects not having received any money were thus informed of their losing status.

Resumé of Procedural Instructions to the Subjects

The word "begin" was a signal to subjects that the previous hand was finished and that a new hand was to commence immediately. Following the word "begin," subjects deposited their fifty-cent pieces through the vertical slot, concentrated for 5 seconds, made a choice of the "yes" or "no" switches regarding their outcome expectancy on the upcoming hand, and the game began. The hand continued until all subjects had indicated they no longer wanted any more cards, at which time the experimenter said "game" and subjects then pushed all their cards through the vertical slot to the experimenter. This same procedure was repeated 35 times for all subjects. However, subjects were not aware as to exactly how many hands had been played at any given point in the experiment, nor did they know precisely when the game would end.

Dependent Measure

The dependent measure was the number of times during the experimental session that subjects kept the card they should have returned to the experimenter, thus enabling them to win the hand. The experiment was designed so as to present each subject with four opportunities to cheat during a session; thus, as far as each subject was concerned, the machine had mistakenly dealt two cards at once only four times in 35 hands. In reality, the experimenter dealt all cards but synchronized his dealing with the onset and termination of the machine-generated sound effects.

The method for providing subjects with a cheating opportunity was quite simple. However, complications arose in determining precisely *when* this opportunity should present itself. We decided to present a subject with an opportunity to cheat when the following conditions could be satisfied: *(a)* If she (the subject) had guessed "yes"; *(b)* when she possessed the same amount of money as the other subjects; *(c)* if she had not previously received more opportunities to cheat than the other subjects; *(d)* when her ESP hit rate was near chance level.

The separate stacks of "cheating cards" were prearranged so that the first two cards totaled 11–14 points, the third put the total over 21, and the fourth, if substituted for the third, brought the total to 19–21 points. Thus, when subjects received two cards at once they were faced with a dilemma: if they did not cheat, they would lose the hand; if they did cheat, they would almost certainly win. Cheating, therefore, was made relatively safe from exposure by having the cards dealt by a machine and also enabled subjects to net $1. The behavioral measure of cheating was whether or not subjects returned to the experimenter the card that was actually theirs and kept the bottom card which enabled them to win. The remaining two subjects in such a game were dealt cards from the general deck. If the subject had cheated, she was always declared the winner on that hand and was given the three fifty-cent pieces. This subject, of course, lost if she did not cheat. The other two subjects, in this hand, were always dealt a hand less than 21 or at times one of them was dealt a hand exceeding 21. If a subject did *not* cheat, the other subject with the score closest to and under 21 was declared the winner. The experimenter used scoreboards to keep track of how often a subject had won a hand, how often each had been given a cheating opportunity, and whether or not a subject had cheated. The scoreboard also provided for an evaluation of trial effects.

Following the card game, all subjects were asked to be seated at a table in the same room. They then filled out a questionnaire consisting of a check on the experimental manipulations and several filler items. Subjects were then debriefed completely. The purpose of the experiment was explained and subjects were assured that the results of the personality test were preprogrammed and had no relationship to their actual test scores.

RESULTS AND DISCUSSION

Analyses of variance on continuous data were all nonsignificant, although the mean differences were of the order hypothesized (mean cheats: LSE = 1.87, NSE = 1.54, HSE = 1.07). Frequency analyses, however, produced significant chi-squares. Subjects were divided according to whether they never cheated or cheated on at least one occasion. Table 19.1 shows a 2 × 3 contingency table chi-square with $df = 2$. Note that 13 people who were given negative feedback cheated at least once, while there were only 6 cheaters among the positive-feedback subjects. The chi-square proved to be significant at beyond the .05 level ($\chi^2 = 7.00, p < .05$). Another chi-square was computed to evaluate the cheating differences between just the high and low self-esteem groups. This chi-square with $df = 1$ also proved to be significant after the correction for continuity had been made ($\chi^2 = 5.17, p < .03$).

Taken as a whole, the data indicate that whether or not an individual cheats is influenced by the nature of the self-relevant feedback he received. People who learned uncomplimentary information about themselves showed a far greater tendency to cheat (on at least one occasion) than individuals who received positive information about themselves. This suggests that individuals with low self-esteem are more prone to commit immoral acts than individuals with high self-esteem, at least when the immoral act is instrumental in producing immediate material gain. Moreover, the number of people cheating in each of the above groups fell on either side of the neutral condition. Although neither experimental condition was significantly different from the control, it is important to note that in the high self-esteem condition there was a greater trend toward honest behavior than in the control, whereas in the low self-esteem condition there was a greater trend toward cheating than in the control.

Our interpretation of the results hinges upon our contention that the manipulation employed in the experiment made subjects feel good about themselves or bad about themselves. In short, we contend that the feedback the subjects received had some impact (however temporary) upon their level of self-esteem. This interpretation is bolstered by our check on the manipulation which indicated that LSE subjects felt worse about themselves than either NSE or HSE subjects. However, since

TABLE 19.1
Number of people cheating at least
once as a function of self-esteem

Condition	Cheat	Never cheat
LSE	13	2
NSE	9	6
HSE	6	9

Note: $\chi^2_{LHN} = 7.00, df = 2, p < .05.$
$\chi^2_{LH} = 5.17, df = 1, p < .03.$

the manipulation check occurred subsequent to the card game, this difference might be due to the cheating behavior rather than the self-esteem manipulation.

There is some additional evidence which is also consistent with our interpretation. This involves the cheating behavior of subjects in terms of their *chronic levels* of self-esteem. Although it was not our intention to measure chronic self-esteem, one can extract a rough measure by looking at the self-concept scores on the CPI, which all subjects filled out as part of the cover story of the experiment. According to these measures, people of high, medium, and low self-esteem had been almost equally distributed among experimental conditions. The following data emerge: In the no feedback (NSE) condition, slightly more "low chronics" cheat than "high chronics." Also, as one might expect, the greatest percentage of cheaters falls among the low chronics who were given negative feedback; the smallest percentage of cheaters falls among the high chronics who were given positive feedback. The small number of subjects in each cell makes statistical analysis of these data unfeasible. The most one can say about these results is that they are consistent with our interpretation of the overall data on the basis of the experimental treatments themselves.

It should be emphasized that one of the unique aspects of this study is the nonspecific nature of the self-concept manipulation. The subjects were not told anything about themselves which would lead them to infer that they were moral-honest or immoral-dishonest people. Rather, they were told things designed to reduce their self-esteem in general. The social implications of these findings may be of some importance. Our results suggest that people who have a high opinion of themselves are less prone to perform any activities which are generally dissonant with their opinion. Similarly, it may be easier for a person with a low self-concept to commit acts of a criminal nature. Moreover, it may be that a common thread running through the complex variables involved in successful socialization (Sears, Maccoby, and Levin, 1957) is that of different development of self-esteem. Granted that most children become aware of what behavior is approved (moral) or disapproved (immoral), the development of high self-esteem in the individual may be crucial in his choosing a moral rather than an immoral mode of behaving.

This discussion is highly speculative to say the least. Further experimentation is necessary before the validity of our reasoning can be determined. One reason for the note of caution is the fact that it is difficult to perform an experiment involving complex human cognitions, emotions, and behavior which leaves us with a single, untarnished explanation for the results. This experiment is no exception. One conceivable alternative interpretation concerns aggressiveness: the subjects in the LSE condition, because they received a negative evaluation, may have been angry at the evaluator and, consequently, may have cheated as a way of punishing him. We attempted to eliminate this possibility in two ways: (a) We separated the experimenter who ran the ESP experiment from the evaluator (a member of the Counseling Center). Toward this end, the experimenter appeared ignorant of and uninterested in these evaluations; it was made to seem to be strictly between the subject and the Counseling Center. (b) The subjects were playing against other subjects rather than against "the house." Thus, when an individual cheated, she was clearly not hurting the experimenter; rather, she was unjustly taking money from a fellow college student.

Perhaps a more compelling explanation involves compensation. The subjects in the low self-esteem situation may, in effect, be saying "Well, I may not have done well on that personality test, but at least I'm going to see to it that I win some money." This explanation is quite different from the one that holds that it is easier to cheat because such behavior is consistent with feelings of low self-esteem. Note, however, that the "compensation" explanation applies only to the subjects in the low self-esteem condition. Thus, this alternative explanation would have been weakened if the subjects in the high self-esteem condition had cheated less than those in the control condition. But as the reader will recall, although these data were in a direction favoring consistency theory, they were not statistically significant. Thus, until further research is performed on this problem, compensation remains a possible explanation.

A final piece of unclarity should be mentioned. We predicted that people in the LSE condition would *cheat* and people in the HSE condition would *not cheat* because we felt that such actions would reflect a consistency between self-esteem and behavior. But *cheating* is merely one of many ways in which a person's behavior could show consistency with low or high self-esteem. For example, in the present situation a LSE subject could try to *lose;* being a loser might be considered as consistent with a low self-esteem. It should be noted that the experimenters took special pains to assure the subjects that they could not lose money. In this situation it seems reasonable to assume that being a loser simply means having bad luck—not being a bad person or even a poor person (financially). We selected cheating as our dependent variable because we felt that it is an unambiguously unethical piece of behavior. Although losing at cards is not pleasant, it does not seem as bad, especially since a loss of money is not involved. The data indicate that our reasoning was correct—that if a sizable number of LSE subjects had sought to lose, our data would have failed to reach significance.

References

Aronson, E., and Carlsmith, J. M. Performance expectancy as a determinant of actual performance. *Journal of Abnormal and Social Psychology,* 1962, **62,** 178–182.

Bramel, D. A. Dissonance theory approach to defensive projection. *Journal of Abnormal and Social Psychology,* 1962, **64,** 121–129.

Rogers, C. R. *Client-centered therapy.* Boston: Houghton-Mifflin, 1951.

Sears, R. R., Maccoby, E. E., and Levin, H. *Patterns of child rearing.* Evanston, Ill.: Row-Peterson, 1957.

Wilson, D. T. Ability evaluation, postdecision dissonance, and co-worker attractiveness. *Journal of Personality and Social Psychology,* 1965, **1,** 486–489.

20

Using Cognitive Dissonance to Encourage Water Conservation

Chris Ann Dickerson, Ruth Thibodeau,
Elliot Aronson, and Dayna Miller

In a field experiment on water conservation, we aroused dissonance in patrons of the campus recreation facility by making them feel hypocritical about their showering habits. Using a 2 × 2 factorial design, we manipulated subjects' "mindfulness" that they had sometimes wasted water while showering, and then varied whether they made a "public commitment" urging other people to take shorter showers. The "hypocrisy" condition—in which subjects made the public commitment after being reminded of their past behavior—was expected to be dissonance-arousing, thereby motivating subjects to increase their efforts to conserve water. The results were consistent with this reasoning. Compared to controls, subjects in the hypocrisy condition took significantly shorter showers. Subjects who were merely reminded that they had wasted water, or who only made the public commitment, did not take shorter showers than control subjects. The findings have implications for using cognitive dissonance as means of changing behavior in applied settings, especially those in which people already support the desired goal, but their behavior is not consistent with those beliefs.

Policy makers frequently attempt to modify behavior in a community often by instituting information-based persuasive campaigns. These appear in various forms including broadcast announcements, newspaper advertisements, signs, mailings, and flyers. In recent years, drought has prompted administrators at the University of California at Santa Cruz (UCSC) to launch a major campaign of just this sort. Campus newspapers contained advertisements from the Water Conservation Office; flyers were posted on public bulletin boards and appeared in mailboxes. Specifically, the UCSC program encouraged people to think of water as a valuable resource and to adopt conservation-oriented behaviors such as flushing toilets less

Reprinted with permission from the authors and *Journal of Applied Social Psychology*, 1992, Vol. 22, No. 11, 841–854. Copyright © 1992 by V. H. Winston & Son, Inc. All rights reserved.

The first author was supported by a National Science Foundation graduate fellowship while completing this research.

often, stopping the flow whenever possible while brushing teeth or washing dishes, and taking shorter, more efficient showers.

The effectiveness of these types of persuasive messages and information campaigns is not certain. One experiment (Aronson and O'Leary, 1983) found that prominent signs asking people to take shorter showers produced mixed results. Indeed, if the message is too heavy-handed, it can even create a backlash. For example, although some subjects in the Aronson and O'Leary study reduced their water use, others showed their annoyance by sabotaging the signs and taking inordinately *long* showers. Moreover, even if people are initially persuaded by signs or flyers that conservation is worthwhile, there is controversy regarding the potency of such straightforward, and sometime "coercive," appeals. They can produce attitude change, but the effects are frequently short-lived (Aronson, 1980).

Similarly, even when messages praising the value of water conservation are successful in changing people's attitudes, there is no guarantee that new attitudes will translate into new behaviors. Social psychologists have long been aware that the link between attitudes and behavior is problematic (e.g., Wicker, 1969). Thus, simply persuading people that conservation is beneficial might not result in reduced consumption. For example, Bickman (1972) interviewed 500 people about their attitudes concerning responsibility for removing litter. Although 94% of the subjects expressed favorable attitudes toward removing litter, only 2% actually picked up litter that had been intentionally left outside of the experimental setting by the experimenter.

We reasoned that a more effective means of promoting water conservation on campus might involve dissonance-generated self-persuasion, rather than informational or coercive appeals to save water. The motivating influence of cognitive dissonance has been shown to promote changes in attitudes as well as behavior (Aronson, 1969, 1980; Brehm and Wicklund, 1976; Freedman, 1965). Dissonance-related techniques have been utilized successfully in a number of applied situations: for example, to improve weight loss (Axsom and Cooper, 1981), reduce snake phobia (Cooper, 1980; Cooper and Axsom, 1982), and as a component of programs designed to promote energy conservation (e.g., Gonzales, Aronson, and Costanzo, 1988). Moreover, Pallak and his colleagues have demonstrated that dissonance-related interventions can produce enduring behavior change. Longitudinal studies have shown that a public commitment manipulation can cause people to reduce their energy consumption for six months or more (Pallak, Cook, and Sullivan, 1980; Pallak and Cummings, 1976; Pallak, Sullivan, and Cook, 1976).

As formulated by Festinger (1957), dissonance theory proposes that when a person holds two cognitions that are psychologically inconsistent, the person will experience cognitive dissonance, an unpleasant drive state akin to hunger or thirst. Once dissonance is aroused, an individual is motivated to reduce it, primarily through attitudinal or behavioral changes designed to reestablish consistency. Soon after Festinger's initial conceptualization, Aronson (1960, 1968) proposed that dissonance theory makes its clearest predictions when expectancies about the self are involved—that is, when people have done something that violates their self-concepts. Most of us share certain general beliefs about ourselves: for example, that we are good, moral, competent individuals. Therefore, choosing to engage in a behavior that is at odds with these important beliefs about the self should produce dissonance.

Given the central role of the self-concept in dissonance arousal, Aronson (1980) has argued that dissonance-related persuasion is likely to be much more effective than straightforward persuasive appeals. In a typical persuasion situation, such as those involving informational campaigns, people change their opinions because they have been convinced by an external source to do so. An unfortunate feature of this type of attitude change is that it is often impermanent. For example, if I change my attitude because I hear a persuasive argument supporting one stance, I am likely to change it again if I hear a better argument supporting another position. There is very little of myself invested in the attitude.

In contrast, dissonance-generated persuasion is highly involving because it entails a challenge to a person's self-concept. Dissonance would occur, for example, if I believed I was a moral person, and then found myself in the uncomfortable position of having done something I considered immoral. To reduce this dissonance, I would need to rethink, or "justify," my actions in order to make them more consistent with my self-concept—typically through changes in relevant attitudes or behaviors. This subtle form of self-persuasion is powerful because the individual's self-concept is directly engaged in the process of attitudinal or behavioral change (Aronson, 1980).

Perhaps the most dramatic demonstration of dissonance-related persuasion is evidenced in the counter-attitudinal advocacy paradigm (e.g., Cohen, 1962; Festinger and Carlsmith, 1959; Nel, Helmreich, and Aronson, 1969). In this procedure, subjects are induced, under conditions of high choice or low incentive, to persuade others to believe something that they themselves do not believe. These subjects subsequently come to believe their own rhetoric; that is, they reduce dissonance by persuading *themselves* that their counter-attitudinal statements were, in fact, a reflection of their true beliefs.

The counter-attitudinal advocacy paradigm, by definition, requires that experimenters induce people to defend a position that they were initially against. This requirement posed a problem for our effort to harness the power of the technique to promote water conservation. Conservation is an example of an "apple-pie and motherhood" issue that everybody already believes in, even though not everyone practices. Recently, however, Aronson and his colleagues (see Aronson, 1992) have developed a modified version of the procedure so that it can be used in pro-attitudinal situations. The new technique involves creating feelings of hypocrisy. This is accomplished by inducing subjects to encourage other people to perform certain worthwhile behaviors. Subjects are then reminded that, on occasion, their own behavior has not been consistent with those goals. Essentially, subjects are confronted with the realization that they do not always practice what they preach. This realization is expected to generate dissonance because being a hypocrite would be inconsistent with most people's self-concepts as persons of integrity. As a result, subjects should be motivated to reduce dissonance by behaving in a manner more consistent with their espoused attitudes.

In an experiment on AIDS prevention, Aronson, Fried, and Stone (1991) explored the dissonance-arousing properties of this new procedure. Using a 2 × 2 factorial design, they induced feelings of hypocrisy regarding condom use. All subjects wrote pro-attitudinal speeches advocating condom use during all sexual encounters. Then, half the subjects simply rehearsed the arguments of the speech. The rest videotaped their prepared speeches, which they believed were going to be shown to high school students as part of an AIDS prevention program. Before taping their speeches, however, half the subjects were also reminded of the occasions when they had failed to use condoms in the past. Thus, all subjects believed that condom use was important, and all had composed a speech arguing that point. However, only those who both made a videotape and were reminded that they had engaged in unsafe sexual behavior were expected to feel hypocritical. These subjects were expected to reduce dissonance by strengthening their intentions to use condoms in the future. Aronson et al.'s (1991) results were consistent with this reasoning. Compared to subjects in the other conditions, those who received the hypocrisy manipulation expressed significantly greater intentions to increase their use of condoms, relative to their past behavior.

The results of this experiment are provocative in suggesting that a "hypocrisy" manipulation can arouse dissonance. Moreover, a follow-up experiment was conducted (Stone, Aronson, Crain, Winslow, and Fried, 1992), using a behavioral measure rather than self-reported behavioral intentions. Specifically, in each of the above conditions, subjects were subsequently given an opportunity to purchase condoms at a huge discount. Fully 83% of the subjects in the hypocrisy condition purchased condoms; this was a significantly greater percentage than in each of the other three conditions.

Did subjects, in fact, increase their condom use as a result of the hypocrisy manipulation? Obviously, it is impossible to know for sure. After all, one cannot follow people into the bedroom to observe their condom-using behavior. However, one *can* follow people into the shower-room—at least at public physical education facilities. The present experiment explores the utility of the hypocrisy-induction procedure in a field setting, using water conservation as the target behavior. In a conceptual replication of Aronson et al. (1991), public commitment endorsing water conservation was crossed with feedback intended to make subjects aware that they had wasted water in the past. After acknowledging that they supported conservation efforts, half the subjects agreed to help persuade other people to conserve water. Additionally, half the subjects were reminded that they did not live up to their own standards, and had sometimes been wasteful. The condition in which subjects both committed publicly to encourage other people to conserve and were reminded that they had wasted water was designed to make subjects feel hypocritical. These subjects were expected to reduce dissonance by reducing their water use while showering.

METHOD

Overview of the Procedure

Female swimmers were recruited as they exited the pool area, on their way to the locker room. A female experimenter (Experimenter 1), posing as a member of a campus water conservation office, approached each potential subject and asked if she could spare a few moments to help with a water conservation project. Then, depending on the experimental condition, subjects either answered some questions, signed a flyer, or both. Subjects were thanked for their participation, and their interaction with the first experimenter was terminated. However, unbeknown to subjects, a second female experimenter (Experimenter 2) was waiting in the shower room where she unobtrusively timed the length of each subject's shower and noted whether subjects turned the water flow off while soaping up.

Experimental Design

Two factors were manipulated: subjects' "mindfulness" of their sometimes wasteful showering habits, and subjects' "commitment" to pro-conservation behaviors. This 2×2 factorial design yielded the following conditions: (1) mindful-plus-commitment (hypocrisy), (2) mindful-only, (3) commitment only, and (4) unmindful/no commitment (no-treatment control). Our primary dependent variable was actual water use, as reflected in the length of the subjects' showers. As a rougher measure of subjects' intentions to conserve water, we also noted whether subjects turned the shower off while applying soap, shampoo, or conditioner.

Subjects

Participants in the study were 80 female swimmers who used the shower after exercising in the campus pool. Females were selected for this study because we intended to gather data only in the women's locker room. We used swimmers because pretesting indicated that swimmers could most reliably be expected to shower and shampoo before leaving the recreational facilities. Although the majority of swimmers used shampoo and/or soap when showering (to remove chlorine from their hair and skin), those few who simply rinsed off under the shower were excluded from the study in order to reduce extraneous within-group variance. This exclusion was minimal and did not occur with differential frequency in any of the treatment conditions.

Experimental Setting

The particular configuration of the shower room is crucial to the design of this field study. The swimming pool and women's locker room are part of the same complex, with direct access to the showers available from poolside. The shower room is a large open room, approximately 15′ wide by 25′ long, without separate shower stalls or curtains. There are 13 showerheads, spaced along the walls of the shower room, and there are usually a number of people showering at any given time during operating hours. Typically, at least two or three other women were using the shower room at the same time as the subject and Experimenter 2. Frequently, there were more then five other women in the shower. These circumstances made it very easy to collect the dependent measures without attracting attention or arousing suspicion. Furthermore, it ensured that Experimenter 2's presence was unlikely to have detectable influence on the subject's behavior.

Procedure

While en route from the pool to the shower room, subjects were approached individually by Experimenter 1, who introduced herself as a representative of the campus water conservation office. After asking the subject if she had a few moments to spare, Experimenter 1 asked the subject whether she was on her way to the shower, and whether she was in favor of water conservation. If subjects answered "yes" to these questions, Experimenter 1 consulted a randomization chart and then introduced the experimental manipulations.

In the mindful-only treatment, she asked subjects to respond verbally to a "survey" consisting of a brief set of questions, such as: (1) When showering, do you ALWAYS turn off the water while soaping up or shampooing? (2) When you take showers, do you ALWAYS make them as short as possible, or do you sometimes linger longer than necessary? (3) In your view, about how long does it take an average person to shower and shampoo, without wasting any water? (4) About how long is your average shower at the Field House? These questions were designed to remind subjects that they had sometimes wasted water while showering.

In the commitment-only treatment, the subject was simply asked to help out with campus conservation efforts by printing her name with a thick black marking pen on a flyer that read: "Please conserve water. Take shorter showers. Turn showers off while soaping up. IF I CAN DO IT, SO CAN YOU!" Experimenter 1 explained that the flyer would be attached to posters that were being created for distribution around campus, and that they were intended to encourage other members of the campus community to conserve water. While making this request, Experimenter 1 drew subjects' attention to the large, colorful "sample" poster on display nearby, and mentioned that another poster was already in place outside of the women's locker room.

In the hypocrisy condition (mindful-plus-commitment), subjects first responded to the brief "mindfulness" survey, then signed the "commitment" flyer as outlined above.

The fourth condition served as a no-treatment control. In essence, the behavior of the subjects in this condition reflects a baseline response to the interventions instituted by the university in an effort to save water. Due to persisting drought conditions in California, UCSC had been quite actively promoting water conservation. Advertisements in the campus newspapers and flyers posted on public bulletin boards urged members of the campus community to reduce their water use. Most pertinent to this study, the university had posted a very large sign inside the actual shower room. The sign read: "Take Shorter Showers. Turn the Water Off While Soaping Up."

Experimenters

Both experimenters were female students. The actions of the two experimenters were carefully coordinated. Experimenter 1 stood near a large doorway leading from the pool deck into the athletic facilities complex. From this vantage point, she was able to intercept all female swimmers who were leaving the pool to enter the locker room. Experimenter 2 sat sunbathing by the pool, near the back door to the woman's locker room. This was approximately 30 feet from Experimenter 1's position. As Experimenter 1 began her interaction with the subject, Experimenter 2 watched, and made sure she could identify the subject later to collect the dependent measures.

As Experimenter 1 approached a potential subject, she asked the subject if she was on her way to the showers, and next, whether she could spare a few moments to participate in a water conservation project. If the subject answered yes to both, Experimenter 1 casually scratched her own knee before continuing the interaction. The knee scratch was a signal to Experimenter 2, who quickly entered the back door of the locker room, and began showering while waiting for the subject. This process enabled Experimenter 2 to remain unaware regarding which manipulation Experimenter 1 had delivered to the subject.

Experimenter 2 was already in the shower room, showering, when the subject entered. Several precautions were taken to guarantee that Experimenter 2 would not influence the subject's behavior. First, as noted above, the setting was a large shower room, and there were frequently a number of women showering. This reduced the possibility that Experimenter 2's presence had any noticeable effect on subjects. Additionally, since Experimenter 2 was often in the shower room for 10 to 15 minutes, she always brought shampoo, conditioner, a shaving razor, and a comb into the shower. These were used as necessary to make her showering appear as natural as possible. Finally, Experimenter 2 always left the water running during her shower. This was to avoid any possibility of influencing subjects to turn their own faucet on and off.

Dependent Measures

Experimenter 2 wore a waterproof sports watch with stopwatch capacity, which she unobtrusively activated as soon as the subject turned on the shower. She also noted whether the subject turned off the shower while applying soap or shampoo. To assess water use accurately, the watch was stopped when the subject turned off the shower and was reactivated if the subject turned it back on to continue her shower.

RESULTS

Manipulation Checks

All subjects answered "yes" to the first question in the survey "Are you in favor of water conservation?"—thus indicating that their attitudes on this issue were positive. In the two conditions in which mindfulness was manipulated, subjects' answers to the brief set of questions confirmed that they were aware of their some-times wasteful showering habits. That is, all subjects replied that: (a) they did not always take the shortest possible showers; (b) they sometimes lingered longer than necessary in the shower; and (c) they did not always turn the shower off while soaping up or shampooing.

Shower Times

A two-way ANOVA was performed on subjects' shower times, measured in seconds (see Table 20.1). No main effects for commitment or mindfulness were obtained, nor was the interaction of the two factors statistically significant, model $F(1, 76) = 1.48$, $p < .26$. However, a planned comparison of mean shower times revealed a significant difference between the hypocrisy group ($M = 220.5$ sec) and the control group ($M = 301.8$ sec), $F(1, 39) = 4.23$, $p < .05$. Means for the commitment-only ($M = 247.7$) and mindfulness-only ($M = 248.3$) groups did not differ from each other, nor did either differ from the control or hypocrisy groups.

TABLE 20.1
Mean shower times (in seconds)

Condition	Mean	SD
Mindful-only	248.3	146.07
Commitment-only	247.7	104.05
Mindful/committed (hypocrisy)	220.5	100.62
Unmindful/uncommitted (control)	301.8	142.32

Turning Off the Shower

We also compared how often subjects in each condition turned off the shower while shampooing or soaping up. An overall chi square analysis yielded a marginally significant difference among all four groups on this dichotomous measure ($x^2 = 7.742$, $df = 3$, $p < .052$) (see Table 20.2). Next, a comparison of the hypocrisy and control groups revealed a significant difference in the expected direction, with hypocrisy subjects turning off the shower more often than control subjects ($x^2 = 4.912$, $df = 1$, $p < .027$).

The frequencies in the hypocrisy condition did not, however, differ from those in the mindful-only and commitment-only conditions. Indeed, the data from these three conditions were identical, with 14 out of 20 subjects in each group turning off the shower, compared to only 7 out of 20 in the control group ($x^2 = 7.742$, $df = 1$, $p < .005$).

TABLE 20.2
Frequency of turning off the shower

Condition	Yes	No
Mindful-only	14	6
Commitment-only	14	6
Mindful/committed (hypocrisy)	14	6
Unmindful/uncommitted (control)	7	13

DISCUSSION

The data from this experiment are consistent with our reasoning that higher levels of dissonance would be aroused for subjects in the hypocrisy condition, leading them to make greater efforts to conserve water than subjects in other conditions. Specifically, it was only subjects in this condition who took significantly shorter showers than subjects in the control condition. Unexpectedly, however, shower times for hypocrisy subjects were not significantly shorter than times for subjects in either the mindful or commitment conditions, both of which fell midway between times for hypocrisy subjects and controls. In addition, subjects in the mindful and commitment conditions were just as likely as those in the hypocrisy condition to turn the water off while showering. In all three conditions, this behavior occurred significantly more often than in the no-treatment condition.

Overall, this pattern of data suggests the possibility that subjects in all three groups were motivated to conserve water, although this effect was strongest for those in the hypocrisy condition. That is, rather than experiencing *no* dissonance, subjects in the mindful and commitment conditions might have experienced some feelings of hypocrisy, albeit of a milder sort than their counterparts in the hypocrisy group. Subjects in the former conditions were exposed to manipulations that could potentially arouse some feelings of hypocrisy. For example, in the commitment condition subjects signed a flyer that stated: "Take shorter showers . . . If I can do it, so can you!" For subjects who had wasted water in the past, this statement might have been experienced as somewhat hypocritical, even without the mindfulness manipulation to heighten its effect. Similarly, subjects in the mindful condition first affirmed their pro-conservation attitudes in the presence of the experimenter (recall that everyone answered "yes" to the initial question: "Are you in favor of water conservation?") and then were made aware of the discrepancy between their attitudes and behavior—that is, the fact that they did not always take the shortest possible showers. This awareness could have aroused mild feelings of hypocrisy, or dissonance, for these subjects.

Why did subjects in these two conditions reduce dissonance by turning the water off, yet did not take shorter showers than controls? One possible reason is that turning the shower off is a fairly vivid and unambiguous way for subjects to demonstrate their commitment to conserve water. As such, it provides a natural "first step" for subjects who are motivated to conserve water, thus affording the clearest and most available route to dissonance reduction. Unlike hypocrisy subjects, however, subjects in the mindful and commitment groups did not take the additional step of significantly reducing the duration of their showers, relative to controls. This finding is consistent with our interpretation that hypocrisy subjects were experiencing the highest levels of dissonance and, as a result, were more motivated to act in accordance with their principles: both by turning off the shower *and* actually using less water. Finally, it should be noted that our primary dependent variable, length of shower, is a true measure of water conservation—unlike turning off the water, which is simply one method of potentially achieving that goal.

Could the effects found in the present experiment be due to some cause other than dissonance arousal? For example, could subjects have taken steps to conserve water simply because their pro-conservation attitudes were made salient by the experimental manipulations? Although our manipulations may have partly served to "prime" subjects' attitudes, we think it is unlikely that the shower-time results are due to the mere effects of attitude accessibility or salience. To begin with, subjects in all three experimental conditions were, in one way or another, reminded of their favorable attitudes toward water conservation prior to taking a shower. Yet, only subjects in the hypocrisy condition showed a significant reduction in their actual water use. In addition, data from the condom experiments discussed earlier (Aronson et al., 1991; Stone et al., 1992) do not support a "priming" interpretation of the present findings. The results of these studies, which employed similar manipulations and were conducted under more controlled laboratory conditions, reflected significantly greater dissonance arousal among hypocrisy subjects compared to all other experimental conditions.

Still it could be argued that in the present study hypocrisy subjects might have experienced a more potent priming effect, given their exposure to both the mindful and commitment manipulations. While this alternative explanation cannot be ruled out, a close look at the details of the procedure makes this interpretation seem less plausible. Specifically, subjects in the hypocrisy condition were treated identically to those in the mindful condition except that the former also signed a leaflet advocating others to conserve water. This leaflet contained no new information above and beyond that already presented in the mindful condition; it simply restated methods of conserving water in the showers. (Indeed, this information is also posted conspicuously in the shower room itself and in other prominent locations within the adjacent locker room.) Thus, it seems doubtful that in the hypocrisy condition this redundant information—presented briefly and only seconds after the more extensive mindfulness manipulation—could have contributed appreciably to any "priming effect" produced by either of the manipulations alone. Rather, we would argue that the impact of signing the leaflet was that it made hypocrisy subjects uncomfortably aware of having preached something they did not always practice, thereby accounting for their greater motivation to conserve water. Future research is necessary, however, to determine conclusively whether these findings are best explained by dissonance arousal or are the effect of increased accessibility of attitudes via priming. In particular, laboratory studies based on the "misattribution of arousal" paradigm in dissonance research (e.g., Zanna and Cooper, 1974) would shed needed light on this issue.

Although a "priming" interpretation cannot be entirely ruled out, taken together with the findings of Aronson et al. (1991) and Stone et al. (1992) our results suggest that feelings of hypocrisy can be dissonance-arousing, thereby motivating people to bring their behavior into closer alignment with their espoused ideals. In addition, in recent years it has been proposed that individuals must produce "foreseeable aversive consequences" in order to experience dissonance (Cooper and Fazio, 1984; see also Thibodeau and Aronson, 1992). Our findings cast doubt on this new formulation of dissonance theory. Any consequences resulting from complying with the experimenter's requests could only serve to promote water conservation—by encouraging other people to save water, and by helping the "Water Conservation Office" with a survey. Far from being an aversive consequence, saving water was something that all subjects in the present study already supported.

Finally, in the present experiment subjects experienced dissonance in a pro-attitudinal advocacy paradigm. This represents a new twist on the counter-attitudinal advocacy manipulation traditionally employed in dissonance research and opens up new opportunities for applying the theory in real-world settings. In particular, interventions along the lines of our hypocrisy manipulation may prove successful in motivating people to act in accordance with their already favorable attitudes toward a given issue, such as water conservation, condom use, recycling, etc. Clearly, using dissonance arousal as a strategy for changing behavior is somewhat more involved than simply hanging signs or posting flyers. As noted earlier, however, research suggests that changes in attitudes and behavior generated by cognitive dissonance tend to be more permanent and may also transfer to new situations, as compared to changes produced by other means of persuasion (Aronson, 1980).

In the long run, then, dissonance-related persuasion may prove to be a cost-effective method for policy makers to employ in a variety of settings, especially those in which the goal is to produce higher levels of consistency between attitudes and beliefs.

References

ARONSON, E. *The cognitive and behavioral consequences of confirmation and disconfirmation of expectancies.* Application for Research Grant submitted to the National Science Foundation, Harvard University, 1960.

ARONSON, E. Dissonance theory: Progress and problems. In R. Abelson, E. Aronson, W. McGuire, T. Newcomb, M. Rosenberg, & P. Tannenbaum (Eds)., *Theories of cognitive consistency: A sourcebook* (pp. 5–27). Chicago: McNally, 1968.

ARONSON, E. The theory of cognitive dissonance: A current perspective. In L. Berkowitz (Ed.), *Advances in experimental social psychology* (Vol. 4, pp. 1–34). New York: Academic Press, 1969.

ARONSON, E. Persuasion via self-justification: Large commitments for small rewards. In L. Festinger, (Ed)., *Retrospection on social psychology* (pp. 3–21). Oxford University Press: Oxford, 1980.

ARONSON, E. The return of the repressed: Dissonance theory makes a comeback. *Psychological Inquiry*, 1992, **3**, 303–311.

ARONSON, E., AND CARLSMITH, J. M. Effect of severity of threat on the valuation of forbidden behavior. *Journal of Abnormal and Social Psychology*, 1963, **66**, 584–588.

ARONSON, E., FRIED, C., AND STONE, J. Overcoming denial: Increasing the intention to use condoms through the induction of hypocrisy. *American Journal of Public Health*, 1991, **18**, 1636–1640.

ARONSON, E., AND O'LEARY, M. The relative effectiveness of models and prompts on energy conservation: A field experiment in a shower room. *Journal of Environmental Systems*, 1983, **12**, 219–224.

AXSOM, D., AND COOPER, J. Reducing weight by reducing dissonance: The role of effort justification in inducing weight loss. In E. Aronson (Ed.), *Readings about the social animal* (3rd ed., pp. 181–196). San Francisco: Freeman, 1981.

BICKMAN, L. Environmental attitudes and actions. *Journal of Social Psychology*, 1972, **87**, 323–324.

BREHM, J., AND WICKLUND, R. *Perspectives on cognitive dissonance.* Hillsdale, NJ: Lawrence Erlbaum Associates, 1976.

COHEN, A. An experiment on small rewards for discrepant compliance and attitude change. In J. Brehm and A. Cohen (Eds.), *Explorations in cognitive dissonance* (pp. 73–78). New York: Wiley, 1962.

COOPER, J. Reducing fears and increasing assertiveness: The role of dissonance reduction. *Journal of Experimental Social Psychology*, 1980, **16**, 199–213.

COOPER, J., AND AXSOM, D. Effort justification in psychotherapy. In G. Weary and H. Mirels (Eds.), *Integrations of clinical and social psychology* (pp. 98–121). New York, Oxford, 1982.

COOPER, J., AND FAZIO, R. A new look at dissonance theory. In L. Berkowitz (Ed.), *Advances in experimental social psychology* (Vol. 17, pp. 229–265). New York: Academic Press, 1984.

FESTINGER, L. *A theory of cognitive dissonance.* Palo Alto, CA: Stanford University Press, 1957.

FESTINGER, L., AND CARLSMITH, J. M. Cognitive consequences of forced compliance. *Journal of Abnormal and Social Psychology*, 1959, **58**, 203–210.

FREEDMAN, J. Long-term behavioral effects of cognitive dissonance. *Journal of Experimental Social Psychology*, 1965, **1**, 145–155.

GONZALES, M., ARONSON, E., AND COSTANZO, M. Using social cognition and persuasion to promote energy conservation: A quasi-experiment. *Journal of Applied Social Psychology*, 1988, **18,** 1049–1066.

NEL, E., HELMREICH, R., AND ARONSON, E. Opinion change in the advocate as a function of the persuasibility of the audience: A clarification of the meaning of dissonance. *Journal of Personality and Social Psychology*, 1969, **12,** 117–124.

PALLAK, M., COOK, D., AND SULLIVAN, J. Commitment and energy conservation. In L. Bickman (Ed.), *Applied Social Psychology Annual* (Vol. 1, pp. 235–253). Beverly Hills: Sage Publications, 1980.

PALLAK, M., AND CUMMINGS, W. Commitment and voluntary energy conservation. *Personality and Social Psychology Bulletin*, 1976, **2,** 27–30.

PALLAK, M., SULLIVAN, J., AND COOK, D. *The long-term effects of commitment on voluntary energy conservation.* Presented at the meeting of the Midwestern Psychological Association, Chicago, 1976.

STONE, J., ARONSON, E., CRAIN, L., WINSLOW, M., AND FRIED, C. *Creating hypocrisy as a means of inducing young adults to purchase condoms.* (In preparation.) University of California at Santa Cruz, 1992.

THIBODEAU, R., AND ARONSON, E. Taking a closer look: Reasserting the role of the self concept in dissonance theory. *Personality and Social Psychology Bulletin*, 1992, **18,** 591–602.

WICKER, A. Attitudes versus actions: The relationship of verbal and overt behavioral responses to attitude objects. *Journal of Social Issues*, 1969, **25,** 41–78.

ZANNA, M., AND COOPER, J. Dissonance and the pill: An attribution approach to studying the arousal properties of dissonance. *Journal of Personality and Social Psychology*, 1974, **29,** 703–709.

21

Self-Theories of Intelligence*

Carol S. Dweck

Why do some very bright individuals do poorly in school and end up achieving little in life? Why do other, seemingly less bright people, rise to the challenges and accomplish far more than anyone ever expected? Much of my career has been devoted to answering these questions, and that's where social psychology comes in.

One of the most important things social psychology has done is to show us how profoundly people's beliefs affect their behavior. This has been shown very clearly in the realm of motivation and achievement. Do people believe their intelligence is a fixed trait or an expandable quality? Do they believe their failures are due to a lack of effort or a lack of ability? Do they believe they are doing a task to learn something new or to show how smart they are? These beliefs are key components of individuals' eagerness to learn, their love of challenge, and their ability to persist and thrive in the face of difficulty. This is why they are key factors in what people achieve—quite apart from their intellectual ability.

The most exciting thing about this is that beliefs can be changed. So, even more important than showing that beliefs matter for people's motivation and achievement, is showing that when you change their beliefs, you change their motivation and achievement. It is sometimes amazing to people who are not social psychologists that what looks like minor belief-changing interventions—teaching students a different view of intelligence, teaching them a different interpretation for failure,

---

*Adapted from: Messages that motivate: How praise molds students' beliefs, motivation, and performance (in surprising ways). In J. Aronson, Ed. (2002), Improving Academic Achievement. New York: Academic Press.

or orienting them toward different reasons for achieving—end up having real effects on their school engagement and achievement. I have seen researchers from other fields be completely baffled by these results because they are used to seeing hugely expensive, large-scale, long-term, multifaceted interventions that yield only small effects. Yet, social psychologists understand the power of a carefully targeted intervention that changes a key belief and refocuses people's motivation in highly productive ways.

THE ROLE OF MOTIVATION IN ACHIEVEMENT

What role does motivation play in achievement? There are many researchers who argue that motivation is the key ingredient not simply in outstanding achievement, but also in extraordinary achievement. Their work suggests that creative genius itself grows out of the ability to sustain intense commitment for very long periods of time in the face of obstacles (Runco, Nemiro & Walberg, 1998; see also Hayes, 1989; Nickerson, 1999; Perkins, 1994; Weisberg, 1986; 1999). They tell us, much to our surprise, that many well-known geniuses were pretty much ordinary bright children who then became obsessed with something and, because of that obsession, ended up making enormous contributions (Howe, 1999; Simonton, 1999). This is true in science: Darwin's father was deeply disappointed in how ordinary his son seemed as a child (Simonton, 1999). It is true in philosophy: John Stuart Mill's father, in fact, was tickled to show that his ordinary child could be trained to be a world-famous philosopher (Howe, 1999). Tolstoy and William James were also seen by some as unexceptional children (Howe, 1999).

Even Mozart, whom we think of as composing in infancy, did not produce really original and noteworthy works until after more than 10 years of nonstop composing (Bloom, 1985; Hayes, 1989; Weisberg, 1999). Most of his early compositions were amateurish hodgepodges of other people's compositions. The same principle applies in athletics as well. We all know the story of how Michael Jordan was cut from his high school basketball team—which only increased his commitment and relentless practice until he became one of the greatest athletes of all time.

Yet, much of society is stubbornly wedded to the idea that accomplishment, especially outstanding accomplishment, is about endowment. After Mozart, Darwin, Michael Jordan, and Tiger Woods practice their skills feverishly and single-mindedly for years and years, we ignore this and instead believe that they were simply born with one-in-a-million ability. When Thomas Edison claimed that genius was 99 percent perspiration, and only 1 percent inspiration, we think he is just being modest. And when we hear that the ringlike structure of benzene came to Kekule, the great chemist, in a dream or that the brilliant poem "Kubla Khan" came to Samuel Taylor Coleridge in an opium-induced delirium, we think "Ah yes, that's genius," forgetting the years of training, commitment, and perseverance that led up to these episodes.

SELF-THEORIES OF INTELLIGENCE

In discussing beliefs that play a key role in motivation, I will focus on one particular kind of belief, namely, people's "theories" about their intelligence. I will begin by describing the two theories of intelligence that people hold: The belief that intelligence is a fixed trait that cannot be developed (which we have called an "entity" theory) vs. the idea that intelligence is a malleable quality, a potential that can be cultivated (which we have called an "incremental" theory). I will then show how these beliefs affect the tasks students will take on, the effort they are willing to exert, their ability to cope with setbacks, and—ultimately—their academic performance.

As you will see, the belief in fixed intelligence can lead even the most able students to worry about how smart they are, to think they're dumb when they fail, to dislike and avoid effort, and to show impaired performance when they face academic difficulty (which even top students can experience when they enter a new school). The belief that intelligence can be developed, in contrast, makes students want to do just that: It leads them to value learning over looking smart, to enjoy effort and challenges, and to thrive in the face of difficulty (see Dweck, 1999).

Which is the correct view of intelligence? Is it fixed or is it something that can be developed? Psychologists have always taken and still take both views. Alfred Binet (1909/1973), the inventor of the IQ test, however, was a radical proponent of the idea that intelligence can be developed. He believed that children's most basic capacity to learn could be transformed through education, and he devoted much of his career to designing educational programs that might do that. Today, more and more psychologists are taking the view that intelligence or important components of it can be developed through motivation and learning (Brown & Campione, 1996; Perkins, 1995; Resnick, 1983; Sternberg, 1985). My work does not directly address the question of the true nature of intelligence, but it does show the critical importance of what people believe about intelligence. Let's now look at the motivational worlds created by the two different beliefs.

THE BELIEF IN FIXED INTELLIGENCE

What Is the Student's Goal?

When students believe that their intelligence is fixed what is it they want most to accomplish through their academic work? The answer is they want to look smart. Since intelligence is such a deeply valued commodity and they only have a fixed amount of it, they want to feel as though they have the right amount. In many studies with grade school, junior high school, and college students, we give students a choice between a challenging task where they can learn important new things and a "safer" task where they can look smart. Most students with the fixed view take the task that will make them look smart (Dweck & Leggett, 1988; Stone & Dweck,

1998). This means that rather than risk making errors, they will sacrifice valuable learning opportunities.

A recent study shows exactly how self-defeating this can be. At the University of Hong Kong (the premier institution of higher learning in Hong Kong), all classes, class assignments, and exams are in English. But not all students come to the university knowing much English. In this study (Hong, Chiu, Dweck, Lin & Wan, 1999), we assessed new students' theories about their intelligence and we obtained their scores on their English proficiency exams. We then asked them if they would be willing to take a remedial English course if the faculty offered it. Students who had low English proficiency and believed in malleable intelligence said yes, but students with low English proficiency and a fixed view of intelligence did not. They were not willing to expose their ignorance or risk errors—even though, by not doing so, they were putting their academic career in jeopardy.

What Does Failure or Difficulty Mean?

You might think that students who believe in fixed intelligence would form an opinion of their intelligence and stick to it, but this isn't the case. Why not? Because, although they believe intelligence is fixed, intelligence is an invisible, internal thing that they can't really observe directly—so they just have to guess its level from their performance. This means that one day students may think their fixed ability is high because they've done well, but the next day think it's low because they haven't.

We have found over and over that students who believe in fixed intelligence see academic setbacks as meaning something very negative about their intellectual abilities (Dweck & Sorich, 1999; Henderson & Dweck, 1990; Mueller & Dweck, 1998; Stone & Dweck, 1998; cf. Grant-Pillow & Dweck, 2003). This is even true of bright students at top schools.

In one study (Dweck & Sorich, 1999), we asked junior high school students to imagine that they really liked a new class they were taking in school. They studied for the first test, but did really poorly. What would they feel and what would they think? They told us they would feel stupid and would think "I'm just not good at this subject" and "I wasn't smart enough." One test had the power to define them.

What would they do? Work harder? Guess again.

What Do They Believe About Effort?

Other students believe that effort can compensate for lower ability, that you can get to the same place by working that much harder—but not these students. They tell us that if you don't have ability, forget it. Specifically, they agree that: "If you're not good at a subject, working hard won't make you good at it" and "It doesn't matter how hard you work—if you're smart you'll do well; if you're not smart, you won't."

So what *would* they do after doing poorly on that test? Compared to students with the malleable view, the students with a fixed view of intelligence agree more with the following: "I would spend *less* time on the subject from now on," and "I would try to cheat on the next test." If effort doesn't work, these are, sadly, the options they see for themselves.

I believe there is no more damaging view for students than the belief that effort is unnecessary (if you're smart) and ineffective (if you're not).

What Happens to Performance?

The need to prove your intelligence can be highly motivating when things are going well, but it does not serve students well when the going gets tougher. To examine this, we have done several large studies of students making the transition to junior high school (Dweck & Sorich, 1999; Henderson & Dweck, 1990). This is when students leave the cocoon of grade school in which teachers have time to be more nurturant, the work is more individualized, and the grading tends to be more generous. Suddenly, students find themselves in a new, more impersonal world with harder work and more stringent grading. This is a particular threat to students with the fixed view, whose intelligence is now on line.

In each of our studies, we have found that this is a time when their grades and achievement test scores suffer compared to their classmates who hold the more malleable view. Regardless of their past achievement, students with the fixed view are more likely to show lower academic performance. Some students who were among the highest achievers before are now in trouble.

Now let's look now at the alternative.

THE BELIEF IN MALLEABLE INTELLIGENCE

What Is Their Goal?

When students believe their intelligence is a potential that they can develop, they focus—not so much on looking smart—but on challenges and learning. When we offer *them* a choice of tasks, they reject the task that would simply make them look smart, in favor of the task that allows them to learn something new, even with a risk of errors.

They agree with statements like these: "It is much more important for me to learn things in my classes than it is to get the best grades," and "I like schoolwork I can learn from even if I make a lot of mistakes." For these students, the name of the game is not the quick fix of outdoing others, but rather personal mastery over time: "I feel successful when I improve in school even if other students get a higher score than me."

What Does Failure or Difficulty Mean?

It sends a message about your effort or strategy, not your fixed ability. Mistakes are simply a natural part of learning, and something that give you information about what to do next. Failure, while never a welcome event, is also signal to do something. When these students get a disappointing grade, they tell us they'd get information about what went wrong, engage in remedial work, and study more the next time (Dweck & Sorich, 1999; Grant-Pillow & Dweck, 2003; Hong et al., 1999). In other words, they take the bull by the horns and work toward improvement in the future.

What Does Effort Mean?

Everything. For these students, effort is what powers their ability and allows them to use it to the fullest. Even geniuses, they believe, have to work hard for their accomplishments. In this, they are in sync with Thomas Edison and his 99 percent perspiration. They also believe that even if you're not so good at something, effort will certainly help you achieve, for effort is the way to overcome setbacks. In short, they agree: "The harder your work at something, the better you will be at it" (Dweck & Sorich, 1999).

What Happens to Performance?

In line with their emphasis on challenge, effort, and learning, these students are able to do well as they make difficult educational transitions. As I've reported, they outshine their classmates with the fixed view in grades and achievement test scores as they confront the challenges of a new school (Dweck & Sorich, 1999; Henderson & Dweck, 1990). Even some students who had not done that well before in school blossom at this time (Henderson & Dweck, 1990).

CAN THEORIES OF INTELLIGENCE BE CHANGED?

Yes, they can. Even though when people's theories are left alone, they tend to be fairly stable, people can be taught a different view.

In a number of experiments, psychologists have tested the effects of orienting students toward a malleable view of ability (by telling them that the ability required by the task could be learned over time with practice or effort) versus a fixed view of ability (by telling them that the ability is inborn, or is one that you either have or don't have) (Aronson, 1998; Jourden, Bandura & Banfield, 1991; Tabernero & Wood, 1999; Wood & Bandura, 1989). These studies have found that when individuals are given the malleable view, they choose more challenging goals for themselves, they maintain confidence and high effective persistence in the face of setbacks, and they end up outperforming those who are given the fixed view. What's also interesting is that the students given the malleable view maintain their interest in the activity even when they're experiencing difficulty.

In a fascinating study designed to test the effects of a self-theory intervention, Joshua Aronson, Carrie Fried, and Catherine Good (Aronson, Fried & Good, 2002) taught college students a malleable view of their intelligence and looked at the impact of this on their actual engagement and achievement in school. Students who were taught this theory, especially the minority students, showed greater engagement with their studies and higher grade-point averages than groups of comparable students who were not. This study shows what a profound effect a short belief-changing experience can have on a student's academic life.

Aronson and Good (2002) also performed a self-theory intervention with minority students in junior high school as part of computer skills class. For the students in the experimental group, the mentors conveyed the view that intelligence is expandable, and helped each student design a Web page that advocated this view. At the end of the year, they compared the performance of the experimental and control groups on statewide standardized achievement tests. The results showed that the students in the malleable theory intervention earned higher achievement test scores in both math and reading than students in the control group. Although the malleable manipulation helped all students, it was particularly beneficial to females in math. In the malleable condition, the gender gap in math, evident in the control group, disappeared.

Recently, we completed a theory-changing intervention with at-risk junior high school students who had been showing sharp declines in achievement (Blackwell, Dweck & Trzesniewski, 2003). As in the Aronson & Good study, students in the experimental group (who received instruction in the theory of malleable ability) and students in the control group both received training in important academic skills and knowledge. However, only students in the experimental group were taught the idea that learning changes the brain and makes you smarter. By the end of the semester, students in the experimental group earned significantly higher math grades than those in the control group and, according to their teachers (who did not know which group students were in), showed marked changes in academic motivation. The malleable theory appeared to energize students to use the new skills they had learned.

Most academic interventions simply try to strengthen the skills that vulnerable students are thought to lack, for example, by teaching them study skills or by tutoring them in the subjects that present difficulty. Yet this does not appear to be enough. In all of the three studies just described, the students in the control group either already had equivalent skills or were given all of the same skill-boosting programs as the experimental group. In each case, only those who experienced the belief-changing intervention showed changes in motivation, put their skills to work for them, and displayed gains in achievement.

Aside from direct interventions, there are also some common practices that can—inadvertently—alter students' theories about their intelligence.

THE EFFECTS OF PRAISE

A few years ago, Melissa Kamins, Claudia Mueller, and I began to wonder if some very common and very well-meant practices might be having unwanted effects on students. We started thinking about how students with the fixed view of intelligence were so fixated on their intelligence and so concerned with how their performance measures them. Well, we thought, when you praise students' intelligence after a job well done, isn't that telling them that intelligence is what it's all about and isn't it telling them that their intelligence can be measured directly from their performance?

Now, of course, this isn't what people mean to do when they praise intelligence. They mean to boost students' confidence and motivate them to do well in the future. In fact, in a survey of parents that we conducted, over 80 percent of parents agreed that it was *necessary* to praise children's ability to make them feel good about themselves. However, to see what intelligence praise *really* does, we conducted a series of studies. To foreshadow our findings, I will tell you that the power of intelligence praise was astounding to us.

In six studies (Mueller & Dweck, 1998; see also Kamins & Dweck, 1999, for studies with younger children), we gave 5th-grade children interesting puzzlelike problems to solve. These problems were part of a popular nonverbal IQ test. The first set of problems they worked on were challenging but well within their range, and virtually all children did really well. After this success, children received one of three forms of praise. One-third of the children were given intelligence praise: "You must be smart at these problems." One-third were given effort praise: "You must have worked hard at these problems." And one-third of the children were simply told that they had done really well, but were not praised for their ability or their effort. Remember, all three groups of students were really the same when they came into the study. The only thing that differed was one sentence of the praise feedback they received. Next, they all received far more difficult problems, on which they did more poorly (so we could assess the impact of this difficulty on their subsequent motivation and performance). Finally, all children received another set of the easier (but challenging) problems.

First, we found that students who were given intelligence praise actually now bought into the fixed view of intelligence more than the students who were given the effort praise. Thus, the intelligence praise per se seemed to imply that the adult was judging some deep-seated ability that dwelt within them, and the effort praise seemed to imply that skills are more acquirable and can be expanded through effort.

What goals did students want to pursue following the initial praise? The majority of the intelligence-praised students chose a task that would allow them to look smart and rejected a challenging task that would allow them to learn a lot but wouldn't necessarily make them look good. The effort-praised students did completely the opposite: as many as 80 to 90 percent of them preferred the task that would allow them to learn a lot and rejected the task that would just make them look smart. So, intelligence praise, rather than making students eager for challenge and learning, did just the opposite. It was effort praise that made students eager to jump right in and learn.

What did failure mean to them? If praising students' intelligence did in fact teach them to measure themselves from their performance, then they should measure themselves from their poorer performance on the second set of problems—and that's what they did. When asked to rate different explanations for why they had trouble with those problems, intelligence-praised students agreed strongly with: "I'm not good enough at the problems," and "I'm not smart enough." What the intelligence praise gave them, one experience with difficulty took away. The effort-praised students hardly blamed their ability at all. Instead they agreed strongly with: "I didn't work hard enough," something they could easily remedy.

How did the difficulty affect children's enjoyment of the task? We assessed this by asking students how much fun they thought the problems were and how much they liked working on them. When students answered these questions right after the praised success, students from all groups thought the task was great fun. And when the effort-praised students were asked these questions after the hard problems, impressively, the difficulty did not change their enjoyment one bit; they really seemed engaged and challenged. But the enjoyment of the intelligence-praised students declined significantly after the difficulty (as did their desire to take the problems home to practice). In short, effort praise, but not intelligence praise, allowed students to maintain their interest and commitment.

What happened to performance? In four studies, we tracked students' performance over the three sets of problems, and looked at what happened from the first set (where all three groups had done equally well) to the third set (that was equivalent to the first set in difficulty, but came after the hard second set). The effort-praised students did the best of the three groups on the final set, and they improved significantly from the first set to the third. This means that their continued involvement and effort paid off. They actually became better ("smarter") at the problems.

In contrast, the intelligence-praised students did the worst of the three groups on the last set of problems, and *declined* significantly from the first to the third set. So, not only does this mind-set lead to self-denigration and loss of enjoyment in the face of difficulty, but it also leads to impaired performance.

This is not to say that students didn't enjoy the intelligence praise. To the contrary. When students received the intelligence praise, they often displayed a proud, satisfied smile that they didn't show in the other conditions. However, that smile of satisfaction was short-lived, as a host of concerns soon overwhelmed them. In contrast, the effort praise, although perhaps not as thrilling initially, had a host of beneficial effects. By the way, we meant the effort praise to stand for a category of praise—process praise—where the emphasis is on what students put into their work to achieve an admirable result. The praise could as easily refer to their strategies and the like, not just sheer effort.

FEEDBACK IN THE REAL WORLD

How might these trait-versus-process messages be communicated to kids in the real world? Chauncy Lennon and I (Dweck & Lennon, 2001) began thinking seriously about this issue when he called to my attention a very strange finding from a large-scale study of thousands of students across the country: The more time parents spent with their children on homework, the less well the students did! Now, of course, it might be the case that parents felt they had to spend more time with poorer students. But it also could be that spending a lot of time with students on their homework sends them the message that they're not capable. So, we started thinking about all the good things parents do that can send their kids a trait message—or that can send their kids a process message—and we developed a questionnaire to ask beginning junior high school students about this.

We developed a series of scenarios in which we asked students to imagine that their parents did something. Here is an example: "Imagine that your parents offer to help you with your schoolwork. Why would they do this?" We then offered them a series of four reasons to rate. Each reason represented a trait message ("They are worried that I'm not smart enough to figure it out on my own") or a process message ("They want to make sure I learn as much as I can from my schoolwork"). The trait messages focused on judgments of smartness-dumbness or goodness-badness, whereas the process messages focused on learning, challenge, effort, strategies, and understanding things. Here's another example.

"Suppose that your parents are very excited when you bring home some good grades. Why would they be this way?" Trait message: "They think it means I'm smart in school." Process message: "They think I worked hard to get good grades." We included positive trait messages like this so that it wouldn't just be that the trait-focused messages were ones that were more negative.

We then looked at what these trait-versus-process messages predicted. First, the trait message predicted a more fixed theory of intelligence, whereas the process message predicted a more malleable theory. The messages also predicted students' effort beliefs, their explanations for failure, and their grades across their transition to junior high school.

Of course, we don't know from these findings whether there are real differences in parents' messages that are causing these differences or whether students who already have a fixed theory just interpret their parents' practices differently from students who have a malleable theory. Our findings from the studies on intelligence-versus-effort praise show that adults' practices *can* have a direct effect on children's beliefs and motivation. However, both possibilities would be interesting and we are looking at this question in our current studies (Pomerantz & Dweck, 2003).

(MORE) IMPLICATIONS

Our findings on trait-versus-process feedback tell a consistent story. They show that practices focussing students on judgments of their intelligence can lead to a belief in fixed intelligence with all of its vulnerabilities. On the other hand, practices that focus students on such things as effort, challenge, or strategies can lead to a belief in malleable intelligence with all of its benefits. Let's look at some of the implications of these findings.

One thing that excites me about these findings is that the process message is pretty easy to incorporate into existing practices. A teacher, for example, may be very structured or unstructured, very autocratic or democratic, very warm or formal—it doesn't matter. A process message can fit into any of these styles.

The same thing is true for parents. In some cultures, the parents rule the roost and children must simply comply. In other cultures, there is a higher premium on understanding the child's point of view and in having a more equal give-and-take between parent and child. Still, a process message can be integrated into either style without asking parents to develop a whole new philosophy of child-rearing that may or may not fit with their culture.

Learning Is Nice, But Aren't Performance Goals also Important?

I've talked about how students with the malleable theory of intelligence value learning something new (a learning goal) over validating their intelligence through their performance (a performance goal). But given our society, are performance goals also important? Yes, they are.

To my mind, it's the balance that counts—keeping a balance between valuing learning and performance. Let's face it: Grades often matter a lot, and many students who want to go on to top schools need good grades. Problems arise when students come to care so much about their performance that they sacrifice important learning opportunities and limit their intellectual growth—as they do with a fixed theory of intelligence.

Problems also arise when students equate their grades with their intelligence or their worth. This can be very damaging, for when they hit difficulty, they may quickly feel inadequate, become discouraged, and lose their ability or their desire to perform well in that area.

For me, the best mix is a combination of a) valuing learning and challenge, and b) valuing grades but seeing them as merely an index of your current performance, not a sign of your intelligence or worth (see Grant-Pillow & Dweck, 2003).

Students who are taught that their performance simply measures their current skills can still relish learning and challenges, for mistakes and setbacks would not be undermining them. By the way, this stance characterizes many top athletes. They are *very* outcome-oriented during a game or match, but they do not see a negative outcome as reflecting their underlying skills or potential to learn. Moreover, in between games they are very learning-oriented. They review tapes of their past game, they try to learn from their mistakes, they talk to their coaches about how to improve, and they work ceaselessly on new skills.

What About "Gifted" Labels and Programs?

Calling a student gifted can be just like intelligence praise. This means that labeling kids as gifted can sometimes do more harm than good by feeding into a fixed theory of intelligence. The label "gifted" implies that students have received some magical quality (the gift) that makes them special and more worthy than others. Some students are in danger of getting hung up on this label. They may become so concerned with deserving the label and so worried about losing it—that is, they may become so concerned with bolstering their fixed, superior intelligence—that they may lose their love of challenge and learning. They may begin to prefer only things they can do easily and perfectly, thus limiting their intellectual growth.

In line with what I discussed earlier, psychologists who study creative geniuses point out that the single most important factor in creative achievement is willingness to put in tremendous amounts of effort and to sustain this effort in the face of obstacles. It would be a pity if by labeling students as gifted, we limited their creative contributions.

However, we can prevent this by making clear to students that "gifted" simply means that if they work hard and keep on learning and stretching themselves, they will be capable of noteworthy accomplishments. Of course, that is true of many people, not just those considered gifted.

What About Girls?

Girls, especially bright girls, have traditionally underestimated themselves and shied away from challenges. Don't they *need* a message that they're smart?

As I have shown, the way to motivate students and to give them more lasting motivation and confidence is not by telling them they're smart, but by focusing them on the processes that create achievement. In fact, my great fear is that in our zeal to bolster the confidence of girls (and minority students as well), we have lavished intelligence praise upon them, thereby making them perhaps even more vulnerable than they were before.

PYGMALION AND THE MALLEABLE THEORY

The idea of beliefs affecting behavior was dramatically demonstrated in the original "Pygmalion in the Classroom" studies by Rosenthal and Jacobson (1968). It was *teachers'* beliefs and *teachers'* behavior that were influenced, but the impact was on students' achievement.

At the beginning of a school year, teachers were told that some students in their classes had the potential to blossom intellectually. These students had in fact been randomly selected, but by the end of the year, especially in the younger grades, many of these students actually showed marked gains in achievement.

This study is often interpreted to mean that when teachers think students are smart, they treat them differently. But teachers were not told that the students were simply smart. They were given a malleable theory of those students' intelligence, and it may well be the malleable theory of intelligence that produced the results. This would mean that it is not only students' theories of intelligence that matter, but teachers', too (see Dweck, 2001).

CONCLUSION

I have shown that self-theories about intelligence can play a central role in motivation and achievement by orienting individuals toward different goals, different interpretations of outcomes, different views of effort, and different ways of coping with difficulty. I have also shown how these theories can be shaped by experience, and how interventions that teach a malleable theory of intelligence can boost motivation and achievement. Just as social psychologists have long known, changing a key belief such as this can have a surprisingly large impact in a surprisingly short time. The task ahead is to identify other key beliefs that affect motivation and effective functioning in other areas of people's lives.

References

ARONSON, J. (1998). *The Effects of conceiving ability as fixed or improvable on responses to stereotype threat.* Unpublished manuscript, University of Texas.

ARONSON, J., FRIED, C., & GOOD, C. (2002). Reducing the Effects of Stereotype Threat on African American College Students by Shaping Theories of Intelligence. *Journal of Experimental Social Psychology* **38,** 113–125.

ARONSON, J., & GOOD, C. (2002). *Reducing Vulnerability to stereotype threat in adolescents by shaping theories of intelligence.* Unpublished manuscript, New York University.

BINET, A. (1909/1973). *Les idées modernes sur les enfants* [Modern ideas on children]. Paris: Flamarion.

BLACKWELL, L. S., DWECK, C. S., & TRZESNIEWSKI, K. (2003). *Implicit theories of intelligence predict achievement across an adolescent transition: A longitudinal study and an intervention.* Unpublished manuscript, Columbia University.

BLOOM, B. S. (1985). *Developing talent in young people.* New York: Ballantine.

BROWN, A. L., & CAMPIONE, J. C. (1996). Psychological theory and the design of innovative learning environments: On procedures, principles, and systems. In L. Schauble & R. Glaser (Eds.), *Innovations in learning: New environments for education,* 289–325). Mahwah, NJ: Erlbaum.

DWECK, C. S. (1999). *Self-theories and goals: Their role in motivation, personality, and development.* Philadelphia: Taylor & Francis/Psychology Press.

DWECK, C. S. (2001). The development of ability conceptions. In A. Wigfield and J. Eccles (Eds.). *The development of achievement motivation.*

DWECK, C. S. & LEGGETT, E. L. (1988). A social-cognitive approach to motivation and personality, *Psychological Review* **95**, 256–273.

DWECK, C. S., & LENNON, C. (April 2001). Person versus process-focused parenting styles. Symposium paper presented at the Biennial Meeting of the Society for Research in Child Development, Minneapolis, MN.

DWECK, C. S. & SORICH, L. (1999). Mastery-oriented thinking. In C. R. Snyder (Ed.). *Coping.* New York: Oxford University Press.

GRANT-PILLOW, H. & DWECK, C. S. (in press). Clarifying achievement goals and their impact. *Journal of Personality and Social Psychology.*

HAYES, J. R. (1989). Cognitive processes in creativity. In J. Glover, R. Ronning, & C. Reynolds (Eds.), *Handbook of creativity.* New York: Plenum.

HENDERSON, V., & DWECK, C. S. (1990). Achievement and motivation in adolescence: A new model and data. In S. Feldman and G. Elliott (Eds.), *At the threshold: The developing adolescent.* Cambridge, MA: Harvard University Press.

HONG, Y., CHIU, C., DWECK, C. S., LIN, D., & WAN, W. (1999). A test of implicit theories and self-confidence as predictors of responses to achievement challenges. *Journal of Personality and Social Psychology* **77**, 588–599.

HOWE, M. J. (1999). Prodigies and creativity. In R. J. Sternberg (Ed.), *Handbook of creativity.* New York: Cambridge University Press.

JOURDEN, F. J., BANDURA, A., & BANFIELD, J. T. (1991). The impact of conceptions of ability on self-regulatory factors and motor skill acquisition. *Journal of Sport and Exercise Psychology* **13**, 213–226.

KAMINS, M., & DWECK, C. S. (1999). Person versus process praise: Implications for contingent self-worth and coping. *Developmental Psychology* **35**, 835–847.

MUELLER, C. M. & DWECK, C. S. (1998). Intelligence praise can undermine motivation and performance. *Journal of Personality and Social Psychology* **75**, 33–52.

NICKERSON, R. S. (1999). Enhancing creativity. In R. J. Sternberg (Ed.), *Handbook of creativity.* New York: Cambridge University Press.

PERKINS, D. N. (1994). Creativity: Beyond the Darwinian paradigm. In M. A. Boden (Ed.), *Dimensions of creativity.* Cambridge, MA: MIT Press.

PERKINS, D. N. (1995). *Outsmarting IQ: The emerging science of learnable intelligence.* New York: Free Press.

POMERANTZ, E., & DWECK, C. S. (in progress). Trait vs. process-focused parenting.

RESNICK, L. B. (1983). Mathematics and science learning: A new conception. *Science,* 477.

ROSENTHAL, R., & JACOBSON, L. (1968). *Pygmalion in the classroom: Teacher expectation and pupils' intellectual development.* New York: Holt, Rinehart & Winston, 1968.

RUNCO, M. A., NEMIRO, J., & WALBERG, H. J. (1998). Personal explicit theories of creativity. *Journal of Creative Behavior* **32**, 1–17.

SIMONTON, D. (1999). *Origins of genius: Darwinian perspectives on creativity.* New York: Oxford.

STERNBERG, R. J. (1985). *Beyond IQ.* New York: Cambridge University Press.

STONE, J., & DWECK, C. S. (1998). *Theories of intelligence and the meaning of achievement goals.* Unpublished manuscript, Columbia University.

TABERNERO, C., & WOOD, R. E. (1999). Implicit theories versus the social construal of ability in self-regulation and performance on a complex task. *Organizational Behavior and Human Decision Processes* **78**, 104–127.

WEISBERG, R. W. (1986). *Creativity: Genius and other myths.* New York: Freeman.

———(1999). Creativity and knowledge: A challenge to theories. In R. J. Sternberg (Ed.), *Handbook of creativity.* New York: Cambridge.

WOOD, R., & BANDURA, A. (1989). Impact of conceptions of ability on self-regulatory mechanisms and complex decision-making. *Journal of Personality and Social Psychology* **56**, 407–415.

VI

HUMAN AGGRESSION

22

The Effects of Observing Violence

Leonard Berkowitz

Experiments suggest that aggression depicted in television and motion picture dramas, or observed in actuality, can arouse certain members of the audience to violent action.

An ancient view of drama is that the action on the stage provides the spectators with an opportunity to release their own strong emotions harmlessly through identification with the people and events depicted in the play. This idea dates back at least as far as Aristotle, who wrote in *The Art of Poetry* that drama is "a representation . . . in the form of actions directly presented, not narrated; with incidents arousing pity and fear in such a way as to accomplish a purgation of such emotions."

Aristotle's concept of catharsis, a term derived from the Greek word for purgation, has survived in modern times. It can be heard on one side of the running debate over whether or not scenes of violence in motion pictures and television programs can instigate violent deeds, sooner or later, by people who observe such scenes. Eminent authorities contend that filmed violence, far from leading to real violence, can actually have beneficial results in that the viewer may purge himself of hostile impulses by watching other people behave aggressively, even if these people are merely actors appearing on a screen. On the other hand, authorities of equal stature contend that, as one psychiatrist told a Senate subcommittee, filmed violence is a "preparatory school for delinquency." In this view emotionally immature individuals can be seriously affected by fighting or brutality in films, and disturbed young people in particular can be led into the habit of expressing their aggressive energies by socially destructive actions.

Until recently neither of these arguments had the support of data obtained by controlled experimentation; they had to be regarded, therefore, as hypotheses, supported at best by unsystematic observation. Lately, however, several psychologists have undertaken laboratory tests of the effects of filmed aggression. The greater control obtained in these tests, some of which were done in my laboratory at the University of Wisconsin with the support of the National Science Foundation, provides a basis for some statements that have a fair probability of standing up under continued testing.

First, it is possible to suggest that the observation of aggression is more likely to induce hostile behavior than to drain off aggressive inclinations; that, in fact, motion picture or television violence can stimulate aggressive actions by normal people as well as by those who are emotionally disturbed. I would add an important qualification: such actions by normal people will occur only under appropriate conditions. The experiments point to some of the conditions that might result in aggressive actions by people in an audience who had observed filmed violence.

Second, these findings have obvious social significance. Third, the laboratory tests provide some important information about aggressive behavior in general. I shall discuss these three statements in turn.

Catharsis appeared to have occurred in one of the first experiments, conducted by Seymour Feshbach of the University of Colorado. Feshbach deliberately angered a group of college men; then he showed part of the group a filmed prizefight and the other students a more neutral film. He found that the students who saw the prizefight exhibited less hostility than the other students on two tests of aggressiveness administered after the film showings. The findings may indicate that the students who had watched the prizefight had vented their anger vicariously.

That, of course, is not the only possible explanation of the results. The men who saw the filmed violence could have become uneasy about their own aggressive tendencies. Watching someone being hurt may have made them think that aggressive behavior was wrong; as a result they may have inhibited their hostile responses. Clearly there was scope for further experimentation, particularly studies varying the attitude of the subjects toward the filmed aggression.

Suppose the audience were put in a frame of mind to regard the film violence as justified—for instance because a villain got a beating he deserved. The concept of symbolic catharsis would predict in such a case that an angered person might enter vicariously into the scene and work off his anger by thinking of himself as the winning fighter, who was inflicting injury on the man who had provoked him. Instead of accepting this thesis, my associates and I predicted that justified film aggression would lead to stronger rather than weaker manifestations of hostility. We believed

FIGURE 22.1
Typical experiment tests reaction of angered man to filmed violence. Experiment begins with introduction of subject *(white shirt)* to a man he believes is a co-worker but who actually is a confederate of the author's. In keeping with pretense that experiment is to test physiological reactions, student conducting the experiment takes blood-pressure readings. He assigns the men a task and leaves; during the task, the confederate insults the subject. Experimenter returns and shows filmed prizefight. Confederate leaves; experimenter tells subject to judge a floor plan drawn by confederate and to record opinion by giving confederate electric shocks. Shocks actually go to recording apparatus. The fight film appeared to stimulate the aggressiveness of angered men. (Photographs by Gordon Coster.)

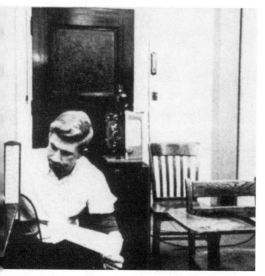

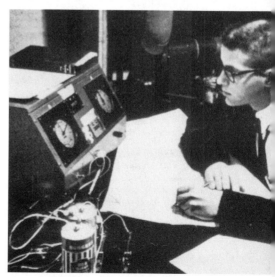

that the rather low volume of open hostility in the Feshbach experiment was attributable to film-induced inhibitions. If this were so, an angered person who saw what appeared to be warranted aggression might well think he was justified in expressing his own hostile desires.

To test this hypothesis we conducted three experiments. Since they resulted in essentially similar findings and employed comparable procedures, I shall describe only the latest. In this experiment we brought together two male college students at a time. One of them was the subject; the other was a confederate of the experimenter and had been coached on how to act, although of course none of this was known to the subject. Sometimes we introduced the confederate to the subject as a college boxer and at other times we identified him as a speech major. After the introduction the experimenter announced that the purpose of the experiment was to study physiological reactions to various tasks. In keeping with that motif he took blood-pressure readings from each man. Then he set the pair to work on the first task: a simple intelligence test.

During this task the confederate either deliberately insulted the subject—for example, by remarks to the effect that "You're certainly taking a long time with that" and references to "cow-college students" at Wisconsin—or, in the conditions where we were not trying to anger the subject, behaved in a neutral way toward him. On the completion of the task the experimenter took more blood-pressure readings (again only to keep up the pretense that the experiment had a physiological purpose) and then informed the men that their next assignment was to watch a brief motion picture scene. He added that he would give them a synopsis of the plot so that they would have a better understanding of the scene. Actually he was equipped with two different synopses.

To half of the subjects he portrayed the protagonist of the film, who was to receive a serious beating, as an unprincipled scoundrel. Our idea was that the subjects told this story would regard the beating as retribution for the protagonist's misdeeds; some tests we administered in connection with the experiment showed that the subjects indeed had little sympathy for the protagonist. We called the situation we had created with this synopsis of the seven-minute fight scene the "justified fantasy aggression."

The other subjects were given a more favorable description of the protagonist. He had behaved badly, they were told, but this was because he had been victimized when he was young; at any rate, he was now about to turn over a new leaf. Our idea was that the men in this group would feel sympathetic toward the protagonist; again tests indicated that they did. We called this situation the "less justified fantasy aggression."

Then we presented the film, which was from the movie *Champion;* the seven-minute section we used showed Kirk Douglas, as the champion, apparently losing his title. Thereafter, in order to measure the effects of the film, we provided the subjects with an opportunity to show aggression in circumstances where that would be a socially acceptable response. We separated each subject and accomplice and told the subject that his co-worker (the confederate) was to devise a "cre-

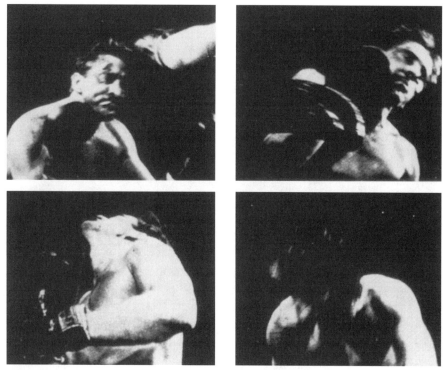

FIGURE 22.2
Filmed aggression shown in author's experiments was from the motion picture *Champion* and included these scenes in which Kirk Douglas receives a bad beating. Watchers had been variously prepared; after showing, they were tested for aggressive tendencies. (Astor Pictures, Inc.)

ative" floor plan for a dwelling, which the subject would judge. If the subject thought the floor plan was highly creative, he was to give the co-worker one electric shock by depressing a telegraph key. If he thought the floor plan was poor, he was to administer more than one shock; the worse the floor plan, the greater the number of shocks. Actually each subject received the same floor plan.

The results consistently showed a greater volume of aggression directed against the anger-arousing confederate by the men who had seen the "bad guy" take a beating than by the men who had been led to feel sympathy for the protagonist in the film (Fig. 22.3). It was clear that the people who saw the justified movie violence had not discharged their anger through vicarious participation in the aggression but instead had felt freer to attack their tormenter in the next room. The motion picture scene had apparently influenced their judgment of the propriety of aggression. If it was all right for the movie villain to be injured aggressively, they seemed to think, then perhaps it was all right for them to attack the villain in their own lives—the person who had insulted them.

Another of our experiments similarly demonstrated that observed aggression has little if any effectiveness in reducing aggressive tendencies on the part of an

Annoying co-worker   Neutral co-worker

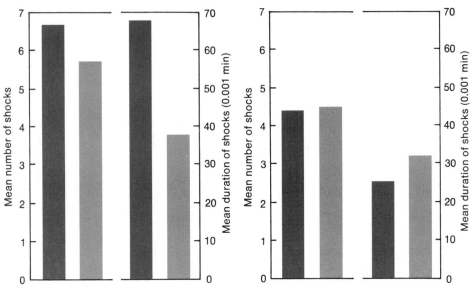

FIGURE 22.3
Responses of subjects invited to commit aggression after seeing prizefighting film varied according to synopsis they heard beforehand. One *(dark gray)* called Douglas' beating deserved; the other *(light gray)* said it was undeserved. After the film the subjects were told they could give electric shocks to an annoying or neutral co-worker based on his "creativeness" in doing a task. Seeing a man receive what had been described as a well-deserved beating apparently lowered restraints against aggressive behavior.

observer. In this experiment some angered men were told by another student how many shocks they should give the person, supposedly in the next room, who had provoked them. Another group of angered men, instead of delivering the shocks themselves, watched the other student do it. Later the members of both groups had an opportunity to deliver the shocks personally. Consistently the men who had watched in the first part of the experiment now displayed stronger aggression than did the people who had been able to administer shocks earlier. Witnessed aggression appeared to have been less satisfying than self-performed aggression.

Our experiments thus cast considerable doubt on the possibility of a cathartic purge of anger through the observation of filmed violence. At the very least, the findings indicated that such a catharsis does not occur as readily as many authorities have thought.

Yet what about the undoubted fact that aggressive motion pictures and violent athletic contests provide relaxation and enjoyment for some people? A person who was tense with anger sometimes comes away from them feeling calmer. It seems to me that what happens here is quite simple: He calms down not because he has discharged his anger vicariously but because he was carried away by the events he witnessed. Not thinking of his troubles, he ceased to stir himself up and his anger dissipated. In addition, the enjoyable motion picture or game could have cast a pleasant glow over his whole outlook, at least temporarily.

The social implications of our experiments have to do primarily with the moral usually taught by films. Supervising agencies in the motion picture and television industries generally insist that films convey the idea that "crime does not pay." If there is any consistent principle used by these agencies to regulate how punishment should be administered to the screen villain, it would seem to be the talion law: an eye for an eye, a tooth for a tooth.

Presumably the audience finds this concept of retaliation emotionally satisfying. Indeed, we based our "justified fantasy aggression" situation on the concept that people seem to approve of hurting a scoundrel who has hurt others. But however satisfying the talion principle may be, screenplays based on it can lead to socially harmful consequences. If the criminal or "bad guy" is punished aggressively, so that others do to him what he has done to them, the violence appears justified. Inherent in the likelihood that the audience will regard it as justified is the danger that some angered person in the audience will attack someone who has frustrated *him,* or perhaps even some innocent person he happens to associate with the source of his anger.

Several experiments have lent support to this hypothesis. O. Ivar Lövaas of the University of Washington found in an experiment with nursery school children that the youngsters who had been exposed to an aggressive cartoon film displayed more aggressive responses with a toy immediately afterward than a control group shown a less aggressive film did. In another study Albert Bandura and his colleagues at Stanford University noted that pre-school children who witnessed the actions of an aggressive adult in a motion picture tended later, after they had been subjected to mild frustrations, to imitate the kind of hostile behavior they had seen.

This tendency of filmed violence to stimulate aggression is not limited to children. Richard H. Walters of the University of Waterloo in Ontario found experimentally that male hospital attendants who had been shown a movie of a knife fight generally administered more severe punishment to another person soon afterward than did other attendants who had seen a more innocuous movie. The men in this experiment were shown one of the two movie scenes and then served for what was supposedly a study of the effects of punishment. They were to give an electric shock to someone else in the room with them each time the person made a mistake on a learning task. The intensity of the electric shocks could be varied. This other person, who was actually the experimenter's confederate, made a constant number of mistakes, but the people who had seen the knife fight gave him more intense punishment than the men who had witnessed the nonaggressive film. The filmed violence had apparently aroused aggressive tendencies in the men and, since the situation allowed the expression of aggression, their tendencies were readily translated into severe aggressive actions.

These experiments, taken together with our findings, suggest a change in approach to the manner in which screenplays make their moral point. Although it may be socially desirable for a villain to receive his just deserts at the end of a motion picture, it would seem equally desirable that this retribution should not take the form of physical aggression.

The key point to be made about aggressiveness on the basis of experimentation in this area is that a person's hostile tendencies will persist, in spite of any satisfaction he may derive from filmed violence, to the extent that his frustrations and aggressive habits persist. There is no free-floating aggressive energy that can be released through attempts to master other drives, as Freud proposed, or by observing others as they act aggressively.

In fact, there have been studies suggesting that even if the angered person performs the aggression himself, his hostile inclinations are not satisfied unless he believes he has attacked his tormentor and not someone else. J. E. Hokanson of Florida State University has shown that angered subjects permitted to commit aggression against the person who had annoyed them often display a drop in systolic blood pressure. They seem to have experienced a physiological relaxation, as if they had satisfied their aggressive urges. Systolic pressure declines less, however, when the angered people carry out the identical motor activity involved in the aggression but without believing they have attacked the source of their frustration.

I must now qualify some of the observations I have made. Many aggressive motion pictures and television programs have been presented to the public, but the number of aggressive incidents demonstrably attributable to such shows is quite low. One explanation for this is that most social situations, unlike the conditions in the experiments I have described, impose constraints on aggression. People are usually aware of the social norms prohibiting attacks on others, consequently they inhibit whatever hostile inclinations might have been aroused by the violent films they have just seen.

Another important factor is the attributes of the people encountered by a person after he has viewed filmed violence. A man who is emotionally aroused does not necessarily attack just anyone. Rather, his aggression is directed toward specific objectives. In other words, only certain people are capable of drawing aggressive responses from him. In my theoretical analyses of the sources of aggressive behavior I have suggested that the arousal of anger only creates a readiness for aggression. The theory holds that whether or not this predisposition is translated into actual aggression depends on the presence of appropriate cues: stimuli associated with the present or previous instigators of anger. Thus if someone has been insulted, the sight or the thought of others who have provoked him, whether then or earlier, may evoke hostile responses from him.

An experiment I conducted in conjunction with a graduate student provides some support for this train of thought. People who had been deliberately provoked by the experimenter were put to work with two other people, one a person who had angered them earlier and the other a neutral person. The subjects showed the greatest hostility, following their frustration by the experimenter, to the co-worker they disliked. He, by having thwarted them previously, had acquired the stimulus quality that caused him to draw aggression from them after they had been aroused by the experimenter.

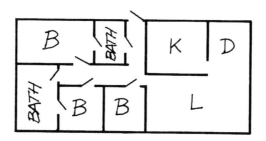

Subject	A	B	C	D	E	F	G	H
Number of shocks	6	3	8	3	6	7	5	4
Duration (0.001 min)	46	38	76	10	120	49	60	28

FIGURE 22.4
Task by annoying co-worker supposedly was to draw a floor plan. Actually, each subject saw the floor plan shown here. The subject was asked to judge the creativeness of the plan and to record his opinion by pressing a telegraph key that he thought would give electric shocks to the co-worker; one shock for a good job and more for poor work. Responses of eight subjects who saw prizefight film are shown; those in boldface type represent men told that Douglas deserved his beating; those in lightface type, men informed it was undeserved.

My general line of reasoning leads me to some predictions about aggressive behavior. In the absence of any strong inhibitions against aggression, people who have recently been angered and have then seen filmed aggression will be more likely to act aggressively than people who have not had those experiences. Moreover, their strongest attacks will be directed at those who are most directly connected with the provocation or at others who either have close associations with the aggressive motion picture or are disliked for any reason.

One of our experiments showed results consistent with this analysis. In this study male college students, taken separately, were first either angered or not angered by *A*, one of the two graduate students acting as experimenters. *A* had been introduced earlier either as a college boxer or as a speech major. After *A* had had his session with the subject, *B*, the second experimenter, showed the subject a motion picture: either the prizefight scene mentioned earlier or a neutral film. (One that we used was about canal boats in England; the other, about the travels of Marco Polo.)

We hypothesized that the label "college boxer" applied to *A* in some of the cases would produce a strong association in the subject's mind between *A* and the boxing film. In other words, any aggressive tendencies aroused in the subject would be more likely to be directed at *A* the college boxer than at *A* the speech major. The experiment bore out this hypothesis. Using questionnaires at the end of the session as the measures of hostility, we found that the deliberately angered subjects directed more hostility at *A*, the source of their anger, when they had seen the fight film and he had been identified as a boxer. Angered men who had seen the neutral

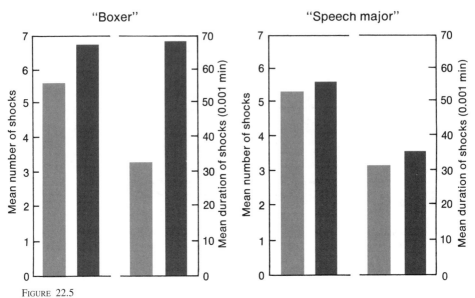

FIGURE 22.5

Co-workers introduction also produced variations in aggressiveness of subjects. Co-worker was introduced as boxer or as speech major; reactions shown here are of men who were angered by co-worker and then saw either a fight film *(dark gray)* or neutral film *(light gray)*. Co-worker received strongest attacks when subjects presumably associated with fight film.

film showed no particular hostility to *A* the boxer. In short, the insulting experimenter received the strongest verbal attacks when he was also associated with the aggressive film. It is also noteworthy that in this study the boxing film did not influence the amount of hostility shown toward *A* when he had not provoked the subjects.

A somewhat inconsistent note was introduced by our experiments, described previously, in "physiological reactions." Here the nonangered groups, regardless of which film they saw, gave the confederate more and longer shocks when they thought he was a boxer than when they understood him to be a speech major (see Fig. 22.6). To explain this finding I assume that our subjects had a negative attitude toward boxers in general. This attitude may have given the confederate playing the role of boxer the stimulus quality that caused him to draw aggression from the angered subjects. But it could only have been partially responsible, since the insulted subjects who saw the neutral film gave fewer shocks to the boxer than did the insulted subjects who saw the prizefight film.

Associations between the screen and the real world are important. People seem to be emotionally affected by a screenplay to the extent that they associate the events of the drama with their own life experiences. Probably adults are less strongly influenced than children because they are aware that the film is make-believe and so can dissociate it from their own lives. Still, it seems clear from the experiments I have described that an aggressive film can induce aggressive actions

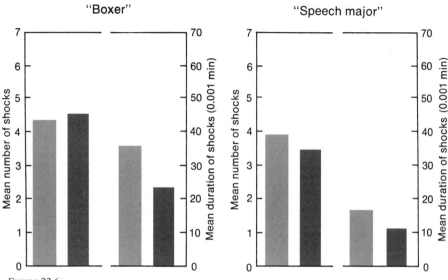

Figure 22.6
Similar test, varied by the fact that the co-worker behaved neutrally toward the subjects and therefore presumably did not anger them, produced these reactions. The greater number of shocks given to the co-worker introduced as a boxer than to the one introduced as a speech major apparently reflected a tendency to take a generally negative attitude toward persons identified as boxers.

by anyone in the audience. In most instances I would expect that effect to be short-lived. The emotional reaction produced by filmed violence probably dies away rather rapidly as the viewer enters new situations and encounters new stimuli. Subjected to different influences, he becomes less and less ready to attack other people.

Television and motion pictures, however, may also have some persistent effects. If a young child sees repeatedly that screen heroes gain their ends through aggressive actions, he may conclude that aggression is desirable behavior. Fortunately screenplays do not consistently convey that message, and in any event the child is exposed to many other cultural norms that discourage aggression.

As I see it, the major social danger inherent in filmed violence has to do with the temporary effects produced in a fairly short period immediately following the film. For that period, at least, a person—whether an adult or a child—who had just seen filmed violence might conclude that he was warranted in attacking those people in his own life who had recently frustrated him. Further, the film might activate his aggressive habits so that for the period of which I speak he would be primed to act aggressively. Should he then encounter people with appropriate stimulus qualities, people he dislikes or connects psychologically with the film, this predisposition could lead to open aggression.

What, then, of catharsis? I would not deny that it exists. Nor would I reject the argument that a frustrated person can enjoy fantasy aggression because he sees characters doing things he wishes he could do, although in most cases his inhibitions restrain him. I believe, however, that effective catharsis occurs only when an angered person perceives that his frustrater has been aggressively injured. From this I argue that filmed violence is potentially dangerous. The motion picture aggression has increased the chance that an angry person, and possibly other people as well, will attack someone else.

References

BANDURA, ALBERT, ROSS, DOROTHEA, AND ROSS, SHEILA A. Imitation of film-mediated aggressive models. *Journal of Abnormal and Social Psychology,* Vol. 66, No. 1, pp. 3–11; January, 1963.

BERKOWITZ, LEONARD. *Aggression: a social psychological analysis.* McGraw-Hill Book Company, 1962.

BERKOWITZ, LEONARD, AND RAWLINGS, EDNA. Effects of film violence on inhibitions against subsequent aggression. *Journal of Abnormal and Social Psychology,* Vol. 66, No. 5, pp. 405–412; May, 1963.

SCHRAMM, WILBUR, LYLE, JACK, AND PARKER, EDWIN B. *Television in the lives of our children.* Stanford University Press, 1961.

WALTERS, RICHARD H., THOMAS, EDWARD LLEWELLYN, AND ACKER, C. WILLIAM. Enhancement of punitive behavior by audio-visual displays. *Science,* Vol. 1236, No. 3519, pp. 872–873; June 8, 1962.

23

The Facilitation of Aggression by Aggression: Evidence Against the Catharsis Hypothesis

Russell G. Geen, David Stonner, and Gary L. Shope

Ninety male subjects were either attacked or treated in a more neutral manner by a male confederate. On a subsequent maze-learning task, one third of the subjects shocked the confederate, one third observed as the experimenter shocked the confederate, and one third waited for a period of time during which the confederate was not shocked. Finally, all subjects shocked the confederate as part of a code-learning task. Subjects who had been attacked and had shocked the confederate during the maze task delivered shocks of greater intensity on the code task than did subjects in the other two conditions, and the former subjects also experienced a greater reduction in diastolic blood pressure than did the latter. The results contradict the hypothesis of aggression catharsis and are discussed in terms of feelings of restraint against aggressing that a subject experiences after committing an aggressive act.

The idea of aggression catharsis is popular both in conventional wisdom and in psychological writing. Certainly it seems to make sense that attacking an enemy allows the attacker to purge himself of hostility and anger toward his victim. Furthermore, in both psychoanalytic theory (e.g., Schafer, 1970) and the frustration–aggression hypothesis (Dollard et al., 1939), the notion is expressed that aggression leads to a release of aggressive drive or instigation, so that further acts of violence are rendered less probable. This point of view stipulates a fairly simple cause–effect model: Instigation produces aggressive arousal, which motivates an aggressive response, which in turn reduces arousal. The end result is a declining level of aggression.

Reprinted with permission from the authors and *The Journal of Personality and Social Psychology,* Vol. 31, No. 4, 1975. Copyright © 1975 by the American Psychological Association. This study was supported by National Science Foundation Grant GS 2748 to the first author.

Largely because of this cause–effect assumption, however, the catharsis hypothesis has encountered troubles on empirical, methodological, and theoretical levels. Although some investigators have reported results that support the notion of catharsis (e.g., Doob, 1970; Feshbach, 1955; Thibaut and Coules, 1952), many others have made findings that contradict it (e.g., deCharms and Wilkins, 1963; Freeman, 1962; Kahn, 1966; Mallick and McCandless, 1966). Still other studies not directly concerned with catharsis have reported a tendency for subjects to *increase* progressively the intensity of electric shocks administered to an antagonist over a series of trials (Buss, 1966b; Geen, 1968). One reason for the lack of conclusiveness that characterizes data on aggression may be caused by more than just lowered aggressive instigation. If the experimental situation is structured in such a way, for example, that aggressive behavior produces feelings of guilt or anxiety in the subject, intensity of aggression may decline not because of reduced instigation but because of increased restraints (e.g., Baron, 1971; Geen, 1970). Perhaps subtle differences in experimental conditions in some of the studies cited above led to varying degrees of inhibitions against aggressing, thus producing the conflicting results. Finally, the catharsis hypothesis can be questioned on theoretical grounds: Because reduction in aggressive arousal may actually represent the termination of an aversive state, it is not at all obvious why such a reduction should reduce the probability of occurrence of the aggressive response that precedes it. On the contrary, it can be argued that lowered aggressive arousal may actually reinforce aggression (Berkowitz, 1970).

Some of the matters discussed here may have been involved in a study by Doob and Wood (1972), which was reported while the present experiment was in progress. In their experiment, Doob and Wood found apparent evidence for aggression catharsis: Angry subjects who aggressed against an antagonist twice were less punitive in their second attack than similarly angered subjects who aggressed only once. A slight tendency toward reduced aggression was also observed among subjects who, prior to their own aggressing, had witnessed the experimenter attacking their adversary. Although Doob and Wood did not present their findings as clearcut evidence for catharsis and suggested that the results could have been due to a process of restoration of equity, they did not mention as a possible explanation increased restraints against aggressing in the groups showing reduced aggression. Their procedures contained two features that could have led to strong inhibitions against aggressing following aggressive responses, however. First, the confederate who sustained the subject's attacks was always a female, and the subjects were both male and female. Buss (1966a) has shown that both male and female subjects, and especially females, tend to reduce the intensity of attacks on a female victim when they suspect that they have hurt her. Doob and Wood's subjects may have believed that they were causing some pain to the confederate and thus held back in later attacks on her. Second, the confederate aroused the subject to attack through verbal badgering and insult, whereas the subject's mode of attacking the confederate was at all times electric shock. It is not difficult to imagine the subject concluding that the confederate had more than paid for her insults by being shocked one time and thus holding back on hurting her further. The subject may have still harbored considerable resentment toward the antagonist but may have been restrained from aggressing by a fear of guilt over further unwarranted aggression. The experimental situation was therefore structured in such a way that aggression could have produced stimuli that inhibited subsequent aggression by the subject. Finally, the Doob and Wood study did not include any measure of arousal, which could have shed some light on the state of aggressive drive characteristic of the subject before and after aggression.

The present experiment, which was designed and begun before the appearance of the Doob and Wood (1972) article, adventitiously avoided some of the potential sources of inhibition implicit in that study. Subjects were all males, as was the confederate. Buss (1966a) has shown that males do not show marked decreases in aggression against other males over a series of shocks, even when they have evidence that the shocks are causing suffering. In addition, subjects were aroused to aggression by electric shocks and later retaliated with shocks. Finally, systolic and diastolic blood pressure were measured at several points during the session. Otherwise the study was similar to the Doob–Wood experiment. The subject was either attacked or not attacked by a confederate; he then either attacked the confederate himself, observed the confederate being attacked by the experimenter, or waited for a period of time during which the confederate was not attacked. Finally subjects in every condition attacked the confederate.

METHOD

Subjects

Subjects were 90 males recruited from an introductory psychology class, with each student receiving a point toward his course grade for participating. Subjects were randomly assigned to the six treatment conditions.

Procedure

The experimenter described the experiment to the subject, and to a confederate who posed as a subject, as one on the effects of punishment on learning. It was explained that one of the men, to be selected by chance, would perform on two types of learning problem, one involving maze learning and the other deciphering of a code, with threat of punishment as a motive in each case. By means of a rigged lottery, the confederate was designated as the one to work on the learning problem under threat of punishment. The two men were thereupon isolated from each other in separate booths which allowed auditory, but not visual, communication. The subject's booth contained the panel of an aggression machine, with 10 shock buttons. The experimenter then said that before the learning problems could begin, it was necessary to discover the degree of similarity that existed between the "learner" and the other person (the subject), who would at some points in the experiment play the role of a teacher; this was justified by the assertion that similarity between teacher and learner is an important variable in the learning process. The first measurement of blood pressure was made just after these instructions had been given.

The subject was then given a set of 12 cards, each bearing an attitude statement on some controversial issue. The subject was instructed to read the statement aloud and state whether he agreed or disagreed with it. The confederate was instructed to express agreement with the subject by saying "I agree" and to register disagreement by giving the subject an electric shock. The rationale for this treatment was that the effects of disagreement between people are most acute when the situation is a highly stressful one, such as threat of shock would produce. The confederate then proceeded to give the subject either (a) two mild shocks following 2 of the statements and no shocks after the other 10 statements (no attack condition) or (b) fairly strong shocks following 8 statements, two mild ones after 2 other statements, and no shocks after the remaining 2 statements, and no shocks after the remaining 2 statements (attack condition). Previous studies (e.g., Geen and Stonner, 1973) have shown that these treatments arouse reliably different levels of anger in subjects. Blood pressure was again measured just after the shocks had been given.

The experimenter then announced that the first task, maze learning, would begin and called the attention of the subject and the confederate to a console in the room visible from both cubicles. Among a panel of light on this console were a red one, a green one, and a white one. The experimenter explained that the onset of the white light signaled the beginning of a trial. Each trial was said to consist of a run through an electronically simulated maze by the learner designate (the confederate), who would express his decision at each of the choice points by pressing one of two switches. If the learner made a correct choice, the green light on the console would go on, but if he made an error the red one would go on. Two thirds of the subjects were told that the red light signaled that the learner was to receive a shock, after which he would go on to the next choice point. The remaining third were told nothing about shocks (and thus comprised the no shocks condition). Of those subjects who were informed that a shock was to be given for each choicepoint error, half were told that the experimenter would give the shock (experimenter shocks condition), whereas the other half were instructed to deliver a constant-intensity shock themselves (subject shocks condition). The subject was told to give shocks by pressing the number 5 button on his panel. Ten trials were run, in which the confederate made 20 errors according to a prearranged schedule. A third measure of blood pressure followed.

The experimenter then explained that the second and final learning task would begin. Again, the confederate was given a learning task, this one consisting of translating an alphabetical code into numerals according to an abstract principle, which the learner was required to discover. The subject was instructed to present trigrams from a list by pressing combinations of switches from among five on his panel labeled A through E. The subject was informed that he would learn only whether the learner had correctly encoded the information or whether he had made an error. A correct response was said to govern the onset of a green light on the subject's panel and an error to control a red light on the same panel. The subject was instructed to give the confederate a shock of any intensity from 1 to 10 by pressing the appropriate button on his panel; he was told that the intensity of the shock increased across the series of buttons. The confederate then proceeded to make 10 errors over a series of 16 trials, following a standard schedule. The intensity and duration of each shock supposedly given to the confederate were measured electronically. The fourth and final measurement of blood pressure was made just after the shock series had ended.

After completing the fourth measurement of blood pressure, the experimenter asked the subject and the confederate to fill out a short questionnaire on which they could express their overall impressions of the experiment. The questionnaire consisted of several ratings scales on which were described (a) the subject's mood—how happy, angry, excited, and anxious he felt; (b) how much he liked the confederate; (c) how much he had held back and restrained himself in shocking the confederate on the code-learning task. Each scale consisted of a continuous 100-mm line, which the subject checked. Finally the experimenter interviewed each subject in order to discover whether the deceptions had been successful. A total of 11 subjects were able to at least approximately verbalize the true nature of the study. These subjects were eliminated from analysis and replaced by other subjects randomly drawn from the same population. The true nature of the experiment was fully discussed by the experimenter and the subject at the end of each session.

RESULTS

Effectiveness of Attack

Ratings of anger made by the subject just after being shocked by the confederate were used as the basis for inferring the effectiveness of the attack manipulation. Subjects who had received 10 shocks reported a mean anger rating of 55.1 (on a 100-mm scale on which 0 represented maximum anger and 100 represented minimum anger), whereas subjects who had received 2 shocks reported a mean rating of 78.3. This difference was significant, F (1, 88) = 13.88, $p < .01$. The treatment used to induce different levels of instigation to aggression was therefore judged to be successful.

Shock Intensity

The mean intensities of shocks given by subjects to the confederate during the code-learning task are reported in Table 23.1. An analysis of variance showed main effects for the attack variable, $F(1, 84) = 26.10$, $p < .001$, and the variable regarding treatment of the confederate during the maze-learning task, $F(2, 84) = 5.93$, $p < .01$. The latter of the two main effects was due primarily to an interaction between the two variables, $F(2, 84) = 3.56$, $p < .05$. Comparisons among means further reveal that subjects in the attack–subject shocks condition gave *stronger* shocks than did those in both the attack–no shocks and the attack–experimenter shocks conditions.

Blood Pressure

Data regarding systolic and diastolic blood pressure were analyzed separately. Although systolic pressure failed to manifest any differences across conditions, treatment effects on diastolic pressure were found. The data were analyzed as a set of three change scores per subject: (a) from baseline to just after the attack–no attack treatment, (b) from that treatment to just after the first attack on the confederate by the subject or experimenter (or the absence of such an attack), and (c) from that treatment to just after the subject himself attacked. These are labeled, respectively, d_{12}, d_{23}, and d_{34} in Table 23.2, which shows the relevant change scores.

No differences were found across the five conditions in baseline diastolic pressure, $F(5, 84) < 1.00$. Analysis of the d_{12} scores indicated that subjects in the attack condition experienced a greater elevation in diastolic pressure (in millimeters of mercury, Hg) than those in the no attack condition (5.92 mm Hg vs. -1.67 mm Hg: $F(1, 84) = 29.12$, $p < .01$. The analysis of the d_{23} scores revealed that subjects in the attack–subject shocks condition experienced a decrease in diastolic pressure to slightly below baseline level, while those in the attack–experimenter shocks condition manifested a slight increase, and those in the attack–no shocks condition re-

TABLE 23.1
Mean intensities of shocks given by subjects on the
code-learning task

Treatment of confederate on code-learning task	Treatment of subject by confederate	
	Attack	No attack
Subject shocks	6.65_a	3.92_{bc}
Experimenter shocks	4.13_{bc}	3.62_c
No shocks	5.20_b	3.20_c

Note: Cells having common subscripts are not significantly different at the .05 level by a Duncan multiple-range test.

TABLE 23.2
Mean diastolic blood pressure changes for the six treatment conditions

Treatment condition	Mean diastolic pressure change		
	$d_{12}{}^a$	$d_{23}{}^b$	$d_{34}{}^c$
Attack–subject shocks	$+6.66_a$	-8.80_a	-1.20_b
Attack–experimenter shocks	$+5.53_a$	$+1.83_c$	-10.67_a
Attack–no shocks	$+5.56_a$	-1.30_{bc}	-6.57_{ab}
No attack–subject shocks	-3.27_b	-1.87_{bc}	-1.07_b
No attack–experimenter shocks	-1.83_b	-1.80_{bc}	-3.53_b
No attack–no shocks	$+.10_b$	-6.60_{ab}	$-.07_b$

Note: Cells having common subscripts within time periods are not significantly different at the .05 level by a Duncan multiple-range test.

[a]Refers to the change in diastolic pressure during the time period from baseline to just after the attack–no attack treatment.

[b]Refers to the change in diastolic pressure during the time period from the attack–no attack treatment to just after the first attack on the confederate by the subject or experimenter (or the absence of such an attack).

[c]Refers to the change in diastolic pressure during the time period from just after the first attack on the confederate by the subject or experimenter (or the absence of such an attack) to just after the subject himself attacked.

vealed a slight decrease. Subjects in the no attack condition showed a moderate decrease in blood pressure. These data produced a significant interaction between the two variables, $F(2, 84) = 6.82, p < .01$. Analysis of the d_{34} scores showed main effects for both the attack, $F(1, 84) = 10.33, p < .01$, and treatment of confederate, $F(2, 84) = 3.15, p < .05$, variables. Both effects are due primarily to the fact that subjects in the attack–experimenter shocks condition experienced a greater drop in diastolic pressure than subjects in any other condition.

Questionnaire Data

Two of the items on the final questionnaire yielded significant differences across conditions.[1] One asked the subject the following question: "On the basis of what you know about the other subject in the experiment, what are your general feelings about him?" The subject replied to this item by marking a 100-mm line ancored at the low end by the statement "I liked him very much" and at the high end by the statement "I didn't like him at all." The results showed that subjects in the attack–subject shocks condition expressed significantly greater dislike for the confederate than did those in the attack–experimenter shocks condition, 45.8 vs. 32.3; $t(18) = 2.73, p < .05$, and slightly more dislike than those in the attack–no shocks condition, 45.8 vs. 36.1; $t(18) = 1.98, p < .10$. Thus, in verbally expressed hostility,

---

[1]None of the other scales from the final questionnaire yielded significant differences across conditions. These scales are not discussed further.

as in physical aggression, subjects were more intense after aggressing than after not aggressing. In response to the questionnaire item "How much did you hold back in shocking the other subject during the code-learning task," subjects again marked a 100-mm line extending from the statement "I held back a lot" (at the low end) to "I didn't hold back at all" (at the high end). The results indicated that subjects in the attack–subject shocks condition reported feeling less restrained than those in both the attack–experimenter shocks, 70.13 vs. 29.20; $t(18) = 4.93$, $p < .01$, and attack–no shocks, 70.13 vs. 48.21; $t(18) = 3.22$, $p < .01$, conditions. This indicates that the attack–subject shocks condition, relative to the other two attack conditions, lowered inhibitions against aggression in the subjects.

DISCUSSION

The findings of the present experiment provide no support for the hypothesis of aggression catharsis and suggest instead that when an experimental situation is arranged to minimize restraints against aggression, the opposite of catharsis occurs. The study also shows that aggressive behavior was followed by a reduction in blood pressure for all three groups of previously attacked subjects: Men in the subject shocks condition experienced decreased pressure after the maze task in which they aggressed, whereas men in the experimenter shocks and no shocks conditions experienced decreased pressure following the learning task, in which they aggressed for the first time. The finding that reduced arousal in the subjects of the attack–subject shocks condition was in turn followed by a high level of aggression rather than a low level casts doubt on the simple cause–effect assumption mentioned earlier in this article. Activity that we may call "physiological catharsis" does follow aggression, as previous reports have shown (e.g., Hokanson and Burgess, 1962), but this cardiovascular change is associated with relatively strong aggressiveness. The results reported here are consistent with those of Kahn (1966), who showed that verbal aggression was followed by both reduced arterial pressure and a high degree of verbal hostility. Our findings, like Kahn's, suggest that future studies of aggression catharsis should include measures of both behavioral aggression and physiological arousal, since we cannot simply assume that decreased arousal brings about a lowered instigation to aggress.

Two explanations of the findings of the present study seem plausible. One is that aggression, by lowering arousal, causes a person to feel relatively at ease. The person may interpret his relaxed condition as being due to the aggression he has just committed and may therefore experience a weakening of socialized restraints against further violence. Our data support this interpretation by showing that aggression is followed by a lowering of motivation to hold back in shocking. The other plausible explanation of our data is that subjects in the attack–subject shocks condition, having aggressed once against the confederate on the maze-learning task, felt compelled to behave consistently by continuing to attack him on the subsequent code-learning phase of the experiment. Doob and Wood (1972) have proposed that such consistency-seeking behavior is enhanced by a high degree of similarity between the first occasion for aggression and the second, such as similarity in the means of aggression used by the subject. Thus, the fact that the subject used electric shock to attack the confederate on both occasions in the present study could have facilitated the subject's need to be equally violent in both. The data from this experiment also showed that men in the attack–subject shocks condition tended to express greater verbal hostility on the final questionnaire than did those in the other two attack groups. This, too, may indicate that subjects acted out of a need to maintain consistency. Perhaps committing violence against another person creates a feeling of need to justify the violent act, and one means of justification is derogation of the victim (see Glass, 1964). The data from this experiment do not allow us to test directly whether the subject's need for consistency underlies the failure to find evidence of catharsis, however, and this possibility remains an intriguing subject for future research.

References

BARON, R. A. Aggression as a function of magnitude of victim's pain cues, level of prior anger arousal, and aggressor–victim similarity. *Journal of Personality and Social Psychology,* 1971, **18,** 48–54.

BERKOWITZ, L. Experimental investigations of hostility catharsis. *Journal of Consulting and Clinical Psychology,* 1970, **35,** 1–7.

BUSS, A. H. The effect of harm on subsequent aggression. *Journal of Experimental Research in Personality,* 1966, **1,** 249–255. (a)

BUSS, A. H. Instrumentality of aggression, feedback, and frustration as determinants of physical aggression. *Journal of Personality and Social Psychology,* 1966, **3,** 153–162. (b)

deCHARMS, R., AND WILKINS, E. J. Some effects of verbal expression of hostility. *Journal of Abnormal and Social Psychology,* 1963, **66,** 462–470.

DOLLARD, J., DOOB, L., MILLER, N. E., MOWRER, O. H., AND SEARS, R. R. *Frustration and aggression.* New Haven, Conn.: Yale University Press, 1939.

DOOB, A. N. Catharsis and aggression: The effect of hurting one's enemy. *Journal of Experimental Research in Personality,* 1970, **4,** 291–296.

DOOB, A. N., AND WOOD, L. Catharsis and aggression: The effects of annoyance and retaliation on aggressive behavior. *Journal of Personality and Social Psychology,* 1972, **22,** 156–162.

FESHBACH, S. The drive-reducing function of fantasy behavior. *Journal of Abnormal and Social Psychology,* 1955, **50,** 3–12.

FREEMAN, E. Effects of aggressive expression after frustrations on performance: A test of the catharsis hypothesis. Unpublished doctoral thesis, Stanford University, 1962.

GEEN, R. G. Effects of frustration, attack, and prior training in aggressiveness upon aggressive behavior. *Journal of Personality and Social Psychology,* 1968, **9,** 316–321.

GEEN, R. G. Perceived suffering of the victim as an inhibitor of attack–induced aggression. *Journal of Social Psychology,* 1970, **81,** 209–215.

GEEN, R. G., AND STONNER, D. Context effects in observed violence. *Journal of Personality and Social Psychology,* 1973, **25,** 145–150.

GLASS, D. C. Changes in liking as a means of reducing cognitive discrepancies between self-esteem and aggression. *Journal of Personality,* 1964, **32,** 531–539.

HOKANSON, J. E., AND BURGESS, M. The effects of three types of aggression on vascular process. *Journal of Abnormal and Social Psychology,* 1962, **64,** 446–449.

KAHN, M. The physiology of catharsis. *Journal of Personality and Social Psychology,* 1966, **3,** 278–286.

MALLICK, S. K., AND McCANDLESS, B. R. A study of catharsis of aggression. *Journal of Personality and Social Psychology,* 1966, **4,** 591–596.

SCHAFER, R. Requirements for a critique of the theory of catharsis. *Journal of Consulting and Clinical Psychology,* 1970, **35,** 13–17.

THIBAUT, J. W., AND COULES, J. The role of communication in the reduction of interpersonal hostility. *Journal of Abnormal and Social Psychology,* 1952, **47,** 770–777.

24

Peacetime Casualties: The Effects of War on the Violent Behavior of Noncombatants

Dane Archer and Rosemary Gartner

Violence by the State is strangely absent from most discussions of the problem of violence. Books about aggression, for example, often treat topics ranging from hormones to homicidal criminals without mentioning capital punishment, the shooting of looters, the beating of protesters, or even that most impressive form of "official" violence: war. This last omission is particularly astonishing, since the unrivaled mortality of wars is both well documented (Singer and Small, 1972) and reasonably contemporary—including the killing of at least 46,000 young American men between 1963 and 1973, in addition to the much greater death toll of other nations involved in the Vietnam War.

Why, then is official violence nearly invisible in discussions of murder and aggression? The most obvious explanation is that wars and other forms of official violence are unique in that they wear the mantle of governmental legitimacy. When aircraft bomb a village, when the United States CIA hires assassins to kill foreign leaders, when a policeman shoots a looter, when a prison firing squad kills a convicted murderer, and when National Guardsmen use lethal weapons to break up a protest, the killings that occur are the result of orders (see Marx, 1970). These orders originate in a hierarchical organization; they are issued by appointed or elected officials and are carried out collectively by uniformed deputies who perform the actual killing. In each case the resulting homicides are described as necessary to

Reprinted (with minor changes) with permission from the authors and Jossey-Bass, Inc., Publishers, from I. L. Kutash, S. B. Kutash, and L. B. Schlesinger (eds.), *Violence: Perspectives of Murder and Aggression,* San Francisco: Jossey-Bass, 1978, 219–232.

This project and the development of the 110-Nation Comparative Crime Data File were supported by NIMH Grant MH 27427 from the Center for Studies of Crime and Delinquency and by a Guggenheim fellowship to the first author. Responsibility for the findings and interpretations in this paper belongs, of course, to the authors alone.

accomplish some official objective—to stop the spread of an alien ideology, to stem the destruction of private property, to deter potential murderers of the future, or to control opponents of governmental policy. Official violence may also be justified as retaliatory—a response to "illegal" violence or the alleged threat of illegal violence. Official killings, therefore, differ from illegal violence in that they result from governmental orders, are usually performed by several agents acting collectively, and are justified as instrumental to some higher purpose. These differentiating features are the basis of the legitimation of official violence.

This process of legitimation is clearly successful in the sense that large numbers of citizens appear to regard government violence as acceptable and unproblematic. Evidence of a public mandate for official violence is easily found. In a 1968 survey, for example, 57 percent of a national sample agreed with the statement "Any man who insults a policeman has no complaint if he gets roughed up in return" (Gamson and McEvoy, 1972, p. 336). The public mandate for official violence includes even the extreme act of homicide. In another 1968 survey, by the Gallup organization, respondents were asked to react to the fact that the mayor of a large city had ordered police to shoot looters on sight during race riots; 61 percent of the men interviewed said that this was the "best way" to deal with the problem of looting. In 1969 roughly half of the American people (48 percent) also thought that shooting was the best way to handle student protests on campus (Kahn, 1972, p. 48). This tolerance of official violence may explain the persistent public perception of riots and rioters as violent—despite the fact that the number of people killed by authorities during civil disorders has consistently exceeded the number of people killed by rioters by approximately ten to one (Couch, 1968).

Public support for official violence is so pervasive that the definition of violence is itself affected. In a 1969 survey, for example, 30 percent of a national sample said that "police beating students" was *not* an act of violence, and an astonishing 57 percent said that "police shooting looters" was *not* an act of violence (Blumenthal et al., 1972, p. 73). The semantics of the label *violence,* therefore, clearly reflect the perceived legitimacy of the actor and not merely the nature of his or her act. The same 1969 survey asked respondents what violent events were of greatest concern to them. Even though the survey occurred during the Vietnam War, only 4 percent of those interviewed mentioned war.

One consequence of the legitimation of official violence, therefore, is the creation of a reservoir of public support. For at least large numbers of Americans, it is clear that even the extreme act of homicide is not regarded as violence—if the homicide carries the stamp of government authority. Widespread deference to government violence may explain the intensity of public reaction to the concept of war crimes, including the trial of Lieutenant William Calley during the Vietnam War (Kelman and Lawrence, 1972). In view of citizen support for official killing, it is perhaps not surprising that public discussions of violence are generally limited to "criminal" violence.

The invisibility of official violence in scientific discussions of aggressions, however, is somewhat more disturbing. Since social scientists are also citizens, it is possible that they too have been captured by the process of legitimation and that they—like many other citizens—no longer think of governmental homicides as violence. For example, wars are generally discussed in political terms in scholarly circles, and political opponents of a war are the only ones who label wartime killings as "murders." Since social scientists are trained to try to regard behavior in a value-free manner, however, it is curious that there has not been more critical discussion of those acts of homicide that happen to have government auspices. Perhaps we are all, scientists included, socialized to accept the State's monopoly on legitimate violence—and perhaps this socialization influences our curiously selective use of the label *violence.*

This tendency to see official violence as legitimate seems limited, however, to the acts of our own government. As an extreme example, wartime practices in Nazi Germany had official government auspices and seem to have enjoyed legitimacy among most contemporary German citizens—including many scientists and intellectuals—but not among citizens of other nations. Even though socialization leads us to defer to governmental violence, therefore, a kind of moral ethnocentrism may restrict this deference to only the acts of our own government. Official acts of violence may enjoy perceived legitimacy inside a government's borders but not outside them.

There may also be structural explanations for the scientific neglect of official violence, however, and this possibility is particularly worrisome. Since social scientists operate in an institutional context, governments may be exerting a disproportionate influence on research agendas for the study of violence. The structure of scientific research itself may therefore create a lamentable "blind spot" concerning governmental violence. Unhappily, case studies of this scientific blind spot are easy to find. For example, when Governor Ronald Reagan of California announced his controversial proposal to establish a Center for the Study of Violent Behavior at UCLA, Earl Brian, the state's secretary of health and welfare, held a press briefing to describe the mission of the proposed center. When asked by a reporter whether the forms of violence studied by the violence center would include war, Dr. Brian replied, "I hadn't thought about war."

Another fascinating illustration of the way official violence can be defined to preclude scientific consideration is described in Short's (1975) excellent account of the history of the National Commission on the Causes and Prevention of Violence. Since Short served as codirector of research (with Marvin E. Wolfgang) for this important presidential commission, his narrative is as well informed as it is interesting. The national commission initially adopted a neutral definition of violence, one that concentrated on the nature of violent acts themselves: "the threat or use of force that results, or is intended to result, in the injury or forcible restraint or intimidation of persons, or the destruction or forcible seizure of property" (Short, 1975, p. 68). Early in the life of the commission, this neutral definition of violence prompted commission researchers to cast a wide net. The commission's *Progress Report,* for example, outlined the scope of the investigation: "There is no implicit value judgment in this definition. The maintenance of law and order falls within it, for a policeman may find it necessary in the course of duty to threaten or use force, even to injure or kill an individual. Wars are included within this definition, as is some punishment of children. It also includes police brutality, the violence of the Nazis, and the physical abuse of a child" (Commission *Progress Report*, p. 3; cited in Short, 1975, p. 68). Even though official violence, such as wars and police brutality, was clearly included in the commission's initial agenda, this emphasis all but disappeared in the commission's subsequent research. For example, by the time its *Final Report* was issued, the commission was concentrating on "all illegal violence" (Short, 1975, p. 69). The insertion of the adjective *illegal* is of pivotal importance, since the actions of governments are—by definition—seldom perceived as illegal. This change of emphasis in the work of a prestigious national investigation had the effect of shifting attention to the acts of "deviant" individual criminals, members of rioting mobs, and assassins. At the same time, this rather traditional focus on illegal violence excluded the acts of governments from consideration—even though the commission conducted its investigations at the very height of the Vietnam War. In fact, Short indicates that some commission researchers had suggested creating a task force on war to go along with the seven task forces on other topics. This idea was abandoned, according to Short, because of the "potentially explosive nature of such a direct focus on war in general and on the conflict in Indochina in particular" (p. 71). Even though much of the commission's research was excellent and even of permanent value, it is still troublesome that the commission was apparently influenced to concentrate on those acts of violence of greatest concern to government—a concern that did not, of course, include the violent acts of government itself.

For all these reasons, discussions of the problem of violence—in both popular and scientific publications—have centered almost exclusively on illegal or "deviant" violence. This prejudice is clearly reflected in language. The term *murder* is almost always reserved for the acts of individual criminals, and even the more neutral word *homicide* is almost never used to describe killings committed by government officials. During wartime, for example, governments use terms like *casualties, body counts,* or even just *losses* to refer to actions that are really—despite these pastel euphemisms—violent homicides. When officials take lives in peacetime, words like *execution* again camouflage the fact that a killing takes place. Only the opponents of a government's violence refuse to participate in this banal vocabulary. Opponents of a war, for example, accuse government officials of "murderous" policies and refer to soldiers as "killers."

We believe that the scientific neglect of official violence needs to be remedied. It is clear that "deviant" violence has in the past monopolized the attention of researchers interested in violence. We believe that this monopoly is scientifically shortsighted, for two reasons. First of all, acts of official violence may turn out to be particularly pernicious, since they are the only forms of violence that carry the prestige and authority of the State. Second, many important and exciting questions about official violence await answers: What kinds of citizens support government violence most strongly? What kinds of government justifications of violence (such as wars or executions) are most effective in legitimating such violence? Do young children regard government violence, such as wartime killing, as "wrong"? At what developmental age are children socialized to accept government violence? Are people at various stages of "moral development" differentially supportive or critical of official violence? Do violent "criminals" support government violence more strongly than a matched group of noncriminals? How do the deputies who carry out official violence justify their behavior to themselves? What kinds of arguments are most effective with juries in death penalty cases? Are Americans more supportive or tolerant of official violence than citizens of relatively nonviolent societies like England? This research agenda is clearly both rich and relatively unexplored.

CONSEQUENCES OF VIOLENCE BY THE STATE

For the past several years, we have been interested in the consequences of violence by the State. Specifically, we wondered whether the most impressive form of official violence, war, tends to increase the level of violence in a society after the war is over. There are rather compelling theoretical reasons to suspect that wars might produce a legacy of postwar violence. For example, there is now incontrovertible evidence that social learning or "modeling" mediates many forms of aggression and violence (Bandura, 1973). Although most research in this area has used either experiments or causal regression techniques to assess the effects of watching media violence, "modeling" theory also appears to provide the best explanation of the apparently contagious patterning of specific murder methods, airplane hijackings, and terrorism (Bandura, 1973, pp. 101–107). The basic tenet of social learning theory is that acts of media violence and real violence can provide a model or script that increases the likelihood of imitative violence. In addition, research indicates that aggressive models appear to be most influential when they are seen as rewarded for their aggression.

If the violent acts of real or fictional individuals can compel imitation, it seems to us very possible that official violence like war could also provide a script for the postwar acts of individuals. Wars, after all, carry the full authority and prestige of the State, and wars also reward killing in the sense that war "heroes" are decorated and lionized in direct proportion to the number of their wartime homicides. Wars also carry, of course, objectives and rationalizations unique to each war—securing the Crimea, humbling the Boers, stopping fascism, deterring communism, and so on. But what all wars have in common—when they are stripped of their idiosyncratic circumstances—is the unmistakable moral lesson that homicide is an acceptable, or even praiseworthy, means to certain ends. It seems likely that this moral lesson will not be lost on at least some of the citizens in a warring nation. Wars, therefore, contain in particularly potent form all the ingredients necessary to produce imitative or modeled violence: great numbers of violent homicides, official auspices and legitimation, and conspicuous praise and rewards for killing and killers.

Even though there are theoretical reasons to expect wars to provide an imitated model for postwar killing, a rigorous test of this legitimation hypothesis is fraught with complications. At first glance, there are a number of intriguing observations in support of the hypothesis. For example, during the Vietnam War the United States murder and nonnegligent manslaughter rate more than doubled—from 4.5 (per 100,000 persons) in 1963 to 9.3 in 1973 (Archer and Gartner, 1976b). This single case of an astonishing increase cannot be regarded as persuasive evidence of a violent legacy of war, of course, because there were many other social and demographic changes in the United States during this decade. A definitive test of the legitimation hypothesis requires a large number of cases, so that the changes in homicide rates in many warring societies can be assessed. In addition, it is important to disentangle the two very different questions included in the legitimation hypothesis: (1) the empirical question of whether, in general, homicide rates do increase after wars and (2) the more interpretive question of what wartime variables could actually cause such increases.

Although writers and social scientists have long suspected that war leaves a violent legacy, a general test of this suspicion has not been possible in the past. The central obstacle to such a test has been the unavailability of the necessary records on national rates of homicide over time. Without a large archive of annual homicide rates for many nations, it has not been possible to test the legitimation hypothesis. Over a period of three years, we have collected a Comparative Crime Data File (CCDF) containing annual rates of homicide and other offenses for 110 nations and 44 major international cities for the period 1900–1970 (see Archer and Gartner, 1976b; see also Archer et al., 1978; Archer and Gartner, 1977).

The creation of the CCDF makes it possible for the first time to attempt a general answer to the question of whether violence by the State increases subsequent violence by individuals. Our basic research design involves a comparison of homicide rate changes in combatant societies with the changes in a control group of noncombatant nations. This controlled comparison is designed to guard against the possibility that homicide increases might be universal over a given period. Only if wars produce consistent increases in postwar homicide rates, therefore, will the changes in combatant nations differ from those in noncombatant nations during the same years. Since wartime mobilization renders the data uninterpretable for war years themselves, we chose as the two periods of comparison the five years prior to a war and the five years after (Archer and Gartner, 1976b). Records of national participation in wars were obtained from an encyclopedic inventory published by Singer and Small (1972). The rich historical data in the CCDF made it possible to examine homicide rate changes after fourteen wars and, since several nations were involved in some wars, after a total of fifty "nation-wars" (one nation in one war). These changes, and the changes in thirty control cases uninvolved in these wars, are shown in Table 24.1.

Our analysis demonstrates that warring nations were more likely to experience homicide rate increases than nations not involved in war. A majority of the combatant nations experienced homicide rate increases of at least 10 percent, while a majority of the uninvolved nations experienced homicide rate *decreases* of greater than 10 percent. Many of the homicide rate increases in warring nations were very large; in several cases the nation's prewar homicide rate more than doubled. The legitimation hypothesis is, therefore, consistent with the results in Table 24.1. Wars do produce a postwar legacy of increased homicide rates.

Even though the difference between combatant and noncombatant nations is striking, this comparison is actually a very conservative test of the legitimation hypothesis. Along with many other changes, wars produce dramatic changes in the age and sex structure of a nation's population. The numbers of young men killed in twentieth-century wars have often been staggering. At the end of World War I, for example, out of every thousand men who were between 20 and 45 at the war's outbreak, 182 died in France, 166 in Austria, 155 in Germany, 101 in Italy, and 88 in Britain (von Hentig, 1947, p. 349). Since young men are universally overrepresented in homicide offense rates (Wolfgang and Ferracuti, 1967), these wartime losses remove from a nation's population precisely those who are statistically most likely to commit homicide in the postwar years. In addition, the postwar baby booms, particularly after large wars, also tend to reduce postwar homicide rates by inflating the population denominator on which they are calculated.

The implications of these conservative artifacts can be summarized easily: If one corrects for the wartime depletion of young men and the surge of postwar babies, warring nations experienced homicide increases even greater than those shown in Table 24.1. For example, France is shown as having a negligible homicide rate increase of 4 percent after World War I and is classified as an unchanged case in Table 24.1. If one controls for France's appalling wartime losses, however, the observed postwar homicide rate can only be considered as an impressive increase. The fact that combatant nations still showed increases much more frequently than the noncombatant nations in Table 24.1, despite the conservative effect of these demographic changes, is therefore particularly impressive.

The nation-wars in Table 24.1 varied considerably in length of wartime involvement and number of men killed. The warring nations in our study, therefore, received different "doses" of war. In terms of the legitimation hypothesis, nations with the greatest wartime mortality are exposed to a larger scale of legitimate killing than other nations. Using the information provided by Singer and Small (1972), we were able to classify nation-wars according to the amount of war experienced by each. The classification we used was whether a nation had fewer or more than five hundred battle deaths per million prewar population. This control procedure produces even more dramatic results and again runs counter to what one would expect from population changes alone. The nations that were heavily impacted by war-time killing suffered postwar homicide increases with particular consistency; 79 percent of these nations experienced homicide rate increases, and only 21 percent had decreases. We interpret this result as an internal validation of

TABLE 24.1
Homicide Rate Changes in Combatant and Control Nations After World War I, World War II, the Vietnam War, and Eleven Other Wars

			Homicide Rate Change (%)		
	Decrease	%	Unchanged (<|10%|)	%	Increase	%

	Decrease	%	Unchanged (<|10%|)	%	Increase	%
Combatant Nations	Australia (I)	-23	England (I)	-5	Belgium (I)	24
	Canada (I)	-25	France (I)	4	Bulgaria (I)	22
	Hungary (I)	-57	S. Africa (I)	-1	Germany (I)	98
	Finland (II)	-15	Canada (II)	6	Italy (I)	52
	N. Ireland (II)	-83	Australia (VN)	7	Japan (I)	12
	U.S. (II)	-12	Korea (VN)	6	Portugal (I)	47
	India (1962 Sino-Ind)	-14	Philippines (VN)	9	Scotland (I)	50
	Israel (1956 Sinai)	-58	Egypt (1956 Sinai)	-2	U.S. (I)	13
	Italy (1896 It-Eth)	-15	Egypt (1967 6-Day)	-4	Australia (II)	32
	Italy (1935 It-Eth)	-44	France (1884 Sino-Fr)	0	Denmark (II)	169
			India (1965 2nd Kash)	6	England (II)	13
			Japan (1904 Russo-Jap)	-9	France (II)	51
			Japan (1932 Manch)	-8	Italy (II)	133
					Japan (II)	20
					Netherlands (II)	13
					New Zealand (II)	313
					Norway (II)	65
					Scotland (II)	11
					S. Africa (II)	104
					New Zealand (VN)	50
					Thailand (VN)	14
					U.S. (VN)	42
					Hungary (1956 Russo-H)	13
					Israel (1967 6-Day)	14
					Japan (1894 Sino-Jap)	15
					Jordan (1967 6-Day)	35
					Pakistan (1965 2nd Kash)	13

Control Nations					
Norway (I)	−37	Ceylon (I)	8	Finland (I)	124[a]
Ceylon (II)	−19	Chile (I)	−3	Thailand (I)	112[a]
Chile (II)	−67	Netherlands (I)	−2	Colombia (II)	34
El Salvador (II)	−20	Thailand (1932 Manch)	7	Sweden (II)	14
Ireland (II)	−22	Ceylon (1962 Sino-Ind)	−4	Turkey (II)	12
Switzerland (II)	−42			Canada (VN)	11
Thailand (II)	−17			England (VN)	23
Burma (VN)	−17			Taiwan (VN)	37
Indonesia (VN)	−23			Ceylon (1965 2nd Kash)	11
Japan (VN)	−23				
Austria (1956 Russo-H)	−13				
Burma (1965 2nd Kash)	−13				
France (1896 Italo-Eth)	−13				
Switzerland (1935 It-Eth)	−22				
Turkey (1956 Sinai)	−33				
Turkey (1967 6-Day)	−19				

[a]Finland and Thailand are both included as control cases for World War I because these two nations were not identified as combatants by Singer and Small (1972). However, the wisdom of classifying these nations as noncombatants during this period is far from clear. Finland underwent something of an "internal" or civil war in 1918, and Thailand actually sent troops to the Allied cause during World War I.

Source: Archer and Gartner (1976b).

the overall finding in Table 24.1, since the nations most likely to show homicide increases are precisely those nations that experienced the largest "amounts" of war.

The answer to the first of the two questions prompted by the legitimation hypothesis is therefore unambiguous. Warring nations are more likely than nonwarring nations to experience postwar surges in individual acts of homicide. The increases occur despite massive wartime losses of young men and are particularly common among nations whose wartime involvement is unusually deadly. It is still a separate matter, of course, to test the second half of the legitimation hypothesis: What is it about wars that actually produces these increases in postwar violence? For example, there has been a long history of speculation about whether veterans of wars are more likely than other citizens to commit acts of violence (Archer and Gartner, 1976a). This fear appears to surface after each war. For example, attorney Clarence Darrow (1922, p. 218) attributed post-World War I crime increases to the returned veterans, whom he described as "inoculated with the universal madness," and Lifton (1973, p. 32) made this more recent prediction about Vietnam veterans: "Some are likely to seek continuing outlets to a pattern of violence to which they have become habituated, whether by indulging in antisocial or criminal behavior or by offering their services to the highest bidder." The basic idea behind this speculation is that the military socializes men to be both more accepting of and more proficient at killing and that this experience may increase the likelihood that veterans will use violence even after the war is over.

A number of spectacular case studies appear to lend substance to the image of the violent veteran. For example, some soldiers who rode with Quantrill's guerrillas during the American Civil War became well known for their postwar lawlessness; they were Jesse and Frank James and the Younger brothers. There are also many recent examples. In 1949 a combat veteran named Howard Unruh went on a rampage in Camden, New Jersey, and killed twelve people with a souvenir pistol— Unruh had won marksman and sharpshooter ratings during World War II. During the Vietnam War, a soldier named Dwight Johnson killed about twenty enemy soldiers and was awarded the Congressional Medal of Honor; several months after his return home to Detroit, he was shot and killed while trying to rob a grocery store. Case studies prove very little by themselves, of course, and the more general question is whether the acts of violent veterans can explain the homocide increases we have observed in postwar societies. Since most nations, including the United States, do not maintain records on the military experience of persons arrested for homicide, it is difficult to determine whether veterans are overrepresented in homicide statistics. Even if the number of homicides committed by veterans were known, it is not clear what rate we would compare this with, since veterans and nonveterans differ in many ways in addition to military experience. An indirect approach to this question involves comparisons between two types of veterans, combat and noncombat; and recent research has not found unusually high rates of offenses or violence among combat veterans (Borus, 1975). In the absence of firm evidence, the image of the violent veteran may be more myth than reality. The persistence of the myth is probably due, in part, to the nature of the training that soldiers receive. Civilians may have deep-seated misgivings about teaching soldiers to kill, and they may fear that it is easier to unleash violence than to rein it in again.

We have found evidence that the hypothesis of the violent veteran, despite its popularity, cannot explain the postwar homicide increases observed in warring nations. The key answer to this question is our finding that postwar increases in violence have occurred among groups who could not have been combat veterans. During the Vietnam War, for example, violence increased precipitously for United States men and women; between 1963 and 1973 homicide arrests increased 101 percent for men and 59 percent for women. We have also obtained data from other nations on postwar offense rates for men and women, and it is clear that postwar rates of violence increase for both sexes. As a final bit of evidence, postwar homicide rates also increase among all age groups, and not just among the young veteran age cohort.

In summary, postwar increases in homicide rates are both common and pervasive. They occur after large and small wars, in victorious as well as defeated nations, in nations with improved postwar economies and nations with worsened economies, among veterans and nonveterans, among men and women, and among offenders in several age groups. We believe that these homicide rate increases cannot be explained by artifacts or by other social changes that happen to coincide with wars. Instead, we think that this finding reveals a potential linkage between the violence of governments and the violence of individuals. This linkage is mediated, we believe, by a process of legitimation in which wartime homicide becomes a high-status, rewarded model for subsequent homicides by individuals. Wars provide concrete evidence that homicide, under some conditions, is acceptable in the eyes of a nation's leaders. This wartime reversal of the customary peacetime prohibition against killing may somehow influence the threshold for using homicidal force as a means of settling conflict in everyday life. There is even some independent evidence of the mechanisms by which governmental violence can permeate the private lives of citizens in warring societies; for example, Huggins and Straus (1975) have shown that fictional violence in children's literature reaches a dramatic maximum in war years.

Even though social scientists have in the past amassed impressive experimental evidence that violence can be produced through imitation or modeling, they have in general neglected the possibility that government—with its vast authority and resources—might turn out to be the most potent model of all. This powerful influence of governments on private behavior seems to be what Justice Louis Brandeis had in mind when he wrote in 1928: "Our government is the potent, the omnipresent teacher. For good or ill, it teaches the whole people by its example. Crime is contagious. If the government becomes a lawbreaker, it breeds contempt for the law."

The astonishing neglect of official violence in the social sciences has almost certainly resulted from the curious tendency of both citizens and scientists to avoid labeling the acts of governments—including even the extreme act of homicide—as violence. This deference to the legitimacy of governments has resulted in the near omission of wars and other forms of official homicide from discussions of violence. The new finding that wars cause surges in postwar homicide rates suggests that this omission is lamentable and that the violent acts of individuals may in part be catalyzed by the violent times in which governments cause them to live.

References

ARCHER, D., AND GARTNER, R. The myth of the violent veteran. *Psychology Today,* Dec. 1976, 94–96, 110–111. (a)

ARCHER, D., AND GARTNER, R. Violent acts and violent times: A comparative approach to postwar homicide rates. *American Sociological Review,* 1976, **41,** 937–963. (b)

ARCHER, D., AND GARTNER, R. Homicide in 110 Nations: The development of the comparative crime data file. *International Annals of Criminology,* 1977, **16,** 109–139.

ARCHER, D., GARTNER, R., AKERT, R., AND LOCKWOOD, T. Cities and homicide: A new look at an old paradox. In R. F. Tomasson (ed.), *Comparative studies in sociology.* Vol. 1. Greenwich, Conn.: JAI Press, 1978 (now *Comparative Social Research*).

BANDURA, A. *Aggression: A social learning analysis.* Englewood Cliffs, N.J.: Prentice-Hall. 1973.

BLUMENTHAL, M. D., KAHN, R. L., ANDREWS, F. M., AND HEAD, K. B. *Justifying violence.* Ann Arbor: University of Michigan Press, 1972.

BORUS, J. F. The reentry transition of the Vietnam veteran. *Armed Forces and Society,* 1975, **2,** 97–114.

COUCH, C. Collective behavior: An examination of stereotypes. *Social Problems,* 1968, **15,** 310–321.

DARROW, C. *Crime and its causes.* New York: Crowell, 1922.

GAMSON, W. A., AND MCEVOY, J. Police violence and its public support. In J. F. Short and M. E. Wolfgang (eds.), *Collective violence,* Chicago: Aldine, 1972.

HUGGINS, M. D., AND STRAUS, M. A. Violence and the social structure as reflected in children's books from 1850 to 1970. Paper presented at 45th annual meeting of the Eastern Sociological Society, 1975.

KAHN, R. L. Violent man: Who buys bloodshed and why. *Psychology Today,* June 1972. **6**(1), 46–48, 83.

KELMAN, H. C., AND LAWRENCE, L. H. American response to the trial of Lt. William L. Calley. *Psychology Today,* June 1972, **6**(1), 41–45, 78–81.

KOHLBERG, L. The cognitive-developmental approach to socialization. In D. A. Goslin (ed.), *Handbook of socialization theory and research.* Chicago: Rand McNally, 1969.

MARX, G. T. Civil disorder and the agents of social control. *Journal of Social Issues,* 1970, **26,** 19–57.

SHORT, J. F. The National commission on the causes and prevention of violence: Reflections on the contributions of sociology and sociologists. In M. Komarovsky (ed.), *Sociology and public policy: The case of presidential commissions.* New York: Elsevier, 1975.

SINGER, J. D. AND SMALL, M. *The wages of war, 1816–1965: A statistical handbook.* New York: Wiley, 1972.

TURIEL, E., AND ROTHMAN, G. R. The influence of reasoning on behavioral choices at different stages of moral development. *Child Development,* 1972, **43,** 741–756.

VON HENTIG, H. *Crime: Causes and conditions.* New York: McGraw-Hill, 1947.

WOLFGANG, M. E., AND FERRACUTI, F. *The subculture of violence.* London: Tavistock, 1967.

25

Deindividuation and Anger-Mediated Interracial Aggression: Unmasking Regressive Racism

Ronald W. Rogers and Steven Prentice-Dunn

A factorial experiment investigated the effects of deindividuation, anger, and race-of-victim on aggression displayed by groups of whites. Deindividuating situational cues produced an internal state of deindividuation that mediated aggressive behavior. Deindividuation theories were extended by the finding that the internal state of deindividuation was composed not only of the factors Self-Awareness and Altered Experience, but also Group Cohesiveness, Responsibility, and Time Distortion. As predicted, nonangered whites were *less* aggressive toward black than white victims, but angered whites were *more* aggressive toward blacks than whites. Interracial behavior was consistent with new, egalitarian norms if anger was not aroused, but regressed to the old, historical pattern of racial discrimination if anger was aroused. This pattern of interracial behavior was interpreted in terms of a new form of racism: regressive racism.

Mob violence that has occurred since the time of the Roman republic has been attributed typically to short-term economic motives and political issues (cf. Rude, 1964). Economic and political motives, however, were inadequate to explain the torture, mutilation, and burning that frequently occurred in outbursts of interracial violence. Lynch mobs convinced social scientists that "the fundamental need was for a better understanding of the causes underlying the resort to mob violence" (Southern Commission on the Study of Lynching, 1931, p. 5). The major purpose of the present experiment was to examine interracial aggression within a group context, especially a context conducive to deindividuation.

Reprinted with permission from the authors and *Journal of Personality and Social Psychology,* 1981, Vol. 41, No. 1, 63–67. Copyright © 1981 by the American Psychological Association, Inc.

The authors gratefully acknowledge Kevin O'Brien, Henry Mixon, George Smith, and Rod Walls for their assistance in collecting the data.

Deindividuation is a process in which antecedent social conditions lessen self-awareness and reduce concern with evaluation by others, thereby weakening restraints against the expression of undesirable behaviors (e.g., Diener, 1977; Zimbardo, 1970). Prentice-Dunn and Rogers (1980) provided the first confirmation of deindividuation theory's major assumption that deindividuating situational cues produce an internal state of deindividuation that mediates the display of aggressive behavior. The deindividuating cues lowered self-awareness and altered cognitive and affective experiences. This deindividuated state weakened restraints against behaving aggressively that are normally maintained by internal and external norms of social propriety. In the present study, therefore, we hypothesized that deindividuating situational cues would produce more aggression than individuating cues, and that an internal state of deindividuation would mediate the effects of deindividuating cues on antisocial behavior.

Many problematic forms of interracial conflict occur in group contexts. The major contribution to our understanding of interracial aggression has come from the Donnersteins' research program (cf. Donnerstein and Donnerstein, 1976), which has focused on situations involving one aggressor and one victim; no published studies have examined interracial aggression displayed by a *group* of whites toward a black individual. The present experiment examined interracial aggression in a group setting in which angry aggressors were deindividuated. This social situation approximates many naturalistic situations.

Studies of interracial aggression have consistently shown that the strength of aggression directed toward a different-race victim varies as a function of, for example, potential censure (Donnerstein and Donnerstein, 1973), threatened retaliation (Donnerstein, Donnerstein, Simon, and Ditrichs, 1972), and the victim's expression of suffering (Baron, 1979; Griffin and Rogers, 1977). Donnerstein and Donnerstein (1976) have reported that, in a variety of conditions, white subjects manifest less direct aggression toward black than white victims. Griffin and Rogers (1977) interpreted their white subjects' more lenient treatment of blacks than whites in terms of "reverse discrimination" (cf. Dutton, 1976): To avoid appearing prejudiced, whites treated blacks more favorably (i.e., less aggressively) than they treated whites.

Reverse discrimination is the overt manifestation of white people's viewing themselves as egalitarian and feeling threatened by the prospect of appearing prejudiced. Blacks would not be expected to display reverse discrimination, and studies of blacks' aggression have confirmed they do not (Wilson and Rogers, 1975). Both blacks' and whites' behavior, however, can be traced to the same underlying source: Both races seem to be "reacting against the older, traditional patterns for their races" (Griffin and Rogers, 1977, p. 157).

For whites, the historical pattern of appropriate behavior toward blacks was racial discrimination and inferior treatment. Although whites may have negative attitudes on several specific issues such as blacks' economic gains (Ross, Vanneman, and Pettigrew, 1976) and race riots (Davis and Fine, 1975), survey data indicate that the new norm is an egalitarian view of the races (Brigham and Wrightsman, in press; Campbell, 1971; Taylor, Sheatsley, and Greeley, 1978). This new norm is especially prevalent among college students. Surveys at the university where the present study was conducted confirmed that the current norm among white students is an unprejudiced, egalitarian view of the races (Rosenberg).[1] Theoretically, reverse discrimination is a product of this relatively new egalitarian view of blacks (Dutton, 1976).

For blacks, the historical pattern of appropriate interracial behavior was to inhibit aggression toward whites and to displace it to fellow blacks. The new norms favor more militancy, antiwhite attitudes, and overt hostility toward whites (Caplan, 1970; Wilson and Rogers, 1975). The new norms for blacks and whites represent dramatic departures from the deep-rooted values of the past. Both races have been found to act on these new norms if they are not emotionally aroused by a verbal insult. Thus, blacks are more aggressive towards white than black targets (Wilson and Rogers, 1975), and whites are more aggressive toward white than black targets (Griffin and Rogers, 1977).

But what happens to behavior based on these new norms if the aggressors are insulted? Baron (1979) reported a three-way interaction effect among race-of-victim, insult, and pain cues. An examination of the conditions comparable to those to be studied in the present experiment (i.e., Baron's no-pain-cues condition) indicated that when white subjects were not insulted, black victims received less aggression than white victims (i.e., reverse discrimination); if insulted, the level of aggression expressed toward blacks increased, but did not significantly differ from the level directed toward the white victims.

Since we wish to understand interracial aggression in general and not merely whites' behavior toward blacks, let us also examine blacks' aggression toward whites. To interpret the interracial aggressive behavior of blacks, Wilson and Rogers (1975) suggested that emotional arousal produced a regression to a chronologically earlier mode of responding. The data from that experiment were interpreted as evidence that blacks' behavior could be understood as a product of "the conflict between new militant norms and the residue of oppression" (p. 857). Anger-mediated aggression should not be as firmly under the cognitive control of new norms of in-group solidarity and pride. The black students had been exposed to the traditional values of in-group rejection and out-group preference for many years before the appearance of the Black Power movement. They undoubtedly retained some residual symptoms. Thus, when they became emotionally aroused, the new values, which had not been fully internalized, gave way to the older, more traditional pattern. Similarly, the young white adults in the present study had been exposed during their socialization to the older tradition of belief in black inferiority.

The foregoing considerations converge to suggest an interaction between race-of-victim and insult variables. If whites are not angered, we predicted that they would display reverse discrimination, directing weaker attacks against blacks than against whites. If angered, we hypothesized that whites would regress to the traditional pattern, displaying more aggression toward blacks than toward whites.

---

[1]Rosenberg, J. *Racial attitudes of undergraduate students.* Unpublished manuscript, University of Alabama, 1980.

One class of deindividuation theories suggests that victim characteristics (e.g., different race) become less salient under conditions of deindividuation. For Festinger, Pepitone, and Newcomb (1952), the defining characteristic of deindividuation is that individuals are not paid attention to as individuals. As elaborated by Zimbardo (1970), deindividuated behavior is not under the controlling influence of usual discriminative stimuli; it is "unresponsive to features of the situation, the target, the victim" (p. 259). Based upon this theoretical position, any differential treatment of different-race victims should vanish when group members become deindividuated. On the other hand, Diener's (1980) theory of less extreme forms of deindividuation postulates that crowd members are *more* responsive to external stimuli as a result of the focus of attention shifting away from the self. It is plausible to infer that any differential treatment of different-race victims should be enhanced by deindividuation. Therefore, the present study was designed to test these two alternative predictions.

Verbal attack, or insult, is a potent and well-established antecedent of aggression in dyadic situations involving one aggressor and one victim (see review by Baron, 1977); however, the effects of anger in a group context have not been investigated. Virtually all studies of deindividuation and aggression have involved unprovoked aggression. Yet, anger adds an important theoretical and applied dimension to our understanding of mob violence. It was hypothesized that insult, or anger arousal, would facilitate the expression of aggression among members of small groups.

One class of deindividuation theories postulates that deindividuated behavior is not influenced by usual discriminative stimuli. It may be derived from these theories that prior insult would have less impact on deindividuated than individuated group members. On the other hand, it may be derived from Diener's (1980) theory that "because self-regulation is minimized or eliminated the deindividuated person is more susceptible to the influences of immediate stimuli, emotions [e.g., anger], and motivations" (p. 211, italics added).

There are several limitations to deriving predictions of interaction effects from these two classes of deindividuation theories. First, neither theory explicitly states how the variables of insult or different-race victim would interact with deindividuation. Thus, other interpretations are possible. Second, the form of the interaction effect may vary as a function of the strength of the deindividuation state. The present study is certainly not an experimentum crucis, but perhaps it can shed light on the interaction of deindividuation and anger-mediated interracial aggression.

METHOD

Design and Subjects

A 2 × 2 × 2 factorial design was employed with three between-subjects manipulations: (a) deindividuating cues versus individuating cues, (b) white versus black victim, and (c) no insult versus insult. Ninety-six male introductory psychology students participated in the experiment to earn extra credit. Twelve subjects were randomly assigned to each cell.

Apparatus

The shock apparatuses were modified Buss aggression machines connected to a polygraph. Each of the four aggression machines had 10 pushbutton switches that could be depressed to deliver "shocks" of progressively increasing intensity. Of course, shocks were not actually delivered. A Grason-Stadler noise generator (Model 901A) was used to produce white noise in the deindividuating cues condition.

Procedure

The procedure was highly similar to one we had used previously (Prentice-Dunn and Rogers, 1980). Subjects arrived in groups of five; four were naive participants and one was our assistant. The study was explained as a combination of two experiments. The subjects had signed up for an experiment entitled "Behavior Modification" and were to be tested together. Our assistant, ostensibly another introductory psychology student, had volunteered for a study labeled "Biofeedback." After the experimenter determined who had volunteered for each topic, the biofeedback subject was sent to another room to receive detailed instructions for the biofeedback study.

After hearing explanations of the concepts of behavior modification and biofeedback, the four white behavior modifiers were told that the response of interest in both studies was heart rate. It was indicated that the biofeedback subject would be attempting to maintain his heart rate at a predesignated, high level. Whenever his heart rate fell below the predetermined level, the behavior modifiers would administer an electric shock. The purpose of having groups of four behavior modifiers was explained as an attempt to establish a laboratory analog of a ward at the local state hospital where behavior modifiers actually worked in small groups.

We explained to all subjects that they received their extra credit points for simply showing up and that they could discontinue at any time. Each subject was asked if he had any questions about or any objections to the use of electric shock. All questions were answered and no one declined to participate. In addition, written informed consent was obtained. Two mild sample shocks were administered to the behavior modifiers (i.e., the subjects) via finger electrode. The shocks were from Switches 4 (.3 mA) and 6 (.45 mA) on the aggression machine and each lasted for 1 sec. These samples were administered to convince the subjects that the apparatus really worked and to give them some idea of the shocks they would be delivering.

The behavior modification subjects were then taken to an adjoining room, seated at aggression machines with partitions that blocked observation of others' responses (thus, responses were experimentally independent), and given instructions for operating the shock apparatus. Each time the biofeedback subject's heart rate fell below the predetermined level, a signal light would be illuminated on their panels. It was explained that the higher the level chosen and the longer the switch was depressed, the stronger the shock administered would be. The "shock" received by the biofeedback subject was alleged to be the average of the intensities and durations selected by the four behavior modifiers.

The final instruction given to the subjects was that any of the 10 shock switches would be sufficient for the purposes of the experiment. It was explained that the equipment had been designed with different shock intensities because we had not known how strong the shocks would have to be to increase heart rate. We explained we had discovered that the different shocks all had equal effects on the biofeedback subject's heart rate, so the naive subjects could choose any intensity they wished on each trial. These instructions were designed to eliminate any potential altruistic motivation, and they made clear that use of the lowest possible intensity on every trial would fulfill the requirements of the experiment. Use of any intensity greater than "1" would only result in additional pain to the biofeedback subject.

Each group was presented with 20 signal lights over the course of the experiment. The interval between the appearance of any two signals was initially chosen randomly, ranging from 20–50 sec. The intervals were then held constant across subsequent trials.

The experimenter then left to bring the biofeedback subject from a waiting room to the experimental room. The doors were left open, so that subjects heard the final instructions given by the experimenter to the biofeedback subject about his role. Thus, the naive subjects would easily hear, but not see, their future victim.

Experimental Manipulations

The first manipulation attempted to differentiate maximally between deindividuating situational cues and individuating ones. In the *deindividuating* cues condition, the experimenter did not address subjects by name. They were informed that the shocks they used were of no interest to the experimenter and that he would not know which intensities and durations they selected (anonymity to the experimenter). Subjects were further informed that they would not meet or see the biofeedback subject (anonymity to the victim). The experimenter indicated that he assured full responsibility for the biofeedback subject's well-being (no responsibility for harm-doing). Finally, white noise was played at 65 dB (SPL) in the dimly lit room under the guise of eliminating any extraneous noise from the hall or other experimental rooms (arousal). Prentice-Dunn and Rogers (1980) have shown that such manipulations decrease the subjects' feelings of identifiability and self-awareness.

In the *individuating* cues condition, the subjects wore name tags and were addressed on a first-name basis. As in Zimbardo's (1970) study, the "unique reactions" of each subject were emphasized, and the experimenter expressed his interest in the shock intensities and durations used by the subjects. Subjects were informed that they would meet the biofeedback subject on completing the study. It was emphasized that the biofeedback subject's well-being was the responsibility of each individual behavior modifier. The room was well-lit and no white noise was broadcast.

A second independent variable, race of victim, was manipulated through the use of four experimental assistants, two whites and two blacks. Assistants were assigned to the treatment cells randomly, with the exception that they appeared an equal number of times in each treatment combination. Analyzing this "assistants" factor as an additional variable in the factorial design yielded no main or interaction effects. Thus, the data from the assistants of each race were pooled in the analyses reported below.

The third independent variable was introduced when the behavior modifiers overheard a conversation in an adjoining room between the experimenter and the biofeedback subject. This conversation took place immediately after the naive subjects received their instructions. This insult manipulation was operationalized as a series of questions and answers between the experimenter and the biofeedback subject (i.e., our assistant). Care was taken that the insulting remarks applied to all of the subjects and were devoid of any racial content or connotation. In the *insult* condition, the biofeedback subject, when asked if he objected to the behavior modifiers shocking him, responded that the equipment looked complicated and he wondered if people who appeared as dumb as the behavior modifiers did could follow instructions properly. When the experimenter reiterated the biofeedback subject's option to withdraw from the experiment, the biofeedback subject answered that he hoped the behavior modifiers were not as stupid as they appeared. Finally, when asked by the experimenter if he knew the behavior modifiers, the biofeedback subject said that he didn't know them personally, but that he knew their type; he could tell that they thought they were "hot stuff." In the *no insult* condition, the biofeedback subject simply stated that he had no objections to these particular behavior modifiers shocking him.

Postexperiment Session

Following the last shock trial, subjects completed a questionnaire containing manipulations-check items (10-point Likert rating scales) and 17 items tapping an internal state of deindividuation. A second questionnaire assessed suspicions about the experiment. Five subjects suspected that shocks were not actually delivered, two subjects correctly guessed the race-of-victim hypothesis, and four subjects believed that the insult manipulation was staged. These subjects were deleted from the data analyses. The data in this unequal n design were analyzed with the complete least squares model recommended by Overall, Spiegel, and Cohen (1975) because this model meets the criterion of estimating the same parameters as those estimated in an orthogonal design. After each experimental session, each subject was thanked and given a full debriefing that was based on Mills' (1976) recommendations. Finally, a questionnaire was given to each student in a stamped envelope addressed to the Psychology Department's Committee on Ethics. These anonymous responses were returned by 58% of the subjects. 98% of the respondents understood why the deception had been necessary and did not resent it. One subject (2% of the sample) indicated that he did not think the deception was necessary, and another subject stated that his participation had not been voluntary. Neither of these two subjects explained their responses in the space provided on the questionnaire. Fortunately, both of these students, along with every other respondent (100% of the sample), indicated that (a) the experiment should be allowed to continue and (b) that they would be willing to participate in another similar experiment.

RESULTS

Aggression

Deindividuating cues.   A multivariate analysis of variance was performed on the sums of the shock intensity scores and the shock duration scores. This analysis yielded a main effect associated with the situational cues manipulation, Wilks's lambda (Λ) = .843, $F(2, 152) = 6.79$, $p < .001$. Univariate analyses of variance disclosed main effects for the situational cues variable on both shock intensity, $F(1, 77) = 12.01$, $p < .001$, and on shock duration, $F(1, 77) = 5.37$, $p < .03$. Compared to subjects in the individuating cues condition, subjects exposed to the deindividuating cues used higher shock intensities ($Ms = 5.3$ and 6.4, respectively) for longer durations ($Ms = 1.6$ & 2.8 sec, respectively). Neither of the two predicted 2-way interaction effects with deindividuating cues were significant ($Fs < 1$).

Insult and race.   To determine if the insult manipulation had been successful, an analysis of variance was performed on the sum of the two items assessing anger toward the victim. The only significant effect was that the insulted groups ($M = 5.1$) expressed much more anger than the noninsulted groups ($M = 1.9$), $F(1, 77) = 29.71$, $p < .0001$. A multivariate analysis of variance indicated that the insulted groups expressed more aggression toward the victim than the noninsulted groups, $\Lambda = .904$, $F(2, 152) = 3.97$, $p < .02$. More importantly, the multivariate analysis of variance revealed a Race $\times$ Insult interaction effect, $\Lambda = .912$, $F(2, 152) = 3.59$, $p < .03$. The aggression centroids are shown in Figure 25.1. Univariate analyses of variance yielded identical interaction effects for both the intensity data, F (1.77) = 4.63, $p < .04$, and the duration data, $F(1, 77) = 4.57$, $p < .04$. A Duncan's multiple-range test ($p < .05$) yielded an identical pattern of results for both measures. As may be seen in Figure 25.1, when white subjects were not insulted, they expressed less aggression toward black than white victims; however, if the white subjects were insulted, they expressed more aggression against black than white victims. There were no other significant main or interaction effects on the aggression data.

Internal State of Deindividuation

Prior research (Diener, 1979; Prentice-Dunn and Rogers, 1980) had established that a subjective state of deindividuation is composed of at least two factors, Self-Awareness and Altered Experience. The 17 items in the Prentice-Dunn and Rogers (1980) study that loaded greater than .4 on only one of these factors were included in the post-experiment questionnaire. Although the present study differed from the former one in that half of the subjects had been emotionally aroused by an insult and in that half aggressed against a different-race victim, an initial principal-axes factor analysis with varimax rotation yielded two factors highly similar to those previously reported. However, five eigenvalues were greater than unity, hence five factors were rotated to a varimax solution. This solution accounted for an additional 26% of the variance. The factor loadings that are greater than or equal to .4 on only one of the factors are shown in

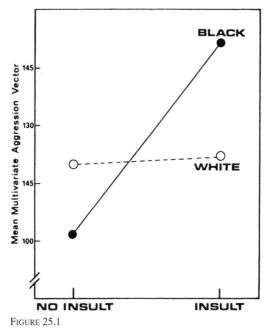

FIGURE 25.1
Aggression as a function of insult and race of victim.

Table 25.1. This factor structure, although not predicted, is readily interpretable. The first factor, which is composed of four items from the original Self-Awareness factor, is highly similar to Fenigstein, Scheier, and Buss' (1975) and Buss' (1980) concept of Public Self-Consciousness coefficient (alpha = .72). The items loading on this factor are highly similar to Fenigstein et al.'s items (e.g., "I'm concerned about what other people think of me.") The original Altered Experience factor decomposed into the second, third, and fourth factors. The second factor might still be labeled Altered Experience (alpha = .62). The third factor represents another facet of altered experiencing, but refers specifically to Time Distortion (alpha = .35). The fourth factor is composed of items traditionally used to measure cohesiveness, thus, it is labeled Group Cohesiveness (alpha = .61). The final factor might be labeled Responsibility (alpha = .69); it reflected the degree to which all group members, including the subject himself, had responsibility for harmdoing. The remaining two items loaded on more than one factor. The question assessing a feeling of togetherness among group members loaded on both the Group Cohesion and Altered Experience factors. Finally, the item measuring inhibition loaded on both the Public Self-Awareness and Altered Experience factors.

TABLE 25.1
Factor loadings on the rotated factors

Factor	Loading
Factor I (Public Self-Awareness)	
Concerned with what experimenter thought of me	.78
Concerned with what victim thought of me	.78
Concerned with what other group members thought of me	.71
Felt self-conscious	.50
Factor 2 (Altered Experience)	
Emotions were different from normal	.69
Thinking was somewhat altered	.65
Felt aroused	.59
Factor 3 (Group Cohesiveness)	
Liked other group members	.70
Session was enjoyable	.65
Willing to volunteer for another study with same group	.77
Factor 4 (Time Distortion)	
Thoughts were concentrated on the moment	.69
Time seemed to go quickly	.67
Factor 5 (Responsibility)	
I had responsibility for harm-doing	.83
Responsibility was shared	.84

Note. These five factors accounted for 13%, 14%, 13%, 9%, and 10% of the variance, respectively.

To replicate our previous study, we asked whether the original two factors could discriminate between the individuating and deindividuating cues conditions. The sums of each subject's raw scores on the Self-Awareness items and the Altered Experience items were submitted to a multivariate analysis of variance. A significant difference was obtained between the two situational cues conditions, $\Lambda = .882$, $F(2, 164) = 5.34$, $p < .006$. Subjects in the deindividuating cues condition had higher scores on the Altered Experience factor ($M = 65.8$) than subjects in the individuating cues condition ($M = 62.8$), but lower scores on the Self-Awareness factor ($Ms = 33.1$ & 38.5, respectively). A multivariate analysis of variance comparing the two situational cues conditions on the five factors also yielded a significant main effect, $\Lambda = .801$, $F(5, 79) = 3.91$, $p < .004$.

Deindividuation and Aggression

The correlation matrix among the original two factors of the internal state of deindividuation and shock intensity was decomposed into components corresponding to paths. This analysis attempted an exact replication of previous findings that there was a causal path from Altered Experience and Self-Awareness to shock intensity. The coefficients were .29 and $-.20$, respectively, confirming the previous structural model.

There was no strong a priori theoretical model that postulated relationships among our three independent variables, the five components of an internal state of deindividuation, and the dependent measures of shock intensity and duration. Therefore, no path analysis was performed. However, a multiple regression analysis was performed using the five factors to predict aggression (sum of shock intensity and duration). All of the relationships were in the expected direction, but the only statistically significant predictor of aggression was Group Cohesiveness (standardized partial regression coefficient = .25, $p < .05$).

DISCUSSION

Deindividuation

The results of the present experiment replicated and extended previous findings (Prentice-Dunn and Rogers, 1980) that deindividuating situational cues produce an internal state of deindividuation that mediates aggression. We had suggested previously that different configurations of stimulus conditions might produce different factor structures of the deindividuation state. Although the present data are only suggestive, the Self-Awareness and Altered Experience components may be differentiated into more precise aspects of deindividuation. First, the original Self-Awareness factor may reduce to Public Self-Awareness, which focuses on reactions of others to oneself (Buss, 1980; Fenigstein et al., 1975). The self-awareness literature has demonstrated that reductions in self-awareness are associated with increased feelings of deindividuation (Ickes, Layden, and Barnes, 1978) and with increased aggression (Scheier, Feningstein, and Buss, 1974). Diener, Lusk, De-Four, and Flax (1980) pointed out that self-awareness is not a unitary phenomenon, but may have several facets.

Our original Altered Experience factor may be differentiated into three independent factors. One factor contained only items assessing altered thinking and altered feelings, accompanied by increased arousal. Although we shall retain the label Altered Experience for this factor, it is interesting to note its similarity to Fenigstein et al.'s (1975) and Buss' (1980) concept of private self-awareness. Private self-awareness refers to the *process* of being conscious of one's thoughts and feelings, whereas the Altered Experience factor refers to a *product* of that awareness. Another interesting facet of the original Altered Experience factor may be found in the Time Distortion factor, which reflected a concentration on the "here and now" that seemed to pass more rapidly than it actually did. Perhaps the most readily interpretable new factor to emerge was Group Cohesiveness, which was the best predictor of aggressive behavior. Finally, the data suggested that feelings of responsibility may be another component of the subjective state of deindividuation.

It is important to emphasize that these data only suggest the existence of these additional factors for several reasons: (a) the ratio of subjects to items was only 5:1; (b) there were a small number of items per factor (2–4); and (c) partially due to the small number of items, the mean reliability coefficient was a modest .60. Future research that overcomes these problems is obviously required before we can confidently accept these additional components of a deindividuated state. Taken together, the available data indicate that the internal state of deindividuation is composed of at least two factors, Self-Awareness and Altered Experience, which may be differentiated into more refined subcomponents that reliably distinguish individuating from deindividuating situations.

Neither of the two alternative forms of a Deindividuation × Race or Deindividuation × Insult interaction effect were obtained. It was surprising that deindividuation did not interact with the race variable. Donnerstein and Donnerstein (1976) found that race interacted with anonymity, potential retaliation, and censure, all of which were manipulated in the individuation–deindividuation independent variable. These interactions were produced by whites' fear of high levels of retaliation from blacks. In the present study, however, whites reported the same level of expected counteraggression from blacks ($M = 6.3$ on a 10-point scale) and whites ($M = 6.4$).[2] Thus, the state of deindividuation neither made group members hyper-responsive to immediate stimuli nor oblivious to them. A similar finding had been obtained for high- versus low-aggressive models (Prentice-Dunn and Rogers, 1980). The models had the same effect in the individuating and deindividuating conditions. One of the next steps in constructing a theory of deindividuation will

[2]The authors wish to thank Ed Donnerstein for suggesting this interpretation.

be to reexamine and refine general propositions that a state of deindividuation will render a person more (or less) responsive to environmental cues. An important conceptual and empirical task is to identify the specific classes of environmental stimuli to which a state of deindividuation would make a group member more or less responsive.

Interracial Aggression

The Race × Insult interaction effect (see Figure 25.1) indicated that nonangered white subjects aggressed more against same-race victims than against different-race victims; in contrast, angered white subjects aggressed more against different-race victims than same-race victims. The interaction effect was stronger in the present study than in Baron's (1979). A key difference between the two experiments was whether the aggressors were acting alone or in a group. Clearly, the interaction emerges more strongly within a group setting. As Miller and Dollard (1941) noted, "People in a crowd behave as they would otherwise, only more so" (p. 218).

If whites were not insulted, they engaged in reverse discrimination (cf. Dutton, 1976) and behaved consistently with current norms. Similarly, noninsulted blacks act consistently with current norms for their race (Wilson and Rogers, 1975). When emotionally aroused, however, the whites' behavior was consistent with the older, traditional pattern of discrimination against blacks. When emotionally aroused, blacks also act consistently with their traditional pattern (Wilson and Rogers, 1975). This finding is but one specific manifestation of Sargent's (1948) thesis that anger can lead to several overt responses, one of which is regression to more primitive behaviors.

When emotionally aroused, both blacks (Wilson and Rogers, 1975) and whites (present study) regress to chronologically earlier modes of appropriate racial behavior. This pattern of interracial aggression could aptly be labeled *regressive racism.* Although racism may be defined to include beliefs of inferiority of a different race, we prefer to adopt the definition of racism as simply the differential treatment of people based solely on their race (P. Katz, 1976). Regressive racism differs in at least two important ways from the two other major forms of individual racism. First, both the dominative and aversive racists (cf. Kovel, 1970) firmly believe in the inferiority of blacks; they never embraced the new egalitarian norms. Thus, they would not exhibit reverse discrimination. Second, the concepts of dominative and aversive racism have been applied almost exclusively to whites. Regressive racism, on the other hand, may be found in the members of any race. To a large extent, black and white Americans take a Janus-faced view of interracial encounters, one face looking forward but the other face focusing grimly on the past.

Katz and his colleagues (e.g., Katz and Glass, 1979) could interpret the Race × Insult interaction effect as evidence of ambivalence-amplification. Although the data from our program of interracial aggression may be consistent with either the regressive racism or ambivalence-amplification interpretations, there are three major problems with the latter analysis of our data. First, ambivalence-amplification assumes that an individual cannot cope with mixed feelings: that a different-race person's behavior that threatens our positive or negative attitudes *must* be resolved by enhancing behavior that will confirm one aspect of our feelings and suppress the other. There is no direct evidence for this assumption. It is more intuitively compelling to believe that people can act on a mixture of positive and negative feelings toward other people. Second, there is no evidence to support the proposed mediating process, whether it is labeled threat to self-esteem, guilt, distress over inequity, or dissonance. Several of Katz's studies (especially Katz, Glass, Lucido, and Farber, 1979) have tested the ambivalence-amplification hypothesis that ambivalence heightens guilt and that the ensuing behavior reduces guilt. Despite the great difficulties of measuring this mediator, Katz's studies have found no supporting evidence. Furthermore, the present study included an item assessing guilt feelings in the postexperiment questionnaire. The data analyses indicated that the independent variables did not differentially affect guilt, nor did the subjects' behavior reduce guilt. Third, it is very difficult for the ambivalence-amplification hypothesis to account for blacks' aggressive behavior (Wilson and Rogers, 1975). In contrast, the concept of regressive racism can account for the behavior of both whites and blacks.

Additional support for and an extension of the concept of regressive racism may be found in the research from the Donnersteins' program. An interaction effect highly similar to the one displayed in Figure 25.1 has been reported between the race-of-victim variable and (a) anonymity-to-victim (Donnerstein et al., 1972), (b) threatened retaliation (Donnerstein et al., 1972), and (c) potential censure (Donnerstein and Donnerstein, 1973). Thus, in Figure 25.1, if the two points on the abcissa labeled "no-insult" and "insult" were to be relabeled (a) "nonanonymous" and "anonymous," (b) "retaliation" and "no-retaliation," or (c) "potential censure" and "no censure," the same interaction would be present.

Crosby, Bromley, and Saxe (1980) interpreted the Donnersteins' findings as revealing that antiblack hostility is actually pervasive, but subtle and covert. The Donnersteins reported that whites were very hostile toward blacks in those conditions in which their negative behavior could not be detected or punished. These latter conditions (anonymity, no retaliation, no censure) are well-established *disinhibitors* of aggression that increase aggressive responding. The present study disclosed that a well-established *instigator* of aggression, anger arousal, produced the same effect as the disinhibitors. Perhaps regressive racism is revealed not only by emotional arousal, but also by a host of variables that disinhibit or instigate aggression. Moreover, regressive racism may be revealed whenever unprejudiced values are not fully internalized (one case of incomplete internalization occurs when the unprejudiced values are relatively new). Regressive racism may be a sufficiently inclusive concept to give coherence to a variety of interracial behavior. Interpreting the Donnersteins' data in terms of regression racism is speculative, and perhaps this extension of the concept goes too far. The concept of regressive racism, however, accounts quite well for anger-mediated interracial aggression.

Both the blacks and whites in our studies and the whites in the Donnersteins' studies have been highly sensitive to the race of their victim. Sadly, neither whites nor blacks accorded the other race egalitarian treatment. Awaiting us, black and white together, is the fire next time; it is smoldering in the regressive racist.

References

BARON, R. A. *Human aggression.* New York: Plenum Press, 1977.

BARON, R. A. Effects of victim's pain cues, victim's race, and level of prior instigation upon physical aggression. *Journal of Applied Social Psychology,* 1979, **9,** 103–114.

BRIGHAM, J., AND WRIGHTSMAN, L. *Contemporary issues in social psychology* (4th ed.). Monterey, Calif.: Brooks/Cole, in press.

BUSS, A. H. *Self-consciousness and social anxiety.* San Francisco: Freeman, 1980.

CAMPBELL, A. *White attitudes toward black people.* Ann Arbor: University of Michigan, Institute for Social Research, 1971.

CAPLAN, N. The new ghetto man: A review of recent empirical studies. *Journal of Social Issues,* 1970, **26,** 59–73.

CROSBY, F., BROMLEY, S., AND SAXE, L. Recent unobtrusive studies of black and white discrimination and prejudice: A literature review. *Psychological Bulletin,* 1980, **87,** 546–563.

DAVIS, E., AND FINE, M. The effects of the findings of the U.S. National Advisory Commission on Civil Disorders: An experimental study of attitude change. *Human Relations,* 1975, **28,** 209–227.

DIENER, E. Deindividuation: Causes and consequences. *Social Behavior and Personality,* 1977, **5,** 143–155.

DIENER, E. Deindividuation, self-awareness, and disinhibition. *Journal of Personality and Social Psychology,* 1979, **37,** 1160–1171.

DIENER, E. Deindividuation: The absence of self-awareness and self-regulation in group members. In P. Paulus (Ed.), *The psychology of group influence.* Hillsdale, N.J.: Erlbaum, 1980.

DIENER, E., LUSK, R., DEFOUR, D., AND FLAX, R. Deindividuation: Effects of group size, density, number of observers, and group member similarity on self-consciousness and disinhibited behavior. *Journal of Personality and Social Psychology,* 1980, **39,** 449–459.

DONNERSTEIN, E., AND DONNERSTEIN, M. Variables in interracial aggression: Potential ingroup censure. *Journal of Personality and Social Psychology,* 1973, **27,** 143–150.

DONNERSTEIN, E., AND DONNERSTEIN, M. Research in the control of interracial aggression. In R. Geen and E. O'Neal (Eds.), *Perspectives on aggression.* New York: Academic Press, 1976.

DONNERSTEIN, E., DONNERSTEIN, M., SIMON, S., AND DITRICHS, R. Variables in interracial aggression: Anonymity, expected retaliation, and a riot. *Journal of Personality and Social Psychology,* 1972, **22,** 236–245.

DUTTON, D. G. Tokenism, reverse discrimination, and egalitarianism in interracial behavior. *Journal of Social Issues,* 1976, **32,** 93–108.

FENIGSTEIN, A., SCHEIER, M. F., AND BUSS, A. H. Public and private self-consciousness: Assessment and theory. *Journal of Consulting and Clinical Psychology,* 1975, **43,** 522–527.

FESTINGER, L., PEPITONE, A., AND NEWCOMB, T. Some consequences of deindividuation in a group. *Journal of Abnormal and Social Psychology,* 1952, **47,** 382–389.

GRIFFIN, B. Q., AND ROGERS, R. W. Reducing interracial aggression: Inhibiting effects of victim's suffering and power to retaliate. *Journal of Psychology,* 1977, **95,** 151–157.

ICKES, W., LAYDEN, M. A., AND BARNES, R. D. Objective self-awareness and individuation: An empirical link. *Journal of Personality,* 1978, **46,** 146–161.

KATZ, I., AND GLASS, D. An ambivalence-amplification theory of behavior toward the stigmatized. In W. G. Austin and S. Worchel (Eds.), *The social psychology of intergroup relations.* Monterey, Calif.: Brooks/Cole, 1979.

KATZ, I., GLASS, D., LUCIDO, D., AND FARBER, J. Harmdoing and victim's racial or orthopedic stigma as determinants of helping behavior. *Journal of Personality,* 1979, **47,** 340–364.

KATZ, P. Racism and social science: Towards a new commitment. In P. Katz (Ed.), *Towards the elimination of racism.* New York: Pergamon Press, 1976.

KOVEL, J. *White racism: A psychological history.* New York: Pantheon, 1970.

MILLER, N., AND DOLLARD, J. *Social learning and imitation.* New Haven, Conn.: Yale University Press, 1941.

MILLS, J. A. A procedure for explaining experiments involving deception. *Personality and Social Psychology Bulletin,* 1976, **2,** 3–13.

OVERALL, J. E., SPIEGEL, D. K., AND COHEN, J. Equivalence of orthogonal and nonorthogonal analysis of variance. *Psychological Bulletin,* 1975, **82,** 182–186.

PRENTICE-DUNN, S., AND ROGERS, R. W. Effects of deindividuating situational cues and aggressive models on subjective deindividuation and aggression. *Journal of Personality and Social Psychology,* 1980, **39,** 104–113.

ROSS, J. M., VANNEMAN, R. D., AND PETTIGREW, T. F. Patterns of support for George Wallace: Implications for racial change. *Journal of Social Issues,* 1976, **32,** 69–91.

RUDE, G. *The crowd in history.* New York: Wiley, 1964.

SARGENT, S. S. Reaction to frustration—A critique and hypothesis. *Psychological Review,* 1948, **55,** 108–114.

SCHEIER, M. F., FENIGSTEIN, A., AND BUSS, A. H. Self-awareness and physical aggression. *Journal of Experimental Social Psychology,* 1974, **10,** 264–273.

Southern Commission on the Study of Lynching. *Lynchings and what they mean.* Atlanta, G.: Author, 1931.

TAYLOR, D. G., SHEATSLEY, P. B., AND GREELEY, A. M. Attitudes toward racial integration. *Scientific American,* 1978, **238**(6), 42–49.

WILSON, L., AND ROGERS, R. W. The fire this time: Effects of race of target, insult, and potential retaliation on black aggression. *Journal of Personality and Social Psychology,* 1975, **32,** 857–864.

ZIMBARDO, P. G. The human choice: Individuation, reason, and order versus deindividuation, impulse, and chaos. In W. J. Arnold and D. Levine (Eds.), *Nebraska Symposium on Motivation* (Vol. 17). Lincoln: University of Nebraska Press, 1970.

26

Predictors of
Naturalistic Sexual Aggression

Neil M. Malamuth

This research integrated within a theoretical and empirical framework varied predictor factors pertaining to males' sexual aggression against women. The selection of predictors was guided by theorizing that sexual aggression is caused by the interaction among multiple factors, including those creating the motivation for the act, those reducing internal and external inhibitions, and those providing the opportunity for the act to occur. The predictor factors assessed were sexual arousal in response to aggression, dominance as a motive for sexual acts, hostility toward women, attitudes accepting of violence against women, psychoticism, and sexual experience. A measure assessing self-reported sexual aggression (primarily among acquaintances) in naturalistic settings served as the dependent measure. The subjects were 155 males. As expected, nearly all the predictor factors significantly related to sexual aggression. In addition, much better prediction of such aggression was achieved by a combination of these factors than by any one individually. It was also found that including interactions among these predictors yielded a regression equation that was more successful in relating to sexual aggression than an equation using an additive combination only. The relevance of these data to the causes and prediction of violence against women is discussed.

Within the last decade, there has been increasing research on the causes of male sexual aggression against women, particularly rape. As described later, most of this research attempted to identify individual factors that may predict such aggression. More recently, however, there has been growing recognition of the need for multifactorial models.

The theoretical guidance for the present research was provided at the general level by Bandura's social learning theory of aggression (1973, 1978) and by vari-

Reprinted with permission from the author and *The Journal of Personality and Social Psychology,* Vol. 50, No. 5, 1986. Copyright © 1986 by the American Psychological Association.

This research was facilitated by grants from the Social Sciences and Humanities Research Council (SSHRC) of Canada. Portions of this article were presented at the 1985 meeting of the International Society for Research on Aggression in Parma, Italy.

The author is particularly grateful to L. Rowell Huesmann for constructive suggestions. Thanks are also expressed to Daniel Linz, Steven Penrod, and James V. P. Check for their helpful suggestions.

ous applications of it to sexual aggression (e.g., Earls, 1983; Malamuth, 1983b; Marshall and Barbaree, 1984). Also providing theoretical guidance was a recent model of the causes of child sexual abuse (Finkelhor, 1984; Finkelhor and Araji, 1983) and its extension by Russell (1984) to sexual aggression. These theories have several features in common. Most important, they emphasize that to understand the causes of sexual aggression it is essential to consider the role of multiple factors, such as those creating the motivation to commit the act, those reducing internal and external inhibitions that might prevent it from being carried out, and those providing the opportunity for the act to occur. Some of these multifactorial models propose additive (e.g., Earls, 1983) and others propose interactive (e.g., Bandura, 1978; Finkelhor, 1984; Malamuth, 1983b) combinations of the causal factors.

The research reported here compared empirically three alternative theoretical models regarding the causes of sexual aggression: The Single Factor model suggests that sexual aggression results from a single factor (e.g., hostility). The Additive model posits multiple factors combining in an additive manner (Earls, 1983). The Interactive model asserts that multiple factors (i.e., motivation, disinhibitory and opportunity) interact to produce sexual aggression, particularly at high levels. Although the dependent measure used here primarily assesses sexual aggression between acquaintances, as noted later, I suggest that considerable similarity may exist among the causes of such aggression and that committed against nonacquaintances.

In studying self-reported naturalistic sexual aggression, six predictors were used in the present study.[1] Three were intended to assess the motivation to commit sexual aggression. These were sexual arousal in response to aggression, the desire to be sexually dominant or powerful, and hostility toward women. In addition, two variables were included primarily to measure factors that may overcome internal and external inhibitions. These consisted of attitudes condoning sexual aggression and of antisocial personality characteristics. Finally, sexual experience was assessed because if a person did not engage in sexual acts generally, then the "opportunity" for sexual aggression would not exist. As discussed later, an additional reason for including this dimension relates to differences in the degree and nature of sexual experiences between relatively sexually aggressive and nonaggressive men. The following discussion expands on the rationale for the selection of the various predictors and describes previous research pertaining to each.

SEXUAL RESPONSIVENESS TO RAPE

The most widely studied response designed to differentiate rapists from nonrapists has been the penile tumescence rape index, a ratio of sexual arousal to rape por-

---

[1]The term *predictor* is used here in the statistical sense and does not necessarily imply a temporal or causal relation with the criterion (or dependent) variable.

trayals compared with arousal to consenting sex portrayals (Abel, Barlow, Blanchard, and Guild, 1977). With this index, a man whose penile tumescence to rape is similar to or greater than his tumescence to consenting depictions is considered to have some inclination to rape (see Quinsey, in press, for a review).

DOMINANCE

The view has been widely expressed that the desire to dominate women is an important motive of sexual aggression both at the cultural (Brownmiller, 1975; Sanday, 1981) and individual (e.g., Scully and Marolla, 1985) levels. Based on clinical interviews with convicted rapists, Groth (1979) concluded that in all cases of forcible rape, three components are present: power, anger, and sexuality. Groth (1979) distinguished among several types of rapists depending on the primary element characterizing their motivation: the power rapist, the anger rapist, and the sadistic rapist. The most common type among the convicted rapists studied by Groth (i.e., 55 percent) was the power rapist. Here he suggests that the offender's desire is to conquer and sexually dominate his victim.

HOSTILITY TOWARD WOMEN

The second most frequent type of rapist, according to Groth (1979) (i.e., about 40 percent of those he studied) is the anger rapist, characterized by his hostility to women. In the present research, hostility toward women was studied primarily for its possible motivating functions. However, it may also discriminate between men who would and those who would not be inhibited by women's suffering from and resistance to sexual aggression. Research on the consequences of victims' reactions to nonsexual aggression indicates that the aggressors' hostile feelings may be a very important determinant. For those feeling relatively low hostility, the victim's suffering and resistance is likely to be unpleasant and therefore inhibit aggression (Geen, 1970; Rule and Leger, 1976). In contrast, for those with relatively high hostility, the victim's suffering may actually be reinforcing and thereby encourage further aggression in the face of resistance (Baron, 1974, 1977; Feshbach, Stiles, and Bitter, 1967; Hartmann, 1969).

ATTITUDES FACILITATING AGGRESSION

Burt (1978, 1980) theorized that certain attitudes that are widely accepted in Western culture but are particularly held by rapists and potential rapists play an important role in contributing to sexual violence by acting as "psychological releasers or neutralizers, allowing potential rapists to turn off social prohibitions against injuring or using others" (1978, p. 282). She developed several scales to measure attitudes that directly and indirectly support aggression against women. Data consistent with Burt's theorizing indicate that male college students' levels of sexual aggression are correlated with attitudes condoning violence against women (e.g., Koss, Leonard, Beezley, and Oros, 1985). In addition, it has been found that convicted rapists have relatively high acceptance of violence against women (e.g., Scully and Marolla, 1984).

ANTISOCIAL PERSONALITY CHARACTERISTICS/PSYCHOTICISM

Rapaport and Burkhart (1984) recently suggested that, although certain factors may provide a context for coercive sexual behavior, the actual expression of aggression occurs only if the subject also has certain personality or characterological deficits. Although these investigators did not directly test this proposition, convicted rapists do sometimes show elevated scores on measures of psychopathic/antisocial characteristics (Armentrout and Hauer, 1978; Rada, 1977). Koss and Leonard (1984) point out, however, that a major problem in these studies has been the failure to control for demographic variables that could cause spurious elevation. Koss and Leonard (1984) found only very weak and/or nonsignificant relations in various studies assessing possible links between measures of psychopathy and sexual aggression among men from the general population.

SEXUAL EXPERIENCE

As noted earlier, assessment of sexual experience may be useful to include in the prediction of sexual aggression due to *opportunity* or access. If powerful factors (e.g., religious convictions) prevented a person from participating in sexual relationships generally, he might not be sexually aggressive even if he has a high proclivity for such behavior. Particularly in the case of nonstranger sexual aggression, it is likely that the willingness and opportunity to engage in sexuality per se is an important factor distinguishing those who will and those who will not express an inclination to sexually aggress in actual behavior.

In addition to the opportunity function, an assessment of sexual experience was included in the present research in light of Kanin's (1957, 1983, 1984) studies of college males who have engaged in various degrees of sexual aggression. He found that more sexually aggressive men are more likely to view sexuality as a means of establishing their self-worth and as an arena for "conquest." They were also found to be more sexually experienced at younger ages, but less likely to view these experiences as satisfactory. Similar data with convicted rapists were recently reported by Langevin, Paitich, and Russon (1985).

PREDICTING LABORATORY AGGRESSION

Malamuth (1983a) assessed the extent to which two of the factors described earlier predicted males' laboratory aggression against women. Males' penile tumescence to rape portrayals as compared with mutually consenting depictions and their attitudes condoning violent acts such as rape and wife battering were assessed in one session. About a week later, subjects participated in what they believed was a totally unrelated experiment. In it they were first angered by a female confederate of the experimenter. Later, they could choose to aggress against her via the administration of aversive noise and other responses. It was found that the degree of both men's attitudes facilitating aggression and of their sexual arousal to rape predicted significantly the amount of their laboratory aggression against the woman. In assessing one aspect of these findings, Malamuth and Check (1982) successfully replicated the relation between attitudes condoning aggression against women and laboratory aggression measured several days later in an ostensibly unrelated context.

THE PRESENT RESEARCH

The present study assessed empirically the prediction of sexual aggression in naturalistic settings using the factors described earlier. Sexual aggression was measured by a self-report inventory developed by Koss and Oros (1982). This measure asks male subjects whether they have engaged in a wide range of coercive sexual activities, ranging from trying to get intercourse by "threatening" to end the relationship, to actually using physical force, such as twisting a woman's arm, to coerce her into intercourse.

It is important to note that the two types of aggression measures used in our research program complement each other well, having opposite advantages and disadvantages. The advantage of the laboratory assessment of aggression (Malamuth, 1983a, 1984b; Malamuth and Check, 1982) is that it is an "objective" measure that does not rely on subjects' self-reports. However, it assesses behavior in a setting that some argue is artificial and low in ecological validity (e.g., Kaplan, 1983). The measure of naturalistic aggression has the advantage of assessing behavior occurring in nonartificial settings. Its disadvantage is in being a self-report measure. Consequently, considerable confidence in the validity of the relations would be gained if the predictors related to both of these aggression measures. Of course, although some similarity may be expected, conceptually there are also important differences between aggression in the laboratory, which does not contain any overt sexual elements (i.e., administering aversive noise to a person in the next room), and aggression in natural settings which occurs within a sexual context.

The factors studied in the present investigation are based on theory and research conducted either with convicted rapists or with subjects from the general population, particularly college students. One of the issues that the current data pertain to is the assertion (see Russell, 1984; Scully and Marolla, 1985) that similar factors contribute to both the type of sexual aggression committed by incarcerated rapists (usually against nonacquaintances) and the type that does not receive legal attention, particularly that committed against acquaintances. If variables derived from work with convicted rapists and with sexual aggressors in the general population can be integrated within a unified empirical and theoretical framework, the findings will provide a firmer basis for understanding the causes of sexual aggression in both populations.

Based on the theory and research described, three interrelated questions were investigated in the present research:

1. Would the predictor factors relate significantly to naturalistic aggression against women?

2. If the factors related to sexual aggression against women, would they provide "redundant prediction" or would a combination of factors predict better than each alone?

3. If a combination of factors were superior, would the Additive or the Interactive models provide the best prediction of naturalistic aggression?

METHOD

Overview of Design

One hundred and fifty-five males participated in the first phase of the research. In this phase subjects completed various scales, including all the predictors except for the sexual arousal measure, as well as the dependent measure of sexual aggression.

The second phase consisted of the assessment of sexual arousal in response to rape portrayals and to consenting depictions. Ninety-five of those participating in Phase 1 also participated in Phase 2.

Subjects

Subjects were recruited from various sources: Several university courses, announcements displayed on university campuses and at a city summer employment center, and via newspaper ads.

The initial descriptions of the research indicated that applicants at or over the age of 18 were needed to participate in various unrelated experiments. They were told that they may sign up for a general subject pool. Experimenters would then select subjects from this list and invite them to participate in specific experiments. Participants were paid about $5.50 per hour.

When contacted by the different experimenters conducting each phase (presented to subjects as independent experiments), potential subjects were given general descriptions of the procedures and measures used. For example, in Phase 2 they were informed that genital measures of sexual arousal would be used. It was emphasized in each phase that subjects could leave at any time and that there would be no penalty whatsoever nor would any explanation be required. Subjects were paid upon arrival at each study and were told that they could keep the money irrespective of whether they completed the experiment or not. As an additional safeguard, an ombudsman, who was a Professor of Law, was hired for the project. All subjects were given his name and phone number upon signing up for the subject pool. They were told that he was completely independent of the staff conducting the research and that they could voice any complaints to him. No complaints were ever made.

At the end of Phase 2 subjects were given debriefings. They included segments emphasizing the horror of rape and presented several points designed to dispel rape myths. The effectiveness of such debriefings in counteracting some potential negative effects of exposure to sexually violent stimuli has been demonstrated in several studies (Check and Malamuth, 1984; Donnerstein & Berkowitz, 1981; Linz, 1985; Malamuth and Check, 1984).

Although subjects' names were not obtained, various background information that was gathered (e.g., date of birth) enabled exact matching of responses across the two research phases. The purpose of leading subjects to believe that these were independent studies was to reduce "demand characteristics" (Orne, 1962) and/or undue self-consciousness that might affect honest responding. Similar procedures have been used successfully in other studies (e.g., Malamuth, 1983a; Malamuth and Check, 1981). The two research phases were completed within 2 months for virtually all subjects.

Obtaining background information enabled a general description of the sample. Subjects were asked about their age, marital status, whether they were students, their major, religious affiliation, and their frequency of attendance of church or other religious institution. These variables were selected on the basis of previous research (e.g., Koss et al., 1985; Schulz, Bohrnstedt, Borgatta, and Evans, 1977) showing that factors such as religiousness and age may affect college students' sexual and sexually aggressive behavior. If the regression analyses reported later are computed by first partialing out the background factors, the relations are at least as strong as those reported without such partialing.

The average age of the 155 male subjects was 23, with a range from 18 to 47 years. Sixty-six percent of the sample were between the ages of 18 to 22, 24 percent between the ages of 23 to 30, and the remaining 10 percent were above the age of 30. Eighty-seven percent of the sample were single, 8 percent were married, and the remaining 5 percent were separated or divorced. Eighty percent were university students, 20 percent were not. Of the students, 21 percent majored in the "pure" sciences, 13 percent in engineering, and 23 percent in the humanities and the social sciences (including psychology). The remainder were distributed over a wide range of majors or as yet undeclared. Twenty percent were Catholics, 32 percent Protestants, 8 percent Jewish, and the remaining 40 percent listed no specific religious affiliation. Fifteen percent indicated that they visit a religious institution (e.g., church) at least once a week, 11 percent at least once a month, 8 percent approximately every two months, and the remaining 56 percent seldom or never.

Phase 1: Materials and Procedure

In the first phase, subjects completed a questionnaire administered by a male experimenter. While filling out this measure they were seated sufficiently apart to ensure confidentiality of responses. Embedded within other items on this questionnaire were the following measures:

Dominance as sexual motive.   Part of a measure developed by Nelson (1979) assessed the function of or motivations for engaging in sexual acts. This measure asks respondents the degree to which various feelings and sensations are important to them as motives for sexual behavior. Nelson (1979) presented data concerning the reliability and validity of this scale, which yields scores on several functions of sexuality. The present study used the dominance segment (eight items) of the power function (composed of the dominance and submissiveness segments). This dominance component refers to the degree to which feelings of control over one's partner motivate sexuality (e.g., "I enjoy the feeling of having someone in my grasp"; "I enjoy the conquest"). It yielded an alpha coefficient of .78.

Hostility.   The Hostility Toward Women (HTW) scale (30 items) was recently developed by Check and Malamuth, 1983 (see also Check, Malamuth, Elias, and Barton, 1985). Data concerning its reliability and validity were presented by Check (1985). Examples of items are "Women irritate me a great deal more than they are aware of," and "When I look back at what's happened to me, I don't feel at all resentful towards the women in my life." In the present study it had an alpha coefficient of .89.

Attitudes facilitating violence.   The attitude measure used in this study was the Acceptance of Interpersonal Violence (AIV) against women scale developed by Burt (1980). Five of its six items measure attitudes supporting violence against women, whereas the sixth concerns revenge. An example of an item is "Sometimes the only way a man can get a cold woman turned on is to use force." This scale was selected because it measures attitudes that *directly* condone the use of force in sexual relationships. Two other scales developed by Burt (1980) assessing attitudes *indirectly* supportive of sexual aggression, the Rape Myth Acceptance and the Adversarial Sexual Beliefs scales, were also used. The findings with these measures were very similar to those with the AIV, but as expected the relations with sexual aggression were somewhat weaker. The results presented in this article are for the AIV scale only. It had an alpha coefficient of .61, which is similar to that originally reported by Burt (1980).

Antisocial characteristics/psychoticism.

The Psychoticism (P) scale of the Eysenck Personality Questionnaire (EPQ) was used (Eysenck, 1978). As Eysenck makes abundantly clear, this scale purports to reflect a variable that stretches through the normal, nonpsychiatric population.

There were three reasons for selecting this particular measure to assess antisocial tendencies. First, Eysenck (1978) hypothesized that psychoticism may be particularly associated with interest in impersonal sex and in sexual aggression. He also reports the findings of an unpublished study that sex offenders are relatively high P scorers. Second, reviews of the literature pertaining to this measure (e.g., Claridge, 1983) concluded that rather than being a measure of psychoticism in the clinical sense, this scale primarily assesses antisocial traits that may relate to aggression. Third, recent research (Barnes, Malamuth, and Check, 1984; Linz, 1985) suggests that this measure may be particularly useful in predicting some sexually aggressive responses.

The alpha coefficient obtained herein was .49. Although Eysenck (1978) had originally reported relatively high alpha coefficients, other researchers have recently reported similar relatively low levels of internal consistency as found here (e.g., McCrae and Costa, 1985). Nevertheless, this measure was retained in the current analyses with the recognition that relatively low levels of internal consistency reduce the likelihood of obtaining statistically significant relations with other variables (Cohen and Cohen, 1983).

Sexual experience.

The Sexual Behavior Inventory (SBI: Bentler, 1968) was used to assess sexual experience in conventional heterosexual acts. Subjects indicated whether they had engaged in various sexual behaviors including kissing, fondling of breasts, intercourse, and oral sex. The alpha coefficient for this scale was .97.

Naturalistic sexual aggression.

As noted earlier, the self-report instrument used to measure sexual aggression was developed by Koss and Oros (1982). It assesses a continuum of sexual aggression including psychological pressure, physical coercion, attempted rape, and rape. Subjects are asked to respond to a sexual experience survey consisting of nine circumstances pertaining to the use of aggression in the context of sexuality (e.g., sexual, oral, or anal intercourse).[2] An example of an item is "I have had sexual intercourse with a woman when she didn't want to because I used some degree of physical force (twisting her arm, holding

---

[2]Although the scale used by Koss and Oros (1982) contains 10 items, 1 item judged ambiguous was not used in the analyses here. It asks whether the subject ever became so sexually aroused that he could not stop himself even though the woman did not want to. The ambiguity is in the lack of information regarding what sexual acts occurred and what type of coercion may have been used.

her down, etc.)." Respondents reply on a *true* versus *false* scale. Koss and Oros (1982) and Koss and Gidycz (1985) presented data regarding the reliability and validity of this scale. In the present study, it had an alpha coefficient of .83.

Phase 2: Materials and Procedure

In the second research phase, sexual arousal in response to rape and to mutually consenting depictions was assessed. In keeping with the accepted methodology and the empirical data in this area (e.g., Abel et al., 1977; Earls and Marshall, 1983), the primary assessment was direct genital arousal measured by penile tumescence. Subjects were seated in a comfortable chair located in a sound attenuated and electrically shielded room equipped with an intercom. Penile tumescence was measured by a mercury-in-rubber strain gauge (Davis Inc., New York City), a device recommended in analyses of various instruments (Laws, 1977; Rosen and Keffe, 1978). Changes in penile diameter that resulted in resistance changes in the mercury column of this strain gauge were amplified through a Wheatstone Bridge and recorded on a polygraph.

For comparison of consistency with the physiological measure, self-reported sexual arousal was assessed on an 11-point scale ranging from 0% (*not at all*) to 100% (*very*) in units of 10 percent. Subjects indicated their arousal immediately after reading each story.

Upon arrival at the laboratory, the subject was greeted by a male experimenter. He then was given a sheet reiterating the information provided on the phone regarding the sexual content of some stimuli and the use of genital arousal measures. After signing a consent form, which emphasized that the subject was free to leave at any time without any penalty and without having to provide any reason to the experimenter, he was escorted to the sound attenuated room. Further instructions were taped, although an intercom was available if communication between the subject and the experimenter was necessary.

The subject was instructed to place the penile gauge on. Following a baseline period, he was told to open a numbered envelope and read the story. Arousal to the stories was monitored by the polygraph in the adjoining room. After the subject read each story and indicated his sexual arousal on a scale, a resting period was interposed to ensure that arousal returned to baseline levels before proceeding to the next story.

There were three depictions read in order. The first described a woman masturbating. Its primary purpose was to generate some initial level of sexual arousal in light of data (Kolarsky and Madlafousek, 1977) suggesting that arousal levels are better differentiated if presented following the elicitation of some sexual arousal rather than immediately following the first baseline period. Additionally, this story was intended to strengthen the credibility of the experimental instructions that the research concerned responses to various types of stimuli. The second and third written stories depicted rape and mutually consenting sex, respectively. They were virtually identical to those used by Abel et al. (1977).

"Rape indices" were computed for each subject following Abel et al. (1977) by dividing maximum arousal to rape by maximum arousal to consenting sex for the tumescence data and for self-reported arousal.[3]

RESULTS

Volunteers Versus Nonvolunteers

Comparisons were made between the 95 volunteers for the second research phase and the 60 who did not volunteer. These comparisons used the 5 predictors assessed in the first phase and the measure of sexual aggression. No significant differences or effects approaching significance were obtained in either a multivariate analysis of variance or in univariate analyses of variance (ANOVAS).

Intercorrelations Among Predictors

Simple Pearson correlations among the predictors are presented in Table 26.1. In general, these data are highly consistent with previous findings (e.g., Malamuth, 1983a; 1984a; Malamuth and Check, 1983), as well as revealing relations not examined in earlier studies. The tumescence index of sexual arousal (i.e., arousal to rape contrasted with arousal to nonrape) was highly correlated with the similar index based on self-reported arousal. To a large degree, these two sexual arousal indices showed similar relations with the other variables: Both indices were significantly associated with the dominance motive and neither related significantly to psychoticism nor to sexual experience. Although the reported arousal index significantly correlated with hostility toward women and with AIV, the tumescence index showed a marginally significant effect with hostility and no significant correlation with AIV.

The dominance motive related significantly to all of the other predictors, except for sex experience, where a marginally significant correlation occurred. Hostility toward women correlated with AIV and revealed a marginally significant relation with psychoticism. Hostility showed a nonsignificant inverse relation with sexual experience. AIV did not relate to either psychoticism or to sexual experience, nor were these two variables related to each other.

---

[3]In some previous research (e.g., Malamuth, 1983a) a difference rather than a ratio score was used. The ratio was used here in keeping with the commonly accepted procedure. The findings are very similar if the difference score is used.

TABLE 26.1
Simple correlations among the predictor variables and sexual aggression[a]

Predictors and dependent variable	1	2	3	4	5	6	7	8
Motivation predictors								
1. TUMRAPE	—	.66****	.25***	.19*	.13	.07	.06	.43****
2. REPRAPE		—	.23**	.26***	.22**	.06	.15	.33***
3. DOM			—	.37****	.36****	.19**	.15*	.38****
4. HTW				—	.37****	.16*	−.11	.30****
Disinhibiting predictors								
5. AIV					—	.08	−.08	.38***
6. PSYCH						—	−.03	.15*
Opportunity predictor								
7. SEXEXP							—	.32****
Dependent variable								
8. SEXAGG								—

Note: TUMRAPE = tumescence arousal to rape index; REPRAPE = reported arousal to rape index; DOM = dominance motive; HTW = hostility toward women scale; AIV = acceptance of interpersonal violence (against women) scale; PSYCH = psychoticism scale; SEXEXP = sexual experience measure; SEXAGG = sexual aggression.

[a]$n = 155$, except with sexual arousal measures where $n = 95$. *$p < .10$. **$p < .05$. ***$p < .02$. ****$p < .001$.

Naturalistic Aggression

The last column of Table 26.1 shows simple correlations between the predictors and self-reported naturalistic sexual aggression. All the predictors related significantly to sexual aggression, except for psychoticism which showed a marginally significant correlation.

Multiple regression analyses were conducted to address the issue of the combined success of the predictors to relate to sexual aggression. As recommended by Cohen and Cohen (1983), all the predictors were centered at their mean, a linear transformation that reduces multicollinearity that may occur with products such as interaction terms. In this analysis, I sought to compare the Single Factor, Additive, and the Interactive models. For the 155 participants in Phase 1, this regression analysis included dominance, hostility toward women, AIV, psychoticism, and sexual experience. For the 95 participants in both research phases, analyses were conducted with the addition of tumescence rape index.

The regression analyses were performed in the following way: To test the Single Factor model versus the Additive model, each predictor was "forced entered" as a main effect and its unique contribution (i.e., that not shared with any other predictors) to the dependent variable was assessed by squared semipartial correlations (Cohen and Cohen, 1983). The results clearly showed that the predictors did not, in general, provide redundant information, but that their combined prediction was

TABLE 26.2
Multiple regression analyses on sexual aggression without tumescence index ($n = 155$)

Predictor	Without interactions		With interactions	
	Beta[a]	sr[2b]	Beta[a]	sr[2b]
DOM	.153	.017*	.078	.005
HTW	.198	.030**	.147	.017**
AIV	.205	.033***	.210	.032***
PSYCH	.073	.005	.102	.010
SEXEXP	.340	.109****	.257	.058****
HTW × PSYCH	—	—	.150	.022**
HTW × AIV × SEXEXP	—	—	.334	.092****
HTW × DOM × AIV × SEXEXP	—	—	.313	.078****
Multiple				
R	.547****		.673****	
R^2	.300		.453	

Note: DOM = dominance motive; HTW = hostility toward women scale; AIV = acceptance of interpersonal violence (against women) scale; PSYCH = psychoticism scale; SEXEXP = sexual experience measure.
  [a]Standardized regression coefficient.
  [b]Squared semipartial correlation coefficient indicating unique contribution of predictor variable to dependent variable.
  *$p < .06$. **$p < .05$. ***$p < .01$. ****$p < .0001$.

considerably greater than that achieved by any variable alone. More specifically, when the entire sample was used ($n = 155$) the HTW, AIV, and sex experience variables all had significant, unique contributions to the regression equation, whereas the unique contribution of dominance was marginally significant (see left columns of Table 26.2). The psychoticism variable did not make a significant, unique contribution. As indicated on the left side of Table 26.2, the Multiple R yielded by this equation assessing additive effects was .547.

When the regression analysis assessing additive effects was performed on the 95 participants in both research phases, the Multiple R was .619 (see left side of Table 26.3). As indicated in this table, the tumescence rape index, AIV, HTW and sex experience contributed significant, unique variance, whereas the dominance and psychoticism predictors did not.

Although these data show that a combination of predictor variables is superior to individual ones, an additional regression analysis compared the Interactive versus the Additive models for combining predictors. Although the Interactive model contends that several factors must interact for relatively high levels of sexual aggression to occur, the use of more than one variable within a given theoretical category (e.g., both the sexual arousal in response to aggression and hostility toward women variables were included as motivational factors) did not enable precise specification of which interaction set would best test this model. Rather than preferring a

TABLE 26.3
Multiple regression analyses on sexual aggression with tumescence index ($n = 95$)

Predictor	Without interactions		With interactions	
	Beta[a]	sr^{2b}	Beta[a]	sr^{2b}
TUMRAPE	.329	.100***	.206	.026**
DOM	.085	.006	.170	.017*
HTW	.209	.032*	.037	.001
AIV	.207	.035*	.168	.022*
PSYCH	.027	.001	.016	.000
SEXEXP	.267	.066**	.111	.010
AIV × EXEXP	—	—	.166	.025**
TUMRAPE × DOM × AIV × PSYCH	—	—	.200	.029**
TUMRAPE × DOM × HTW × AIV	—	—	.493	.151****
TUMRAPE × DOM × HTW × AIV × SEXEXP	—	—	.445	.158****
Multiple				
R	.619****		.865****	
R²	.383		.748	

Note: TUMRAPE = tumescence arousal to rape index; DOM = dominance motive; HTW = hostility toward women scale; AIV = acceptance of interpersonal violence (against women) scale; PSYCH = psychoticism scale; SEXEXP = sexual experience measure.
[a]Standardized regression coefficient
[b]Squared semi-partial correlation coefficient indicating unique contribution of variable.
*$p < .05$. **$p < .005$. ***$p < .001$. ****$p < .0001$.

particular interaction, all possible interactions (i.e., the crossproducts) were allowed "free entry" in a stepwise process after the "forced entry" of the main effects.[4]

The resulting equation for the 155 subjects yielded a Multiple R of .673 (see right side of Table 26.2). Contributing significant unique variance were a two-way interaction between the HTW and psychoticism, a three-way interaction among HTW, AIV, and sex experience and a four-way interaction that contained these three variables as well as dominance (see Table 26.2). A hierarchical comparison of the model with the interactions ($R^2 = .453$) versus the model with the main effects only ($R^2 = .300$) yielded a significant effect, $F(3, 146) = 9.99$, $p < .001$.

With the 95 subjects participating in both research phases, the regression equation including interactions yielded a Multiple R of .865 (see right side of Table 26.3). The squared semipartial correlation coefficients indicated that contributing

[4]Some statisticians might test the Interaction model by a fully hierarchical approach in which regression models with higher order interactions are assessed only in comparison to nested models including all the lower order interactions. The difference in such an approach as contrasted to that used here (i.e., allowing "free entry" to all the interactions) concerns only which interactions are most appropriate to include in the model and not whether some interactions account for additional variance.

unique variance were a two-way interaction between AIV and sex experience, a four-way interaction among the tumescence index, dominance, AIV, and psychoticism, a four-way interaction among the tumescence index, dominance, HTW, and sex experience, as well as a five-way interaction containing these four variables and AIV (see right columns of Table 26.3). A comparison of the models with and without the interactions yielded a highly significant difference, $F(4, 84) = 12.86$, $p < .001$. The results for both samples, therefore, indicate that a regression model containing interactive relations among the predictors is preferable to a model containing additive relations only.

To directly assess whether the tumescence rape index provided additional predictive information, it was necessary to compare regression models with and without this variable for the same 95 subjects. This comparison indicated that the regression model with this variable (Multiple $R = .865$) was significantly better than without it (Multiple $R = .600$), $F(3, 85) = 16.45, p < .001$.

To illustrate and further examine the data, the following analysis was performed: For each predictor a relatively high score was defined as above the median of its distribution. Subjects were then divided according to the number of predictors for which they scored *high* and *low*. This approach is analogous to classifying a characteristic as present or not by defining presence as a relatively high score. A person scoring above the median on all the variables would be considered as possessing all the characteristics. In keeping with the regression results, for the 155 subjects the dominance, HTW, AIV, psychoticism, and sex experience predictors were used for this classification, whereas for the 95 subjects these variables as well as the tumescence rape index were used.

Figure 26.1 shows the average level of sexual aggression according to this classification scheme, with the top graph showing the results for the entire sample of 155 subjects and the bottom graph for the 95 participants in the two research phases. In both instances, ANOVAS performed on these data yielded highly significant ($p < .0001$) effects. Comparisons among means were performed using the Scheffé test (Scheffé, 1953) for groups differing substantially in size and the Tukey test (Tukey, 1953) for those of similar size. These comparisons indicated that the highest levels in both graphs were significantly different ($p < .05$) from all others and that the second highest levels differed significantly from some of the lowest levels. Trend analyses showed that a cubic term fitted the curve within statistical error for the sample of 155 subjects, whereas a quintic term fitted the curve for the 95 participants in both research phases. ANOVAS comparing average sexual aggression within each level of this classification scheme (e.g., those scoring high on one set of four predictors vs. those scoring high on a different set of four predictors) supported the rationale of classifying subjects according to the number of predictors on which they scored relatively high: For both samples, no significant differences were found within each classification level. It should be noted, however, that the relatively small numbers in each cell reduced the likelihood of finding such differences.

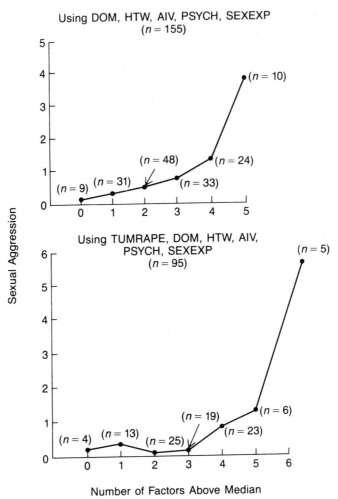

FIGURE 26.1
Mean levels of sexual aggression as a function of number of factors on which subjects scored above median.

DISCUSSION

The data provided the following answers to the three questions posed earlier: First, in the simple correlation analyses all the predictors except psychoticism were significantly related to naturalistic aggression, and psychoticism showed a marginally significant relation. Second, the predictors did not, on the whole, provide "redundant information" in that a combination of them was superior to any individual ones for predicting levels of sexual aggressiveness. Third, the data were more consistent with the Interactive than with the Additive model of combining the predictors. Regression equations containing interactive effects accounted for a significantly greater percentage of the variance (45 percent for the 155 subjects and 75 percent for the 95 subjects) than equations containing additive effects only (30 percent and 45 percent, respectively). However, it may be that a modified version of the Interactive model that also incorporates additive effects would best account for the data. Multifactorial models in other areas of research (e.g., Faraone and Tsuang, 1985) may provide useful guides in the development of such a model.

Additional analyses were conducted classifying subjects according to the number of predictors on which they scored relatively high (i.e., above the median). A curve was found indicating that with an increasing number of predictors with high scores, greater levels of sexual aggression occurred. The data pattern appeared to show a synergistic process whereby the combined action of several variables yielded considerably higher levels of sexual aggression than would be expected by the additive combination of them.

Malamuth and Check (1985b) attempted a partial replication of the research reported here. They administered to 297 males the same measures used here, except for the sexual arousal indices and for psychoticism. The results replicated very successfully the present conclusions: The predictors related significantly to sexual aggression, a combination of predictors was superior to individual ones, and an equation including interactions was preferable to an additive one only. Further, classifying subjects according to the number of predictors on which they scored relatively high showed the same general relation reported here, although the slope of the line was somewhat less steep. This appeared to be due, at least in part, to a lower proportion of subjects in that study at the very high levels of sexual aggression as compared with the present or earlier studies.

Malamuth (1984b) recently assessed the ability of a number of the predictors used in the present research (i.e., tumescence rape index, self-reported arousal to rape index, dominance, AIV, and psychoticism) to predict laboratory aggression against female and against male targets. Laboratory aggression was measured in a procedure similar to that used by Malamuth (1983a). The results showed that except for the penile tumescence measure (which was in the expected direction but not statistically significant), all the predictors significantly related to aggression against females. The data for male targets were more ambiguous, suggesting no or possibly weak relations with the predictors. On the basis of this study and earlier work (Malamuth, 1983a; Malamuth and Check, 1982), it is apparent that the same predictors found here to relate to self-reported naturalistic sexual aggression also relate in similar ways to laboratory aggression against women.[5]

The present findings suggest a high degree of similarity between some factors contributing to stranger and to acquaintance rape. Although we did not specifically

---

[5]Some subjects in the research measuring laboratory aggressiveness also participated in the present research. This enabled assessing the relation between laboratory aggression and a composite of six items from the measure of naturalistic sexual aggression that concern the use of force or aggression. (The other three items refer to psychological tactics such as "saying something you don't mean.") Reported naturalistic aggression correlated significantly with both laboratory aggression against males, $r(47) = .25, p < .04$, one-tailed, and against female targets, $r(38) = .31, p < .025$, one-tailed.

ask subjects whether they knew their victims, based on earlier studies using the same measure (see Koss and Leonard, 1984), it seems very likely that the vast majority of the sexually aggressive acts reported were in acquaintance situations. Yet, some of the same factors theorized and/or found to contribute to stranger rape (e.g., sexual arousal in response to aggression, dominance motivation, hostility toward women) related to sexual aggression among the subjects studied here.

The results suggest that the presence of any predictor alone is unlikely to result in high levels of sexual aggression. This conclusion may be particularly relevant to research focusing on sexual arousal in response to aggression. Although measures assessing such arousal (i.e., the tumescence rape index) have been used in the diagnosis and treatment of rapists (Quinsey, in press), there are considerable data showing that within the general population a substantial percentage of men show arousal patterns similar to those of known rapists (e.g., Malamuth, Check, and Briere, 1986). The present results are supportive of the view that sexual arousal in response to aggression is one of the factors that may create an inclination to aggress against women. They also indicate clearly that other factors must be present before such an arousal pattern will lead to aggressive behavior. The findings point to the types of variables that should be included in clinical and research assessments.

The data also provide important information pertaining to recent research on the effects of sexually aggressive mass media stimuli. In several studies (e.g., Linz, 1985; Malamuth and Check, 1981, 1985a) exposure to certain types of media stimuli changed men's attitudes about aggression against women, including rape. Some (e.g., Vance, 1985) have downplayed the social significance of such findings by asserting that attitudes of this type have not been shown to actually relate to aggressive behavior. The present data extend earlier laboratory findings (Malamuth, 1983a, 1984b; Malamuth and Check, 1982) in showing that the same scales used to measure the impact of media exposure on attitudes (e.g., the AIV scale) are useful predictors, in combination with other factors, of actual aggression in naturalistic and in laboratory settings. Although causal relations cannot be inferred on the basis of such correlational data alone, the findings are consistent with a theoretical model hypothesizing that media depictions contribute to changes in attitudes and that these may, under certain conditions, be one of the contributing factors affecting actual aggressive behavior (see Malamuth and Briere, in press).

An important goal for future research is to further develop and empirically test varied multifactorial models regarding the causes of sexual aggression. These models should attempt to define the causal links among the predictor variables in addition to their influences on sexual aggression. Structural equation modeling with latent variables (e.g., Bentler and Bonett, 1980; Kenny and Judd, 1984) may be particularly suited for this purpose. As well, such models should incorporate two conceptual elements suggested by the present data in combination with earlier work (e.g., Malamuth, 1984a). First, rather than adopting an "all or none" approach, sexual aggressiveness should be conceptualized along a continuum encompassing both differing degrees of inclinations to aggress and differing levels of actual aggressive behavior. Second, in attempting to understand the causes of relatively high levels of this continuum, emphasis should be placed on analyzing crucial configurations of multiple interacting factors (i.e., motivational, disinhibitory and opportunity) rather than on searching for a single or even the primary causal factor.

References

ABEL, G. G., BARLOW, D. H., BLANCHARD, E., AND GUILD, D. The components of rapists' sexual arousal. *Archives of General Psychiatry*, 1977, **34**, 895–903.

ARMENTROUT, J. A., AND HAUER, A. L. MMPIs of rapists of adults, rapists of children, and nonrapist sex offenders. *Journal of Clinical Psychology*, **34**, 330–332.

BANDURA, A. *Social learning theory:* Englewood Cliffs, NJ: Prentice-Hall, 1973.

BANDURA, A. Social learning theory of aggression. *Journal of Communication*, 1978, **3**, 12–19.

BARNES, G., MALAMUTH, N. M., AND CHECK, J. V. P. Personality and sexuality. *Personality and Individual Differences*, 1984, **5**, 159–172.

BARON, R. A. Aggression as a function of victim's pain cues, level of prior anger arousal, and exposure to an aggressive model. *Journal of Personality and Social Psychology*, 1974, **29**, 117–124.

BARON, R. A. *Human aggression.* New York: Plenum, 1977.

BENTLER, P. M. Heterosexual behavior assessment-1: Males. *Behaviour Research and Therapy*, 1968, **6**, 21–25.

BENTLER, P. M., AND BONETT, D. G. Significance tests and goodness of fit in the analysis of covariance structures. *Psychological Bulletin*, 1980, **88**, 588–606.

BROWNMILLER, S. *Against our will: Men, women and rape.* New York: Simon and Schuster, 1975.

BURT, M. R. Attitudes supportive of rape in American culture. *Hearing of the 95th Congress, 2nd Session, House Committee on Science and Technology, Subcommittee, Domestic and International Scientific Planning, Analysis, and Cooperation, Research Into Violent Behavior: Sexual Assaults*, 277–322. Washington, DC: U.S. Government Printing Office, 1978.

BURT, M. R. Cultural myths and support for rape. *Journal of Personality and Social Psychology*, 1980, **38**, 217–230.

CHECK, J. V. P. *The Hostility Toward Women Scale.* Unpublished doctoral dissertation, University of Manitoba, Winnipeg, Canada, 1985.

CHECK, J. V. P., AND MALAMUTH, N. M. *The Hostility Toward Women Scale.* Paper presented at the Western Meetings of the International Society for Research on Aggression, Victoria, Canada, 1983.

CHECK, J. V. P., AND MALAMUTH, N. M. Can participation in pornography experiments have positive effects? *The Journal of Sex Research*, 1984, **20**, 14–31.

CHECK, J. V. P., MALAMUTH, N. M., ELIAS, B., AND BARTON, S. On hostile ground. *Psychology Today*, 1985, **19**, 56–61.

CLARIDGE, G. The Eysenck Psychoticism Scale. In J. N. Butcher and C. D. Spielberger (Eds.), *Advances in Personality Assessment* (Vol. 2), 71–114. Hillsdale, NJ: Erlbaum, 1983.

COHEN, J., AND COHEN, P. *Applied multiple regression/correlation for the behavioral sciences.* Hillsdale, NJ: Erlbaum, 1983.

DONNERSTEIN, E., AND BERKOWITZ, L. Victim reactions in aggressive-erotic films as a factor in violence against women. *Journal of Personality and Social Psychology,* 1981, **41,** 710–724.

EARLS, C. M. Some issues in the assessment of sexual deviance. *International Journal of Law and Psychiatry,* 1983, **6,** 431–441.

EARLS, C. M., AND MARSHALL, W. L. The current state of technology in the laboratory assessment of sexual arousal patterns. In J. G. Greer and I. R. Stuart (Eds.), *The sexual aggressor: Current perspectives on treatment,* 336–362. New York: Van Nostrand Reinhold, 1983.

EYSENCK, H. J. *Sex and Personality.* London: Open Books, 1978.

FARAONE, S. V., AND TSUANG, M. T. Quantitative models of the genetic transmission of schizophrenia. *Psychological Bulletin,* 1985, **98,** 41–46.

FESHBACH, S., STILES, W. B., AND BITTER, E. The reinforcing effect of witnessing aggression. *Journal of Experimental Research in Personality,* 1967, **2,** 133–139.

FINKELHOR, D. *Child sexual abuse: New theory and research.* New York: The Free Press, 1984.

FINKELHOR, D., AND ARAJI, S. *Explanations of pedophilia: A four factor model.* Durham, NH: University of New Hampshire, 1983.

GEEN, R. G. Perceived suffering of the victim as an inhibitor of attack-induced aggression. *Journal of Social Psychology,* 1970, **81,** 209–215.

GROTH, A. N. *Men who rape: The psychology of the offender.* New York: Plenum, 1979.

HARTMANN, D. P. Influence of symbolically modeled instrumental aggression and pain cues on aggressive behavior. *Journal of Personality and Social Psychology,* 1969, **11,** 280–288.

KANIN, E. J. Male aggression in dating-courtship relations. *American Journal of Sociology,* 1957, **63,** 197–204.

KANIN, E. J. Rape as a function of relative sexual frustration. *Psychological Reports,* 1983, **52,** 133–134.

KANIN, E. J. Date rape: Unofficial criminals and victims. *Victimology: An International Journal,* 1984, **1,** 95–108.

KAPLAN, R. The measurement of human aggression. In R. Kaplan, V. Konecni, and R. Novaco (Eds.), *Aggression in children and youth,* 44–72. The Hague, The Netherlands: Sijthoff & Noordhuff, 1983.

KENNY, D. A., AND JUDD, C. M. Estimating the nonlinear and interactive effects of latent variables. *Psychological Bulletin,* 1984, **96,** 201–210.

KOLARSKY, A., AND MADLAFOUSEK, J. Variability of stimulus effect in the course of phallametric testing. *Archives of Sexual Behavior,* 1977, **6,** 135–141.

KOSS, M. P., AND GIDYCZ, C. A. Sexual Experiences Survey: Reliability and validity. *Journal of Consulting and Clinical Psychology,* 1985, **53,** 422–423.

KOSS, M. P., AND LEONARD, K. E. Sexually aggressive men: Empirical findings and theoretical implications. In N. M. Malamuth and E. Donnerstein (Eds.), *Pornography and sexual aggression,* 213–232. New York: Academic Press, 1984.

KOSS, M. P., LEONARD, K. E., BEEZLEY, D. A., AND OROS, C. J. Nonstranger sexual aggression: A discriminant analysis of psychological characteristics of nondetected offenders. *Sex Roles,* 1985, **12,** 981–992.

KOSS, M. P., AND OROS, C. J. Sexual experiences survey: A research instrument investigating sexual aggression and victimization. *Journal of Consulting and Clinical Psychology,* 1982, **50,** 455–457.

LANGEVIN, R., PAITICH, D., AND RUSSON, A. E. Are rapists sexually anomalous, aggressive or both? In R. Langevin (Ed.), *Erotic preference, gender identity, and aggression in men: New research studies,* 17–38. Hillsdale, NJ: Erlbaum, 1985.

LAWS, D. R. A comparison of the measurement characteristics of two circumferential penile transducers. *Archives of Sexual Behavior,* 1977, **6,** 45–51.

LINZ, D. Sexual violence in the media: Effects on male viewers and implications for society: Unpublished doctoral dissertation, University of Wisconsin, Madison, 1985.

MALAMUTH, N. M. Factors associated with rape as predictors of laboratory aggression against women. *Journal of Personality and Social Psychology,* 1983, **45,** 432–442. (a)

MALAMUTH, N. M. Mediators of aggression: Personality, attitudinal, cognitive and emotional. Paper presented at the Western Meetings of the International Society for Research on Aggression, Victoria, Canada, 1983. (b)

MALAMUTH, N. M. Aggression against women: Cultural and individual causes. In N. M. Malamuth & E. Donnerstein (Eds.), *Pornography and sexual aggression,* 19–52. New York: Academic Press, 1984. (a)

MALAMUTH, N. M. Violence against women: Cultural, individual and inhibitory-disinhibitory causes. Paper presented at the Annual Meetings of the American Psychological Association, Toronto, Canada, 1984. (b)

MALAMUTH, N. M., AND BRIERE, J. (in press). Sexual violence in the media: Indirect effects on aggression against women. *Journal of Social Issues.*

MALAMUTH, N. M., AND CHECK, J. V. P. The effects of mass media exposure on acceptance of violence against women: A field experiment. *Journal of Research in Personality,* 1981, **15,** 436–446.

MALAMUTH, N. M., AND CHECK, J. V. P. *Factors related to aggression against women.* Paper presented at the annual meeting of the Canadian Psychological Association, Montreal, Canada, 1982.

MALAMUTH, N. M., AND CHECK, J. V. P. Sexual arousal to rape depictions: Individual differences. *Journal of Abnormal Psychology,* 1983, **92,** 35–67.

MALAMUTH, N. M., AND CHECK, J. V. P. Debriefing effectiveness following exposure to pornographic rape depictions. *The Journal of Sex Research,* 1984, **20,** 1–13.

MALAMUTH, N. M., AND CHECK, J. V. P. The effects of aggressive pornography on beliefs in rape myths: Individual differences. *Journal of Research in Personality,* 1985, **19,** 299–320. (a)

MALAMUTH, N. M., AND CHECK, J. V. P. *Predicting naturalistic sexual aggression: A replication.* Unpublished manuscript, University of California, Los Angeles, 1985. (b)

MALAMUTH, N. M., CHECK, J. V. P., AND BRIERE, J. Sexual arousal in response to aggression: Ideological, aggressive and sexual correlates. *Journal of Personality and Social Psychology,* 1986, **50,** 330–340.

MARSHALL, W. L., AND BARBAREE, H. E. A behavioral view of rape. *International Journal of Law and Psychiatry,* 1984, **7,** 51–77.

MCCRAE, R. R., AND COSTA, P. T. Comparison of EPI and Psychoticism scales with measures of the five factor model of personality. *Personality and Individual Differences,* 1985, **6,** 587–597.

NELSON, P. A. *A sexual functions inventory.* Unpublished doctoral dissertation, University of Florida, 1979.

ORNE, M. On the social psychology of the psychological experiment: With particular reference to demand characteristics and their implications. *American Psychologist,* 1962, **17,** 776–783.

QUINSEY, V. L. (in press). Sexual aggression: Studies of offenders against women. *International Yearbook on Law and Mental Health.*

RADA, C. M. MMPI profile types of exposers, rapists, and assaulters in a court services population. *Journal of Consulting and Clinical Psychology,* 1977, **45,** 61–69.

RAPAPORT, K., AND BURKHART, B. R. Personality and attitudinal characteristics of sexually coercive college males. *Journal of Abnormal Psychology,* 1984, **93,** 216–221.

ROSEN, R. C., AND KEEFE, F. J. The measurement of human penile tumescence. *Psychophysiology,* 1978, **15,** 366–376.

RULE, B. G., AND LEGER, G. H. Pain cues and differing functions of aggression. *Canadian Journal of Behavioural Science,* 1976, **8,** 213–222.

RUSSELL, D. E. H. *Sexual exploitation: Rape, child sexual abuse and workplace harrassment.* Beverly Hills: Sage Publications, 1984.

SANDAY, P. The socio-cultural context of rape: A cross-cultural study. *Journal of Social Issues,* 1981, **37,** 5–27.

SCHEFFÉ, H. A. A method for judging all possible contrasts in the analysis of variance. *Biometrika,* 1953, **40,** 87–104.

SCHULTZ, B., BOHRNSTEDT, G. W., BORGATTA, E. F., AND EVANS, R. R. Explaining premarital sexual intercourse among college students. *Social Forces,* 1977, **56,** 148–165.

SCULLY, D., AND MAROLLA, J. Convicted rapists' vocabulary of motive: Excuses and justifications. *Social Problems,* 1984, **31,** 530–544.

SCULLY, D., AND MAROLLA, J. "Riding the bull at Gilley's": Convicted rapists describe the rewards of rape. *Social Problems,* 1985, **32,** 251–263.

TUKEY, J. W. *The problem of multiple comparisons.* Unpublished manuscript, Princeton University, 1953.

VANCE, C. S. What does the research prove? *Ms Magazine,* April 1985, p. 40.

VII

PREJUDICE

27

The Nonverbal Mediation
of Self-Fulfilling Prophecies
in Interracial Interaction

Carl O. Word, Mark P. Zanna, and Joel Cooper

Two experiments were designed to demonstrate the existence of a self-fulfilling prophecy mediated by non-verbal behavior in an interracial interaction. The results of Experiment 1, which employed naive, white job interviewers and trained white and black job applicants, demonstrated that black applicants received (a) less immediacy, (b) higher rates of speech errors, and (c) shorter amounts of interview time. Experiment 2 employed naive, white applicants and trained white interviewers. In this experiment subject-applicants received behaviors that approximated those given either the black or white applicants in Experiment 1. The main results indicated that subjects treated like the blacks of Experiment 1 were judged to perform less adequately and to be more nervous in the interview situation than subjects treated like the whites. The former subjects also reciprocated with less proximate positions and rated the interviewers as being less adequate and friendly. The implications of these findings for black unemployment were discussed.

Sociologist Robert Merton (1957), by suggesting that an originally false definition of a situation can influence the believer to act in such a way as to bring about that situation, is generally credited with focusing attention on the phenomenon of the self-fulfilling prophecy. The present investigation is concerned with such a phenomenon in face-to-face, dyadic interactions. In this context it is hypothesized that one person's attitudes and expectations about the other person may influence the believer's actions, which in turn, may induce the other person to behave in a way that confirms the original false definition. Interpersonally, this phenomenon has been documented in schools, with teachers' expectations influencing students' performances, and in psychology laboratories, with experimenters' expectations influencing subjects' responses (cf. Rosenthal, 1971).

Reprinted with permission of the authors and *Journal of Experimental Social Psychology, 10.* Copyright © 1974 by Academic Press, Inc.

This research was supported by N.I.H. Biomedical Research Grants #5 S05 FR07057-04 and #5 S05 RR07057-07.

In the present study attention will be directed toward (1) possible nonverbal mediators of this effect, and (2) the reciprocal performances of the interactants. The focus, in addition, will be on the interaction of black and white Americans with a view toward examining the employment outcomes of black job applicants interviewed by whites.

ATTITUDES AND IMMEDIACY

Mehrabian (1968) has recently reported a series of studies linking attitudes toward a target person and the concomitant nonverbal behavior directed toward that person. The results of these studies have consistently found that closer interpersonal distances, more eye contact, more direct shoulder orientation, and more forward lean are a consequence of more positive attitudes toward an addressee. Mehrabian (1969) has considered such nonverbal behaviors in terms of "immediacy" and has defined immediacy "as the extent to which communication behaviors enhance closeness to and nonverbal interaction with another . . . greater immediacy is due to increasing degrees of physical proximity and/or increasing perceptual availability of the communicator to the addressee" (p. 203).

A related series of studies has been conducted by Kleck and his associates (Kleck, 1968; Kleck, Buck, Goller, London, Pfeiffer and Vukcevic, 1968; Kleck, Ono and Hastorf, 1966) pursuing Goffman's (1963) observation that normals tend to avoid stigmatized persons. They have begun to document what might be called a nonverbal stigma effect. For example, normal interactants were found to terminate interviews sooner (Kleck *et al.,* 1966) and to exhibit greater motoric inhibition (Kleck, 1968) with a handicapped person (i.e., leg amputee), and to employ greater interaction distances with an epileptic stranger (Kleck *et al.,* 1968). This set of studies, then, also suggests that those persons who possess a personal characteristic which is discrediting in the eyes of others are treated with less immediate behaviors. In addition to such discrediting characteristics as a physical disability or a criminal record, Goffman (1963) includes blackness in a white society as a stigmatizing trait.

Thus, a body of data suggests that (1) attitudes toward an individual are linked with nonverbal behavior emitted toward that individual, and (2) positive attitudes lead to more immediate nonverbal behaviors. Two questions that now arise are concerned with whether such behaviors are (1) decoded or understood by the target and (2) reciprocated.

DECODING AND RECIPROCATING IMMEDIACY

Recent studies suggest that such evaluative, nonverbal behaviors are both decoded and reciprocated. Mehrabian (1967) found friendliness ratings of an interviewer varied as a function of the physical interaction distance, and the immediacy of head and body positions given subjects. Eye contact has been extensively investigated. Both Kleck and Nuessle (1968) and Jones and Cooper (1971) found that a high degree of eye contact produced higher evaluations of the communicator and produced more positive evaluations on the part of the subjects than did low eye contact.

Since individuals apparently are able to decode affective components of communications from variations in immediacy behavior, it seems reasonable to expect they would reciprocate such variations. This proposition also has received support. Rosenfeld (1967), for example, found that subjects treated to more smiles and positive head nods did reciprocate with more of each.

Thus individuals apparently decode less immediacy as indicating less friendly behavior and reciprocate with less friendly (i.e., less immediate) behavior of their own. Since individuals seldom are able to monitor their own nonverbal behaviors, they are more likely to attribute the reciprocated immediacy, not to their own, original nonverbal behavior, but instead to some disposition inherent in their cointeractant (cf. Jones and Nisbett, 1971). With this nonverbal reciprocation, then, a self-fulfilling prophecy is born.

WHITE-BLACK INTERACTION IN A JOB
INTERVIEW SETTING

So far we have been concerned with describing possible mechanisms of interpersonal, self-fulfilling prophecies. The discussion now turns to consider such a process in black-white, dyadic interactions. It has been demonstrated time and again that white Americans have generalized, negative evaluations (e.g., stereotypes) of black Americans. This has been shown most recently in our own subject population by Darley, Lewis, and Glucksberg (1972). Such negative evaluations, of course, represent the kind of attitudes that can initiate an interpersonal, self-fulfilling prophecy. The general hypothesis that the present study sought to investigate, therefore, was that whites interacting with blacks will emit nonverbal behaviors corresponding to negative evaluations and that blacks, in turn, will reciprocate with less immediate behaviors. If the context in which the interaction occurs involves a job interview, with the white interviewing the black, such reciprocated behavior may be interpreted as less adequate performance, thus confirming, in part, the interviewer's original attitude.

These general expectations are operationalized by two subhypotheses: First, black, as compared to white, job applicants will receive less immediate nonverbal communications from white job interviewers; second, recipients of less immediate nonverbal communications, whether black or white, will reciprocate these communications and be judged to perform less adequately in the job interview situation than recipients of more positive nonverbal communications. The first hypothesis was tested in Experiment 1, which employed naive, white job interviewers and trained white and black job applicants; the second in Experiment 2, which used naive, white job applicants and trained white job interviewers who were instructed to emit either immediate or nonimmediate cues.

EXPERIMENT 1

METHOD

Overview

In the context of a study on group decision-making white subjects, as representatives of a team in competition with other teams, interviewed both white and black job applicants. The applicants were trained to respond similarly in both the verbal and nonverbal channels. The interview situation itself was arranged to give the subject-interviewers the opportunity to treat their applicants differentially without the knowledge (1) that their own behavior was being monitored, or (2) that race of the applicants was the experimental variable.

Subjects (Interviewers) and Confederates (Applicants and Team Members)

Subject-interviewers were 15 white, Princeton males recruited to participate in a study of group decision-making conducted by Career Services and the Psychology Department. They were informed that the study would last approximately one hour and a half and that they would be paid $2.00 and possibly $5.00 more. One of the subjects was eliminated when he indicated that he was aware of the purpose of the study before the debriefing period. No other subject volunteered this sort of information after intensive probing, leaving an *n* of 14.

Confederate-applicants were two black and three white high school student volunteers referred by their high school counselor. Each was told that the study was concerned with cognitive functioning and that the experimenter was interested in finding out how subjects made up their minds when forced to choose between nearly identical job applicants. All confederates in both experiments were naive with respect to the hypotheses. Intensive probing following the experiment indicated that they did not become aware. The three confederates who served as the subject's "team members" and the experimenter were male Princeton volunteers.

Procedure

Upon arrival the subjects entered a room containing two confederate team members, who introduced themselves and acted friendly. Another confederate entered and acted friendly, as well. Then the experimenter entered, handed out written instructions and answered any questions.

The instructions informed subjects that the four people in the room constituted a team; that they were to compete with four other teams in planning a marketing campaign; and that they needed to select another member from four high school applicants. In order to increase incentive and concern, an additional $5.00 was promised to the team which performed best in the competition. Using a supposedly random draw, the subject was chosen to interview the applicants. He was then handed a list of 15 questions which was to serve as the interview material, told he had 45 minutes to interview all four high school students and taken to the interview room where the first confederate-applicant was already seated.

In order to measure the physical distance that the interviewer placed himself from the applicant, the experimenter upon entering the interview room, feigned to discover that there was no chair for the interviewer. Subjects were then asked to wheel in a chair from an adjoining room.

Subjects were led to believe that there would be four interviews so that the race variable would be less apparent to them. In addition, to eliminate any special effect that might occur in the first and last interview, an a priori decision was made not to analyze the data from the first "warm-up" interview and not to have a fourth interview. The "warm-up" job candidate was always white. Half the subjects then interviewed a black followed by a white applicant; the other half interviewed a white then a black candidate. After completion of the third interview, subjects were told that the fourth applicant had called to cancel his appointment. After the third interview, subjects were paid and debriefed.

Applicant Performance

Confederate-applicants were trained to act in a standard way to all interviewers. First, they devised answers to the 15 questions such that their answers, though not identical, would represent equally qualifying answers. Confederates then rehearsed these answers until two judges rated their performances to be equal. Confederates were also trained to seat themselves, shoulders parallel to the backs of their chairs (10° from vertical) and to make eye contact with the interviewer 50% of the time. A code was devised to signal confederates during their interviews if they deviated from the pose or began to reciprocate the gestures or head nods given them.

Dependent Measures

Immediacy behaviors.   Following Mehrabian (1968, 1969), four indices of psychological immediacy were assessed: (1) Physical Distance between interviewer and interviewee, measured in inches; (2) Forward Lean, scored in 10° units, with zero representing the vertical position and positive scores representing the torso leaning toward the confederate; (3) Eye Contact, defined as the proportion of time the subject looked directly at the confederate's eyes; and (4) Shoulder Orientation, scored in units of 10° with zero representing the subject's shoulders parallel to those of the confederate and positive scores indicating a shift in either direction. Two judges,[1] placed behind one-way mirrors, scored the immediacy behaviors.

More distance and shoulder angle represent less immediate behaviors while more foreward lean and more eye contact represent more immediate behaviors. An index of total immediacy was constructed by summing the four measures, standardized, and weighted according to the regression equation beta weights established by Mehrabian (1969). Final scores of this index represent $(-.6)$ distance + $(.3)$ forward lean + $(.3)$ eye contact + $(-.1)$ shoulder orientation. Positive scores represent more immediate performances.

Related behaviors.   Two related behaviors, which indicate differential evaluations of the applicants (cf. Mehrabian, 1969), were also assessed: (1) Interview length indicates the amount of time from the point the subject entered the interview room until he announced the interview was over, in minutes. This measure was taken by the experimenter. (2) Speech Error Rate, scored by two additional judges from audiotapes, represents the sum of (a) sentence changes, (b) repetitions, (c) stutters, (d) sentence incompletions, and (e) intruding, incoherent sounds divided by the length of the interview and averaged over the two judges. Higher scores represent more speech errors per minute.

RESULTS

Reliabilities and Order Effects

Reliabilities, obtained by correlating the judges' ratings, ranged from .60 to .90 (see Table 27.1). Preliminary analyses also indicated that there were no effects for the order in which confederate-applicants appeared, so that the results are based on data collapsed across this variable.

---

[1]All judges employed in the present research were Princeton undergraduates. Each worked independently and was naive concerning the hypothesis under investigation. Intensive probing indicated that they did not become aware of the hypothesis.

TABLE 27.1
Mean interviewer behavior as a function of race of job applicant; Experiment I

Behavior	Reliability	Blacks	Whites	t^b	p
Total immediacy[a]	—	−.11	.38	2.79	<.02
Distance	.90	62.29 inches	58.43 inches	2.36	<.05
Forward lean	.68	−8.76 degrees	−6.12 degrees	1.09	n.s.
Eye contact	.80	62.71%	61.46%	<1	n.s.
Shoulder orientation	.60	22.46 degrees	23.08 degrees	<1	n.s.
Related behaviors					
Interview length	—	9.42 min.	12.77 min.	3.22	<.01
Speech error rate	.88	3.54 errors/min.	2.37 errors/min.	2.43	<.05

[a]See text for weighing formula, from Mehrabian (1969).
[b]t test for correlated samples was employed.

Immediacy Behaviors

The results, presented in Table 27.1, indicate that, overall, black job candidates received less immediate behaviors than white applicants ($t = 2.79$; $df = 13$; $p < .02$). On the average, blacks received a negative total immediacy score; whites received a positive one. This overall difference is primarily due to the fact that the white interviewers physically placed themselves further from black than white applicants ($t = 2.36$; $df = 13$; $p < .05$). None of the other indices of immediacy showed reliable differences when considered separately.

Related Behaviors

The results for interview length and speech error rate are also presented in Table 27.1. Here it can be seen that blacks also received less immediate behaviors. White interviewers spent 25% less time ($t = 3.22$; $df = 13$; $p < .01$) and had higher rates of speech errors ($t = 2.43$; $df = 13$; $p < .05$) with black as compared to white job candidates.

The results of the first experiment provide support for the hypothesis that black, as compared to white, job applicants receive less immediate nonverbal communications from white job interviewers. Indirectly the results also provide support for the conceptualization of blackness as a stigmatizing trait. The differences in time (evidenced by 12 of 14 interviewers), in total immediacy (evidenced by 10 of 14 interviewers), and in speech error rate (evidenced by 11 of 14 interviewers) argues for an extension of the stigma effect obtained by Kleck and his associates to include black Americans.

EXPERIMENT 2

METHOD

Overview

A second experiment was conducted to ascertain what effect the differences black and white applicants received in Experiment I would have on an applicant's job interview performance. In the context of training job interviewers, subject-applicants were interviewed by confederate-interviewers under one of two conditions. In the Immediate condition, as compared to the Nonimmediate condition, interviewers (1) sat closer to the applicant, (2) made fewer speech errors per minute, and (3) actually took longer to give their interviews. The main dependent measures were concerned with the interview performance of the applicant, both in terms of its judged adequacy for obtaining the job and in terms of its reciprocation of immediacy behaviors.

Subjects (Job Applicants) and Confederates (Interviewers)

Thirty white male Princeton University students were recruited ostensibly to help Career Services train interviewers for an upcoming summer job operation. No subjects were eliminated from the study, leaving an *n* of 15 in each condition. The two confederate-interviewers were also white male Princeton students.

Procedure

Upon arrival each subject was given an instruction sheet which informed him that Career Services had contracted with the Psychology Department to train Princeton juniors and seniors in the techniques of job interviewing and that one of the techniques chosen included videotaping interviewers with job applicants for feedback purposes. The subject was then asked to simulate a job applicant, to be honest, and to really compete for the job, so as to give the interviewer real, lifelike practice. To make the simulation more meaningful, subjects were also informed that the applicant chosen from five interviewed that evening would receive an additional $1.50.

Subjects were taken to the interview room and asked to be seated in a large swivel chair, while the Experimenter turned on the camera. The confederate-interviewer then entered, and assumed either an immediate or nonimmediate position which will be described in more detail below. Exactly five minutes into the interviewing in both conditions, a guise was developed whose result was that the experimenter had to reclaim the chair in which the subject was sitting. The subject was then asked to take a folding chair leaning against the wall and to continue the interview. The distance from the interviewer which the subject placed his new chair was one of the study's dependent measures designed to assess reciprocated immediacy.

When the interview ended, the experimenter took the subject to another room where a second investigator, blind as to the condition of the subject, administered self-report scales and answered any questions. Subject was then paid and debriefed.

Immediacy Manipulation

As in the Kleck and Nuessle (1968) and the Jones and Cooper (1971) studies, systematic nonverbal variations were introduced by specifically training confederates. Two confederate-interviewers alternated in the two conditions. In the Immediate condition, confederates sat at a chair on the side of a table. In the Nonimmediate condition, confederates sat fully behind the table. The difference in distance from the subject's chair was about four inches, representing the mean difference in distance white interviewers gave black and white applicants in Experiment 1.[2]

In addition, the confederate-interviewers in the Immediate condition were trained to behave as precisely as possible like the subject-interviewers in Experiment 1 had acted toward white applicants. In the Nonimmediate condition, interviewers were trained to act as subject-interviewers had acted toward Blacks in Experiment 1. The factors used to simulate the immediacy behaviors found in the first experiment were speech error rate, length of interview and, as has been previously mentioned, physical distance. Eye contact, shoulder orientation and forward lean did not show significant differences in Experiment I and thus were held constant in Experiment 2 (with the levels set at 50% eye contact, 0° shoulder orientation and 20° forward lean).

Dependent Measures

Three classes of dependent variables were collected: (1) judges' ratings of interview performance; (2) judges' ratings of reciprocated immediacy behaviors; and (3) subjects' ratings of their post-interview mood state and attitudes toward the interviewer.

Applicant performance. Applicant interview performance and demeanor were rated by a panel of two judges from videotapes of the interviews. The videotapes were recorded at such an angle that judges viewed only the applicant, not the

---

[2]By having the interviewer sit either behind or at the side of the table, the impact of the four inch difference in distance was intentionally maximized in terms of psychological immediacy.

confederate-interviewer. The judges were merely instructed about the type of job subjects were applying for, and were asked to rate (1) the overall adequacy of each subject's performance and (2) each subject's composure on five (0–4) point scales. High scores, averaged over the judges, represent more adequate and more calm, relaxed performances, respectively.

Reciprocated immediacy behaviors.   Two additional judges, placed behind one-way mirrors as in Experiment 1, recorded subjects' forward lean, eye contact, and shoulder orientation in accordance with the procedures established by Mehrabian (1969). Distance was directly measured after each interview, and represents the distance, in inches, from the middle of the interviewer-confederate's chair to the middle of the subject's chair, after the interruption. Speech errors were scored by another panel of two judges from audiotapes of the interviews, also according to Mehrabian's (1969) procedures. High scores represent more speech errors per minute.

Applicant mood and attitude toward the interviewer.   After the interview, subjects filled out a series of questionnaires designed to assess their mood state and their attitudes toward the interviewer. Following Jones and Cooper (1971), subjects' moods were expected to vary as a function of immediacy conditions. The mood scale adapted from that study was employed. It consisted of six polar adjectives (e.g., happy-sad) separated by seven-point scales. Subjects were asked to respond to each pair according to "the way you feel about yourself."

Two measures of subjects' attitudes toward the interviewer were collected. First, subjects were asked to rate the friendliness of the interviewer on an 11-point scale, with zero representing an "unfriendly" and 10 representing a "friendly" interviewer, respectively. Second, in order to assess subjects' attitudes concerning the adequacy of the interviewer as an individual, they were asked to check the six adjectives best describing their interviewer from a list of 16 drawn from Gough's Adjective Checklist. Final scores represent the number of positive adjectives chosen minus the number of negative adjectives checked.

RESULTS

Reliabilities and Interviewer Effects

Reliabilities, obtained by correlating judges' ratings, ranged from .66 to .86 (see Table 27.2). Preliminary analyses also indicated that there were no effects for interviewers, so that the results presented are based on data collapsed across this variable.

TABLE 27.2
Mean applicant responses under two conditions of interviewer immediacy; Experiment 2

Response	Reliability	Nonimmediate	Immediate	F	P
Applicant performance					
Rated performance	.66	1.44	2.22	7.96	<.01
Rated demeanor	.86	1.62	3.02	16.46	<.001
Immediacy behaviors					
Distance	—	72.73 inches	56.93 inches	9.19	<.01
Speech error rate	.74	5.01 errors/min.	3.33 errors/min.	3.40	<.10
Self reported mood and attitudes					
Mood	—	3.77	5.97	1.34	n.s.
Interviewer friendliness	—	4.33	6.60	22.91	<.001
Interviewer adequacy	—	−1.07	1.53	8.64	<.01

Applicant Performance

It was predicted from an analysis of the communicative functions of nonimmediacy that applicants would be adversely affected by the receipt of nonimmediate communications. Those effects were expected to manifest themselves in less adequate job-interview performances.

Subjects in the two conditions were rated by two judges from video-tapes. The main dependent measure, applicant adequacy for the job, showed striking differences as a function of immediacy conditions (see Table 27.2). Subjects in the Nonimmediate condition were judged significantly less adequate for the job ($F = 7.96$; $df = 1/28$; $p < .01$). Subjects in the Nonimmediate condition were also judged to be reliably less calm and composed ($F = 16.96$; $df = 1/28$; $p < .001$).

Reciprocated Immediacy Behaviors

Following Rosenfeld (1967) among others, it was expected that subjects encountering less immediate communications would reciprocate with less immediate behaviors of their own. This expectation was supported by both the measures of physical distance and speech error rate (see Table 27.2).

Subjects in the Immediate condition, on the average, placed their chairs eight inches closer to the interviewer after their initial chair was removed; subjects in the Nonimmediate conditions placed their chairs four inches further away from their interviewer. The mean difference between the two groups was highly significant ($F = 9.19$; $df = 1/28$; $p < .01$).

As in Experiment 1 mean comparisons for the forward lean, eye contact, and shoulder orientation measures of immediacy did not reach significance. The combination of these measures, using the weighting formula devised by Mehrabian

(1969), however, was reliably different (means of $-.29$ and $.29$ in the Nonimmediate and Immediate conditions, respectively; $F = 5.44$; $df = 1/28$; $p < .05$).

The rate at which subjects made speech errors also tended to be reciprocated with subjects in the Nonimmediate condition exhibiting a higher rate than subjects in the Immediate condition ($F = 3.40$; $df = 1/28$; $p < .10$).

Applicant Mood and Attitude Toward the Interviewer

It was expected that subjects receiving less immediate (i.e., less positive) communication would (1) feel less positively after their interviews, and (2) hold less positive attitudes toward the interviewer himself. These expectations were only partially supported (see Table 27.2). Although subjects in the nonimmediate condition reported less positive moods than subjects in the immediate condition, this difference was not statistically reliable.

Subjects in the less immediate condition did, however, rate their interviewers to be less friendly ($F = 22.91$; $df = 1/28$; $p < .001$) and less adequate overall ($F = 8.64$; $df = 1/28$; $p < .01$) than subjects in the more immediate condition.

DISCUSSION

Results from the two experiments provide clear support for the two subhypotheses, and offer inferential evidence for the general notion that self-fulfilling prophecies can and do occur in interracial interactions.

The results of Experiment 1 indicated that black applicants were, in fact, treated to less immediacy than their white counterparts. Goffman's (1963) conception of blackness as a stigmatizing trait in Anglo-American society is, thus, given experimental support—insofar as that classification predicts avoidance behaviors in interactions with normals. These results may also be viewed as extending the stigma effect documented by Kleck and his associates with handicapped persons.

That the differential treatment black and white applicants received in Experiment 1 can influence the performance and attitudes of job candidates was clearly demonstrated in Experiment 2. In that experiment those applicants, treated similarly to the way Blacks were treated in Experiment 1, performed less well, reciprocated less immediacy, and found their interviewers to be less adequate. Taken together the two experiments provide evidence for the assertion that nonverbal, immediacy cues mediate, in part, the performance of an applicant in a job interview situation. Further, the experiments suggest that the model of a self-fulfilling prophecy, mediated by nonverbal cues, (1) is applicable to this setting, and (2) can account, in part, for the less adequate performances of black applicants (cf. Sattler, 1970).

Social scientists have often tended to focus their attention for such phenomena as unemployment in black communities on the dispositions of the disinherited. Such an approach has been termed "victim analysis" for its preoccupation with the wounds, defects and personalities of the victimized as an explanation for social problems (Ryan, 1971). The present results suggest that analyses of black-white interactions, particularly in the area of job-seeking Blacks in white society, might profit if it were assumed that the "problem" of black performance resides not entirely within the Blacks, but rather within the interaction setting itself.

References

DARLEY, J. M., LEWIS, L. D., AND GLUCKSBERG, S. Stereotype persistence and change among college students: one more time. Unpublished Manuscript, Princeton University, 1972.

GOFFMAN, E. *Stigma: notes on the management of spoiled identity.* Englewood Cliffs, New Jersey: Prentice-Hall, 1963.

JONES, R. E., AND COOPER, J. Mediation of experimenter effects. *Journal of Personality and Social Psychology,* 1971, **20,** 70–74.

JONES, E. E., AND NISBETT, R. E. The actor and the observer: divergent perceptions of the causes of behavior. In E. E. Jones, D. E. Kanouse, H. H. Kelley, R. E. Nisbett, S. Valins and B. Weiner (Eds.), *Attribution: perceiving the causes of behavior.* New York: General Learning Press, 1971.

KLECK, R. E. Physical stigma and nonverbal cues emitted in face-to-face interactions. *Human Relations,* 1968, **21,** 19–28.

KLECK, R., BUCK, P. L., GOLLER, W. L., LONDON, R. S., PFEIFFER, J. R., AND VUKCEVIC, D. P. Effects of stigmatizing conditions on the use of personal space. *Psychological Reports,* 1968, **23,** 111–118.

KLECK, R. E., AND NUESSLE, W. Congruence between indicative and communicative functions of eye contact in interpersonal relations. *British Journal of Social and Clinical Psychology,* 1968, **7,** 241–246.

KLECK, R. E., ONO, H., AND HASTORF, A. H. The effects of physical deviance upon face-to-face interaction. *Human Relations,* 1966, **19,** 425–436.

MEHRABIAN, A. Orientation behaviors and nonverbal attitude communication. *Journal of Communication,* 1967, **17,** 324–332.

MEHRABIAN, A. Inference of attitudes from the posture, orientation, and distance of a communicator. *Journal of Consulting and Clinical Psychology,* 1968, **32,** 296–308.

MEHRABIAN, A. Some referents and measures of nonverbal behavior. *Behavior Research Methods and Instrumentation,* 1969, **1,** 203–207.

MERTON, R. K. *Social theory and social structure.* New York: Free Press, 1957.

ROSENFELD, H. M. Nonverbal reciprocation of approval: an experimental analysis. *Journal of Experimental and Social Psychology,* 1967, **3,** 102–111.

ROSENTHAL, R. Teacher expectations. In G. S. Lesser (Ed.), *Psychology and the educational process.* Glenview, Illinois: Scott, Foresman, 1971.

RYAN, W. *Blaming the victim.* New York: Pantheon, 1971.

SATTLER, J. Racial "experimenter effects" in experimentation, testing, interviewing, and psychotherapy. *Psychological Bulletin,* 1970, **73,** 136–160.

28

The Effect of Stereotype Threat on the Standardized Test Performance of College Students

Joshua Aronson, Claude M. Steele,
Moises F. Salinas and Michael J. Lustina

"The objective test is a common touchstone. It gives all students who take it the same chance, asks them to run the same race—even though they have had different economic backgrounds, different educational, cultural, and social opportunities."
    —Henry Chauncy, first President of the Educational Testing Service

"For some reason I didn't score well on tests. Maybe I was just nervous. There's a lot of pressure on you, knowing that if you fail, you fail your race."
    —Texas State Senator Rodney Ellis in a 1997 interview.

No one questions the fact that members of certain minority groups like African-Americans and Latinos typically score less well than European-Americans on tests that aim to measure either basic intelligence or scholastic achievement. On widely used tests such as the standard IQ test and college entrance exams such as the Scholastic Aptitude Test (SAT), African-Americans and Latinos typically score a standard deviation lower than whites (e.g., Herrnstein & Murray, 1994). This means, for example, that on average, an African-American testee will score 15 points lower than the average white testee on the IQ test, and 100 points lower on the SAT. These are well established, virtually lawful patterns of performance that appear on nearly every test of academic ability.

Author Note: Much of the research reported here was presented at a talk by the first author entitled "Stereotype Threat and the Academic Underperformance of African Americans and Latinos," at the Tenth Annual Convention of the American Psychological Society, Washington D.C., May, 1998. We thank Elliot Aronson and Stacey Rosenkrantz for helpful comments on this manuscript.

But where do these differences come from? What can be done to address them? These have been some of the most hotly debated and politically charged discussions among psychologists and in the popular culture (e.g., Herrnstein & Murray, 1994; Jacoby & Glauberman, 1995; Neisser, 1986). On one end of the spectrum are the "nativists," who view the tests as unbiased indicators of ability or achievement, and thus interpret lower scores as reflective of inherently lower intelligence endowed by genetics (e.g., Herrnstein & Murray, 1994; Jensen, 1969; 1980). At the other end are those who see the tests as culturally biased, in that they contain items that are worded or framed in a way that require specialized knowledge or familiarity of areas that are alien to certain subcultures of society, such as poor or minority students (e.g., Eells, et al., 1952; Owen, 1985; Hafner & White, 1981). Considerable research on test bias has been conducted that casts doubt on claims of cultural bias (see Jensen, 1980, for a review) and many attempts to "de-bias" the tests—for example, by having them constructed by minority group members—have not been successful (Neisser, et al., 1996; Sattler & Gwynn, 1982). The race gaps persist and the controversy about what they mean continues.

Despite the abundance of research and discussion on the content of the tests, relatively little attention in this debate has been paid to the *testing situation* itself—that is, how the social context of testing might *feel* different to members of different social groups, and how such differences could influence performance. From the social psychologist's perspective, the lack of emphasis on the testing situation is odd given the emphasis our field has placed on environmental factors in analyzing human behavior. The research reported here explored the possibility that the standardized test performance of African-Americans and other minorities results not from bias inherent in the test, or inability inherent in the individual, but rather, from extra psychological burden arising from the testing situation. Namely, we argue that awareness of widely known negative stereotypes that allege low ability in these groups puts the minority test-taker in an uncomfortable social psychological predicament.

The predicament is this: the mere existence of a devaluing stereotype means that anything one does, or any of one's features that conform to it, makes the stereotype more plausible as a self-characterization, in the eyes of others, and perhaps even in one's own eyes. This predicament is most likely experienced as a self-evaluative apprehension, a burden of suspicion that can be troubling and disruptive to individuals to whom negative stereotypes could conceivably apply (Aronson, Quinn, & Spencer, 1998; Steele, 1997; Steele & Aronson, 1995). Importantly, it is a predicament that could apply to the member of any group, not merely members of ethnic minorities. Thus, under specific conditions, images elicited by the terms "dumb jock" or "absent-minded professor," for example, can establish in the athlete or college teacher the apprehension that these negative labels fit. When the stereotype alleges important negative qualities, this apprehension can have critically disruptive effects.

Thus, consider an African-American or Latino student trying to solve difficult items on a test or called upon in class to answer a complex question. As for anyone, low performance in such situations could bring with it disappointment, discouragement, and embarrassment. But the stereotype alleging African-American or Latino intellectual inferiority poses for the black or Latino student the additional risk of confirming a deeply negative, racial inferiority, a suspicion of being unalterably limited and not fitting or belonging in an academic setting. We call this apprehension "stereotype threat," and hypothesize that it can meaningfully hinder performance on challenging cognitive tasks, such as standardized tests.

Stereotype threat could conceivably undermine performance through a number of well-documented processes. Studies of "test-anxiety," for example, show how the fear of poor performance can interfere with a person's ability to execute complicated mental tasks, either by simply diverting mental attention (e.g., Bond, 1982; Carver & Scheier, 1981; Sarason, 1972; Wine, 1971), or, alternatively, by prompting a self-esteem protective withdrawal of effort (e.g., Hormuth, 1986; Geen, 1985). Our argument, then, is that the situation of being evaluated—by a teacher, a test, an audience, and so on—in a situation where ability stereotypes are relevant, simply makes performance a more "high-stakes" endeavor for the minority group member, intensifying test anxiety and distraction, which are certain to interfere with performance.

The hypothesis in all the experiments to be reported was quite straightforward: if performance on difficult standardized tests is hindered by stereotype threat, then conditions that reduce stereotype threat should improve performance. The first two experiments (Steele & Aronson, 1995) tested this hypothesis with African-American college students taking a test of their verbal abilities. The third experiment (Aronson & Salinas, 1998) expanded this hypothesis to Latinos. The fourth experiment (Aronson, et al., 1998) tested the hypothesis that anyone—even members of non-minority groups—can suffer from stereotype threat.

EXPERIMENT 1

Procedure

African-American and Caucasian Stanford University undergraduates took a difficult test comprised of items from the verbal portion of the Graduate Record Exam (GRE). Participants were randomly assigned to one of two conditions. In the "stereotype threat" condition ($n = 20$) the students took the test under conditions designed to maximize any apprehensions they might have about confirming a stereotype alleging lower intellectual ability among members of their group. Specifically, we told them that the reason we were giving them the test was that we were interested in a precise measure of their verbal ability. They were further told that when the test was over, we would give them feedback on how they performed, pointing out their "strengths and weaknesses."

The remaining participants ($n = 20$) were in the "no stereotype threat" condition. They took the test under conditions designed to minimize stereotype threat. Specifically they were told that we were not interested in evaluating their ability, but rather, that we wanted to better understand the "psychology of verbal problem solving." They were also told they would receive feedback, but they were told that the feedback would be aimed at familiarizing them with the kinds of problems that typically appear on standardized tests.

Both groups were asked to try as hard as they could to complete as many of the 24 problems as possible in the allotted time (25 minutes).

We predicted that because there exists a widely known negative stereotype about their group's intellectual ability, African-Americans would feel much like Senator Ellis reported feeling in the quote that began this chapter. Namely, they would feel "a lot of pressure" to disconfirm the stereotype. This pressure, we predicted, would have an adverse effect on their test performance. Thus, we predicted that the African-Americans would perform less well in the stereotype threat condition than in the no stereotype threat condition.

Results and Discussion

The dependent measure in this study was the number of problems participants correctly solved. To correct for any preexisting preparational differences, we analyzed their scores with an analysis of covariance (ANCOVA), using each participant's self-reported verbal SAT score as the covariate. The corrected means are presented in Figure 28.1 (page 404).

As Figure 28.1 shows, our predictions about the effect of stereotype threat on test performance were confirmed. When the test was presented as diagnostic of participants' verbal abilities, it had a markedly significant effect on the performance of the African-American students, but had no effect whatsoever on the performance of the Caucasian students. When presumably threatened by the evaluative scrutiny of the stereotype threat condition, the African-American students' scores plummeted. But in the no stereotype threat condition—where any concerns about fulfilling the stereotype were nullified by the explicitly nonevaluative setting—they solved almost twice as many of the problems correctly.

The results of subsequent studies (Aronson & Salinas, 1998; Steele & Aronson, 1995) aimed at understanding what caused this underperformance—whether it was caused by anxiety, distraction, or the withdrawal of effort—pointed the causal arrow away from effort withdrawal and in the direction of a combination of anxiety and distraction. Moreover, these studies strongly suggested important cognitive consequences of making test performance explicitly evaluative of ability. Specifically, we found that African-Americans in the stereotype threat conditions were more likely to be thinking about the stereotypes regarding their group (as measured by subtle measures of stereotype activation) than were their counterparts in a nonevaluative testing

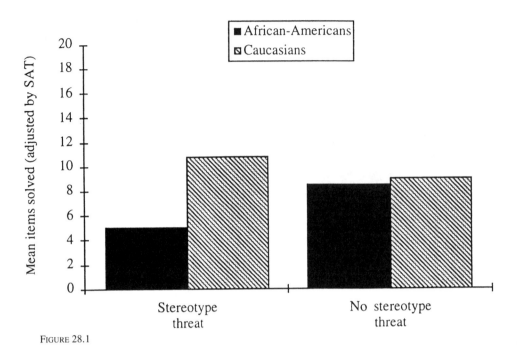

■ African-Americans
◨ Caucasians

Mean items solved (adjusted by SAT)

20
18
16
14
12
10
8
6
4
2
0

Stereotype
threat

No stereotype
threat

FIGURE 28.1

situation. In other words, making the situation evaluative brought to mind stereotypes about their group, and along with it, further analysis suggested, the motivation
to disprove those stereotypes, in part by trying *harder* to perform well on the test.

Several key questions remained. We were fairly confident that a highly evaluative testing situation could arouse a concern with fulfilling the negative stereotype,
and that this could in turn undermine performance. But, in addition, we were curious as to whether or not stereotype threat, in and of itself—in the absence of the
test being explicitly evaluative of ability—would be sufficient to disrupt the performance of African-Americans on a difficult test. We had shown that evaluative
scrutiny lowers the performance of African-Americans and that it also arouses
stereotypes, but this did not prove that the stereotype threat undermined their performance. We conducted a second experiment to address this question.

EXPERIMENT 2

Procedure

The procedure in this experiment was identical to the no stereotype threat conditions of the previous experiment. Participants were African-American or Caucasian Stanford undergraduates who were asked to take a test but were told that the

purpose was not to evaluate their abilities. Stereotype threat was manipulated in this experiment by making half of the participants aware that we might be paying attention to their race, and presumably that race could be of import to the purposes of the study. This was done by asking all participants to fill out a brief demographic questionnaire, which asked them to indicate their sex, their major of study, their year in school, and so on. In the stereotype threat condition, we asked them to indicate their race, in the no stereotype threat condition, we did not. In all other respects the conditions were identical. We predicted that making race salient would have a performance debilitating effect on the African-American participants, but not upon the Caucasians.

Results and Discussion

As shown in Figure 28.2, this was precisely what happened. Paralleling the results of Experiment 1, African-Americans performed just as well as the Caucasian students when they took the test under no stereotype threat conditions but performed considerably less well when stereotype threat was induced by making race salient. Follow-up measures in this study and others using the race-salience manipulation suggested that the stereotype threat manipulation caused African-Americans to become more anxious than their white or non-stereotype threatened counterparts, thus offering at least a partial explanation for why they were less able to solve the problems under stereotype threat.

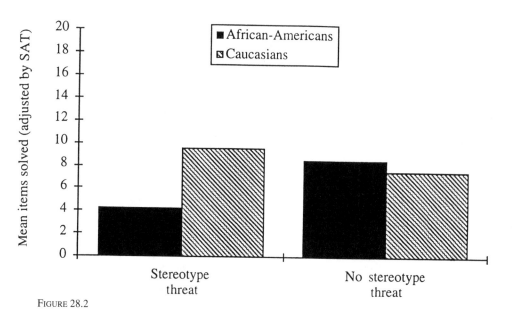

FIGURE 28.2

Making race salient depressed African-Americans' performance even when the test was not presented as a measure of their ability. It did so, it seems reasonable to assume, by making the stereotype mentally available, and thus creating the anxiety-provoking predicament of trying to disprove its implication of low ability. Much research has shown similar effects—demonstrating how adding extra motivation to perform well on extremely difficult tasks that require full concentration can create a "choking under pressure" effect (see Baumeister & Showers, 1986, for a review).

In the next 2 experiments, we performed a conceptual replication of the basic effect of stereotype threat on standardized test performance. These replications were conducted with two questions in mind. First, to what other groups might these processes apply? As we suggested earlier, stereotype threat is a form of situational threat, that, in theory, could befall the member of any group, so long as the person feels at risk of confirming a negative stereotype. Second, what other ways of manipulating stereotype threat might be sufficient to undermine standardized test performance?

Some answers to these questions have come from recent research conducted by Spencer, Steele, and Quinn (in press) who demonstrated how conceptually similar manipulations to those we just discussed can undermine the performance of women taking difficult tests of their math abilities. In our own research, we wanted to take this a step further—to test the generality of the stereotype threat formulation. Thus, Experiment 3, in this series, examines the verbal GRE performance of Latinos. Rather than manipulating stereotype threat by varying the amount of evaluative scrutiny or the salience of race, we did so by raising the issue of "cultural bias" on standardized tests. We also conducted the study in a group setting designed to approximate the look and feel of an actual standardized test-taking situation.

EXPERIMENT 3

Procedure

We recruited 144 Caucasian and 56 Latino male and female undergraduates from the University of Texas, who participated for course credit. Participants were assigned to one of several testing sessions composed of ethnically diverse groups of at least 20 individuals. Each individual was assigned at random to either a stereotype threat or a no stereotype threat condition. In both conditions, participants were given a test booklet that contained two standard sections of a GRE verbal test, each containing 27 items. As in previous studies, the test was presented as a measure of verbal ability, but we did not tell them they would be evaluated following the test. Placed in between the first and second section of the verbal test was a short questionnaire that asked participants to make a few ratings about the first part of the test—how difficult the problems were, how many items they thought they had solved, and so on. This questionnaire contained the experimental manipulation that distinguished the two conditions. In the stereotype threat condition, we added an additional question which read: "tests like this are sometimes considered to be biased against certain groups (e.g., women, ethnic minorities). How biased do you think tests like these are?" They were asked to rate the degree of bias on a seven-point Likert scale. The questionnaire in the no stereotype threat condition did not include this question. In all other respects, the two conditions were identical.

We hypothesized that by asking students to consider the bias inherent in the test, participants in the stereotype threat condition, like their counterparts in previous studies, would become preoccupied with fulfilling the stereotype, which in turn would undermine their performance on the second half of the test.

Results and Discussion

Our analysis of the number of items solved suggests this indeed happened. To correct for any preexisting differences in preparation, we analyzed their scores on the second half of the test with an ANCOVA, using their scores on the first half as a covariate. As Figure 28.3 shows, raising the issue of test bias had no effect on the performance of the Caucasian participants, but had a significantly negative effect on the Latinos. This finding suggests that Latinos, like African-Americans and women on tests of math, can be significantly hindered by stereotype threat.

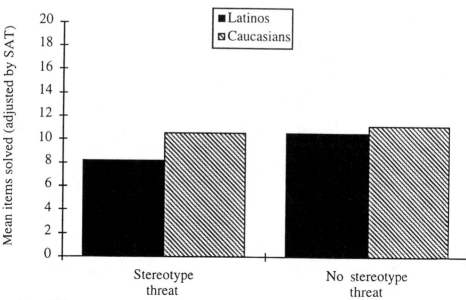

FIGURE 28.3

One obvious question is what mediated this underperformance. Did the bias question make participants more anxious or did it provide them with an easy excuse for not trying? Follow-up studies (see Aronson & Salinas, 1998) suggested that anxiety, not effort withdrawal, was to blame for the lower performance in the stereotype threat condition.

Aside from extending the range of stereotype threat effects to another ethnic group and a new manipulation, this study raises an intriguing possibility regarding beliefs about test bias. Crocker and Major's (1989) research on "attributional ambiguity" demonstrates how minority group members may employ such beliefs about bias as an attempt to protect their feelings of self-worth from the implications of low performance or from negative feedback. Thus, the Crocker and Major analysis shows that the ability to write off standardized tests as biased can protect self-esteem. In a similar vein, our own earlier research found that, under stereotype threat conditions, African Americans tend to inflate their ratings of the degree of bias contained in standardized tests (Steele & Aronson, 1995). What this last experiment adds to the picture is the demonstration that using claims of bias as a defense mechanism is a double-edged sword: Although it protects self-esteem, it simultaneously interferes with performance.

Despite the rather consistent support for the stereotype threat formulation in all these studies, one important theoretical question remains unanswered: to what extent does the experience of stereotype threat depend upon being a member of an actual minority group? In each of the studies, one could conceivably argue that the participants who experienced stereotype threat underperformed because they possessed some trait-like inferiority—the result of a long history of being the target of a stereotype—that was merely brought to the surface by reminding them of the stereotype. Such a hypothesis follows from the "looking-glass-self" view of personality (e.g., Cooley, 1956; Mead, 1934) which suggests that stigmatizing treatment could result in a stigmatized personality. Indeed, this was precisely the view of social scientists whose opinions proved to be pivotal in the 1954 Supreme Court case that ended racial segregation in the schools (*Brown* v. *Board of Education*)—they saw internalized inferiority as a necessary consequence of prejudicial treatment (Allport, 1954; Cook, 1979; Gerard, 1983).

Is there something special about being African-American or Latino, or female that makes these test-takers underperform when confronted with stereotypes about their group? We doubt it. In our view, stereotype threat is a process that people feel when they want to disprove the negative expectations that others may hold about them. Thus, by this definition, virtually anyone could be made to underperform on a difficult intellectual test if they were exposed to a stereotype that predicted underperformance for their group.

We suspect that there is an additional necessary condition for stereotype threat to occur—what we refer to as "domain identification." Domain identification is the degree to which one cares about the ability domain to which the stereotype applies. In order to be threatened by a stereotype alleging low ability, the individual needs to care enough about the ability to want the stereotype not to be true. In each of the studies we have reported thus far, the necessary conditions were presumably met. By dint of their status as African-Americans or Latinos, all of the students were targets of a stereotype alleging low scholastic ability. And because most college students need to have adequate verbal abilities, low performance on a verbal test should be at least somewhat threatening.

To test the hypothesis that anyone in a stereotype threat situation would score lower on a test of their abilities, we conducted an experiment that examined the intellectual test performance of a social group we predicted would be highly unlikely to have internalized stereotype-based feelings of intellectual inferiority—white males selected on the basis of their high mathematical abilities. If these highly skilled majority-group members could be threatened by a stereotype alleging their relative inferiority in math, then it seems reasonable to assume that ingrained feelings of inferiority need not be involved in stereotype threat.

EXPERIMENT 4

Procedure

The participants in this experiment were white male students enrolled in a calculus course at the University of Texas at Austin. Three weeks prior to the experimental session these students filled out a questionnaire during class regarding their math abilities and their math-related attitudes. Using the responses to this questionnaire, we were able to draw two groups of equally able math students who differed only in the degree to which they reported caring about mathematics. Thus, the experiment took the form of a 2 × 2 factorial design. The factors were math identification of the participant (high vs. low) and experimental condition (stereotype threat vs. no stereotype threat).

Both groups were run simultaneously in several group test administrations for which students were given extra credit in their calculus course. All students took the same 15-item test. The problems were drawn from the math subject GRE test practice booklets that pilot testing revealed to be at the upper limit of these students' abilities and were presented as a measure of their math abilities. Stereotype threat was manipulated by introducing the experiment (by written instructions) as an exploration of why Asian students consistently outperformed all other groups on standardized tests of this sort. In the no stereotype threat condition, no mention of the Asian stereotype was made. We predicted that the students would perform worse when exposed to the stereotype, but that this effect would be most pronounced for the students who cared a great deal about their math abilities.

Results and Discussion

The means for the test performance are presented in Figure 28.4. It is clear that stereotype threat interfered with students' performance on the test, but only among those who were identified with their math abilities. Indeed, for those who were less identified, the stereotype threat actually boosted their performance. This pattern of data not only confirmed the prediction that stereotype threat can affect non-minorities, it also provides very clear evidence of the critically important role of domain-identification in mediating the effects of stereotypes on performance. Follow-up data in this experiment strongly suggested that the underperformance was not due to the withdrawal of effort. If anything, participants appeared to be trying too hard.

Apparently, one need not be a minority to be bothered by stereotypes. White males enrolled in a calculus class clearly do not fit the profile of the "target of a stereotype" or "the disadvantaged minority student." They are not normally considered at risk to be stereotyped against, looked down upon because of their race, or targeted by low performance expectations. Indeed, one could argue that, for all intents and purposes, there is no stereotype suggesting that "white men can't do math," at least not in the same way that there is about women and math, about African-Americans and Latinos and intelligence, and so on. That is, if people are asked to list all the stereotypes they are aware of regarding white people, "bad at math" will not make the list (Aronson & Disko, 1998). Nonetheless, when placed in a situation where a negative stereotype about another group's superiority is made relevant, these highly skilled white males appeared to experience much the

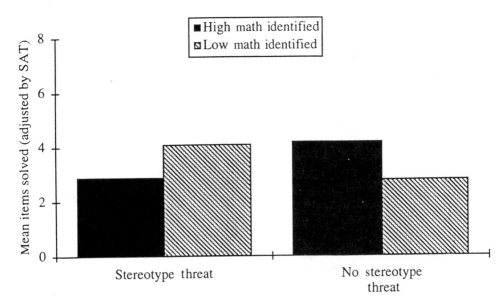

FIGURE 28.4

same psychological predicament as the African-American students, women, Latinos, and the elderly in past stereotype threat experiments—and their test performance suffered as a result.

CONCLUSION AND IMPLICATIONS

In our view, the combined effect of stereotypes and identification should raise some serious questions about the fairness of standardized tests. In most academic situations the relationship between identification and achievement will be linear—the more one cares about doing well, the harder one will study, the more regularly one will attend class, and so on.

But, high stakes tests like the SAT are a different matter because, as our last experiment showed, test takers can be penalized simply for caring too much. We might well question the over-reliance on standardized tests as gateways to higher education, particularly when other measures exist which do not subtract points for possessing the very qualities that predict higher performance once they get there.

The results of these experiments strongly suggest that standardized tests like the SAT, the GRE and the LSAT do not ask all people to "run the same race." Even in the absence of culturally biased items, there appear to be considerable obstacles thrown in the path of groups who are targeted by stereotypes. Perhaps tests are not culturally biased in the sense of containing items that in-and-of-themselves put minority students at a disadvantage. But the testing situation itself may be unfair to those students who are unlucky enough to find themselves targeted by a stereotype.

References

ALLPORT, G. *The nature of prejudice.* New York: Doubleday, 1954.

ARONSON, J., & DISKO, D. Frequency of stereotypes about blacks, whites, Asians and Latinos. Unpublished raw data, University of Texas, Austin, 1998.

ARONSON, J., & SALINAS, M. F. Stereotype threat, attributional ambiguity, and Latino underperformance. Unpublished manuscript, University of Texas, 1998.

ARONSON, J., LUSTINA, M., KEOUGH, K., BROWN, J. L., & STEELE, C. M. Inducing stereotype threat in the non-stereotyped. Manuscript submitted for publication, 1998.

ARONSON, J., QUINN, D., & SPENCER, S. Stereotype threat and the academic underperformance of minorities and women. In J. Swim and C. Stangor (Eds.), *Prejudice: The target's perspective.* San Diego: Academic Press, 1998.

BAUMEISTER, R. F., & SHOWERS, C. J. A review of paradoxical performance effects: Choking under pressure in sports and mental tests. *European Journal of Social Psychology,* 1986, **16**(4), 361–383.

BOND, C. F. Social facilitation: A self-presentation view. *Journal of Personality and Social Psychology,* 1982, **42**, 1042–1050.

CARVER, C. S., & SCHEIER, M. F. *Attention and self-regulation: A control-theory approach to human behavior.* New York: Springer-Verlag, 1981.

COOK, S. W. Social science and school desegregation: Did we mislead the Supreme Court? *Personality & Social Psychology Bulletin,* 1979, **5**(4), 420–437.

COOLEY, C. H. *Human Nature and the Social Order.* New York: Free Press, 1956.

CROCKER, J., & MAJOR, B. Social stigma and self-esteem: The self-protective properties of stigma. *Psychological Review,* 1989, **96**(4), 608–630.

EELLS, K., DAVIS, A., HAVIGHURST, R. J., HERRICK, V. E., & TYLER, R. W. *Intelligence and cultural differences: A study of cultural learning and problem solving.* Chicago: University of Chicago Press, 1952.

GEEN, R. G. Evaluation apprehension and response withholding in solution of anagrams. *Personality and Individual Differences,* 1985, **6**, 293–298.

GERARD, H. School desegregation: The social science role. *American Psychologist,* 1983, **38**, 869–878.

HAFNER, A. L., & WHITE, D. Bias in mental research. *Harvard Educational Review,* 1981, **51**(4), 577–585.

HERRNSTEIN, R. J., & MURRAY, C. *The bell curve. Intelligence and class structure in American life.* New York: Free Press, 1994.

HORMUTH, S. E. Lack of effort as a result of self-focused attention: An attributional ambiguity analysis. *European Journal of Social Psychology,* 1986, **16**, 181–192.

JACOBY J., & GLAUBERMAN, N. *The bell curve debate.* New York: Random House, 1995.

JENSEN, A. R. How much can we boost I.Q. and scholastic achievement? *Harvard Educational Review,* 1969, **39**, 1–123.

JENSEN, A. R. *Bias in mental testing.* New York: Free Press, 1980.

NEISSER, U. New answers to an old question. In U. Neisser (Ed.), *The school achievement of minority children.* Hillsdale: Lawrence Erlbaum, 1986.

NEISSER, U., BOODOO, G., BOUCHAR, T. J., JR., BOYKIN, A. W., & others. Intelligence: Knowns and unknowns. *American Psychologist,* 1996, **51**(2), 77–101.

OWEN, D. *None of the above: Behind the myth of scholastic aptitude.* Boston: Houghton Mifflin, 1985.

SARASON, I. G. Experimental approaches to test anxiety: Attention and the uses of information. In Spielberger, C. D. (Ed.), *Anxiety: Current Trends in Theory and Research, 2.* New York: Academic Press, 1972.

SATTLER, J. M., & GWYNNE, J. White examiners generally do not impede the intelligence test performance of Black children: To debunk a myth. *Journal of Consulting & Clinical Psychology,* 1982, **50**(2), 196–208.

SPENCER, S. J., STEELE, C. M., & QUINN, D. M. The effect of stereotype threat on women's math performance. *Journal of Experimental Social Psychology,* in press.

STEELE, C. M., & ARONSON, J. Stereotype threat and the intellectual test performance of African-Americans. *Journal of Personality & Social Psychology,* 1995, **69**(5), 797–811.

WINE, J. Test anxiety and direction of attention. *Psychological Bulletin,* 1971, **76**, 92–104.

29

Experiments in Group Conflict

Muzafer Sherif

What are the conditions which lead to harmony or friction between groups of people? Here the question is approached by means of controlled situations in a boys' summer camp.

Conflict between groups—whether between boys' gangs, social classes, "races" or nations—has no simple cause, nor is mankind yet in sight of a cure. It is often rooted deep in personal, social, economic, religious and historical forces. Nevertheless, it is possible to identify certain general factors which have a crucial influence on the attitude of any group toward others. Social scientists have long sought to bring these factors to light by studying what might be called the "natural history" of groups and group relations. Intergroup conflict and harmony is not a subject that lends itself easily to laboratory experiments. But in recent years there has been a beginning of attempts to investigate the problem under controlled yet life-like conditions, and I shall report here the results of a program of experimental studies of groups which I started in 1948. Among the persons working with me were Marvin B. Sussman, Robert Huntington, O. J. Harvey, B. Jack White, William R. Hood and Carolyn W. Sherif. The experiments were conducted in 1949, 1953 and 1954; this article gives a composite of the findings.

We wanted to conduct our study with groups of the informal type, where group organization and attitudes would evolve naturally and spontaneously, without formal direction or external pressures. For this purpose we conceived that an isolated summer camp would make a good experimental setting, and that decision led us to choose as subjects boys about eleven or twelve years old, who would find camping natural and fascinating. Since our aim was to study the development of group relations among these boys under carefully controlled conditions, with as little interference as possible from personal neuroses, background influences or prior

Reprinted with permission from the author and *Scientific American,* Vol. 195, No. 5, 1956 (Scientific American Offprint 454).

experiences, we selected normal boys of homogeneous background who did not know one another before they came to the camp.

They were picked by a long and thorough procedure. We interviewed each boy's family, teachers and school officials, studied his school and medical records, obtained his scores on personality tests and observed him in his classes and at play with his schoolmates. With all this information we were able to assure ourselves that the boys chosen were of like kind and background: all were healthy, socially well-adjusted, somewhat above average in intelligence and from stable, white, Protestant, middle-class homes.

None of the boys was aware that he was part of an experiment on group relations. The investigators appeared as a regular camp staff—camp directors, counselors and so on. The boys met one another for the first time in buses that took them to the camp, and so far as they knew it was a normal summer of camping. To keep the situation as lifelike as possible, we conducted all our experiments within the framework of regular camp activities and games. We set up projects which were so interesting and attractive that the boys plunged into them enthusiastically without suspecting that they might be test situations. Unobtrusively we made records of their behavior, even using "candid" cameras and microphones when feasible.

We began by observing how the boys became a coherent group. The first of our camps was conducted in the hills of northern Connecticut in the summer of 1949. When the boys arrived, they were all housed at first in one large bunkhouse. As was to be expected, they quickly formed particular friendships and chose buddies. We had deliberately put all the boys together in this expectation, because we

FIGURE 29.1
Members of one group of boys raid the bunkhouse of another group during the first experiment of the author and his associates, performed at a summer camp in Connecticut. The rivalry of the groups was intensified by the artificial separation of their goals. (Photograph by Muzafer Sherif.)

wanted to see what would happen later after the boys were separated into different groups. Our object was to reduce the factor of personal attraction in the formation of groups. In a few days we divided the boys into two groups and put them in different cabins. Before doing so, we asked each boy informally who his best friends were, and then took pains to place the "best friends" in different groups as far as possible. (The pain of separation was assuaged by allowing each group to go at once on a hike and campout.)

As everyone knows, a group of strangers brought together in some common activity soon acquires an informal and spontaneous kind of organization. It comes to look upon some members as leaders, divides up duties, adopts unwritten norms of behavior, develops an *esprit de corps.* Our boys followed this pattern as they shared a series of experiences. In each group the boys pooled their efforts, organized duties and divided up tasks in work and play. Different individuals assumed different responsibilities. One boy excelled in cooking. Another led in athletics. Others, though not outstanding in any one skill, could be counted on to pitch in and do their level best in anything the group attempted. One or two seemed to disrupt activities, to start teasing at the wrong moment or offer useless suggestions. A few boys consistently had good suggestions and showed ability to coordinate the efforts of others in carrying them through. Within a few days one person had proved himself more resourceful and skillful than the rest. Thus, rather quickly, a leader and lieutenants emerged. Some boys sifted toward the bottom of the heap, while others jockeyed for higher positions.

We watched these developments closely and rated the boys' relative positions in the group, not only on the basis of our own observations but also by informal sounding of the boys' opinions as to who got things started, who got things done, who could be counted on to support group activities.

As the group became an organization, the boys coined nicknames. The big, blond, hardy leader of one group was dubbed "Baby Face" by his admiring followers. A boy with a rather long head became "Lemon Head." Each group developed its own jargon, special jokes, secrets and special ways of performing tasks. One group, after killing a snake near a place where it had gone to swim, named the place "Moccasin Creek" and thereafter preferred this swimming hole to any other, though there were better ones nearby.

Wayward members who failed to do things "right" or who did not contribute their bit to the common effort found themselves receiving the "silent treatment," ridicule or even threats. Each group selected symbols and a name, and they had these put on their caps and T-shirts. The 1954 camp was conducted in Oklahoma, near a famous hideaway of Jesse James called Robber's Cave. The two groups of boys at this camp named themselves the Rattlers and the Eagles.

Our conclusions on every phase of the study were based on a variety of observations, rather than on any single method. For example, we devised a game to test the boys' evaluations of one another. Before an important baseball game, we set up a target board for the boys to throw at, on the pretense of making practice for the game more interesting. There were no marks on the front of the board for the boys to judge objectively how close the ball came to a bull's-eye, but, unknown to them, the board was wired to flashing lights behind so that an observer could see exactly where the ball hit. We found that the boys consistently overestimated the performances by the most highly regarded members of their group and underestimated the scores of those of low social standing.

The attitudes of group members were even more dramatically illustrated during a cook-out in the woods. The staff supplied the boys with unprepared food and let them cook it themselves. One boy promptly started to build a fire, asking for help in getting wood. Another attacked the raw hamburger to make patties. Others prepared a place to put buns, relishes and the like. Two mixed soft drinks from flavoring and sugar. One boy who stood around without helping was told by others to "get to it." Shortly the fire was blazing and the cook had hamburgers sizzling. Two boys distributed them as rapidly as they became edible. Soon it was time for the watermelon. A low-ranking member of the group took a knife and started toward the melon. Some of the boys protested. The most highly regarded boy in the group took over the knife, saying, "You guys who yell the loudest get yours last."

When the two groups in the camp had developed group organization and spirit, we proceeded to the experimental studies of intergroup relations. The groups had had no previous encounters; indeed, in the 1954 camp at Robber's Cave the two groups came in separate buses and were kept apart while each acquired a group feeling.

Our working hypothesis was that when two groups have conflicting aims—i.e., when one can achieve its ends only at the expense of the other—their members will become hostile to each other even though the groups are composed of normal well-adjusted individuals. There is a corollary to this assumption which we shall consider later. To produce friction between the groups of boys we arranged a tournament of games: baseball, touch football, a tug-of-war, a treasure hunt and so on. The tournament started in a spirit of good sportsmanship. But as it progressed good feeling soon evaporated. The members of each group began to call their rivals "stinkers," "sneaks" and "cheaters." They refused to have anything more to do with individuals in the opposing group. The boys in the 1949 camp turned against buddies whom they had chosen as "best friends" when they first arrived at the camp. A large proportion of the boys in each group gave negative ratings to all the boys in the other. The rival groups made threatening posters and planned raids, collecting secret hoards of green apples for ammunition. In the Robber's Cave camp the Eagles, after a defeat in a tournament game, burned a banner left behind by the

FIGURE 29.2
Members of both groups collaborate in common enterprises during the second experiment, performed at a summer camp in Oklahoma. At the top, the boys of the two groups prepare a meal. In the middle, the two groups surround a water tank while trying to solve a water-shortage problem. At the bottom, the members of one group entertain the other. (Photographs by Muzafer Sherif.)

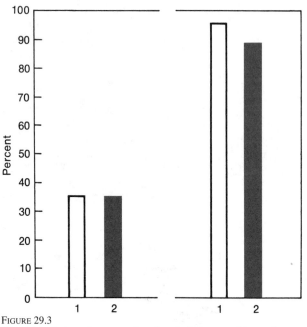

FIGURE 29.3
Friendship choices of campers for others in their own cabin are shown for Red Devils *(white)* and Bulldogs. *(gray)*. At first, a low percentage of friendships were in the cabin group *(left)*. After five days, most friendship choices were within the group *(right)*.

Rattlers; the next morning the Rattlers seized the Eagles' flag when they arrived on the athletic field. From that time on name-calling scuffles and raids were the rule of the day.

Within each group, of course, solidarity increased. There were changes: one group deposed its leader because he could not "take it" in the contests with the adversary; another group overnight made something of a hero of a big boy who had previously been regarded as a bully. But morale and cooperativeness within the group became stronger. It is noteworthy that this heightening of cooperativeness and generally democratic behavior did not carry over to the group's relations with other groups.

We now turned to the other side of the problem: How can two groups in conflict be brought into harmony? We first undertook to test the theory that pleasant social contacts between members of conflicting groups will reduce friction between them. In the 1954 camp we brought the hostile Rattlers and Eagles together for social events: going to the movies, eating in the same dining room and so on, But far from reducing conflict, these situations only served as opportunities for the rival groups to berate and attack each other. In the dining-hall line they shoved each other aside, and the group that lost the contest for the head of the line shouted "Ladies first!" at the winner. They threw paper, food and vile names at each other at the tables. An Eagle bumped by a Rattler was admonished by his fellow Eagles to brush "the dirt" off his clothes.

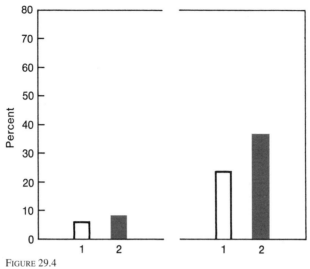

FIGURE 29.4

During conflict between the two groups in the Robber's Cave experiment, there were few friendships between cabins *(left)*. After cooperation toward common goals had restored good feelings, the number of friendships between groups rose significantly *(right)*.

We then returned to the corollary of our assumption about the creation of conflict. Just as competition generates friction, working in a common endeavor should promote harmony. It seemed to us, considering group relations in the everyday world, that where harmony between groups is established, the most decisive factor is the existence of "superordinate" goals which have a compelling appeal for both but which neither could achieve without the other. To test this hypothesis experimentally, we created a series of urgent, and natural, situations which challenged our boys.

One was a breakdown in the water supply. Water came to our camp in pipes from a tank about a mile away. We arranged to interrupt it and then called the boys together to inform them of the crisis. Both groups promptly volunteered to search the water line for the trouble. They worked together harmoniously, and before the end of the afternoon they had located and corrected the difficulty.

A similar opportunity offered itself when the boys requested a movie. We told them that the camp could not afford to rent one. The two groups then got together, figured out how much each group would have to contribute, chose the film by a vote and enjoyed the showing together.

One day the two groups went on an outing at a lake some distance away. A large truck was to go to town for food. But when everyone was hungry and ready to eat, it developed that the truck would not start (we had taken care of that). The boys got a rope—the same rope they had used in their acrimonious tug-of-war—and all pulled together to start the truck.

These joint efforts did not immediately dispel hostility. At first the groups returned to the old bickering and name-calling as soon as the job in hand was

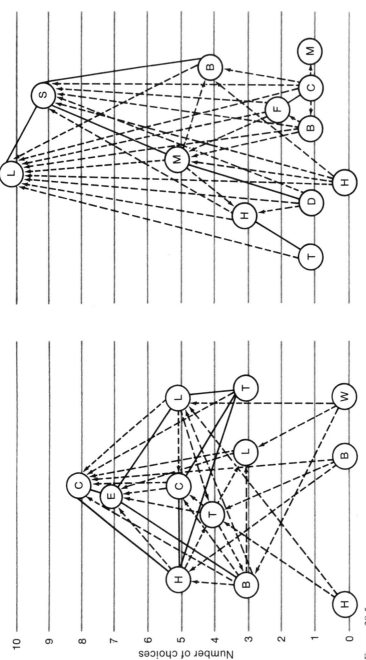

FIGURE 29.5
Sociograms represent patterns of friendship choice within the fully developed groups. One-way friendships are indicated by broken arrows; reciprocated friendships, by solid lines. Leaders were among those highest in the popularity scale. Bulldogs (*left*) had a close-knit organization with good group spirit. Low-ranking members participated less in the life of the group but were not rejected. Red Devils (*right*) lost the tournament of games between the groups. They had less group unity and were sharply stratified.

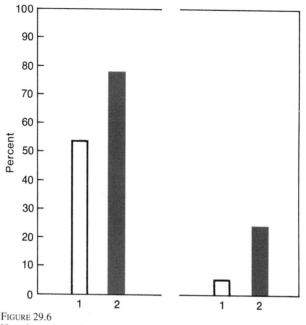

FIGURE 29.6
Negative ratings of each group by the other were common during the period of conflict *(left)* but decreased when harmony was restored *(right)*. The graphs show percentage who thought *all* (rather than *some* or *none*) of the other group were cheaters, sneaks, and so forth.

finished. But gradually the series of cooperative acts reduced friction and conflict. The members of the two groups began to feel more friendly to each other. For example, a Rattler whom the Eagles disliked for his sharp tongue and skill in defeating them became a "good egg." The boys stopped shoving in the meal line. They no longer called each other names, and sat together at the table. New friendships developed between individuals in the two groups.

In the end the groups were actively seeking opportunities to mingle, to entertain and "treat" each other. They decided to hold a joint campfire. They took turns presenting skits and songs. Members of both groups requested that they go home together on the same bus, rather than on the separate buses in which they had come. On the way the bus stopped for refreshments. One group still had five dollars which they had won as a prize in a contest. They decided to spend this sum on refreshments. On their own initiative they invited their former rivals to be their guests for malted milks.

Our interviews with the boys confirmed this change. From choosing their "best friends" almost exclusively in their own group, many of them shifted to listing boys in the other group as best friends (see Fig. 29.4). They were glad to have a second chance to rate boys in the other group, some of them remarking that they had changed their minds since the first rating made after the tournament. Indeed they had. The new ratings were largely favorable (see Fig. 29.6).

Efforts to reduce friction and prejudice between groups in our society have usually followed rather different methods. Much attention has been given to bringing members of hostile groups together socially, to communicating accurate and favorable information about one group to the other, and to bringing the leaders of groups together to enlist their influence. But as everyone knows, such measures sometimes reduce intergroup tensions and sometimes do not. Social contacts, as our experiments demonstrated, may only serve as occasions for intensifying conflict. Favorable information about a disliked group may be ignored or reinterpreted to fit stereotyped notions about the group. Leaders cannot act without regard for the prevailing temper in their own groups.

What our limited experiments have shown is that the possibilities for achieving harmony are greatly enhanced when groups are brought together to work toward common ends. Then favorable information about a disliked group is seen in a new light, and leaders are in a position to take bolder steps toward cooperation. In short, hostility gives way when groups pull together to achieve overriding goals which are real and compelling to all concerned.

Reference

SHERIF, MUZAFER, AND SHERIF, CAROLYN W. *Groups in harmony and tension.* Harper & Brothers, 1953.

30

Jigsaw Groups and the Desegregated Classroom: In Pursuit of Common Goals

Elliot Aronson and Diane Bridgeman

The desegregated classroom has not produced many of the positive results initially expected by social scientists some 25 years ago. It is argued that one of the major reasons for this failure is the overemphasis on competitiveness at the expense of interdependence in the classroom. In short, students in most classrooms very rarely cooperate with each other in pursuit of common goals. In this article, we describe a program of research in which elementary school students are "forced" to spend part of their classroom time mastering material in an interdependent structure. The results indicate that such structured interdependence increases the self-esteem, the morale, the interpersonal attraction, and the empathy of students across ethnic and racial divisions, and also improves the academic performance of minority students without hampering the performance of the ethnic majority.

There were high hopes when the Supreme Court outlawed school segregation a quarter of a century ago. If black and white children could share classrooms and become friends, it was thought that perhaps they could develop relatively free of racial prejudice and some of the problems that accompany prejudice. The case that brought about the court's landmark decision was that of *Brown v. Board of Education;* the decision reversed the 1896 ruling *(Plessy v. Ferguson)* that held that it was permissible to segregate racially, as long as equal facilities were provided for both races. In the *Brown* case, the court held that psychologically there could be no such thing as "separate but equal." The mere fact of separation implied to the minority group in question that its members were inferior to those of the majority.

The Brown decision was not only a humane interpretation of the Constitution, it was also the beginning of a profound and exciting social experiment. As Stephan

---

Reprinted with permission of the authors and Division 8 of the American Psychological Association and of Sage Publications, Inc., from *Personality and Social Psychology Bulletin,* Vol. 5, No. 4, 1979, pp. 438–466.

(1978) has recently pointed out, the testimony of social psychologists in the *Brown* case, as well as in previous similar cases in state supreme courts, suggested strongly that desegregation would not only reduce prejudice but also increase the self-esteem of minority groups and improve their academic performance. Of course the social psychologists who testified never meant to imply that such benefits would accrue automatically. Certain preconditions would have to be met. These preconditions were most articulately stated by Allport in his classic, *The Nature of Prejudice,* published the same year as the Supreme Court decision:

> Prejudice . . . may be reduced by equal status contact between majority and minority groups in the pursuit of common goals. The effect is greatly enhanced if this contact is sanctioned by institutional supports (i.e., by law, custom or local atmosphere), and provided it is of a sort that leads to the perception of common interests and common humanity between members of the two groups [Allport, 1954, p. 281].

THE EFFECTS OF DESEGREGATION

A quarter of a century after desegregation was begun, an assessment of its effectiveness is not encouraging. One of the most careful and thoroughgoing longitudinal studies of desegregation was the Riverside project conducted by Gerard and Miller (1975). They found that long after the schools were desegregated, black, white, and Mexican-American children tended not to integrate but to hang together in their own ethnic clusters. Moreover, anxiety increased and remained high long after desegregation occurred. These trends are echoed in several other studies. Indeed, the most careful, scholarly reviews of the research show few if any benefits (see St. John, 1975; Stephan, 1978). For example, according to Stephan's review, there is no single study that shows a significant increase in the self-esteem of minority children following desegregation; in fact, in fully 25 percent of the studies, desegregation is followed by a significant decrease in the self-esteem of young minority children. Moreover, Stephan reports that desegregation reduced the prejudice of whites toward blacks in only 13 percent of the school systems studied. The prejudice of blacks toward whites *increased* in about as many cases as it decreased. Similarly, studies of the effects of desegregation on the academic performance of minority children present a mixed and highly variable picture.

What went wrong? Let us return to Allport's prediction: Equal status contact in pursuit of common goals, sanctioned by authority, will produce beneficial effects. We will look at each of these three factors separately.

Sanction by Authority

In some school districts there was clear acceptance and enforcement of the ruling by responsible authority. In others the acceptance was not as clear. In still others (especially in the early years) local authorities were in open defiance of the law. Pettigrew (1961) has shown that desegregation proceeded more smoothly and with less violence in those localities where local authorities sanctioned integration. But such variables as self-esteem and the reduction of prejudice do not necessarily change for the better even where authority clearly sanctions desegregation. While sanction by authority may be necessary, it is clearly not a sufficient condition.

Equal Status Contact

The definition of equal status is a trifle slippery. In the case of school desegregation, we would claim that there is equal status on the grounds that all children in the fifth grade (for example) have the same "occupational" status; that is, they are all fifth grade students. On the other hand, if the teacher is prejudiced against blacks, he may treat them less fairly than he treats whites, thus lowering their perceived status in the classroom (see Gerard and Miller, 1975). Moreover, if, because of an inferior education (prior to desegregation) or because of language difficulties, black or Mexican-American students perform poorly in the classroom, this could also lower their status among their peers. An interesting complication was introduced by Cohen (1972). While Allport (1954) predicted that positive interactions will result if cooperative equal status is achieved, expectation theory, as developed by Cohen, holds that even in such an environment biased expectations by both whites and blacks may lead to sustained white dominance. Cohen reasoned that both of these groups accepted the premise that the majority group's competence results in dominance and superior achievement. She suggested that alternatives be created to reverse these often unconscious expectations. According to Cohen, at least a temporary exchange of majority and minority roles is therefore required as a prelude to equal status. In one study (Cohen and Roper, 1972), black children were instructed in building radios and in how to teach this skill to others. Then a group of white children and the newly trained black children viewed a film of themselves building the radios. This was followed by some of the black children teaching the whites how to construct radios while others taught a black administrator. Then all the children came together in small groups. Equal status interactions were found in the groups where black children had taught whites how to construct the radios. The other group, however, demonstrated the usual white dominance. We will return to this point in a moment.

In Pursuit of Common Goals

In the typical American classroom, children are almost never engaged in the pursuit of common goals. During the past several years, we and our colleagues have systematically observed scores of elementary school classrooms and have found that, in the vast majority of these cases, the process of education is highly competitive. Children vie with one another for good grades and the respect of the teacher. This occurs not only during the quizzes and exams but also in the informal give and take of the classroom, where children typically learn to raise their hands (often frantically) in response to questions from the teacher, groan when someone else is called upon, and revel in the failure of their classmates. This pervasive competitive atmosphere unwittingly leads the children to view one another as foes to be heckled and vanquished. In a newly desegregated school, all other things being equal, this atmosphere could exacerbate whatever prejudice existed prior to desegregation.

A dramatic example of dysfunctional competition was demonstrated by Sherif et al. (1961) in the classic "Robber's Cave" experiment. In this field experiment, the investigators encouraged intergroup competition between two teams of boys at a summer camp; this created fertile ground for anger and hostility even in previously benign, noncompetitive circumstances—like watching a movie. Positive relations between the groups were ultimately achieved only after both groups were required to work cooperatively to solve a common problem.

It is our contention that the competitive process interacts with "equal status contact." That is to say, whatever differences in ability that existed between minority children and white children prior to desegregation are emphasized by the competitive structure of the learning environment; furthermore, since segregated school facilities are rarely equal, minority children frequently enter the newly desegregated school at a distinct disadvantage, which is made more salient by the competitive atmosphere.

It was this reasoning that led Aronson and his colleagues (1975, 1978a) to develop the hypothesis that interdependent learning environments would establish the conditions necessary for the increase in self-esteem and performance and the decrease in prejudice that were expected to occur as a function of desegregation. Toward this end they developed a highly structured method of interdependent learning and systematically tested its effects in a number of elementary school classrooms. The aim of this research program was not merely to compare the effects of cooperation and competition in a classroom setting. This had been ably demonstrated by other investigators dating as early as Deutsch's (1949) experiment. Rather, the intent was to devise a cooperative classroom structure that could be utilized easily by classroom teachers on a long-term sustained basis and to evaluate the effects of this intervention via a well-controlled series of field experiments. In short, this project is an action research program aimed at developing and evaluating a classroom atmosphere that can be sustained by the classroom teachers long after the researchers have packed up their questionnaires and returned to the more cozy environment of the social psychological laboratory.

The method is described in detail elsewhere (Aronson et al., 1978a). Briefly, students are placed in six-person learning groups. The day's lesson is divided into six paragraphs such that each student has one segment of the written material.[1] Each student has a unique and vital part of the information, which, like the pieces of a jigsaw puzzle, must be put together before any of the students can learn the whole picture. The individual must learn his own section and teach it to the other members of the group. The reader will note that in this method each child spends part of her time in the role of expert. Thus, the method incorporates Cohen's findings (previously discussed) within the context of an equal status contact situation.

Working with this "jigsaw" technique, children gradually learn that the old competitive behavior is no longer appropriate. Rather, in order to learn all of the material (and thus perform well on a quiz), each child must begin to listen to the others, ask appropriate questions, and in other ways contribute to the group. The process makes it possible for children to pay attention to one another and begin to appreciate each other as potentially valuable resources. It is important to emphasize that the motivation of the students is not necessarily altruistic; rather, it is primarily self-interest, which, in this case, happens also to produce outcomes that are beneficial to others.

EXPERIMENTS IN THE CLASSROOM

Systematic research in the classroom has produced consistently positive results. The first experiment to investigate the effects of the jigsaw technique was conducted by Blaney et al. (1977). The schools in Austin, Texas, had recently been desegregated, producing a great deal of tension and even some interracial skirmishes throughout the school system. In this tense atmosphere, the jigsaw technique was introduced in 10 fifth grade classrooms in seven elementary schools. Three classes from among the same schools were also used as controls. The control classes were taught by teachers who, while using traditional techniques, were rated very highly by their peers. The experimental classes met in jigsaw groups for about forty-five minutes a day, three days a week for six weeks. The curriculum was basically the same for the experimental and control classes. Students in the jigsaw groups showed significant increases in their liking for their groupmates both within and across ethnic boundaries. Moreover, children in jigsaw groups showed a significantly greater increase in self-esteem than children in the control classrooms. This was true for Anglo children as well as for ethnic minorities. Anglos and blacks showed greater liking for school when taught in the jigsaw classrooms than when studying in traditional classrooms. (The Mexican-American students showed a tendency to like school *less* in the jigsaw classes; this will be discussed shortly.)

These results were essentially replicated by Geffner (1978) in Watsonville, California—a community consisting of approximately 50 percent Anglos and 50 percent Mexican-Americans. As a control for the possibility of a Hawthorne effect,

---

[1]The method works best with discrete, continuous written material (like social studies), but it has been successfully utilized with mathematics and language arts as well.

Geffner compared the behavior of children in classrooms using the jigsaw and other cooperative learning techniques with that of children in highly innovative (but not interdependent) classroom environments as well as with traditional classrooms. Geffner found consistent and significant gains within classrooms using jigsaw and other cooperative learning techniques. Specifically, children in these classes showed increases in self-esteem as well as increases in liking for school. Negative ethnic stereotypes were also diminished. That is, children increased their positive general attitudes toward their own ethnic group as well as toward members of other ethnic groups to a far greater extent than did children in traditional and innovative classrooms.

Changes in academic performance were assessed in an experiment by Lucker, et al. (1977). The subjects were 303 fifth and sixth grade students from five elementary schools in Austin, Texas. Six classrooms were taught in the jigsaw manner, while five classrooms were taught traditionally by competent teachers. For two weeks children were taught a unit on colonial America taken from a fifth grade textbook. All children were then given the same standardized test. The results showed that Anglo students performed just as well in jigsaw classes as they did in traditional classes ($\overline{X}$ = 66.6 and 67.3 respectively); minority children performed significantly better in jigsaw classes than in traditional classes ($\overline{X}$ = 56.6 and 49.7 respectively).[2] The difference for minority students was highly significant. Only two weeks of jigsaw activity succeeded in narrowing the performance gap between Anglos and minorities from more than 17 percentage points to about 10 percentage points. Interestingly enough, the jigsaw method apparently does *not* work a special hardship on high ability students: Students in the highest quartile in reading ability benefited just as much as students in the lowest quartile.

UNDERLYING MECHANISMS

Increased Participation

We have seen that learning in a small interdependent group leads to greater interpersonal attraction, self-esteem and liking for school, more positive inter-ethnic and intra-ethnic perceptions, and, for ethnic minorities, an improvement in academic performance. We think that some of our findings are due to more active involvement in the learning process under conditions of reduced anxiety. In jigsaw, children are required to participate. This increase in participation should enhance interest, which would result in an improvement in performance as well as an increased liking for school—all other things being equal. But all other things are sometimes not equal. For example, in the study by Blaney et al. (1977), there was some indication from our observation of the groups that many of the Mexican-

---

[2]The mean scores have been converted to percentage of correct answers.

American children were experiencing some anxiety as a result of being required to participate more actively. This seemed to be due to the fact that these children had difficulty with the English language, which produced some embarrassment in working with a group dominated by Anglos. In a traditional classroom, it is relatively easy to "become invisible" by remaining quiet and refusing to volunteer. Not so in jigsaw. This observation was confirmed by the data on liking for school. Blaney et al. found that Anglos and blacks in jigsaw classrooms liked school better than those in the traditional classrooms, while for Mexican-Americans the reverse was true. This anxiety could be reduced if Mexican-American children were in a situation in which it was not embarrassing to be more articulate in Spanish than in English. Thus, Geffner (1978), working in a situation in which both the residential and school population was approximately 50 percent Spanish-speaking, found that Mexican-American children (like Anglos and blacks) increased their liking for school to a greater extent in the cooperative groups than in traditional classrooms.

Increases in Empathic Role-taking

Only a small subset of our results is attributable to increases in active participation in and of itself. We believe that people working together in an interdependent fashion increase their ability to take one another's perspective. For example, suppose that Jane and Carlos are in a jigsaw group. Carlos is reporting and Jane is having difficulty following him. She doesn't quite understand because his style of presentation is different from what she is accustomed to. Not only must she pay close attention, but, in addition, she must find a way to ask questions that Carlos will understand and that will elicit the additional information she needs. In order to accomplish this, she must get to know Carlos, put herself in his shoes, empathize.

Bridgeman (1977) tested this notion. She reasoned that taking one another's perspective is required and practiced in jigsaw learning. Accordingly, the more experience students have with the jigsaw process, the greater will their role-taking abilities become. In her experiment, Bridgeman administered a revised version of Chandler's (1973) role-taking cartoon series to 120 fifth grade students. Roughly half of the students spent eight weeks in a jigsaw learning environment while the others were taught in either traditional or innovative small group classrooms. Each of the cartoons in the Chandler test depicts a central character caught up in a chain of psychological cause and effect, such that the character's subsequent behavior is shaped by and fully comprehensible only in terms of the preceding events. In one of the sequences, for example, a boy who has been saddened by seeing his father off at the airport begins to cry when he later receives a gift of a toy airplane similar to the one that had carried his father away. Midway into each sequence, a second character is introduced in the role of a late-arriving bystander who witnesses the resultant behaviors of the principal character but is not privy to the causal events. Thus, the subject is in a privileged position relative to the story character, whose role the subject is later asked to assume. The cartoon series measures the degree to which the subject is able to set aside facts known only to him or herself and adopt a perspective measurably different from his or her own. For example, while the subject knows why the child in the above sequence cries when he receives the toy airplane, the mailman who delivered the toy is not privy to this knowledge. What happens when the subject is asked to take the mailman's perspective?

After eight weeks, students in the jigsaw classrooms were better able to put themselves in the bystander's place than students in the control classrooms. For example, when the mailman delivered the toy airplane to the little boy, students in the control classrooms tended to assume that the mailman knew the boy would cry; that is, they behaved as if they believed that the mailman knew that the boy's father had recently left town on an airplane—simply because they (the subjects) had this information. On the other hand, students who had participated in a jigsaw group were much more successful at taking the mailman's role—realizing that he could not possibly understand why the boy would cry upon receiving a toy airplane.

Attributions for Success and Failure

Working together in the pursuit of common goals changes the "observer's" attributional patterns. There is some evidence to support the notion that cooperation increases the tendency for individuals to make the same kind of attributions for success and failure to their partners as they do to themselves. In an experiment by Stephan et al. (1978), it was found (as it has been in several experiments by others) that when an individual succeeds at a task, he tends to attribute his success dispositionally (e.g., skill), but when he fails he tends to make a situational attribution (e.g., luck). Stephan et al. went on to demonstrate that individuals engaged in an *interdependent* task make the same kinds of attributions to their partner's performance as they do to their own. This was not the case in competitive interactions.

Effects of Dependent Variables on One Another

It is reasonable to assume that the various consequences of interdependent learning become antecedents for one another. Just as low self-esteem can work to inhibit a child from performing well, anything that increases self-esteem is likely to produce an increase in performance among underachievers. Conversely, as Franks and Marolla (1976) have indicated, increases in performance should bring about increases in self-esteem. Similarly, being treated with increased attention and respect by one's peers (as almost inevitably happens in jigsaw groups) is another important antecedent of self-esteem, according to Franks and Marolla. There is ample evidence for a two-way causal connection between performance and self-esteem (see Covington and Beery, 1976; Purkey, 1970).

OTHER COOPERATIVE TECHNIQUES

In recent years a few research teams utilizing rather different techniques for structuring cooperative behavior have produced an array of data consistent with those resulting from the jigsaw technique. For example, Cook and his colleagues (1978) have shown that interracial cooperative groups in the laboratory underwent a significant improvement in attitudes about people of other races. In subsequent field experiments, Cook and his colleagues found that interdependent groups produced more improved attitudes toward members of previously disliked racial groups than was present in noninterdependent groups. It should be noted, however, that no evidence for generalization was found; that is, the positive change was limited to the specific members of the interdependent group and did not extend to the racial group as a whole.

Johnson and Johnson (1975) have developed the "Learning Together" model, which is a general and varied approach to interdependent classroom learning. Basically, Johnson and Johnson have found evidence for greater cross-ethnic friendship ratings, greater self-esteem, and higher motivation in their cooperative groups than in control conditions. They have also found increases in academic performance.

In a different vein, Slavin (1978) and DeVries, Edwards, and Slavin (1978) have developed two highly structured techniques that combine within-group cooperation with across-group competition. These techniques, "Teams Games and Tournaments" (TGT) and "Student Teams Achievement Divisions" (STAD), have consistently produced beneficial results in lower class, multi-racial classrooms. Basically, in TGT and STAD, children form heterogeneous five-person teams; each member of a team is given a reasonably good opportunity to do well by dint of the fact that she competes against a member of a different team with similar skills to her own. Her individual performance contributes to her team's score. The results are in the same ball park as jigsaw: Children participating in TGT and STAD groups show a greater increase in sociometric, cross-racial friendship choices and more observed cross-racial interactions than control conditions. They also show more satisfaction with school than the controls do. Similarly, TGT and STAD produce greater learning effectiveness among racial minorities than do the control groups.

It is interesting to note that the basic results of TGT and STAD are similar to those of the jigsaw technique in spite of one major difference in procedure: While the jigsaw technique makes an overt attempt to minimize competition, TGT and STAD actually promote competitiveness and utilize it across teams—within the context of intrateam cooperation. We believe that this difference is more apparent than real. In most classrooms where jigsaw has been utilized, the students are in jigsaw groups for less than two hours per day. The rest of the class time is spent in a myriad of process activities, many of which are competitive in nature. Thus, what seems important in both techniques is that *some* specific time is structured around cooperativeness. Whether the beneficial results are produced *in spite* of a surrounding atmosphere of competitiveness or *because* of it is the task of future research to determine.

CONCLUSIONS

We are not suggesting that jigsaw learning or any other cooperative method constitutes the solution to our interethnic problems. What we have shown is that beneficial effects occur as a result of structuring the social psychological aspects of classroom learning so that children spend at least a portion of their time in pursuit of common goals. These effects are in accordance with predictions made by social scientists in their testimony favoring desegregating schools some 25 years ago. It is important to emphasize the fact that the jigsaw method has proved effective even if it is employed for as little as 20 percent of a child's time in the classroom. Moreover, other techniques have produced beneficial results even when interdependent learning was purposely accompanied by competitive activities. Thus, the data do not indicate the desirability of either placing a serious limit on classroom competition or interfering with individually guided education. Interdependent learning can and does coexist easily with almost any other method used by teachers in the classroom.

References

ARONSON, E., STEPHEN, C., SIKES, J., BLANEY, N., AND SNAPP, M. *The Jigsaw Classroom.* Beverly Hills: Sage Publications, 1978. (a)

ARONSON, E., BRIDGEMAN, D. L., AND GEFFNER, R. The effects of a cooperative classroom structure on students' behavior and attitudes. In D. Bar-Tal and L. Saxe (eds.), *Social Psychology of Education: Theory and Research.* Washington, D.C.: Hemisphere, 1978. (b)

BLANEY, N. T., STEPHAN, C., ROSENFIELD, D., ARONSON, E., AND SIKES, J. Interdependence in the classroom: A field study. *Journal of Educational Psychology,* 1977, **69,** 139–146.

BRIDGEMAN, D. L. Enhanced role taking through cooperative interdependence: A field study. *Child Development,* 1981, **52,** 1231–1238.

CHANDLER, M. J. Egocentrism and antisocial behavior: The assessment and training of social perspective-taking skills. *Developmental Psychology,* 1973, **9,** 326–332.

COHEN, E. Interracial interaction disability. *Human Relations,* 1972, **25**(1), 9–24.

COHEN, E., AND ROPER, S. Modification of interracial interaction disability: An application of status characteristics theory. *American Sociological Review,* 1972, **6,** 643–657.

COOK, S. W. Interpersonal and attitudinal outcomes in cooperating interracial groups. *Journal of Research and Development in Education,* 1978.

COVINGTON, M. V., AND BEERY, R. G. *Self-Worth and School Learning.* New York: Holt, Rinehart & Winston, 1976.

DEUTCSH, M. An experimental study of the effects of cooperation and competition upon group process. *Human Relations,* 1949, **2,** 199–231.

DeVries, D. L., Edwards, K. J., and Slavin, R. E. Bi-racial learning teams and race relations in the classroom: Four field experiments on Teams–Games–Tournament. *Journal of Educational Psychology,* 1978.

Franks, D. D., and Marolla, J. Efficacious action and social approval as interacting dimensions of self-esteem: A tentative formulation through construct validation. *Sociometry,* 1976, **39,** 324–341.

Geffner, R. A. The effects of interdependent learning on self-esteem, inter-ethnic relations, and intra-ethnic attitudes of elementary school children: A field experiment. Unpublished Doctoral Thesis, University of California, Santa Cruz, 1978.

Gerard, H., and Miller, N. *School Desegregation.* New York: Plenum, 1975.

Johnson, D. W., and Johnson, R. T. *Learning Together and Alone.* Englewood Cliffs, N.J.: Prentice-Hall, 1975.

Lucker, G. W., Rosenfield, D., Sikes, J., and Aronson, E. Performance in the interdependent classroom: A field study. *American Educational Research Journal,* 1977, **13,** 115–123.

Pettigrew, T. Social psychology and desegregation research. *American Psychologist,* 1961, **15,** 61–71.

Purkey, W. W. *Self-Concept and School Achievement.* Englewood Cliffs, N.J.: Prentice-Hall, 1970.

Sherif, M., Harvey, O. J., White, J., Hood, W., and Sherif, C. *Intergroup Conflict and Cooperation: The Robber's Cave Experiment.* Norman, Okla.: University of Oklahoma Institute of Intergroup Relations, 1961.

Slavin, R. E. Student teams and achievement divisions. *Journal of Research and Development in Education,* 1978.

Stephan, C., Presser, N. R., Kennedy, J. C., and Aronson, E. Attributions to success and failure in cooperative, competitive and interdependent interactions. *European Journal of Social Psychology,* 1978, **8,** 269–274.

Stephan, W. G. School desegregation: An evaluation of predictions made in *Brown v. Board of Education. Psychological Bulletin,* 1978, **85,** 217–238.

St. John, N. *School Desegregation: Outcomes for Children.* New York: John Wiley and Sons, 1975.

31

Branch Rickey, Jackie Robinson, and the Social Psychology of Affirmative Action

Anthony R. Pratkanis and Marlene E. Turner

April 10, 1947, was a remarkable day in the history of management. The setting was old Ebbets Field in Brooklyn, N.Y. More than 14,000 baseball fans were on hand to see the Brooklyn Dodgers play their top minor-league ballclub, the Montreal Royals, in one of the preseason's last exhibition games.

At the top of the sixth inning, Dodger announcer Red Barber read the following statement from Dodger President Branch Rickey for fans listening on the radio: "The Brooklyn Dodgers today purchased the contract of Jackie Roosevelt Robinson from the Montreal Royals. He will report immediately." Five days later Robinson donned uniform No. 42 to become the first black American since 1887 to play baseball in the all-white major leagues.

When Rickey hired Robinson, he inaugurated history's first affirmative-action program.

By affirmative action, we mean the proactive removal of discriminatory barriers and the promotion of institutions leading to integration of in- and out-groups. This definition may strike some as odd; in common parlance, affirmative action has come to mean a "quota" system. This confuses one possible tactic (among many) with what should be an overall objective of integration.

From *Across the Board,* July/August, 1994, pp. 42–47. Reprinted by permission of the authors and The Conference Board. First published under the title *Mr. Rickey Has His Way.*

What is most remarkable about Rickey's effort is its sweeping success. He changed the face of baseball and turned his team into a winning and profitable franchise. For more than 40 years, social psychologists have studied how best to implement desegregation plans, and Rickey's desegregation of the Dodgers remains the best illustration of those principles, which still can be used to improve the effectiveness of affirmative-action programs.

THE PSYCHOLOGY OF INEVITABLE CHANGE

One factor that increases the likelihood of successful integration is the feeling that change is inevitable—that the out-group member (in this case, black Americans) will be joining the in-group members (white major-leaguers) in the very near future, and nothing can be done to prevent it. The psychology of the inevitable works because it forces the prejudiced individual to bring his attitudes in line with the new reality. By contrast, when leaders oppose or give only halfhearted support to affirmative action, opposition is encouraged.

How did Rickey use the psychology of the inevitable? During 1947 spring training, Dodger Manager Leo Durocher found out that some Dodger players—Dixie Walker, Eddie Stanky, Kirby Higbe, and Bobby Bragan—were drawing up a petition to warn that they would never play alongside Robinson. Durocher gathered the team and told them: "Well, boys, you know what you can do with that petition. You can wipe your ass with it. I hear Dixie Walker is going to send Mr. Rickey a letter asking to be traded. Just hand him the letter, Dixie, and you're gone. Gone! I don't care [what color the guy is]. I am the manager, and I say he plays."

The next night, Rickey called the dissident players to his hotel suite and lectured them on Americanism. Several felt ashamed and gave ground. At the request of Walker and Higbe, who persisted in their objections to Robinson, Rickey arranged trades; when Walker quickly changed his mind, his trade was canceled. Higbe (who, interestingly, believed as late as 1967 that he had acted correctly) was sold to the last-place Pittsburgh Pirates.

Walker, Stanky, and Bragan later became some of Robinson's strongest supporters. In 1965, Bragan sat next to Robinson at Rickey's funeral. As he recalled in Maury Allen's *Jackie Robinson: A Life Remembered:* "We shook hands warmly. I don't think either of us thought anything about it, or of the past. It was a new time. I changed. Jackie changed. The world changed."

ESTABLISHING EQUAL-STATUS CONTACT

At the time Rickey was planning to bring a black American to baseball, many believed that blacks and whites could not develop close interpersonal relationships. Social psychologists disagreed, identifying the "equal-status contact" hypothesis: Positive intergroup relations can occur when members of the two groups: a) possess equal status, b) seek common goals, c) are cooperatively dependent on each other, and d) interact with positive support of authorities, laws, or customs.

To Rickey, who was privy to social-science thinking, the typical ballclub does or (more often) could meet those four conditions. Each playing position has equal status; teams seek a common goal (the pennant); each player is mutually dependent on teammates to reach the goal; and the owner and manager can provide the positive support of authority.

The task of Dodger management was to keep the team on track toward its superordinate goal. Dodger management reminded the white players of how close they had come the previous season to qualifying for the World Series and that the missing component might be Robinson's speed on the base paths. As Durocher repeatedly told the white players in spring training, "He'll put money in your pocket, boys."

Dixie Walker's behavior shows the results of equal-status contact. A short time into the 1947 season, Walker approached Robinson in the batting cage and spoke his first words to him: "Ah think you'd be better able to handle that curveball if you didn't stride so far." Walker later showed the rookie how to hit behind the runner. When asked why, he replied, "I saw things in this light: When you're on a team, you got to pull together to win." At the end of the 1947 season, Walker credited Robinson with putting the Dodgers in the race.

THE PEE WEE REESE PRINCIPLE

One factor that perpetuates prejudice is a norm—a rule or expectation used to guide behavior (e.g., whites don't play baseball with blacks; women can't handle top-management positions). Norms draw their power from the belief that everyone else supports the norm and that social sanctions will result if the norm is transgressed.

The most effective way to change a norm is to violate it, puncturing the reality the norm creates. By hiring Robinson, Rickey took the first step toward breaking the norms of prejudice. Others displayed support: Brooklyn fans wore "I'm for Robinson" buttons; Dodger sportswriters wrote sympathetic articles; players such as Pirate Hank Greenberg supported Robinson when Pittsburgh fans verbally abused him.

One Dodger stands out in his actions to break the norms of prejudice—eventual Hall-of-Famer Harold "Pee Wee" Reese. In spring training, Reese refused to sign the anti-Robinson petition, surprising teammates who expected a Southern boy would "know better." Reese was the first Dodger to kid Robinson and to dine with him off the field. After Reese broke the ice, others grew friendlier.

One Reese-Robinson incident has acquired legendary status. Early in the 1947 season, the Dodgers traveled to Ohio to play the Cincinnati Reds. Thousands from Reese's boyhood home of Kentucky jammed Crosley Field to hurl racial slurs. The hatemongering continued into the bottom of the first inning, when the Dodgers took the field. Reese left his shortstop position and walked the 120 feet over to first base, where Robinson stood.

Reese smiled at Robinson and spoke a few words; Robinson smiled back. With all eyes on the pair, Reese casually placed his arm around Robinson's shoulder. The stands were silent. Reese's action punctured the norm of anti-black racism and broke another common myth as well: that all whites are racists and incapable of change.

NONVIOLENT RESISTANCE

Robinson and Rickey first met August 28, 1945 in Rickey's office, where the owner broke the news: "I've sent for you because I'm interested in you as a candidate for the Brooklyn National League club. I think you can play in the major leagues. . . . What I don't know is whether you have the guts."

For the next three hours, Rickey described the situations that Robinson would face as a black American entering an all-white league—the segregated hotels and restaurants, what his wife would hear in the stands, the abuse he would take on the field. Rickey got into Robinson's face, yelling insults and racial slurs, asking Robinson what he would do if a player spiked him during a game and said, "How do you like that, nigger boy?" Robinson asked, "Mr. Rickey, do you want a Negro who's afraid to fight back?" Rickey answered, "I want a ballplayer with guts enough not to fight back."

Why did Rickey, nicknamed "the Mahatma," place so much emphasis on nonviolence? First, Rickey feared a spiral of violence—between 1900 and 1949, 33 major race riots rocked U.S. towns, many near baseball parks.

Second, and perhaps more importantly for today's manager, nonviolence alters the social dynamics. If Robinson were not to fight back, then it became his Dodger teammates' responsibility to stand up for him, which they did on many occasions, most notably a run-in with the St. Louis Cardinals. After two previous spiking incidents, Enos Slaughter hit a grounder that was tossed to Robinson at first base, and deliberately spiked him on the back of the leg. The Dodgers immediately poured out of the dugout to protest, threatening the Cardinals with "dire consequences" if attacks continued.

The lesson: Don't leave it to the newcomer alone to defend his right to be in the organization; co-workers and management must share this burden.

One effective means of attitude change is to reverse perceptions and present the world through another's viewpoint. Seeing the world as another sees it provides an opportunity to receive new information and to challenge old ways of seeing. Rickey succeeded in getting the Dodgers to see the world through Robinson's eyes.

The Dodgers' baptism by fire occurred April 22, when the Philadelphia Phillies came to town for a three-game series. Phillies Manager Ben Chapman began screaming racial slurs at Robinson: "Hey, nigger, why don't you go pickin' cotton?" Soon his team joined in: "Hey, coon, do you always smell so bad?" and then they would flap their hands as if something stunk.

The abuse continued into the second game of the series. Feelings on the Dodger bench were tense. Most likely, the white Dodgers had never experienced prejudice before, and now they started to get the full treatment: "Hey, you carpet-baggers, how's your little Reconstruction period getting along?"

Toward the end of the second game, the white Dodgers exploded. Eddie Stanky was the first off the bench, demanding of the Phillies what type of man would say such things. Dixie Walker—yes, the former petitioner Dixie Walker—was next to support Robinson. Although the Phillies' abuse persisted for several years, it was much diminished.

For the record, the Dodgers swept the series, with Robinson scoring the winning run in the first and third games and adding an insurance run in the second game. Branch Rickey was beside himself with glee and could not resist the opportunity to lecture Ben Chapman. As he later told Harvey Frommer in *Rickey and Robinson: The Men Who Broke Baseball's Color Barrier* (MacMillan): "When Chapman and the others poured out that string of unconscionable abuse, he solidified and unified 30 men, not one of whom was willing to see someone kick around a man who had his hands tied behind his back."

INDIVIDUATING THE NEW GROUP MEMBER

One problem that occurs when an out-group member joins an in-group is the continued use of stereotypes—the person is not seen as Jackie Robinson but as a Negro ballplayer. The use of stereotypes promotes in-group favoritism and makes it easier to dislike the new employee since he is seen as a vague category and not a flesh-and-blood human being.

One solution to this problem is to encourage the treatment of the new group member as an *individual*. Introduce the new employee as a unique person with special skills, experience, and qualities that will add new depth to the organization. Don't introduce him as one manager of a major hospital-supply company did a new employee: "It is good she is a woman and even better that she is black—but it would have been best of all if she was disabled too."

Rickey felt that through the "intimacy" of baseball and the heat of competition, the white Dodgers would come to know and like Robinson. Since baseball fans would have no opportunity to interact personally with him, Rickey called on media friends to "introduce" Robinson as an individual of accomplishment in sports, academics, and the military. In 1950 Robinson contributed greatly to the individuation effort by starring in *The Jackie Robinson Story*.

Through the psychology of the inevitable, Rickey put great pressure on the white Dodgers to change their prejudices. He coupled this with a positive means of coming to terms with racism—forgiveness and redemption. In Rickey's Methodist theology, redemption means the transformation of the person; one hates the sin but loves the sinner.

When Rickey saw signs that a white player was "coming around," he would place that player in a new role of authority—a position that would involve interacting with and serving black Americans. Social scientists call this cooptation, or providing the opponent with a new role complete with new information, role expectations, and social pressures that increase identification with the organization's goals.

A case in point is Bobby Bragan, the Dodgers' expendable second-string catcher. Rickey could easily have washed his hands of him after Bragan's participation in the petition drive, but he felt Bragan needed time to think and that someday he would learn he was wrong. In 1948, Rickey appointed Bragan manager of the Dodger farm club in Fort Worth, Texas. Monte Irvin, one of the New York Giants' first black players, described it this way: "After a year or so, Bragan realized how wrong his attitude was. Later he went out of his way to help black ballplayers."

Rickey was not above using even the bitter Chapman incident to promote his cause. The Phillies' attack on Robinson and the other Dodgers drew a public outcry. Worried about his and his team's image, Chapman issued a statement—and an insincere apology—that he was riding Robinson as he would any rookie. Rickey took the opportunity to stage a photo of Chapman with Robinson that appeared in every major newspaper's sports pages.

UNDO THE PERCEPTION
OF PREFERENTIAL SELECTION

Many white Americans doubted Jackie Robinson's ability to make it in the major leagues. Star pitcher Bob Feller said, "If he were a white man, I doubt they would even consider him big-league material." When Robinson had an off-day because of a sore shoulder, a reporter commented, "Had he been white, the Royals would have dropped him immediately."

New York Yankees General Manager Larry McPhail said that the level of Robinson's ability, "were he white, would make him eligible for a trial with, let us say, the Brooklyn Dodgers' Class B farm at Newport News." McPhail also believed black Americans, in general, could not compete in the white leagues without considerable training. "A major-league player must have something besides natural ability. He must also have a competitive attitude and discipline"—implying that blacks lacked these characteristics.

The fact that Jackie Robinson was perceived as preferentially selected for the Dodgers should alert us to one potential problem of affirmative action—it can lead to the (mis)perception that the recipient was hired just because he was black (or a woman, etc.) and can't necessarily do the job.

Of course, in Robinson's case the perception was ridiculous. In 1946, with the Montreal Royals, Robinson won the International League batting championship with a .349 average, scored 113 runs, was chosen the league's Most Valuable Player, and went on to lead the club to victory in the Little World Series. If Robinson did not qualify for a chance in the majors, then no minor-league player that year did.

Social psychologists have identified three general reasons why affirmative action can be perceived as preferential selection. The first is simple racism. As McPhail's quote indicates, some believed that black Americans lack certain essential abilities. If they lacked the ability, then why did they get the job? The answer: It must be preferential selection.

Second, some affirmative-action procedures may be seen as violating norms of universality and procedural justice or fairness. Finally, white resistance to affirmative action is higher among those who feel relatively deprived. In such cases, attitudes toward affirmative action serve a scapegoating function—the dissatisfied individual blames black Americans for his problems.

The perception of affirmative action as preferential selection can have negative consequences for the beneficiary as well. Considerable research has shown that women who feel they were preferentially selected for a desired position give lower self-evaluations of their abilities and skills. Others in the organization can pick up on this "second-class" status, thereby creating a two-tiered organization.

But managers do not have to let the misperception of preferential selection go unchecked. Rickey and his assistants followed seven guidelines in countering this misperception:

- Establish unambiguous, explicit, and focused qualifications criteria to be used in the selection decision (the baseball box score);
- Be certain that selection procedures are perceived as fair (Robinson paid his dues in the minors);

- Provide specific information testifying to the competencies of the new hire (Rickey's and Durocher's confidence in Robinson's ability; Robinson's season with Montreal);
- Emphasize the recipient's contributions to the team (Durocher claimed Robinson would get the Dodgers in the pennant drive);
- Develop socialization strategies that deter feelings of helplessness (the minor leagues and "Dodgertown");
- Reinforce the fact that affirmative action is not preferential selection (Rickey repeatedly told Robinson that he would have to make it on his own—in the box score and with his teammates—and not to depend on the owner for help); and
- Refocus the helping effort away from the recipient by identifying and communicating the social barriers preventing integration (everyone was aware of the color bar).

Removing Institutional Barriers

Out-groups are excluded from the in-group by more than just interpersonal prejudice; certain institutional practices can also restrict the choices of an out-group member. Institutional barriers can include inferior schools in minority-populated areas, the lack of day-care for working parents, limited job opportunities in poor areas, laws restricting new housing, insistence on traditional career paths, the flow of information in "old boy" networks, and tracking out-groups into certain careers.

One institution that posed a particular problem for Rickey was many towns' segregated housing and dining facilities. Black Americans, even star ballplayers, were not allowed to stay in most hotels nor to eat in most restaurants. Rickey discovered the significance of this practice during spring training in 1946, when Robinson was isolated from his team. In 1947, Rickey attempted a temporary and costly measure: The Dodgers held spring training in Havana, Cuba—a racially desegregated country. (Ironically, Rickey paid for his Cuban spring training with the money from the sale of petition organizer Kirby Higbe.)

In 1948, Rickey opened "Dodgertown," fulfilling his dream of a "college of baseball." In Dodgertown, black and white players could room together, eat together, and train together without the pressure of local segregation laws. It is interesting to note that long after the repeal of segregation, Dodgertown and its many imitators remain in operation because such camps are useful in creating team cohesion. There is a lesson to be learned: The creative removal of institutions serving as out-group barriers can also improve the lot of the in-group.

WHY DID RICKEY DO IT?

Branch Rickey hardly fits today's stereotype of an "advocate for affirmative action"—a wide-eyed liberal, out of touch with reality. Rickey was a lifelong conservative, a Republican, a staunch Christian, and above all else, a strong believer in capitalism. He was also a shrewd business leader with an eye on the bottom line. In the 1930s, he made the St. Louis Cardinals into one of baseball's winningest and most profitable franchises through an innovative training program—the development of the "farm" system of minor-league clubs.

A Final Box Score

Branch Rickey stayed with the Brooklyn Dodgers through 1950, moving to Pittsburgh and building a farm system that would help the Pirates win the 1960 World Series. After retiring in 1955, Rickey continued to speak out for integration, serving as chairman of President Eisenhower's commission to promote racial harmony (a precursor to the Equal Opportunity Employment Commission). Two years after his 1965 death, Rickey received baseball's highest honor: induction into the National Baseball Hall of Fame and Museum.

Jackie Robinson played for the Dodgers for 10 years—a period baseball writers call the golden Brooklyn decade. In that 10-year period, the Dodgers won six National League pennants, won the World Series in 1955, and took opponents to the wire in two pennant races. Robinson was named baseball's Rookie of the Year in 1947, won the league batting title and was named Most Valuable Player in 1949, and was named to the National League All-Star team six consecutive years. He batted .311 lifetime and held the fielding mark for second basemen playing 150 or more games, with a .992 percentage.

In 1962, Robinson was elected to the Hall of Fame—along with Bob Feller, who years before had publicly questioned Robinson's ability. The two were the first players in baseball history elected in their first year of eligibility, and their Cooperstown plaques are displayed side by side.

—A.R.P. and M.E.T.

So why did Rickey hire Robinson? Rickey gave two answers:

First, for the good of his Dodgers. As Rickey told an aide: "The greatest un-tapped reservoir of raw material in the history of the game is the black race! The Negroes will make us winners for years to come, and for that I will happily bear being called a bleeding heart and a do-gooder and all that humanitarian rot." Rickey was right—the Dodgers were perennial contenders, and the gates swelled. His genius lay in recognizing the advantages of affirmative action when most other owners felt that hiring a black American would send baseball into financial ruin.

Second, his Christian faith led Rickey to conclude that affirmative action was a moral imperative. To illustrate his point, he often told the story of coaching his college team in 1904, when the team hotel refused to admit one player, Charley Thomas, because he was black. Rickey finally convinced the manager to place a cot in his room for Thomas to sleep on—as the hotel would do for any black servant. That night Thomas cried in bed, pulling at his skin, "It's my black skin, Mr. Rickey. . . . If I could pull it off I'd be like everybody else." The incident haunted Rickey for more than 40 years, and he vowed to do whatever he could to see that other Americans did not have to face the bitter humiliation heaped on Thomas.

Rickey's two reasons for affirmative action may strike some as odd; after all, you can't serve God and mammon. But Rickey saw no contradiction. For him, capitalism works best when barriers are removed and free enterprise can operate. Expanding the labor market means lower labor costs, a greater pool of talent to choose from, and ultimately a superior product. Capitalism requires a society where all can compete fairly. In this case, the moral imperative merely underscored the mission's importance.

VIII

LIKING, LOVING, AND INTERPERSONAL SENSITIVITY

32

"Playing Hard to Get": Understanding an Elusive Phenomenon

Elaine Walster (Hatfield), G. William Walster,
Jane Piliavin, and Lynn Schmidt

According to folklore, the woman who is hard to get is a more desirable catch than the woman who is too eager for an alliance. Five experiments were conducted to demonstrate that individuals value hard-to-get dates more than easy-to-get ones. All five experiments failed. In Experiment VI, we finally gained an understanding of this elusive phenomenon. We proposed that two components contribute to a woman's desirability: *(a)* how hard the woman is for the subject to get and *(b)* how hard she is for other men to get. We predicted that the selectively hard-to-get woman (i.e., a woman who is easy for the subject to get but hard for all other men to get) would be preferred to either a uniformly hard-to-get woman, a uniformly easy-to-get woman, or a woman about which the subject has no information. This hypothesis received strong support. The reason for the popularity of the selective woman was evident. Men ascribe to her all of the assets of uniformly hard-to-get and the uniformly easy-to-get women and none of their liabilities.

According to folklore, the woman who is hard to get is a more desirable catch than is the woman who is overly eager for alliance. Socrates, Ovid, Terence, the *Kama Sutra,* and Dear Abby all agree that the person whose affection is easily won is unlikely to inspire passion in another. Ovid, for example, argued:

> Fool, if you feel no need to guard your girl for her own sake, see that you guard her for mine, so I may want her the more. Easy things nobody wants, but what is forbidden is tempting. . . . Anyone who can love the wife of an indolent cuckold, I should suppose, would steal buckets of sand from the shore. [pp. 65–66.]

When we first began our investigation, we accepted cultural lore. We assumed that men would prefer a hard-to-get woman. Thus, we began our research by interviewing college men as to why they preferred hard-to-get women. Predictably,

---

This research was supported in part by National Science Foundation Grants GS 2932 and GS 30822X and in part by National Institute for Mental Health Grant MH 16661.

Reprinted with permission from the authors and *The Journal of Personality and Social Psychology,* Vol. 26, No. 1, 1973. Copyright © 1973 by the American Psychological Association.

the men responded to experimenter demands. They explained that they preferred hard-to-get women because the elusive woman is almost inevitably a valuable woman. They pointed out that a woman can only afford to be "choosy" if she is popular—and a woman is popular for some reason. When a woman is hard to get, it is usually a tip-off that she is especially pretty, has a good personality, is sexy, etc. Men also were intrigued by the challenge that the elusive woman offered. One can spend a great deal of time fantasizing about what it would be like to date such a woman. Since the hard-to-get woman's desirability is well recognized, a man can gain prestige if he is seen with her.

An easy-to-get woman, on the other hand, spells trouble. She is probably desperate for a date. She is probably the kind of woman who will make too many demands on a person; she might want to get serious right away. Even worse, she might have a "disease."

In brief, nearly all interviewees agreed with our hypothesis that a hard-to-get woman is a valuable woman, and they could supply abundant justification for their prejudice. A few isolated men refused to cooperate. These dissenters noted that an elusive woman is not always more desirable than an available woman. Sometimes the hard-to-get woman is not only hard to get—she is *impossible* to get, because she is misanthropic and cold. Sometimes a woman is easy to get because she is a friendly, outgoing woman who boosts one's ego and insures that dates are "no hassle." We ignored the testimony of these deviant types.

We then conducted five experiments designed to demonstrate that an individual values a hard-to-get date more highly than an easy-to-get date. All five experiments failed.

Theoretical Rationale

Let us first review the theoretical rationale underlying these experiments.

In Walster, Walster, and Berscheid (1971) we argued that if playing hard to get does increase one's desirability, several psychological theories could account for this phenomenon:

>   1. Dissonance theory predicts that if a person must expend great energy to attain a goal, one is unusually appreciative of the goal (see Aronson and Mills, 1959; Gerard and Mathewson, 1966; Zimbardo, 1965). The hard-to-get date requires a suitor to expend more effort in her pursuit than he would normally expend. One way for the suitor to justify such unusual effort is by aggrandizing her.
>   2. According to learning theory, an elusive person should have two distinct advantages: *(a)* Frustration may increase drive—by waiting until the suitor has achieved a high sexual drive state, heightening his drive level by introducing momentary frustration, and then finally rewarding him, the hard-to-

get woman can maximize the impact of the sexual reward she provides (see Kimball, 1961, for evidence that frustration does energize behavior and does increase the impact of appropriate rewards). *(b)* Elusiveness and value may be associated—individuals may have discovered through frequent experience that there is more competition for socially desirable dates than for undesirable partners. Thus, being "hard to get" comes to be associated with "value." As a consequence, the conditional stimulus (CS) of being hard to get generates a fractional antedating goal response and a fractional goal response, which leads to the conditioned response of liking.

3. In an extension of Schachterian theory, Walster (1971) argued that two components are necessary before an individual can experience passionate love; *(a)* He must be physiologically aroused; and *(b)* the setting must make it appropriate for him to conclude that his aroused feelings are due to love. On both counts, the person who plays hard to get might be expected to generate unusual passion. Frustration should increase the suitor's physiological arousal, and the association of "elusiveness" with "value" should increase the probability that the suitor will label his reaction to the other as "love."

From the preceding discussion, it is evident that several conceptually distinct variables may account for the hard-to-get phenomenon. In spite of the fact that we can suggest a plethora of reasons as to why playing hard-to-get strategy might be an effective strategy, all five studies failed to provide any support for the contention that an elusive woman is a desirable woman. Two experiments failed to demonstrate that outside observers perceive a hard-to-get individual as especially "valuable." Three experiments failed to demonstrate that a suitor perceives a hard-to-get date as especially valuable.

Walster, Walster, and Berscheid (1971) conducted two experiments to test the hypothesis that teenagers would deduce that a hard-to-get boy or girl was more socially desirable than was a teenager whose affection could be easily obtained. In these experiments high school juniors and seniors were told that we were interested in finding out what kind of first impression various teenagers made on others. They were shown pictures and biographies of a couple. They were told how romantically interested the stimulus person (a boy or girl) was in his partner after they had met only four times. The stimulus person was said to have liked the partner "extremely much," to have provided no information to us, or to have liked the partner "not particularly much." The teenagers were then asked how socially desirable both teenagers seemed (i.e., how likable, how physically attractive, etc.). Walster, Walster, and Berscheid, of course, predicted that the more romantic interest the stimulus person expressed in a slight acquaintance, the less socially desirable that stimulus person would appear to an outside observer. The results were diametrically opposed to those predicted. The more romantic interest the stimulus person expressed in an acquaintance, the *more* socially desirable teenagers judged him to be. Restraint does not appear to buy respect. Instead, it appears that "All the world *does* love a lover."

Lyons, Walster, and Walster (1971) conducted a field study and a laboratory experiment in an attempt to demonstrate that men prefer a date who plays hard to get.

Both experiments were conducted in the context of a computer matching service. Experiment III was a field experiment. Women who signed up for the computer matching program were contacted and hired as experimenters. They were then given precise instructions as to how to respond when their computer match called them for a date. Half of the time they were told to pause and think for 3 seconds before accepting the date. (These women were labeled "hard to get.") Half of the time they were told to accept the date immediately. (These women are labeled "easy to get.") The data indicated that elusiveness had no impact on the man's liking for his computer date.

Experiment IV was a laboratory experiment. In this experiment, Lyons et al. hypothesized that the knowledge that a woman is elusive gives one indirect evidence that she is socially desirable. Such indirect evidence should have the biggest impact when a man has no way of acquiring *direct* evidence about a coed's value or when he has little confidence in his own ability to assess value. When direct evidence is available, and the man possesses supreme confidence in his ability to make correct judgments, information about a woman's elusiveness should have little impact on a man's reaction to her. Lyons et al. thus predicted that when men lacked direct evidence as to a woman's desirability, a man's self-esteem and the woman's elusiveness should interact in determining his respect and liking for her. Lyons et al. measured males' self-esteem via Rosenberg's (1965) measure of self-esteem. Rosenfeld's (1964) measure of fear of rejection, and Berger's (1952) measure of self-acceptance.

The dating counselor then told subjects that the computer had assigned them a date. They were asked to telephone her from the office phone, invite her out, and then report their first impression of her. Presumably the pair would then go out on a date and eventually give us further information about how successful our computer matching techniques had been. Actually, all men were assigned a confederate as a date. Half of the time the woman played hard to get. When the man asked her out she replied:

> Mmm [slight pause] No, I've got a date then. It seems like I signed up for that Date Match thing a long time ago and I've met more people since then—I'm really pretty busy all this week.

She paused again. If the subject suggested another time, the confederate hesitated only slightly, then accepted. If he did not suggest another time, the confederate would take the initiative of suggesting: "How about some time next week—or just meeting for coffee in the Union some afternoon?" And again, she accepted the next invitation. Half of the time, in the easy-to-get condition, the confederate eagerly accepted the man's offer of a date.

Lyons et al. predicted that since men in this blind date setting lacked direct evidence as to a woman's desirability, low-self-esteem men should be more receptive to the hard-to-get woman than were high-self-esteem men. Although Lyons et al.'s manipulation checks indicate that their manipulations were successful and their self-esteem measure was reliable, their hypothesis was not confirmed. Elusiveness had no impact on liking, regardless of subject's self-esteem level.

Did we give up our hypothesis? Heavens no. After all, it had only been disconfirmed four times.

By Experiment V, we had decided that perhaps the hard-to-get hypothesis must be tested in a sexual setting. After all, the first theorist who advised a woman to play hard to get was Socrates; his pupil was Theodota, a prostitute. He advised:

> They will appreciate your favors most highly if you wait till they ask for them. The sweetest meats, you see, if served before they are wanted seem sour, and to those who had enough they are positively nauseating; but even poor fare is very welcome when offered to a hungry man. [Theodota inquired] And how can I make them hungry for my fare? [Socrates' reply] Why, in the first place, you must not offer it to them when they have had enough—but prompt them by behaving as a model of Propriety, by a show of reluctance to yield, and by holding back until they are as keen as can be; and then the same gifts are much more to the recipient than when they're offered before they are desired [see Xenophon, p. 48.]

Walster, Walster, and Lambert (1971) thus proposed that a prostitute who states that she is selective in her choice of customers will be held in higher regard than will be the prostitute who admits that she is completely unselective in her choice of partners.

In this experiment, a prostitute served as the experimenter. When the customer arrived, she mixed a drink for him; then she delivered the experimental manipulation. Half of the time, in the hard-to-get condition, she stated, "Just because I see you this time it doesn't mean that you can have my phone number or see me again. I'm going to start school soon, so I won't have much time, so I'll only be able to see the people that I like the best." Half of the time, in the easy-to-get condition, she did not communicate this information. From this point on, the prostitute and the customer interacted in conventional ways.

The client's liking for the prostitute was determined in two ways: First, the prostitute estimated how much the client had seemed to like her. (Questions asked were, for example, How much did he seem to like you? Did he make arrangements to return? How much did he pay you?) Second, the experimenter recorded how many times within the next 30 days the client arranged to have sexual relations with her.

Once again we failed to confirm the hard-to-get hypothesis. If anything, those clients who were told that the prostitute did not take just anyone were *less* likely to call back and liked the prostitute less than did other clients.

At this point, we ruefully decided that we had been on the wrong track. We decided that perhaps all those practitioners who advise women to play hard to get are wrong. Or perhaps it is only under very special circumstances that it will benefit one to play hard to get.

Thus, we began again. We reinterviewed students—this time with an open mind. This time we asked men to tell us about the advantages *and* disadvantages of hard-to-get *and* easy-to-get women. This time replies were more informative. According to reports, choosing between a hard-to-get woman and an easy-to-get woman was like choosing between Scylla and Charybdis—each woman was uniquely desirable and uniquely frightening.

Although the elusive woman was likely to be a popular prestige date, she presented certain problems. Since she was not particularly enthusiastic about you, she might stand you up or humiliate you in front of your friends. She was likely to be unfriendly, cold, and to possess inflexible standards.

The easy-to-get woman was certain to boost one's ego and to make a date a relaxing, enjoyable experience, but . . . Unfortunately, dating an easy woman was a risky business. Such a woman might be easy to get, but hard to get rid of. She might "get serious." Perhaps she would be so oversexed or overaffectionate in public that she would embarrass you. Your buddies might snicker when they saw you together. After all, they would know perfectly well why you were dating *her.*

The interlocking assets and difficulties envisioned when they attempted to decide which was better—a hard-to-get or an easy-to-get woman—gave us a clue as to why our previous experiments had not worked out. The assets and liabilities of the elusive and the easy dates had evidently generally balanced out. On the average, then, both types of women tended to be equally well liked. When a slight difference in liking did appear, it favored the easy-to-get woman.

It finally impinged on us that there are *two* components that are important determinants of how much a man likes a woman: *(a)* How hard or easy she is for him to get, and *(b)* how hard or easy she is for *other men* to get. So long as we were examining the desirability of women who were hard or easy for everyone to get, things balanced out. The minute we examined other possible configurations, it became evident that there is one type of woman who can transcend the limitations of the uniformly hard-to-get or the uniformly easy-to-get woman. If a woman has a reputation for being hard to get, but for some reason she is easy for the subject to get, she should be maximally appealing. Dating such a woman should insure one of great prestige; she is, after all, hard to get. Yet, since she is exceedingly available to the subject, the dating situation should be a relaxed, rewarding experience. Such a *selectively* hard-to-get woman possesses the assets of both the easy-to-get and the hard-to-get women, while avoiding all of their liabilities.

Thus, in Experiment VI, we hypothesized that a selectively hard-to-get woman (i.e., a woman who is easy for the subject to get but very hard for any other man to get) will be especially liked by her date. Women who are hard for everyone—including the subject—to get, or who are easy for everyone to get—or control women, about whom the subject had no information—will be liked a lesser amount.

METHOD

Subjects were 71 male summer students at the University of Wisconsin. They were recruited for a dating research project. This project was ostensibly designed to determine whether computer matching techniques are in fact more effective than is random matching. All participants were invited to come into the dating center in order to choose a date from a set of five potential dates.

When the subject arrived at the computer match office, he was handed folders containing background information on five women. Some of these women had supposedly been "randomly" matched with him; others had been "computer matched" with him. (He was not told which women were which.)

In reality, all five folders contained information about fictitious women. The first item in the folder was a "background questionnaire" on which the woman had presumably described herself. This questionnaire was similar to one the subject had completed when signing up for the match program. We attempted to make the five women's descriptions different enough to be believable, yet similar enough to minimize variance. Therefore, the way the five women described themselves was systematically varied. They claimed to be 18 or 19 years old; freshmen or sophomores; from a Wisconsin city, ranging in size from over 500,000 to under 50,000; 5 feet 2 inches to 5 feet 4 inches tall; Protestant, Catholic, Jewish or had no preference; graduated in the upper 10 to 50 percent of their high school class; and Caucasians who did not object to being matched with a person of another race. The women claimed to vary on a political spectrum from "left of center" through "moderate" to "near right of center"; to place little or no importance on politics and religion; and to like recent popular movies. Each woman listed four or five activities she liked to do on a first date (i.e., go to a movie, talk in a quiet place, etc.).

In addition to the background questionnaire, three of the five folders contained five "date selection forms." The experimenter explained that some of the women had already been able to come in, examine the background information of their matches, and indicate their first impression of them. Two of the subject's matches had not yet come in. Three of the women had already come in and evaluated the subject along with her four other matches. These women would have five date selection forms in their folders. The subject was shown the forms, which consisted of a scale ranging from "definitely do *not* want to date" (-10) to "definitely want to date" ($+10$). A check appeared on each scale. Presumably the check indicated how much the woman had liked a given date. (At this point, the subject was told his identification number. Since all dates were identified by numbers on the forms, this identification number enabled him to ascertain how each date had evaluated both him and her four other matches.)

The date selection forms allowed us to manipulate the elusiveness of the woman. One woman appeared to be uniformly hard to get. She indicated that though she was willing to date any of the men assigned to her, she was not enthusiastic about any of them. She rated all five of her date choices from $+1$ to $+2$, including the subject (who was rated 1.75).

One woman appeared to be uniformly easy to get. She indicated that she was enthusiastic about dating all five of the men assigned to her. She rated her desire to date all five of her date choices $+7$ to $+9$. This included the subject, who was rated 8.

One woman appeared to be easy for the subject to get but hard for anyone else to get (i.e., the selectively hard-to-get woman). She indicated minimal enthusiasm for four of her date choices, rating them from +2 to +3, and extreme enthusiasm (+8) for the subject.

Two women had no date selection forms in their folders (i.e., no information women).

Naturally, each woman appeared in each of the five conditions.

The experimenter asked the man to consider the folders, complete a "first impression questionnaire" for each woman, and then decide which *one* of the women he wished to date. (The subject's rating of the dates constitute our verbal measure of liking; his choice in a date constitutes our behavioral measure of liking.)

The experimenter explained that she was conducting a study of first impressions in conjunction with the dating research project. The study, she continued, was designed to learn more about how good people are at forming first impressions of others on the basis of rather limited information. She explained that filling out the forms would probably make it easier for the man to decide which one of the five women he wished to date.

The first impression questionnaire consisted of three sections:

Liking for various dates.   Two questions assessed subject's liking for each woman: "If you went out with this girl, how well do you think you would get along?"—with possible responses ranging from "get along extremely well" (5) to "not get along at all" (1)—and "What was your overall impression of the girl?"—with possible responses ranging from "extremely favorable" (7) to "extremely unfavorable" (1). Scores on these two questions were summed to form an index of expressed liking. This index enables us to compare subject's liking for each of the women.

Assets and liabilities ascribed to various dates.   We predicted that subjects would prefer the selective woman, because they would expect her to possess the good qualities of both the uniformly hard-to-get and the uniformly easy-to-get woman, while avoiding the bad qualities of both her rivals. Thus, the second section was designed to determine the extent to which subjects imputed good and bad qualities to the various dates.

This section was comprised of 10 pairs of polar opposites. Subjects were asked to rate how friendly–unfriendly, cold–warm, attractive–unattractive, easy-going–rigid, exciting–boring, shy–outgoing, fun-loving–dull, popular–unpopular, aggressive–passive, selective–nonselective each woman was. Ratings were made on a 7-point scale. The more desirable the trait ascribed to a woman, the higher the score she was given.

Liabilities attributed to easy-to-get women.   The third scale was designed to assess the extent to which subjects attributed selected negative attributes to each woman. The third scale consisted of six statements:

> She would more than likely do something to embarrass me in public.
> She probably would demand too much attention and affection from me.

She seems like the type who would be too dependent on me.
She might turn out to be too sexually promiscuous.
She probably would make me feel uneasy when I'm with her in a group.
She seems like the type who doesn't distinguish between the boys she dates. I probably would be "just another date."

Subjects were asked whether they anticipated any of the above difficulties in their relationship with each woman. They indicated their misgivings on a scale ranging from "certainly true of her" (1) to "certainly not true of her" (7).

The experimenter suggested that the subject carefully examine both the background questionnaires and the date selection forms of all potential dates in order to decide whom he wanted to date. Then she left the subject. (The experimenter was, of course, unaware of what date was in what folder.)

The experimenter did not return until the subject had completed the first impression questionnaires. Then she asked him which woman he had decided to date.

After his choice had been made, the experimenter questioned him as to what factors influenced his choice. Frequently men who chose the selectively easy-to-get woman said that "She chose me, and that made me feel really good" or "She seemed more selective than the others." The uniformly easy-to-get woman was often rejected by subjects who complained "She must be awfully hard up for a date—she really would take anyone." The uniformly hard-to-get woman was once described as a "challenge" but more often rejected as being "snotty" or "too picky."

At the end of the session, the experimenter debriefed the subject and then gave him the names of five actual dates who had been matched with him.

RESULTS

We predicted that the selectively hard-to-get woman (easy for me but hard for everyone else to get) would be liked more than women who were uniformly hard to get, uniformly easy to get, or neutral (the no information women). We had no prediction as to whether or not her three rivals would differ in attractiveness. The results strongly support our hypothesis.

Dating Choices

When we examine the men's choices in dates, we see that the selective woman is far more popular than any of her rivals (See Table 32.1.) We conducted a chi-square test to determine whether or not men's choices in dates were randomly distributed. They were not ($\chi^2 = 69.5$, $df = 4$, $p < .001$). Nearly all subjects preferred to date the selective woman. When we compare the frequency with which her four rivals (combined) are chosen, we see that the selective woman does get far more than her share of dates ($\chi^2 = 68.03$, $df = 1$, $p < .001$).

TABLE 32.1
Men's Choices in a Date

Item	Selectively hard to get	Uniformly hard to get	Uniformly easy to get	No information for No. 1	No information for No. 2
Number of men choosing to date each woman	42	6	5	11	7

We also conducted an analysis to determine whether or not the women who are uniformly hard to get, uniformly easy to get, or whose popularity is unknown, differed in popularity. We see that they did not ($\chi^2 = 2.86$, $df = 3$).

Liking for the Various Dates

Two questions tapped the men's romantic liking for the various dates: *(a)* "If you went out with this woman, how well do you think you'd get along?"; and *(b)* "What was your overall impression of the woman?" Scores on these two indexes were summed to form an index of liking. Possible scores ranged from 2 to 12.

A contrast was then set up to test our hypothesis that the selective woman will be preferred to her rivals. The contrast that tests this hypothesis is of the form $\Gamma_1 = 4\mu$ (selectively hard to get) -1 (uniformly hard to get -2μ (neutral). We tested the hypothesis $\Gamma_1 = 0$ against the alternative hypothesis $\Gamma_1 \neq 0$. An explanation of this basically simple procedure may be found in Hays (1963). If our hypothesis is true, the preceding contrast should be large. If our hypothesis is false, the resulting contrast should not differ significantly from 0. The data again provide strong support for the hypothesis that the selective woman is better liked than her rivals ($F = 23.92$, $df = 1/70$, $p < .001$).

Additional Data Snooping

We also conducted a second set of contrasts to determine whether the rivals (i.e., the uniformly hard-to-get woman, the uniformly easy-to-get woman, and the control woman) were differentially liked. Using the procedure presented by Morrison (1967) in chapter 4, the data indicate that the rivals are differentially liked ($F = 4.43$, $df = 2/69$). As Table 32.2 indicates, the uniformly hard-to-get woman seems to be liked slightly less than the easy-to-get or control woman.

In any attempt to explore data, one must account for the fact that observing the data permits the researcher to capitalize on chance. Thus, one must use simultaneous testing methods so as not to spuriously inflate the probability of attaining statistical significance. In the present situation, we are interested in comparing the means of a number of dependent measures, namely the liking for the different

TABLE 32.2
Men's Reactions to Various Dates

Item	Type of date			
	Selectively hard to get	Uniformly hard to get	Uniformly easy to get	No information
Men's liking for dates	9.41[a]	7.90	8.53	8.58
Evaluation of women's assets and liabilities				
Selective[b]	5.23	4.39	2.85	4.30
Popular[b]	4.83	4.58	4.65	4.83
Friendly[c]	5.58	5.07	5.52	5.37
Warm[c]	5.15	4.51	4.99	4.79
Easy Going[c]	4.83	4.42	48.2	4.61
Problems expected in dating	5.23[d]	4.86	4.77	4.99

[a]The higher the number, the more liking the man is expressing for the date.
[b]Traits we expected to be ascribed to the selectively hard-to-get and the uniformly hard-to-get dates.
[c]Traits we expected to be ascribed to the selectively hard-to-get and the uniformly easy-to-get dates.
[d]The higher the number the *fewer* the problems the subject anticipates in dating.

women in the dating situation. To perform post hoc multiple comparisons in this situation, one can use a transformation of Hotelling's t^2 statistic, which is distributed as F. The procedure is directly analogous to Scheffé's multiple-comparison procedure for independent groups, except where one compares means of a number of dependent measures.

To make it abundantly clear that the main result is that the discriminating woman is better liked than each of the other rivals, we performed an additional post hoc analysis, pitting each of the rivals separately against the discriminating woman. In these analyses, we see that the selective woman is better liked than the woman who is uniformly easy to get ($F = 3.99$, $df = 3/68$), than the woman who is uniformly hard to get ($F = 9.47$, $df = 3/68$), and finally, than the control women ($F = 4.93$, $df = 3/68$).

Thus, it is clear that although there are slight differences in the way rivals are liked, these differences are small, relative to the overwhelming attractiveness of the selective woman.

Assets and Liabilities Attributed to Dates

We can now attempt to ascertain *why* the selective woman is more popular than her rivals. Earlier, we argued that the selectively hard-to-get woman should occupy a unique position; she should be assumed to possess all of the virtues of her rivals, but none of their flaws.

The virtues and flaws that the subject ascribed to each woman were tapped by the polar–opposite scale. Subjects evaluated each woman on 10 characteristics.

We expected that subjects would associate two assets with a uniformly hard-to-get woman: Such a woman should be perceived to be both "selective" and "popular." Unfortunately, such a woman should also be assumed to possess three liabilities—she should be perceived to be "unfriendly," "cold," and "rigid." Subjects should ascribe exactly the opposite virtues and liabilities to the easy-to-get woman: Such a woman should possess the assets of "friendliness," "warmth," and "flexibility," and the liabilities of "unpopularity" and "lack of selectivity." The selective woman was expected to possess only assets: She should be perceived to be as "selective" and "popular" as the uniformly elusive woman, and as "friendly," "warm," and "easygoing" as the uniformly easy woman. A contrast was set up to test this specific hypothesis. (Once again, see Hays for the procedure.) This contrast indicates that our hypothesis is confirmed ($F = 62.43$, $df = 1/70$). The selective woman is rated most like the uniformly hard-to-get woman on the first two positive characteristics and most like the uniformly easy-to-get woman on the last three characteristics.

For the reader's interest, the subjects' ratings of all five women's assets and liabilities are presented in Table 32.2.

Comparing the Selective and the Easy Women

Scale 3 was designed to assess whether or not subjects anticipated fewer problems when they envisioned dating the selective woman than when they envisioned dating the uniformly easy-to-get woman. On the basis of pretest interviews, we compiled a list of many of the concerns men had about easy women (e.g., "She would more than likely do something to embarrass me in public.").

We, of course, predicted that subjects would experience more problems when contemplating dating the uniformly easy woman than when contemplating dating a woman who was easy for *them* to get, but hard for anyone else to get (i.e., the selective woman).

Men were asked to say whether or not they envisioned each of the difficulties were they to date each of the women. Possible replies varied from 1 (certainly true of her) to 7 (certainly not true of her). The subjects' evaluations of each woman were summed to form an index of anticipated difficulties. Possible scores ranged from 6 to 42.

A contrast was set up to determine whether the selective woman engendered less concern than the uniformly easy-to-get woman. The data indicate that she does ($F = 17.50$, $df = 1/70$). If the reader is interested in comparing concern engendered by each woman, these data are available in Table 32.2.

The data provide clear support for our hypotheses: The selective woman is strongly preferred to any of her rivals. The reason for her popularity is evident. Men ascribe to her all of the assets of the uniformly hard-to-get and the uniformly easy-to-get women, and none of their liabilities.

Thus, after five futile attempts to understand the "hard-to-get" phenomenon, it appears that we have finally gained an understanding of this process. It appears that a woman can intensify her desirability if she acquires a reputation for being hard-to-get and then, by her behavior, makes it clear to a selected romantic partner that she is attracted to him.

In retrospect, especially in view of the strongly supportive data, the logic underlying our predictions sounds compelling. In fact, after examining our data, a colleague who had helped design the five ill-fated experiments noted that, "That is exactly what I would have predicted" (given his economic view of man). Unfortunately, we are all better at postdiction than prediction.

References

ARONSON, E., AND MILLS, J. The effect of severity of initiation on liking for a group. *Journal of Abnormal and Social Psychology,* 1959, **67,** 31–36.

BERGER, E. M. The relation between expressed acceptance of self and expressed acceptance of others. *Journal of Abnormal and Social Psychology,* 1952, **47,** 778–782.

GERARD, H. B. AND MATHEWSON, G. C. The effects of severity of initiation and liking for a group: A replication. *Journal of Experimental Social Psychology,* 1966, **2,** 278–287.

HAYS, W. L. *Statistics for psychologists.* New York: Holt, Rinehart, 1963.

KIMBALL, G. A. *Hilgard and Marquis' conditioning and learning.* New York: Appleton-Century-Crofts, 1961.

LYONS, J., WALSTER, E. AND WALSTER, G. W. Playing hard-to-get: An elusive phenomenon. University of Wisconsin, Madison: Author, 1971. (Mimeo)

MORRISON, D. F. *Multivariate statistical methods.* New York: McGraw-Hill, 1967.

OVID. *The art of love.* Bloomington: University of Indiana Press, 1963.

ROSENBERG, M. *Society and the adolescent self image.* Princeton, N.J.: Princeton University Press, 1965.

ROSENFELD, H. M. Social choice conceived as a level of aspiration. *Journal of Abnormal and Social Psychology,* 1964, **68,** 491–499.

WALSTER, E. Passionate love. In B. I. Murstein (Ed.), *Theories of attraction and love.* New York: Springer, 1971.

WALSTER, E., WALSTER, G. W., AND BERSCHEID, E. The efficacy of playing hard-to-get. *Journal of Experimental Education,* 1971, **39,** 73–77.

WALSTER, G. W., AND LAMBERT, P. Playing hard-to-get: A field study. University of Wisconsin, Madison: Author, 1971. (Mimeo)

XENOPHON. *Memorabilia.* London: Heinemann, 1923.

ZIMBARDO, P. G. The effect of effort and improvisation on self persuasion produced by role-playing. *Journal of Experimental Social Psychology,* 1965, **1,** 103–120.

33

The Search for a Romantic Partner: The Effects of Self-Esteem and Physical Attractiveness on Romantic Behavior

Sara B. Kiesler and Roberta L. Baral

What do people look for in a romantic partner? Observations of everyday life suggest one "common sense" assumption: that people prefer romantic partners who are attractive and socially desirable. Yet if the person himself were truly objective, he would consider what is most practical. That is, what is the probability of a successful outcome for attempts to win various alternative partners? While attainment of a very attractive partner might be very rewarding, the chances of actually "catching" such a person are likely to be somewhat lower than are the chances of winning a less attractive partner. Hence, if one is only moderately or low attractive himself, his most realistic initial choice would be based on both the wish to maximize attractiveness of a partner and the likelihood of positive outcome. This hypothesis, of course, is not new. For example, "exchange theories" (Homans, 1961; Thibaut and Kelley, 1959) assume that people estimate potential "costs" and "rewards" when choosing others.

Reprinted with permission from the authors. Selection from *Personality and Social Behavior*, Kenneth J. Gergen and David Marlowe, eds. Copyright © 1970, Addison-Wesley Publishing Company, Inc., Chapter 8, pp. 155–165. Reprinted by permission of Addison Wesley Longman.

The present study was supported by United States Public Health Grant MH-131-33-01 to the senior author, and by National Science Foundation Grants GE6156 and GY832 to the Yale University Culture and Behavior Honors Major, directed by Charles A. Kiesler. The junior author and experimenter were participants in the National Science Foundation Undergraduate Research Program.

The authors would like to thank the following persons for their extensive cooperation: H. Richardson Moody, Jr., who was the experimenter; Lola Libby, who was a confederate; and Charles A. Kiesler, who gave considerable aid in the analysis and editorial phases of the study.

For the average sort of person, then, realistic behavior should entail his choosing a person who is not extremely attractive. Yet "average" and "below average" people do not always choose those who are actually moderate or low in favorability. A study by Walster et al. (1966) provides an example. At a college dance, dates were randomly matched in order to study the relationship of physical attractiveness to romantic behavior. In general, the investigators found that the more attractive the female date, the better liked she was and the more the man said he would like to date her, *regardless* of his *own* physical attractiveness. Furthermore, the same finding held for women. The more attractive the male date, the more he was liked and wanted as a date again, regardless of the woman's own attractiveness.

The question arises, however, why the moderately and low attractive person in the Walster et al. study tended to choose the most attractive partner (instead of a more "realistic" partner). One possibility is that subjects over-evaluated their own attractiveness. First, the subjects may have assumed that the computer has paired them on the basis of similarity, thus making it easy to believe that they were fairly equal in attractiveness to the very attractive partners. Second, all the subjects were dressed up and prepared to present their best face. In such a context, it may have been easy to distort personal attributes and end up with relatively high "self-esteem." Even if subjects did not misperceive their own physical attractiveness, they could have felt that their intelligence or personality made up for any deficiency in physical attractiveness. If they did, indeed, exaggerate their own positive attributes, then their behavior was realistic in that both chances of success and maximization of attractiveness were considered. Each one merely ended up choosing someone of *objectively* higher attractiveness.

That people do overevaluate themselves in many situations has long been known (see Crowne and Marlowe, 1964). For example, a prior success experience should raise a person's self-esteem and feelings of worthiness (e.g., Aronson and Carlsmith, 1962). In the romantic-behavior situation, then, certain situational conditions that raise self-esteem may be of some importance in affecting what the romantic behavior will be. We have assumed that one effect will be on the person's perceptions of a potential partner. Thus, if self-esteem is high, he will perceive a highly attractive person as attainable and will choose that person.

Let us now consider what happens when self-esteem is lowered. For instance, if a person is presented with evidence that he is not overintelligent, then it is harder for him to distort his self-image in a favorable direction. Unlike the person with high self-esteem, the person with low self-esteem should perceive the very attractive partner as relatively dissimilar and "hard to get." He should then choose someone not so desirable.

We propose, then, that the self-esteem variable will influence who seems to be a realistic choice. In the present study, our hypothesis was: The *lower* the self-esteem, the lower would be the attractiveness of a chosen romantic partner. Thus we predicted that moderately attractive males with high self-esteem would tend to choose and like very attractive females, but with low self-esteem they would tend to choose only moderately attractive females.

In order to test our hypothesized interaction between self-esteem and attractiveness of the partner, an experiment was designed in which two levels of self-esteem, high and low, and two levels of physical attractiveness of a female, high and moderate, were orthogonally varied. Male subjects were first led to believe that they were doing very well or rather poorly on an intelligence test. We assumed that the former condition would lead to temporarily high self-esteem and encourage overevaluation of self, and that the latter condition would lead to a temporary lowering of self-esteem and would discourage overevaluation of self. The subjects were then exposed to a female of very high or only moderate physical attractiveness. Subsequently, observations were made of the subjects' romantic behavior.

METHOD

Subjects

Subjects were 43 male volunteers ranging in age from 19 to 37. They were recruited from institutions in the New Haven, Connecticut, area, including Southern Connecticut College, Yale Medical School, Yale College, New Haven College, and local libraries. The subjects were mostly undergraduate and graduate students, but included among them were also a few men in various occupations (e.g., high school teacher). Of the 43 subjects, 6 were excluded from the final analysis: 1 for suspicion, 1 for knowing one of the confederates previously, 2 because they were married, and 2 because they were engaged. The subjects were paid $1.50 for their participation.

Procedure

The subjects were recruited for a one-hour study on "intelligence testing." As each subject arrived he was ushered into an ordinary faculty office at Yale University by a male experimenter. The experimenter told the subject that he was perfecting and establishing norms for a new intelligence test, which had already been successfully used on "hundreds" of students. He emphasized that the test was already very accurate and reliable, and that it predicted "success in life." He then asked the subject to take the test orally, explaining that it consisted of five parts, which would be presented sequentially.

Self-Esteem Manipulation

The subjects were randomly assigned to the low or high self-esteem condition. In both conditions the "test" was the same. Subjects were first required to repeat from memory long lists of numbers; in a second part, they were asked to define words. To reduce initial variance in performance, the test was made extremely difficult. For instance, some of the words to be defined were fictitious (e.g., "sympanic").

The manipulation of high self-esteem was accomplished by conveying to the subject the impression that his performance was better than that of most subjects. At preprogrammed intervals the experimenter nodded; at others he told the subject that other subjects had had much more trouble with the questions. In addition, the number task was made somewhat easier by reading the numbers with some rhythm. Thus performance was actually a little better in the high-self-esteem condition than in the low-self-esteem condition.

In the low-self-esteem condition, the experimenter attempted to convey the impression that the subject's performance was inferior. At intervals he frowned and looked away or mentioned that other subjects had performed better. At other intervals he asked the subject if he felt "relaxed enough."

After the "second part" of the test, the experimenter suggested a break. He then gave the subject a short questionnaire, saying that it was a "Psychology Department questionnaire administered to all subjects in studies at Yale." This questionnaire was designed to check on the self-esteem manipulation.

When the subject had filled out the questionnaire, the experimenter stood up and said he "hadn't eaten all day and really needed a cup of coffee." Low-self-esteem subjects were told that "maybe a break will help you." High-self-esteem subjects were told that "since you are doing so well we have plenty of time." The experimenter asked the subject to come with him to get a cup of coffee. Just before they left the room, the experimenter "noticed" a telephone message on his desk and remarked that "he'd better take care of it soon." This sequence was performed in order to prepare the subject for the experimenter's eventual departure.

Meeting the Potential Romantic Partner

The experimenter took the subject to a small canteen in the same building and bought the coffee. As he turned to sit down, he appeared to recognize a girl seated at one of the tables and approached her. This girl was actually one of two confederates used in the study. The experimenter greeted the confederate and asked her if she was working in the building during the summer. She was then introduced to the subject as a coed at a nearby college who was doing summer work for a psychologist, and a preprogrammed conversation began.

After a minute, the experimenter excused himself, telling the subject that "now would be a good time to make that phone call." He was gone for ten minutes, during which the confederate engaged the subject in further conversation (asking him what he did, what his likes and dislikes were, etc.). The experimenter then returned and, acting displeased, told the subject that since his "fiancée really needs the car" he would have to break off the experiment. He apologized, paid the subject, and left. The confederate then continued talking with the subject (on prearranged topics), either for a half hour or until the subject attempted to leave or asked her for a date, whichever came first.

Physical Attractiveness Manipulation

The female confederate, one of two chosen because they were highly attractive, appeared in one of two attractiveness conditions, "high" or "moderate." Both confederates appeared in both conditions in random sequence. In the high-attractiveness condition, each confederate wore becoming make-up and fashionable clothing designed to enhance her initial attractiveness. In the moderate-attractiveness condition, an attempt was made to reduce somewhat the confederate's initial attractiveness. She wore heavy glasses and no makeup, and her hair was pulled back with a rubber band. Her skirt and blouse clashed and were arranged sloppily.

During the interaction the confederates attempted to act exactly the same in all encounters. They were friendly, accepting, and interested throughout. To reduce bias, they were not informed of the self-esteem condition the subjects were in.

The Dependent Variable: Romantic Behavior

After the experimenter "concluded" the experiment and during the following half hour, the confederate recorded the frequency of behavior falling into certain prescribed categories of "romantic behavior." The categories included asking for a date, asking for information that presumably would lead to a date (e.g., asking for the confederate's phone number), offering to buy a snack or coffee for her, offering her a cigarette or mint already on hand, complimenting her, and, finally ignoring her when, at the end of the prescribed time, she said she should "get back to work" (called "ignoring the first cue to leave"). At first, it was intended also to measure the amount of time the subject stayed with the confederate, but this measure turned out to be unreliable since the confederate had to stop the experiment if the subject asked her a date. It should be noted, however, that the majority (80 percent) did not attempt to leave before the time was up.

At the end of the experimental session, the confederate completely debriefed the subject and in particular emphasized the real nature of the intelligence tes⸱ After the debriefing, the subject was asked to rate the confederate on her attractiveness, using a 100-point scale.[1]

---

[1]Although this attempt to check on the attractiveness manipulation has very limited validity, giving it during the experiment would have incurred suspicion. Informal pretest observations by a group of five persons not in the experiment supports our contention that the manipulation was effective. In fact, two judges described the "moderate" confederate as "low" in attractiveness.

RESULTS

Effectiveness of the Manipulations

Subjects were asked two questions to check on the self-esteem manipulation. These were: "How would you describe your present emotional feelings?" (on a scale from "very happy" to "very sad"); and "How good do you personally feel your performance is in the task required in the present study?" (on a scale from "excellent" to "poor"). Both scales were arbitrarily scored from 1 to 20, the higher the score, the lower the self-esteem. According to analyses of variance performed on these data, subjects in the high-self-esteem condition tended to feel better than did low-self-esteem subjects ($F = 3.89$, $df = 1, 33$, $p < .10$), and they felt their performance was better ($F = 13.17$, $df = 1, 33$, $p < .01$). Thus, while the generalized mood response to the manipulation was somewhat weaker than the more direct measure of self-esteem (felt adequacy of performance), the manipulation seemed to have been effective overall.

The manipulation of physical attractiveness of the confederate was also effective at the 0.01 level (although one must have reservations about our measure).

There were no systematic differences among conditions of subject attractiveness, according to ratings made by the experimenter and confederates.

To check on possible differences between the two confederates, all data on romantic behavior (described in detail below) were subjected first to three-way analyses of variance (self-esteem $\times$ attractiveness $\times$ confederate). These analyses revealed significant tendencies for one confederate to elicit more romantic behavior than the other. However, there were no interactions of confederate with any independent variable. Thus the data for both confederates were combined for the analyses presented below.

Comparisons were also made between the first half of the experiment and the last half to check on possible confederate bias as a result of learning to recognize cues distinguishing high-self-esteem subjects from low-self-esteem subjects. However, the analysis indicated that there was no difference between phases of the experiment. In addition, a check of confederate descriptions of subjects indicated that they were unable to guess above chance levels the subjects' experimental condition.

Romantic Behavior

We predicted an interaction such that high-self-esteem subjects would display more romantic behavior toward the highly attractive confederate, whereas low-self-esteem subjects would display more romantic behavior toward the moderately attractive confederate. To test this prediction, we first summed the frequency of romantic behavior in each behavioral category for each subject. Any subject could get a score of 0 or 1 in each category except the "asked for date" category, in which he could obtain a score of 2 if he asked for two dates. Thus a subject's romantic behavior "score" could range from 0 to 7. The mean scores for each condition are graphically presented in Figure 33.1. Because the data were distributed in skewed fashion, the scores were transformed to produce a more normal distribution [X = log (X + 2)]. These data were then subjected to an analysis of variance. According to the analysis of variance, the hypothesized interaction between self-esteem and attractiveness was supported ($F = 5.34$; $df = 1, 33$; $p < .05$). Thus high-self-esteem subjects tended to choose the highly attractive girl, while low-self-esteem subjects tended to prefer the moderately attractive girl, as predicted.

Table 33.1 presents a breakdown of the data for each romantic-behavior category. For purposes of simplification, the percentage of subjects in each condition who displayed each type of romantic behavior (i.e., the percentage who got a score of 1 in each category) is presented. These data are exactly equivalent to the frequency data, except in the "asked for date" category, where percentages for number of subjects asking for at least one date and percentages for number of dates over total possible (two per subject) are presented separately.

The data in Table 33.1 indicate that of the 14 appropriate comparisons, 12 are in the predicted direction. Within the high-self-esteem conditions, romantic behavior is greater with the highly attractive confederate than with the moderately attractive confederate for all categories but one (asking for information). Within the low-self-esteem conditions, romantic behavior tends to be greater with the moderately attractive confederate than with the highly attractive confederate for all categories but one (offering to buy). These single comparisons are not significantly different

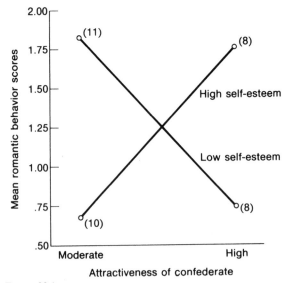

FIGURE 33.1
Romantic behavior toward another as function of self-esteem.

TABLE 33.1
Percentage of Subjects Displaying Each Type of Romantic Behavior

	Experimental condition			
	High self-esteem		Low self-esteem	
Romantic Behavior	Moderately attractive confederate (N = 10)	Highly attractive confederate (N = 8)	Moderately attractive confederate (N = 11)	Highly attractive confederate (N = 8)
Asked for date (at least one)	20	25	36	25
Asked for date (% dates of total possible)	10	19	27	13
Offered to buy coffee, etc.	0	25	18	25
Offered cigarette, gum, mint	10	25	27	0
Expressed compliments	0	25	18	0
Ignored first cue to leave	10	25	45	12
Asked for information— phone number, address, etc.	30	25	18	12

by themselves, but the overall consistency of the results for different romantic behaviors seems to provide some additional confidence in our hypothesis.

DISCUSSION

Our results indicate that self-esteem will affect which romantic partners are chosen: Low self-esteem will lead to choice of a partner lower in attractiveness than will high self-esteem. We interpret these results as indicating *not* that high-self-esteem persons are less "realistic" or "practical," but rather that the possession of high self-esteem changes what the person believes is a realistic or practical choice. Thus our interpretation of the effect of self-esteem on romantic behavior leans heavily on the assumption that changes in perceptions of the self affect perceptions of the chances of success or failure (i.e., probable payoff) when making a romantic choice. If a highly attractive person is perceived as much more attractive than oneself, as when one has low self-esteem, then the chances of success with that person will be perceived as relatively low. If a highly attractive person is perceived as similar in attractiveness to oneself, as when one has high self-esteem, then the chances of success will be seen as relatively high.

What if, in some way, we could have made subjects believe that choosing the confederate (in all conditions) would not entail any risk of rejection or failure? First, we should find subjects choosing the highly attractive confederate more than the moderately attractive confederate—maximizing attractiveness without having to consider possible failure. However, a recent study by Walster (1965) suggests a further difference: low-self-esteem persons may have a higher need for affection than high-self-esteem persons and, moreover, may be less demanding of perfection (will rate someone as more attractive than will high-self-esteem persons). Thus their attempts to secure acceptance—given no chance of failure—should be more intense than those of high-self-esteem persons. The Walster study bears out these predictions. Female subjects who had already been asked out by a male confederate liked him more when they had low self-esteem than when they had high self-esteem. In sum then, we conclude that our results will obtain only when the chances of failure are unknown or known to be relatively high.

One further point should be considered. It is possible that, when giving the intelligence test, the experimenter manipulated acceptance of the subject, as well as perceived intellectual worthiness. If so, our low-self-esteem subjects may have felt socially rejected, as well as less intellectually capable. This would support another explanation of our results, that is, that the low-self-esteem subject liked the highly attractive girl less because she disconfirmed his expectation of himself as an undesirable person. We attempted to avoid this possibility by having the experimenter act friendly and accepting to all subjects, but only with another experiment, in which various manipulations of self-esteem are used, can this explanation be totally rejected.

References

ARONSON, E., AND CARLSMITH, J. M. Performance expectancy as a determinant of actual performance. *Journal of Abnormal Social Psychology,* 1962, **65,** 178–182.

CROWNE, D. P., AND MARLOWE, D. *The Approval Motive: Studies in Evaluative Dependence.* New York: Wiley, 1964.

HOMANS, G. C. *Social Behavior: Its Elementary Forms.* New York: Harcourt, Brace and World, 1961.

THIBAUT, J. W., AND KELLEY, H. H. *The Social Psychology of Groups.* New York: Wiley, 1959.

WALSTER, E. The effect of self-esteem on romantic liking. *Journal of Experimental Social Psychology,* 1965, **1,** 184–197.

WALSTER, E., ARONSON, V., ABRAHAMS, D., AND ROTTMAN, L. Importance of physical attractiveness in dating behavior. *Journal of Personality and Social Psychology,* 1966, **4,** 508–516.

34

Social Perception and Interpersonal Behavior: On the Self-Fulfilling Nature of Social Stereotypes

Mark Snyder, Elizabeth Decker Tanke, and Ellen Berscheid

This research concerns the self-fulfilling influences of social stereotypes on dyadic social interaction. Conceptual analysis of the cognitive and behavioral consequences of stereotyping suggests that a perceiver's actions based upon stereotype-generated attributions about a specific target individual may cause the behavior of that individual to confirm the perceiver's initially erroneous attributions. A paradigmatic investigation of the behavioral confirmation of stereotypes involving physical attractiveness (e.g., "beautiful people are good people") is presented. Male "perceivers" interacted with female "targets" whom they believed (as a result of an experimental manipulation) to be physically attractive or physically unattractive. Tape recordings of each participant's conversational behavior were analyzed by naive observer judges for evidence of behavioral confirmation. These analyses revealed that targets who were perceived (unknown to them) to be physically attractive came to behave in a friendly, likeable, and sociable manner in comparison with targets whose perceivers regarded them as unattractive. It is suggested that theories in cognitive social psychology attend to the ways in which perceivers create the information that they process in addition to the ways that they process that information.

> Thoughts are but dreams
> Till their effects be tried
>
> —William Shakespeare, *The Rape of Lucrece*

Reprinted with permission of the authors and *The Journal of Personality and Social Psychology,* Vol. 35, No. 9, 1977. Copyright © 1977 by the American Psychological Association.

Research and preparation of this manuscript were supported in part by National Science Foundation Grants SOC 75-13872, "Cognition and Behavior: When Belief Creates Reality," to Mark Snyder and GS 35157X, "Dependency and Interpersonal Attraction," to Ellen Berscheid. We thank Marilyn Steere, Craig Daniels, and Dwain Boelter, who assisted in the empirical phases of this investigation; and J. Merrill Carlsmith, Thomas Hummel, E. E. Jones, Mark Lepper, and Walter Mischel, who provided helpful advice and constructive commentary.

Cognitive social psychology is concerned with the processes by which individuals gain knowledge about behavior and events that they encounter in social interaction, and how they use this knowledge to guide their actions. From this perspective, people are "constructive thinkers" searching for the causes of behavior, drawing inferences about people and their circumstances, and acting upon this knowledge.

Most empirical work in this domain—largely stimulated and guided by the attribution theories (e.g., Heider, 1958; Jones and Davis, 1965; Kelley, 1973)—has focused on the processing of information, the "machinery" of social cognition. Some outcomes of this research have been the specification of how individuals identify the causes of an actor's behavior, how individuals make inferences about the traits and dispositions of the actor, and how individuals make predictions about the actor's future behavior (for reviews, see Harvey, Ickes, and Kidd, 1976; Jones et al., 1972; Ross, 1977).

It is noteworthy that comparatively little theoretical and empirical attention has been directed to the other fundamental question within the cognitive social psychologist's mandate: What are the cognitive and behavioral consequences of our impressions of other people? From our vantage point, current-day attribution theorists leave the individual "lost in thought," with no machinery that links thought to action. It is to this concern that we address ourselves, both theoretically and empirically, in the context of social stereotypes.

Social stereotypes are a special case of interpersonal perception. Stereotypes are usually simple, overgeneralized, and widely accepted (e.g., Karlins, Coffman, and Walters, 1969). But stereotypes are often inaccurate. It is simply not true that all Germans are industrious or that all women are dependent and conforming. Nonetheless, many social stereotypes concern highly visible and distinctive personal characteristics, for example, sex and race. These pieces of information are usually the first to be noticed in social interaction and can gain high priority for channeling subsequent information processing and even social interaction. Social stereotypes are thus an ideal testing ground for considering the cognitive and behavioral consequences of person perception.

Numerous factors may help sustain our stereotypes and prevent disconfirmation of "erroneous" stereotype-based initial impressions of specific others. First, social stereotypes may influence information processing in ways that serve to bolster and strengthen these stereotypes.

Cognitive Bolstering of Social Stereotypes

As information processors, humans readily fall victim to the cognitive process described centuries ago by Francis Bacon:

> The human understanding, when any proposition has been once laid down . . . forces everything else to add fresh support and confirmation. . . . it is the peculiar and per-

petual error of the human understanding to be more moved and excited by affirmatives than negatives [pp. 23–24].

Empirical research has demonstrated several such biases in information processing. We may overestimate the frequency of occurence of confirming or paradigmatic examples of our stereotypes simply because such instances are more easily noticed, more easily brought to mind, and more easily retrieved from memory (see Hamilton and Gifford, 1976; Rothbart et al., unpublished). Evidence that confirms our stereotyped intuitions about human nature may be, in a word, more cognitively "available" (Tversky and Kahneman, 1973) than nonconfirming evidence.

Moreover, we may fill in the gaps in our evidence base with information consistent with our preconceived notions of what evidence should support our beliefs. For example, Chapman and Chapman (1967, 1969) have demonstrated that both college students and professional clinicians perceive positive associations between particular Rorschach responses and homosexuality in males, even though these associations are demonstrably absent in real life. These "signs" are simply those that comprise common cultural stereotypes of gay males.

Furthermore, once a stereotype has been adopted, a wide variety of evidence can be interpreted readily as supportive of that stereotype, including events that could support equally well an opposite interpretation. As Merton (1948) has suggested, ingroup virtues ("We are thrifty") may become out-group vices ("They are cheap") in our attempts to maintain negative stereotypes about disliked outgroups. (For empirical demonstrations of this bias, see Regan, Straus, and Fazio, 1974; Rosenhan, 1973; Zadny and Gerard, 1974).

Finally, selective recall and reinterpretation of information from an individual's past history may be exploited to support a current stereotype-based inference (see Loftus and Palmer, 1974). Thus, having decided that Jim is stingy (as are all members of his group), it may be all too easy to remember a variety of behaviors and incidents that are insufficient one at a time to support an attribution of stinginess, but that taken together do warrant and support such an inference.

Behavioral Confirmation of Social Stereotypes

The cognitive bolstering processes discussed above may provide the perceiver with an "evidence base" that gives compelling cognitive reality to any traits that he may have erroneously attributed to a target individual initially. This reality is, of course, entirely cognitive: It is in the eye and mind of the beholder. But stereotype-based attributions may serve as grounds for predictions about the target's future behavior and may guide and influence the perceiver's interactions with the target. This process itself may generate behaviors on the part of the target that erroneously confirm the predictions and validate the attributions of the perceiver. How others treat us is, in large measure, a reflection of our treatment of them (see Bandura,

1977; Mischel, 1968; Raush, 1965). Thus, when we use our social perceptions as guides for regulating our interactions with others, we may constrain their behavioral options (see Kelley and Stahelski, 1970).

Consider this hypothetical, but illustrative, scenario: Michael tells Jim that Chris is a cool and aloof person. Jim meets Chris and notices expressions of coolness and aloofness. Jim proceeds to overestimate the extent to which Chris's self-presentation reflects a cool and aloof disposition and underestimates the extent to which this posture was engendered by his own cool and aloof behavior toward Chris, that had in turn been generated by his own prior beliefs about Chris. Little does Jim know that Tom, who had heard that Chris was warm and friendly, found that his impressions of Chris were confirmed during their interaction. In each case, the end result of the process of "interaction guided by perceptions" has been the target person's *behavioral confirmation* of the perceiver's initial impressions of him.

This scenario makes salient key aspects of the process of behavioral confirmation in social interaction. The perceiver (either Jim or Tom) is not aware that his original perception of the target individual (Chris) is inaccurate. Nor is the perceiver aware of the causal role that his own behavior (here, the enactment of a cool or warm expressive style) plays in generating the behavioral evidence that erroneously confirms his expectations. Unbeknownst to the perceiver, the reality that he confidently perceives to exist in the social world has, in fact, been actively constructed by his own transactions with and operations upon the social world.

In our empirical research, we proposed to demonstrate that stereotypes may create their own social reality by channeling social interaction in ways that cause the stereotyped individual to behaviorally confirm the perceiver's stereotype. Moreover, we sought to demonstrate behavioral confirmation in a social interaction context designed to mirror as faithfully as possible the spontaneous generation of impressions in everyday social interaction and the subsequent channeling influences of these perceptions on dyadic interaction.

One widely held stereotype in this culture involves physical attractiveness. Considerable evidence suggests that attractive persons are assumed to possess more socially desirable personality traits and are expected to lead better lives than their unattractive counterparts (Berscheid and Walster, 1974). Attractive persons are perceived to have virtually every character trait that is socially desirable to the perceiver: "Physically attractive people, for example, were perceived to be more sexually warm and responsive, sensitive, kind, interesting, strong, poised, modest, sociable, and outgoing than persons of lesser physical attractiveness" (Berscheid and Walster, 1974, p. 169). This powerful stereotype holds for male and female perceivers and for male and female stimulus persons.

What of the validity of the physical attractiveness stereotype? Are the physically attractive actually more likable, friendly, and confident than the unattractive? Physically attractive young adults are more often and more eagerly sought out for social dates (Dermer, 1973; Krebs and Adinolphi, 1975; and Walster, et al., 1966). Even as early as nursery school age, physical attractiveness appears to channel social interaction: The physically attractive are chosen and the unattractive are rejected in sociometric choices (Dion and Berscheid, 1974; Kleck, Richardson and Ronald, 1974).

Differential amount of interaction with the attractive and unattractive clearly helps the stereotype persevere, for it limits the chances for learning whether the two types of individuals differ in the traits associated with the stereotype. But the point we wish to focus upon here is that the stereotype may also channel interaction so that it behaviorally confirms itself. Individuals may have different styles of interaction for those whom they perceive to be physically attractive and for those whom they consider unattractive. These differences in interaction style may in turn elicit and nurture behaviors from the target person that are in accord with the stereotype. That is, the physically attractive may actually come to behave in a friendly, likable, sociable manner—not because they necessarily possess these dispositions, but because the behavior of others elicits and maintains behaviors taken to be manifestations of such traits.

Accordingly, we sought to demonstrate the behavioral confirmation of the physical attractiveness stereotype in dyadic social interaction. In order to do so, pairs of previously unacquainted individuals (designated, for our purposes, as a perceiver and a target) interacted in a getting-acquainted situation that had been constructed to allow us to control the information that one member of the dyad (the male perceiver) received about the physical attractiveness of the other individual (the female target). To measure the extent to which the actual behavior of the target matched the perceiver's stereotype, naive observer judges, who were unaware of the actual or perceived physical attractiveness of either participant, listened to and evaluated tape recordings of the interaction.

METHOD

Participants

Fifty-one male and 51 female undergraduates at the University of Minnesota participated, for extra course credit, in a study of "the processes by which people become acquainted with each other." Participants were scheduled in pairs of previously unacquainted males and females.

The Interaction Between Perceiver and Target

To insure that participants would not see each other before their interactions, they arrived at separate experimental rooms on separate corridors. The experimenter informed each participant that she was studying acquaintance processes in social relationships. Specifically, she was investigating the differences between those initial interactions that involve nonverbal communication and those, such as telephone conversations, that do not. Thus, she explained, the participant would engage in a telephone conversation with another student in introductory psychology.

Before the conversation began, each participant provided written permission for it to be tape recorded. In addition, both dyad members completed brief questionnaires concerning such information as academic major in college and high school of graduation. These questionnaires, it was explained, would provide the partners with some information about each other with which to start the conversation.

Activating the perceiver's stereotype.   The getting-acquainted interaction permitted control of the information that each male perceiver received about the physical attractiveness of his female target. When male perceivers learned about the biographical information questionnaires, they also learned that each person would receive a snapshot of the other member of the dyad, because "other people in the experiment have told us they feel more comfortable when they have a mental picture of the person they're talking to." The experimenter then used a Polaroid camera to photograph the male. No mention of any snapshots was made to female participants.

When each male perceiver received his partner's biographical information form, it arrived in a folder containing a Polaroid snapshot, ostensibly of his partner. Although the biographical information had indeed been provided by his partner, the photograph was not. It was one of eight photographs that had been prepared in advance.

Twenty female students from several local colleges assisted (in return for $5) in the preparation of stimulus materials by allowing us to take Polaroid snapshots of them. Each photographic subject wore casual dress, each was smiling, and each agreed (in writing) to allow us to use her photograph. Twenty college-age men then rated the attractiveness of each picture on a 10-point scale.[1] We then chose the four pictures that had received the highest attractiveness ratings ($M = 8.10$) and the four photos that had received the lowest ratings ($M = 2.56$). There was virtually no overlap in ratings of the two sets of pictures.

Male perceivers were assigned randomly to one of two conditions of perceived physical attractiveness of their targets. Males in the attractive target condition received folders containing their partners' biographical information form and one of the four attractive photographs. Males in the unattractive target condition received folders containing their partners' biographical information form and one of the four unattractive photographs. Female targets knew nothing of the photographs possessed by their male interaction partners, nor did they receive snapshots of their partners.

---

[1]The interrater correlations of these ratings of attractiveness ranged from .45 to .92, with an average interrater correlation of .74.

The perceiver's stereotype-based attributions. Before initiating his get-ting-acquainted conversation, each male perceiver rated his initial impressions of his partner on an Impression Formation Questionnaire. The questionnaire was con-structed by supplementing the 27 trait adjectives used by Dion, Berscheid, and Walster (1972) in their original investigation of the physical attractiveness stereo-type with the following items: intelligence, physical attractiveness, social adept-ness, friendliness, enthusiasm, trustworthiness, and successfulness. We were thus able to assess the extent to which perceivers' initial impressions of their partners reflected general stereotypes linking physical attractiveness and personality char-acteristics.

The getting-acquainted conversation. Each dyad then engaged in a 10-minute unstructured conversation by means of microphones and headphones con-nected through a Sony TC-570 stereophonic tape recorder that recorded each par-ticipant's voice on a separate channel of the tape.

After the conversation, male perceivers completed the Impression Formation Questionnaires to record final impressions of their partners. Female targets ex-pressed self-perceptions in terms of the items of the Impression Formation Ques-tionnaire. Each female target also indicated, on 10-point scales, how much she had enjoyed the conversation, how comfortable she had felt while talking to her part-ner, how accurate a picture of herself she felt that her partner had formed as a result of the conversation, how typical her partner's behavior had been of the way she usually was treated by men, her perception of her own physical attractiveness, and her estimate of her partner's perception of her physical attractiveness. All partici-pants were then thoroughly and carefully debriefed and thanked for their contribu-tion to the study.

Assessing Behavioral Confirmation

To assess the extent to which the actions of the target women provided behav-ioral confirmation for the stereotypes of the men perceivers, eight male and four female introductory psychology students rated the tape recordings of the getting-acquainted conversations. These observer judges were unaware of the experimen-tal hypotheses and knew nothing of the actual or perceived physical attractiveness of the individuals on the tapes. They listened, in random order, to two 4-minute segments (one each from the beginning and end) of each conversation. They heard *only* the track of the tapes containing the target women's voices and rated each woman on the 34 bipolar scales of the Impression Formation Questionnaire as well as on 14 additional 10-point scales; for example, "How animated and enthusiastic is this person?," "How intimate or personal is this person's conversation?," and "How much is she enjoying herself?," "Another group of observer judges (three males and six females) performed a similar assessment of the male perceivers' behavior based upon only the track of the tapes that contained the males' voices.[2]

RESULTS

To chart the process of behavioral confirmation of social stereotypes in dyadic social interaction, we examined the effects of our manipulation of the target women's apparent physical attractiveness on (a) the male perceivers' initial impressions of them, and (b) the women's behavioral self-presentation during the interaction, as measured by the observer judges' ratings of the tape recordings.

The Perceivers' Stereotype

Did our male perceivers form initial impressions of their specific target women on the basis of general stereotypes that associate physical attractiveness and desirable personalities? To answer this question, we examined the male perceivers' initial ratings on the Impression Formation Questionnaire. Recall that these impressions were recorded *after* the perceivers had seen their partners' photographs, but *before* the getting-acquainted conversation.[3] Indeed, it appears that our male per-

---

[2]We assessed the reliability of our raters by means of intraclass correlations (Ebel, 1951), a technique that employs analysis-of-variance procedures to determine the proportion of the total variance in ratings due to variance in the persons being rated. The intraclass correlation is the measure of reliability most commonly used with interval data and ordinal scales that assume interval properties. Because the measure of interest was the mean rating of judges on each variable, the between-rater variance was not included in the error term in calculating the intraclass correlation. (For a discussion, see Tinsley and Weiss, 1975, p. 363.) Reliability coefficients for the coders' ratings of the females for all dependent measures ranged from .35 to .91 with a median of .755. For each dependent variable, a single score was constructed for each participant by calculating the mean of the raters' scores on that measure. Analyses of variance, including the time of the tape segment (early vs. late in the conversation) as a factor, revealed no more main effects of time or interactions between time and perceived attractiveness than would have been expected by chance. Thus, scores for the two tape segments were summed to yield a single score for each dependent variable. The same procedure was followed for ratings of male perceivers' behavior. In this case, the reliability coefficients ranged from .18 to .83 with a median of .61.

[3]These and all subsequent analyses are based upon a total of 38 observations, 19 in each of the attractive target and unattractive target conditions. Of the original 51 dyads, a total of 48 male-female pairs completed the experiment. In each of the remaining three dyads, the male participant had made reference during the conversation to the photograph. When this happened, the experimenter interrupted the conversation and immediately debriefed the participants. Of the remaining 48 dyads who completed the experimental procedures, 10 were eliminated from the analyses for the following reasons: In 4 cases the male participant expressed strong suspicion about the photograph; in 1 case, the conversation was not tape recorded because of a mechanical problem; and in 5 cases, there was a sufficiently large age difference (ranging from 6 to 18 years) between the participants that the males in these dyads reported that they had reacted very differently to their partners than they would have reacted to an age peer. This pattern of attrition was independent of assignment to the attractive target and unattractive target experimental conditions ($\chi^2 = 1.27$, *ns*).

ceivers did fashion their initial impressions of their female partners on the basis of stereotyped beliefs about physical attractiveness, multivariate $F(34, 3) = 10.19$, $p < .04$. As dictated by the physical attractiveness stereotype, men who anticipated physically attractive partners expected to interact with comparatively sociable, poised, humorous, and socially adept women; by contrast, men faced with the prospect of getting acquainted with relatively unattractive partners fashioned images of rather unsociable, awkward, serious and socially inept women, all F's (1, 36) $< 5.85, p < .025$.

Behavioral Confirmation

Not only did our perceivers fashion their images of their discussion partners on the basis of their stereotyped intuitions about beauty and goodness of character, but these impressions initiated a chain of events that resulted in the behavioral confirmation of these initially erroneous inferences. Our analyses of the observer judges' ratings of the women's behavior were guided by our knowledge of the structure of the men's initial impressions of their target women's personality. Specifically, we expected to find evidence of behavioral confirmation only for those traits that had defined the perceivers' stereotypes. For example, male perceivers did not attribute differential amounts of sensitivity or intelligence to partners of differing apparent physical attractiveness. Accordingly, we would not expect that our observer judges would "hear" different amounts of intelligence or sensitivity in the tapes. By contrast, male perceivers did expect attractive and unattractive targets to differ in sociability. Here we would expect that observer judges would detect differences in sociability between conditions when listening to the women's contributions to the conversations, and thus we would have evidence of behavioral confirmation.

To assess the extent to which the women's behavior, as rated by the observer judges, provided behavioral confirmation for the male perceivers' stereotypes, we identified, by means of a discriminant analysis (Tatsuoka, 1971), those 21 trait items of the Impression Formation Questionnaire for which the mean initial ratings of the men in the attractive target and unattractive target conditions differed by more than 1.4 standard deviations.[4] This set of "stereotype traits" (e.g., sociable, poised, sexually warm, outgoing) defines the differing perceptions of the personality characteristics of target women in the two experimental conditions.

We then entered these 21 stereotype traits and the 14 additional dependent measures into a multivariate analysis of variance. This analysis revealed that our observer judges did indeed view women who had been assigned to the attractive target condition quite differently than women in the unattractive target condition,

---

[4]After the 21st trait dimension, the differences between the experimental conditions drop off sharply. For example, the next adjective pair down the line has a difference of 1.19 standard deviations, and the one after that has a difference of 1.02 standard deviations.

$Fm(35, 2) = 40.0003$, $p < .025$. What had initially been reality in the minds of the men had now become reality in the behavior of the women with whom they had interacted—a behavioral reality discernible even by naive observer judges, who had access *only* to tape recordings of the women's contributions to the conversations.

When a multivariate analysis of variance is performed on multiple correlated dependent measures, the null hypothesis states that the vector of means is equal across conditions. When the null hypothesis is rejected, the nature of the difference between groups must then be inferred from inspection of group differences on the individual dependent measures. In this case, the differences between the behavior of the women in the attractive target and the unattractive target conditions were in the same direction as the male perceivers' initial stereotyped impressions for fully 17 of the 21 measures of behavioral confirmation. The binomial probability that at least 17 of these adjectives would be in the predicted direction by chance alone is a scant .003. By contrast, when we examined the 13 trait pairs that our discriminant analysis had indicated did *not* define the male perceivers' stereotype, a sharply different pattern emerged. Here, we would not expect any systematic relationship between the male perceivers' stereotyped initial impressions and the female targets' actual behavior in the getting-acquainted conversations. In fact, for only 8 of these 13 measures is the differences between the behavior of the women in the attractive target condition in the same direction as the men's stereotyped initial impressions. This configuration is, of course, hardly different from the pattern expected by chance alone if there were no differences between the groups (exact binomial $p = .29$). Clearly, then, behavioral confirmation manifested itself only for those attributes that had defined the male perceivers stereotype; that is, only in those domains where the men believed that there did exist links between physical attractiveness and personal attributes did the women come to behave differently as a consequence of the level of physical attractiveness that we had experimentally assigned to them.

Moreover, our understanding of the nature of the difference between the attractive target and the unattractive target conditions identified by our multivariate analysis of variance and our confidence in this demonstration of behavioral confirmation are bolstered by the consistent pattern of behavioral differences on the 14 additional related dependent measures. Our raters assigned to the female targets in the attractive target condition higher ratings on *every* question related to favorableness of self-presentation. Thus, for example, those who were thought by their perceivers to be physically attractive appeared to the observer judges to manifest greater confidence, greater animation, greater enjoyment of the conversation, and greater liking for their partners than those women who interacted with men who perceived them as physically unattractive.[5]

---

[5]We may eliminate several alternative interpretations of the behavioral confirmation effect. Women who had been assigned randomly to the attractive target condition were not in fact more physi-

In Search of Mediators of Behavioral Confirmation

We next attempted to chart the process of behavioral confirmation. Specifically, we searched for evidence of the behavioral implications of the perceivers' stereotypes. Did the male perceivers present themselves differently to target women whom they assumed to be physically attractive or unattractive? Because we had 50 dependent measures[6] of the observer judges' ratings of the males—12 more than the number of observations (male perceivers)—a multivariate analysis of variance is inappropriate. However, in 21 cases, univariate analyses of variance did indicate differences between conditions (all p's $< .05$). Men who interacted with women whom they believed to be physically attractive appeared (to the observer judges) more sociable, sexually warm, interesting, independent, sexually permissive, bold, outgoing, humorous, obvious, and socially adept than their counterparts in the unattractive target condition. Moreover, these men were seen as more attractive, more confident, and more animated in their conversation than their counterparts. Further, they were considered by the observer judges to be more comfortable, to enjoy themselves more, to like their partners more, to take the initiative more often, to use their voices more effectively, to see their women partners as more attractive, and, finally, to be seen as more attractive by their partners than men in the unattractive target condition.

It appears, then, that differences in the level of sociability manifested and expressed by the male perceivers may have been a key factor in bringing out reciprocating patterns of expression in the target women. One reason that target women who had been labeled as attractive may have reciprocated these sociable overtures is that they regarded their partners' images of them as more accurate, $F(1, 28) = 6.75, p < .02$, and their interaction style to be more typical of the way men generally treated them, $F(1, 28) = 4.79, p < .04$, than did women in the unattractive target

---

cally attractive than those who were assigned randomly to the unattractive target condition. Ratings of the actual attractiveness of the female targets by the experimenter revealed no differences whatsoever between conditions, $t(36) = .00$. Nor, for that matter, did male perceivers differ in their own physical attractiveness as a function of experimental condition, $f(36) = .44$. In addition, actual attractiveness of male perceivers and actual attractiveness of female targets within dyads were independent of each other, $r(36) = .06$.

Of greater importance, there was no detectable difference in personality characteristics of females who had been assigned randomly to the attractive target and unattractive target conditions of the experiment. They did not differ in self-esteem as assessed by the Janis–Field–Eagly (Janis and Field, 1973) measure, $F(1, 36) < 1$. Moreover, there were no differences between experimental conditions in the female targets' self-perceptions as reported after the conversations on the Impression Formation Questionnaire (*Fm* < 1). We have thus no reason to suspect that any systematic, pre-existing differences between conditions in morphology or personality can pose plausible alternative explanations of our demonstration of behavioral confirmation.

[6]Two dependent measures were added between the time that the ratings were made of the female participants and the time that the ratings were made of the male participants. These measures were responses to the questions, "How interested is he in his partner?" and "How attractive does he think his partner is?"

condition.[7] These individuals, perhaps, rejected their partners' treatment of them as unrepresentative and defensively adopted more cool and aloof postures to cope with their situations.

DISCUSSION

Of what consequence are our social stereotypes? Our research suggests that stereotypes can and do channel dyadic interaction so as to create their own social reality. In our demonstration, pairs of individuals got acquainted with each other in a situation that allowed us to control the information that one member of the dyad (the perceiver) received about the physical attractiveness of the other person (the target). Our perceivers, in anticipation of interaction, fashioned erroneous images of their specific partners that reflected their general stereotypes about physical attractiveness. Moreover, our perceivers had very different patterns and styles of interaction for those whom they perceived to be physically attractive and unattractive. These differences in self-presentation and interaction style, in turn, elicited and nurtured behaviors of the target that were consistent with the perceivers' initial stereotypes. Targets who were perceived (unbeknownst to them) to be physically attractive actually came to behave in a friendly, likable, and sociable manner. The perceivers' attributions about their targets based upon their stereotyped intuitions about the world had initiated a process that produced behavioral confirmation of those attributions. The initially erroneous attributions of the perceivers had become real: The stereotype had truly functioned as a self-fulfilling prophecy (Merton, 1948).[8]

We regard our investigation as a particularly compelling demonstration of behavioral confirmation in social interaction. For if there is any social–psychological process that ought to exist in "stronger" form in everyday interaction than in the psychological laboratory, it is behavioral confirmation. In the context of years of social interaction in which perceivers have reacted to their actual physical attractiveness, our 10-minute getting-acquainted conversations over a telephone must seem minimal indeed. Nonetheless, the impact was sufficient to permit outside observers who had access only to one person's side of a conversation to detect manifestations of behavioral confirmation.

---

[7]The degrees of freedom for these analyses are fewer than those for other analyses because they were added to the experimental procedure after four dyads had participated in each condition.

[8]Our research on behavioral confirmation in social interaction is a clear "cousin" of other demonstrations that perceivers' expectations may influence other individuals' behavior. Thus, Rosenthal (1974) and his colleagues have conducted an extensive program of laboratory and field investigation of the effects of experimenters' and teachers' expectations on the behavior of subjects in psychological laboratories and students in classrooms. Experimenters and teachers led to expect particular patterns of performance from their subjects and pupils act in ways that selectively influence or shape those performances to confirm initial expectations (e.g., Rosenthal, 1974).

Might not other important and widespread social stereotypes—particularly those concerning sex, race, social class, and ethnicity—also channel social interaction so as to create their own social reality? For example, will the common stereotype that women are more conforming and less independent than men (see Broverman, et al., 1972) influence interaction so that (within a procedural paradigm similar to ours) targets believed to be female will actually conform more, be more dependent, and be more successfully manipulated than interaction partners believed to be male? At least one empirical investigation has pointed to the possible self-fulfilling nature of apparent sex differences in self-presentation (Zanna and Pack, 1975).

Any self-fulfilling influences of social stereotypes may have compelling and pervasive societal consequences. Social observers have for decades commented on the ways in which stigmatized social groups and outsiders may fall "victim" to self-fulfilling cultural stereotypes (e.g., Becker, 1963; Goffman, 1963; Merton, 1948; Myrdal, 1944; Tannenbaum, 1938). Consider Scott's (1969) observations about the blind:

> When, for example, sighted people continually insist that a blind man is helpless because he is blind, their subsequent treatment of him may preclude his even exercising the kinds of skills that would enable him to be independent. It is in this sense that stereotypic beliefs are self-actualized [p. 9].

And all too often it is the "victims" who are blamed for their own plight (see Ryan, 1971) rather than the social expectations that have constrained their behavioral options.

Of what import is the behavioral confirmation process for our theoretical understanding of the nature of social perception? Although our empirical research has focused on social stereotypes that are widely accepted and broadly generalized, our notions of behavioral confirmation may apply equally well to idiosyncratic social perceptions spontaneously formed about specific individuals in the course of every day social interaction. In this sense, social psychologists have been wise to devote intense effort to understanding the processes by which impressions of others are formed. Social perceptions are important precisely because of their impact on social interaction. Yet, at the same time, research and theory in social perception (mostly displayed under the banner of attribution theory) that have focused on the manner in which individuals process information provided them to form impressions of others may underestimate the extent to which information received in actual social interaction is a product of the perceiver's own actions toward the target individual. More careful attention must clearly be paid to the way in which perceivers *create* or *construct* the information that they process in addition to the way in which they *process* that information. Events in the social world may be as much the *effects* of our perceptions of those events as they are the *causes* of those perceptions.

From this perspective, it becomes easier to appreciate the perceiver's stubborn tendency to fashion images of others largely in trait terms (e.g., Jones and Nisbett, 1972), despite the poverty of evidence for the pervasive cross-situational consistencies in social behavior that the existence of "true" traits would demand (e.g.,

Mischel, 1968). This tendency, dubbed by Ross (1977) as the "fundamental attribution error," may be a self-erasing error. For even though any target individual's behavior may lack, overall, the trait-defining properties of cross-situational consistency, the actions of the perceiver himself may produce consistency in the samples of behavior available to that perceiver. Our impressions of others may cause those others to behave in consistent traitlike fashion for us. In that sense, our trait-based impressions of others are veridical, even though the same individual may behave or be led to behave in a fashion perfectly consistent with opposite attributions by other perceivers with quite different impressions of that individual. Such may be the power of the behavioral confirmation process.

References

BACON, F. *[Novum organum]* (J. Devey, ed.). New York: P. F. Collier & Son, 1902. (Originally published, 1620.)

BANDURA, A. *Social learning theory.* Englewood Cliffs, N.J.: Prentice Hall, 1977.

BECKER, H. W. *Outsiders: Studies in the sociology of deviance.* N.Y.: Free Press, 1963.

BERSCHEID, E., AND WALSTER, E. Physical attractiveness. In L. Berkowitz (ed.) *Advances in experimental social psychology.* Vol. 7. New York: Academic Press, 1974.

BROVERMAN, I. K., VOGEL, S. R., BROVERMAN, D. M., CLARKSON, F. E., AND ROSENKRANTZ, P. S. Sex-role stereotypes: A current appraisal. *Journal of Social Issues,* 1972, **28,** 59–78.

CHAPMAN, L., AND CHAPMAN, J. The genesis of popular but erroneous psychodiagnostic observations. *Journal of Abnormal Psychology,* 1967, **72,** 193–204.

CHAPMAN, L., AND CHAPMAN, J. Illusory correlations as an obstacle to the use of valid psychodiagnostic signs. *Journal of Abnormal Psychology,* 1969, **74,** 271–280.

DERMER, M. *When beauty fails.* Unpublished doctoral dissertation, University of Minnesota, 1973.

DION, K. K., AND BERSCHEID, E. Physical attractiveness and peer perception among children. *Sociometry,* 1974 **27**(1), 1–12.

DION, K. K., BERSCHEID, E., AND WALSTER, E. What is beautiful is good. *Journal of Personality and Social Psychology,* 1972, **24,** 285–290.

EBEL, R. L. Estimation of the reliability of ratings. *Psychometrika,* 1951, **16,** 407–424.

GOFFMAN, E. *Stigma: Notes on the management of spoiled identity.* Englewood Cliffs, N.J.: Prentice-Hall, 1963.

HAMILTON, D. L., AND GIFFORD, R. K. Illusory correlation in interpersonal perception: A cognitive basis of stereotypic judgments. *Journal of Experimental Social Psychology,* 1976, **12,** 392–407.

HARVEY, J. H., ICKES, W. J., AND KIDD, R. F. *New directions in attribution research.* Hillsdale, N.J.: Erlbaum, 1976.

HEIDER, F. *The psychology of interpersonal relations.* New York: Wiley, 1958.

JANIS, I., AND FIELD P. Sex differences and personality factors related to persuasibility. In C. Hovland and I. Janis (eds.), *Personality and persuasibility.* New Haven, Conn.: Yale University Press, 1973.

JONES, E. E., AND DAVIS K. E. From acts to dispositions: The attribution process in person perception. In L. Berkowitz (ed.), *Advances in experimental social psychology.* Vol. 2. New York: Academic Press, 1965.

JONES et al. *Attribution: Perceiving the causes of behavior.* Morristown, N.J.: General Learning Press, 1972.

JONES, E. E., AND NISBETT, R. E. The actor and the observer: Divergent perceptions of the causes of behavior. In E. Jones, D. Kanouse, H. Kelley, S. Valins, and B. Weiner (eds.),

Attribution: Perceiving the causes of behavior. New York: General Learning Press, 1972.

KARLINS, M., COFFMAN, T. L., AND WALTERS, G. On the fading of social stereotypes: Studies in three generations of college students. *Journal of Personality and Social Psychology,* 1969, **13**, 1–16.

KELLEY, H. H. The process of causal attribution. *American Psychologist,* 1973, **28**, 107–128.

KELLEY, H. H., AND STAHELSKI, A. J. The social interaction basis of cooperators' and competitors' beliefs about others. *Journal of Personality and Social Psychology,* 1970, **16**, 66–91.

KLECK, R. E., RICHARDSON, S. A., AND RONALD, L. Physical appearance cues and interpersonal attraction in children. *Child Development,* 1974, **45**, 305–310.

KREBS, D., AND ADINOLPHI, A. A. Physical attractiveness, social relations, and personality style. *Journal of Personality and Social Psychology,* 1975, **31**, 245–253.

LOFTUS, E., AND PALMER, J. Reconstruction of automobile destruction. *Journal of Verbal Learning and Verbal Behavior,* 1974, **13**, 585–589.

MERTON, R. K. The self-fulfilling prophecy. *Antioch Review,* 1948, **8**, 193–210.

MISCHEL, W. *Personality and assessment.* New York: Wiley, 1968.

MYRDAL, G. *An American dilemma.* New York: Harper & Row, 1944.

RAUSH, H. L. Interaction sequences. *Journal of Personality and Social Psychology,* 1965, **2**, 487–499.

REGAN, D. T., STRAUS, E., AND FAZIO, R. Liking and the attribution process. *Journal of Experimental Social Psychology,* 1974, **10**, 385–397.

ROSENHAN, D. L. On being sane in insane places. *Science,* 1973, **179**, 250–258.

ROSENTHAL, R. *On the social psychology of the self-fulfilling prophecy: Further evidence for pygmalion effects and their mediating mechanisms.* New York: M.S.S. Information Corp. Modular Publications, 1974.

ROSS, L. The intuitive psychologist and his shortcomings: Distortions in the attribution process. In L. Berkowitz (ed.), *Advances in experimental social psychology.* Vol. 10. New York: Academic Press, 1977.

ROTHBART, M., FULERO, S., JENSEN, C., HOWARD, J., AND BIRRELL, P. *From individual to group impressions: Availability heuristics in stereotype formation.* Unpublished manuscript, University of Oregon, 1976.

RYAN, W. *Blaming the victim.* New York: Vintage Books, 1971.

SCOTT, R. A. *The making of blind men.* New York: Russell Sage, 1969.

TANNENBAUM, F. *Crime and the community.* Boston: Ginn, 1938.

TATSUOKA, M. M. *Multivariate analysis.* New York: Wiley, 1971.

TINSLEY, H. E. A., AND WEISS, D. J. Interrater reliability and agreement of subjective judgments. *Journal of Counseling Psychology,* 1975, **22**, 358–376.

TVERSKY, A., AND KAHNEMAN, D. Availability: A heuristic for judging frequency and probability. *Cognitive Psychology,* 1973, **5**, 207–232.

WALSTER, E., ARONSON, V., ABRAHAMS, D., AND ROTTMAN, L. Importance of physical attractiveness in dating behavior. *Journal of Personality and Social Psychology,* 1966, **4**, 508–516.

ZADNY, J., AND GERARD, H. B. Attributed intentions and informational selectivity. *Journal of Experimental Social Psychology,* 1974, **10**, 34–52.

ZANNA, M. P., AND PACK, S. J. On the self-fulfilling nature of apparent sex differences in behavior. *Journal of Experimental Social Psychology,* 1975, **11**, 583–591.

35

Some Evidence for Heightened Sexual Attraction Under Conditions of High Anxiety

Donald G. Dutton and Arthur P. Aron

Male passersby were contacted either on a fear-arousing suspension bridge or a non–fear-arousing bridge by an attractive female interviewer who asked them to fill out questionnaires containing Thematic Apperception Test pictures. Sexual content of stories written by subjects on the fear-arousing bridge and tendency of these subjects to attempt postexperimental contact with the interviewer were both significantly greater. No significant differences between bridges were obtained on either measure for subjects contacted by a male interviewer. A third study manipulated anticipated shock to male subjects and an attractive female confederate independently. Anticipation of own shock but not anticipation of shock to confederate increased sexual imagery scores on the Thematic Apperception Test and attraction to the confederate. Some theoretical implications of these findings are discussed.

There is a substantial body of indirect evidence suggesting that sexual attractions occur with increased frequency during states of strong emotion. For example, heterosexual love has been observed to be associated both with hate (James, 1910; Suttie, 1935) and with pain (Ellis, 1936). A connection between "aggression" and sexual attraction is supported by Tinbergen's (1954) observations of intermixed courting and aggression behaviors in various animal species, and a series of experiments conducted by Barclay have indicated the existence of a similar phenomenon in human behavior. In one study, Barclay and Haber (1965) arranged for stu-

Reprinted with permission of the authors and *Journal of Personality and Social Psychology,* Vol. 30, No. 4, 1974. Copyright © 1974 by the American Psychological Association.

This research was supported by University of British Columbia Research Committee Grant 26 9840 to the first author and National Research Council Postdoctoral Fellowship 1560 to the second author.

dents in one class to be angered by having their professor viciously berate them for having done poorly on a recent test; another class served as a control. Subsequently, both groups were tested for aggressive feelings and for sexual arousal. A manipulation check was successful, and the angered group manifested significantly more sexual arousal than did controls ($p < .01$) as measured by explicit sexual content in stories written in response to Thematic Apperception Test (TAT)-like stimuli. Similar results were obtained in two further studies (Barclay, 1969, 1970) in which fraternity and sorority members were angered by the experimenter. The 1970 study employed a female experimenter, which demonstrated that the aggression–sexual arousal link was not specific to male aggression; the 1969 study provided additional support for the hypothesis by using a physiological measure of sexual arousal (acid phosphatase content in urine samples).

Barclay has explained his findings in terms of a special aggression–sexuality link and has cited as support for his position Freud's (1938) argument that prehistoric man had to physically dominate his potential mates and also a study by Clark (1952) in which increased sexual arousal produced by viewing slides of nudes yielded increased aggression in TAT responses. Aron (1970), on the other hand, argued that an aggression–sexuality link exists, but it is only a special case of a more general relationship between emotional arousal of all kinds and sexual attraction. To demonstrate this point, he designed a study in which instead of anger, residual emotion from intense role playing was the independent variable. In this experiment, each of 40 male subjects role played with the same attractive female confederate in either a highly emotional or a minimally emotional situation. Subjects enacting highly emotional roles included significantly more sexual imagery in stories written in response to TAT-like stimuli ($p < .01$) and indicated significantly more desire to kiss the confederate ($p < .05$) than did subjects in the control condition. One possible explanation is suggested by Schachters' theory of emotion (Schachter, 1964; Schachter and Singer, 1962). He argued that environmental cues are used, in certain circumstances, to provide emotional labels for unexplained or ambiguous states of arousal. However, it is notable that much of the above-cited research indicates that a sexual attraction–strong emotion link may occur even when the emotions are unambiguous. Accordingly, taking into account both the Schachter position and findings from sexual attraction research in general, Aron (1970) hypothesized that strong emotions are relabeled as sexual attraction whenever an acceptable object is present, and emotion-producing circumstances do not require the full attention of the individual.

The present series of experiments is designed to test the notion that an attractive female is seen as more attractive by males who encounter her while they experience a strong emotion (fear) than by males not experiencing a strong emotion. Experiment 1 is an attempt to verify this proposed emotion–sexual attraction link in a natural setting. Experiments 2 and 3 are field and laboratory studies which attempt to clarify the results of Experiment 1.

EXPERIMENT 1

METHOD

Subjects

Subjects were males visiting either of two bridge sites who fit the following criteria: (a) between 18 and 35 years old and (b) unaccompanied by a female companion. Only one member of any group of potential subjects was contacted. A total of 85 subjects were contacted by either a male or a female interviewer.

Site

The experiment was conducted on two bridges over the Capilano River in North Vancouver, British Columbia, Canada. The "experimental" bridge was the Capilano Canyon Suspension Bridge, a 5-foot-wide, 450-foot-long, bridge constructed of wooden boards attached to wire cables that ran from one side to the other of the Capilano Canyon. The bridge has many arousal-inducing features such as *(a)* a tendency to tilt, sway, and wobble, creating the impression that one is about to fall over the side; *(b)* very low handrails of wire cable which contribute to this impression; and *(c)* a 230-foot drop to rocks and shallow rapids below the bridge. The "control" bridge was a solid wood bridge further upriver. Constructed of heavy cedar, this bridge was wider and firmer than the experimental bridge, was only 10 feet above a small, shallow rivulet which ran into the main river, had high handrails, and did not tilt or sway.

Procedure

As subjects crossed either the control or experimental bridge, they were approached by the interviewer.[1]

Female interviewer.   The interviewer explained that she was doing a project for her psychology class on the effects of exposure to scenic attractions on creative expression. She then asked potential subjects if they would fill out a short questionnaire. The questionnaire contained six filler items such as age, education, prior visits to bridge, etc., on the first page. On the second page, subjects were instructed to write a brief, dramatic story based upon a picture of a young woman covering her face with one hand and reaching with the other. The instructions and the picture

---

[1]The interviewers were not aware of the experimental hypothesis in order to prevent unintentional differential cueing of subjects in experimental and control groups.

(TAT Item 3GF) employed were adapted from Murray's (1943) *Thematic Apperception Test Manual.* A similar measure of sexual arousal has been employed in the Barclay studies (1969, 1970; Barclay and Haber, 1965), and in other sex-related experiments (Aron, 1970; Clark, 1952; Leiman and Epstein, 1961). The particular TAT item used in the present study was selected for its lack of obvious sexual content, since projective measures of sexual arousal based on explicit sexual stimuli tend to be highly sensitive to individual differences due to sexual defensiveness (Clark and Sensibar, 1955; Eisler, 1968; Leiman and Epstein, 1961; Lubin, 1960). If the subject agreed, the questionnaire was filled out on the bridge.

Stories were later scored for manifest sexual content according to a slightly modified version of the procedure employed by Barclay and Haber (1965). Scores ranged from 1 (no sexual content) to 5 (high sexual content) according to the most sexual reference in the story. Thus, for example, a story with any mention of sexual intercourse received 5 points; but if the most sexual reference was "girl friend," it received a score of 2; "kiss" counted 3; and "lover," 4.

On completion of the questionnaire, the interviewer thanked the subject and offered to explain the experiment in more detail when she had more time. At this point, the interviewer tore the corner off a sheet of paper, wrote down her name and phone number, and invited each subject to call, if he wanted to talk further. Experimental subjects were told that the interviewer's name was Gloria and control subjects, Donna, so that they could easily be classified when they called. On the assumption that curiosity about the experiment should be equal between control and experimental groups, it was felt that differential calling rates might reflect differential attraction to the interviewer.

Male interviewer.   The procedure with the male interviewer was identical to that above. Subjects were again supplied with two fictitious names so that if they phoned the interviewer, they could be classified into control or experimental groups.

RESULTS

Check on Arousal Manipulation

Probably the most compelling evidence for arousal on the experimental bridge is to observe people crossing the bridge. Forty percent of subjects observed crossing the bridge walked very slowly and carefully, clasping onto the handrail before taking each step. A questionnaire was administered to 30 males who fit the same criteria as the experimental subjects. Fifteen males on the experimental bridge were asked, "How fearful do you think the average person would be when he crossed this bridge?" The mean rating was 79 on a 100-point scale where 100 was equal to extremely fearful. Fifteen males on the control bridge gave a mean rating of 18 on the same scale ($t = 9.7$, $df = 28$, $p < .001$, two-tailed). In response to the question

"How fearful were you while crossing the bridge?" experimental-bridge males gave a rating of 65 and control-bridge males a rating of 3 ($t = 10.6$, $p < .001$, $df = 28$, two-tailed). Hence, it can be concluded that most people are quite anxious on the experimental bridge but not on the control bridge. To prevent suspicion, no checks on the arousal of experimental subjects could be made.

Thematic Apperception Test Responses

Female interviewer.   On the experimental bridge, 23 of 33 males who were approached by the female interviewer agreed to fill in the questionnaire. On the control bridge, 22 of 33 agreed. Of the 45 questionnaires completed, 7 were unusable either because they were incomplete or written in a foreign language. The remaining 38 questionnaires (20 experimental and 18 control) had their TAT stories scored for sexual imagery by two scorers who were experienced with TAT scoring. (Although both were familiar with the experimental hypothesis, questionnaires had been coded so that they were blind as to whether any given questionnaire was written by a control or experimental subject.) The interrater reliability was +.87.

Subjects in the experimental group obtained a mean sexual imagery score of 2.47 and those in the control group, a score of 1.41 ($t = 3.19$, $p < .01$, $df = 36$, two-tailed). Thus, the experimental hypothesis was verified by the imagery data.

Male interviewer.   Twenty-three out of 51 subjects who were approached on the experimental bridge agreed to fill in the questionnaire. On the control bridge 22 out of 42 agreed. Five of these questionnaires were unusable, leaving 20 usable in both experimental and control groups. These were rated as above. Subjects in the experimental group obtained a mean sexual imagery score of .80 and those in the control group, .61 ($t = .36$, *ns*). Hence the pattern of result obtained by the female interviewer was not reproduced by the male interviewer.

Behavioral Data

Female interviewer.   In the experimental group, 18 of the 23 subjects who agreed to the interview accepted the interviewer's phone number. In the control group, 16 out of 22 accepted (see Table 35.1). A second measure of sexual attraction was the number of subjects who called the interviewer. In the experimental group 9 out of 18 called, in the control group 2 out of 16 called ($X^2 = 5.7$, $p < .02$). Taken in conjunction with the sexual imagery data, this finding

TABLE 35.1
Sexual attraction under conditions of high anxiety
Behavioral responses and thematic apperception test imagery scores for each experimental group

Interviewer	No. filling in questionnaire	No. accepting phone number	No. phoning	Usable questionnaires	Sexual imagery score
Female					
Control bridge	22/23	16/22	2/16	18	1.41
Experimental bridge	23/33	18/23	9/18	20	2.47
Male					
Control bridge	22/42	6/22	1/6	20	61
Experimental bridge	23/51	7/23	2/7	20	80

suggests that subjects in the experimental group were more attracted to the interviewer.

Male interviewer.   In the experimental group, 7 out of 23 accepted the interviewer's phone number. In the control group, 6 out of 22 accepted. In the experimental group, 2 subjects called; in the control group, 1 subject called. Again, the pattern of results obtained by the female interviewer was not replicated by the male.

Although the results of this experiment provide prima facie support for an emotion–sexual attraction link, the experiment suffers from interpretative problems that often plague field experiments. The main problem with the study is the possibility of different subject populations on the two bridges. First, the well-advertised suspension bridge is a tourist attraction that may have attracted more out-of-town persons than did the nearby provincial park where the control bridge was located. This difference in subject populations may have affected the results in two ways. The experimental subjects may have been less able to phone the experimenter (if they were in town on a short-term tour) and less likely to hold out the possibility of further liaison with her. If this were the case, the resulting difference due to subject differences would have operated *against* the main hypothesis. Also, this difference in subject populations could not affect the sexual imagery scores unless one assumed the experimental bridge subjects to be more sexually deprived than controls. The results using the male interviewer yielded no significant differences in sexual imagery between experimental and control subjects; however, the possibility still exists that sexual deprivation could have interacted with the presence of the attractive female experimenter to produce the sexual imagery results obtained in this experiment.

Second, differences could exist between experimental and control populations with respect to personality variables. The experimental population might be more predisposed to thrill seeking and therefore more willing to chance phoning a strange female to effect a liaison. Also, present knowledge of personality theory does not allow us to rule out the combination of thrill seeking and greater sexual imagery. Accordingly, a second experiment was carried out in an attempt to rule out any differential subject population explanation for the results of Experiment 1.

EXPERIMENT 2

METHOD

Subjects

Subjects were 34 males visiting the suspension bridge who fit the same criteria as in Experiment 1.

Procedure

The chief problem of Experiment 2 was choosing a site that would allow contact with aroused and nonaroused members of the same subject population. One possibility was to use as a control group suspension-bridge visitors who had not yet crossed the bridge or who had just gotten out of their cars. Unfortunately, if a substantial percentage of this group subsequently refused to cross the bridge, the self-selecting-subject problem of Experiment 1 would not be circumvented. Alternatively, males who had just crossed the bridge could be used as a control. The problem with this strategy was that this group, having just crossed the bridge, may have felt residual anxiety or elation or both, which would confound the study. To avoid this latter problem, control subjects who had just crossed the bridge and were sitting or walking in a small park were contacted at least 10 minutes after crossing the bridge. This strategy, it was hoped, would rule out residual physiological arousal as a confounding factor. Except that a different female experimenter was used in Experiment 2 and no male interviewer condition was run, all other details of the study were identical to Experiment 1.

RESULTS

Check on Arousal Manipulation

As with Experiment 1, no arousal manipulation check was given to experimental subjects in order not to arouse suspicion about the real intent of the experiment. Data for a group of nonexperimental subjects of the same age and sex as experimental subjects are reported in Experiment 1.

Thematic Apperception Test Responses

In the experimental group, 25 of 34 males who were approached agreed to fill in the questionnaire. In the control group, 25 out of 35 agreed. Of the 50 questionnaires completed, 5 were unusable because they were incomplete. The remainder (23 experimental and 22 control) were scored for sexual imagery as in Experiment 1. The interrater reliability in Experiment 2 was + .79.

Subjects in the experimental group obtained a mean sexual imagery score of 2.99 and those in the control group, a score of 1.92 ($t = 3.07$, $p < .01$, $df = 36$, two-tailed). Thus the experimental hypothesis was again verified by the imagery data.

Behavioral Data

In the experimental group, 20 of the 25 subjects who agreed to the interview accepted the interviewer's phone number. In the control group, 19 out of 23 accepted. In the experimental group, 13 out of 20 called, while in the control group, 7 out of 23 phoned ($X^2 = 5.89$, $p < .02$). Thus the behavioral result of Experiment 1 was also replicated.

Experiment 2 enables the rejection of the notion of differential subject populations as an explanation for the control–experimental-bridge differences for female interviewers in Experiment 1. However, some additional problems in the interpretation of the apparent anxiety–sexual attraction link require the superior control afforded by a laboratory setting.

First, although the female experimenter was blind to the experimental hypothesis and her behavior toward the subjects was closely monitored by the experimenter, the possibility of differential behavior toward the subjects occurring was not excluded. Distance of the interviewer from the subjects was controlled in both Experiments 1 and 2, but more stable nonverbal forms of communication (such as eye contact) could not be controlled without cueing the female interviewer to the experimental hypothesis.

Second, even if the interviewer did not behave differentially in experimental and control conditions, she may have appeared differently in the two conditions. For example, the gestalt created by the experimental situation may have made the interviewer appear more helpless or frightened, virtually a "lady in distress." Such would not be the case in the control situation.

If this different gestalt led to differences in sexual attraction, the apparent emotion–sexual arousal link might prove artifactual. Accordingly, a laboratory experiment was run in which tighter control over these factors could be obtained. This experiment involved a 2 × 2 factorial design, where *(a)* the male subject expected either a painful or nonpainful shock (subject's emotion was manipulated) and *(b)* the female confederate also expected either a painful or nonpainful shock (the lady-in-distress gestalt was manipulated).

EXPERIMENT 3

METHOD

Subjects

Eighty male freshmen at the University of British Columbia took part in this experiment. All subjects were volunteers.

Much of the initial phase of the procedure was patterned after that used in Schachter's (1959) anxiety and affiliation research. Subjects entered an experimental room containing an array of electrical equipment. The experimenter welcomed the subject and asked him if he had seen another person who looked like he was searching for the experimental room. The experimenter excused himself "to look for the other subject," leaving the subject some Xeroxed copies "of previous studies in the area we are investigating" to read. The articles discussed the effects of electric shock on learning and pain in general.

The experimenter reentered the room with the "other subject," who was an attractive female confederate.[2] The confederate took off her coat and sat on a chair three feet to the side and slightly in front of the subject. The experimenter explained that the study involved the effects of electric shock on learning and delivered a short discourse on the value and importance of the research. At the end of this discourse, the experimenter asked if either subject wanted out of the experiment. As expected, no subject requested to leave.

The experimenter then mentioned that two levels of shock would be used in the experiment, describing one as quite painful and the other level as a "mere tingle, in fact some subjects describe it as enjoyable," and concluded by pointing out that the allocation of subjects to shock condition had to be "completely random so that personality variables won't affect the outcome." At this point, the experimenter asked both subjects to flip a coin to determine which shock level they would receive.[3] Hence, the subject reported "heads/tails," the confederate reported "heads/tails," and the experimenter said, "Today heads receives the high shock level." The ex-

---

[2] The female confederate knew that the study involved sexual attraction but did not know the experimental hypothesis. Her every action in the experimental room was carefully rehearsed to avoid any possibility of differential behavior among experimental conditions. Spacing of the confederate's chair from the subject's was carefully controlled, and the confederate was instructed to avoid any eye contact with the subject after their initial introduction. Hence, eye contact was restricted to the confederate's entering the room and returning to her chair after removing her coat. Both the confederate's and the subject's chairs faced the same direction (toward the experimenter), so that eye contact was easily avoided. In addition, the confederate's chair was somewhat closer to the experimenter than was the subject's chair, so that the subject could see the confederate while the experimenter delivered the instructions.

[3] Toward the end of the experiment, the confederate was told to report either the same result as the subject or a different result (of the coin flip) to facilitate obtaining equal *ns* for experimental conditions as quickly as possible.

TABLE 35.2
Reported anxiety in experimental conditions

Subject expects:	Female con-federate to get strong shock	Female con-federate to get weak shock	No female confederate
Strong shock	3.17	3.05	3.80
Weak shock	2.42	2.28	

Note: n per cell = 20.

perimenter then described the way in which the shock series would take place, the method of hooking subjects into electrodes, etc.

The experimenter then asked if the subjects had any questions, answered any that arose, and then said:

> It will take me a few minutes to set up this equipment. While I'm doing it, I would like to get some information on your present feelings and reactions, since these often influence performance on the learning task. I'd like you to fill out a questionnaire to furnish us with this information. We have two separate cubicles down the hall where you can do this—you will be undisturbed and private, and I can get this equipment set up.

The confederate then got up, walked in front of the subject to her coat, which was hanging on the wall, rummaged around for a pencil, and returned to her chair. The experimenter then led the subject and the confederate to the cubicles, where they proceeded to fill out the questionnaires.

RESULTS

A three-part questionnaire constituted the dependent measure of this study. Part 1 (feelings about the experiment included a check on the anxiety manipulation, Part 2 (feelings toward your co-subject) included two attraction questions found to be most sensitive in experimental situations of this sort (Aron, 1970), and Part 3 included the TAT picture used in Experiments 1 and 2, which was again scored for sexual imagery.

Anxiety

Anxiety was measured by the question "How do you feel about being shocked?" (cf., Schachter, 1959) to which subjects could respond on a 5-point scale where scores greater than 3 indicated dislike. (The greater the score, the greater the anxiety.) Table 35.2 presents the results on this measure. In conditions where the subject anticipated receiving a strong shock, subjects reported significantly more anxiety than in conditions where the subject anticipated receiving a weak shock

TABLE 35.3
Attraction ratings by experimental condition

Subject expects:	Female confederate to get strong shock	Female confederate to get weak shock
Strong shock	3.7	3.4
Weak shock	2.9	2.7

Note: Strongest attraction rating is 5.

($t = 4.03$, $p < .001$, $df = 39$, one-tailed). In conditions where the subject anticipated receiving a strong shock with the female co-subject present, subjects reported significantly less anxiety than in a control condition ($n = 20$), where two male subjects were run ($t = 2.17$, $p < .025$, $df = 19$, one-tailed). No significant differences in the subject's anxiety occurred as a function of the confederate receiving a strong versus a weak shock (see Table 35.2).

Attraction to Confederate

Two questions assessed attraction to the confederate in this study: *(a)* How much would you like to ask her out for a date? and *(b)* how much would you like to kiss her? (An alternative set of questions was provided for those subjects who ostensibly had a male copartner. The experimenter instructed subjects in this condition to overlook these.) Attraction ratings were established by taking the mean rating made by subjects on these two questions. Table 35.3 shows the results, by condition, of those ratings. A 2 × 2 analysis of variance revealed a significant main effect for subjects anticipating strong shock to themselves on attraction ratings ($F = 22.8$, $p < .001$). Subjects' expectations of strong versus weak shock to the female confederate produced no significant increase in attraction ($F = 2.61$, *ns*). (There was no significant interaction.) Hence, the lady-in-distress effect on attraction did not seem to appear in this study.

Thematic Apperception Test Responses

Sexual imagery scores on the TAT questionnaire were obtained as in Experiments 1 and 2 and are shown in Table 35.4. In the present study, sexual imagery was higher when the subject expected strong shock but only when the female confederate also expected strong shock ($F = 4.73$, $p < .05$). When the female confederate expected weak shock, differences in sexual imagery scores as a function of strength of shock anticipated by the subject failed to achieve significance ($F = 4.22$, $P = .07$).

TABLE 35.4
Sexual imagery scores by experimental condition

Subject expects:	Female confederate to get strong shock	Female confederate to get weak shock
Strong shock	2.27	2.19
Weak shock	1.52	1.69

Note: Strongest imagery score is 5.

GENERAL DISCUSSION

The results of these studies would seem to provide a basis of support for an emotion–sexual attraction link. The Barclay studies (Barclay, 1969, 1970; Barclay and Haber, 1965) have already demonstrated such a link for aggression and sexual arousal, and the present findings seem to suggest that the link may hold for fear as well. Indeed, the present outcome would seem to be particularly satisfying in light of the very strong differences obtained from the relatively small subject populations, and because these results were obtained, in Experiments 1 and 2, outside of the laboratory in a setting in which real-world sexual attractions might be expected to occur.

The strong result of Experiment 3 supports the notion that strong emotion per se increases the subject's sexual attraction to the female confederate. Brehm, Gatz, Goethals, McCrimmon, and Ward (1967) obtained results consistent with Experiment 3 in a similar study. They also had male subjects threatened by impending electric shock in two experimental groups and not threatened in the control group. They obtained an F significant at the 5 percent level for differences between the threat and no-threat groups.

The theoretical implications of these results are twofold. In the first place, they provide additional support in favor of the theoretical positions from which the original hypothesis was derived: the Schachter and Singer (1962) tradition of cognitive labeling of emotions and the Aron (1970) conceptual framework for sexual attraction processes. In the second place, these data seem to be inconsistent with (or at least unpredictable by) standard theories of interpersonal attraction. Both the reinforcement (Byrne, 1969) and the cognitive consistency (Festinger, 1957; Heider, 1958) points of view would seem to predict that a negative emotional state associated with the object would *decrease* her attractiveness; and neither theory would seem to be easily capable of explaining the arousal of a greater sexual emotion in the experimental condition of the present experiments.

Although the present data support the cognitive relabeling approach in general, they are consistent with more than one interpretation of the mechanics of the process. The attribution notions of Nisbett and Valins (1972), self-perception theory (Bem, 1972), and role theory (Sarbin and Allen, 1968) can all provide possible explanations for the anxiety–sexuality link. A further possible explanation is that heightened emotion, instead of being relabeled as sexual, serves merely to disinhibit the expression of preexistent sexual feelings. It is known that inhibition and sexual defensiveness influence sexual content in TAT stories (Clark, 1952), and this alternative cannot be ruled out by the present data. Yet another alternative suggested by Barclay (personal communication, 1971), is that the aggression–sexuality and anxiety–sexuality links may be independent phenomena and not necessarily subcases of a general emotion–sexuality link.

Some evidence for the mechanics of the anxiety–sexual arousal link in the current research may be obtained from the fear ratings made by subjects in Experiment 3. When subjects anticipated receiving a strong shock and the female confederate was present during the anxiety manipulation, subjects reported significantly less fear than when no potential sexual object was present ($t = 2.17$, $df = 19$, $p <$ .025). Since the questionnaires were filled out in private in both groups, it is unlikely that subjects' reporting merely reflects appropriate behavior in the presence of the opposite or same sex. One possible explanation for this result is that, having relabeled anxiety as sexual arousal, the subject is less likely to feel anxious. A more conclusive explanation of the mechanics of the anxiety–sexual arousal link must await the conclusion of present laboratory studies designed specifically to investigate this problem. However, regardless of the interpretation of the mechanics of this link, the present research presents the clearest demonstration to date of its existence.

References

ARON, A. Relationship variables in human heterosexual attraction. Unpublished doctoral dissertation, University of Toronto, 1970.

BARCLAY, A. M. The effect of hostility on physiological and fantasy responses. *Journal of Personality,* 1969, **37,** 651–667.

BARCLAY, A. M. The effect of female aggressiveness on aggressive and sexual fantasies. *Journal of Projective Techniques and Personality Assessment,* 1970, **34,** 19–26.

BARCLAY, A. M., AND HABER, R. N. The relation of aggressive to sexual motivation. *Journal of Personality,* 1965, **33,** 462–475.

BEM, D. Self-perception theory. In L. Berkowitz (ed.), *Advances in experimental social psychology.* Vol. 6. New York: Academic Press, 1972.

BREHM, J. W., GATZ, M., GOETHALS, G., McCRIMMON, J., AND WARD, L. Psychological arousal and interpersonal attraction. Unpublished manuscript, Duke University, 1967.

BYRNE, D. Attitudes and attraction. In I. L. Berkowitz (ed.), *Advances in experimental social psychology.* Vol. 4. New York: Academic Press, 1969.

CLARK, R. A. The projective measurement of experimentally induced levels of sexual motivation. *Journal of Experimental Psychology,* 1952, **44,** 391–399.

CLARK, R. A., AND SENSIBAR, M. R. The relationship between symbolic and manifest projections of sexuality with some incidental correlates. *Journal of Abnormal Social Psychology,* 1955, **50,** 327–334.

EISLER, R. M. Thematic expression of sexual conflict under varying stimulus conditions. *Journal of Consulting and Clinical Psychology,* 1968, **32,** 216–220.

ELLIS, H. *Studies in the Psychology of Sex.* New York: Random House, 1936.

FESTINGER, L. *A theory of cognitive dissonance.* Evanston, Ill.: Row, Peterson, 1957.

FREUD, S. *Basic writings.* New York: Modern Library, 1938.

HEIDER, F. *The psychology of interpersonal relations.* New York: Wiley, 1958.

JAMES, W. *The principles of psychology.* Vol. 2. New York: Holt, 1910.

KELLY, H. Attribution theory in social psychology. In D. Levine (ed.), *Nebraska Symposium on Motivation: 1967,* Lincoln: University of Nebraska Press, 1967.

LEIMAN, A. H., AND EPSTEIN, S. Thematic sexual responses as related to sexual drive and guilt. *Journal of Abnormal and Social Psychology,* 1961, **63,** 169–175.

LUBIN, B. Some effects of set and stimulus properties on T.A.T. stories. *Journal of Projective Techniques,* 1960, **24,** 11–16.

MURRAY, H. A. *Thematic Apperception Test manual.* Cambridge, Mass.: Harvard University Press, 1943.

NISBETT, R., AND VALINS, S. *Perceiving the causes of one's own behavior.* New York: General Learning Press, 1972.

SARBIN, T. R., AND ALLEN, V. L. *Role theory: Handbook of social psychology.* Reading, Mass.: Addison-Wesley, 1968.

SCHACHTER, S. *The psychology of affiliation.* Stanford, Calif.: Stanford University Press, 1959.

SCHACHTER, S. The interaction of cognitive and physiological determinants of emotional state. In L. Berkowitz (ed.), *Advances in experimental social psychology.* Vol. 1. New York: Academic Press, 1964.

SCHACTER, S., AND SINGER, J. E. Cognitive, social and physiological components of the emotional state. *Psychological Review,* 1962, **69,** 379–399.

SUTTIE, I. D. *The origins of love and hate.* London: Kegan Paul, 1935.

TINBERGEN, N. The origin and evolution of courtship and threat display. In J. S. Huxley, A. C. Hardy, and E. B. Ford (eds.), *Evolution as a process.* London: Allen & Unwin, 1954.

36

Keeping Track of Needs and Inputs of Friends and Strangers

Margaret S. Clark, Judson R. Mills,
and David M. Corcoran

Proceeding from the distinction between communal and exchange relationships drawn in previous work, it was hypothesized that keeping track of the needs of a friend would be greater than keeping track of the needs of a stranger and that keeping track of a stranger's inputs into a joint task would be greater than keeping track of the inputs of a friend. These hypotheses were tested in an experiment in which the number of times subjects looked at lights (which never changed) was the dependent measure. In the "needs" condition, a change in the lights meant the other person needed help (which the subject could not provide). In the "inputs" condition, a change in the lights meant the other had made a substantial contribution to a joint task. In support of the hypotheses, it was found that the number of looks at the lights in the "needs" condition was significantly greater when the other was a friend than a stranger, while the number of looks in the "inputs" condition was significantly greater when the other was a stranger than a friend.

A distinction has been drawn by Clark and Mills (1979; Mills and Clark, 1982) between communal relationships, in which members benefit each other on the basis of needs or to demonstrate general concern for each other's welfare, and exchange relationships, in which members benefit each other in response to specific benefits received in the past or expected in the future. Some of the most important support for this distinction has come from research demonstrating that *(a)* members of exchange relationships, but not communal relationships, keep track of individual inputs into joint tasks for which there will be a reward (Clark, 1984) and *(b)* members of communal relationships are more likely than members of exchange relationships to keep track of the other's needs if there is no clear opportunity for

---

Reprinted with permission from the authors and Sage Publications, Inc. Selection from *Personality and Social Psychology Bulletin,* Vol. 15, No. 4, 1989. Copyright © 1989 by Sage Publications, Inc.

This research was supported by National Institute of Mental Health Grant R01 MH40390 and by National Science Foundation Grant BNS-8807894. We thank Carolyn Muchant Taraban for her help in conducting the data analyses.

the other to reciprocate, even when they cannot respond to the other's needs (Clark, Mills, and Powell, 1986).

The present study was designed with two purposes in mind. In the earlier work indicating that persons in communal relationships are more likely to keep track of the other's needs than persons in exchange relationships (Clark et al., 1986), keeping track of the other's needs was measured by how many times the subjects checked a box for notes from the other requesting help (Study 1) or looked at lights indicating whether the other was experiencing difficulty on a task (Study 2). It might be argued that high scores on these measures indicated something other than concern for the other's welfare, something more general. That is, the differences might have resulted from greater interest in *everything* about the other in a communal relationship.

In the present study we attempted to demonstrate that persons in communal relationships are more interested in keeping track of the needs of the other but not in *all* types of information about the other. To accomplish this, we investigated whether members of communal relationships would be more likely than members of exchange relationships to look at lights when the lights indicated whether the other had a need but not when the lights indicated whether the other had made a substantial contribution to a joint task for which there would be a reward.

Our second goal was to demonstrate that the Clark et al. (1986) finding of greater attention to needs in communal than in exchange relationships also occurs when ongoing, established communal relationships are contrasted with exchange relationships. In the Clark et al. (1986) studies, manipulations were used to lead subjects to desire either an exchange or a communal relationship with someone they were meeting for the first time. Moreover, to date our experimental program of research on the distinction between exchange and communal relationships has examined established communal relationships in only one series of studies (i.e., Clark, 1984). That is, Clark (1984) found not only that subjects led to desire a communal relationship were less likely to keep track of inputs into joint tasks than subjects led to desire an exchange relationship (Study 1) but also that members of ongoing friendships are less likely to keep track of inputs into such tasks than pairs of strangers are (Studies 2 and 3). In order to demonstrate that the effect found in the Clark et al. (1986) research on keeping track of needs also occurs in established communal relationships, in the present study we examined whether members of ongoing friendships would be more likely to keep track of each other's needs than pairs of strangers would.

Such a demonstration, of course, depends on the assumption that ongoing friendships do tend to be communal relationships—in other words, relationships in which people feel a special responsibility for the needs of the other and give benefits in response to those needs. This assumption seemed justified on the basis of prior studies that have indicated, for example, that people believe needs should be taken into account when money is divided between friends to a greater extent than when it is divided between strangers (Lamm and Schwinger, 1980, 1983) and that friends are perceived to be more obligated to help each other than strangers are (Bar-Tal, Bar-Zohar, Greenberg, and Herman, 1977). It is also supported by a finding that providing help in the form of confidant and emotional support is a particularly sensitive positive indicant of whether a relationship will become one that its participants refer to as a close friendship (Hays, 1985). Finally, it ought to be noted that the present study itself will provide a test of this assumption.

In addition to the two primary goals just outlined, because our experiment also included conditions allowing for a conceptual replication of the earlier finding that members of exchange relationships are more likely to keep track of individual inputs into joint tasks for which there will be a reward than members of communal relationships (Clark, 1984), we predicted that we would replicate those findings.

In sum, our two primary goals were to demonstrate that *(a)* although people in communal relationships are more attentive to the other's needs, they are not more attentive to *everything* about the other and *(b)* our earlier results revealing greater attentiveness to needs when subjects are led to expect a communal relationship than when they are led to expect an exchange relationship would be paralleled by a finding that people in ongoing communal relationships are more likely to keep track of each other's needs than strangers are. In addition, we expected to be able to conceptually replicate the Clark (1984) findings of greater attention to inputs into joint tasks in exchange than in communal relationships.

The specific hypotheses tested were:

1. Members of ongoing friendships will be more likely to keep track of each other's needs than pairs of strangers.
2. Pairs of strangers will be more likely to keep track of each other's inputs into joint tasks for which there will be a reward than members of ongoing friendships.

METHOD

Overview

Subjects in an experiment ostensibly on task performance were paired either with their friend or with a stranger who was the friend of a different subject. They were left to wait alone while the person with whom they were paired supposedly worked on a task. Subjects in the "needs" condition had been instructed that lights in their room would change whenever the other person needed help (which the subject could not provide). Subjects in the "inputs" condition had been instructed that the lights would change whenever the other made a substantial contribution to a joint task for which there would be a joint reward. The number of times the subject looked toward the lights (which never changed) was observed by an experimenter who was unaware whether the observed subject had been assigned to the "needs" or to the "inputs" condition.

Subjects

Forty-two college students, 28 males and 14 females, served as subjects and received either credit toward fulfilling a course requirement or $3.00 in pay in exchange. Each subject signed up with a friend, and both members of each pair of friends were randomly assigned to either the "communal" (friends) or the "exchange" (strangers) condition. In addition, each subject was randomly assigned to either the "inputs" or the "needs" condition (with the exception of members of the final few pairs, who, prior to arriving for the study, were assigned to the "inputs" or "needs" condition in such a way as to best balance the number of male and female subjects as well as the sex composition of pairs among the four conditions).[1] Two additional students were run, but they were not counted as subjects, nor were their data included in any analyses, because, as will be explained in more detail under Procedure, their behavior interfered with collection of the dependent measure. One of these subjects had been assigned to the communal/inputs condition, the other to the communal/needs condition.

Procedure

After signing up for a questionnaire study on friendship along with a friend, each subject was contacted by phone and informed that the study on friendship had been completed. However, the caller continued, subjects were still needed for another study, on task performance. The experimenter secured each person's consent to participate in the new study. Then that person and his or her friend were scheduled to participate in the new study, either together or paired with the members of a different pair of friends.[2]

Upon arrival, each of the two scheduled subjects was greeted by the male experimenter and taken to a different room. The subject to be run first was taken into the experimental room and seated at a desk facing one wall. Mounted on the lid of a mailbox on the opposite wall from the desk were two small lights, one green and one red. The experimenter began by explaining that the research being conducted that day was part of a collaborative project between some faculty members in the psychology department and some faculty members in the university's business school. It involved studying workers' strategies and performances. One factor that might influence strategy selection on tasks was whether a person worked in the same room with another person or in a separate room. During the current session, the two subjects would be working in separate rooms.

At this point the experimenter handed the subject a packet of pages filled with rows of numerals and a set of written instructions in a manila folder. He explained that the task involved searching the matrices for certain sequences of four digits, which were specified on a separate list that would be provided shortly. The four-digit numbers were supposedly embedded horizontally, vertically, or diagonally, as well as forward or backward, in the matrices. The subject and his or her partner would take turns at this task. The partner was to work on his or her packet first and search for numbers for 15 min. Then the subject would work on a different packet for 15 min. While the partner took his or her turn, the subject was to simply relax in his or her room. There was a stack of magazines in the room, and the subject was told to look through them if he or she wished. The subject was given a set of written instructions to read, and the experimenter left the room, supposedly to instruct the other subject.

The first half of the written instructions reiterated what the experimenter had just said; the second half was used to manipulate the "needs" versus "inputs" variable. Because the instruction sheet was placed in a manila folder that the experimenter picked up from a stack of randomly ordered folders, the experimenter was able to remain unaware whether the subject had been assigned to the "needs" or the "inputs" condition.

In the "needs" condition, the second section of the instructions, entitled "Explanation of the Lights," noted that in a different condition of the study the experimenters were interested in keeping track of when participants felt they were having difficulty with the task and needed help. This was done by having the participant press a button if and when that participant felt he or she was in need of help. Each time the other person felt he or she was in need of help, he or she would press a button, a green light in the subject's room would turn off, and a red light would turn on. The experimenter could then record exactly when this took place. All this, the instruction sheet explained, was irrelevant to the subject's version of the task, except that for purposes of control the experimenter wanted to keep conditions as comparable as possible. For that reason, even though the lights were not needed that day, the other person would press a button every time he or she needed help, and the red light would then come on in the subject's room. In the conditions being currently run, though, the instructions stated, it was not necessary for the subject to observe the lights or to do anything should they change from green to red.

In the "inputs" condition, the first section of the instructions was identical to that in the "needs" condition. The second section noted that it was important to keep subjects' motivation high in order for them to do well on the task. Therefore, a reward based on the subject's and his or her partner's performance would be given after their completion of the task. The size of the reward would be determined by how well they did as a pair. For every 10 number sequences each person found, the pair would receive a monetary bonus. At the completion of the task, the person "with a red star at the top of his/her page" would be given the entire reward to divide. Who had this star supposedly had been determined by the flip of a coin. Because it was not specified on which page this star would appear, it was ambiguous to the subject whether the subject or the partner would be dividing the reward. Following this was a section labeled "Explanation of the Lights." It explained that in a different condition of the study the experimenters were interested in recording exactly when participants found 10 sequences on a single page. When the other person found 10 sequences on a single page, he or she would press a button, the green light in the subject's room would turn off, and the red light would turn on. The experimenter could then record exactly when this took place. All this was supposedly irrelevant to the subject's version of the task except that for purposes of control the experimenter wanted to keep conditions as comparable as possible. For that reason, even though the lights were not needed that day, the other person would press a button every time he or she found 10 sequences on a single page, and then the red light would come on in the subject's room. In the conditions currently being run, though, it was not necessary for the subject to observe the lights or to do anything should they change from green to red.

The subject was left in the experimental room to wait while the experimenter supposedly went next door to start the partner on his or her task. In fact, the experimenter had previously given the first subject's partner an "individual" filler task to complete, after which, that other subject was led to believe, there would be another task involving both subjects. Instead of going to the partner's room, the experimenter immediately entered a room adjacent to the experimental room and observed the subject through a one-way mirror for 10 min (beginning within 10 sec of leaving the experimental room). The experimenter counted the times the subject turned away from his or her desk to observe the lights on the opposite side of the room. To reduce potential suspicion, all but the very edge of the one-way mirror was covered with a poster on the subject's side. After 10 min the experimenter reentered the experimental room, administered a suspicion check, and then debriefed the subject.

After the first subject had been run, the experimenter escorted him or her into a different room, brought the second subject into the experimental room with the lights, and repeated the same procedure with that subject. No subject indicated suspicions at the conclusion of the study.

As mentioned above, two students who were run were not counted as subjects because their behavior prevented the experimenter from collecting the dependent measure as planned. During the 10-min observation period, these two subjects lifted the top of the mailbox (thereby obscuring the lights mounted on the lid) and looked into the box.

RESULTS

The dependent measure was the number of times the subject looked at the lights. The mean number of looks at the lights in each condition appears in Table 36.1. As can be seen, the means fell in the expected pattern. As predicted from our first hypothesis, friends looked at the lights more often than strangers did in the "needs" condition but not in the "inputs" condition. As predicted from our second hypothesis and the results of Clark (1984), in the "inputs" condition strangers looked at the lights more often than friends did.

A test for homogeneity of variance between the four conditions revealed a significant departure from equality of variance, $F(MAX)$ (4, 12) = 20.70, $p < .01$.

TABLE 36.1
Mean number of looks at the lights

	Relationship type	
Meaning of lights	Friend	Stranger
Inputs	Mean = 1.31	Mean = 3.78
	SD = 2.14	SD = 2.49
	Range = 0–7	Range = 1–8
	(n = 13)	(n = 9)
Needs	Mean = 4.36	Mean = 1.00
	SD = 5.57	SD = 1.22
	Range = 0–20	Range = 0–3
	(n = 11)	(n = 9)

Therefore, prior to conducting further analyses, the data were subjected to a transformation of the form $x = \log(x + 1)$ followed by a check to see whether there were still significant departures from homogeneity of variance. There were not, $F(MAX)$ (4, 12) = 2.22, n.s. A 2 × 2 (Relationship Type × Meaning of Lights) between-subjects analysis of variance was then conducted on the transformed data. As expected, this analysis of variance yielded a significant interaction between Relationship Type and Meaning of Lights, $F(1, 38) = 16.35$, $p < .001$. Neither the main effect of Relationship Type, $F(1, 38) = 0.04$, nor the main effect of Meaning of Lights, $F(1, 38) = 0.03$, was significant. The analysis of variance was followed by planned comparisons to test our specific predictions. As expected, the difference between the behavior of friends and strangers in the "needs" condition was significant, $F(1, 38) = 7.15$, $p < .01$, as was the difference between the behavior of friends and strangers in the "inputs" condition, $F(1, 38) = 9.31$, $p < .01$.

It might be asked whether the observed effects were due to one or two extreme scores. Whereas the range of number of looks for 41 of the 42 subjects was 0 to 8 looks, there was one extreme score (20 looks) in the communal/needs condition. However, even if this score is truncated to a score of 8 (the next-highest score) and the 2 × 2 ANOVA on the transformed data is repeated, the predicted interaction between Relationship Type and Meaning of Lights remains significant, $F(1, 38) = 17.02$, $p < .001$. Moreover, the planned comparisons between the communal/inputs and exchange/inputs conditions, $F(1, 38) = 10.62$, $p < .01$, and between the communal/needs and exchange/needs conditions, $F(1, 38) = 6.70$, $p < .01$, also remain significant.[3]

DISCUSSION

The results provide support for the hypothesis that keeping track of the needs of a friend will be greater than keeping track of the needs of a stranger. When a change in the lights meant the other needed help, the number of looks at the lights was significantly greater when the other was a friend than when the other was a stranger. It is important to note that the subjects were not able to provide help to the other in the "needs" condition.

As mentioned above, this study had two goals. One was to show that our earlier finding (Clark et al., 1986) that subjects desiring communal relationships are more likely to keep track of the other's needs than subjects desiring exchange relationships if there is no clear opportunity for the other to reciprocate was not due to greater interest in *everything* about the other in a communal relationship. The finding in the present study that friends were significantly more likely than strangers to look at the lights when a change meant that the other had a need but *not* when it meant the other had made a substantial contribution to a joint task rules out the interpretation that persons in a communal relationship are more interested in everything about the other. This, of course, does not mean that needs are the only things about the other to which members of communal relationships will be more likely to attend than members of exchange relationships. For instance, our theoretical position would also lead us to expect them to be more attentive to such things as the other's liking for them and the other's attentiveness to *their* needs (both of which might indicate whether the other shared the subject's interest in a communal relationship). Our point is simply that the greater attention to needs when a communal relationship is desired, observed by Clark et al. (1986), is not indicative of communal subjects' indiscriminate interest in everything about the other.

Our second goal was to show that the Clark et al. (1986) finding of more attention to the other's needs when a communal rather than an exchange relationship was expected would also occur in ongoing, established friendships (assumed to be communal in nature), compared with relationships between strangers who had no reason to expect to see each other again (assumed to be exchange in nature). Therefore, rather than manipulating desire for a communal or an exchange relationship as in past studies, the behavior of members of existing friendships was contrasted with that of pairs of strangers. The finding that members of ongoing friendships looked at the lights more often in the "needs" condition than pairs of strangers provides valuable evidence of keeping track of needs in ongoing communal relationships. At the same time, it provides evidence supporting our initial assumption that friendships do tend to be communal relationships while relationships between strangers do not. This finding also fits well with a wider prior literature on friendship supporting the assumption that friendships tend to be communal relationships. That literature shows, for instance, that people are more likely to say needs ought to be taken into account when money is divided between friends than when it is divided between strangers (Lamm and Schwinger, 1980, 1983), subjects feel friends are more obligated to help them than strangers are (Bar-Tel et al., 1977), observers react to a friend's success with more positive feelings and failure with more negative feelings than they do to a stranger's success or failure (Finney and Helm, 1982), and providing help in the form of confidant and emotional support is a particularly sensitive indicant of whether a relationship develops into one that its members refer to as a close friendship (Hays, 1985).

In addition to these primary goals, the present study included conditions permitting a conceptual replication of an earlier finding (Clark, 1984) that members of exchange relationships would be more likely to keep track of each other's inputs into a joint task for which there would be a reward than members of communal relationships. The results in the two "inputs" conditions did fall in the predicted pattern, with a significantly greater number of looks at the lights when the other was a stranger than a friend. Thus, the secondary goal of providing a conceptual replication of the Clark (1984) findings was also met.

Notes

1. Following assignment of subjects to conditions, the communal/inputs condition contained seven male subject/male other pairs, two male subject/female other pairs, two female subject/male other pairs, and two female subject/female other pairs; the communal/needs condition, eight male/male, one male/female, one female/male, and one female/female; the exchange/inputs condition, three male/male, two male/female, one female/male, and three female/female; and the exchange/needs condition, three male/male, two male/female, two female/male, and two female/female.
2. Although we did not include a specific manipulation check on whether our pairs of resulting friends really were more likely to be friends than our pairs of resulting strangers, we have used an identical procedure for sign-up/assignment of subjects to conditions in another study in which such a check was included (Clark & Muchant, 1988). At the conclusion of that study subjects orally rated the closeness of their relationship with a partner on a 1 (*not at all close*) to 7 (*very close*) scale. A t test revealed that the closeness ratings in the friends' condition ($M = 5.48$) were significantly higher than those in the strangers' condition ($M = 1.06$), $t(29) = -19.76$, $p < .0001$.
3. Questions also might be raised regarding whether there were any effects of sex of the subject, sex of the other, and/or sex composition of the pair. No predictions regarding these variables were made; nonetheless, an additional 2 (Sex of Subject) $\times$ 2 (Sex of Other) $\times$ 2 (Relationship Type) $\times$ 2 (Meaning of Lights) analysis of variance was performed on the transformed data. It revealed no significant main or interaction effects (nor any with a probability level below .10) involving sex of the subject or sex of the other. In connection with the lack of such effects, however, it should be noted that an insufficient number of subjects were included in the study to test the effects of four different variables and their interactions with much power. Consequently, any firm conclusions regarding how sex of the subject, sex of the other, or sex composition of the pair (tested by the interaction of sex of the subject and sex of the other) might influence (or not influence) the observed pattern of results should await further research.

References

BAR-TAL, D., BAR-ZOHAR, Y., GREENBERG, M. S., AND HERMAN, M. Reciprocity behavior in the relationship between donor and recipient and between harm-doer and victim. *Sociometry,* 1977, **40,** 293–298.

CLARK, M. S. Record keeping in two types of relationships. *Journal of Personality and Social Psychology,* 1984, **47,** 549–557.

CLARK, M. S., AND MILLS, J. R. Interpersonal attraction in exchange and communal relationships. *Journal of Personality and Social Psychology,* 1979, **51,** 333–338.

CLARK, M. S., MILLS, J. R., AND POWELL, M. Keeping track of needs in communal and exchange relationships. *Journal of Personality and Social Psychology,* 1986, **51,** 333–338.

CLARK, M. S., AND MUCHANT, C. B. *Reactions to and willingness to express emotion in communal and exchange relationships.* Manuscript submitted for publication, 1988.

FINNEY, P. D., AND HELM, B. The actor-observer relationship: The effect on actors' and observers' responsibility and emotion attributions. *Journal of Social Psychology,* 1982, **117,** 219–225.

HAYS, R. B. A longitudinal study of friendship development. *Journal of Personality and Social Psychology,* 1985, **48,** 909–924.

LAMM, H., AND SCHWINGER, T. Norms concerning distributive justice: Are needs taken into consideration in allocation decisions? *Social Psychology Quarterly,* 1980, **43,** 425–429.

LAMM, H., AND SCHWINGER, T. Need consideration in allocation decisions Is it just? *Journal of Social Psychology,* 1983, **119,** 205–209.

MILLS, J. R., AND CLARK, M. S. Exchange and communal relationships. In L. Wheeler (Ed.), *Review of personality and social psychology* (Vol. 3, pp. 225–234). Beverly Hills, CA: Sage, 1982.

Name Index

Subject Index